TRICHINOPOLY GAZETTEER

TRICHINOPOLY GAZETTEER

BY

LEWIS MOORE

VOLUME 1

COSMO PUBLICATIONS

2000 INDIA

Trichinopoly Gazetteer

First COSMO Print 2000

ISBN 81-7755-080-2 (set)

Published by
MRS. RANI KAPOOR
for COSMO PUBLICATIONS Div. of
GENESIS PUBLISHING PVT. LTD.
24-B, Ansari Road,
Darya Ganj,
New Delhi-110 002, INDIA

Printed at
Mehra Offset Press

PREFACE.

THE Government of Madras were pleased in May 1873 to accept an offer made by me to compile a Manual of the Trichinopoly District. My transfer to Madura District in 1875, and other causes that it is not necessary to particularize, have delayed the completion of the work considerably beyond the time by which I had hoped to be able to finish it.

I have not been as fortunate in receiving contributions from other District Officers as some of my predecessors in the task of compiling District Manuals. I have, however, much pleasure in thanking Surgeon W. G. King for a paper on the Diseases of the District, and Mr. W. A. Symonds for one on Jails.

LEWIS MOORE.

28*th June* 1878.

CONTENTS.

CHAPTER I.

GENERAL FEATURES OF THE DISTRICT AND DESCRIPTIVE NOTICES OF THE SEVERAL TALUQS.

CHAPTER II.

GEOLOGY AND SOILS.

CHAPTER III.

FLORA AND FAUNA.

CHAPTER IV.

CLIMATE AND DISEASES, CIVIL HOSPITALS AND DISPENSARIES.

CHAPTER V.

POPULATION.

CHAPTER VI.

POLITICAL HISTORY OF TRICHINOPOLY, PART I.

(FROM THE FOUNDING OF THE CHÓLA KINGDOM TILL THE FALL OF THE NÁYAK DYNASTY.)

CHAPTER VII.

POLITICAL HISTORY OF TRICHINOPOLY, PART II.

(FROM THE FALL OF THE NÁYAK DYNASTY TILL THE RAISING OF THE SIEGE OF TRICHINOPOLY AND THE DEATH OF CHANDA SAHIB IN 1752.)

CHAPTER VIII.

POLITICAL HISTORY OF TRICHINOPOLY, PART III.

(FROM THE RAISING OF THE SIEGE OF TRICHINOPOLY AND THE DEATH OF CHANDA SAHIB IN 1752 TILL THE TREATY BETWEEN THE ENGLISH AND FRENCH IN 1754.)

CHAPTER IX.

POLITICAL HISTORY OF TRICHINOPOLY, PART IV.

(FROM THE TREATY BETWEEN THE FRENCH AND ENGLISH IN 1754 TILL THE ACQUISITION OF THE DISTRICT BY THE ENGLISH IN 1801.)

CHAPTER X.

REVENUE HISTORY OF TRICHINOPOLY, PART I.

(FROM THE ACQUISITION OF THE DISTRICT BY THE ENGLISH TILL THE INTRODUCTION OF THE REVISED SETTLEMENT.)

CHAPTER XV.

UBLIC WORKS DEPARTMENT. THE ANICUTS. RAILWAYS.

CHAPTER XVI.

LOCAL FUNDS.

CHAPTER XVII.

MUNICIPALITIES.

CHAPTER XVIII.

POLICE AND JAILS.

CHAPTER XIX.

CIVIL AND CRIMINAL JUSTICE.

CHAPTER XX.

EDUCATION.

CHAPTER XXI.

ANCIENT TEMPLES AND BUILDINGS.

CHAPTER XXII.

PUDUKOTTAI.

APPENDIX.

STATISTICS.

MANUAL

OF THE

TRICHINOPOLY DISTRICT.

CHAPTER I.

GENERAL FEATURES OF THE DISTRICT AND DESCRIPTIVE NOTICES OF THE SEVERAL TALUQS.

Position and Boundaries of the District.—Mountains and Hills.—Rivers. TRICHINOPOLY TALUQ—General Features.—Cultivation.—Rates of Assessment.—Irrigation. — Revenue. — Communications. — Public Bungalows. — Fairs and Markets.—Principal Towns, Trichinopoly, Srírangam, Lálgudi. MUSIRI TALUQ—General Features.—Cultivation.—Rates of Assessment.—Irrigation.—Revenue.—Communications.—Public Bungalows.—Fairs and Markets.—Principal Towns, Musiri, Turaiyúr. THE PACHAMALAI HILLS — General Features. — Natural Products.—Area and Population.—Assessment. KULITTALAI TALUQ—General Features.—Cultivation.—Rates of Assessment.—Irrigation.— Revenue.—Communications.—Public Bungalows.—Fairs and Markets.—Principal Towns, Kulittalai, Manapparai. PERUMBALÚR TALUQ—General Features.—Cultivation.—Irrigation.—Rates of Assessment.—Revenue.—Communications.—Public Bungalows. — Fairs. — Principal Towns, Perumbalúr, Válikandapuram. UDAIYÁRPÁLAYAM TALUQ—General Features.—Cultivation.—Rates of Assessment.—Irrigation.—Revenue.—Communications.—Principal Towns, Jeyamkondasólapuram, Ariyalúr, Udaiyárpálayam, Kílapaluvúr.

CHAPTER I. GENERAL FEATURES, &c.

Position and boundaries of the district.

TRICHINOPOLY[1] District lies between 10° 37′ and 11° 31′ North latitude and 78° 13′ and 79° 37′ East longitude, and has an area of 3,583 square miles. It is bounded on the north-west and north by the Collectorate of Salem, on the north and north-east by South Arcot, on the east and south-east by Tanjore, on the south by the Pudukóttai State and Madura, and on the west by Coimbatore. The district is at present divided into five taluqs, Trichinopoly, Musiri, Kulittalai, Perumbalúr and Udaiyárpálayam, of which Musiri, Perumbalúr and Udaiyárpálayam lie to the north and

(1) Properly Tirisiráppalli, the city of the three-headed (*Rákshasa*).—Dr. CALDWELL's *Dravidian Grammar*, page 485.

CHAPTER I. GENERAL FEATURES, &c.

Kulittalai to the south of the Cauvery,[2] while Trichinopoly is divided by that river into two almost equal portions.

Mountains and hills.

The surface of the country is generally very flat. It is, however, broken here and there by a number of protruding masses of crystalline rock, bosses of gneiss, of which the Trichinopoly rock in the centre of the fort, and the Golden Rock near the Central Jail are the best known. There are, however, many others scattered over the district, of which that known as Ratnagiri, in the limits of Siváyam village near Kulittalai, and Perumálmalai, not far from Turaiyúr, may be instanced as the most remarkable. The only hills of any importance in the district are the Pachamalais, which lie between the northern portions of the Musiri and Perumbalúr Taluqs, and extend into Ahtúr Taluq in the Salem District. The altitude of these hills is, however, by no means great, being generally not more than about 2,000 feet above the level of the sea, and they are very feverish and unhealthy. A narrow valley separates these hills from another range, the Kollimalais, which is of considerably greater elevation, reaching in some parts to about 3,500 feet. This range, however, does not extend into Trichinopoly District, but merely forms the boundary between it and Salem. The south and south-west portions of the Kulittalai Taluq, and especially the Kadavúr Zemindári, are more uneven and hilly than the rest of the district, but they are not traversed by any range of hills worthy of special note.

Rivers.

The river Cauvery and its branch the Coleroon[3] constitute the only important hydrographic features of this part of the country. The former of these rivers enters the district at its western extremity and traverses it from west to east. It forms the boundary between the Kulittalai and Musiri Taluqs, and then flows through Trichinopoly Taluq. At about eleven miles to the west of the town of Trichinopoly it separates into two branches, one of which, flowing south-east, retains the name of Cauvery, while the

---

(2) Properly Kávéri. Stated by Dr. Caldwell to be so called from Kávér, turmeric, on account of its muddy color. Dr. Caldwell also suggests the possibility of the origin of the name Kávéri from the Dravidian Kávi (காவி), red ochre, or Ká (Kâvi), a grove, and éru, a river (Telugu), or éri, a sheet of water (Tamil).—*Dravidian Grammar*, page 456. The river Cauvery is mentioned in Ptolemy's Geography as **Χάβηρος**.

(3) Properly Kollidam (கொல்லிடம்), the place of slaughter. I have not been able to discover the origin of this name. The current tradition regarding it is as follows : One of the Chóla kings is said to have built the great Vishnu temple in Srírangam island, and to have employed many laborers at the work. When it was finished he had not the means to pay the men their wages, so he inveigled them into boats, which were upset as soon as they had reached the middle of the river now known as the Coleroon. Hence the river was called Kollidam, or the place of slaughter.—TAYLOR, *Oriental MSS.*, Vol. III, page 522.

other, running to the north-east, is termed the Coleroon. These rivers almost rejoin at a distance of about ten miles to the east of Trichinopoly Town, near the village of Kóviladi in Tanjore District, where it has been found necessary to separate them by an artificial bank. The portion of land enclosed by the two rivers is known as the island of Srírangam, famous for its extensive pagoda dedicated to Vishnu. To the west of this island the Cauvery is called the Agunda or Broad Cauvery. After its separation from the Cauvery, the Coleroon flows in a north-east direction through the taluq of Trichinopoly, and further on forms the boundary between the Udaiyárpálayam Taluq and the Tanjore District. The river Vellár forms the northern boundary of a portion of the district, separating Perumbalúr Taluq from South Arcot, but it does not flow through any portion of it. A few villages in the extreme west of Kulittalai Taluq are irrigated from the Ambrávati, which forms the boundary between that taluq and Coimbatore. A detailed descriptive account of each taluq in the district will now be given.

CHAPTER I. GENERAL FEATURES, &c.

TRICHINOPOLY.

General features.

Trichinopoly Taluq is divided into two almost equal portions by the river Cauvery, which crosses its entire length from west to east. Prior to the introduction of Mr. Pelly's scheme in 1861, the portion of the present taluq lying to the north of the river was termed the Lálgudi, and that to the south the Kónád Taluq. The area of the taluq is 519 square miles, its greatest length from east to west being about 36 miles and its greatest breadth from north to south about 30 miles. Of the 436 villages in the taluq, 386 are held on ryotwári tenure, and 50 are inám. There are no zemindári villages in it. The portions of the taluq along the Cauvery are irrigated by numerous channels from that river and are very fertile. The remainder of the taluq is, as a rule, unirrigated, and is, in many parts, sandy and hilly. It is, however, on the whole very flat, and there are no mountains or hills of any importance to be found in it. To the south of the taluq there are 15 villages, known as the Iluppúr Division, separated from the rest of the district by the Pudukóttai Territory, which completely surrounds them.

Cultivation.

The soil of the greater portion of the fields irrigated by the Cauvery and its channels has been enriched by alluvial deposit and is most productive. Mr. Puckle, however, who, when engaged in drawing up a scheme for the revision of the revenue system of the district had great opportunities of observing the nature of the soil in different localities, was of opinion that in some of the irrigated villages it had been much impoverished by an excessive

CHAPTER I. GENERAL FEATURES, &C.

mixture of river-sand deposited during the frequent inundations to which the taluq was subject before it was properly embanked.[4] As regards the villages in the taluq to the north of the Cauvery, Mr. Puckle considered that, from the upper anicut to the Madras trunk road (No. 3), the soil was light and sandy and the irrigation good, but not first-rate, while, from the same road as far as Lálgudi, the soil was richer and the irrigation excellent.[5] In the Iluppúr Division the soil is hard and gravelly, interspersed with tracts of land so impregnated with saltpetre as to be almost bare of vegetation. There is, however, a considerable amount of cultivation carried on under tanks and wells in this portion of the taluq.

Paddy is the principal grain grown in the taluq, no less than 68,000 acres being cultivated with it every year. The most important dry grains are chólum, varagu and cumbu; oil-seeds, rági, gram and dholl are also grown to a less extent, while a considerable quantity of land, especially in the villages to the north of the Coleroon, is cultivated with sugar-cane, indigo and cotton. A large amount of rice is exported every year from Trichinopoly principally to Madura and Tanjore. The dry grains grown in the taluq are not sufficient to supply the local demand, and these grains are therefore imported to a slight extent. The staple food, however, of the mass of the population of the taluq is rice. Statement No. 7-A, given in the appendix, shows the extent of land in the taluq cultivated with each of the principal grains in Fasli 1285.

Rates of assessment.

The rates of assessment on irrigated land in Trichinopoly Taluq vary from 1 Rupee to Rupees 7-8-0. The mass of the fields irrigated by the Cauvery and its channels are charged either Rupees 5 or Rupees 6 per acre, while tank-irrigated lands pay, as a rule, Rupees 2-8-0. The dry rates range between 4 Annas and Rupees 3-8-0, more than two-thirds of the land of this description in the taluq being assessed at 1 Rupee per acre or less.

Irrigation.

The principal sources of irrigation are the Cauvery and its channels. The following statement gives certain details regarding the villages irrigated by the most important of these channels:—

(4) Paragraph 15 of Appendix B attached to Mr. Puckle's letter as Deputy Director of Revenue Settlement, to the Director, dated 28th October 1860.

(5) Deputy Director, to Director, dated 30th May 1865, paragraph 20.

CHAPTER I. GENERAL FEATURES, &c.

Number.	Names of Channels.	No. of Villages irrigated.	Ayakat (Irrigable Area). Government. Extent.		Assessment.		Inám. Extent.		Assessment.	
			ACRES.	CTS.	RS.	A.	ACRES.	CTS.	RS.	A.
1	Uyyakondán ..	89	16,457	21	91,751	5	2,179	25	5,336	0
2	Elanda Vattalai ..	7	1,919	82	10,100	12	7	14	19	8
3	Ayyan Váykkál ..	66	9,855	43	54,136	6	518	21	1,983	15
4	Peravala do. ..	97	12,964	59	48,815	10	701	27	1,448	12
5	Náttu do. ..	15	3,335	35	18,572	14	123	85	335	9

The principal tanks are Kúttappár with an ayakat of 498 acres, paying a yearly assessment of Rupees 1,562; Kiliyúr, ayakat 808 acres, assessment Rupees 2,039; and Válavandánkóttai, the tank into which the Uyyakondán channel finally flows, ayakat 654 acres, assessment Rupees 2,150. Statement No. 4, given in the appendix, shows the extent of land cultivated under each source of irrigation, and the assessment charged on it.

Revenue.

The following statement shows the revenue derived from each of the different sources in Trichinopoly Taluq for the last five years:—

Items.	Fasli 1281, 1871-72.	Fasli 1282, 1872-73.	Fasli 1283, 1873-74.	Fasli 1284, 1874-75.	Fasli 1285, 1875-76.
	RS.	RS.	RS.	RS.	RS.
Land Revenue ..	4,07,180	4,30,737	4,27,560	4,34,786	4,33,844
Miscellaneous ..	23,368	21,217	15,475	22,100	23,522
Abkári	89,300	98,100	98,100	98,100	35,050*
Stamps	3,667	4,638	22,900	27,806	33,184
Road Fund	31,550	31,776	31,902	31,604	31,463

Communications.

The South Indian Railway runs across the taluq from west to east, the stations on it being Elamanúr, Trichinopoly Fort, Trichinopoly Junction, and Tiruvarambúr. Of the two stations in Trichinopoly itself the former is close to the native part of the town, while the latter is at no great distance from the cantonment where the European residents live. The same railway also enters the taluq at its south-western extremity and runs through it as far as Trichinopoly Junction, the only station on this portion of the line in this taluq being Kolattúr.

The following are the principal roads in the taluq: Road No. 3, the Madras trunk road, runs from Trichinopoly almost due

* This refers to toddy alone, as, since Fasli 1284, the right to vend arrack throughout the whole district has been sold in one farm, and as it is therefore impossible to show the revenue derived on account of the sale of this commodity in each taluq.

CHAPTER I. GENERAL FEATURES, &c.

north as far as the limits of the Perambalúr Taluq. It is in excellent order, and metalled and bridged throughout. This road crosses two fine bridges over the Cauvery and Coleroon. The former of these has 32 arches of 49 feet span each, and its total length is 1,936 feet. It was built in 1849 at a cost of about a lakh of rupees. The bridge over the Coleroon has also 32 arches, but they are of 60 feet span, and its length is 2,685 feet. It was constructed in 1852 at a cost of about 1½ lakhs. At a distance of a few hundred yards from the north end of the bridge over the Coleroon, Road No. 4 branches off from the Madras trunk road, and runs in a north-eastern direction across the taluq, passing through Lálgudi and Pullambádi. It is in good order, and metalled and bridged throughout the portion of it that is in Trichinopoly Taluq. Road No. 1 also leaves the trunk road at the same point as that just mentioned, and, running in a westerly direction, enters the Musiri Taluq close to the upper anicut; it is in good order, and metalled and bridged throughout. It crosses the Ayyár, which is at that point the boundary between Musiri and Trichinopoly Taluq, by means of an iron girder bridge which was erected in 1873 at a cost of Rupees 72,868. Road No. 2 branches off from this road at a distance of about a mile from the Coleroon bridge, and passing through Mannachanellúr, runs through Musiri Taluq and thence to Ahtúr in Salem District. Roads Nos. 9 and 10, from Trichinopoly to Madura and Dindigul respectively, run through a portion of the south-western part of the taluq. The former of these is kept in good order, and is metalled and bridged. The latter is not bridged in some places, and is not, as a rule, kept in first-rate repair. The traffic on these roads has been greatly diminished since the opening of the southern extension of the South India Railway in 1875. Road No. 11, the Karúr road, runs along the south bank of the Cauvery from Trichinopoly to the boundary of the Kulittalai Taluq. It is in good order, and metalled and bridged throughout. Road No. 5 leaves the Madras trunk road in the Srírangam island, and runs *viâ* the grand anicut in the Tanjore District to Combaconum. Road No. 7, the Tanjore road from Trichinopoly to Tanjore, *viâ* Tiruvarambúr, is one of the oldest roads in the district, having been made in 1849. It is in good order, and metalled and bridged throughout. Road No. 19 runs from Pullambádi on Road No. 4 to Aramanaikurichi on the bank of the Coleroon. Road No. 20 from Sirudaiyúr on Road No. 4, passes through Lálgudi and goes on to Sengaraiyúr on the Coleroon. It is intended to extend this road along the Coleroon bank by the Nandaiyár anicut and Tirumalavádi, till it joins the road already constructed along the bank of that river from the lower anicut as far as a village named Vappúr in Udaiyárpálayam Taluq. Road No. 21 extends from Samayapuram on the

Madras trunk road to Irungalúr, the head-quarters of an S. P. G. Mission. Road No. 8 runs from Trichinopoly to Pudukóttai Only six miles of this road are in the Trichinopoly District, and these are metalled and kept in good order. Road No. 6 extends from Trichinopoly to Combaconum, *via* Sarkárpálayam. Of this road only five miles run through Trichinopoly Taluq, while the rest is in Tanjore District. Road No. 23 passes from Trichinopoly to Allituraí, a village to the south-west of the head quarters of the district. It is hoped that funds may be provided in time to enable the Local Fund Board to push on this road as far as Tógamalai, a village in Kulittalai Taluq on Road No. 25.

Public bungalows.

The only public bungalow in the taluq at present is the one in the Trichinopoly cantonment, which is under the management of the Municipality. Three other buildings, formerly used as public bungalows, situated at Tuvágudi on the Tanjore road, at Samayapuram on the Madras trunk road, and at Nágamangalam on the Madura road, are at present under the charge of the Public Works Department. The question of transferring these buildings to the Local Fund Board is under the consideration of Government. In addition to these there was formerly a public bungalow at Sirugambúr, not far from the upper anicut, but, as it is off the line of road, it is of no use; and for this reason the Local Fund Board in 1877 declined to take over charge of it. It is now rapidly falling into ruins.

Fairs and markets.

Weekly fairs are held at the following places in Trichinopoly Taluq: at Uraiyúr in the Trichinopoly Municipality every Sunday; at Tuvágudi and Pirattiyúr on Monday; and at Kolattúr on Tuesday; at Puliyúr, Sirugambúr and in a tope in Sirudaiyúr, on Road No. 4, close to the Lálgudi Deputy Tahsildar's Office on Friday; and at Samayapuram and Iluppúr every Saturday.

Principal towns.

The most important towns and villages in the taluq are Trichinopoly, population 73,893; Srírangam, population 11,271; Lálgudi, population 4,355; Pullambádi, population 3,371; Iluppúr, population 2,968, and Mannachanellúr, population 2,960.

—Trichinopoly.

A lengthened account of the capital of the district is not necessary here, as all the information that it has been found possible to collect regarding its past history is given in Chapters VI to IX, and as an account of its present condition, together with a summary of the efforts that have been made of late years towards the improvement of the town, are given in the chapter on the municipalities in the district. Trichinopoly Fort is situated on the right bank of the Cauvery, about a mile south of that river, and at a distance in a direct line of 56 miles from the sea at its nearest point. The fort is a rectangular figure, measuring about a mile by half a mile.

CHAPTER I. GENERAL FEATURES, &c.

Till recently it was surrounded by ramparts and a ditch; the walls have now been completely levelled and the ditch filled in. The entire space enclosed by the fort is densely populated. The streets in this part of the town are narrow, but have been on the whole regularly laid out. Inside the fort is the Trichinopoly Rock, which rises abruptly out of the plain to a height of 273 feet above the level of the street at its foot. An account of the temple and other buildings on this rock is given in the chapter on ancient temples and buildings. A few hundred yards to the south of the rock is the building known as the Nawáb's palace, which was restored in 1873 at a cost of Rupees 36,181, according to a suggestion made by Lord Napier when he visited Trichinopoly in 1871 as Governor of Madras. The building now affords accommodation for the offices of the Tahsildar, District Munsif, Town Sub-Magistrate, District Registrar, and the Municipal Birth and Death Registrar. The Fort Police Station is also located in a portion of the building. It was originally intended that the Audience Hall should be converted into a Municipal Office, but the Commissioners declined to purchase it, and it is now made use of as a Normal School-house. Between the rock and the north-west entry to the fort, known as the Main Guard Gate, there is a handsome *teppakulam* in the houses round which the officers of the garrison lived during the stirring times when Trichinopoly was first a military station. One of these houses is still pointed out as having been Lord Clive's house, but whether he ever lived in it or not may well be doubted. The Tahsildar's Office was till quite recently located in an old mantapam a few yards to the north of the *teppakulam*, where the Town Munsif still holds his court.

The portion of the town where the troops are stationed, and where the civil and military officers reside, known as the cantonment, is situated about 1½ miles south of the fort. During the time for which Trichinopoly has been a military station the site of the cantonment has gradually been entirely changed. At first, as already stated, the officers lived round the *teppakulam* in the fort, and this portion of the town was not completely abandoned by the military till quite recently. In Dr. Ranking's Report on the Civil and Military Station of Trichinopoly, written by him as Sanitary Commissioner in 1867, it is stated that the guard formerly kept up at what is still known as the Main Guard had been abolished only quite recently, and it is strongly urged in the same report that the arsenal, which up till then had been stationed in the fort at the foot of the rock, should be removed to the cantonment, and all the native guards withdrawn from the fort. This suggestion was carried out in 1869. The first Collectors of

Trichinopoly held their offices in Uraiyúr[6] and also lived there, and to this part of the town the greater portion of the troops in the station appear to have been removed shortly after our first occupation of Trichinopoly. For a considerable time the pagoda in Uraiyúr was occupied by troops, but it was eventually relinquished on the earnest entreaties of its priests and managers.[7] The Uraiyúr parade ground is still to be seen, although the officers' quarters, mess houses, &c., with which it was surrounded have entirely disappeared. After they had remained in this portion of the town for many years, the troops were moved to the site they now occupy, which is from every point of view greatly superior to the one which has been abandoned. With the exception of the lines in Puttúr occupied by a Native Infantry regiment, all the troops in the garrison are now stationed to the south of the Uyyakondán irrigation channel. The military force quartered in Trichinopoly consists at present of one battery of Artillery, a detachment of European Infantry, and three Native Infantry regiments. Of these two Native regiments are quartered to the extreme south-east of the cantonment, while the third occupies the Puttúr lines to the north-west, the European troops being stationed in the centre.

CHAPTER I GENERAL FEATURES, &c.

The Collector's Office is held in a building formerly used as a dwelling house, but which has been considerably enlarged and improved since it was purchased by Government. It is a commodious building, and on the whole well suited for the purposes to which it is applied. The Municipal Office is located in a small building close to it in the same compound. The Court of the District and Session Judge is held in a large building close to the Uyyakondán channel, which was also formerly a private residence. The Cantonment Magistrate and Small Cause Court Judge holds his office in the same building as the District Judge.

—Srírangam.

Srírangam is situated almost in the centre of the island of the same name, and about two miles north of Trichinopoly. The greater portion of the houses in the town are inside the walls of the temple, of which a full account is given in the chapter on ancient temples and buildings. An account of the Srírangam Municipality will be found in the chapter on municipalities. The Trichinopoly Taluq School, the only school of this description in the district, is held in Srírangam.

—Lálgudi.

Lálgudi, the head-quarters of the Deputy Tahsildar of the taluq, is situated twelve miles north-east of Trichinopoly on Road No. 20,

(6) Dr. Caldwell says that this name means literally "The city of habitation." It is mentioned in Ptolemy's Geography as 'Ορθοῦρα.—CALDWELL'S *Dravidian Grammar*, Introduction, pages 17 and 96.

(7) Letter from Collector of Trichinopoly to Board of Revenue, dated November 27th, 1803.

CHAPTER I. GENERAL FEATURES, &c.

and at a distance of about half a mile from the point where it branches off from Road No. 4. The country round the village is highly irrigated and very fertile, and, as it is studded with tamarind, cocoanut and other trees, it has a green and cheerful appearance. In 1873 an office was built for the Deputy Tahsildar, on the new standard plan, within the limits of Sirudaiyúr village, at the place where Roads Nos. 4 and 20 meet. A sub-jail is attached to the building, and two latrines, a cooking room, an hospital building, and a ryots' shed have been erected in the compound round the central office building. The cost of the office and the several out-houses was Rupees 15,063. The hospital shed having been found to be perfectly useless for the object for which it had been intended, was converted into a building which it was proposed should serve as an office for the Special Sub-Registrar who is stationed at Lálgudi. This officer, however, has now been given a room in the main building, and has consequently not availed himself of the shed intended for him. The Police Station is located in Lálgudi itself, in the building formerly used as an office by the Magistrate. There is a Middle-class Anglo-Vernacular School at Lálgudi, which is well attended. Lálgudi seems to have been at one time fortified to some extent, for it is mentioned in Orme's History[8] as a mud fort. No traces of the walls are now to be found.

MUSIRI.

General features.

Musiri Taluq lies entirely to the north of the Cauvery. Its area is 667 square miles. The villages in this taluq along the north bank of the Cauvery, being well irrigated by channels from that river, are very fertile. The centre and northern portions of the taluq are, as a rule, unirrigated. In addition to the Cauvery, the only rivers of any importance in the taluq are the Ayyár and the Karaipottánár; the former of these rises in a gorge between the Pachamalais and Kollimalais, and receiving numerous tributaries from both these ranges of hills, after a course of about 30 miles falls into the Cauvery near the upper anicut. Of the tributaries of this river the best worth mentioning is the Taligai. The Karaipottánár flows through the Káttuputtúr mittah and a number of Government villages situated at the extreme west end of the taluq, and falls into the Cauvery.

The surface of the taluq is, as a rule, flat, the only range of hills in it being the Pachamalais, which separate it from Perambalúr Taluq. The Kollimalais form its boundary at the north-west corner, but they are entirely in the Salem District. South-west of the Kollimalais there is another hill, the Talamalai, which forms the

---

(8) ORME's *History of Hindustan*, Vol. I, page 222.

boundary of the district at one point, although it lies entirely outside it. This hill is frequently visited by Europeans from Trichinopoly, as the climate is much cooler than that of the plains, while the view from the summit is beautiful. Mr. Onslow, when Collector of Trichinopoly, had a small bungalow built on the top of this hill, and was in the habit of spending a portion of the hot weather there every year. On leaving the district he sold this bungalow to his late butler, whom he had appointed Tahsildar of Musiri, by whom it was sold to the Káttuputtúr mittahdar. The building is now completely in ruins. There is another small hill, not far from Musiri, called Tiruvéngimalai, that may be mentioned. It is situated a little north to the road from Musiri to Salem, and about three miles from the former place. It is about 270 feet high, and has a temple on the top, leading up to which there is a flight of 500 steps. A good view of the valley of the Cauvery may be obtained from the summit of this hill.

There is one zemindári in the taluq, that of Turaiyúr, which comprises 33 villages, and pays a merely nominal peishcush of only Rupees 700 a-year. The Káttuputtúr mittah in the south-western corner of the taluq has already been mentioned. It is the only estate of this description in the district, and was transferred from Salem in 1851. It comprises eight villages, and pays an annual peishcush of Rupees 15,901-7-11.

Cultivation.

The portion of the Musiri Taluq lying along the Cauvery River possesses a most fertile soil and excellent means of irrigation. The country north of the valley of the Cauvery and south of the Pachamalai hills is very uniform in character. The soil is black in the hollows, and red on the higher levels and in the neighborhood of the hills. Water is to be found, as a rule, near the surface, and both tanks and wells abound, especially in the Turaiyúr Zemindári. The principal grains grown in the taluq are paddy, chólum, cumbu, rági and horse-gram; varagu is found here and there, but it is not extensively cultivated. The staple food of the people in the villages all along the Cauvery is paddy. Further north dry grains, especially chólum and cumbu, are largely consumed. Statement No. 7-A in the appendix shows the extent of land in the taluq cultivated with each of the principal grains in Fasli 1285.

Rates of assessment.

The rates of assessment on irrigated lands range from 1 Rupee to Rupees 7, the greater portion of these lands being charged either Rupees 4-8-0, Rupees 5 or Rupees 6. The dry rates vary from 6 Annas to Rupees 3-8-0, one half of these lands in the taluq being assessed at 1 Rupee.

Irrigation

The principal sources of irrigation are the Cauvery, Ayyár and Karaipottánár. The following statement gives some details regard-

CHAPTER I. GENERAL FEATURES, &c.

ing the villages in the taluq irrigated by the more important of the channels from the Cauvery :—

No.	Name of Channel.	No. of Villages irrigated.	Ayakat.			
			Extent.		Assessment.	
			ACRES.	CTS.	RS.	A.
1	Náttuváykkál	9	1,850	97	10,915	3
2	Strínivásanallúr Channel	2	328	33	2,388	14
3	Tottiyam Periya Váykkál	8	1,311	99	8,012	9
4	Tottiyam Chinna Váykkál ..	12	1,562	69	10,139	7
5	Sípiláputtúr Channel ..	2	688	83	4,528	2

There are 53 tanks in the taluq, of which the most important are Jambéri, which has an ayakat of 1,147 acres, paying an assessment of 5,768 Rupees a year; the large irrigation tank in the Turaiyúr Zemindári, close to the head-quarter village, ayakat 386½ cawnies, assessment Rupees 3,066; Tirutalaiyúr tank, ayakat 614 acres, assessment Rupees 2,182; and Murungakalattúr, ayakat 766 acres, assessment Rupees 2,557. Statement No. 4, given in the appendix, shows the extent of land cultivated under each source of irrigation in the taluq and the assessment charged on it.

Revenue.

The following table gives the revenue derived from the different sources in the taluq during the last five years :—

Items.	Fasli 1281, 1871-72.	Fasli 1282, 1872-73.	Fasli 1283, 1873-74.	Fasli 1284, 1874-75.	Fasli 1285, 1875-76.
	RS.	RS.	RS.	RS.	RS.
Land Revenue ..	2,90,462	3,02,211	3,05,561	3,08,883	3,04,000
Miscellaneous ..	19,492	17,422	11,586	17,354	22,950
Abkári ..	17,500	15,200	15,200	15,200	1,650*
Stamps ..	5,905	6,922	7,600	7,012	7,281
Road Fund ..	28,506	28,346	28,138	28,585	28,507

Communications.

There is no line of railway through any portion of the taluq. The station on the South Indian Railway at Kulittalai is, however, almost exactly opposite the taluq head-quarters, and, as there is a ferry across the river at this point, there is a considerable amount of traffic from the taluq by this station. The Lálápéttai Station is very similarly situated with respect to Tottiyam, as there are ferries across the river from Kattapalli to Sípiláputtúr and from Katlai to Aiyalúr. The following are the principal lines of road in the taluq: Road No. 1 enters the taluq

* This refers to toddy alone, for the reason given in the notice of Trichinopoly Taluq.

at its eastern extremity and crosses it from east to west, passing through the head-quarters of the taluq and Tottiyam. From Tottiyam it runs in a north-west direction till it enters the Namakal Taluq of the Salem District, the last village in Musiri being Harikistnavári. It is in good order, and metalled and bridged throughout. Road No. 13 runs from Musiri direct to Turaiyúr, a distance of 18 miles. It is metalled and, with a few not very important exceptions, bridged throughout. A fine bridge on this road was built in 1873 over the Ayyár at Kannanúr, formerly the head-quarters of the Turaiyúr Taluq. Road No. 2 enters the taluq at its south-eastern corner and running right across it *viâ* Turaiyúr, enters the Ahtúr Taluq in the Salem District at its north-western extremity. This road is metalled, and is in fair order. Road No. 12 from Síppiláputtúr to Válayapatti in Salem District *viâ* Káttuputtúr. This road is under construction, the portion from Káttuputtúr to the border of the Trichinopoly District having alone been finished. It is hoped that it may be possible to induce the Salem Local Fund Board to extend it from the point where it enters their circle to Válayapatti on Road No. 1. It has been proposed to extend Road No. 13 from Turaiyúr to Perambalúr. At present there is only a bandy-track, which in wet weather is almost impassable, between these two important villages.

Public bungalows. There are at present no public bungalows in the taluq. The building at Tottiyam, on Road No. 1, formerly used as a public bungalow, on the abolition of the old Public Bungalow Fund, was handed over to the Public Works Department to be used as a store-shed and inspection bungalow. The question of transferring this building from that department to the Local Fund Board is under consideration. There was formerly a public bungalow at Musiri, but that building is now used by the Head Assistant Collector as an office.

Fairs and markets. The following are the weekly fairs held in the taluq: at Chettikulam, at the foot of Subramaniaswámi hill, on Sunday, and at Eragudi on the same day; at Tottiyam on Tuesday; at Musiri on Wednesday; at Kannanúr, on the bank of the Ayyár river, on Thursday; and at the foot of Perumálmalai near Turaiyúr on Saturday.

Principal towns. The most important villages in the taluq are—Musiri, population 4,018; Nágayanallúr, population 3,337; Uppiliyapuram, population 3,234; Tiruppangal, an Inám village, population 3,489; Káttuputtúr, in the mittah of the same name, population 4,331; Turaiyúr, the residence of the zemindár of the same name, population 6,308; and Kírambúr and Sikkitambúr in the same zemindári, population 4,445 and 3,670 respectively. Of these villages Musiri and Turaiyúr are the only places of any importance.

CHAPTER I. GENERAL FEATURES, &c. —Musiri.

Musiri, the head-quarters of the Tahsildar of the taluq, is a moderate, sized village, situated on the Cauvery, almost exactly opposite to Kulittalai. Since 1867 it has also been the head-quarters of the Head Assistant Collector and Magistrate, whose division comprehends the two taluqs of Musiri and Kulittalai. It is also the head-quarters of the officer of the Public Works Department in charge of No. 2 Range. Musiri is a neat and healthy village, but it is a place of no importance whatever, and was selected as the divisional officer's head-quarters probably because of its central position in the division. The taluq office is an old one. It is, however, in good order, and the accommodation in it is sufficient. A sub-jail, with a latrine and cooking-room and an hospital building, now used as a resting-place for persons who come to the office, were added to the building in 1872. The Police Station was in a small thatched building opposite the taluq office till quite lately, but it has now been removed into the centre-room in the sub-jail building. In 1874 the Local Fund Board determined to open a small hospital in Musiri, and built a thatched house for the Hospital Assistant in charge. The dispensary is at present held in a portion of the old public bungalow, but it is intended eventually to locate it in a suitable building, which it is proposed to erect as soon as the necessary funds are forthcoming. The Local Fund Board has promised to assist, and it is hoped that it may be possible to raise a considerable sum from the wealthy landholders in and about the village. An imposing-looking Roman Catholic Chapel was built here in 1876. In the same year the Local Fund Board did a good deal towards the general improvement of the village: dust-bins and latrines were erected, the principal roads were gravelled, culverts were built, and the side-drains cleared out. Up to this the condition of the village roads had been very bad. In 1875 three flights of steps leading down to the Cauvery for the convenience of the villagers in washing and getting drinking-water were built by funds raised by the Tahsildar from local subscriptions, assisted by the Local Fund Board.

—Turaiyúr.

Turaiyur, the head-quarters of a Deputy Tahsildar and Sub-Magistrate, is the largest village in the taluq. The head-quarters of the old Turaiyúr Taluq was Kannanúr, a village six miles from Turaiyúr on the road to Musiri. The office in Turaiyúr was formerly held in an old mantapam, but a new building, on the standard plan, was erected in 1874 a little to the south of the village, by the side of the road from Musiri. There is a sub-jail attached to the office, and in the compound two latrines, one for the use of the prisoners in the sub-jail and one for the general public, a cooking-room, and a shed for persons who come to the office to wait in, have been built. The cost of the several buildings, including compensation for the land taken up for them, was Rupees 12,043.

There is an Anglo-Vernacular Grant-in-Aid School, which is held in a building belonging to the zemindár. A good deal was done for the improvement of the village in 1876. The large *teppakulam*, the water of which is used by the greater part of the villagers for drinking, was cleared out at the expense of the villagers with the assistance of the zemindár, two latrines were built near the town by the Local Fund Board, and the roads were put in order. Not far from the *teppakulam* just mentioned, there is a very fine irrigation tank, which, however, is unfortunately very much out of repair at present. In the centre of this tank there is a curious and picturesque building three stories high, in which the zemindárs used formerly to live for short periods when the tank was full of water. It is now out of repair and rapidly falling into ruins. The house in which the zemindár lives is an ordinary building, of no interest whatever either from an historical or architectural point of view. The house in which the zemindárs formerly lived was pulled down by the present owner in 1868 because he had quarrelled with his adoptive mother who used to live there, and in consequence had taken a dislike to the building.

THE PACHAMALAI HILLS.

General features.

The Pachamalai, or Green Hills, are situated partly in Musiri and partly in Perumbalúr Taluq. A small portion of the range is in Salem District. These hills are the most important in the district, but they do not reach a greater elevation than about 2,000 feet, or in some parts 2,500 feet above the level of the sea. Their greatest length from north to south is about 20 miles, measuring to the extremities of the spurs at either end. In shape the range has a slight resemblance to an hour-glass, being nearly cut in two by ravines of great size and depth opening to the north-east and south-west. Of the two parts into which the range is thus divided, the north-eastern is the larger, and, as a rule, reaches a higher level than the south-eastern. Besides the rambling shape of the range, its most striking physical feature is the great steepness of the western slopes compared with those on the east, which are rarely precipitous, and are broken by several long spurs which project far into the low country.[9] The climate of the Pachamalais is notoriously feverish and unhealthy. No inhabitant of the plains, whether Native or European, can sleep a night on them without being almost certain to get a bad attack of fever.

Natural products.

As the hills are ascended from the Musiri side they are found to be covered on the slopes with jungle, consisting principally of usilai (*Acacia amara*) ; higher up the jungle becomes denser, and bamboo trees are to be seen intermixed with dense masses of

(9) Memoirs of the Geological Survey of India, Vol. IV, Part II, page 16.

Chapter I. General Features, &c.

thorny bushes. On the summit there are, in parts, forests of considerable extent, consisting of véngai (*Pterocarpus marsupium*), teak (*Tectona grandis*), blackwood (*Dalbergia latifolia*), and sandalwood (*Santalum album*). In the interior the hills are covered with a dense jungle with bamboos through it. Round the scattered villages to be found on the hills patches of land have been cleared, in which cumbu, chólum, rági, varagu, castor-oil, pumpkins and beans are cultivated in small quantities. The jack tree (*Artocarpus integrifolius*) is also extensively grown in these villages. The system of cultivation is the same as is found to prevail on other hill-ranges A few acres of jungle are burnt and cleared, the ground scratched up, and a few seeds scattered. The first season a fair crop is obtained, the second year the crop is inferior, and in the third season it is scarcely worth gathering. The field is then deserted and another patch cleared in the same manner, the relinquished land not being returned to till ten or twelve years have elapsed. If the hills are ascended from Arumbavár in the Perumbalúr Taluq, a dense bamboo jungle with véngai and small teak trees through it will be met with.[10] In addition to what has been already mentioned, the principal products of the hills are gall-nuts, a bark called vémbádam-pattai, from which a red dye is extracted, the fruit of the hill gooseberry (*Rhodomyrtus tomentosa*) and honey.

Area and population.

The hills have never been surveyed, and their area cannot be ascertained with any approach to accuracy. In Fasli 1286 (1876-77) 5,179 acres were held on puttah, but this does not by any means represent the area over which cultivation extends, as under the system of cultivation prevailing there, an account of which has been already given, the same land is cultivated for not more than two or three years running, and is then allowed to lie fallow. As a rule, about an equal extent of land is taken up and relinquished each year. For example, in Fasli 1281 lands assessed at Rupees 1,087 were abandoned and lands paying Rupees 1,037 newly taken up. There are three villages on the hills: Vannádu, with 27 hamlets attached to it; Tembaranádu, with 20 hamlets; and Kómbai, with 6 hamlets. The population of these villages, according to the census of 1871, amounted to 13,413 persons. It is very doubtful, however, if this return can be depended on, as it was taken by the village karnams, who very seldom visit the hills, and most certainly made no attempt to go through the villages, house to house, on the occasion of the census being taken.

Assessment.

The cultivated land on the hills is divided into two classes: ulavukádu, land capable of being ploughed, and punalkádu, or

(10) Letter from Deputy Conservator of Forests to Collector, No. 253, dated 5th February 1873.

CHAPTER I. GENERAL FEATURES, &c.

land which cannot be ploughed and the cultivation of which is carried on by grain being dribbled in among trees and rocks wherever a few feet of soil is to be found. The former of these descriptions of land pays 8 Annas and the latter 4 Annas an acre. The produce of the hill forests, excluding grain and the produce of the fruit-trees, was formerly rented out by Government, but latterly a seigniorage has been collected by rangers appointed for the purpose on all fuel, charcoal, bamboos, &c. brought down from the hills. By this means Rupees 3,089-4-2 were realized in the five years from 1868 to 1873. The hill-tribes are allowed to cut whatever wood they may require for domestic purposes. A tax is also raised on the honey produced on the hills, from which about 60 Rupees a year is collected.

KULITTALAI.

General features.

The Kulittalai Taluq lies altogether to the south of the river Cauvery, which forms its northern boundary and separates it from Musiri Taluq. It is the largest taluq in the district, having an area of 930 square miles; its greatest length from north to south is 44 miles, and its greatest breadth from east to west 23 miles. A narrow strip of land in this taluq, running along the Cauvery and varying in breadth from one to two miles, is irrigated directly by channels from that river and is very fertile. With this exception, however, the taluq is, as a general rule, unirrigated and the soil by no means productive.

The northern and central portions of the taluq are flat, while the west and south-west are hilly in parts, and present a somewhat varied aspect. The wildest part of the taluq, and, indeed, of the whole district, is the Kadavúr Zemindári, which lies to the extreme south-west of the taluq. The village of Kadavúr is situated in the south of the zemindári, and is completely surrounded by hills, none of which, however, attain to any great altitude. Although all this portion of the taluq is covered with hills, there is no range of any importance to be found in it. The principal one is that called Semmalai, running through the south-western portion of the taluq, the most remarkable peak in which is that known as Tékkamalai. Two of the large bosses of gneiss with which the district is studded are to be found in Kulittalai Taluq; one of these, called Ratnagiri, is within the limits of Siváyam village, close to the road from Kulittalai to Manapparai, and about five miles distant from the former place. A flight of 952 steps leads up to the top of this hill, which commands a magnificent view of the surrounding country. There is a small temple dedicated to Siva on the summit, an inscription on which states that these steps and the wall round the temple were constructed in S. S. 1710

CHAPTER I. GENERAL FEATURES, &c.

(A.D. 1788). The other, close to Tógamalai, does not rise to nearly so great a height. The southern portion of the taluq, consisting of the zemindári of Marungápuri and 32 Government villages, comprised the old Manapparai Taluq, and was transferred from Madura to Trichinopoly in 1856.

Cultivation.

In the portion of the taluq irrigated by the Cauvery the soil is very fertile, as it is enriched by river-deposit. In the few villages to the extreme west of the taluq, irrigated by the Ambrávati, the soil is not so good, as that river does not appear to possess the fertilizing qualities of the Cauvery. The supply is also irregular and scanty, and the land has constantly to be left waste for want of water. In the centre and south of the taluq the soil is very poor, and is impregnated to a great extent with soda and saltpetre. The principal grains grown in the taluq are rice, chólum and cumbu; rági, horse-gram, varagu and dholl are also cultivated, but not to as great an extent as the other grains just mentioned. In the irrigated portions of the taluq rice is the staple food of the inhabitants, but in the Manapparai Division the people, as a rule, live on chólum and cumbu. But little grain is exported from, or imported into, the taluq. Statement No. 7-A, given in the appendix, shows the actual extent of land cultivated with each description of grain in the taluq in Fasli 1285.

Irrigation.

The principal sources of irrigation in the taluq are the Cauvery, Ambrávati and Mámundi rivers. The following statement gives some particulars regarding the villages irrigated by the principal channels from the Cauvery :—

No.	Names of Channels.	No of Villages irrigated.	Ayakat. Government Lands. Extent.		Assessment.	
			ACRES.	CTS.	RS.	A.
1	Marudúr Náttu Váykkál	21	5,526	89	37,423	14
2	Mahádánapuram do.	4	945	68	6,707	1
3	Kristnarayapuram Náttu Váykkál ..	6	1,227	30	7,353	6
4	Katlai Váykkál	4	1,587	67	3,834	7
5	Nangapuram Váykkál	4	2,041	99	10,848	14

There are 307 tanks in the taluq; none of them, however, are of any great importance. The two largest tanks in the taluq are Maravanúr, with an ayakat of 378 acres, paying an assessment of Rupees 957 per annum; and Sevalúr (supplied from the Mámundi river), ayakat 266 acres, assessment Rupees 666. Both these tanks are in the Manapparai Division. There are a large number of tanks, some of which are of considerable size, in this division; but they are, as a general rule, much silted up and in bad order, and, owing to the deficiency of their water-supply, it would not pay to repair them. Only a small portion of the ayakat under these tanks is, as a rule, cultivated, and of the crops sown a large part is withered every year. The cultivators are a hardy race, but they are miserably poor and have been impoverished by frequent bad seasons. In fact a good season in Manapparai, either for the dry crops or the wet under tanks, is a very rare occurrence.

Statement No. 4, given in the appendix, shows the extent of land under the several sources of irrigation in the taluq, and the assessment charged on it.

Rates of assessment.

The rate of assessment charged on wet lands in the taluq range from 1 Rupee to Rupees 6-8-0 per acre, the greater portion of the irrigated fields under the Cauvery being charged Rupees 5, 5-8-0, or 6, while those under the Ambrávati are assessed at Rupees 2-8-0. The rates on dry lands vary from 14 Annas to Rupees 2-12-0, almost one half of the lands of this nature in the taluq being charged only 6 Annas per acre.

Revenue.

The following table gives the revenue derived from the different sources in the Kulittalai Taluq for the last five years :—

Items.	Fasli 1281, 1871-72.	Fasli 1282, 1872-73.	Fasli 1283, 1873-74.	Fasli 1284, 1874-75.	Fasli 1285, 1875-76.
	RS.	RS.	RS.	RS.	RS.
Land Revenue ..	1,78,172	1,85,654	1,86,419	1,85,367	1,85,720
Miscellaneous ..	23,834	12,315	9,586	10,399	11,630
Abkári	12,500	11,104	11,100	11,100	2,030*
Stamps	9,829	11,450	15,253	18,112	24,351
Road Fund	22,937	18,620	22,633	22,031	21,737

Communications.

The Kulittalai Taluq is on the whole well provided with roads and other means of communication, and is especially fortunate in being traversed in two directions by a railway. The line from Erode to Trichinopoly runs through the taluq from west to east, and has stations within its limits at Katalai, Lálápéttai and Kulittalai. The southern portion of the South Indian Railway crosses the taluq from north-east to south-west, running through the Manapparai Division. The stations on the line in Kulittalai Taluq are Manapparai and Vaiyampatti. The following are the roads at present kept up in the taluq: Road No. 11, from Trichinopoly to Karúr, known as the Karúr road, crosses the taluq from east to west, running through the Kasbah station. This road is metalled and bridged throughout. Road No. 25, from

* This refers to toddy alone, for the reason already given.

CHAPTER I. GENERAL FEATURES, &c.

Kulittalai to Kóvilpatti *viâ* Manapparai. This road is metalled throughout and is fairly well provided with bridges and culverts, except that a bridge is required over the Mámundi river at the point where this road and the Dindigul road meet and cross this river about a mile north of Manapparai. Road No. 10, from Trichinopoly to Dindigul, known as the Dindigul road, traverses the south-eastern portion of the taluq, running through Manapparai: It is metalled throughout, but a few more bridges are much required on it. The Madura road, No. 9, from Trichinopoly to Madura, also traverses a small portion of the south-eastern extremity of the taluq, running through Kóvilpatti and Tuverankurichi. A small branch road has been lately constructed by the Local Fund Board, leading from the Madura road to Marungápuri, the place of residence of the zemindár of the same name. There are remains of what must have been once a fine road from Manapparai to Tuverankurichi *viâ* Puttánattam. This road runs through that portion of the taluq that was transferred from Madura, and it is generally believed that it is one of the many roads that were laid out under the orders of Mr. Blackburn, when Collector of that district. It also appears to be on the whole probable that the main road from Trichinopoly to Madura formerly took this line. In 1877 the portion of this road from Manapparai to Puttánattam was put in order by the Local Fund Board, and it has been proposed that, as soon as funds are available, the remainder should be repaired as far as Tuverankurichi. In 1876 a short road, intended as a railway feeder, was made from the Dindigul road to the Vaiyampatti railway station. There are no roads in the Kadavúr Zemindári. There are two bandy tracks, each about nine miles long, leading to Kadavúr village, one of which runs from Vaiyampatti, and the other from Aiyalúr in Madura District. These tracks are utterly impassable to spring carts, and it is only with great difficulty that an ordinary country-cart can be got over them.

Public bungalows.

There are public bungalows in the taluq kept up for the accommodation of travellers at Kóvilpatti and Tuverankurichi on the Madura road, and at Manapparai on the Dindigul road. The buildings at Manavási on the Karúr road and Pudupálayam, close to the road from Kulittalai to Manapparai, and about 1½ miles from the former village, are at present under the charge of the Public Works Department. In addition to these, there were formerly public bungalows at Nangapuram and Kalpatti. The former of these buildings is on the old Karúr road, which crosses the taluq at a distance of about one mile south of the present line. When the old line was abandoned it became of no use, and was accordingly sold. The bungalow at Kalpatti was handed over to the Police Department to be used as a station-house in 1876.

Fair and markets.

The following are the weekly fairs held in the several villages in the taluq: on Sunday at Pothampatti in the Kadavúr Zemindári, Kóvilpatti in the Marungápuri Zemindári and at Kulittalai itself; on Monday at Valanádu in the Marungápuri Zemindári, Nangapuram and Chintámanipatti in the Kadavúr Zemindári; on Tuesday at Kattapalli, close to the Katalai railway station, Aniyappúr and Puttánattam; on Wednesday at Manapparai, Nadupatti (near Kalpatti), and Kosúr; on Thursday at Periyapatti; on Friday at Tógamalai and Pálaviduthi in the Kadavúr Zemindári; on Saturday at Siváyam, Elangákurichi and Tuverankurichi.

Principal towns.

The largest towns in the taluq are Mahádánapuram, population 6,016; Vaiganallár, attached to Kulittalai, population 3,048; Nangapuram, population 4,264; Sevalúr, of which Manapparai, the head-quarters of the Deputy Tahsildar, is a hamlet, population 3,113; Reddiyapatti, of which Elangákurichi is a hamlet, population 2,752; Kílappagudi, in the Kadavúr Zemindári, population 3,915. The largest village in the Marungápuri Zemindári, according to the census returns, is Ponnampatti, of which Tuverankurichi is a hamlet, population 2,566; Kulittalai, the head-quarters of the Tahsildar of the taluq, has a population of only 1,398; but, if the population of Vaiganallúr, Manattattai, Muttubúpálasamudram and the Inám Village Kadambarkóvil, which are attached to Kulittalai, and in reality form with it one town, are added, the total is raised to 7,071.

—Kulittalai.

Kulittalai, the head-quarters of the Tahsildar of the taluq and a railway station, is situated on the river Cauvery. The greater part of the land round the village is highly cultivated, and there are numerous clumps of cocoanut and other trees in and about it. This gives the place a green and fresh appearance, especially as the village is one of the neatest and best laid out in the district. The village streets are on the whole good. In 1876-77 the Local Fund Board had a number of them gravelled and the side-drains cleared out. In the same year a good deal was done for the sanitation of the town, and two latrines and thirty dust-bins were built. The Tahsildar's Office is prettily situated in an open piece of ground, surrounded by cocoanut trees, close to the Karúr road, between Kulittalai and Kadambarkóvil. It was built in 1875, according to the new standard plan, at a cost of Rupees 28,616-7-8. A sub-jail is attached to it, and in the compound there are a ryot's shed, a sub-jail, cooking-room and latrine, and a public latrine. The old taluq office in the centre of the village is used as the Anglo-Vernacular Grant-in-Aid School-house. The Police Station is close to it. Kulittalai is the head-quarters of a District Munsif, whose jurisdiction extends over the taluqs of Musiri and Kulittalai

CHAPTER I. GENERAL FEATURES, &c.

and a portion of Trichinopoly. His court is held in a building formerly used as a private dwelling house, for which a monthly rent is paid. Up to 1874 the Tahsildars of Musiri and Kulittalai were Sub-Registrars for their respective taluqs. In that year the registration work was taken from them, and a special Sub-Registrar appointed, with jurisdiction over the whole of the two taluqs, exclusive of the portions under the Sub-Registrars at Turaiyúr and Manapparai. His head-quarters are at Kulittalai.

—Manapparai.

Manapparai, the head-quarters of the Deputy Tahsildar of the taluq, is a hamlet of Sevalúr and a very small village, with a population of only 318 persons. It is, however, a station on the South Indian Railway Extension Line, and this, added to the fact that it is the Deputy Tahsildar's head-quarters, has of late made the place of some little importance. The Deputy Tahsildar's Office is built on the old standard plan. A sub-jail forms a portion of the building, and there are an hospital shed and a sub-jail, cooking-room, and latrine in the office compound. The Police Station is located in the Deputy Tahsildar's Office, and the lines are close to it. There is a chattram in the village, which was repaired by the Local Fund Board in 1874, and is of great use to travellers. Up to 1877 the village site and all the land round Manapparai were grown over with prickly-pear to an extent scarcely to be equalled in any other village in the district. In that year, however, the plant was completely removed, and the village has now a cheerful and neat appearance. The public bungalow in Manapparai is the only one in the district that was not built by the English. It has a lofty circular dome, and resembles in its style of architecture the large hall in the building in Trichinopoly, known as the Nawáb's palace. It is, however, of course, on a much smaller scale. The building appears to be of Hindu origin, and is said to have been built by Mangammál[11] as a chattram.

Seven miles north-east of Manapparai, and about two miles off the Dindigul road in the village of Kuppanárpatti, a hamlet of Periyapatti, the remains of a small military station are to be found, which appear worthy of mention. The ruins consist of two buildings, evidently once used as barracks for European troops and quarters for their officers, stables, a magazine, a guard-room, and three wells. The ground on which these buildings have been erected rises considerably above the surrounding plain, and is about 10 acres in extent. It is evident that it was once fortified to some degree, and it is probable that it was an outlying-station from the garrison in Trichinopoly, used to keep the wild tribes in the zemindáries in order.

(11) Mangammál governed Madura and Trichinopoly as regent towards the close of the Náyak dynasty.

CHAPTER I.
GENERAL FEATURES, &c.

PERAMBALUR.

General features.

Perambalúr Taluq lies between Musiri and Udaiyárpálayam Taluqs, and to the north of Trichinopoly Taluq, by which it is bounded on the south, while the river Vellár forms its northern boundary and separates it from Salem and South Arcot Districts. It has an area of 690 square miles, its greatest breadth from west to east being 21 miles and its length from north to south 42 miles. The general aspect of the taluq is flat, the north-western portion being, however, more rugged and hilly than the rest. There are no mountains or hills in it of any importance, with the exception of the Pachamalais, which separate it from Musiri and run for a short distance into the taluq. Twenty-two villages of the Ariyalúr Zemindári are in Perambalúr, but the rest of the taluq, with the exception of nine inám villages, is held directly under Government on ryotwári tenure.

Cultivation.

From the Pachamalai hills along the banks of the Vellár and stretching up as far as the Udaiyárpálayam Taluq, there is a continued plain of black cotton soil, in which there are large tracts of stiff black clay. In the southern portion of the taluq bordering on Trichinopoly, the country is rocky and the soil, as a rule, poor. Perambalúr is one of the Kádárambam, or upland taluqs, and there is but little irrigated land in it. Only two villages are directly irrigated by channels from the Vellár, but the tanks in a few other villages get their supply from this river. There are two affluents of the Vellár that irrigate a small portion of the taluq. Across one of these, the Kallár, two calingulas have been built for the irrigation of Vembávúr and Kottattúr villages. The other, the Chinnár, rises in the Pachamalai hills in the limits of Ládapuram village, and falls into the Vellár at Kalingaráyanallúr. Across it three calingulas have been built, from which water is taken off for the supply of the tanks in some of the neighboring villages. There is a considerable extent of cultivation under tanks in the taluq. The most important of these tanks are the Attiyúr tank, with a cultivated area under it of 607 acres, paying a yearly assessment of Rupees 3,411 ; Okalúr tank, ayakat 649 acres and assessment Rupees 4,645 ; and the tank in Arumbávúr, ayakat 398 acres and assessment Rupees 2,136. Statement No. 4, given in the appendix, shows the extent of land under each source of irrigation, and the assessment charged on it. Less rice is grown in Perambalúr than in any other taluq in the district. The principal dry grains cultivated there are varagu, rági and cumbu. 24,000 acres are under cotton, being half of the total area on which this crop is raised in the whole district. Chólum, dholl and horse-gram are also grown to a slight extent. Statement No. 7-A, given in the appendix, shows the extent of land in the taluq cultivated with all the principal crops in Fasli 1285.

CHAPTER I. GENERAL FEATURES, &c.

Rates of assessment.

The rates of assessment charged on wet lands in Perambalúr vary from Rupees 1-12-0 to Rupees 7-4-0, only 23 acres, however, being assessed at the higher rate, while the mass of the irrigated land in the taluq pays 4 Annas an acre. The rates on dry lands range between 4 Annas and Rupees 3-8-0, the great bulk of the land of this description being charged at rates varying from 7 Annas to Rupees 1-12-0.

Revenue.

The following table gives the revenue derived from the several sources of irrigation in Perambalúr Taluq in the last five years :—

Items.	Fasli 1281, 1871-72.	Fasli 1282, 1872-73.	Fasli 1283, 1873-74.	Fasli 1284, 1874-75.	Fasli 1285, 1875-76.
	RS.	RS.	RS.	RS.	RS.
Land Revenue ..	2,41,553	2,26,440	2,26,061	2,25,173	2,35,494
Miscellaneous ..	10,972	20,573	13,148	14,522	18,369
Abkári	12,801	8,000	8,003	8,003	530*
Stamps	14,056	12,731	25,599	20,687	17,934
Road Fund	20,309	20,137	18,159	19,079	20,014

Communications.

There are only two roads of any importance in Perambalúr. Road No. 3, from Trichinopoly to Madras, traverses the taluq from south to north, passing through Perambalúr and Válikandapuram villages. It is in good order, and metalled and bridged throughout. Road No. 15 connects Ariyalúr and Perambalúr, and then crossing through the north-west portion of the taluq, enters the Ahtúr Taluq in Salem District. It is not metalled or bridged, and, as it runs for the most part through cotton soil, it is by no means a pleasant road to travel over in the rainy season.

Public bungalows.

There are at present no public bungalows in the taluq. The question of transferring the bungalows at Toramangalam, close to Perambalúr, and Válikandapuram, which are at present under the Public Works Department, to the Local Fund Board is under consideration. There was formerly another public bungalow at Úttattúr, a village in the south of the taluq, on the old trunk road to Madras. When, however, the line of the road was changed, this bungalow became of no use to travellers, and it was accordingly sold in 1861 to the S. P. G. Mission at Irungalúr, by whom it is used as a place of worship.

Fairs.

Weekly fairs are held at the following places in Perambalúr Taluq : at Siruvachúr every Monday; at Perambalúr itself on Tuesday; and at Kristnapuram on Wednesday.

Principal towns.

The most important villages in Perambalúr Taluq are Kurumbalúr, population 5,112; Perambalúr, population 3,186; Arumbávúr, population 2,466; and Válikandapuram, population 1,165.

* This refers to toddy alone, for the reasons already given.

Kurumbalúr, the largest town in the taluq, is situated at a distance of about five miles from Perambalúr. It is noted for the ornamental vessels and plates of brass and zinc inlaid with silver and copper that are made there. Perambalúr, the head-quarters of the Tahsildar of the taluq, is situated almost in the centre of the taluq on the old trunk road (No. 3) from Trichinopoly to Madras. The Taluq Office is on the old plan, and is the worst in the district. An estimate has been sanctioned for the construction of a new office, but the building has not as yet been commenced. Perambalúr is also the head-quarters of a District Munsif, whose jurisdiction extends over Udaiyárpálayam and Perambalúr Taluqs. The village is considered an unhealthy one and is greatly disliked by native officials. They principally complain of the water-supply, which is very indifferent. Válikandapuram, the place that saw Váli, was the head-quarters of a taluq that comprised the northern portion of the present Perambalúr Taluq till the introduction of Mr. Pelly's scheme in 1861. It is now an unimportant village, although sacred in the eyes of Hindus as the place where legends say that Ráma met Váli when on his way to Ceylon. It is frequently mentioned in Orme's History as one of the most important forts on the main road from Madras to Trichinopoly.

UDAIYÁRPÁLAYAM.

General features.

The Udaiyárpálayam Taluq lies to the extreme north-east of the district. It is bordered on the north and south by the rivers Vellár and Coleroon respectively, on the east by the Chidambaram Taluq in South Arcot, and on the west by Perambalúr Taluq. Its area is 777 square miles, its greatest breadth from south-west to north-east being 45 miles, and its greatest length from north to south 29 miles. The general aspect of the taluq is flat, and there are no mountains or even hills of any importance to be found in it. Of the total area of the taluq 222 square miles are included in the Udaiyárpálayam and Ariyalúr Zemindáries, of which the former is entirely in this taluq, while the latter is divided between it and Perambalúr.

Cultivation.

The soil in Udaiyárpálayam is for the most part a mixture of red sand and clay. There are, however, strips of black soil running along the banks of the Vellár and Coleroon rivers, and to the west of the taluq and throughout the greater part of the Ariyalúr Zemindári the soil is black cotton, thinly spread over a substratum of limestone. About 13,750 acres in the taluq are covered with a jungle of low brushwood. There is but little wet cultivation in the taluq. The principal dry grains raised are varagu, cumbu and rági, and of these the two former are the staple food of the people. Dholl, horse-gram, gingelly oil seed and indigo are

CHAPTER I. GENERAL FEATURES, &c.

also grown. Statement No. 7-A, given in the appendix, shows the extent of land in the taluq cultivated with each of the principal grains in Fasli 1285. There is but little exportation or importation of grain, but large quantities of firewood are carried for sale from different parts of the taluq to Combaconum and other villages in Tanjore District. To such an extent indeed is the exportation of this article carried on, that the jungles with which the country is covered, especially those in the Udaiyárpálayam Zemindári, are rapidly becoming denuded.

Rates of assessment —Irrigation.

The rates of assessment on irrigated lands in the taluq vary from Rupees 2-4-0 to Rupees 5. The Ponnéri channel from the Coleroon irrigates 17 villages, the greater part of the land under it being assessed at Rupees 3-12-0. The Kandrádittam channel, taken off at the Nandaiyár anicut in Trichinopoly Taluq, irrigates seven villages. The tank-irrigated lands in the taluq, which are, as a rule, poor, are for the most part assessed at 3—4 an acre. The most important of these tanks are the Kandrádittam tank, with an ayakat of 749 acres, paying an assessment of Rupees 2,654 per annum; the tank in Srípurandán village, ayakat 411 acres, assessment Rupees 1,765; and Sukra tank in Kámarasavalli village, ayakat 551 acres, assessment Rupees 1,644. An anicut is under construction across the Vellár at Peländorai, which will irrigate four villages in this taluq. There are near the village of Gangaikandapuram the remains of what must have been once a magnificent tank scarcely inferior to the Víránam tank in South Arcot District. The embankment of this gigantic reservoir, extending almost across the taluq from north to south, and about 16 miles in length, is still to be seen. It appears to have been supplied with two channels, one from the Coleroon, which entered it at the southern end, and another smaller one from the Vellár, which flowed in at the north end. Traces of these channels remain, but the tank has been abandoned for years, and the bed is now almost entirely over-grown with jungle. An account of a remarkable pagoda near Gangaikandapuram is given in Chapter XXI, Statement No. 4, given in the appendix, shows the extent of land cultivated under each source of irrigation, and the assessment charged on it. The rates of dry assessment in this taluq vary from 10 Annas to Rupees 3-8-0, more than two-thirds of the dry land being charged 1 Rupee per acre. The dry lands in the taluq are, as a rule, indifferent. There are, however, some lands along the Coleroon bank and the South Arcot frontier, where the soil being compounded of black sand and loam, is superior to those found in the rest of the taluq.

Revenue.

The following table gives the revenue derived from the different sources of irrigation in the taluq during the last five years :—

CHAPTER I.
GENERAL FEATURES, &c.

Items.	Fasli 1281, 1871-72	Fasli 1282, 1872-73.	Fasli 1283, 1873-74.	Fasli 1284, 1874-75.	Fasli 1285, 1875-76.
	RS.	RS.	RS.	RS.	RS.
Land Revenue. ..	2,14,295	2,11,944	2,15,278	2,17,759	2,10,852
Miscellaneous ..	10,929	16,922	10,910	13,295	21,396
Abkári	14,508	8,001	8,000	8,001	530*
Stamps	1,773	1,667	1,969	2,378	2,911
Road Fund	19,663	19,312	22,059	23,080	23,185

Communications.

The following are the principal roads in the taluq : Road No. 6, from Trichinopoly to Mannárgudi in South Arcot, traverses the taluq from west to east, passing through Kílapaluvúr, Udaiyárpálayam, Jeyamkondasólapuram, and Gangaikandapuram; Road No. 15, from Tirumánúr to Kristnápuram in the Perambalúr Taluq, on the confines of the Ahtúr Taluq in Salem District, crosses the taluq from south to north-west. It starts from Tirumánúr on the Coleroon, and passes through Kílapaluvúr and Ariyalúr ; Road No. 17, from Madanakurichi *viâ* Jeyamkondasólapuram to Rajéndrapatnam, also traverses the taluq from south to north; Road No. 18, the Combaconum trunk road, from Combaconum to Madras, crosses the eastern extremity of the taluq. This is the only road in the taluq that is metalled. Road No. 20 runs along the bank of the Coleroon, from the lower anicut as far as Vappúr. It is intended that this road should eventually be extended as far as Sengaraiyúr in Trichinopoly Taluq, so as to meet the road from Sirudaiyúr to that village. There are no public bungalows in the taluq. There are only two weekly fairs in this taluq ; one of these is held every Sunday at Ariyalúr, and the other every Monday at Jeyamkondasólapuram.

The most important villages in the taluq are Udaiyárpálayam, population 5,879; Ariyalúr, population 5,852; Jeyamkondasólapuram, population 2,729; Vilandai, population 3,263, and Kílapaluvúr, population 1,750.

Principal town—Jeyamkondasólapuram.

Jeyamkondasólapuram or the city of the Victorious Chóla, the head-quarters of the Tahsildar of the taluq, is situated on Road No. 6, about five miles north-east of Udaiyárpálayam. The village is an unimportant one, and the people in it are poor. The Tahsildar's Office is on the old standard plan, but a new sub-jail and out-houses have been built round it recently. The Taluq Sheristadar is Sub-Registrar for the whole taluq. There are two curious Jain figures to be seen in the village, an account of which is given in Chapter XXI.

—Ariyalúr.

Ariyalúr is a more important place. It is the head-quarters of the Deputy Collector and Magistrate of the district, whose charge comprises the taluqs of Perambalúr and Udaiyárpálayam.

* This refers to toddy alone, for the reasons already given.

CHAPTER I. GENERAL FEATURES, &c.

It is also the chief village in the Ariyalúr Zemindári and the residence of the zemindár. The so-called palace in which he lives is, however, a miserable building, almost in ruins. A commodious office was built for the Deputy Collector in Ariyalúr in 1875, at a cost of Rupees 4,098-9-11. Up till then that officer had to hold his court in an old mantapam. There is also a Branch Post Office and a Local Funds School in the village. The Local Fund Board have recently opened a small Branch Dispensary there under the medical supervision of an Hospital Assistant. Ariyalúr is a healthy town, but its appearance is dreary, and there is nothing of any interest connected with it. A considerable extent of the village site was covered with prickly-pear up till 1876, when it was removed by the Local Fund Board.

—Udaiyárpálayam.

Udaiyárpálayam is the place of residence of the zemindár of the same name. It is also the head-quarters of the Public Works Department Officer in charge of No. 3 Range, which consists of the taluq of Udaiyárpálayam alone. The village is a large one, but it is badly built, and there is nothing worthy of notice about it. What is known as the palace of the zemindár is an uninteresting building of no architectural beauty whatever.

—Kílapaluvúr.

Kílapaluvúr is situated on Road No. 6, and is distant 22 miles from Lálgudi and 23 from Jeyamkondasólapuram. It was formerly the head-quarters of a taluq, and is now of the Deputy Tahsildar of Udaiyárpálayam Taluq, which was transferred here from Rajéndrapatnam in 1873. The Deputy Tahsildar holds his court in a building on the old standard plan, formerly used as the taluq office. A sub-jail on the new plan and out-houses have been recently built near it. Kílapaluvúr is a small village, with nothing of historical or archæological interest about it. It is, however, prettily situated, and is a pleasanter camping-place than most of the villages in the taluq.

CHAPTER II.

GEOLOGY AND SOILS.

Introductory.—Part I, Plant-beds.—Part II, Úttattúr Group, Coral-reef Limestone.—Part III, Úttattúr Group, Úttattúr Beds.—Part IV, Trichinopoly Group.—Part V, Ariyalúr Group.—Part VI, Post-cretaceous Rocks (Cuddalore Sandstone).—Part VII, Metamorphic Rocks.—Part VIII, Crystalline Rocks.—Part IX, Superficial Deposits and Soils.—Part X, Economic Geology.

CHAPTER II. GEOLOGY AND SOILS.

Of the geology of Trichinopoly but little was known before the investigations of the officers of the Geological Survey of India in that part of the country commenced. Indeed, the Reverend Dr. Muzzy, of Madura, appears to have been the only geologist who travelled over the Trichinopoly District before their arrival, and his observations, however valuable, were almost necessarily fragmentary, his attention having been directed to the mineralogy and petrology of the district rather than to the elucidation of its geological structure. The Geological Survey of India began their researches in Trichinopoly in 1857, and concluded them in 1860. The following pages have been abridged, with slight alterations, from Volume IV, Part I, of their Memoirs by Mr. H. F. Blandford, and Part II by Messrs. W. King and R. Bruce Foote.

General conformation of the country.

The general geological conformation of the country is very simple. The greater part of the area is occupied by metamorphic rocks belonging to the gneiss family, and resting on these are three great groups of sedimentary rocks belonging to different geological periods, and overlying each other in regular succession from west to east. The first of these great groups belongs to the cretaceous era. Resting upon these cretaceous rocks are, secondly, a group of rocks whose exact age has not as yet been determined owing to the absence of organic remains, but which are provisionally distinguished as the post-cretaceous rocks. Resting on these again are the beds of the fluvio-marine alluvium of the coast and river deltas. The sedimentary formations form great bands, running in a north-east by north to south-west by south direction, and widening generally as they extend southward.

Sedimentary rocks.

The igneous and older sedimentary rocks of the district, as regards their classification and mode of occurrence, will be described first. These sedimentary rocks comprise several distinct groups of deposits resting unconformably on each other and representing, in broken sequence, a long geologic period. As developed in Trichinopoly District they are five in number, three of which are

CHAPTER II. GEOLOGY AND SOILS.

undoubtedly of cretaceous age. Taken in descending order they may be enumerated as follow:—

Tertiary	.. ..	Cuddalore Sandstones,
Cretaceous	.. ..	The Ariyalúr Group, The Trichinopoly Group,
Doubtful	.. ..	The Úttattúr Group, The Úttattúr Plant-beds: plant remains and other fossils,

and to these may be added a very remarkable and interesting formation, the "coral-reef limestone," which occurs at a few points at the base of the Úttattúr Group, apparently formed under somewhat different conditions, but physically associated with it.

The lowest and therefore oldest beds, the "Plant-beds," are seen in the neighbourhood of Úttattúr, in the south of the Perambalúr Taluq, cropping out irregularly from beneath the base of the Úttattúr Group, and occupying the south-western corner of the sedimentary area. From this point, if we proceed either eastward across the strike, or north-eastward along the general boundary of the sedimentary rocks, we meet with all the members of the above series successively overlapping each other, and dipping at a low angle with much regularity to the east. The highest group, a mass of coarse, ferruginous grits of unknown thickness, which has been termed the Cuddalore Sandstones, occupies a large area to the north-east, including nearly the whole of the Udaiyárpálayam Taluq. A few outliers of those rocks are scattered here and there over the cretaceous rocks to the west of the principal formation, and are, in general, easily recognizable by their coarse grain, their mottled colors, and the universal absence of any fossil remains.

PART I.—PLANT-BEDS.

Extent and position of the plant-beds.

The oldest of the stratified portion of the series are, as has already been stated, the plant-beds of Úttattúr, and of these a description will now be given. The small group of shales and sandstones, which have been designated the Úttattúr plant-beds, are seen at several points cropping out in five or six separate patches from beneath the beds of the Úttattúr Group. Altogether they extend about 12 miles in a north and south direction, being finally overlapped by the Úttattúr Group at Kalppádi on the north, and near Neykulam, a few miles south of Úttattúr, in the opposite direction. As a distinct group they are of small extent and of little importance, but they become of much interest owing to the nature of their fossil contents, which, with a few doubtful exceptions, consist of plant-impressions, principally *Palæo zamia*, all in a very fragmentary condition, and, owing to the softness of their shaly and sandy matrix, very readily obliterated by friction or carriage. The position of these plant-beds proves only that they are older than the Úttattúr Group, which is probably of middle-cretaceous age. Anything beyond this must be determined by other evidence.

First noticed at Úttattúr.

These plant-beds were first noticed in the neighbourhood of Úttattúr, where the lowest beds are well seen in a little ravine about a mile to the east of the building, formerly used as a public bungalow, near that village. At this spot they appear cropping out from beneath the soft yellow gypseous clays of the Úttattúr Group, which for some distance form the left bank of the nullah, while a thick greenstone dyke, against the denuded face of which the latter were originally deposited, courses along the right bank, It is at the extremity of this dyke, where two small branches of the nullah meet, that the plant-beds crop out; and in the broken ground, drained by the upper branches of the nullah, the coarse sandstones, with intercalated bands of soft white and grey shale of which they consist, are exceedingly well exposed. The bottom bed is a coarse ferruginous sand, containing pebbles and large blocks of gneiss, the latter always much decomposed. It is, indeed, a noteworthy fact that at this locality, and, indeed, generally where the plant-beds rest on the gneiss, the latter rock is decomposed to a considerable distance, and frequently to such an extent that, where the foliation is well marked, the decomposed gneiss has been mistaken for a bedded micaceous sandstone. Elsewhere, in the country immediately around, this decomposition of the gneiss is not usual, and it is also rarely seen where beds of the other groups rest on that rock.

Beds succeeding the conglomerates.

The conglomerates are succeeded by a series of fine micaceous shales, alternating with sandy shales and coarse semi-consolidated sands similar to that which forms the matrix of the boulder bed. These beds are exposed in section in the banks of several little ravines, and dip generally at an angle of five or six degrees away from the gneiss, but without much regularity as regards direction. In the finer beds, especially the soft grey micaceous shales, the impressions of *Palæo zamia* fronds are tolerably abundant, the venation being well exhibited in freshly-broken specimens. The vegetable matter has entirely disappeared, and the softness of the shale is such that it is almost impossible to pack specimens for carriage without somewhat obliterating the more delicate parts of the impressions. Near the bottom is a band of ferruginous sand, similar to several which are intercalated in the shales, in which, together with some small pebbles of gneiss, several of an indurated clay, evidently derived from some earlier formed bed, were found. This cannot, however, be regarded as proving the former existence of a more ancient sedimentary formation. The fragments are

CHAPTER II. GEOLOGY AND SOILS.

small and few in number, and identical in appearance with some thin bands intercalated in the sands with which they occur. In thin shallow deposits where the level of the water, owing to local circumstances, is fluctuating—and such may well have been the conditions under which the plant-beds were formed—nothing is more common than to see these deposits of mud, which have been laid bare to the sun and dried afterwards, broken up and embedded in a subsequent deposit.

Mr. Blandford has described in detail some other plant-beds similar to that just noticed, discovered by him in several other villages in the Perambalúr Taluq, and also in Neykulam in Musiri Taluq. It does not, however, appear to be necessary to repeat his description of these beds here.

PART II.—ÚTTATTÚR GROUP, CORAL-REEF LIMESTONE.

The peculiar formation that has been designated coral-reef limestone occurs in isolated ridges and bosses at several points along the boundary of the cretaceous rocks, the lowest beds of which are heaped around it, and occasionally, in a great measure, formed of its debris. It rests sometimes on the plant-beds, and sometimes, and more frequently, on the gneiss or on the lowest beds of the Úttattúr Group, and appears to belong exclusively to the earliest portion of the Úttattúr period, during which the clays and argillaceous limestone of the Úttattúr Group, abounding in the various forms of cretaceous cephalopoda, indicate the existence of a moderately deep sea.

Limestone at Tiruppattúr.

About a mile to the south of Tiruppattúr in the Musiri Taluq and to the east of the shallow nullah that flows down from that village, a broad rocky ridge, rising several feet above the level of the surrounding land, marks the boundary of the cretaceous rocks. The rock of which this ridge is composed differs strikingly, both in structure and external appearance, from the ordinary sedimentary rocks of the district. It is a compact splintery limestone of a pale pink or cream color, sonorous and brittle under the hammer, and breaking with a more or less conchoidal fracture with equal facility in any direction. In general it exhibits no distinct bedding, but occasionally a thick slab-like structure is perceptible over a limited area. Small irregular cavities sometimes occur in it, which are partially or wholly filled with crystallized calc spar. Externally the rock is much eroded and often deeply honey-combed by the action of the atmosphere; it is sometimes pale, sometimes black on the surface, and rarely exhibits to the naked eye any trace of organic structure. In some places it contains a few small bivalves and corals, and occasionally a coarsely-ribbed picten of a species peculiar to this rock. In other parts, and especially towards the base, it exhibits a mass of irregular white streaks, from a few lines to two or three inches in thickness, preserving an irregular parallelism to each other and never intersecting. No organic structure is perceptible in these streaks to the naked eye, and the rock shows no tendency to break along them in preference to any other direction; but an occasional weathered surface shows that they are corals of various species of *Astræa*, seen in section, evidently *in situ*, and embedded with the rock on which they successively grew.

Form and extent of the Tiruppattúr Ridge.

The total length of the Tiruppattúr Ridge is about half a mile. It is divided in the middle by a small nullah, and in the interval are deposited some soft grey shales much resembling those of the plant-beds, but which appear to belong to the Úttattúr Group. On the western half of the ridge they lap round the base, and are seen in a small field drain resting against the highly inclined face of the rock at angles of 20° to 30°, with one or two lenticular calcareous bands at their base, enclosing a few pebbles of the limestone. About fifty yards from the limestone they are covered up by the coarse conglomerate that occurs at the base of the Trichinopoly Group, and this latter also is full of pebbles and boulders of the limestone. In the interval between the two main divisions of the ridge, a small isolated boss of the limestone, which has probably been separated from the main ridge by denudation, is exposed in a little gully which cuts through the Úttattúr shales, and the latter are clearly seen dipping away in all directions from the boss. Passing to the north-east along the boundary of the Úttattúr Group, we meet with a few masses of limestone similar to that above described on the old Madras road not far from Neykulam, close to an old ruined temple. So far as can be made out, these appear to be surrounded by the Úttattúr clays, which occur quite at the base of the group, and are exposed in the gullies close by. Their relations are not, however, very clearly seen, as the limestone only is visible, except in one instance, projecting above the soil.

Neykulam Ridge.

Kárai Ridge.

Again, about a mile to the north-east of Kárai in the Perambalúr Taluq, a prominent ridge of limestone is met with, part of which presents the characters of the coral-reef limestone, and part evidently belongs to the Úttattúr Group. The ridge, which rises some 20 or 30 feet above the average level of the soft shales around it, runs at right angles to the general strike of the Úttattúr beds, the limestone beds of the latter having been deposited around a ridge similar to that of Tiruppattúr, and concealing a great part of its surface. The coral-reef limestone is thus only exposed at its western extremity, where the Úttattúr beds have been removed by denudation, and where it rests apparently on some calcareous shales, the relations of which are by no means clear. It is full of corals, principally of various forms of *Astræadæ*, among which a

CHAPTER II. GEOLOGY AND SOILS.

Dimorphastrœa is very common, and which stand out prominently on the weathered surface of the limestone, their lamella sharp and distinct, reminding one of the silicified corals of the English mountain limestone. The overlying limestone beds of the Úttattur Group, the mineral characters of which are quite local, and due evidently to their material being derived principally from the old coral reef, are also full of corals, and except that they are distinctly bedded and dip concordantly with the overlying shales, are scarcely to be distinguished from the massive limestone on which they rest.

Sirukambúr Ridge.

Again, near Sirukambur in the Trichinopoly Taluq, on the north bank of that branch of the Ayyár river which flows past the village, there is a range of little bosses of coral-reef limestone. They are very small, the largest being only 30 feet across, and appear to rest on a mass of gypseous shales, which in mineral character are undistinguishable from the local shales of the Úttattúr Group, while they are certainly unconformable on the plant-beds close by. So far as the dip of the shales can be relied on, they appear to underline the limestone. Moreover, on the opposite side of the limestone, and where the limestone is absent, on the shales, there rests a bed of conglomerate limestone, full of Úttattúr fossils, and containing fragments of the coral limestone, whereas neither fossils nor pebbles occur in the shales below. This bed of limestone, which is very conspicuous, may be traced across the nullah striking to the south-east, and the shales beneath it, somewhat changed in mineral character, are also well exposed to the south of the nullah, where they undoubtedly overlie the Varaguppádi Ridge. It would seem, therefore, as if the coral-reef limestone were partly of subsequent formation to the lowest beds of the Uttattúr Group, in which, as shall be seen presently, small local unconformities, indicating irregular deposition, are of very frequent occurrence.

All the coral-reef limestone ridges hitherto described occur unquestionably at the base of the Úttattúr Group, either resting on gneiss or on the plant-beds, or possibly, in one or two cases, on some of the first-formed deposits of the Úttattúr Group.

Limestone Ridges at Kallakkudi.

We now pass on to the limestone at Kallakkudi, a village on the confines of the Udaiyárpálayam Taluq, which is in all respects the finest example met with of this peculiar rock. It forms a broken ridge or series of ridges, about 3½ miles long, extending along the edge of the cretaceous rocks from near Pullambádi to a point about a mile and a half north of Kallakkudi. Of the main ridge, that part immediately to the north of Kallakkudi is most clearly exposed, and is that in which the peculiar characteristics of this singular formation are best to be studied. Its greatest width is about 250 yards. It rises with a gentle slope from the gneiss, presenting a rugged surface of close-packed limestone masses. Towards its base no definite structure is perceptible, the great protruding hummocks being pitted and honey-combed into a variety of irregular forms by the action of the weather, but, in the middle and upper parts, a very distinct bedded structure is manifested in the arrangement of the masses, although there is no corresponding change in the mineral character of the rock.

At the summit of the slope the rock disappears beneath regur, and a short distance beyond this the Trichinopoly beds, resting on the limestone, are seen wherever broken ground exposes the underlying rocks. The rock of which the greater part of the ridge is composed bears a close resemblance to that of Tiruppattúr. The streaked coralliferous variety is occasionally seen towards the base, and elsewhere the rock is either white or of a pale flesh or yellow color. The first of these three varieties presents rather an earthy or chalky fracture, and, so far as can be judged by the eye unaided by chemical tests, would seem to be an almost pure indurated calcareous mud. This, however, is never seen in large masses, but only in the interior of blocks of the flesh-colored variety, which is hard and subcrystalline, being, in fact, the white rock altered by the infiltration of a calcareous solution. The third mentioned variety is the most common, and derives its color from the admixture of an ochreous clay, similar to that which occurs so largely in the bedded deposits of the Úttattúr Group. In this variety, which occurs both at the base and in the higher parts of the ridge, fossils are occasionally found, and sometimes a great part of the stone consists of comminuted shells. Close to the bottom a few pebbles of gneiss, apparently derived from the underlying boulder-bed, are occasionally met with.

Fossils found in the Kallakkudi Ridge.

The fossils noticed are not very numerous, but are of interest as tending to confirm the view of the Úttattúr age of the limestone; they consist of—

Corals	1	species.	
Rhynchonella ..	1	,,	
Ostrea	1	,,	elongated and plicated like *O. larva,* much resembling a species common in the Úttattúr Group.
Pecten	1	,,	the large-ribbed species noticed at Tiruppattúr.
Belemnites	1	,,	not determinable.

Following the outcrop of the Trichinopoly beds to the north-west, another patch of the coral limestone is met with at the south of the nullah that drains the Kallakkudi Valley. It is low and flat and resembles in all respects the limestone of the lower part of the Kallakkudi Ridge, the streaked coralliferous rock being common both *in situ* and in the boulders of the rock, which are enclosed in the overlying Trichinopoly conglomerates. It is, in fact, the base of a ridge, the upper part of which has probably been denuded. The southern edge of the Kallakkudi Ridge terminates somewhat abruptly, and the Trichinopoly beds are exposed in one or two little nullahs dipping away from it usually at a high angle. Adjoining the camping-ground at Kallakkudi, at a distance of about 200 yards from the main ridge, we meet with another small ridge of limestone, on which the village is partly built, consisting in part of the coralliferous form of the limestone. A break of about a mile then intervenes, which is occupied by the boulder-bed, and we then come to the Vadugapéttai Ridge, which extends for about a mile to the bank of the Pullambádi nullah. The rock of this ridge is much concealed by the soil, and the summit close to the village, which is the most elevated point for many miles round, is thickly covered with an isolated patch of ferruginous sand, similar to that which occupies the high ground of the Udaiyárpálayam jungles. Some of the rock is, however, exposed on the western slope, and, close to the village, the same variation in the character of the rock is observable which obtains elsewhere. The coralliferous form of the limestone occurs only at the base of the ridge, where the corals are very abundant, and the rock massive in structure and honey-combed on the surface. The upper part, on the other hand, exhibits, when viewed on the ground, a decided bedded structure; and when broken, a subcrystalline fracture, being composed of broken corals, shells, &c., cemented into a compact limestone.

Further patches of limestone.

Pisolitic limestone.

At the base of this ridge a peculiar rock of a pisolitic structure occurs in great quantity. It is made up of small pisiform nodules formed by the deposition of successive coats of calcareous matter round fragments of the limestone, and cemented together by similar material generally into a compact stone, with occasional irregular cavities. It is probably formed in part beneath the soil, where the latter is thin, for, in a section exposed in a small quarry in the Trichinopoly beds (here also limestone), a layer of the pisolitic rock, about six inches thick, was found beneath the cotton soil, and resting on about two feet of little rolled fragments of the different varieties of the limestone.

Structure of the pisolitic rock.

The nuclei of the individual nodules are most frequently mere grains, and the nodules vary from the size of a pea to that of a hazelnut; but sometimes the rock is made up of limestone fragments of all sizes, up to four or five inches in diameter, and not unfrequently masses of the pisolite itself are seen imbedded in a more recent formation of a similar nature. This rock, although more abundant here than elsewhere, is by no means peculiar to this ridge. Limestone blocks, both of the coral-reef and purer sedimentary varieties, are also occasionally found with a similar calcareous coating, one or two inches thick, in which the pisolitic structure is largely seen, and where it is difficult to imagine that any accumulation of calcareous matter could take place mechanically or chemically.

Age of the pisolitic rock. That this rock is of sub-aerial and recent formation there can be little doubt, for it occurs coating the limestones in situations where no accumulation of water is possible. Moreover, in a specimen presented by Mr. Cunliffe to the Geological Museum, a specimen of *Hellix fallaciosa*, one of the commonest living snails of the country, was thoroughly embedded. There is, however, some difficulty in understanding how successive coats of calcareous matter could be deposited round a number of nuclei so as to form pisolite, if the nodules were not freely suspended in the formative fluid.

PART III.—ÚTTATTÚR GROUP. ÚTTATTÚR BEDS.

Extent of the Úttattúr Group. The Úttattúr Group is the lowest of the three main subdivisions comprised in the great fossiliferous series of Trichinopoly above the plant-beds. It occupies a strip of country about 30 miles in length and 3 or 4 miles in average width, and extends in a north-east direction from the neighbourhood of the village of Tiruppattúr in the Musiri Taluq, to within a few miles of the river Vellár, where it is overlapped by the Ariyalúr Group just before the entire series disappears beneath the great deposits of regur and alluvium which occupy the valley of that river. Along the whole of its western boundary it rests with undisturbed stratification either on the gneiss or on the plant-beds and coral-reef limestone, but on the south, where it abuts against the confines of the granitic region of Tachankurichi, a village in the Trichinopoly Taluq, it is cut off by a system of little parallel faults and concealed beneath the beds of the Trichinopoly Group. That it originally extended far to the westward and southward of its present limits seems very probable when we regard the lithologic characters of the existing formation and the evidences of extensive denudation afforded by the abundance of its debris in the conglomerates of the higher groups. No traces of it have, however, been found anywhere to the westward or southward of its present area, and on the north-east, in the district of South Arcot, it is equally wanting.

Lithological character of the group. In lithologic character the Uttattúr beds present much variety. Fine silts, calcareous shales, and sandy clays, frequently concretionary and more or less tinted with ochreous matter, predominate throughout the group, and, as far north as Kerudamangalam and

Kárai in the Perambalúr Taluq, constitute almost the entire bulk of the deposit. To the north of these villages limestone bands become intercalated in the lower or western part of the group, and sands, grits and conglomerates in the upper or eastern part; these changes in mineral character being accompanied by a great enrichment of the fauna in the one case and an impoverishment in the other. Conglomerates are of rare occurrence in the lower part of the group. Indeed, except in the immediate neighbourhood of the coral reefs, scarcely anything that can be called a conglomerate is to be met with in the bottom beds, which consist of soft shales formed of the finest sediment, and resting at varying angles and with most irregular stratification, on the uneven gneiss bottom.

Gypsum not contemporaneous.

Gypsum occurs in most of the argillaceous beds, and is, to a certain extent, characteristic of the Úttattúr Group. No interstratified bands of this mineral, or any that could be regarded as of contemporaneous formation, have, however, been met with. It either forms plates of irregular thickness intercalated in the beds and filling cracks in the clays and shales with which it is associated, or it is found segregated in concretions and occasionally replacing the original shells around casts of *Nautili*, *Ammonites*, and some of the thick-shelled mollusca. In all cases it appears to have crystallised out subsequently to the formation and partial desiccation of the enclosing strata, and has probably been introduced by waters infiltered from the surface.

Stratification.

The stratification of the Úttattúr Group, although tolerably regular on the whole, and exhibiting a general dip to the south-west, presents many anomalies which lead to the conclusion that it is by no means due to regular superposition of sediment deposits on a horizontal sea-bottom, but rather to the banking of successive layers of sedimentary matter; the dip of which is, with few exceptions, due to the shelving form of the banks on which they were formed.

Fauna of the Úttattúr Group.

The fauna of the Úttattúr Group is especially rich. Its principal characteristic is the abundance and variety of its cephalopoda, and in this respect it may be held to equal, if not to surpass, the remarkable fauna of the Valudaiyár beds of Pondicherry. The forms, however, are nearly all different, and for the most part peculiar to this group. One or two species of *Ammonites*, and possibly one of *Ancyloceras* (*Hamites*, Forbes) occur in the Úttattúr beds, but, as a rule, the *Ammonites* bear more resemblance to upper-cretaceous species and are in some cases identical with green sand and even white chalk forms of Europe. Some few of them also pass through into the Trichinopoly Group, but the number of these does not appear to exceed a very few species.

The specific development of the genus *Ammonite* is not the only instance of the richness of the cephalopod fauna. *Ancyloceras*,

Scaphites, *Turrilites*, (*Hamites ?*), *Ptychoceras*, and *Baculites* all furnish representatives. *Nautilus* also is represented by seven species and a great abundance of individuals, while of *Belemnites* (the only *Dibranchiate* genus) only three species have been distinguished.

The remaining classes of the mollusca, the *Gasteropoda*, *Conchifera* and *Brachiopoda*, are all well represented, as will be seen by the following provisional generic list. Those, the species of which are numerous, are marked with an asterisk, and a great abundance of individuals is noted by the mark †.

Gasteropoda.

* Rostellaria.†
* Fuses.
Voluta.
* Natica.†
Nerinœa.
Turritella.
Turbo.
Phasianella.
Pleurotomaria.†
Dentalium.†
Cerithium.
Patella.
Emarginula.
Cinulia.
Acteonella.
Tornatella.

Conchifera.

* Ostrea.†
* Pecten.†
Lima.
Spondylus.†
Plicatula.
Inoceramus.†
Pinna.
* Arca.†
Pectunculus.
Nucula.
Leda (*doubtful*).
Trigonia.
Radiolites.
* Cardium.
* Cytherea.
Teredo.

Brachiopoda.

Terebratula.
Rhynchonella
Crania.

The above list is, in all probability, very imperfect, as may be expected from the nature of the materials from which it has been drawn up, and it is likely that there are many omissions which will become apparent when the collections are fully examined. Such as it is, however, it is characteristically cretaceous. The presence of such genera as *Cinulia*, *Acteonella* and *Radiolites*, and the great abundance of *Inocerami*, no less than the absence of most genera especially characteristic of oolitic or tertiary times, fully respond to the indications afforded by the cephalopoda of the cretaceous age of the fauna.

Other forms of life. Of other forms of life there are many instances. Corals of several species occur in the lower beds, many of them derived from the wreck of the reef limestone, but some also of contemporaneous origin. Of *Annelids* also there are several species, some of them peculiar to, and very characteristic of, the group.

CHAPTER II. GEOLOGY AND SOILS.

Wherever they occur they are always in great abundance, and are very characteristic of certain beds. Of the crustacea no examples have been met with. The "crustacean" remains mentioned by Dr. Muzzy as occurring in great abundance in the *Belemnite* clays of Úttattúr are concretionary nodules, as are also the fossil turtles mentioned by the same observer. The remains of vertebrate animals are also very scarce, the vertebra and teeth of a shark and a few bones of doubtful nature being the only instances of their occurrence.

Plants.

Plant remains in the form of drift-wood, sometimes bored by the teredo, abound in certain parts of the group. The wood is cycadaceous and exogenous.

PART IV.—TRICHINOPOLY GROUP.

Extent of the Trichinopoly Group.

The Trichinopoly Group, the middle sub-division of the cretaceous series in the Trichinopoly District, is, like the Úttattúr Group, confined to that district, where it occupies a narrow strip of country between the Úttattúr and Ariyalúr Groups. Its greatest width 3½ miles, is near its southern extremity, where, overlapping the faulted boundary of the Úttattúr beds, it rests immediately on the gneiss extending down to the alluvial plain of the Cauvery. Its width diminishes gradually as it stretches northward; thinning out, and not apparently overlapped, until all trace of it is lost beneath the cotton-soil in the north of the district, beyond which we find the Ariyalúr Group resting on the Úttattúr beds. It is, therefore, distinctly unconformable to the Úttattúr Group, but it is not strikingly so except at its southern extremity, where the latter group had suffered some disturbance in the interval preceding the formation of the Trichinopoly Group; while, with respect to the Ariyalúr Group, no decided unconformity of bedding is to be detected, owing possibly to the want of good sections at the junction of the two. The distinction between them rests at present solely on the evidence of the fossils, coupled with the fact that the Ariyalúr beds extend beyond the Trichinopoly Group and rest on the gneiss at both extremities of the latter group.

Physical conditions of the deposits of the southern part of the group.

The Trichinopoly beds are even more characteristically than those in the Uttattúr Group the deposits of a shallow sea. As far north as Kerudamangalam in the south of the Perambalúr Taluq the stratification presents the greatest irregularity, an irregularity evidently due to the shifting of currents, and yet, owing to the fine and regular lamination of the beds over large areas, most puzzling to the geologist, who, having followed an apparently regular series of stratified deposits for a distance of a mile or more, suddenly meets with an inexplicable unconformity which baffles all his attempts to trace it out, and which is yet of such magnitude that it is only after the constant repetition of such failures that he can convince himself that he has to deal with the local irregularities of a drifted deposit. The difficulty of gaining a clue to the real state of things is the greater that, in the area within which these irregularities are the greatest, fossils are scarce, and those met with are by no means characteristic, belonging to such species as are either common to other groups, or so closely resemble Úttattúr and Ariyalúr species, that, without a more critical knowledge of them than can be gained in the field, it is impossible to accept them with confidence as indicative of the Trichinopoly Group. As regards lithologic character, there is but little to distinguish these from the underlying Úttattúr beds, or from the lowest beds of the Ariyalúr Group, except in one peculiarity which the conglomerates of the Trichinopoly series have in common with the Ariyalúr beds, but which is not met with in those of the Úttattúr Group.

Peculiarity of the Trichinopoly and Ariyalúr conglomerates.

A broad band of barren stony ground, marked with conspicuous ridges of bare rock, pink and glittering with abraded quartz and felspar, stretches for many miles along the north flank of the alluvial valley of the Cauvery, its course coinciding with that of the river and of the gneiss folia and bedding over the whole of the low country between the Kollimalais and the hills in the Madura District. Of the rocks composing this ridge no fragments have been met with in the conglomerates of the Úttattúr Group, which consist exclusively of the debris of the gneiss and coral-reef limestone, and it is probable that the Úttattúr sea therefore stretched far up the present Cauvery valley, and that, if the granite was exposed anywhere in the land of the epoch, it must have been too far away to the westward to admit of recognizable traces of it being carried to the existing deposits of the area. The faulting which occurred at the close of the Úttattúr period must have brought this ridge above the level of the sea; and accordingly the conglomerates of both the Trichinopoly and Ariyalúr Groups are full of pebbles of felspar, quartz, and the granite itself, and also of the highly-foliated hornblende schists which are associated with the granite, and do not occur elsewhere in the neighbourhood. In the two later groups, also, frequent masses of loose unstratified gravel, composed almost exclusively of granitic debris, are found; and in some places beds of rolled pebbles, almost without any admixture of finer materials, composed of the quartz of this rock mixed with gneiss pebbles, and closely resembling in its features of accumulation an ordinary recent shingle-beach. The greater part of the Trichinopoly beds, however, consist of fine sands and clays with infiltrated kunkur much resembling those which constitute some of the southern Úttatúr beds, and bands of limestone of the

CHAPTER II. GEOLOGY AND SOILS.

different varieties met with in the Úttattúrs are also occasionally intercalated, though less common.

Northern portion of the group.

Between Alundalaippúr and Kerudamangalam, two villages in the south of the Perambalúr Taluq, or rather in the country to the east of these places, the beds begin to assume a definite strike parallel to the longitudinal axis of the group. Regular bands of shell limestone become intercalated in the lower beds, and hence to the northern termination of the group, regularly stratified alternations of sands and sandy clays and shales, with bands of shell limestone, calcareous grit and conglomerate, constitute the whole of the group with unimportant exceptions.

Fauna.

The fauna of the Trichinopoly Group is, as might be expected from the peculiarities of its stratification, characterised by an abundance of shallow-water forms. A generic list of the fossils collected in this group by the Geological Survey is given by Mr. Blandford in the Geological Survey Memoirs, but it does not appear to be necessary to insert it here, as a list of those discovered in the Úttattúr Group has already been given, and as those found in the Ariyalúr Group, considered by Mr. Blandford to be of great interest, will be noticed further on.

Fossil flora.

The fossil flora of the Trichinopoly beds is, like that of the associated groups, remarkable for the preponderance, if not the almost exclusive occurrence, of exogenous or cycadeous forms, as indicated by the wood which is abundant in the lower beds of the group and is met with in drifted logs of many feet in length. Not a single undoubted specimen of endogenous wood was found among the numerous specimens noticed in the field.

PART V.—ARIYALÚR GROUP.

Extent of the group.

The extent of the Ariyalúr Group in the Trichinopoly District alone considerably exceeds that of both the groups previously treated of, and, unlike them, it extends beyond the limits of the district and occupies a large area to the north of the Vellár in the South Arcot District. In Trichinopoly it occupies a broad strip of country in the Perambalúr and Udaiyárpaláyam Taluqs, extending from the banks of the Vellár nearly to those of the Coleroon, and comprising an area of about 200 square miles. In the vicinity of the latter river it is concealed by superficial deposits (regur and alluvium), and at Tanjore, where the older rocks reappear to the south of the Cauvery delta, these consist of the Cuddalore sandstones, a group of doubtful age, but newer than the cretaceous rocks upon which they rest in Trichinopoly and South Arcot.

Lithological features.

Much of the Ariyalúr beds are concealed beneath cotton soil, and sections are even rarer in these beds than in those of the older groups. They consist in great part of white unfossiliferous sands and green argillaceous sands with casts of small fossils in the unconsolidated matrix. Bands of calcareous grit and nodular calcareous shales are frequent in the lower beds, and these abound in fossils, and similar shales reappear in some of the higher beds.

Zonal sub-divisions.

Indeed, although there are no very definite boundaries between the sub-divisions of the group, there are in the Ariyalúr Group of Trichinopoly three tolerably well-defined zones, the lower and uppermost of which are fossiliferous and characterised by distinct fauna, while the middle zone, consisting chiefly of white and grey sands, is almost without fossils. These zones pass into each other in South Arcot, but it will be convenient to observe the distinction in describing the more extensive deposits of Trichinopoly.

Conglomerates.

Conglomerates are of comparatively rare occurrence in the group, and except near its southern boundary, those frequent irregularities of bedding, which characterize a large part of the Trichinopoly Group, are not met with. The dip of the beds is generally very low, the highest (6°) only prevails in the lower beds of the group, where they rest on Trichinopoly beds. Elsewhere dips of 2° and 3° are prevalent, the inclination being towards the north-east. At its northern and southern extremities the group rests on gneiss, overlapping the older groups on which it rests in the interval. Its thickness is not easily ascertainable, but not only its low angle of dip, but also the fact that the gneiss bottom protrudes through the beds at more than one spot, more than a mile from the boundary of the group, warrant the inference that its thickness is nowhere very great, probably not exceeding 1,000 feet.

Source of materials.

The constituents of the Ariyalúr beds were derived in part from the granitic band of Tachankurichi, in part from the gneiss; and a few pebbles of yellow marl, in the conglomerate beds, show that the older, probably the Úttattúr beds, were also undergoing denudation to some extent at the time of its formation. As compared with the lower groups, the bedding of the Ariyalúr Group is very uniform, and the beds thick and homogeneous.

Fauna.

The fauna of the Ariyalúr Group is one of great interest. That of the lower beds includes many of the commonest forms of the Trichinopoly fauna, and a few of these range through a large part of the group, but are associated with a large proportion of new and peculiar forms, and, as a whole, the fauna offers many striking points of contrast to those of the lower groups. It is essentially *upper cretaceous*, and in many points reminds one

CHAPTER II. GEOLOGY AND SOILS.

strongly of that of the white chalk of Europe, especially in the abundance of *Bryozoa*, *Echinida*, *Brachiopoda*, and small *Corals*, and the occurrence of such forms as *Crania* and *Marsupites*, both of which are absent in the lower groups. *Ammonites* are common in the lower beds, chiefly of peculiar species, but including a few, such as *A. Sugata*, Forbes, and *A. Mantelli*, which have passed up from the lower groups. *Nautili* are numerous both in species and individuals, all of them peculiar to the group as regards our Indian formation, but including some European forms, notably *N. Bouchardianus*, *N. Clementinus* and *N. Danicus*. The occurrence of this last in the highest beds only in Trichinopoly, is remarkable, not only in the mere fact of its occurrence, but also in its association with an *ovulum*, and a fauna having as much of tertiary as of a cretaceous aspect, and peculiar to the beds in question.

Hamites, *Baculites* and possibly *Turrilites* reappear in the lower part of the Ariyalúr, having been nearly or entirely absent from the Trichinopoly deposits, and *Radiolites* of more than one species are extremely abundant at a particular zone; squaloid teeth (*Lamna*, *&c.*) are found in some of the lower beds, but the most remarkable and interesting occurrence is that of remains of the *Megalosaurus*, a reptile which in Europe has not been found to range above the Wealden formation. These remains consisted of bones in so bad a state of preservation, however, as to have little recognizable form, and one tooth, upon the discovery of which the identification of the reptile therefore rests.

Fossil wood is not uncommon in the fossiliferous beds of the Ariyalúr Group, but is less abundant than in the Trichinopoly beds. Its nature has not been ascertained.

The following generic list of fossils, drawn up, as in previous cases, from field-lists, will convey a general idea of the character of the fauna :—

VERTEBRATA.

Reptilia.
Megalosaurus.

Pisces.
Squaloid teeth.
Lamna.
Corax.
Otodus.
Oxyrhina.
Odontaspis.

ARTICULATA.

Crustacean claws.

Annelids (*Serpula*, *Spirorbis*, *&c.*)

MOLLUSCA.

Cephalopoda.

Nautilus.*
Ammonites.*
Baculites.
Turrilites.
Hamites.

Brachiopoda.

Terebratula.*
Rhynchonella.
Crania.

Gasteropoda.

Rostellaria.
Pyrula.
Fusus.
Voluta.*
Ovulum.
Natica *
Pyramidella.
Chemnitzia.
Cerithium.
Nerinœa.
Turritella.
Scalaria.
Solarium.
Nerita.
Turbo.
Trochus.
Rotella ?
Pleurotomaria.
Cinulia.
Acteonella.
Bulla.
Cylichna ? or a new genus.

Conchifera.

Ostria.*
Pecten.*
Lima.
Spondylus.*
Plicatula.
Vulsella.
Perna.
Inoceramus.*
Pinna.
Mytilus.
Modiola.
Arca.*
Pectunculus.
Trigonia.
Radiolites.*
Cardium.*
Lucina.
Corbis.
Cyprina.
Astarte.
Crassatilla.
Opis.
Cardita.
Cytherea.
Corbula.
Pholadomya.

BRYOZOA.*

Radiata.

Echinodermata.
Spatangus * or Micaster.
Nuclcolites.*
Catopygus.
Cidaris ?
Echinus ?
Marsupites.
Crinoid stems.
Polypiaria.
Fungia.
Turbinolia, &c.

PROTOZOA.

Foraminifera.

PLANTÆ.

Fossilwood, sp. ?

Chapter II. Geology and Soils.

In the above list only the genera most abundant in individuals have been marked with an asterisk, the data being insufficient to make it possible to note specific abundance also.

Part VI.—Post-Cretaceous Rocks (Cuddalore Sandstones).

This name has been assigned by Mr. Blandford to an important series of rocks resting immediately on the cretaceous formations found in the South Arcot and Trichinopoly Districts.

Areas in which these rocks occur.

This series of rocks occurs in four distinct areas, separated by the valleys of the Pennár, Vellár, and Cauvery rivers. The four areas are, in all probability, parts of a great continuous deposit over the eastern side of the Karnatic, which was cut through, and in great part denuded away, during the formation of the valleys now occupied by the above-named rivers. They have the form of low table-lands or plateau, terminating in low but abrupt headlands on their northern and eastern sides, around which the beds of the present alluvium have been deposited.

On the south side of the Cauvery the Cuddalore series appears to rest immediately on the metamorphic rocks; the cretaceous beds, if they ever covered those parts, having been in great part, if not entirely, denuded away previously to the deposition of the post-cretaceous formations.

Age of the rocks.

Owing to the absence of any fossil remains, the exact age of this rather extensive formation is as yet undecided, fossil traces not offering sufficient data whereby to refer these beds to well-determined horizons amongst the recognized tertiary or quarternary formations.

As indicated by the name "Cuddalore sandstones," this series of rocks consists mainly of more or less ferruginous sandstones associated with mottled grits, containing numerous cavities filled with clay and occasionally beds of clay. Resting upon these, occurs very generally a highly ferruginous conglomerate deposit of indurated clay, well known as laterite. This laterite is, in many places, apparently inseparable from the soft mottled grits, and seems to pass downward into them by imperceptible gradations.

Laterite deposits.

The laterite deposits occur very generally on the top of the grits series without any apparent unconformity. Notwithstanding, however, this intimate association of the laterite with the grits, there appears to be an unconformity when their relation over a larger area is considered, and this we shall endeavour to illustrate after having considered the general lithological character of the deposits. This brown ferruginous deposit, usually called laterite, occurs in two forms over the district as a regular aqueous deposit of great extent, or as the effects of decomposition *in situ* of highly ferruginous rocks.

The latter variety has been observed in two or three localities south of the Cauvery as an assemblage of blocks in the beds of streams, where a small quantity of water almost constantly remains; and that it is essentially decomposed gneiss *in situ*, is evident, since the foliation is distinctly visible, as well as the gradual change from a dark reddish brown friable surface of sandy clay to the true rock internally, the folia of quartz still remaining as needles or ridges in the decomposed parts of the block.

The laterite proper consists essentially of an agglomeration of little rounded particles, cemented together by a ferruginous sandy clay, the little nodules or concretions being more distinct in their form towards the upper surface, where they become darker in color, gradually changing from yellowish-red to dark brown or black, eventually becoming quite polished, and assuming a semi-metallic lustre. Generally these consist of ferruginous sandy clay, concretionary in structure, but in many cases they are composed of iron ore, showing a grey metallic surface when broken; grains of sand also are frequently included in the mass, which sometimes assumes a true conglomeratic character. The matrix or cementing material increases in quantity from the interior of the bed to the surface, the latter being harder and less friable than the interior, which is clayey. In its least compact form this formation occurs as a gravel-like accumulation of small rounded pellets of impure, clayey, brown haematite, for which the very suitable name of "pisiform lateritic gravel" has been proposed by Dr. Oldham. Beds or large nests of pale yellow and white clay occur with the laterite, and would seem to indicate an underlying variety or lithomarge, but no section has been found sufficiently deep to show the relation between the clay and the underlying rock, which is gneiss.

Pisolitic and tubiform character.

Where the deposit is thoroughly exposed on all sides, the vertical section shows a regular pisiform structure throughout, accompanied by tubiform cavities, though of a more ferruginous character towards the upper surface. It is mainly on the sides and under-surfaces of blocks that the tubiform character is seen; the upper showing it less frequently. Of the cause of these tubiform vermicular cavities no altogether satisfactory solution has yet been offered, nor have the phenomena observed suggested any as yet unobserved cause to which to attribute them.

Conglomeratic laterite.

Though of so uniform a structure over a great part of its extent, the laterite becomes highly conglomeratic in many places, especially in the outlying patches south and south-east of

CHAPTER II. GEOLOGY AND SOILS.

Trichinopoly. Here, as on the brigade-ground and a mile and a half south of the race-course, it encloses subangular fragments of quartz and gneiss of sizes varying from that of a small pebble to pieces of three or four inches in diameter. At times the quantity of these is so great that in the latter locality they almost make a pavement, having, as it were, its seams or joints of laterite. A conglomerate of quartz fragments is, however, the most ordinary form. Occasionally, the laterite is a coarse deposit of small particles of quartz in a matrix of ferruginous sandy clay.

Physical features of the laterite country.

The laterite characterizes the country over which it is developed by its peculiarly flat or table-land surfaces, which are sometimes of great extent. Where the ground rises above the general level this deposit laps round it, leaving an island of the subjacent rock, or, where parallel streams have worn their way as they flowed down from the higher grounds, the laterite is found denuded from all but the low ridges between the streams, showing its scarped edges in contour lines along the sides and around the heads of the valleys. Most interesting examples on a small scale, of this last feature, are observable to the south of the Trichinopoly race-course.

Unconformity of laterite and grits.

The probable unconformity of the laterite to the mottled grits of Tanjore and Vallam is assumed for the following reason, that the laterite greatly overlaps the grits, stretching for many miles westward over the gneiss rocks in the direction of Trichinopoly. Of the existence of the overlap there can be no doubt whatever, as the contact of the laterite and gneiss is exposed to view in many places.

Location of the laterite.

Crossing the great bay of alluvium which runs south for some miles from the Erumbísvaram Rock, there is a large patch of laterite conglomerate which commences about a quarter of a mile north of the new Trichinopoly road, crosses the old road a little south-east of the Golden Rock, and, making a bend like the lower limb of an S, terminates a few hundred yards west of Sandepéttai-malai and about $1\frac{1}{4}$ mile south of the Fakir's rock at Trichinopoly. Westward of the Kóraiyár, an affluent of the Cauvery near Trichinopoly, no lateritic conglomerate appears.

This laterite a true sedimentary formation.

There can be little doubt that this laterite south-east of Trichinopoly is a true sedimentary formation like the laterite of Tanjore and Vallam, and is not to be ranked among the sub-aerial pseudo-laterites, such as those of the Nílagiris and Shevaroys, which have resulted solely from the oxidization of weathered ferruginous materials, and mainly from the hornblendic or amphibolitic rocks of those mountains. Should it be imagined, however, that it is a laterite formed by the decomposition of the gneiss rock *in situ*, there are several valid objections to that supposition, and it will most likely be established when the country around Pudukóttai shall have been surveyed to be of the same age as, and a continuation of, the laterite lying on the mottled grits of Vallam and Tanjore.

Objections to the decomposition *in situ* theory.

The objections to the application of the decomposition *in situ* theory in this case, are principally three :—

1*st.*—The underlying gneiss rock, when exposed, is almost invariably quite fresh and undecomposed in contact with the bed of lateritic conglomerate; whereas, had decomposition *in situ* been the cause of the latter formation, there would be evidences of such decomposition in the shape of only partially decomposed portions of gneiss at the line of junction. Such, however, is scarcely ever the case.

2*nd.*—The formation of such masses of ferruginous rock could only take place by the decomposition of a rock containing an abundance of iron among its constituents, as, for instance, very hornblendic gniess, &c. ; but in this area highly ferruginous varieties of gneiss are almost unknown, quartzose or felspatho-quartzose gneiss forming the great mass of the country.

3*rd.*—The position of the bed of laterite and its conglomeratic structure containing rounded and subangular fragments of quartz, are two points, both of which are opposed to the decomposition *in situ* hypothesis. The occurrence of rounded fragments, almost pebbles, of quartz in the conglomerate cannot be explained by supposing the edges to have been blunted by weathering; but there is no difficulty in obtaining an explanation if the phenomenon is referred to a process of attrition previous to deposition, the whole of the materials composing the laterite appearing to have been conveyed from a distance.

PART VII.—METAMORPHIC ROCKS.

Gneissose Rocks.

General character of the gneiss.

a. Varieties of Gneiss.—The metamorphic series, as developed in the country here treated of, embraces a great succession of gneissose rocks of various kinds, chiefly of the hornblendic varieties, and of crystalline limestone in comparatively small quantity. This series constitutes the bottom rocks of the country, no older formation having been discovered, and is overlaid successively by cretaceous rocks, the Cuddalore sandstones, and superficial deposits of alluvium, &c. The different members of this series have undergone great contortion in some districts and have been broken through by numerous granite veins and traversed by dykes of greenstone and other trappean rocks, and by veins of quartz.

CHAPTER II. GEOLOGY AND SOILS.

Syenitoid gneiss.

A very common and widely distributed form of these rocks is that of a dark-grey, hard, compact, massive, syenitoid gneiss, of quartz, hornblende, and felspar, in which the constituent minerals are pretty evenly distributed. It is this general type of rock which mainly constitutes the different mountain-masses in this part of the country. Allied to this type there is another in which hornblende occurs, only to a very limited extent, being often almost entirely absent. This is a massive quartzo-felspathic gneiss of a pale grey or buff color, and for the most part distinctly foliated. This variety is more particularly developed in that portion of the Trichinopoly District lying to the south of the Cauvery.

Quartzo-felspathic gneiss.

Quartzite.

Quartzites or quartzose gneiss occur only in one or two localities, as for example close to Neyvéli in the Musiri Taluq.

Hornblende schists and rock.

Hornblende schist alternates very frequently with the quartzo-felspathic variety of the gneiss. Hornblende occasionally predominates to such an extent as to constitute a regular hornblende rock, in which any trace of foliation is generally most obscure, rendering the rock very like many igneous rocks. The bedded or banded structure of the mass, however, alternating as it does with the same structure in other varieties of the metamorphic series, readily determines the true nature of the rock.

Chlorite schists.

Chlorite schists are to be found in the direction of Kannanúr in the Musiri Taluq, and, among these chloritic schists, beds containing garnet in abundance occur at Tulaiyanattam and Pudupatti in the same taluq.

Quasi-porphyritic gneiss.

Associated with these chloritic rocks is a considerable development of a quasi-porphyritic gneiss, highly quartzose, with imperfectly formed crystals of drab, pink, or purplish felspar, these imperfect crystals disseminated in the general matrix, and frequently causing the mass at first sight to have much the appearance of a conglomerate; the foliation, however, is almost invariably well marked. A similar rock appears at Káttupputtúr in the south-western portion of the Musiri Taluq, and also at different localities between this and the places noted above, indicating the extension of beds of this variety across the country.

South of the Cauvery gneiss of a similar character has been observed, but not to so great an extent, at Manikanda Choultry, eight miles south-west of Trichinopoly, and again further to the west at Rachándár-Tirumalai. At the former of these places the irregularly porphyritic character of the rock is not so apparent, the felspar having become segregated as it were into bodies of an almond shape, which are arranged closely and sinuously together in lines parallel to the foliation. Many of these segregated portions are binary compounds of quartz and felspar. These are some of the most marked varieties of the gneissose rocks in the district.

b. Crystalline Limestone.—This rock is of rare occurrence in this district, being found only at a few places. It may be seen at Neyvéli on the left bank of the Ayyár, in the Musiri Taluq, and at Kallupatti in the Kulittalai Taluq. In the same taluq bands of limestone, extending over a length of more than 12 miles, and stretching far into the district of Coimbatore, are to be found. Four of these bands may be seen at a spot about 16 miles south of Karúr. From this point they stretch in continuous lines in an east north-east direction to a large boss of gneiss, around which two of the limestone bands make a slight bend or curve and then pursue their original course, although occasionally covered up and concealed by alluvium and gneiss debris to a point south-west of Kíranúr in the Kadavúr Zemindári. A great number of small bands cross the old boundary bank between the districts of Coimbatore and Trichinopoly, but these are eventually united into thicker beds or spread out into rocky surfaces of thirty or forty yards in width, which disappear beneath the alluvial deposits of the two streams running to the north, and reappear as a nearly-equal number of beds crossing the country further to the east. Two beds also occur about two miles to the north-east of these at Kíranúr, one of which was traceable only for a mile or so in a continuous line.

Color and texture of limestone. Variations in the color and texture of the limestone in this locality are pretty frequent. Nearly pure white marble, both fine and coarse-grained, was observed lying immediately round one side of a boss of gneiss noticed in this part of the country, while on the opposite side was a largely crystallized variety, in which separate crystals of carbonate of lime (calcite) were easily distinguishable, generally of a pink color. A beautiful pink variety, admirably adapted for marble slabs on account of its close texture and absence of folia of foreign minerals, is of frequent occurrence in several bands. East of Kíranúr also there is a bluish-colored band.

Included minerals. Other minerals, such as chlorite and mica, enter more or less into the composition of most of the limestone of this part of the country, but in some beds these are very rare and sometimes totally absent. When occurring to any extent, they form laminæ running through the mass of the rock. Chlorite occurs largely in some of the pink limestone, dotting the surface with bright green, while glittering scales of yellow mica replace this mineral in the white varieties of the limestone. Detached pieces of gneiss and nests of quartz sometimes occur enclosed in the limestone, but these are very rare.

CHAPTER II. GEOLOGY AND SOILS.

Economic value of limestone.

Although limestone occurs largely in the south-west part of this district close to many villages, some of which are even built upon the wider expanses of the rock, it does not appear to be used in any way by the people, excepting as a stone on which to sharpen their knives and hatchets. They prefer the more stubborn gneiss as a building stone for their temples, and the more readily-collected little fragments of *kunkur* for lime. They admit the superiority of the stone-lime, but say that a basketful of the ordinary kind is quite good enough for their work. At Neyvéli in Musiri Taluq fine masses of limestone have been quarried, but for no other purpose than to enable the workmen to get more easily at the bed of quartzite which is adjacent on the northern side. The limestone, however, is undoubtedly a valuable material, and might with advantage be used when obtainable in sufficient quantity. As a material for building it is lighter than any of the gneiss rocks, and the finer varieties are not exceeded in durability by any of these. Neyvéli is only seven miles from the Cauvery, down which river the stone could be carried in boats to Trichinopoly or into the Tanjore District. Indeed during the freshes in the river, the stone could be loaded close to Neyvéli, where the Ayyár passes the village.

Foliation and strike.

Details of Metamorphic Country.—Over the whole area surveyed the lamination of the metamorphic rocks is distinctly visible, although more decidedly in the magnetic iron-beds than in the hornblende rocks and schists. The general direction of this foliated structure is, for the southern and central parts of the area, east, north-east and west, south-west, but in the northern part it tends to the north-east, north-east by north, and even north north-east. Great and frequent alterations are, however, as might be expected, observable in the neighbourhood of igneous rocks, as long the south bank of the Cauvery, around the north-west of Togamalai, and in various parts of the country where the strata give evidence of their having undergone immense pressure and consequently extensive disturbance and distortion. Local changes in direction over a small area are very frequently met with, but the original direction is almost immediately reassumed.

Jointing.

Two principal systems of jointing were observed, one running north, south, varying 5° or 10° to the east or west, and the other running east, north-east, west, south-west. There are also occasional cases of a system having a north-west, south-east direction. The north and south line of jointing is most constant and distinct, that running east, north-east, west, south-west, being often coincident with the foliation. In the latter case, the constancy of the dip, about 70° southwards of the planes of jointing, was quite sufficient to distinguish it from the foliation. These various systems are very well displayed round the base of the Pachamalais, and the faces of many of the finest precipices of the other mountain groups coincide with some of the chief places of jointing.

Joint fissure channels for trap.

In some of the regions of trappean intrusion the fissures of jointing have been the channels along which the dykes have been formed, as in the set of dykes in the neighbourhood of Válikandapuram, where the north-south system appears to have been the line of least resistance, only three dykes in that locality being parallel to the east, north-east, west, south-west line.

Sedimentary origin of the gneiss.

The sedimentary origin of the gneiss, as far as true bedding offers any proof, is very apparent in many localities. In the country round the Talaimalai Hill, Táttaiyangárpéttai and Turaiyúr, in connection with the magnetic iron beds running from the Talaimalai into the Kollimalais, such a structure is very well exemplified. Beds of hornblende rock, quartzose gneiss, occasionally false-bedded, and hornblende schist, dipping at various angles, are easily traceable for miles across the level country as streaks of pale and dark rock, as well as on the faces of a few sharp ridges and conical hills. The Talaimalai is composed of highly-inclined beds, the hardest of which run up to form the precipitous peaks which render the hill so characteristic from all sides of the country. Again, Pagalavádi Hill to the south of Turaiyúr, when viewed from the west, shows the different beds dipping south-east by south at an angle of 50°. Standing on any of the thick hornblendic beds half-way up this hill, one may trace its descent to the plain, where it runs along eastward for miles, indicated by a dark run of angular debris between similar rows of various width, but of lighter color.

Relation of the beds to each other.

As regards the succession or relation to each other of the different series of beds or bands of the metamorphic rocks, very little can be made out at present, except conclusions drawn from local observations.

The foliation, or, in other words, the indication of strike of the rock masses, over the area now under consideration is, on the whole, from west to east, with a tendency always to curve round more to the north-east, until a nearly north-by-east direction is attained at the northern edge of the area. The relation of the beds may then be studied, to a certain extent, by commencing at the southern limit and taking them according to their succession northwards.

Beds of the Cauvery Valley.

In the valley of the Cauvery it appears that the rocks of this region are composed of two series, which extend along the valley as three bands in a nearly east—west direction, the most southerly and narrowest being one of hornblendic rocks and schists. Alongside of this is a broad belt of quartzose and quartzo-felspathic gneiss, associated on its northern edge with an extensive and nearly parallel development of granitic rocks. North of this comes the third band, which is very similar in its constituent beds to the first, namely, a hornblendic and schistose series, with intercalated beds of quartzose gneiss, and this borders the great band of massive syenitoid gneiss of the Kollimalais and Pachamalais.

Neglecting the slight changes in the direction of the dip of the bedding which have been observed in those localities where the intrusion of igneous matter has taken place, there is a very decided connection between the inclination of the beds and these different bands of rock described above. North of the Cauvery, and nearly up to the foot of the Kollimalais, the rocks have a general dip northwards, while about six miles south of the river, where the corresponding band of hornblendic rocks comes in, the dip is reversed, and the beds which lie between that and the northern part of the Madura District dip generally to the south. The region of quartzo-felspathic gneiss, lying between these two bands of the hornblendic series, shows the same change in dip on its two edges, thus indicating a great anticlinal fold, of which this middle band is the nucleus.

Around Trichinopoly the country does not present so uniform a character in the dip of its rock-beds, while immediately south of the Pachamalais, as well as west of the Talaimalai and the Kollimalais, the outcrops of strata traverse the country in great curves, which are distinctly traceable for many miles.

Physical features.

The physical features of the country, in which the two divisions of gneiss are described as occurring, differ considerably. The peculiar rounded bosses and hills, so common on the banks of the Cauvery and south of it, *e.g.*, the Trichinopoly Rock, the Golden Rock, Erumbísvaram Pagoda Rock, Retnagiri near Siváyam, and the rock at Tógamalai are all composed of quartzo-felspathic gneiss, and owe their present form in great part to the hardness and mode of weathering of this variety of gneiss. Great part of the surface of these bosses has been quarried as building material for the religious edifices erected on them, and the workmen have taken advantage of the readiness with which the stone may be split off in concentric surfaces. The country around these hills is undulating and rounded in its surface, except where igneous rocks occur, when it becomes more rugged in character. The region of hornblendic gneiss, on the other hand, with its frequently alternating beds of schist and quartzo-felspathic gneiss, is diversified by numerous ridges and conical hills surrounded by an almost level country.

PART VIII.—CRYSTALLINE ROCKS.

Of rocks of igneous or quasi-igneous origin, two classes are represented within the Trichinopoly District, namely,—

(*a*) Trap-rocks.
(*b*) Granites (quartz veins).

Rocks of the first class are extensively developed in numerous dykes which traverse the country pretty generally in various directions, while those of the second class are confined more especially to the southern part of the area.

(*a*) *Trap Rocks.*—By far the greater number of the dykes met with consist of coarse-grained black or bluish (or greenish) block, and very hard, tough, basaltic trap, but without olivine, except in a very few cases.

Associated locally with this rock, as thin strings running into the adjacent gneiss, and often even permeating the coarser rock itself, is a fine-grained bluish-black trap, which is generally more split up by jointing than the basaltic or coarser variety.

Columnar structure has not been observed well marked, but jointing is often developed to a great extent, frequently producing polygonal blocks, which sometimes pass into the common ball form so frequently seen in weathered dykes. The same systems of jointing as are seen in the gneissic rocks are, with slight variations, seen in the trap. Columnar structure.

Green Stone or *Diarite* has been observed in several cases in which the rock was markedly porphyritic. One case occurred at the edge of a spread of laterite about a mile south-east by south of the Tuvágudi Travellers' Bungalow on the road between Trichinopoly and Tanjore. Another may be seen about six miles south-south-west of Trichinopoly, associated with some large veins of granite and quartz.

The distribution of the dykes is very irregular; none of any size are met with south of the granite region on the north bank of the Cauvery, while all over the country occupied by the "granitoid gneiss" the trap-dykes are few in number and small in size. Absence of dykes south of the Cauvery.

The general mineral character of by far the greater number of the trap-dykes is identical; they consist generally of a rather coarse-grained, but exceedingly hard and tough, block basalt-like mass, hardly ever containing recognizable crystals of any foreign substance. Mineral character of dykes.

In a few cases the fresh fracture showed a greyish lustre, due apparently to numerous small crystals of a felspathic mineral.

Of the age of the trap-dykes, all that is known is that they are pre-cretaceous. The evidence of this is found in the case of the Geological age of the dykes.

CHAPTER II. GEOLOGY AND SOILS.

green-stone dykes of Úttattúr, all of which disappear under the cretaceous rocks without in the least affecting them. Had the dykes been formed by intrusion of the trappean rocks after deposition of the beds of the cretaceous system, the latter must inevitably have shown signs of alteration at the point of junction even if they had not been penetrated themselves by the eruptive masses. From the great similarity of mineral character, it does not seem rash to argue the probability of the dykes, *generally*, being of pre-cretaceous age.

(*b*) *Granites and Quartz Veins.*—The greatest development of granite in the Trichinopoly District occurs along the north bank of the Cauvery, in a band stretching from the neighbourhood of Irungalúr, in the Trichinopoly Taluq, as far west as Karúr, and in all probability beyond that point. This band is from 4 to 6 miles wide, measuring from the edge of the alluvium northwards, and is made up of reefs of granite which run generally in a north-east-by-north direction. The rock appears to have been intruded between the planes of bedding of the gneiss. It is, as a rule, largely crystallized with but little mica and very large felspar (orthoclase) crystals of a rich salmon color.

Binary granite.

A very common form of granite throughout the Trichinopoly District is a binary variety, consisting of felspar and quartz, in which the felspar is usually of a white or yellowish-white color; though typical granite (quartz, felspar and mica) is of frequent occurrence. About seven or eight miles south-south-east of Trichinopoly, there is a very fine vein of this last, in which the crystals of felspar are very large, some of them being four or five inches in diameter, with the mica occurring in long flat prisms of two-and-a-half inches in length. This vein, like another of identical character at Neyvéli, a few yards south of the crystalline limestone, shows two structures; the sides of the vein are irregularly crystallized, while internally it assumes the structure of graphic granite. Of the granite and quartz veins met with elsewhere, only a few require any separate mention on account of their having distinguishing features.

Crystal cavities in quartz.

In several instances the quartz was found to be full of cavities, which had evidently contained rhombic crystals of some accessory mineral, possibly carbonate of iron. Occasionally a rusty-looking mass of decomposed matter is found remaining in the corners of the cavities, which suggests the idea of its being the remnant of decay of the crystals which originally filled the cavities. In no case was any distinctly recognizable substance found occupying the cavities.

Besides these distinct and probably latest intrusions of granite among the metamorphic rocks, there are distributed all over the valley of the Cauvery, from Karúr to Trichinopoly, and beautifuly displayed on the numerous bosses and hummocks of quartzo-felspathic gneiss of that region, thin strings and veins of granite, varying from a few inches to a foot in thickness; and of these there are two systems, one of which very often crosses the other. In the newer the walls of the veins are distinctly marked, while in the other the lines of separation are seen with difficulty, these having been obliterated by remetamorphism. Enclosed fragments of gneiss torn off by the granite during its intrusion are by no means unfrequent.

Enclosed fragments of granite veins.

A very interesting example of this last feature may be seen in one of the most prominent granite ridges near Sinna Vangáram, about three miles from Samayapuram in Trichinopoly Taluq, where a mass of well-foliated gneiss of irregular shape, but several feet in length, is visible, imbedded in the mass of the pink granite.

Again, in the large and extended outburst of granite which has taken place north-east of Tógamalai, Kulittalai Taluq, immense masses of hornblendic schist, 30 or 40 square yards in extent, appear to have been, as it were, floated about, while their ragged edges are lengthened out until felspar, quartz, mica, and hornblende have been twisted into a thin rope of different-colored strands. In all cases the laminæ of felspar appear to have been lengthened out and twisted to a greater extent than those of the other minerals.

PART IX.— SUPERFICIAL DEPOSITS AND SOILS.

Among superficial deposits there are three more especially deserving of notice, because, though they often occupy merely the position of surface soils, they frequently also attain to such extent and thickness as really to demand the rank of geological formations; and, further, they are almost peculiar to India. These are *laterite*, *cotton soil*, and *kunkur*. In the country at present described laterite occurs more particularly associated with the post-cretaceous rocks, and on this account this rock has been described in the portion of this chapter relating to them. The peculiar phenomena observed in connection with cotton soil will be touched upon when treating of soils considered with reference to agriculture.

Kunkur.

The greyish white calcareous deposit, generally known under the name of kunkur, occurs commonly over the whole country, generally as little grains or concretions, or small agglomerations of such in the soil; very often also as a travertin-like deposit on the surface of the rocks in river-beds, where it occasionally forms the matrix of coarse conglomerates and breccias. Less frequently it is to be seen as the result of decomposition *in situ*.

CHAPTER II. GEOLOGY AND SOILS.

Two forms of kunkur.

This rock in some respects resembles laterite in its mode of occurrence. It exists in like manner under two different forms, which are the result of deposition from water in the one case, and of decomposition of the rock *in situ* in the other.

Concretionary kunkur.

The first form is kunkur proper, and is more commonly observable as a semi-concretionary deposit of a white, grey, or light-brown color on the surfaces and in the joints of rocks, particularly on the rocks or in the beds of streams. The concretions are essentially composed of carbonate of lime in a matrix of the same mineral, but small grains of quartz and gneiss often replace these. Another form of occurrence is that of single pisolitic grains, or small accumulations of these, in the different soils, and cotton soil is so largely impregnated with it in some localities that it almost loses its distinctive character as "regur." The ordinary "chunam" is made from the small nodular concretions. The conglomeratic form of kunkur is not of very frequent occurrence to any large extent, but it may be well seen in the banks of the river Taligai, a few miles south of the low ridge, which forms the junction between the Kollimalais and the Pachamalais. Here for about two miles the banks consist of thick masses of conglomerate, in which fragments of almost every variety of rock of the neighbourhood may be detected. The conglomerate not unfrequently forms cliffs running along the water-side at a very equal level, and presenting the appearance of quays of artificial construction. Much more rare than the conglomerate cliffs are cliffs of concretionary limestone formed by infiltration of calcareous matter held in solution into sandy soil. Where the infiltration process has been active, a rude, branching, and faintly coral-like mass of kunkur concretions becomes solid a yard or two higher up in the section, while in a downward direction the branches become disconnected, and further down still the kunkur occurs only in pellets imbedded in the red sand. The horizontal extension of such aggregations of kunkur are generally limited to a few square yards, where the infiltration has been but trifling; only a few rudely cylindrical concretions may be seen in a vertical position.

Kunkur from decomposition *in situ*.

The form of kunkur resulting from the decomposition of gneiss *in situ* has only been observed to any extent in sections exposed by the digging of wells, and these are mostly in the neighbourhood of alluvial deposits, such as the cultivated flats below tank bunds and spreads of cotton soil, the difficulty in these cases being to find a fresh section. At Ranganádapuram, a few miles north of Turaiyúr, the following section was found in a recently dry tank: at the surface, cotton soil containing grains of kunkur; this, after a foot or so in depth, gradually changed into a white semi-compact kunkury marl, having small grains of gneiss and quartz in it. There was about two feet of this, when another gradual change into true gneiss *in situ* appeared. In this space of change, from kunkury marl to gneiss, there were remains of folia with fragments of undecomposed gneiss in position, having their laminæ parallel to the true direction of foliation. A like change is also often observable on the banks of streams, where the gneiss is decomposed into a white calcareous rock of marly appearance for some inches from the surface which still retains foliation marks and undecomposed laminæ of quartz and mica, and occasionally sporadic garnets.

The greatest development of both of the above forms of kunkur has been observed, as might be expected, where hornblendic gneiss or basaltic trap prevail, there being about seven per cent. of lime in hornblendic rock, while as much as nine per cent. of the same mineral occurs in some basalts. Kunkur is generally of a dirty white color where pure, but the presence of iron renders it brown or reddish in hue. It occasionally assumes a pisolitic or botryoidal form, and is thin reddish-brown or dark-brown color, and very compact.

Age of kunkur.

As regards the age of this deposit, as far as has been seen, it would appear to be essentially recent, and there can be little doubt that the formation of all the varieties of kunkur mentioned above is now in progress in every part of the country where the calceferous rocks are being acted on by atmospheric agencies.

Kunkur pebbles, formed by the wearing down of angular fragments or of large concretions, may be found in the upper courses of several of the large rivers and streams in considerable quantity.

Soils.—Under this head are included, irrespective of their origin, those formations, generally but slightly coherent, which form the upper surface of the country, and therefore come under the hands of the agriculturists.

Four classes of soils.

The various soils which occur throughout the district may be conveniently referred to the following four classes:—

I. Red soils.
II. Alluvial soils.
III. Black soils.
IV. Mixed soils.

These will be treated of in succession according to their relative importance as they are arranged above.

Red soil: Lál.

I. First in importance, because covering by far the greatest area, is the "Red soil" or Lál, which is for the most part a sandy soil, and is perhaps most typically seen on and in the neighbour-

CHAPTER II. GEOLOGY AND SOILS.

hood of the Cuddalore Sandstones, where it is, on the whole, either the result of the weathering of the sands *in situ*, or a loose deposit of materials derived from the adjacent rocks. There it is a highly-ferruginous soil, but occasionally clayey, and then of pale yellow and greyish-brown color, and, on the whole, not very productive. Generally it is thinly spread over the surface, as in the Udaiyár-pálayam Taluq, but instances have been observed where it attains a thickness of four feet or more. It is, as a rule, very fine grained, but becomes coarser towards the bottom, where a thin layer of rounded quartz pebbles is of frequent occurrence.

The surface is often hardened or caked, the furrows, even in freshly-ploughed fields, becoming compact after some days' exposure.

Red soil, especially the sandy variety, covers by far the greater area in the metamorphic regions. Around the foot of each of the mountain-ranges the red soil occurs in a belt, a mile or two in width, forming a deposit of fine red sand, having a caked surface, like that observed in the soil covering the grits.

It is generally four or five feet deep, but much greater thickness is often observable in the peculiarly deep and narrow gullies which have been worn in the deposit by the streams.

The *Lál* is in many cases nothing more than the result of the decomposition of the underlying, or closely adjoining, rocks of the metamorphic series, which are all more or less ferruginous, and have a more irregular texture than the grits.

Fertility of coarse arenaceous soils.

The red and sandy soils are very largely cultivated for, and appear to be admirably adapted to, the growth of dry-grain crops.

Connection of red soil with underlying rocks.

With regard to the connection of the red soil with the underlying rocks, it may be observed that where granite and quartz abound a coarse dry soil of reddish or brown color prevails, as is the case over the greater part of the Trichinopoly District south of the Cauvery. Where hornblendic rocks prevail, the soil shows rapid alternations of red of all shades, some very bright, others toned by an admixture of brown. The presence of magnetic iron-beds renders the soil generally of a very dark-red or reddish-brown.

Origin of the red soils.

Of the origin of the red soils but little can be said. A great part, and probably by far the greatest part, is formed by the docomposition of more or less ferruginous rocks, especially the hornblendic varieties. Mr. Blandford considered them to have been chiefly formed in or on the sides of lagoons, a supposition which, however, in the opinion of Messrs. King and Foote, did not appear to be borne out by the facts of the case generally, though to certain beds of limited area such an origin might be attributed.

The red soils occurring on the several ranges of mountains which are evidently formed by weathering of the underlying rocks, cannot be distinguished by the eye from the *Lál* of the plains, and in both, the variation of the amount of ferruginous matter may be constantly seen to be dependent upon the nature of the underlying rocks.

II. Second in point of area are the *alluvial soils.*

Position of the alluvium.

Deposition of alluvium has taken place along the whole seaboard of this part of Southern India, forming a continuous belt varying in breadth, which, in a westerly direction, runs up the valleys of the three main rivers and of their tributaries; while all along the edge of the seaward belt, and occasionally further inland, ridges of sand have been formed by the winds prevalent in these localities.

Alluvium of the Cauvery.

The alluvium of the Cauvery extends over a very wide area, occupying a considerable part of the Trichinopoly District, and by far the larger half of Tanjore, and it strikes up in a northerly direction to join the alluvium of the Vellár in the South Arcot District.

The delta.

The delta commences at the head of Srírangam Island, ten miles west-north-west of Trichinopoly, where the Coleroon branches off, forming the most northerly of the many channels by which the water reaches the sea.

Northern boundary.

The northern boundary of the alluvial valley is formed by metamorphic rocks which extend eastward, with a short intervening spread of cretaceous rocks, to within nine or ten miles south of Ariyalúr. From this point the cretaceous rocks, succeeded by Cuddalore sandstones, form the boundary; the latter formation gradually landing north and forming a low promontory between the alluvial flats of the Cauvery and Vellár Rivers.

Along the side of the delta, as well as on the north bank of the Cauvery, west of Srírangam Island, the alluvial boundary, owing to the more gentle rise of the country (except in the neighbourhood of the rugged granitic ridges of Irungalúr, and the spread of granitoid metamorphic rocks to the eastward) and the uniform character of the rocks across which the tributaries have worn their way, extends for a good distance up the courses of these rivers. On the south side the boundary is much less sinuous, the streams having more the nature of torrents than of rivers; the country through which they flow rising rather rapidly and being more rugged than that on the left bank of the Cauvery.

Cultivation of the alluvium.

Almost the whole surface of the alluvial plain is under wet cultivation. In many places the limit of this cultivation coincides with the boundary of the alluvium; in others it has crossed and covered up the natural line of boundary, rendering the exact determination and laying down of the saem a matter of great difficulty and sometimes an impossibility. In the case of the tributary streams from the north, this difficulty occurs pretty frequently, for bunds have been built across the streams at various points, so as to form tanks, and these, with the artificial channels running parallel to the river, have assisted in the formation of alluvial flats extending often a mile or more beyond the true boundary.

Alluvial soils.

Nature of the Alluvial Soils.—Two principal varieties of soil occupy by far the greater part of the surface of the delta, and are very nearly equal in extent of development first, dark humus; second, pale yellow sandy soil.

The dark humus occurs chiefly above and about the head of the delta, the seaboard and adjacent country having a decidedly sandy character; many parts indeed, if not irrigated, would speedily become a perfect desert. The humus is, where dry, not unlike cotton-soil in appearance, but less friable; when wet it has considerable plasticity without, however, in general, assuming a clayey character. The sandy districts, when well irrigated, are by no means unfertile, though vegetation has not quite the same unbounded luxuriance as on the dark soil. Clayey beds are very rare.

Cotton soil.

III. *Black Soils.*—Cotton soil (or regur), as the name implies, is one in which cotton is grown. But it does not follow that this vegetable product is only grown on such a soil; indeed, it is oftener and better cultivated on a dark-grey soil, in which there is a considerable amount of calcareous matter (kunkur).

Cotton soil near Válikandapuram and Settikulam.

In the neighbourhood of Válikandapuram, there are some extensive spreads of cotton soil flanking the north-east side of the Pachamalais. It is also found to the south of these mountains where there is a large spread immediately south and west of Settikulam.

In the Turaiyúr Valley.

In the Turaiyúr Valley, between the Kollimalais and Pachamalais, regur occurs, in several detached and rounded patches, about three miles north-west of Kannanúr, at Badarpéttai, four or five miles south of Uppiliyapuram and at Ammapatti, three miles south of Turaiyúr.

Varieties of regur.

The very black soil lies, as far as has been observed, on the higher undulations of the comparatively flat country. It is generally of a very dark-brownish black color, with occasionally greyish or bluish shades. The mineral composition of cotton soil varies considerably, some varieties being so sandy as to constitute a clayey loam, while others are marly, or still more rarely form a very stiff clay, all agreeing, as a rule, in the absence of coarse mineral particles.

In dry weather the surface is seamed with gaping cracks, which break it up into irregular polygonal figures, and the soil is then very friable, but in wet weather it becomes a highly tenacious mud.

Many of the larger cracks extend three or four feet in depth, and, where numerous, render the ground unsafe for rapid riding.

Organic matter in regur.

According to existing chemical analysis, there is very little organic matter in this soil, the mean result of observations being about four per cent.

Agricultural value.

Regur is principally devoted to the cultivation of cotton, but dry grains are also extensively raised on it.

Mixed soils.

IV. The least important of the four classes of soils that have been mentioned above is that of the mixed *soils* which occupy a small area, comparatively speaking, in the country now treated of. In this class the various transitions between red, black, sandy, and white soils and vegetable mould are included. These transitions are generally met with at the borders of great spreads of the several pure soils which commonly appear to graduate into each other, a process greatly assisted by the turning up of the soils in agricultural processes. In many cases the transition is very gradual and insensible, and it is often very difficult to decide what to consider as an impure variety of a pure soil, or what to class at once as a mixed soil.

Mixed regur soil.

In connection with the regur two classes of mixed varieties may be established.

First.—Soils of organic origin, in which animal life was more prevalent than vegetable life, as proved by the excessive quantity of kunkur formed by decomposition of shells, &c., and subsequent precipitation of the carbonate of lime derived from them. This class is one which undergoes many changes in its composition and texture, according to the greater or lesser amount of kunkur particles which may be distributed through it, becoming of a light grey or even whitish color.

Secondly.—Soils of an origin only in part organic are found, which assume a dark brown or reddish tinge, owing to the admixture of ferruginous matter derived from the rock in the immediate neighbourhood. Some of the transition soils are of great fertility, especially the dark chocolate-colored loams met with at the junction of rich red soils with black soils.

White or salt soil.

The most barren of all the soils is the white or salt soil, generally a mixture of clay and sand in variable proportions, containing considerable quantities of both soda and potash, together with some common salt. These salts are derived from the decomposition of the highly felspathic rocks in the neighbourhood. This white soil is generally met with in hollows or swampy plains, and often contains small but troublesome quicksands.

CHAPTER II. GEOLOGY AND SOILS.

On the south bank of the Cauvery there are several spreads of this white soil, where large nullahs, which have had a rapid course over the different beds of the metamorphic series, suddenly come upon nearly level ground near the edge of the alluvium. The white soil occurs in many places all over the country, but the spreads are very rarely of sufficient extent to be worthy of notice.

Rarity of marls.

As might be expected from the very trifling amount of limestone occurring within the Trichinopoly District, true marls are almost unknown, unless some of the kunkury varieties of cotton soil be regarded as such. If this be done, they are not uncommon in the regur-covered districts before enumerated.

PART X.— ECONOMIC GEOLOGY.

No one can have travelled through any of the districts of Southern India in which large pagodas occur without having been struck by the admirable adaption to architectural purposes of several varieties of gneiss rock, as regards both the size and the durability of the blocks employed independently of their beauty when polished.

Gneiss.

Fine masses of this rock might be obtained from several of the gneiss bosses near Trichinopoly, such as the Erumbísvaram Pagoda Rock, the Golden Rock, and the Trichinopoly Rock itself, in all of which the jointing and foliation appear favorable to the quarrying of large rectangular masses of stone.

Some of the finest carvings in the temple of Srírangam are executed in fine-grained pinkish-colored quartzo-felspathic gneiss, containing a few small crystals of magnetic iron.

The entrance to the rock pagoda at Trichinopoly may likewise be mentioned as showing some fair examples of large-sized carved pillars of gneiss.

Close to the travellers' bungalow at Válikandapuram stands a fine old pagoda, now rapidly falling into ruins, the base of the gópuram and adjoining mantapam of which, as well as a small deep tank surrounded by a covered terrace, show some very beautiful carvings in gneiss on a large scale.

Crystalline limestone.

The crystalline limestones of this area, so far as is known, have never been put to any use in masonry, excepting perhaps a few rough blocks, loosely piled together, in the bund of a tank. If well selected, however, they are not only admirably adapted for general building purposes, but could advantageously be applied to decorative purposes, being susceptible of a high polish. The marble must, however, not be polished in the native method, which generally greatly defaces the stone by choking all the minute cracks between the crystals with some black substance.

The beds at each of the localities enumerated in Part VII are, it is believed, well worth quarrying both for building stones and lime-burning. In the former capacity their superiority to bricks is unquestionable, and they are so much more easily and cheaply dressed than any of the siliceous gneissic rocks that they merit every attention. The beds are, as a rule, singularly free from joints, and blocks of immense size might, in many places, be obtained with very little difficulty. The natives, indeed, do not use the limestone even for the purpose of lime-burning, for which object, of all the various materials available, two only are made use of, viz., kunkur and shells. The intermittent process of burning is the only one practised and the quantity of lime burnt at one operation is usually small, frequently less than a hundred-weight. The kilns are of mud and vary in construction.

Kunkur mortar.

The mortar prepared from kunkur is very hard and lasting. It appears, however, to be but sparingly used in stone edifices. In some of the large pagodas the stones are either laid together without mortar, or so little is used that it is not seen at the surface of the work. The roofs of many of the chattrams and mantapams are constructed of long blocks of gneiss carried on joists of the same rock, which in their turn are borne on the elongated capitals of the square columns, all, so far as can be seen, laid dry without mortar. The best and purest kunkur noticed during the geological survey occurred in the laminated sandy beds of the Trichinopoly group to the west of Kallikkudi. Perhaps equally good is found in similar beds of the Úttattúr group to the east of Terani and Kárai, and the mineral occurs more or less throughout the gypseous clays to the east of Úttattúr, and to the south and south-east of the same place. On the Ariyalúr beds in the east of the district it usually forms a bed of one or two feet in thickness, being probably derived in a great measure from the denuded beds of the group ; and a similar bed frequently occurs in the same position on the surface of the gneiss, where the rock is covered with regur. In the old alluvium of the Vellár and the other large rivers kunkur always occurs to some extent, but it is less abundant in the more recent deposits of the Cauvery Delta. It is probably in a great measure owing to the almost universal distribution of this mineral, and the ease with which it is collected, as much as to its excellence as a material for mortar, that the limestones so abundant throughout the district have been hitherto almost entirely neglected as a source of lime.

Pot-stone vessels.

Vessels of all shapes and sizes are made from blocks of pot-stone or compact steatite. The vessels are cut by means of various chisel-shaped tools, while resting either on a pad of straw and rags or else on the operator's lap.

CHAPTER II. GEOLOGY AND SOILS.

Uses to which trappean rocks are put.

Trap rocks are used only as rough stones for tank-bunds, &c., or as road metal, for which latter purpose they are better than almost any other class of rocks, especially for roads exposed to heavy traffic. In addition to their exceeding hardness and difficulty of working, there is a great objection to their employment as building stones, namely, that in damp climates the basaltic varieties absorb and retain great quantities of moisture.

Laterite.

Laterite, if well selected, offers a fair building stone, and, though apt to wear away soon under heavy traffic, it also makes a good road material, because of its strong binding qualities. It is quarried in various places for both purposes, especially along the road from Trichinopoly to Tanjore.

It is quarried at or a little below the surface, square blocks being picked out with a crow-bar, or the ordinary pick used by the natives, and then left for some time to become hardened. While being quarried the stone is sectile, requiring but little trouble in the dressing, but eventually it becomes quite hard. It is largely employed as a road metal. It is, from its very vesicular character, but rarely susceptible of anything like ornamental carving.

On the subject of the value of laterite as a building stone a considerable diversity of opinion exists amongst those able to form a correct judgment on such a matter—by some its value is greatly extolled, by others it is rejected as a very untrustworthy material,—on account of its very varying degree of resistance to crushing power. The fact is, laterite frequently varies greatly in quality even in different parts of the same bed; hence, in a work in which durability is an object, much circumspection should be used in the selection of the laterite blocks to be employed, which should be neither very sandy nor yet wanting in iron. Where of poor quality the laterite soon crumbles away when exposed to the influence of weather and moisture.

Brick clays.

The only clays used by the natives for brick-making are those of the fluviatile alluvial deposits, and more rarely of the superficial deposits, which cover the gneiss of the low country. The latter are in general but little adapted for the purpose, consisting either of sand, with too small a proportion of clay, or of regur, which, on the other hand, is an almost pure loam. Where the two forms of soil meet and intermingle are the best spots for the purpose of brick-manufacture. It is only in towns and some few large villages that bricks are much used, the huts of the agricultural classes being built of mud with thatched roofs. The native process of brick-making is a rude form of that commonly practised in other countries. The clay, which is always so sandy as to enable the workmen to dispense with the preliminary process of pugging, is mixed by the aid of a shovel with sufficient water to render it a semi-fluid paste, which is rudely and rapidly moulded in a wetted mould, and the bricks, being dried in the sun, are burnt in a kiln in the usual manner. The native bricks are soft and bad, frequently containing cavities and irregular in shape, but this is due to want of proper care in mixing and moulding and to insufficient burning. It is probable that the same clays used by them would yield excellent bricks under an improved process.

Fine clays and pottery materials.

The cretaceous rocks and plant-beds of Trichinopoly yield several fine clays well adapted for the manufacture of pottery and other materials used in the ceramic arts, viz., China stone and kaolin, felspar, flints, and gypsum, are all obtainable within this district. None of these are utilized by the natives, whose pottery (unglazed and porous) is made chiefly from sandy ferruginous clays, which occur at one or two places in the superficial deposits.

Pipe-clay.

A fine pipe-clay occurs in the plant-beds between Terani and Kárai, forming a thick bed, which is exposed in cne of the small feeders of the Terani Tank, about a mile and half to the north-east of the village. The clay is a greyish-white clunch, with a few stains of iron, but, were a pure clay required, the stained parts might be easily separated by hand-picking. This clay when ground and kneaded works well, and when burnt assumes a bluish-white tinge.

Felspar.

The granitic ridge to the north of the Cauvery contains a large quantity of felspar, and this mineral might be easily obtained free from any admixture of quartz. Large quantities are scattered over the stony parts of the ridge, and might be collected at small cost. It is apparently an arthoclase, but it has not yet been analysed.

Flints.

Flints, almost undistinguishable from fragments of English chalk flints, are found at Kurichikulam, in the Udaiyárpálayam Taluq, a few miles south of the Vellár. They occur in the highest exposed part of the cretaceous rocks near the overlap of the Cuddalore beds, and probably form a continuous band running north and south. The country is, however, too thickly covered with soil to admit of the flint-bed being traced throughout. These flints are used by the natives of the surrounding villages for obtaining fire with a steel.

Gypsum.

This mineral is common in many parts of the cretaceous rocks of Trichinopoly, generally in the form of fibrous plates intercalated in the bedding and of no great thickness, more rarely in concretions, and replacing the shells of *Nautili*, *Ammonites*, and other fossils. A pure gypsum, fitted for the preparation of stucco or statuary casts, is with difficulty found, as it almost invariably contains a small proportion of clay, which cannot be separated by washing, and which would destroy its whiteness; but it may be obtained in any desired quantity of sufficient purity for the

CHAPTER II. GEOLOGY AND SOILS.

preparation of moulds, such as are used in the ceramic arts, or indeed for any purpose in which pure whiteness is not essential. It is most abundant in the Úttattúr beds, especially in the belemnite clays to the east of Úttattúr, and in the unfossiliferous clay to the north-east of Maravattúr. At the former place it occurs in fibrous plates of from half an inch to two or three inches in thickness, and may be collected in any quantity in the broken ground between Úttattúr and Kerudamangalam. At Maravattúr it occurs both in the fibrous form and in transparent plates (selenite) and crystals irregularly intercalated in the clays of the lower part of the group. Fragments of great purity may be easily selected, but it cannot be obtained in any quantity free from the argillaceous matrix.

Salt and soda.

Common salt effloresces from the soil and superficial rocks over a considerable area to the north of Lálgudi and is collected by the poorest of the village people for household use. It is very impure, containing apparently a considerable admixture of chloride of calcium, which gives it a disagreeable bitter taste, and which the village people have not the art of separating. It is chiefly collected from the beds of nullahs, where, after a draught of a few weeks, it covers the sand with a thin efflorescence. The surface sand, having been scraped together by the villagers, is lixiviated, and the solution thus obtained evaporated to dryness in the sun on flat stones, round which a run of clay has been made to retain the solution.

Soda is of widespread occurrence in the Trichinopoly District, chiefly on the gneiss and on the alluvium, more rarely on the cretaceous rocks. It is, however, never derived from these latter rocks, but from the decomposition of the many varieties of hornblendic and felspathic gneiss. It occurs in a whitish soil known as "dhobies' earth," which is usually found in marshy places. The earth is collected by washermen, and used instead of soap for washing cloth. The soda is frequently mixed with common salt and probably with other soluble salts.

Iron ores.

The cretaceous rocks contain in several places ferruginous nodules, which mounds of old slags prove to have been worked by the natives at some former period. The greater part of the plains is now too denuded of jungle to allow of fuel being consumed in the production of iron, however abundant its ores may be, and little or no iron is at present made in the Trichinopoly District. The only place where the people have been observed engaged in this manufacture is at Talugai Village in the Musiri Taluq. Ferruginous concretions, which have been at one time worked, occur in the Úttattúr beds to the south of Úttattúr and in the lower beds of the Ariyalúr group to the south of Ariyalúr.

CHAPTER II. GEOLOGY AND SOILS.

Copper ores.

The gneiss in the neighbourhood of Olappádi and Veppúr Villages in the Perumbalúr Taluq shows frequent stains of copper, and in a small nullah to the south of the latter village Mr. Blandford found two or three pieces of cupriferous veinstone, but was unable to discover their origin. The specimens were considerably water-worn; they consisted of quartz with little nests of malachite, red oxide, fahl-erz and native copper, and were of sufficient richness to repay working were there any quantity of ore equally good. The gneiss around was found much penetrated by little cracks filled with quartz and calespar, and it is probable that the veinstone had been derived from one of these of unusually large dimensions.

Ornamental stones.

Under this head may be included the marbles which have been described under the head of limestones, and a few varieties of quartz of no great importance. The only marble worked by the natives as such is the shell marble of Kerudamangalam, a village in the south of the Perambalúr Taluq, of which table-tops, paper-weights, and similar ornaments are manufactured in Trichinopoly. When polished it is of dark-grey color, and is marked, like the well known purbeck stone, with white sections of the included shells.

CHAPTER III.

FLORA AND FAUNA.

FLORA—Cereals.—Fibres.—Tobacco.—Indigo.—Betel-vine.—Vegetables.—Timber and Fruit Trees.

THE FOREST DEPARTMENT—Fuel Reserves.—Plantations.—Proposal to transfer the Pachamalais to the Forest Department.

FAUNA—Feræ Naturæ.—Mammals.—Fish.—Snakes.—Silkworm.

CHAPTER III. FLORA AND FAUNA.

THE flora and fauna of the district have never been described, and I have not been able, either in the Collector's records or elsewhere, to get much assistance towards preparing an account of them. Such information as I have been able to collect will be found in the following pages :—

FLORA.

Cereals.

The most important cereals grown in the district will be first described.

The principal grain grown in the district is rice (*Oryza sativa*), of which there are two main varieties known as Sambá or Pisánam and Kár. Sambá is the best description of rice grown in the district, and is consumed by all the well-to-do classes. It is sometimes a five and sometimes a six months' crop. When grown as a single crop, as it very commonly is, it is sown in July and August and harvested in December and January. When cultivated as a second crop, it is sown in October and November and harvested in March and April. It is sometimes sown broadcast, but, as a rule, is grown first in seed-beds and then transplanted. There are thirteen different kinds of Sambá grown in the district, of which the following are the Tamil names :—Sirumaniyan (six months' crop), Tótakál sambá (five months), Muttu sambá (six months), Vattalkundu sambá (five months), Gerudan sambá (six months), Anantan sambá (five months), Pálaimaniyan (six months), Kaivara sambá (five months), Vangi (six months), Púngár (four months), Sembálai (six months), Perumbisánam (seven months), Irámabanam (seven months).

Kár is an inferior description of paddy, and is eaten principally by the lower classes. It is of four kinds, known as Kódaikár, Senkuruvai, Venkuruvai, and Márikár. Of these the three first are four months' crops, but the last takes five and sometimes six months to reach maturity. Márikár is sown in July and August and harvested in November and December, and the other three description of Kár paddy are, as a rule, sown in November and December and harvested in March and April.

In addition to the above there is a bearded variety of paddy to be found in the district which is called Válán, from the Tamil word Vál, a tail. It is an inferior description of rice, and it is eaten by the laboring classes only. It is sown in February and March and harvested in July and August. In Fasli 1285 (1875-76) 134,007 acres in the district were cultivated with rice.

The following are the dry grains grown in the district :—Rági (*Eleusine coracana*) (Tam. Képpai) is one of the commonest dry grains. It is a four months' crop, and is sown in May, June, July or August, and harvested in September, October, November, or December. It is eaten by all classes in the dry villages, usually in the form of cakes. It is often grown on garden land, and watered by baling from wells. In Fasli 1285 (1875-76) 104,007 acres in the district were cultivated with rági.

Chólum (*Holcus saccharatus*) is extensively grown all over th dry parts of the district, especially in Kulittalai and Musiri Taluqs. It is a four months' crop, and is sown in June or July and harvested in October or November. It is boiled and eaten much in the same manner as rice. In Fasli 1285 (1875-76) 140,176 acres in the district were cultivated with chólum. Cumbu (*Holcus spicatus*) is the dry grain most extensively grown in the district. It is a four months' crop, being sown in July and harvested in November. It is eaten in the same manner as chólum. In Fasli 1285 157,193 acres were cultivated with this grain. Varagu (*Paspalum frumentaceum*) is extensively cultivated in Udaiyárpálayam and Perambalúr Taluqs, and to a less degree in the dry villages in the other taluqs. It is a four months' crop, being sown in May, June or July, and harvested in September, October, and November. It is boiled and eaten like cumbu. In Fasli 1285 (1875-76) 145,803 acres in the district were cultivated with varagu.

Tuvarai (*Cajanus Indicus*) is cultivated to a considerable extent in Musiri Taluq, but not much elsewhere. It is a three months' crop, and is sown in December and harvested in March. When the husks have been removed it is known as dholl (Tam. Paruppu), and is eaten in the form of cakes. It is a favorite flavoring grain. In Fasli 1285 28,028 acres were sown with this grain. Sámai (*Panicum miliaceum*) is extensively grown in Kulittalai Taluq, but is rarely met with in Perambalúr and Udaiyárpálayam. It is a three months' crop, being sown in August or September and harvested in November or December. It is boiled and eaten in the same way as chólum or cumbu. In Fasli 1285 24,809 acres were cultivated with sámai. Ulundu (*Phaseolus radiatus*), black

CHAPTER III. FLORA AND FAUNA.

gram, is but little grown in the district, only 2,372 acres having been cultivated with it in Fasli 1285. The seed is pounded and then made into cakes and eaten. It is a four months' crop, being sown in September and harvested in January.

Tinai (*Panicum Italicum*), or Italian millet, is a three months' crop, being sown in September and harvested in December. It is an inferior description of grain, and is but little cultivated, only 2,372 acres having been sown with it in Fasli 1285.

Mochai (*Dolichos lablab*) is a six months' crop, being sown in July or August and reaped in February and March. It is but little grown, and only 3,934 acres were cultivated with it in Fasli 1285.

Kollu (*Dolichos uniflorus*), or horse-gram, is a four months' crop, being sown in October and reaped in February. It is a precarious crop, as it requires frequent showers, and is destroyed equally by excessive drought or moisture. It is grown to a considerable extent in Kulittalai Taluq, but not much elsewhere. In Fasli 1285 25,022 acres were cultivated with gram.

Kadalai (*Cicer arietinum*), or Bengal gram, is but little cultivated in this district, only 649 acres having been cultivated with it in Fasli 1285. It is a three months' crop, being sown in December and harvested in March. Amanaku (*Ricinus communis*), or castor-oil seed. There are two varieties of the castor-oil plant known as *Fructibus Majoribus* and *Minoribus*. It is from the former of these that the lamp-oil, which is so much used, is made, while the castor-oil used as medicine is prepared from the small-seeded variety. The large-seeded variety is cultivated throughout the dry parts of the district, and 24,321 acres were sown with it in Fasli 1285. It is a six months' crop, being sown in July and harvested in January.

An account of the fibres of the district will now be given.

Fibres.

The cultivation of fibre-producing trees and plants in Trichinopoly District is very limited. The principal descriptions to be found are the following :—The plantain (*Musa paradisiaca*) (Tam. Válai). Although this tree is extensively cultivated, its fibre is made but little use of. The palmyra (*Borassus flabelliformis*) (Tam. Panaimaram). This tree is but rarely to be met with, and but little fibre is made from it. (*Hibiscus cannabinus*) (Tam. Pulicharkírai). This plant is cultivated on dry lands and in gardens, as a rule, along with some description of grain. The fibre is very strong, and is used for making ropes, &c. Tálai (*Pandanus odoratissimus*). The leaves of this plant abound in tough fibres, which are used for matting, &c., cordage. It is not extensively cultivated in the district. Sunn (*Crotalaria juncea*) (Tam. Sanal). The hemp manufactured from this plant is imported into Trichinopoly, but it is not cultivated there to any extent.

Among other useful plants grown in the district the following may be mentioned :—

Tobacco.

Tobacco (*Nicotiana tabacum*) (Tam. Pugaiyilai) is grown to a considerable extent in Kulittalai Taluq, to a less degree in Musiri, Perambalúr, and Udaiyárpálayam, and scarcely at all in Trichinopoly. The total number of acres cultivated with it in Fasli 1285 was 1,261. The average quantity produced per acre is about $1\frac{1}{2}$ candies.

—Method of cultivation.

Tobacco is, as a rule, grown on permanently improved garden land, and a rich alluvial soil is that best suited for its cultivation. The crop requires a considerable amount of water, which is, as a rule, raised to it by baling from wells. Cattle-dung is used to manure it. The seed is not sown broadcast in the fields, but in seed-beds. The seeds are sown about the middle of October, the seedlings transplanted towards the end of November, and the crop generally cut towards the beginning of the following April. As a general rule the plant is not interfered with till it puts forth about ten leaves. These are then left, and all others that may sprout out afterwards are plucked off. When these ten leaves come to maturity the stem on which they are growing is cut down. As a general rule there is no second crop. In some cases, however, after the stems have been cut the roots remaining in the ground are watered, and a fresh crop thus raised. The leaves thus grown are, however, generally small and poor.

—Method of curing adopted.

The following is the account given of the manner in which the tobacco leaves are cured. When the leaves have come to maturity, one day towards evening the cultivators cut down all the plants without, however, removing them from the fields. On the following morning these plants are collected and put in heaps, each containing twenty or thirty. These heaps are covered with varagu straw or sugar-cane stalks. In the evening the straw is removed and the plants are left exposed to the air till the following morning, when they are again covered as before. They are thus covered and uncovered every morning and evening for six or seven days, when they are taken into a house and hung in bundles of four or five tied together with a string and fastened to the beams of the roof. They are left thus for seven or eight days, when they are taken down and placed in heaps of one or one and a half yards in height and covered with straw, weights being placed on the top of them. On the fourth day these heaps are opened and the plants changed to a different spot, when they are again covered and lighter weights placed on them. This is done four times, and the leaves are then taken off from the several stems and strung together in bundles of

CHAPTER III. FLORA AND FAUNA.

sixty or seventy each. These are hung in the shade for three days, after which they are placed in rows and covered with straw, over which light weights are placed. They are left thus for fifteen days, when they are taken out and are then considered fit for use. The manufacture of cigars and cheroots is extensively carried on in Trichinopoly town, but, as the leaf grown in the district is not of a high quality, these are, as a rule, made of imported tobacco, the greater part of which comes from Dindigul. Manufactured tobacco is exported from Trichinopoly to all parts of India.

Cotton (*Gossypum Indicum*) (Tam. Parutti) is extensively cultivated in the karisal or black cotton soil of Perambalúr Taluq, but not much in other taluqs. It is sown in October or November, and the picking is carried on in February and March. In Fasli 1285 46,526 acres were cultivated with cotton. Indigo (*Indigofera tinctoria*) (Tam. Avuri) is but little grown in the district, only 678 acres having been cultivated with it in Fasli 1285. It is sown in October or November and cut in April and May. Betel-vine (*Chavica betel*) (Tam. Vettilai) is extensively grown in the gardens near Trichinopoly town. It is a precarious but most remunerative crop. It requires constant watering and heavy manuring. The vine is generally trained up the agati tree (*Agati grandiflora*). The leaves mixed with lime are masticated by natives of all classes. Turmeric (*Curcuma longa*) (Tam. Manjal) is grown extensively, as it is an almost invariable ingredient in curries. The crop takes about eight months to reach maturity, and requires irrigation. The following are the principal vegetables grown :—Chillies, green and red (*Capsicum annuum*) (Tam. Milakáy); Brinjals (*Solanum melongena*) (Tam. Katirikáy); Cucumber (*Cucumis utilissimus*) (Tam. Velliri); Sweet potato (*Batatas edulis*) (Tam. Vallikilangu); Onions (*Allium cepa*) (Tam. Vengáyam). Garlic (*Allium sativum* (Tam. Vellaipúndu); and various sorts of greens called in Tamil kérai.

The following is a list of the most important fruit and timber trees to be found in the district :—

Botanical Name.	Tamil Name.	Remarks.
Acacia amara ..	Usilai	The wood is strong and close-grained and is used for rice-pounders and in making cattle-pens.
Acacia Arabica ..	Karuvélam ..	*The Babul tree.*—The wood is hard and is used for making carts, ploughs, &c., and largely for firewood. The bark is used as a tonic and the young leaves as an astringent. The tree grows rapidly, and is to be found in all parts of the district, especially in the beds of tanks.
Acacia leucophlœa.	Velvélam	*The Panicled Acacia.*—The wood is hard and is used for building purposes, agricultural implements, and for firewood. The bark is one of the ingredients used in the manufacture of arrack.
Acacia planifrons ..	Sáli	The wood is used in making cattle-pens and for firewood.
Acacia sundra ..	Karungáli ..	The wood is hard and close-grained. It rarely, however, grows to a large size, and is used principally for posts and in making cots.
Ægle marmelos ..	Vilva-maram ..	*The Bel tree.*—The wood is useless. The fruit is nutritious and is used as an alterative. A decoction made from the fruit dried before it is ripe is used in cases of diarrhœa and dysentery.
Agati grandiflora ..	Agati	Principally grown in betel gardens. The bark is bitter and is used as a tonic. The leaves are used as a fodder for cattle and the wood as firewood.
Ailanthus excelsa.	Pínári	The wood is light and not durable. It is used for making planks.
Alangium decapatalum.	Alinji	The wood is handsome and valuable.
Anacardium occidentale.	Muntirikai ..	*The Cashew Nut.*—Oil is made from the nuts, the kernels of which are eaten by all classes. The wood is useless.
Anona squamosa.	Sítá-maram ..	*The Custard Apple tree.*—The leaves when bruised and mixed with salt are applied to tumours in order to ripen them. The fruit is excellent and is eaten by Natives and Europeans. The tree is constantly met with in the gardens in the irrigated parts of the district.
Artocarpus integrifolius.	Pilá-maram ..	*The Jack tree.*—The fruit, which grows to an enormous size and hangs by a peduncle springing from the trunk, is a favorite article of fruit with Natives. It has a sickening and offensive smell. The leaves are given as fodder to goats and other cattle. The wood is much used for making furniture for which it is very well suited.

CHAPTER III.
FLORA AND FAUNA.

Botanical Name.	Tamil Name.	Remarks.
Azadirachta Indica.	Véppa-maram ..	*The Nim or Margosa tree.*—The bark, which has a remarkably bitter taste, is often used as a substitute for cinchona. It is considered by Natives to be a useful tonic in intermittent fevers. It is also the custom among them to cover patients recovering from small-pox with its leaves. The oil extracted from the fruits is extensively used for lamps, oil cakes, &c., and by Natives for bathing purposes. The leaves are used as manure and as fodder for cattle. The wood is hard and very useful for economical purposes, principally because it is proof against insects. It makes an excellent avenue tree.
Bassia longifolia ..	Iluppai	One of the commonest trees in the district. The wood is hard and durable, but not easily worked. Its great merit is that it is not attacked by insects. Oil made out of the ripe fruit is very generally used. The smell of a tope of Iluppai trees at the season when the ripe fruits are falling is most disagreeable.
Bambusa arundinacea.	Múngil	*The Bamboo tree.*—The bamboo is applied to so many useful purposes that it would be difficult to mention an object to which strength and elasticity are requisite and for which lightness is no objection for which its stems are not made use of. It is used largely for building purposes, ladders, basket-boats, rafts, &c. The roots are diluent and the bark is a specific in eruptions. The seed is eaten and is known as bamboo rice.
Bauhinia acuminata	Kokumantárai ..	A large handsome shrub with white flowers which are used by Natives in their religious ceremonies. The wood serves as a fuel.
Bauhinia tomentosa.	Káttumantárai ..	The wood is used as fuel. Native physicians give the dried leaves and young flowers in cases of dysentery.
Borassus flabelliformis.	Panai-maram ..	*The Palmyra tree.*—The saccharine juice obtained by excision from the spadix, or young flowering branch, is when freshly drawn before sunrise of a pleasant sweet taste. After fermentation it becomes an intoxicating drink known as toddy. Jaggery is made from the same juice. The wood is largely used for rafters, joists, &c., being split in the direction of its length. The leaves are ordinarily used for thatching purposes. Strong and durable fibres are made from the petioles of the fronds. The tree is not much grown in this district.
Butea frondosa ..	Púvarasu ..	*The Bastard teak.*—This tree when in blossom has a striking appearance from its scarlet flowers from which a yellow dye is made. The tree reaches no great size and its wood is of little use. It is common throughout the district. What is known commercially as the *Butea kino* is made from a gum which exudes from the wood of this tree.

Botanical Name.	Tamil Name.	Remarks.
Calophyllum inophyllum.	Pinnai	*The Alexandrian Laurel.*—The oil extracted from the fruit is used for lamps and also medicinally. The wood is close-grained and durable and serves for building purposes and as firewood.
Canarium strictum.	Karuppu kungiliyam.	*Black Dammer tree.*—The tree yields a black dammer, which however is not much used. The wood is strong and well suited for building purposes.
Casuarina muricata.	Savukku-maram ..	*The Casuarina tree.*—Considerable quantities of this tree have been planted by the Forest Department chiefly in the padugai (river deposit) land along the Cauvery. The main stems are most useful as posts and the branches make excellent firewood.
Cathartocarpus fistula.	Konnai	*The Pudding Pipe tree.*—The wood is used for rafters and similar purposes and for firewood. The flowers are used by Natives in certain religious ceremonies.
Chloroxylon swietenia.	Kadapavurasu ..	*The Satin-wood tree.*—The wood is hard and durable and is used for building purposes, naves of wheels, axles, &c.
Citrus aurantium.	Kolingi	*The Orange tree.*—The fruit is eaten by all classes. It is not, however, extensively grown in this district.
Cocos nucifera ..	Tenna-maram ..	*The Cocoanut tree.*—To be found all over the irrigated portions of the district. There is scarcely a part of the plant which is not applied to some use by Natives. The nuts are eaten both ripe and unripe, and oil, largely used for culinary purposes and lamps, is made from them; *coir* is the fibrous rind of the nuts and is worked up into mats, cables, &c. Toddy and jaggery are also extracted from the tree in much the same manner as from the palmyra. The wood is strong and durable and is used for building and the leaves for thatching purposes.
Cratæva nurvala..	Mávilingai ..	The leaves, bark, and roots are used medicinally. The wood is soft and easily worked. It is used for making plank and as firewood.
Dalbergia latifolia.	Tótakatti ..	*Black-wood tree.*—The wood is most valuable, and when polished has something of the appearance of rosewood. Chairs, tables, and ornaments of various kinds, especially vases, are made of this wood in Trichinopoly.
Dalbergia sissu ..	Sesha-maram ..	The wood is light, but remarkably strong and durable. It is used for all ordinary economical purposes.
Diospyros cordifolia.	Vakkanai ..	The wood is hard and durable. It is used for firewood.
Eriodendron anfractuosum.	Ilavam	The seeds are embedded in silky cotton, which is used for stuffing beds, cushions, &c. The wood is soft and easily worked.
Erythrina Indica.	Marukkai ..	*The Indian Coral tree.*—The wood is soft and of but little use. The leaves are used as fodder for cattle.
Eugenia jambolana.	Nával	The wood is brittle and not of much value. It is used for firewood and for building purposes.

CHAPTER III. FLORA AND FAUNA.

Botanical Name.	Tamil Name.	Remarks.
Feronia elephantum.	Velám	*The Wood-apple tree.*—The fruit is eaten by all classes. A transparent gum exudes from this tree which resembles gum-arabic and is used by Native physicians in cases of diarrhœa and dysentery. The wood is white, hard, durable, and fine-grained.
Ficus glomerata ..	Péyatti	The wood is used for building purposes. The fruit is eaten by the poorer classes. A juice extracted from the trunk is used by Natives as medicine in cases of diabetis.
Ficus Indica ..	Álai	*The Banyan tree.*—This tree is especially remarkable for the great size to which it constantly grows in the following manner:—A gummy kind of rootlet falls from the branches which, on reaching the ground, forms a support to the branch, and several of these extending and increasing year by year, forming a vast assemblage of pillar-like stems, cover a considerable area round the original trunk. The wood is used for building purposes, making doors, carts, &c. It is brittle, light, and coarse-grained. The fruit is sometimes eaten by the poorer classes. The leaves are commonly used by Hindus when sewed together as plates to eat their food off.
Ficus racemosa ..	Atti	*The Fig tree.*—The fruit is eaten by all classes. The wood is brittle and coarse-grained. The tree is not extensively grown in this district.
Ficus religiosa ..	Arasu	The wood is light and of little use. It however grows very quickly and makes a fair avenue tree. It is to be found all over the district.
Hardwickia binata.	Áchá	The wood is hard, strong, and heavy. It is much used for building purposes.
Inga dulcis ..	Korukápuli ..	*The Manilla Tamarind.*—The fruit is eaten by the poorer classes. The wood is hard, coarse-grained, and brittle. It is used for economical purposes and as firewood.
Maba buxifolia ..	Irumbuli	The berries are edible. The wood is dark-colored, hard, durable, and useful for various economical purposes.
Mangifera Indica.	Má-maram ..	*The Mango tree.*—The wood is hard, close-grained, and durable. The fruit is the best of all Indian fruits and is eaten by Europeans and Natives. Out of the unripe fruit tarts, preserves, pickles, and chatney are made. The tree is common in the irrigated portions of the district. It is best propagated by grafting, but also grows from seed.
Melia Azedarach ..	Malai Vémbu ..	The wood is hard and handsomely marked. It is used for many purposes. Insects will not attack it. The root is nauseous and bitter. When in flower it has some resemblance to the Lilac, and has been called the Persian Lilac.
Memecylon tinctorium.	Kásá	The wood is used for building and firewood. A yellow dye is made from the leaves.

Botanical Name.	Tamil Name.	Remarks.
Mimusops elengi..	Magila-maram ..	The wood is used for building and firewood. The flowers are flagrant and aromatic, and an odoriferous water is distilled from them by Natives.
Morinda umbellata.	Nuná	A yellow dye is extracted from the roots of this tree. The wood is not much used.
Moringa pterygosperma.	Murungai ..	*The Horse Radish tree.*—The wood is useless except as fuel. The root of the tree is like English horse-radish. The leaves, flowers, and raw fruits are eaten by Natives.
Musa paradisiaca.	Válai	*The Plantain or Banana tree.*—The commonest fruit tree in the district, grown in all the irrigated parts. The fruit is eaten by all classes—Native and European. The leaves are used for dressing blisters, and by Natives to eat their food off. The fibre is used as a substitute for hemp.
Nauclea cordifolia.	Manja kadambu ..	The wood is soft, close, even-grained, and easily worked, but not durable. It is, however, useful especially for furniture.
Odina Wodier ..	Otiyam	A gum which exudes from this tree is applied to bruises, ulcers, and wounds. The wood is dark-colored and strong, but it is not of much use for economical purposes.
Phyllanthus emblica.	Nelli	The fruits are eaten by Natives and also used medicinally. The bark is astringent and the dried fruits laxative. The wood is hard and durable.
Pongamia glabra..	Pungai	The oil extracted from the seeds is used by Natives in eruptive diseases and also for lamps. The leaves are eaten by cattle and used for manure. The wood is tough, fibrous, and coarse, and is used as fuel.
Prosopis spicigera.	Vanni	The wood is of a dark-red color, durable, hard, and close-grained. It is very strong and is used for building purposes and as firewood.
Psidium pyriferum.	Koyyá	*The Guava tree.*—The fruit is sweet and is eaten by all classes. Guava jelly made from it is an excellent conserve. The bark of the root is used as an astringent and the wood as firewood. It is grown in all parts of the irrigated taluqs.
Pterocarpus marsupium.	Véngai	The wood is very strong and durable. It is largely used for building purposes and for making carts, &c.
Santalum album ..	Santanam ..	*The Sandal-wood tree.*—The wood is very fragrant and is burnt to perfume temples and dwelling houses. Boxes and ornamental cabinets, &c., are made from it. An oil is extracted from the wood, which is used for various purposes. The tree is to be found on the Pachamalai Hills, but not in great numbers.
Salvadora Persica.	Ugá	The bark is used by Natives for medicinal purposes. The tree is not common in the district.

CHAPTER III.
FLORA AND FAUNA.

Botanical Name.	Tamil Name.	Remarks.
Sapindus emarginatus.	Púvanti	*The Soap-nut tree.*—The wood is close-grained and hard, but not durable. The capsule is considered by Natives to be expectorant. The fruit is used as soap.
Seshbania Ægyptica.	Karumsembai ..	The flowers and leaves are used medicinally and the wood for firewood.
Strychnos nux-vomica.	Etti	*The Poison-nut tree.*—The wood is dark and durable and is safe against white-ants. It is used for building purposes. The root is used in cases of intermittent fever and snake-bites. The seeds are poisonous. They are used medicinally in various ways.
Strychnos potatorum.	Téttá	*The Clearing-nut tree.*—The seeds and fruit are used medicinally. The wood is hard and durable and serves many economical purposes.
Tamarindus Indica.	Puliya-maram ..	*The Tamarind tree.*—The wood is close-grained, very hard, durable, and beautifully-veined. It is used for oil presses, axles of carts, &c. The pulp of the seed-pods is used both as food and medicinally. It contains a large proportion of acid and is an invariable ingredient in curries. The tamarind is grown all over the district and makes a beautiful avenue tree.
Tectona grandis ..	Tékku	*The Teak tree.*—This tree is the most valuable of all the Indian timber trees. It is used for building purposes, furniture, &c. Oil extracted from the wood is used as varnish. The tree is but rarely to be found in the district.
Terminalia alata.	Marutai	The wood is valuable and is much used for building purposes.
Terminalia chebula.	Kudukay	The wood is hard, strong and close-grained. It is used for agricultural and building purposes. Galls found on the leaves are used for various medicinal purposes. The fruit is astringent and is used by Natives in various manufactures.
Thespesia populnea.	Púvarasu	*The Portia tree.*—This tree grows rapidly, and for this reason is often used in roadside avenues. The wood is strong and close-grained, and is used for making furniture. The capsule is filled with a yellow pigment that is used in cases of cutaneous diseases. The bark and leaves are also used medicinally.
Vitex negunda ..	Nocchi	*The fine-leaved Chaste tree.*—The leaves, young shoots, bark, and root are used medicinally. The wood is used for building purposes and as fuel.
Wrightia antidysenterica.	Veppálai ..	*The Conessi-bark tree.*—The wood is hard, close and even-grained. It is used for building purposes and the bark medicinally in cases of dysentery and bowel-complaints.

CHAPTER III. FLORA AND FAUNA.

Botanical Name.	Tamil Name.	Remarks.
Wrightia tinctoria.	Pilá	The wood is close-grained and very white. It is used for building and other economical purposes.
Zyzyphus glabrata.	Karukatá ..	The wood is durable and hard. It is used for building and also for cabinet or ornamental work.
Zyzyphus jujuba.	Elládu	*The Jujube tree.*—The wood is adopted for cabinet and ornamental work. The fruit is largely eaten by Natives.

NOTE.—I have derived much assistance in the preparation of this list from information supplied to me by Mr. Hadfield, Assistant Conservator of Forests. For further particulars regarding the trees mentioned here reference may be made to Colonel HEBER DRURY's *Useful Plants of India* (2nd edition) and Dr. BALFOUR's *Timber Trees of India.*

THE FOREST DEPARTMENT.

The operations of the Forest Department were extended to Trichinopoly in 1871.[1] There are no reserved forests in the district, and the work of the department has, as a rule, been confined to the formation of fuel reserves and plantations.

Fuel Reserves.

The following statement gives certain particulars regarding the fuel reserves up to the 31st March 1877 :—

Name of the Reserve.	Year in which the Reserve was formed.	Area in Acres.	Charges up to 31st March 1877.	Receipts up to 31st March 1877.
			RS.	RS.
Lálápéttai	1871 ..	106	4,620	1,968
Srípurandán	1874 ..	463	1,723	331
Ténmalai	1871 ..	153	1,027	..
Panjamtángi	1871 ..	1,000	1,142	8
Minnakkaradu	1871 ..	1,000	433	..
Tuvágudi	1876 ..	944	144	..
Total ..	..	3,666	9,089	2,307

The Lálápéttai Reserve is in Kulittalai Taluq close to the line of railway. It is padugai land on the Cauvery bank, the principal tree to be found in it being the *Acacia Arabica.* The Srípurandán Reserve is on the Coleroon bank in Trichinopoly Taluq. It is padugai land covered with the *Acacia Arabica.* The Ténmalai Reserve is a hill in Kulittalai Taluq not far from Manapparai and about 2½ miles north of the line of railway from Trichinopoly to

(1) G.O., No. 502 of the 21st March 1871.

CHAPTER III. FLORA AND FAUNA.

Madura. The tree most met with in it is the *Acacia planifrons*. There are also a few satin-wood trees. The Panjamtángi Reserve is another hill in Kulittalai Taluq near Kalpatti and about 2½ miles to the east of the line of railway. The principal tree to be found in it is the *Acacia planifrons*. The Minnakkaradu Reserve is a small hill close to Panjamtángi, about a mile from the railway. The Tuvágudi Reserve is in Trichinopoly Taluq, about 10 miles from Trichinopoly on the Tanjore road, and at a distance of about 2 miles from the railway. The principal trees in it are the *Acacia Arabica* and *Acacia leucophlœa*.

Plantations.

The following is a list of the plantations in the district:—

Name of Plantations.	Taluq in which Plantation is situated.	Year in which the Plantation was formed.	Area.	No. of Trees.	Receipts up to 1st March 1877.	Charges up to 1st March 1877.
					RS.	RS.
Elamanúr ..	Trichinopoly.	1871 ..	84	137,700	9,657	1,549
Kulittalai ..	Kulittalai.	1871 ..	62	69,600	7,390	308
Manattattai ..		1874 ..	10	12,000	1,993	101
Sittalvái ..		1871 ..	110	128,400	6,119	387
Sekkanam ..		1874 ..	92½	84,000	1,961	585
Kattalai ..		1871 ..	52	45,240	6,041	151
Kulamánikkam ..	Udaiyárpálayam.	1874 ..	84½	73,515	2,894	221
Araimanaikurichi ..		1874 ..	32¾	28,492	1,278	176
Káraippákkam ..		1874 ..	29¾	25,882	897	25
Tiruvénganúr ..		1874 ..	14	12,180	575	130
Várappankurichi ..		1874 ..	95½	83,085	972	93
Sáttambádi ..		1874 ..	30¾	26,752	951	47
Pudúr ..		1874 ..	86	149,640	276	275
	..	..	783¾	776,486	41,004	4,048

Most of the tracts planted are padugai lands along the banks of the Cauvery and Coleroon, and, as they are often flooded when there are high freshes in the rivers, the ground is seldom very dry, planting is easy, casualties are few, the growth of the trees is rapid, and the plantations are a decided success. The trees principally grown in the plantations are the *Acacia Arabica* and *Casuarina*, but there is also a mixture of *Inga dulcis*, *Albizzia Lebbek*, *Dalbergia sissu*, *Azadirachta Indica* (Nim), and *Eugenia jambolana*. It is anticipated that the plantations can be felled over every five or six years, but, as the oldest of them are now only a little over four years' growth, it has been considered too soon yet to commence experimental fellings.[2]

Proposal to transfer the Pachamalais to the Forest Department.

In 1876 the Conservator of Forests recommended that the Pachamalais should be handed over to the Forest Department, and

(2) Annual Report on the administration of Forest Department for 1876-77, paragraph 86.

his suggestion was referred to the Collector for report.[3] Mr. Sewell was of opinion that the license system as then worked was sufficient to prevent indiscriminate felling; that the system of cultivation in vogue on the hills (a description of which is given in Chapter I) had not operated to denude the hills of jungle to any serious extent; and that the small number of really good timber trees combined with the difficulties of transport would prevent the jungle becoming a really valuable forest reserve. Under these circumstances, and taking into consideration the difficulty of checking oppression of the hill men by the subordinate establishment which would be entertained by the Forest Department, the Collector deprecated any change being made for the present. In this view the Board concurred. The orders of Government on this question have not yet been received.

FAUNA.

Feræ naturæ.

But few of the larger feræ naturæ are to be found in the district. Elephants are unknown, a tiger now and then makes its appearance in Udaiyárpálayam Taluq, and bears are to be seen on the Pachamalai Hills and in parts of Perambalúr Taluq. The following statement shows the number of deaths reported as caused by wild beasts and snake-bites for five years as well as the amount paid as rewards for killing wild beasts. No rewards are given for the destruction of snakes:—

Years.	No. of Deaths by Wild Beasts.	No. of Deaths by Snake-bites.	Rewards granted for killing Wild Beasts. RS. A. P.
1872	9	217	72 0 0
1873	12	212	312 0 0
1874	14	185	80 0 0
1875	15	167	24 8 0
1876	10	159	112 0 0

There is but little game to be got in the district. A few deer and antelope are to be found in the jungles in Udaiyárpálayam and the zemindáris in the south of Kulittalai Taluq. Snipe, teel, and wild-duck are plentiful, but with exception of these birds there is but little in Trichinopoly to attract the sportsman.

Mammals.

The following is a list of the mammals to be found in the district with their names as identified by Dr. Jerdon in his "Mammals of India":—

(3) G.O., No. 1,605 of the 1st May 1877.

(4) Board's Proceedings, No. 408 of the 15th February 1878.

CHAPTER III.
FLORA AND FAUNA.

Number in Jerdon's Mammals.	Zoological Name.	English Name.	Tamil Name.
6	Inuus silenus	Lion-monkey	Karunkurangu.
9	Macacus radiatus	Madras monkey ..	Kurangu.
11	Loris gracilis	Slender lemur ..	Tévángu.
26	Hipposideros speoris ..	Bat	Vavvál.
69	Sorex cærulescens ..	Common mush shrew.	Múnjúru.
91	Ursus labiatus	Indian black bear ..	Karadi.
100	Lutra nair	Common Indian otter.	Nírnáy.
104	Felis tigris	Tiger	Puli.
113	Do. rubiginosa ..	Rusty-spotted cat ..	Púnai.
115	Do. chaus	Common jungle cat ..	Káttupúnai.
117	Do. jubata	Hunting leopard ..	Síruttai.
121	Vivverra Malaccensis ..	Lesser civet cat ..	Punugu púnai.
123	Paradoxurus musanga.	Common tree cat ..	Maranáy.
129	Herpestes monticolus ..	Long-tailed mungoos.	Kíripillai.
135	Canis pallipes	Indian wolf	Ŏnáy.
136	Do. aureus	Jackal	Nari.
138	Vulpes Bengalensis ..	Indian fox	Kuli nari.
155	Do. palmarum ..	Common-striped squirrel.	Anil.
170	Girbillus Indicus ..	Indian jerboa rat ..	Sekappu eli.
174	Mus bandicota ..	Bandicoot rat	Peruchali.
204	Hystrix leucura ..	Indian porcupine ..	Mulpandri.
208	Lepus nigricollis ..	Black-naped hare ..	Muyal or musal.
215	Sus Indicus	Indian wild boar ..	Káttupandri.
220	Rusa Aristotelis ..	Samber stag	Kadambai.
221	Axis maculatus ..	Spotted deer	Pulli mán.
228	Antelope bezoartica ..	Indian antelope ..	Kalai-mán, Veli-mán.
238	Gavæus gaurus ..	Gaur or wild bull ..	Káttumádu.

Bullocks and buffaloes are the only animals used for agricultural purposes, and these are undersized and of inferior breed.

Fish.

The following are the principal descriptions of fish bought and sold in the Trichinopoly market: *Wallago attu*, Bl., commonly called the fresh-water shark (Tam. *Válai*); *Ophiocephalus marulius*, Ham. Buch., and other Ophiocephalidæ commonly called in English Murrel from the Hindustani name *Maral* (Tam. *Virál*); *Macrones aor*, Ham. Buch., Anglicè cat-fish (Tam. *Killatti*); *Labeo calbasu*, Ham. Buch., and other Labeos sometimes called in English the Rohi from *Labeo Rohita*, Ham. Buch., *Ruhu* in Punjabee, Bangalee and Ooriya (Tam. *Sélkendai*), and prawns. All these are eaten by Europeans. The *Clupea palasah*, C. and V., Anglicè the sable fish or *Hilsa* (Tam. *Ullam*), used to be sold in Trichinopoly, but the anicuts on the Coleroon now prevent its making its appearance so far up the river. The demand for fish in the market is greater than the supply, which, there can be no doubt, has diminished in consequence of the anicuts. Fish may be seen swarming in large numbers below these dams, engaged in constant but vain endeavours to ascend the apron wall.

Snakes.

A list of the snakes in the district was drawn up by me in 1873 under the orders of the Board of Revenue and sent to Dr. Shortt for his remarks. These snakes, classified and described with the assistance of his observations on this list, are given below :—

Tamil Names.	*Description.*
(1.) Nágam. The cobra.	
Karu Nágam	The Pariah or black cobra.
Para nágam	
Sennágam	The Bráhman or red cobra.
Páppára nágam	
Setti nágam	The Merchant cobra, said to be so called from its habit of looking about on all sides when lifting up its head.
Púnágam	The smallest kind of cobra found amongst flowers (extremely venomous).
Talai nágam	A kind of cobra found among leaves.
Nandu tinni nágam	A cobra alleged to live upon crabs.
Kódumbai nágam	A cobra with a short, thin body.
	All these seven kinds of cobras are deadly.
(2.) Sárai	The four varieties given under this head are kinds of the whip or rat snake, the *Pytos mucosis*, erroneously called the male cobra. They are all harmless.
Perunsárai	The largest snake of this description.
Nedunsárai	
Karunsárai	The black sárai.
Manjal sárai	The yellow sárai.
Vensárai	The white sárai.
(3.) Viriyan. The vipers.	
Karudu viriyan	These are called the blood-vipers and are of a reddish color. They are the Russel's or chain viper, *Daboia elegans*, which is venomous.
Udira viriyan	
Iratta viriyan	
Udira mandalam	
Kattu viriyan	The binding viper, so called because its bite causes the joints of the body to become immovable. It is striped, black and white.
Kannádi viriyan	The carpet snake, *Echis carinota.* It is venomous.
Kalludai viriyan	The ass viper, so called on account of the slow manner in which it moves. It grows to a large size and is of a black color. Its bite is not deadly.
Irutalai viriyan ..	The earth snake, *Eryx Johnii.* A very harmless reptile.
Pul viriyan	The grass-adder.
Eri viriyan	The burning viper, so called on account of the burning pain that follows its bite.
(4.) Suruttai. Udu suruttai	A kind of suruttai the bite of which is said to cause swelling.
Nedunsuruttai	The largest kind of suruttai.
Kurunsuruttai	The smallest kind.
Sensuruttai	The yellow kind of suruttai.
Aranaivál suruttai	A kind of suruttai with a tail like that of the green lizard.

CHAPTER III. FLORA AND FAUNA.

Tamil Names.	*Description.*
Iratta suruttai	A kind of suruttai the bite of which is said to cause vomiting of blood, &c.

All these are intended for either the *Echis carinota* or carpet viper, previously mentioned in Group 3, which kills by slow poisoning followed by gangrene or mortification, or for the *Dipsas trignata*, or the broad-headed tree snake, which is harmless.

(5.) Valalai. A snake about 3 feet long and the thickness of a man's finger.

Karu valalai .. .. .. Karumpámbu	The black kind of valalai, called the king of the serpentine tribe.
Sevvalalai	The red kind of valalai.
Iratta valalai	A kind of valalai the bite of which is said to cause vomiting of blood.

All these are the *Bungarus arcuatus*, or white-arched bungarus, a very deadly snake.

(6.) Pudaiyan sembudaiyan	The red kind of pudaiyan.
Karumbudaiyan	The black kind.
Irutalaipudaiyan	A kind of pudaiyan stated by the natives to have a head at each end.
Sirupudaiyan	A small kind of pudaiyan. All these are a species of earth snake, the *Gongylopis coinais*, and are harmless.
(7.) Kombéri-múkkan	Blue tree snake or *Dendrophis picta.* It is also harmless and climbs up trees.
(8.) Pachaipámbu	The common green snake, *Passerita mycterizaris.* It is perfectly harmless.
(9.) Mannulipámbu .. .. .. Irutalaipámbu .. .. .. Kúlaipámbu	These are all names for the common earth-snake, *Eryx Johnii*, mentioned before in Group 3. They are also called the double-headed snake from their stumpy tails. They are quite harmless.
(10.) Malaipámbu	The common rock snake, *Python molurus.* It is harmless.

Silk-worms.

About thirty years ago an attempt was made to cultivate mulberry trees and breed silk-worms in Trichinopoly. An association called "The East Indian Silk Manufacturing Company at Trichinopoly" was formed by a few of the leading East Indians in the town; mulberry trees were planted and silk worms procured from Mysore. The attempt, however, proved a failure. It appears that the scorching dry heat and hot winds that prevail in Trichinopoly during so many months of the year proved destructive to the growth and culture of the silk-worms, and the enterprise was abandoned after a few years' trial.[5]

(5) *Vide* letter, No. 310, of the 11th December 1869, from the Collector of Trichinopoly to the Board of Revenue. In a letter by a pensioned Deputy Collector, Mr. Boalth, which forms an enclosure to the Collector's report, a full account of the experiment is given.

CHAPTER IV.

CLIMATE AND DISEASES, CIVIL HOSPITALS AND DISPENSARIES.

CLIMATE—Seasons.—Effect of the climate on health.—Meteorological statistics. DISEASES—Diseases of the Respiratory system.—Digestive system.—Cancer.—Diseases of the Circulatory system.—Ague.—Rheumatism.—Typhoid fever.—Relapsing fever.—Typhus fever.—Small-pox.—Venereal Diseases.—Leprosy.—Elephantiasis.—Diseases of the skin.—Diseases of the eye.—Diseases of the ear.

CIVIL HOSPITALS AND DISPENSARIES—Municipal Hospital, Trichinopoly.—Municipal Hospital, Srírangam.—Musiri Branch Dispensary.—Ariyalúr Branch Dispensary.—Irungalúr Mission Dispensary.

CLIMATE.

CHAPTER IV. CLIMATE, DISEASES, &c. — Climate.

THE climate of Trichinopoly is characterized by a high mean temperature and a low degree of humidity, while at the same time the extremes of heat and cold are, as a rule, moderate. There is much sun-glare and reflected and radiated heat, and at certain seasons the atmosphere is very sultry and enervating.

—Seasons.

The following is, perhaps, the best division into seasons of the several months of the year in Trichinopoly that can be made :—

Cool—(December, January and February).
Hot—(March, April and May).
Windy—(June, July and August).
Rainy—(September, October and November).

During the cool season (December, January and February) the north-east monsoon prevails. This period, although the pleasantest to the feelings, is the most unhealthy, mainly owing to the very regular occurrence of cholera about the end of October or beginning of November. This latter month ushers in cool mornings, which in December and January become comparatively cold, indeed absolutely cold to old residents. Solar radiation is, however, still high.

The hot season, consisting of the months of March, April and May, is very trying, the range of temperature being high and the atmosphere remarkably dry. The mornings are sultry. The evenings, however, are often rendered comparatively cool by a south-east wind, which sometimes blows with considerable strength, at first bringing up clouds of dust, but soon settling down into a pleasant cool breeze. The nights even at this season are never intensely hot. Sun-glare is very great, and radiation of heat from the bare sandy soil extreme. In this season there are occasional thunder-storms and whirlwinds accompanied with rain, the latter

CHAPTER IV. CLIMATE, DISEASES, &c.

being partial and capricious. These showers break most gratefully the almost intolerable heat of this portion of the year.

During the windy season, consisting of June, July and August, the high winds of the south-west monsoon prevail, blowing with great violence at times. The rainfall varies greatly from year to year, both in the date of its accession and in its amount. As a rule, during the greater part of this period there is a high wind and no rain, and the result is most disagreeable clouds of dust.

The rainy season of September, October and November comprises two close and sultry months (September and October) and one (November) cool and pleasant. Usually about the 15th of October the north-east monsoon sets in, and is often accompanied by electric storms of violence. In September the winds are variable and the evenings generally close and sultry.

Popularly the climate is said to consist of "eight months hot and four hotter." This is somewhat a libel upon it, for taking it all in all, though it is undoubtedly at times very trying and enervating, it is by no means intolerable, and to the feelings of many more endurable than the moist heat of the coast.[1]

—Effect of climate on health.

In April and May Europeans suffer to a considerable degree from the high temperature. This is due to the unvarying character of the climate. The variation in the temperature by night and by day is so slight as not to give sufficient respite from exhausting influences till the dawn of another day brings its burden of heat to be endured.

During the greater part of the year the air is dry, allowing of free skin action ; hence affections of the liver amongst Europeans are rare. Indeed those who in many other stations are martyrs to functional derangements of the liver progress favorably here. Dysentery and diarrhœa are also rare amongst residents. In short, beyond the exhausting influence of constant heat, which is inimical to many constitutions, Trichinopoly may be considered as free from any deleterious influence due to climatic conditions.

Deaths from sunstroke amongst the European soldiers forming the garrison is an almost yearly occurrence during the hottest season of the year, but this may in a great measure be regarded as the result of the well-known carelessness of the men.

It is generally believed that the climate of Trichinopoly town and cantonment has undergone considerable modification of late years, consequent upon the spread of irrigation, the mean annual temperature being lowered and the humidity increased.

There is no reason to regard the climate as being otherwise than healthy for natives.[2]

(1) Report on the Civil and Military Station of Trichinopoly, drawn up in 1867 by Dr. J. L. Ranking, Sanitary Commissioner.

(2) Extract from a Note by Dr. W. G. King.

The following meteorological tables for a series of ten years were obtained from the Trichinopoly Observatory. Statement No. 5, given in the appendix, shows the rainfall in the district for ten years.

CHAPTER IV. CLIMATE, DISEASES, &c. —Meteorological statistics.

Months.	1868.				1869.				1870.				1871.				1872.			
	Dry Maximum.	Mean Dry Bulb.	Maximum in Sun.	Minimum on Grass.	Dry Maximum.	Mean Dry Bulb.	Maximum in Sun.	Minimum on Grass.	Dry Maximum.	Mean Dry Bulb.	Maximum in Sun.	Minimum on Grass.	Dry Maximum.	Mean Dry Bulb.	Maximum in Sun.	Minimum on Grass.	Dry Maximum.	Mean Dry Bulb.	Maximum in Sun.	Minimum or Grass.
January	*	*	*	*	93·3	81·2	139·9	66·6	88·4	80·0	140·3	64·0	82·6	78·4	132·8	58·5	89·8	79·7	137·7	58·2
February	*	*	*	*	95·9	86·2	143·2	67·4	93·0	81·0	140·4	60·1	92·1	83·3	138·0	59·9	94·6	83·4	140·2	59·6
March	*	*	*	*	99·8	90·0	148·6	71·7	96·8	86·7	147·5	66·9	95·5	87·0	139·8	63·7	99·2	87·8	142·2	61·7
April	*	*	*	*	103·1	90·1	145·8	74·7	103·6	92·2	147·8	71·8	101·0	90·2	145·9	70·6	100·5	89·8	142·9	71·3
May	*	*	*	*	103·5	91·9	144·1	75·6	105·7	92·1	146·1	76·1	100·7	90·3	140·7	72·8	102·4	90·6	138·4	72·7
June	100·5	90·5	140·2	79·6	99·7	90·4	139·9	74·6	99·2	88·1	138·6	74·1	99·3	94·5	135·2	73·3	97·6	86·9	131·0	73·2
July	94·5	86·4	136·7	75·0	99·5	88·4	136·0	73·1	97·0	87·2	135·2	72·6	97·1	87·4	134·3	71·8	96·9	86·8	132·8	71·5
August	96·8	90·9	141·8	74·5	95·9	86·3	139·2	71·6	94·2	84·8	136·4	70·9	98·8	88·5	138·8	71·5	95·5	85·6	133·9	71·0
September ...	96·9	88·4	143·7	74·6	95·3	84·5	140·6	71·0	95·3	84·9	133·5	68·8	96·2	85·1	138·1	71·9	94·6	82·7	134·5	69·7
October	90 8	83·6	137·1	71·9	90·4	84·6	135·1	72·9	93·0	83·7	135·2	67·1	92·1	82·1	134·0	67·9	90·7	82·2	133·1	67·5
November ...	89·1	84·0	133·5	67·6	8 5·6	79·2	127·2	66·4	87·1	78·1	128·4	65·4	86·3	79·3	126·0	66·5	86·1	81·0	125·3	66·3
December ...	87·2	80 2	134·7	65·3	86·3	79·1	132·0	63·4	83·4	76·5	130·8	60·6	86·3	79·8	130·8	61·9	86·8	80·0	135·1	66·1
Annual Mean ...	93·7	86·3	138·2	72·6	95·7	86·0	139·2	70·8	94·7	84·6	138·4	68·2	94·0	85·2	136·1	67·5	94·6	84·7	135·6	67·4

Months.	1873.				1874.				1875.				1876.				1877.			
	Dry Maximum.	Mean Dry Bulb.	Maximum in Sun.	Minimum on Grass.	Dry Maximum.	Mean Dry Bulb.	Maximum in Sun.	Minimum on Grass.	Dry Maximum.	Mean Dry Bulb.	Maximum in Sun.	Minimum on Grass.	Dry Maximum.	Mean Dry Bulb.	Maximum in Sun.	Minimum on Grass.	Dry Maximum.	Mean Dry Bulb.	Maximum in Sun.	Minimum on Grass.
January ...	*	*	*	*	88·9	78·7	138·4	*	88·9	79·9	136·7	58·8	90·2	78·0	*	67·2	89·6	80·3	155·7	62·7
February ...	*	*	*	*	92·6	83·3	138·0	*	92·3	82·0	142·4	52·9	96·5	89·3	155·4	61·8	95·0	84·5	155·8	65·3
March	*	*	*	*	*	*	*	*	100·0	90·1	145·7	67·5	100·6	90·3	158·7	68·9	98·4	88·8	159·6	67·6
April	*	*	*	*	*	*	*	*	102·3	91·7	*	71·7	104·6	91·8	161·3	75·4	102·2	91·5	163·8	74·6
May	*	*	*	*	*	*	*	*	104·2	92·6	*	74·7	102·4	91·2	145·5	74·1	101·2	91·9	155·5	74·6
June	*	*	*	*	96·9	91·9	135·9	73·1	96·7	87·3	*	73·6	101·6	90·2	152·8	74·6	100·4	90·6	152·8	74·9
July	98·7	87·7	135·1	72·8	97·1	87·6	135·4	72·2	98·4	89·1	*	74·3	100·1	89·9	153·8	75·5	101·6	91·7	155·4	75·2
August ...	95·9	86·1	130·8	71·0	96·9	88·0	138·8	71·7	98·5	87·6	*	72·3	96·1	86·9	152·4	72·7	100·9	90·4	156·6	74·5
September ...	96·1	88·8	136·2	73·6	92·9	84·5	135·4	70·9	97·4	87·7	*	71·9	96·7	87·6	155·9	71·1	96·3	86·7	155·0	71·6
October ...	89·6	81·7	132·9	68·8	91·2	83·5	138·9	70·3	93·3	82·2	*	68·1	95·8	86·0	158·2	70·3	91·2	85·3	151·2	70·1
November ...	84·7	80·1	136·8	61·8	87·6	81·0	136·4	67·0	87·3	79·5	*	63·4	89·8	82·2	148·8	66·3	94·6	81·7	150·3	68·4
December ...	86·3	81·8	137·9	64·9	85·0	78·1	129·7	61·9	86·8	81·6	*	61·1	86·9	80·4	147·7	62·4	86·2	79·8	145·1	66·6
Annual Mean ...	91·9	84·4	134·9	68·8	92·1	84·1	135·3	69·6	95·5	85·9	141·6	67·5	96·8	87·0	153·7	70·1	96·5	86·8	154·7	70·5

* No observations.

DISEASES.

(*Contributed by* Surgeon W. G. KING, *Civil Surgeon, Trichinopoly*, 1876—78.)

CHAPTER IV. CLIMATE, DISEASES, &c.

The diseases prevalent in the district present no distinctive character from those prevalent generally in India. Ague, rheumatism, syphilis, true and false, gonorrhœa, ophthalmia, phthisis, bronchitis, and anæmia are those most generally found.

Disease of the respiratory system.

Inflammatory diseases of the throat and chest are rare, as might be expected in so equable a climate. Phthisis is not found to any marked extent, but is not uncommonly met with in those of strictly sedentary occupation.

Digestive system.

Under this head diseases causing the greater part of the mortality in the district may be classed. Diarrhœa and dysentery are very common, more markedly so at the onset of the cold season, probably the result of undue exposure; but in ordinary times these diseases are no doubt due to inferior food and impure water. Dyspepsia and functional derangements of the alimentary canal are much met with in consequence of the irritating diet and the extraordinary culinary arrangements of many; a third cause being the habit of neglecting to take food for hours, and the compensatory gorging which ensues.

The prevalence of intestinal worms is very common. Indeed I really do not think I should be far from the truth in stating that in the course of his life, every native at some period or other becomes host to these disgusting guests. Native treatment seems to consist in violent purging by means of various oils. They have, however, unlimited belief in the European medicine santonine. Thread-worms give a small percentage in such cases. I have not seen a case of *Tænia* of any variety in the district, but the *Tænia solium* no doubt exists, as among the lower castes there are not wanting those who eat pork.

Cancer.

This disease in all its forms is found in the district.

Circulatory system.

Heart disease, I may safely affirm, is a most rare affection. This I say on the strength of constant examination of Natives with a view of determining if they are fit to undergo flogging. This is no doubt due to the scarcity, before mentioned, of acute rheumatism. Fatty degeneration of the organ, consonant with other organs of the body, is common. Senile degeneration of the arteries is common. Aneurism is rare.

Ague.

Ague is constantly present throughout the district, but is nearly universally of a mild type, rarely sufficiently marked to require admission of persons to hospital as in-patients. No part of the district is highly malarious, but in the Udaiyárpálayam

Taluq occasionally marked outbreaks have been known. The Pachamalai Hills also have an ill-fame for the prevalence of this disease. On the other hand, in the Central Jail I have not rarely seen severe types of remittent fever, the subjects having no history of previous attacks, whilst nothing to which the source of malaria can be attributed is known in the neighbourhood. An indigenous enlarged spleen is nearly unknown. Such cases, when they have come to my notice, have always been imported from other districts.

—Native treatment.

Quinine is largely used by Native *vydians*, and indeed is one of the two English preparations in which they possess implicit faith (the other drug being chlorodyne). Others during the cold stage use decoctions of stimulating spices, and bedaub the head with preparations of garlic during the hot stage. Drugs are sometimes introduced into the ear.

Rheumatism.

Acute rheumatic fever occurs occasionally, but on the whole is a medical curiosity. Sub-acute rheumatism and affection of solitary joints are of common occurrence.

Typhoid fever.

Undoubted cases of typhoid fever have occasionally come to notice. Thus in 1874-75 and 1876 this disease appeared amongst both Natives and Europeans. In East Indians I have seen characteristic typhoid spots appear not only on the abdomen, but also on the dorsal aspect of the hand.

Relapsing fever. Typhus fever.

Although during the famine of 1876—78 (the most probable time for their appearance) I was on the constant out-look for these diseases, I have never seen a case of either.

Small-pox.

From the records in my possession since the year 1857, I find that this disease has been absent from Trichinopoly in only one year. Indeed no other result than its constant presence can be looked for, when it is remembered that its appearance is esteemed by Natives as a visitation sent by the goddess Mári, which it would be impious to attempt to resist. With a system such as this what is to be expected? Small-pox, once introduced, is to be checked partially by vaccination, and entirely only by the exhaustion of supply of subjects likely to be affected by its influence.[3]

Venereal diseases.

This class of disease is exceedingly common among the Natives of this district, and has apparently existed to its present extent for years past. The result upon the mass of the people is most

(3) Vaccination is fairly well received by the Natives, especially the poorer classes, who are induced to submit to it by the batta of 2 Annas allowed for each person. Any objections that caste Natives, Bráhmans and the well-to-do classes, might urge towards preventing the access of the goddess Mári to their bodies, are fairly put aside by the fact of it being necessary for them to produce a certificate of vaccination when applying for public employment.

CHAPTER IV. CLIMATE, DISEASES, &c.

marked, and syphilitic taint is found to present itself constantly in the treatment of general diseases.

—Native treatment.

The Native treatment of venereal diseases is most disastrous. The various types of the disease are alike subjected to mercurial treatment. The favourite method of giving mercury isby fumigation and inhalation of mercurial vapour, this to an extent sufficient to produce most severe salivation. The result of this treatment is constantly seen in the collapsed nose of the unfortunate syphilitic patient.

Leprosy.

Leprosy is not unfrequently found, but cannot be said to be largely present. It is usually met with among classes subjected to inferior hygiene and diet, both of which conditions, granting the existence of a family taint, I consider favour its development.

—Native treatment.

Preparations of arsenic are used by Musalman physicians.

Elephantiasis.

Elephantiasis is not met with in any frequency.

Madura foot is found amongst the ryots cultivating black-cotton soil. It is not, however, seen with anything like the frequency that it is in the neighbouring district of Madura.

Diseases of the skin.

These diseases are due probably, as in other hot climates, to the activity demanded of the skin. Their great prevalence strikes the most casual observer. No doubt, also, naturally dirty habits among the lower classes give opportunity for the break-down of the skin, whilst among the upper classes the habit of using dirty water for bathing purposes may possibly have something to do with the excessive frequency of diseases of a vegetable parasitic origin. With Natives of even a comparatively educated class, the idea is firmly rooted, that water, being itself a pure substance, cannot be contaminated. In an ordinary village tank the washing of cloths and bodies, and toilette operations of a strictly oriental character, must throw large quantities of organic matter into the water thus used. With the tropical sun, evaporation into a more or less approach to a treacly consistency goes on, as surely in a village tank as in a chemist's laboratory, and thus a mass of all varieties of vegetable and animal matter becomes, in course of time, a solution that can but form a favourable nidus for vegetable parasitic growth. To this cause then, I think, may be safely assigned much of the prevalence of the varieties of ring-worm found disfiguring in patches the bodies of Natives.

Eczema and itch are very common, the former often from long neglect yielding a most exaggerated character, whilst the latter seems to be well-nigh the normal condition of a Native's hand.

Diseases of the eye.

Country sore-eyes or ophthalmia become epidemic almost every year. With ordinary care the disease runs a short course, but aided by Native maltreatment, the result of this affection to the patient is frequently the permanent loss of vision.

—Native treatment.

The most usual course pursued is to place lime on the surrounding orbit.

Naturally all diseases of the eye are found more or less, but certainly the one which is most strikingly common is the existence of senile cataract, co-existing with a far lower average senility than is found to be the case in England. The prevalence of the degeneration known as *Arcus senilis* at a comparatively early age is also remarkable.

Diseases of the ear.

Inflammatory conditions of the external auditory passages, the result of the rough use of pieces of sticks, &c., with occasional injury to internal organs are frequent.

The ear, with Natives, undergoes somewhat unfair play, for they not only constantly amuse themselves by titilating its passage with sticks, but make it the receptacle for supposed remedial agents in various diseases.

Such a thing as a " púchi " or insect occasionally finding its way into the ear, and its subsequent escape being prevented, either by its being half-smashed by the unfortunate host or by his effectually barring the egress, is of course possible. I have been often amused by Natives persisting that they have " púchies " in their ears when there was certainly nothing to be found. I remember on one occasion a troop of about half-a-dozen women came from a distant village to have their ears examined, as they all felt certain that they were inhabited by " púchies."

Civil Hospitals and Dispensaries.

Municipal Hospital, Trichinopoly.—No records exist regarding the history of this institution, originally the civil hospital and public dispensary of the district, previous to 1857. In that year the hospital was located in Puttúr, in a private dwelling-house which Government rented at a cost of Rupees 30 per mensem. This building seems to have afforded sufficient accommodation for the sick, but to have been kept in a bad state of repair.

The attendance of patients as recorded for the year 1857 seems well-nigh incredible when compared with that of subsequent years. The daily average of out-patients is put down at 200. I have however reason to think that the peculiar method that was then adopted for calculating the number of patients was the cause of this apparently high figure. It appears that patients were considered to be " out-patients," whether they attended the hospital or not, as long as they were borne on the books as under treatment. In trivial cases an out-patient may attend but once and never make his appearance again, and there seems to have been no strict rule as to whether the names of such patients should be kept on the books or not. In-patients are stated as giving an average of thirty. This number appears to have included police peons, lock hospital patients and lunatics. Separate accommodation was afforded for females in a small out-building divided into two portions, one of which was devoted to syphilitic cases.

Besides the above hospital, there was at this period a so-called branch dispensary located in a building near the main-guard gate, which did good work in the fort. The number of out-patients attending this institution seems to have been included in the returns of the Puttúr Hospital. This branch institution was a decided success under the management of Native Surgeon Baulu Mudaliyár.

The year 1857 seems to have seen the civil hospital in a more flourishing condition than it has since been till within the last few years; but from that date medical officers record a large annual decrease in the number of patients.

A lock hospital was established in Trichinopoly in 1859, and was at first attached to the civil dispensary, a ward in the building in Puttúr being assigned to diseased females.

In 1861 the usefulness of the civil hospital was greatly curtailed by an order of Government restricting the expenditure on dieting of patients, &c., to the sum of Rupees 80 per mensem. This amount, together with a sum of Rupees 400 raised by voluntary subscriptions, was its only available resources. The reduction in the number of applicants for relief which the above measure produced, became even more marked in 1863, when a rule was introduced that all who were in a position to pay for medicines should do so.

In 1863 it was found necessary to remove the civil dispensary from Puttúr to a rented bungalow close to the Garrison Hospital and just outside the cantonment limits. It did not, however, remain long here, but was again removed to a terraced house in Bímanaiken-pálayam close to the railway crossing. The lock hospital was then established in the building vacated by the dispensary.

The impossibility of keeping up a useful hospital with such inadequate funds was now so strongly felt, that in 1863 the then Collector, aided by a committee of native gentlemen, managed to collect a sum of Rupees 20,000 with a view of endowing and building an hospital. The invested capital of the institution on the 1st April 1877 amounted to Rupees 22,695.

From an annual attendance of 24,000 out-patients recorded in 1857, the numbers steadily decreased till the returns showed a total attendance of only 8,403, while the in-patients amounted to but 123. The cause of this decrease was no doubt the very economical policy pursued by the committee of management, who seem to have restricted the medical officer's expenditure in every possible way.

On the 15th February 1872 the civil dispensary was transferred to the Trichinopoly Municipality, under whose management it has since remained.

The building in Bímanaikenpálayam, to which it has been already stated that the civil dispensary was transferred, is a large well-built house, with well-proportioned rooms, and on the whole fairly suited for an hospital. Its site was, however, found objectionable, as the building is close to the bank of the Uyyakondán channel and on too low a level. Its distance from the fort also greatly lessened its utility. After considerable discussion it was eventually decided to erect a new set of buildings on a portion of the filled-in moat to the south of the fort. The new hospital was opened for the accommodation of patients in 1874.

The present hospital consists of a number of excellently designed buildings, the plan pursued throughout being that of the separate principle. Altogether there are eight buildings, of which the principal one is the male ward, affording accommodation inside to twelve patients; whilst, on account of the existence of large and well-built double verandahs, an equal number could be accommodated outside. The arrangements for aerial space are everything that could be desired. There are also two similar buildings with somewhat smaller verandahs, one of which is used as a female ward and the other for the surgery and out-patient departments.

A narrow line of five compartments, each forming a distinct room, has also been added as a lying-in ward. Each ward has a small courtyard behind it, in which separate cooking and bathing may be carried on in privacy, and without prejudice to caste.

A building on the same principle as the lying-in ward is used for the reception of caste patients. The well-to-do classes can also make use of these wards while under treatment, on payment of a small rent.

The attendance of patients has steadily increased since the opening of the new building. The number of surgical cases treated during the last year (1877) shows that this class of practice is thoroughly appreciated by Natives. Many sufferers travel from long distances to avail themselves of European aid in such cases.[4]

---

(4) The greater part of this account of the Trichinopoly Municipal Hospital is taken from Notes which Surgeon W. G. King was kind enough to draw up for me.

CHAPTER IV.
CLIMATE, DISEASES, &c.

The following statement shows the number of in-door and out-door patients treated in the Municipal Hospital during the year 1876-77 :—

In-door Patients.											Out-door Patients.				
1	2	3	4	5	6		7			8	9	10	11	12	
Total treated during the Year.	Number cured.	Number relieved.	Discharged otherwise.	Died.	Number of Beds available.		Daily Average Number.			Rates of death per cent. of Average Strength.	Number treated.			Average Daily Attendance.	Total Number of Patients, both In-door and Out-door.
					Male.	Female.	Male.	Female.	Total.		Attended personally.	Represented by Friends.	Total.		
815	567	71	650	126	22	13	20	21	32	15	17	239	17739	72	18,592

The total cost of all the hospital buildings up to 1st April 1878 has been Rupees 19,700.

In December 1875 an hospital for lepers, supported by the Municipality with the assistance of the Local Fund Board, was opened in a building to the east of the fort, close to the new boulevard. This building was originally the District Jail, and up to 1871 a Lunatic Asylum. In that year the Trichinopoly Lunatic Asylum was abolished and the patients in it removed to Madras. On the 1st April 1877 twenty-one lepers were under treatment in this hospital, three as out-patients and eighteen as in-patients.

Municipal Hospital, Srírangam.—The proposal to establish a dispensary in Srírangam originated with Surgeon-General Balfour, who, on his visit to the town in 1871, met the temple trustees, spoke to them of the importance of having a dispensary there, and of the benefits which such an institution would confer on the inhabitants and pilgrims, and tried to persuade them to give a portion of the pagoda funds towards this most useful charity. A few months after this the trustees were induced to come forward and offer a subscription of Rupees 300 per annum, which sum now forms one of the sources out of which the dispensary is maintained. This amount was shortly afterwards supplemented by a subscription of about Rupees 500, which was raised at a public meeting convened in Srírangam on the 6th June 1872. It is needless to state that the small annual sum offered by the trustees was quite inadequate to defray the expense of starting and maintaining a dispensary, even on the smallest possible scale. The result was that, when other efforts to raise funds proved unavailing, the project appeared likely to be abandoned. At this crisis the Srírangam Municipal Commissioners came forward, and, at a meeting held on the 10th September 1872, resolved to grant annually Rupees 1,200 from their funds towards its support. They then applied themselves to secure contributions for the dispensary from other sources. An application having been made to the members of the Local Fund Board, they at a meeting held on the 12th September 1872, agreed to grant Rupees 1,500 per annum to the hospital, being the equivalent of the sum received as contributions from the Municipality and the Pagoda Trustees. The Commissioners next appealed to Government, and obtained (G.O., No. 1,446, dated 23rd October 1872) a donation for the dispensary of the necessary surgical instruments and a six months' supply of medicines.[5] The dispensary was opened on the 1st January 1873. At first it was located in a rented house inside the temple walls, where there was no accommodation for in-patients. A set of hospital buildings were, however, shortly afterwards erected outside the walls and close to the southern gate. These buildings were opened for in-patients in March 1874. In 1874 the Princess of Tanjore presented the Municipal Commissioners with a sum of Rupees 2,000 for the erection of an additional ward, and the hospital at present affords accommodation for eighteen male and six female patients. The total cost of the buildings up to the 31st March 1878 has been Rupees 16,500.

CHAPTER IV. CLIMATE, DISEASES, &c.

The annexed statement shows the number of out-patients and in-patients treated in the hospital for a period of three years. The steady increase that there has been in the number of patients is a trustworthy indication of the confidence that the inhabitants of Srírangam, and the pilgrims and others who resort there, are gradually showing in English medicine and treatment.

Years.	Out-Patients.	In Patients.	Total.
1873-74 ..	10,088	5	10,093
1874-75 ..	11,525	175	11,700
1875-76 ..	12,637	207	12,844

Musiri Branch Dispensary.

Branch Dispensaries.—A branch dispensary was opened by the Local Fund Board in Musiri in 1876. The dispensary is located in a room in the old public bungalow. There is no accommodation at present for in-patients, but it is intended to build an hospital with wards for male and female patients before long. 2,820 out-patients were treated at this dispensary in the year 1876-77.

Ariyalúr Branch Dispensary.

A second branch dispensary was opened by the Local Fund Board in Ariyalúr in 1876. A dispensary building is at present under construction by the Local Fund Board, but there is no accommodation for in-patients. 1,240 out-patients were treated at this dispensary in the year 1876-77.

Irungalúr Mission Dispensary.

There is a Mission dispensary at Irungalúr, under the management of the S.P.G. Mission there, to which a grant of Rupees 500 a year is given by the Local Fund Board.

(5) Extracted, with slight alterations, from a report by Native Surgeon Baulu Mudaliyár, who has been in charge of the hospital since it was opened, and to whom its success has been mainly due.

CHAPTER V.

POPULATION.

First attempts at estimating the population of the district.—Manner in which the Census of 1871 was taken.—Results of the Census.—Population and number of houses.—Increase of population.—Sex and nationality.—Proportion of sexes.—Religion.—Distribution of population according to religion.—Caste.—Hindus.—Muhammadans.—Occupation.—Education.—Taluqwar particulars.—Population of towns.—Condition of the people.—Emigration.

CHAPTER V. POPULATION.

First attempts at estimating the population of the district.

THE earliest attempt that appears to have been made to ascertain the population of the district was in Fasli 1231 (1821-22), when it was stated to be 788,196. The next was in Fasli 1246-47 (1836-37), when the population was returned at 552,477, or 235,719 below the figure arrived at fifteen years previously. The results of these early attempts at a census are, however, so untrustworthy that it would be rash to assume that the population of the district really did decrease between 1822 and 1838. Since 1851-52 a quinquennial census of all the districts in the Presidency has been taken, and the following table shows the results thus obtained in Trichinopoly :—

—	Males.	Females.	Total.
Census of 1851-52 (Fasli 1261)	360,325	348,871	709,196
Do. of 1856-57 („ 1266)	414,603	394,977	809,580
Do. of 1861-62 („ 1271)	481,633	457,767	939,400
Do. of 1866-67 („ 1276)	504,245	502,581	1,006,826

Manner in which the Census of 1871 was taken.

All these figures are more or less untrustworthy, and it was not until 1871, when the first detailed census of the Presidency was taken, that returns approaching to accuracy were obtained. The following is a brief account of the manner in which that census was taken :—

The preliminary enumeration was commenced on the 15th of July 1871 and completed by the end of that month, and the second or final enumeration began on the night of the 14th of November 1871 and ended by the evening of the 15th. The Village Karnams and such of the Munsifs as were able to write were charged with taking the census in the villages, and the Clerks in the offices of the Tahsildars and Deputy Tahsildars were employed in the head-quarters of these officers. There was, therefore, no necessity for employing special agents, except in the town of Trichinopoly, where the Municipal Commissioners employed paid men to do the work. Even in the zemindári tracts the work was done by the Karnams and Munsifs. Each taluq was divided into as many groups of villages as there were Revenue Inspectors and Clerks in the Tahsildars' and Deputy Tahsildars' offices, and each official had a group of villages given him, to every one of which he was ordered to go and examine at least three or four houses and compare the results thus obtained with the enumerators' accounts, and wherever any mistake was found the whole village was gone through carefully again, and the Karnams' carelessness taken serious notice of. The Tahsildars and Deputy Tahsildars and the Divisional Officers also examined the returns, visiting three or four villages of each group at random.

Population and number of houses.

According to the final tabulation made in the Census of 1871 the inhabitants of Trichinopoly District numbered 1,200,408 and the houses 210,690. As only 4,683 of these last were deserted, the percentage of inmates to a house was 5·8, varying in different taluqs as shown in the following table. A very small number of dwellings were terraced or tiled :—

Taluqs.	Average Number of Persons to each of the Inhabited Houses.				
	Terraced.	Tiled.	Thatched.	Unknown.	Total.
Trichinopoly	6·5	5·6	5·9	13·9	5·9
Musiri	5·5	4·1	5·9	6·7	5·9
Kulittalai	5·4	4·0	3·9	19·8	3·9
Perambalúr	9·6	10·0	7·4	9·6	7·5
Udaiyárpálayam	5·5	8·4	8·2	7·0	8·2
Total ..	6·4	6·2	5·8	11·9	5·8

Increase of population.

The next table gives the population of the taluqs in 1871, compared with that shown in the quinquennial return for 1866-67, by which it becomes apparent that a net increase of 19·2 took place in the interval :—

Taluqs.	Population as per Quinquennial Return of 1866-67.	Population according to the Census of 1871.	Increase.	Percentage of Increase.
Trichinopoly	255,397	306,461	51,064	20·0
Musiri	226,273	257,174	30,901	13·7
Kulittalai	190,880	228,313	37,433	19·6
Perambalúr	144,072	170,567	26,495	18·4
Udaiyárpálayam ..	190,204	237,893	47,689	25·0
Total ..	1,006,826	1,200,408	193,582	19·2

Sex and nationality.

Particulars of the present population as to sex and nationality for each taluq are given below :—

Taluqs.	Houses.			Population.											
				Children.		Adults.		Total.							
	Inhabited.	Uninhabited.	Total.	Boys under 12 Years of Age.	Girls under 10 Years of Age.	Males.	Females.	Males.	Females.	Hindus.	Muhamadans.	Christians.	Buddhists and Jains.	Others.	Total.
Trichinopoly ..	51,983	2,300	54,283	54,960	49,249	92,231	110,021	147,191	159,270	260,119	15,374	30,915	..	53	306,461
Musiri	43,470	1,617	45,087	47,565	42,879	76,310	90,420	123,875	133,299	249,551	3,490	3,954	..	179	257,174
Kulittalai	58,698	1	58,699	41,781	37,676	71,452	77,404	113,233	115,080	212,782	6,893	8,638	..	..	228,313
Perambalúr	22,849	7	22,856	31,358	28,659	52,479	58,071	83,837	86,730	163,536	4,679	2,198	143	11	170,567
Udaiyárpálayam ..	29,007	758	29,765	44,113	39,291	75,885	78,604	119,998	117,895	229,788	1,588	6,517	..	..	237,893
Total ..	206,007	4,683	210,690	219,777	197,754	368,357	414,520	588,134	612,274	1,115,776	32,024	52,222	143	243	1,200,408

Of the gross population the males numbered 588,134 and the females 612,274, or in the proportion of 104 of the latter to 100 of the former. With slight variations, this proportion was found to prevail in all the taluqs, except Udaiyárpálayam, where the females were in a minority of 2,103.

CHAPTER V. POPULATION. Proportion of sexes.

92·9 per cent. of the people are classed as Hindus, 2·7 as Muhammadans, 4·4 as Christians, only 143 as Buddhists, with a few more who are returned as "Others." The Hindus enrol themselves under religious headings as follows:—

Religion.

—	Population.	Proportion.
Sivites	843,729	75·6
Vishnuvites	270,654	29·2
Lingayets	533	·05
Other Hindus	860	·08
Total ..	1,115,776	100

The Muhammadans are comparatively few, although they established their empire in Trichinopoly during the 17th century. They are returned as—

Soonees	25,511
Shias	3,193
Wahábis	89
Others	3,231

and half of these are settled in Trichinopoly Town alone.

The Christians are numerically much stronger than the Muhammadans. They are arranged under the following heads:—

—	Roman Catholics.	Protestants.	Total.
Europeans	325	298	623
Eurasians	285	345	630
Native Christians	48,889	1,933	50,822
Others	23	124	147
Total ..	49,522	2,700	52,222

Christianity has spread, as a rule, among the lower classes only. Since the commencement of the 17th century Trichinopoly has

CHAPTER V. POPULATION.

been the scene of the labors of a large number of Jesuit priests, of whom the best known was Father Beschi. Of late years they have made but few converts.

The Jains are all found in one taluq, viz., Perambalúr.

Distribution of the population according to religion.

The annexed table gives the proportion in which the population of the district is divided among the several religions :—

Taluqs.	Hindus.				Muhammadans.				Christians.					
									Europeans and Eurasians.		Natives.		Others.	
	Vishnuvites.	Sivites.	Lingayets.	Other Hindus.	Soonees.	Shias.	Wahábis.	Other Muhammadans.	Roman Catholics.	Protestants.	Roman Catholics.	Protestants.	Roman Catholics.	Protestants.
Trichinopoly ..	24·5	75·1	·1	·3	76·3	17·3	·6	5·8	48·9	51·09	95·6	4·4	15·6	84·4
Musiri ..	30·6	69·3	·03	·008	73·3	2·9	..	23·8	..	100·0	92·6	7·4	..	..
Kulittalai ..	19·0	80·9	·05	..	96·6	2·6	..	·8	42·9	57·1	99·4	·6	..	..
Perambalúr ..	29·6	70·3	·03	·008	68·3	3·4	..	28·3	..	100·0	99·09	·9	..	..
Udaiyárpálayam.	18·1	81·8	·02	·008	86·2	5·7	..	8·1	..	..	95·9	4·05	..	..
Total ..	24·2	75·6	·05	·08	79·6	10·0	·6	10·0	48·7	51·3	96·2	3·8	15·6	84·4

Caste.

Statement No. 2, given in the appendix, shows the Hindus in the district, including Native Christians and Buddhists, as divided into the several castes to which they belong, and also the Muhammadans classified as Labbays, Mapilahs, &c.

Hindus.

According to this statement it appears that the Hindu population is mainly composed of four castes, viz., Vannians, Vellálars, Pariahs, and Sátánis, who form rather more than 75 per cent. of the whole. Some castes, such as Kshattriyas, Writers, Potters, Shánárs or Palmyra-climbers, have very few representatives, and but little remark is called for regarding them, save that the Chetties in this district devote themselves to cultivation more than is usual with them. Out of their 6,912 who are employed, 3,927 trade and 2,635 are cultivators and laborers. More than half the Bráhmans are farmers, the same is the case with the Kshattriyas, while the Milkmen have forsaken pastoral for agricultural employ to the extent of upwards of three-fourths of their number. Out of 9,818 Fishermen 8,618 live by cultivation, principally as field-laborers.

In the census returns no less than 122,332 persons are classed as Sátánis. There are, however, in reality, very few Sátánis in Trichinopoly. None are to be found through the district, and only a very limited number—certainly, I should say, not above 1,000—in

Trichinopoly and Sríraangam towns. Mr. Cornish states in his census report that, according to the system of caste classification adopted by the Census Committee, members of the following castes, among many others, were classed as Sátánis, viz., Bairági, Jógi, Pandáram, Tambiran, and Víra Sivas. Of course members of these castes are not really Sátánis, and it is to be regretted that they were classed as such. Even, however, if the members of all the castes mentioned by Mr. Cornish are added to the real Sátánis, the total for Trichinopoly District would not be anything like as high as 122,000. There are in this district a large number of Nayudus and Reddies who are all of Telugu extraction. They, however, are not shown separately in the returns, and it is impossible to say under what head they have been included. 3,674 are entered as Kshattriyas. It is very doubtful, however, if there are any inhabitants of this district who have the slightest claim to be classed under this head.

Among all castes the worship of Siva predominates, with the exception of the Kshattriyas and Shepherds, as the next table shows:—

Caste.	Sivaites.	Vishnavites.	Lingayets.	Other Hindus.	Christians.	Buddhists and Jains.	Total.	Percentage on the preceding Columns. Sivaites.	Vishnavites.	Lingayates.	Other Hindus.	Christians.	Buddhists and Jains.
Bráhman	20,018	11,410	..	..	..	..	31,428	63·7	36·3	..	..	..	..
Kshattriya	680	2,732	..	..	262	..	3,674	18·5	74·4	..	..	7·1	..
Chetti	14,419	6,998	20	..	18	..	21,455	67·2	32·6	·09	..	·08	..
Vellálan	118,220	76,726	25	1	5,881	..	200,853	58·9	38·2	·02	·0005	2·9	..
Idaiyan	19,754	41,350	..	21	106	..	61,231	32·3	67·5	..	·03	·2	..
Kammálan	24,106	2,352	44	..	1,969	..	28,471	84·7	8·2	·2	..	6·9	..
Kanakkan	261	29	..	..	4	..	294	88·8	9·9	..	..	1·3	..
Kaikalan	25,336	8,944	38	..	109	..	34,427	73·6	26·0	·1	..	·3	..
Vánnian	331,070	49,227	11	283	17,676	143	398,410	83·1	12·4	·003	·07	4·4	·04
Kusavan	5,903	376	28	..	125	..	6,432	91·8	5·9	·4	..	1·9	..
Sátáni	96,610	20,627	367	..	4,728	..	122,332	78·9	16·9	·3	..	3·9	..
Sembadavan	22,495	1,716	..	1	162	..	24,374	92·3	7·0	..	·004	·7	..
Shánán	4,528	225	..	6	60	..	4,819	94·0	4·7	..	·1	1·2	..
Ambattan	9,470	3,590	..	13	13	..	13,086	72·4	27·4	..	·1	·1	..
Vannán	9,888	2,225	..	..	184	..	12,297	80·4	18·1	..	..	1·5	..
Others	27,891	18,136	..	..	72	..	46,099	60·5	39·3	..	..	·2	..
Pariahs	113,080	23,991	..	535	19,453	..	157,059	72·0	15·3	..	·3	12·4	..
Total ..	843,729	2,70,654	533	860	50,822	143	1,166,741	72·3	23·2	·05	·08	4·3	·01

Labbays and Sheiks from the bulk of the Muhammadans, and they, like their Hindu brethren, largely affect cultivation as a means of living. Nearly half of them are so engaged. Trade is their next most popular occupation, and employs close on 2,000 of their numbers.

CHAPTER V. POPULATION.

Muhammadans.

Occupation.

Statement No. 2-A given in the appendix shows the occupation of the male population of the Trichinopoly District. It appears from it that the Civil Service of Government is composed chiefly of these four classes :—

Vellálars	721
Vannians	440
Bráhmans	383
Muhammadans	315

It includes also 155 Pariahs.

In the Military Service the four classes noted below predominate :—

Vellálars	861
Muhammadans	590
Vannians	445
Pariahs	443

Of those in learned professions, nearly half are Bráhmans, and no other class need be noticed in this category, except the Barbers, who have 172 of their number so engaged.

The minor professions are filled chiefly by Bráhmans 1,916, Vellálars 1,897, and Vannians 1,071.

Personal service employs 13,572 people, mostly Barbers, Washermen, and Pariahs.

The trading column, though headed by Chetties, does not engross the usual proportion of this caste. Out of the 15,492 merchants there are of—

Chetties	3,927
Vellálars	3,702
Others (Hindus)	2,098
Muhammadans	1,940
Shepherds	903
Vannians	810

The bulk of those who engage in cultivation are Vannians in the south, then came the Vellálars and Pariahs in point of numbers, but it is a favourite occupation with nearly all the castes in this district.

Dress is provided by Weavers and Pariahs in nearly equal numbers, almost to the exclusion of other castes ; food by shepherds and Vannians, the Fishermen doing little in that way. The metal column has always one large figure opposite the Artisans, and so has

CHAPTER V. POPULATION.

the construction. Books call for no remark. Household goods employ Potters firstly, then "Others" and Vellálars.

Laborers are drawn from all ranks, but chiefly the Vannians and Pariahs. The property-holders are nearly half Vellálars.

Out of 2,163 the following classes contribute the largest numbers to the heading "Unproductive":—

Pariahs	536
Vellálars	336
Vannians	269
Bráhmans	155

Education.

Education shows well in Trichinopoly. 6 per cent. of the population, or 72,086 souls, can read and write, of whom only 478 are females. They are classed as follows:—

—	Gross Population.	Number able to read and write.	Proportions.
Hindus	1,115,776	66,049	5·9
Muhammadans	32,024	3,168	9·9
Christians (Natives)	50,822	2,377	4·7
Europeans and Eurasians	1,400	485	34·8
Buddhists and Jains	143	2	1·4
Others	243	5	2·1
Total ..	1,200,408	72,086	6·0

The Muhammadans of this district are more generally educated than the Hindus, and the Native Christians show badly.

Taluqwar particulars.

The annexed statement shows the particulars of the population of each taluq in the district:—

Name of the Taluq.	Hindus (including Native Christians).							Muhammadans.			Europeans.			Eurasians.			Others.			Total.		
	Hindus.		Native Christians.		Total Hindus.																	
	Males.	Females	Males.	Females	Males.	Females	Total.	Males.	Females.	Total.	Males.	Females.	Total.	Males.	Females.	Total.	Males.	Females.	Total.	Males.	Females.	Total.
1	2	3	4	5	6	7	8	9	10	11	12	13	14	15	16	17	18	19	20	21	22	23
1. Trichinopoly ...	124,638	135,481	14,148	15,379	138,786	150,860	289,646	7,548	7,826	15,374	451	165	616	284	341	625	122	78	200	147,191	159,270	306,461
2. Musiri	120,186	129,365	1,904	2,049	122,090	131,414	253,504	1,697	1,793	3,490	1	...	1	...	...	...	87	92	179	123,875	133,299	257,174
3. Kulittalai	105,429	107,353	4,276	4,355	109,705	111,708	221,413	3,522	3,371	6,893	4	...	4	2	1	3	...	...	...	113,233	115,080	228,313
4. Perambalúr ...	80,386	83,293	1,053	1,141	81,439	84,434	165,873	2,390	2,289	4,679	1	1	2	1	1	2	6	5	11	83,837	86,730	170,567
5. Udaiyárpálayam ...	115,864	113,924	3,286	3,231	119,150	117,155	236,305	848	740	1,588	...	...	...	...	...	...	...	...	...	119,998	117,895	237,893
Total ...	546,503	569,416	24,667	26,155	571,170	595,571	1,166,741	16,005	16,019	32,024	457	166	623	287	343	630	215	175	390	588,134	612,274	1,200,408

CHAPTER V. POPULATION.

Population of towns.

There are in the district, according to the Census of 1871, ninety-six towns with a population exceeding 2,000, and of these seven have more than 5,000 inhabitants. In many cases, however, these so-called towns are merely clusters of hamlets, often containing only a few houses each which have been grouped together for purposes of revenue administration.[1]

Condition of the people.

The inhabitants of the portions of the district lying along the rivers are, as a rule, well-to-do, but there are but few wealthy men to be found. In the unirrigated portions of the district the people are poor, but they are on the whole better off than in most of the neighbouring districts owing to the low rates of assessment charged on all Government land in Trichinopoly. The ordinary dress of the people consists of a cotton waist cloth and a second cloth of the same material usually thrown over the shoulders. In towns the houses are, as a rule, built with mud walls and tiled roofs. In Trichinopoly and Srírangam alone are there many houses built of brick. In the villages the people live in thatched hovels. As a rule, no furniture will be found in the houses but a wooden sleeping cot, a bench or two, and number of brass chatties. In the houses of a few wealthy men in the large towns other articles such as chairs, tables, almirahs (wardrobes), &c., are to be seen.

The wages ordinarily received by the different classes of labourers are as follow :—

		A.	P.	
Agricultural day-labourers (male)	..	4	0	per diem.
Do. do. (female)	..	1	8	,,
Other day labourers, coolies (male)	..	3	0	,,
Do. do. (female)	..	1	6	,,
Smiths and Carpenters	..	8	0	,,
Bricklayers	..	7	0	,,

Emigration.

There is no immigration worth mentioning into the district, but there is a considerable amount of emigration out of it, principally of labourers to Ceylon and the Mauritius. As a rule, however, those who leave the country return again to it before very long.

(1) The figures and the greater part of the information contained in the foregoing portion of this chapter are taken from Mr. Cornish's report on the Census of 1871

CHAPTER VI.

POLITICAL HISTORY OF TRICHINOPOLY, PART I.

(FROM THE FOUNDING OF THE CHÓLA KINGDOM TILL THE FALL OF THE NÁYAK DYNASTY.)

The Chóla, Chéra, and Pándya kingdoms.—Allusion to the Chóla kingdom in the Asoka edicts.—Mention of the Chólas in the works of the Greek geographers.—The Chinese Buddhist Pilgrims.—Marco Polo's visit to Southern India.—Impossibility of compiling a list of the Chóla kings.—Rajéndra Chóla, Kulótunga Chóla.—Rámánuja, the founder of the Srí Vaishnava system.—Discussion regarding the date of Sundara Pándya.—Allusions in the Singhalese chronicles to the Chóla kingdom.—Invasions of Ceylon by the Chólas and Pándyas.—Intervention of the Muhammadans.—Malik Káfúr.—Kampana Udeiyár.—Visvanátha Náyakkan gets possession of Madura and Trichinopoly.—Visvanátha fortifies Trichinopoly.—Reign of Tirumala Náyakkan.—Choka Náyakkan removes the capital of the kingdom from Madura to Trichinopoly.—Mangammál's regency.—Description of Trichinopoly in 1719.

CHAPTER VI. POLITICAL HISTORY, PART I.

The Chóla, Chéra, and Pándya kingdoms.

THE first rays of historical light that have been thrown on that portion of Southern India of which the present district of Trichinopoly forms a part show it divided into three kingdoms named after the three dynasties of the Chóla, Chéra, and Pándya kings. The origin of these three kingdoms is entirely lost in obscurity. It may, however, on the whole be considered to have been proved that they existed as early as the fifth century before Christ, and it is certain that they lasted under various forms till the sixteenth century A.D., when the several countries that had been comprised in them fell under the sway of the Náyakkas. Of the history, however, of these kingdoms during this lengthened period we know very little. Native legends indeed regarding them and their rulers exist in abundance, but as materials for history they are utterly worthless, and the few facts that have been satisfactorily established regarding them have been ascertained from the scattered allusions to these kingdoms that are to be found in the works of travellers who have from time to time visited Southern India and from inscriptions. The Tamil tradition regarding the origin of these kingdoms is that Chéran, Chólan, and Pándyan were three royal brothers who lived and ruled in common at Kolkei on the river Támraparni in Tinnevelly. After a time they separated; Pándyan remained in the south, while Chéran and Chólan founded independent kingdoms in the north and west respectively.[1]

---

(1) CALDWELL's *Dravidian Grammar*, Introduction, page 18.

CHAPTER VI.
POLITICAL HISTORY, PART I.

Allusion to the Chóla kingdom in the Asoka edicts.

The earliest extant allusion to the Chóla kingdom is to be found in the edicts promulgated by Asoka, the Buddhist Emperor of Northern India, in the year B.C. 250, where the following passage occurs[2] :—" In all the subjugated territories of the King Priyadasi, the beloved of the gods, and also in the bordering countries as Chóda, Palaya (or Paraya), Satyaputra, Keralaputra, Tambapani it is proclaimed . . ." There appears to be no doubt that the word Chóda in this passage is the same as Chóla, and its presence in this edict proves that the Chóla kingdom existed at least as far back as the third century B.C.[3]

Mention of the Chólas in the works of the Greek geographers.

In Ptolemy's Geography, written about A.D. 130, and also in the *Periplus Maris Erythræi*, the date of which is about A.D. 80, allusions are made to the ancient kingdoms of Southern India. The following words and phrases which occur in these works have been identified, among others, as referring to the Chóla kingdom and the territory comprised in it. Σῶραι νομάδες. 'Αρκάτου βασίλειον Σῶρα—'Ορθοῦρα βασίλειον Σῶρναγος—Παραλία Σωρητῶν and Χαβήρος. In the words Σῶραι, Σῶρα and Σώρναγος there can be but little doubt that the Sóras or Chólas are referred to. It is difficult, however, to say positively what 'Αρκάτου βασίλειον Σῶρα means. On this point Dr. Caldwell remarks : " As General Cunningham has pointed out, Σῶρα is represented as the name of a city where a king called Ἄρκατος reigned. Though this was evidently Ptolemy's meaning, yet one is strongly tempted to suppose that here the names given by the natives of the country to his informants had got transposed. The name Σῶρα is identical with that of the people of the district, whom Ptolemy himself calls Σῶραι νομάδες and Ἄρκατος answers exceedingly well in situation as well as in sound to Arcot, the capital of the Karnatic in Muhammadan times. There is a distinct tradition that the inhabitants of that part of the Chóla or Sóra country which lies between Madras and the ghauts, including Arcot as its centre, were Kurumbars or wandering shepherds—nomads—for several centuries after the Christian era. General Cunningham objects to this identification that Arcot is quite a modern name ; but it must, as Colonel Yule has pointed out, be at least as old as 1340 A.D. for it is mentioned by Ibn Batuta."[4] Dr. Caldwell also points out

---

(2) Professor Wilson's translation, given at page 459 of Mr. TALBOYS WHEELER'S *History of India*, Vol. 3, Appendix I.

(3) On this point Dr. Burnell remarks as follow :—" Prinsep suggested, and no doubt rightly, that Coda refers to the Cóla kingdom in South India ; Professor H. H. Wilson, however, seems to think that these names refer to the north of India ; but, as the Cóla kingdom of the south was always famous, it does not appear necessary to assume another Cóla kingdom in the north as yet unknown.—*Elements of South Indian Paleography*, page 11, note.

(4) *Dravidian Grammar*, Introduction, page 96.

that we know from native poems that the name of the ancient capital of the Chólas was Uraiyúr, at present a suburb of Trichinopoly Town, and that we may safely identify this name with Ptolemy's *'Ορθοῦρα*, the capital of the *Παραλία Σωρητῶν*, and General Cunningham, in his ancient geography, expresses the same opinion.[5] *Παραλία Σωρητῶν* is evidently the coast of the Sóras or Chólas, that is the coast now known as the Coromandel, and *Χαβήρος* may safely be identified as the Cauvery.[6]

As has been already remarked it appears probable that the Chóla kingdom was founded in about the 5th century before Christ. Who, however, the founder was or where he came from it is impossible to state with any certainty. Professor Wilson has given it as his opinion that his name was Tayaman Nale and that he was a settler who came from Oude or some part of Upper Hindustan. This statement is, however, of very doubtful accuracy. No doubt, according to all the native legends and mythical tales, the early kings of this part of the country were sprung from either the Solar or Lunar race and came from some place in the north of the peninsula. Little or no weight can however be attached to these assertions, made in all probability with the sole view of gratifying the pride of descent of some of the later rulers of these countries. As remarked by Dr. Caldwell, "the Aryan immigrants to the south appear to have been generally Bráhmanical priests and instructors rather than Kshattriya soldiers; and the kings of the Pándyas, Chólas, Kalingas, and other Dravidians appear to have been simply Dravidian Chieftains whom their Bráhmanical preceptors and spiritual directors dignified with Aryan titles and taught to imitate and emulate the grandeur and cultivated tastes of the Solar, Lunar, and Agni-kula races of kings."[7] The Chóla and Pándya kings are of course held by Natives to have been Kshattriyas, but there is no evidence that they have the slightest claim to be considered as such. It may appear worthy of remark that their caste title was Déva, the same as that of the Maravas at present.[8]

The Chinese Buddhist pilgrims.

The next notices that we meet of the Chóla kingdom are those made by the famous Chinese traveller, Hiouen-Thsang, in his journal of his pilgrimage. It is, however, rather doubtful if he ever travelled as far south as Trichinopoly or indeed if there are really any allusions to the Chóla kingdom in his journal. On this point General Cunningham remarks as follows: "From Danakakuta Hiouen-Thsang travelled for 1,000 li or 167 miles to Chuliye or

---

(5) *Ancient Geography*, page 551.
(6) CALDWELL'S *Dravidian Grammar*, Introduction, page 27.
(7) *Dravidian Grammar*, Introduction, page 115.
(8) CALDWELL'S *Dravidian Grammar*, page 553.

CHAPTER VI. POLITICAL HISTORY, PART I.

Jholiye, which he describes as a small district only 2,400 li or 400 miles in circuit. To enable us to fix the position of this unknown territory it is necessary to note the pilgrim's subsequent route to the south for 1,500 or 1,600 li, or about 260 miles, to Kánchípura or Conjeveram, the well-known capital of Dravida. Now the distance of Kánchípura from the Kistna is from 240 to 260 miles, so that Choliye must be looked for somewhere along the south bank of that river at 167 miles to the south-west of Dharanikotta. This position corresponds almost exactly with Karnúl which is 230 miles in a direct line to the north-north-west of Conjeveram and 160 west-south-west of Dharanikotta. M. Julien has identified Chóliya with Chóla, which gives its name to Chóla-mandalam or Coromandel. But Chóla was to the south of Dravida, whereas the Chóliya of Hiouen-Thsang lies to the north of it. If we accept the pilgrim's bearings and distances as approximately correct, the position of Chóliya must certainly be looked for in the neighbourhood of Karnúl."[9] He further remarks that an adherence to the text of Hiouen-Thsang involves the total omission of any mention of the famous kingdom of Chóla. Dr. Caldwell has, however, suggested a solution of the difficulty. He remarks that, although it is difficult to identify the country called Chóliya by Hiouen-Thsang with that inhabited by the Chólas, yet that it seems probable that the names are indentical and that we know that the Northern Cirars were ruled by an offshoot of the Chólas in the eleventh century.[10] It therefore on the whole may probably be assumed that, although this traveller never visited Trichinopoly, yet that he traversed portions at all events of the Chóla kingdom. The following abstract of his remarks on the country is taken in great part from Professor Cowell's article on Chinese Buddhist pilgrims in India printed as an appendix to his edition of Elphinstone's History of India. It appears that, after visiting Orissa and Andhra, Hiouen-Thsang went to Dhanakacheka or Mahándhra (Mahendri)—this is evidently the place called Danakakuta by General Cunningham—and thence to Chóla, which he describes as mostly a desert covered with marshes and jungles. The monasteries, he states, were nearly all in ruins, but there were a number of temples, and the heretics who went naked (the *Nirgranthas*) were very numerous. From thence his way lay southward through forests and desert-plains until he reached Dravida and its capital Kánchípura (Conjeveram). He states that in this town there were 100 monasteries with 10,000 monks and 80 temples. Here he met some monks from Ceylon who advised him not to proceed there as the king had just died and as the country was consequently in a disturbed condition. He took

(9) *Ancient Geography*, Vol. I, page 545.
(10) *Dravidian Grammar*, Introduction, page 17.

CHAPTER VI. POLITICAL HISTORY, PART I.

their advice and did not go south of Kánchípura.[11] As he left China in the year 629 A.D. and returned in 645, the date of his visit to the Chóla kingdom can be fixed with sufficient accuracy.

Marco Polo's visit to Southern India.

The next traveller on record who visited the south of India was Marco Polo, the Venetian, whose travels in that country took place in A.D. 1292 or 1293. He does not mention the Chóla kingdom by name, but states that at the time of his visit the south of India was divided into five kingdoms. His remarks are as follows: "When you leave the island of Seilan (Ceylon) and sail westward about sixty miles, you come to the great province of Maabar, which is styled India the greater; it is the best of all the Indies and is on the mainland. You must know that in this province there are five kings, who are own brothers. I will tell you about each in turn. The province is the finest and noblest in the world. At this end of the province reigns one of those five royal brothers, who is crowned a king, and his name is Sonder Bandi Davár. In his kingdom they find very fine and great pearls;"[12] and afterwards, when treating of what he terms the province of Lar whence the Bráhmans come, Marco Polo says that the king of the country who is rich and powerful is eager to purchase stones and large pearls; and that he sends the Abraiaman (Bráhman) merchants into the kingdom of Maabar called Soli, which is the best and noblest province of India, and where the best pearls are found, to fetch him as many of these as they can get, and he pays them double the cost-price for all.[13] In commenting on these passages Colonel Yule points out that Maabar was the name given by the Musalmans in the 13th and 14th centuries to a tract corresponding in a general way to what is now termed the Coromandel Coast. As regards the position of the port of Maabar, visited by Marco Polo at or near which Sonder Bandi seems to have lived- Colonel Yule is inclined to look for it rather in Tanjore than on the gulf of Manar, south of the Ramésvaram shallows. The difficulties in this view are the indication of its being "sixty miles west of Ceylon" and the special mention of the pearl fishery in connexion with it. The pearl difficulty may, however, be solved by the probability that the dominion of Sonder Bandi *extended* to the coast of the gulf of Manar. In addition to this, Marco Polo in the second passage quoted above calls the province of Sonder Bandi *Soli*, which we can scarcely doubt is Chóla or Sóla-désam, *i.e.*, Tanjore and Trichinopoly. He calls it also "the best and noblest

(11) ELPHINSTONE's *History of India*, 5th edition, page 295.

(12) From Colonel Yule's translation of *Marco Polo*, 2nd edition, Vol. II, page 313.

(13) YULE's *Marco Polo*, Vol. II, page 350.

CHAPTER VI. POLITICAL HISTORY, PART I.

province of India," a description which would scarcely suit the coast of Rámnád, but which might be justifiably applied to the well-watered valley of the Cauvery.

Impossibility of compiling a list of the Chóla kings.

It is quite impossible to compile anything approaching to an accurate list of the Chóla kings.[14] In the introduction to his Descriptive Catalogue of the Mackenzie MSS. Professor Wilson has given a list of them, which he states he has drawn up from information obtained from the temples in Conjeveram. The kings mentioned in it are said to have reigned between S.S. 136 and S.S. 830 (A.D. 214 and 908).[15] This list is identical with one given in Prinsep's Antiquities.[16] Prinsep states that the names in it are those of the rajas of the Chóla kingdom which included the country now called the Karnatic below the ghauts and Tanjore. The capitals of this kingdom, it is said, were Arcot in Ptolemy's time, then Uraiyúr, then Combaconum, and lastly Tanjore. This latter statement is, however, of very doubtful accuracy. Besides the one already mentioned Prinsep gives a second list of the Chóla kings, and in addition to these other lists are to be found in Tayor's Oriental MSS. and his Catalogue Raisonné of the Oriental MSS. in the College in Fort St. George. All these lists diverge widely from that given in the Trichinopoly local Purána. I do not, however, consider that there would be any advantage in inserting any of them here, as they are all hopelessly inaccurate and void of any value or interest, either historically or otherwise. The extraordinary discrepancies to be found in these lists, both as regards the names of the kings and the order in which they reigned, raises the presumption that, if they are in any sense whatever to be deemed historically trustworthy, which is more than doubtful, they contain the names of merely petty local chiefs and rulers. The following are the names of the Chóla and Pándya kings that occur most frequently in the inscriptions in the Trichinopoly District, of which I have obtained copies :—Déva Chóla, Sundra Pándya, Rájéndra Chóla, Víra Pándya, Kulótunga Chóla, Kulasékhara, and Karikála Chóla. These inscriptions have unfortunately been of very little use to me for the following reasons :—They almost invariably are accounts of gifts of land, &c., to temples, and the name of the king who was reigning at the time of the gift and the year of his reign in which it was made are, as a general rule, given ; but, as the year in which this took place is not stated either according to the usual computation from the death of Sáliváhana

---

(14) *Vide Elements of South Indian Paleography*, page 37, where Dr Burnell remarks that the list of the Chóla and Pándya kings is quite uncertain.

(15) Introduction to *Descriptive Catalogue of the Mackenzie MSS.*, page 36.

(16) PRINSEP'S *Antiquities*, Vol. II, useful tables, page 279.

CHAPTER VI. POLITICAL HISTORY, PART I.

or any other method, they are of very little use towards establishing the dates of the kings mentioned in them.[17]

Rájéndra Chóla Kulótunga Chóla.

Of the numerous kings that must have ruled over the Chóla kingdom during the twenty centuries for which it appears to have lasted, we can fix the dates of only a very few with anything approaching to certainty. Of these the most important are Rájéndra Chóla, Kulótunga Chóla, Karikála Chóla, and Víra Chóla. Of all the Chóla kings these are probably those of whom most is known. They appear to have lived in the 11th, 12th, and 13th centuries A.D., the period when the Chóla kingdom enjoyed the greatest prosperity, and yet it is most difficult, not only to fix their dates, but even to give the order in which they reigned. First of all as regards Rájéndra. From inscriptions found by Sir Walter Elliot and Dr. Caldwell it would appear that this monarch began to reign about A.D. 1063, and that he was succeeded after a reign of 49 years by Kulótunga, who was probably his son, about A.D. 1112. Rájéndra is shown to have ruled over not only the Chóla but also the Kalinga, and perhaps the Pándya kingdoms. In one of the inscriptions, in which his name has been found, he is termed Rájéndra Chóla Pándya.[18] As Rájéndra and his successor Kulótunga were the patrons of the poet Kambar, and as there is a stanza prefixed to the Tamil Rámáyana of that author, in which it is stated that the work was finished in the year of the Sáliváhana era corresponding to A.D. 886, it has been very generally assumed that Rájéndra must have reigned in the 9th century. Dr. Caldwell, however, has shown good reasons for doubting the genuineness of this stanza,[19] and therefore, in spite of the statement made in it, we may safely put the reigns of Rájéndra and Kulótunga in the end of the 11th and the beginning of the 12th century. Kulótunga Chóla is said to have built the famous temple at Tanjore, but there is very little evidence to prove that such is the case. He appears to have ruled over the whole of the Pándya in addition to the Chóla kingdom without a rival. Vikrama Pándya, called also Vikrama Chóla Pándya, most probably because, like some of his successors, he ruled over the two kingdoms, and Víra Chóla seem to have

(17) Dr. Burnell points out that inscriptions in the Grantha-Tamil character abound in the Tamil country, where there is scarcely a temple of any note which has not acres of wall covered with them, but that it is very unusual to find any with dates that can be identified, most being only in the year of the king's reign or life and genealogical details being very rarely given. He also remarks that, as the Chóla and Pándya kings appear to mention the year of their reign most generally, and the second also, but rarely, the Quilon era, the task of establishing the succession of these dynasties and the dates is likely to prove very formidable.—*Elements of South Indian Paleography*, pages 37 and 56.

(18) CALDWELL'S *Dravidian Grammar*, Introduction, pages 135 and 136.

(19) *Dravidian Grammar*, Introduction, page 134.

CHAPTER VI. POLITICAL HISTORY, PART I.

reigned between Kulótunga and Sundra Pándya,[20] whose date may be considered to have been fixed with tolerable accuracy after considerable discussion, an analysis of which will be given further on. Whether, however, Karikála Chóla, the most famous perhaps of the time, also lived in this interval or before Rájéndra, it is difficult to decide. The difficulty is principally owing to the uncertainty that prevails as to whether Karikála was the king whose persecutions obliged Rámánuja, the famous founder of the Srí Vaishnava system, to flee from the Chóla country. The account given of Rámánuja's life is briefly as follows:—It is said that, in consequence of his having promulgated novel opinions on theological subjects, he was persecuted by the Chóla Rajá, who was a strenuous supporter of the Smártah Bráhmans. Being obliged to flee from this persecution, he took refuge at the court of Peddata, the Jaina king of the Hoisala race, who was converted by him and then assumed the title of Vishnu Vardhana. The Jaina priests were naturally irritated at their king's defection from their creed, and they are said to have engaged in a disputation with Rámánuja on the merits of the rival forms of belief for eighteen years, but to have been in the end completely worsted. After this Rámánuja is said to have lived at Mélkótta, at present one of the chief seats of his followers, for fourteen years, when, the king that had persecuted him having died, he took up his abode at Srírangam (near Trichinopoly), where he is said to have had great success in converting the Jains.[21] Professor Wilson has shown[22] that various traditionary accounts name Karikála as the Chóla king who persecuted Rámánuja, and he has, on what Dr. Caldwell[23] considers to be conclusive evidence, shown that this celebrated preacher lived in the beginning of the 12th century. Karikála's date would be established if we could accept these traditionary accounts. In this, however, there would be some difficulty. Rámánuja appears to have lived before Kambar, as the latter refers to him in one of his poems, and, if therefore Karikála was Rámánuja's persecutor, he must have reigned prior to Kambar's patrons Rájéndra and Kulótunga. This however is very doubtful, as will be seen further on when Sundra Pándya's date is discussed. Karikála probably lived in the 13th century and was a contemporary of Sundra Pándya.

Rámánuja the founder of the Srí Vaishnava System.

Discussion regarding the date of Sundra Pándya.

One of the most important eras in the history of the kingdoms of Southern India is the reign of Sundra Pándya, the last of the old dynasty of the Pándyas and the expeller of the Jains from Madura. If his date can be determined, much light will

(20) CALDWELL'S *Dravidian Grammar*, Introduction, page 140.
(21) BUCHANAN'S *Mysore, Canara, and Malabar*, Vol. I, pages 349 and 350.
(22) Introduction to *Descriptive Catalogue of the Mackenzie MSS.*, page 62.
(23) *Dravidian Grammar*, Introduction, page 136.

be thrown on the confused chronology of this period. A brief analysis of the discussion that has taken place on this point will therefore be given here, as it appears to me that the result of it has been to fix the date of Sundara's reign at the close of the 13th and the commencement of the 14th century A.D. It will be remembered that in his journal of his travels Marco Polo stated that at the time of his visit in A.D. 1292 to this part of India it was ruled over by one of five royal brothers whose name was Sonder Bandi Davár. In the first edition of his Dravidian Grammar Dr. Caldwell remarked that he believed that this monarch was identical with Sundara Pándya. This view has not, however, been adopted by Mr. Nelson in his Manual of the Madura District, where he discusses at considerable length the question of Sundara Pándya's date, and arrives at the conclusion that he reigned in the latter half of the 11th century.[24] Colonel Yule also in the second edition of his translation of Marco Polo's travels states that he is unable to adopt Dr. Caldwell's view. The most important evidence bearing on the point is that contained in the works of the several Muhammadan historians who allude to Sundara Pándya. The principal of these allusions are the following:—Wassáf states that Ma'bar extends from Kaulam to Niláwar (Nellore), and that a few years ago the Devar of this country was Sundara Pandi who had three brothers, each of whom established himself in independence in some different country. In the year 1293 A.D. this monarch died, and was succeeded by his brother. The eminent prince Ṭaki-úd-dín Abdur Rahmán was the Devar's Deputy, Minister, and Adviser, and on his death continued Prime Minister as before.[25] If this passage stood alone, there would be no difficulty in identifying the Sundara Pandi stated in it to have died in 1293 with the Sonder Bandi who was ruling when Marco Polo visited this country in 1292, but what renders the whole question confused and doubtful is that Wassáf afterwards gives the following account of a king of Ma'bar, whom he calls Kales Dewar, in which mention is made of Sundara Pándya, whose date does not suit the prince alluded to by Marco Polo. Kales Dewar, he states, had two sons, of whom one Sundar Pandi, was legitimate and the other, Tira Pandi (Víra Pándya?) illegitimate. As Tira Pandi was remarkable for his shrewdness and intrepidity, the king nominated him as his successor. His brother Sundar Pandi, being enraged at this supersession, killed his father in a moment of rashness and undutifulness towards the close of the year 1310

(24) *Madura Manual*, Part III, pages 54–70.

(25) *The History of India as told by its own Historians*, by Sir H. M. ELLIOT, Vol. III, pages 32–35, and Vol. I, page 69, where Rashid-úd-dín gives the same account.

CHAPTER VI. POLITICAL HISTORY, PART I.

A.D. and placed the crown on his own head in the city of Mardi (Madura ?). He induced the troops who were there to support his interests and had some of the royal treasures, which were deposited there, conveyed to the city of Mankúl (Námakkal ?). He himself accompanied them and marched on in royal pomp with elephants, horses, and treasure. Upon this his brother Tira Pandi, being resolved on avenging his father's blood, followed to give him battle, and on the margin of a lake called Taláchi they came to action. Both brothers, each ignorant of the fate of the other, fled away, but Tira Pandi being unfortunate, and having been wounded, fell into the hands of the enemy and seven elephant-loads of gold also fell to the lot of the army of Sundar Pandi. Manár Barmúl, however, the daughter of Kales Dewar, who had espoused the cause of Tira Pandi, sent him assistance both in men and money, which was attended with a most fortunate result. Sundar Pandi had taken possession of the kingdom, and the army and the treasure were his own, but notwithstanding in the middle of the year 1310 Tira Pandi, having collected an army, advanced to oppose him, and Sundar Pandi, trembling and alarmed, fled from his native country and took refuge under the protection of Alá-úd-dín, Sultan of Delhi, and Tira Pandi became firmly established in his hereditary kingdom. Alá-úd-dín, however, afterwards sent his General Hazárdinári to conquer Ma'bar.[26] By another of these Muhammadan historians, Amir Khusru, it is stated that Sundara Pándya and his brother Bír Pándya (Víra Pándya ?) were fighting together when Alá-úd-dín invaded the country in 1311 A.D. His account of the invasion is as follows: Alá-úd-dín's army under his General Malik Naib, or Malik Káfúr, left Delhi in November 1310, and reduced Dwára Samudra, the capital of the Bellala kings. While on his march to Dwára Samudra, it is said that he arrived at a place called Bandrí where he stayed to make inquiries respecting the countries further on. Here he was informed that the two Rais of Ma'bar, the elder named Bír Pándya and the younger Sundar Pándya, who had up to that time continued on friendly terms, had advanced against each other with hostile intentions, and that Billál Deo, the Rai of Dwára Samudra, on hearing of this fact, had marched for the purpose of attacking their two empty cities and plundering the merchants, but that, on hearing of the advance of the Muhammadan army, he had returned to his own country. After the capture of Dwára Samudra, it is stated that Malik Naib marched to Birdhúl, the capital of the elder of the two Rais—"the yellow-faced Bír." He took the city and destroyed all the temples there. From Birdhúl he advanced to Kham, and thence to Mathra

(26) ELLIOT, Vol. II, pages 52–54.

(Madura), the dwelling place of the younger brother, Sundar Pándya. He found the city empty, as the Rai had fled with his Ranis, leaving two or three elephants behind him. These were captured and the temple in which they had been left burnt. Immediately after this Malik Káfúr returned to Delhi.[27] Colonel Yule is of opinion that Birdhúl here mentioned was the capital of Polo's Sonder Bandi, that it was not far from the Cauvery, and was either Tanjore, Combaconum, or some other city in or near the delta of that river.[28] Colonel Yule points out that, according to the Muhammadan historians, we have two rulers in Má'bar within twenty years bearing the name Sundara Pándya, and for this reason principally he comes to the conclusion that he cannot accept Dr. Caldwell's identification of the Sonder Bandi of Marco Polo and the great Sundara Pándya.[29] In the second edition of his Dravidian Grammar Dr. Caldwell goes fully into the whole subject and answers the objections that have been made to the view put forward by him in his first edition. He remarks that the statements of the Muhammadan historians respecting the first of their two Sundaras do not seem to him irreconcileable with the supposition of the identity of Polo's Sonder with the Sundara Pándya who is mentioned in numerous inscriptions that have been found who impalled the Jains and with whose name the ancient list of Pándya kings breaks suddenly off. If we leave out of account Wassáf's second Sundara, who flees to Delhi in 1310, we find him agreeing with Rashid-úd-dín with respect to the Sundara who died in 1293, the man of four brothers whom we may with very little hesitation identify with Marco Polo's Sonder who was reigning in 1292. He further remarks that he does not think that it is impossible to identify this same Sundara with the Sundara of the inscriptions. "It is clear from both the Muhammadan historians that at the close of the 13th century there reigned in Madura a Sundara Pándya who was Dewar—that is, as they interpreted the title, lord paramount—of Ma'bar, the Pándya Chóla country. He was, it is true, one of four (or five) brothers who had acquired power in different directions, yet still he alone was called Dewar, and said to have been possessed of immense wealth. Polo also, though he speaks of his brothers as 'kings,' yet speaks of Sonder alone as 'a crowned king,' and gives him distinctly the title of Bandi; so that it is evident that in some respects he was regarded as supreme. There is no trace in Sundara's inscriptions of his brothers, or of his power being in any degree shared by them, or of the position he

---

(27) ELLIOT, Vol. III, pages 85–92. See also Vol. III, page 204, where it is stated by another annalist that two Rais in Ma'bar were conquered by Malik Káfúr.

(28) YULE'S *Marco Polo*, Vol. II, page 319.

(29) YULE'S *Marco Polo*, Vol. II, page 317.

CHAPTER VI. POLITICAL HISTORY, PART I.

and they held being one that they had 'acquired,' instead of being one that they had inherited; but these are particulars which would not be likely to make their appearance in inscriptions; and there is nothing in the inscriptions or traditions inconsistent with the supposition that he had brothers who had acquired power together with himself. All that is necessary to stipulate for in order to bring the accounts into agreement is that in some sense he alone should be Pandi Dévar, or lord paramount, so that his name only should appear in the inscriptions, and in this, as it seems to me, no particular difficulty can be involved." Dr. Caldwell finally arrives at the conclusion that, pending the discovery of a dated inscription in which Sundara Pándya is mentioned, he sees no valid reason why we should hesitate to identify the Sundar of the Muhammadan historians both with Polo's Sonder and with the Sundara or Kún Pándya of the Saiva revival.[30] I have obtained copies of a considerable number of inscriptions in the Trichinopoly District in which Sundara Pándya is mentioned. They show clearly that he ruled over this part of the country as well as Madura, but they throw no light on the vexed question of as to the time at which he lived as they are not dated.

Allusions in the Singhalese chronicles to the Chóla kingdom.

Certain passages in the Singhalese chronicles throw a little light on some of the vexed questions regarding Sundara Pándya. Before these, however, are touched on, a short account must be given of the frequent invasions of the island of Ceylon by the Chóla and Pándya kings, which appear to have taken place. The connection between these kingdoms and Ceylon would seem to date from a very remote period, for, according to the Mahâwanso, Vijaya, the first sovereign of Ceylon, married a daughter of the Pándya king about B.C. 543.[31] According to these chronicles the first regular invasion of Ceylon from Southern India was about B.C. 247, when it is stated that "a Damilo named Eláro, of the illustrious 'Uju' tribe, invading the island from the Chóla country for the purpose of usurping the sovereignty and putting to death the reigning king Asélo, ruled the kingdom for forty-four years, administering justice with impartiality to friends and foes."[32] The second invasion took place about one hundred years after the first, and the third was in A.D. 110, when it is stated that the island was invaded by a king who carried away 12,000 Singhalese as slaves to Mysore. The son, however, of the king in whose reign this had occurred, in A.D. 113 avenged the outrage by invading the Chóla kingdom, and brought back not only the

Invasions of Ceylon by the Chólas and Pándyas.

(30) CALDWELL's *Dravidian Grammar*, Introduction, pages 139–143, and Appendix III.

(31) TURNOUR's *Mahâwanso*, Vol. I, pages 51 to 53.

(32) TURNOUR's *Mahâwanso*, Vol. I, page 128.

captives from his own country, but also a number of the Chóla people, whom he established in a part of his own island, where Sir Emerson Tennent states that "the Malabar features are thought to be descernible to the present day."[33] Frequent invasions followed, and Ceylon was never for any length of time free from the incursions of the *Damilos*, as they are called in Páli, that is, the Tamils or Tamulians, up to the end of the 12th century. In A.D. 840 the Pándya king overran the north of Ceylon, plundered the capital, and did not leave the island till he had received a large ransom as the price of his departure. A few years after this the Ceylon monarch assisted the son of the Pándya in an insurrection that he had raised against his father, was successful, and returned to his own kingdom after having plundered Madura. About a hundred years later the king of Ceylon sent an army to the assistance of the Pándyas in a conflict in which they were then engaged with the Chólas. His allies were worsted, and the Chóla king invaded Ceylon, where however he met with no success, his army being repulsed by the mountaineers of Rohuna.[34] In A.D. 1023 the Chólas again invaded Ceylon and carried away the king and queen to their own country as captives, leaving a Chóla viceroy in charge of the island. An army of 10,000 men is said to have been sent to assist this viceroy in subduing Rohuna, but to have been defeated in the attempt. The king died in captivity; on which his son proclaimed himself king of Ceylon under the title of Wikrama Báhu, and was making great preparations for attacking the Chólas when he died. His son Wijayo Bahu, who succeeded him in A.D. 1071, having received pecuniary assistance from the Buddhist Government of Siam, determined to expel the Chólas from his island. After a protracted and desultory warfare a general action was fought under the walls of Pollonnaruwa, the king's capital. The Chólas being defeated, threw themselves into the town, which was carried by storm after a siege of six weeks and given up to the sword. The king's authority was now established over the whole island, and ambassadors arrived at his court from the sovereigns of India and Siam. At the audience granted to them, the precedence was given to the envoy of the king of Siam. Enraged at this, the Chóla monarch cut off the nose and ears of the Singhalese envoy at his court. Each monarch then prepared to invade the territory of the other. The Chóla army embarked first and landed at Mantotte, on the north-west coast of the island near Adam's Bridge, where the Singhalese army was drawn up ready to sail. The Singhalese were defeated, and the Chólas marched at once on their capital, from which the king had fled,

(33) Sir EMERSON TENNENT's *Ceylon*. Fourth Edition. Vol. I, page 397.

(34) TENNENT's *Ceylon*, Vol. I, pages 397-403.

CHAPTER VI. POLITICAL HISTORY, PART I.

took possession of it, and demolished the palace. The king, however, soon reassembled his army, which, under the command of his son, expelled the Chólas from the island. In the forty-fifth year of his reign, or A.D. 1116, this monarch invaded the Chóla country, but was obliged to beat a hasty retreat.[35] Although there are no doubt many inaccuracies in the preceding narrative, yet it is probable that it is on the whole not very far from the truth, for the Singhalese chroniclers are, it must be remembered, most trustworthy, in which they offer a pleasing contrast to their Hindu brethren.

One of the most remarkable names in the list of the kings of Ceylon is that of Parákrama Báhu, who came to the throne in 1153 and reigned up to 1186. It is stated that after he had reduced the whole of his own island to subjection, he turned his attention to the chastisement of Kulasékhara, the Pándya king, for the countenance and aid that he had always afforded to all invaders of Ceylon. He sent a powerful army against this prince under the command of his Minister Lankanátha, who subdued Rámésvaram and the neighbouring provinces, drove the king from his capital, and placed his son Wírapandu (Virá Pándya) on the throne. Kulasékhara made three attempts to recover his kingdom with the aid of the Chóla king. He was however defeated, and the Chóla territory having also been conquered, he was obliged to surrender. He was restored to his kingdom, and the conquered portion of the Chóla country was made a separate principality for Wírapandu.[36] A somewhat different account of this invasion of the south of India by the Singhalese has been given by Mr. Rhys Davids in the Journal of the Asiatic Society of Bengal, where it is stated that the Pándu king of Madura, Parákrama, being terrified by the army with which the Kulasékhara was preparing to attack him, applied for aid to the king of Ceylon, Parákrama Báhu. This monarch sent his General with a large force to slay Kulasékhara, and establish in that kingdom same one who came of the stock of the kings of Pándu. Kulasékhara sent Sundara, the Pándu king, to attack the Singhalese General, who, however, utterly routed him in three pitched battles. Kulasékhara himself was afterwards defeated, and obliged to take refuge in a city which he and his followers barricaded. The Singhalese carried the place by storm, and Kulasékhara was obliged to escape in disguise. On this Víra Pándu was declared king in the city of Madura.[37] According to the Tamil manuscripts Srítála, the Pándya king whom Malik Káfúr conquered was Parákrama, which it will be remarked is the name

(35) TURNOUR's *Maháwanso*, Vol. I, Appendix, page lxv.
(36) TURNOUR's *Maháwanso*, Vol. I, Appendix, page lxvi.
(37) CALDWELL's *Dravidian Grammar*, pages 538 and 539.

given in the above account to the monarch who sent for aid to Ceylon against Kulasékhara. This fact is in support of the view that the Sundara of Marco Polo, of the Muhammadan historians and of the Singhalese chronicles, are one and the same. There is some error, no doubt, about the dates, but the mention of the names of Kulasékhara, Sundara, Víra and Parákrama in the Ceylon chronicles, and of Kales (which it may safely be presumed is Kulasékhara) Sundara and Tira (Víra) in the Muhammadan histories, and of Parákrama in Tamil manuscripts giving an account of the invasion recounted in them, renders it almost certain that the two series of narratives relate to the same transactions.

I have not considered that it would serve any useful purpose to insert any of the numerous fables and stories that are extant regarding the Chóla kings. Whether there is any truth whatsoever in these stories it would be difficult to say; probably there is a little in some of them, but I, at all events, have been quite unable to separate it from the mass of falsehood and absurdity in which it lies buried, and the result of the endeavours made by others to extract something valuable in a historical point of view from these myths is not such as to encourage me to make any similar attempt.

Intervention of the Muhammadans.

There is some difficulty in fixing with absolute certainty the date of the earliest incursion of the Muhammadans into Trichinopoly and the other southern districts of the Madras Presidency. There seems, however, on the whole to be but little doubt that the first Musalman force that ever crossed the Kistna was that led by Malik Káfúr, General of Alá-úd-dín, Emperor of Delhi, in the year A.D. 1310 against Dwárasamudra, the capital of the Billál kingdom. The account of this invasion, given by the Muhammadan historians, has already been noticed. Káfúr is said to have penetrated as far as Rámésvaram, where he erected a mosque.[38] Although Káfúr did not remain long in Southern India, but returned almost at once to Delhi, yet it seems that some of his followers stayed behind him, and that after his departure the Muhammadans, under eight successive chiefs, ruled over Madura and the adjoining countries for forty-eight years, when they were conquered by a General named Kampana Udeiyár. It is very difficult to say who this man was. In the Srítála he is called the General of the King of Mysore, and this view is borne out by his name Udeiyár, which seems originally to have meant a lord of thirty-three villages, and to have been a common title in Mysore for a petty chieftain.[39] In one of the manuscripts translated by Taylor, it is stated that Kampana Udeiyár, a Karnatic man, General of the

Malik Káfúr.

Kampana Udeiyár.

(38) BRIGGS' *Ferishta*, Vol. I, page 373.

(39) WILKS' *History of Mysore*, Vol. I, page 21.

CHAPTER VI. POLITICAL HISTORY. PART I.

forces of the Mysore king, came and cut off and drove away the Muhammadans;[40] but, on the other hand, in another manuscript, an abstract of which is given in the same writer's Catalogue Raisonné, mention is made of a man named Kampana Udeiyár having been about this time the agent of Bukha, the Ráyar of Vijayanagar.[41] Whoever this General was, there can be no doubt that he obtained possession of Trichinopoly and Madura about the year 1372, but that he did not extend his conquest to Tanjore, where the Chóla kings were then reigning. The history of Trichinopoly from this date till Visvanátha obtained the possession of the throne of Madura in 1559 is wrapped in great obscurity. The names, indeed, of the several kings given in the Tamil manuscripts as having ruled the country during that interval, afford almost the sole clue that can be discovered as to their origin. The Srítála says that Kampana Udeiyár was succeeded by his son Embana Udeiyár, and that after him his brother-in-law Porkása Udeiyár reigned. These three Udeiyárs seem to have kept possession of the country for about thirty-three years up to A.D. 1404, when, according to the same Tamil manuscript, the Mysore rulers ceased to reign, and were succeeded by two men named Lekkina Náyakkan and Muthanan Náyakkan. Whether these two ruled jointly or not is not clearly stated, but at all events they held the throne between them up till about A.D. 1451. Who these Náyakkas were it is impossible to say, but it seems on the whole most probable that they came from the Vizianagram kingdom. The Srítála then goes on to relate how, in 1451, one Lakkana Náyakkan came to Madura with four men named Sundara Tól Mahá Vilivánáthi Ráyar, Kaleiyár Somanár, Angátha Perumál, and Matharasa Terumálei Mahá Vilivánáthi Ráyar, the illegitimate children of a Pándya monarch by a dancing girl, whom he appears to have proclaimed as the true Pándyas. These men seem to have ruled the country for the next forty-eight years down to about the year 1500. After that it is stated that one Narasa Náyakkan came to worship at Rámésvaram and got possession of the fort of Madura, how, it is not stated. He remained in the country for only a short time, and was succeeded by another Náyakkan named Tenna, who reigned for fifteen years. After him nine Náyakkas appear to have ruled Madura and Trichinopoly in succession till about 1546, when a man named Vittila Rayar got possession of the throne and held it for the next twelve years. Who he was or where he came from it is impossible to say with certainty, but it is most probable that he was a native of the Vizianagram kingdom. He reigned till 1557, and after him three Náyakkas seem to have ruled the country in the next two

(40) *Oriental MSS.*, Vol. I, page 204.

(41) *Catalogue Raisonné*, Vol. III, page 438.

years. However this may be, there can be no doubt that a Pándya was on the throne in 1559, for it was his expulsion from the kingdom by the Chóla monarch of Tanjore that eventually brought Visvanátha Náyakkan to Madura.

Visvanátha Náyakkan gets possession of Madura and Trichinopoly.

During the period just treated of, about which from want of materials I have been obliged to give only a brief and confused account, there can be but little doubt that Trichinopoly and Madura formed portions of the same kingdom. With the reign of Visvanátha the materials for a much fuller and more accurate history of the country are however available. The manner in which that monarch became the ruler of Madura in 1559, and eventually of Trichinopoly also, will now be briefly related. Towards the close of the 15th century, a Pándya king named Chandra Shékhara appears to have been reigning in Madura. How this happened it is difficult to say. Probably a Náyakkan was the real ruler, but considered it advisable to obtain prestige for his government by conferring the title of king on some descendant of the ancient dynasty of the Pándyas. The Chóla king of Tanjore, Víra Shékhara, invaded the Pándya's country and deposed him, on which he fled to the court of Krishna Ráyar, who was then king of Vizianagram, and besought him to reinstate him on his throne. Krishna Ráyar yielded to his request, and directed one of his Generals, Nágama Náyakkan, to march against the Chóla kings and restore the deposed Pándya. These orders were carried out by Nágama with ease, but as soon as the object of his expedition was accomplished, he seems to have abandoned any idea of handing over the kingdom to Chandra Shékhara, and to have attempted to become himself the ruler of the country. Krishna Ráyar soon discovered his designs and directed his own son, Visvanátha Náyakkan, to march against him. Visvanátha's object in undertaking the charge of this expedition seems to have been to preserve his father from destruction, as he well knew that, if conquered by a stranger, his chance of escaping with his life would be but small. Nágama Náyakkan was easily defeated and was taken prisoner by his son, who, however, soon afterwards obtained a pardon for him from the king. It would appear that at first Visvanátha reinstated the Pándya king on the throne of Madura, retaining all the actual power in his own hands. However this may be, it is certain that soon afterwards he himself became the nominal as well as the actual king of the country. In one of the Tamil manuscripts collected by Mr. Taylor, called the History of the Karnatic Governors, it is stated that the Pándya family almost immediately after their restoration to the throne became extinct by failure of natural heirs.[42] The

(42) *Oriental MSS.*, Vol. II, page 13.

CHAPTER VI. POLITICAL HISTORY, PART I.

accuracy of this statement may, however, well be doubted. Under Visvanátha's strong and judicious government the country of Madura appears to have been increased in prosperity, and his subjects spread themselves into the territories of the Chóla king in the direction of Trichinopoly. The condition of that country was at that time most turbulent, and the roads were infested with robbers. Pilgrims to Srírangam, in consequence, suffered much inconvenience, and were frequently plundered while attempting to reach that shrine. As these thefts took place within the Tanjore boundary, constant disputes were caused by demands made by Visvanátha that the property stolen from his subjects should be restored. Partly in order to remove these difficulties, the king of Madura proposed to give the king of Tanjore the fort of Vallam, taking Trichinopoly from him in exchange. This proposition was acceded to, and Trichinopoly became a portion of the kingdom of the Náyakkas, and remained so till it was taken possession of by Chanda Sahib. It is probable that fear of the Muhammadans may have induced the kings of Tanjore and Madura to come to an amicable settlement of their differences. However this may be, it is evident that the king of Madura must have been at this time much the more powerful of the rival monarchs, for, if not, he could never have been able to persuade his rival to accept the insignificant fort of Vallam in exchange for Trichinopoly. Visvanátha appears to have done much for the improvement of the town and neighbourhood of Trichinopoly. In the Tamil manuscripts already mentioned, it is stated that at a great cost he built a double walled fort round the town, and had a deep moat dug outside the walls. He also erected dwelling-houses within the enclosure thus formed and caused a large *teppakulam*[43] to be dug there. Besides this he built a palace in the town, had the jungles on both sides of the Cauvery cleared away, dug water-courses, rendered a quantity of land that had hitherto been waste fit for cultivation, and induced immigrants from other parts of his kingdom to settle there and till them. He also caused new villages to be built on both banks of the Cauvery, and cleared the country of the robbers with which it was infested. It is further stated that he built Srírangam and other temples, as well as a large number of mantapams and similar edifices.[44] It would appear that up to Visvanátha's reign Uraiyúr was the capital of the country, and that he, if he did not found Trichinopoly, at all events fortified and greatly enlarged it. I have no doubt that the statement above quoted, that he built the wall round the Trichinopoly fort and the large *teppakulam* close to the foot of the rock is

Visvanátha fortifies Trichinopoly.

---

(43) Raft-tank, so called from the rafts, *teppam*, on which the images of the gods are carried round the tank at certain festivals.

(44) TAYLOR's *Oriental MSS.*, Vol. II, pages 16 and 17.

correct, although I am afraid that its present inhabitants would not like to be told that their historic city is so modern. That he built the oldest portions of the famous Vishnu temple in the Sríraṅgam island is certainly not the case, although I fancy that it owes the massive walls that surround it, and some if not all its gópurams to him. Visvanátha died in A.D. 1563, and was succeeded on the throne by his son Kumára Krishnappa. He is stated to have been an able monarch, and in his time the country appears to have been free from disturbance. He died in 1573, and was succeeded by his son Periya Vírappa. This king is said to have strengthened the fortifications of Trichinopoly, and also to have built a fort somewhere near that town. It is impossible, however, to say where the fort was. Mr. Taylor conjectures that it may have been Erumbísvaram, but of this he gives no proof. Periya Vírappa died in 1595, and was succeeded by his eldest son Visvappa Náyakkan. his second son Kumára Krishnappa Náyakkan being named as second in power to him. From this it appears to have been the custom to appoint the younger brother of the king as next to him in authority, with a right to the succession to the crown, in case the regular king had no legitimate heir. This rule naturally before long was productive of serious complications and disputes. At this time, the kingdom of the Náyakkas appears to have included almost the whole of the present district of Trichinopoly, and to have extended as far north as Válikandapuram in the Perambalúr taluq. Visvappa died about 1600, and was succeeded by his brother Kumára Krishnappa, who soon followed him in 1602, leaving as his heir a son of about 7 years of age, named Muttukrishnappa. This boy's uncle however, Kastúri Rangaya, the youngest son of Krishnappa Náyakkan, usurped the throne and remained in possession of it till he was murdered some time afterwards, when the rightful heir, Mutthukrishnappa, succeeded. But little is known about the state of Trichinopoly during his reign. He died in 1609 leaving three sons, Mutthuvírappa, the famous Tirumala Náyakkan, and Kumáramuttu. The crown devolved on the eldest of these, Mutthuvírappa, who reigned till 1623, when he died and was succeeded by Tirumala Náyakkan. During the last ten or twelve years of Mutthuvírappa's reign Trichinopoly seems to have been the capital of the Náyak kingdom, whence it was transferred to Madura by Tirumala. The reason for the change is stated in the Tamil chronicle to have been as follows:—Tirumala Náyakkan had for a long time been suffering from catarrh without any prospect of cure. While on his way to Madura, he stopped at Dindigul, and when there was visited in a vision by the god Sundaréshwara and the goddess Mínákshi, who promised to cure him of his disease if he would transfer his capital to Madura. He accordingly determined to do so, and was soon afterwards restored

Reign of Tirumala Náyakkan.

CHAPTER VI. POLITICAL HISTORY, PART I.

to health. Tirumala was by far the most remarkable of the Náyakkas, but it does not appear that an account of his reign is required in an history of the district of Trichinopoly, as all the principal transactions of it relate more especially to Madura, where he made his capital during the whole of his reign, and as these have already been fully described by Mr. Nelson in his Manual of that district.[45]

Although Tirumala made Madura his capital, yet he did not entirely neglect Trichinopoly, but is stated to have remained there for some time, personally supervising the construction and extension of the fortifications. He also appears to have supplemented the work of enlarging the Srírangam temple begun by Visvanátha, for, in the Tamil manuscripts already mentioned, he is said to have constructed ninety-six ráyar gópurams, of which some were in Srírangam. Tirumala died in A.D. 1659, and was succeeded by his son Muttu Vírappa. Throughout the greater part of the period now treated of, the districts of Madura and Trichinopoly were constantly devastated by incursions of the Muhammadans. To resist these, Muttu Vírappa strengthened the fortifications of Trichinopoly, and garrisoned the town with an increased body of troops. Shortly after his accession to the throne the country was again invaded, and the fort of Trichinopoly threatened. On perceiving, however, that that place had been strengthened, the Musalman Generals drew off their forces in the direction of Tanjore, which they captured They then turned back with a view of attacking Trichinopoly, but their army had become so weakened by famine and pestilence that they were obliged to abandon the idea and retreat from Southern India. Muttu Vírappa died shortly after, and was succeeded by his son Choka Náyakkan, whose first act of any importance was to remove the capital of his kingdom from Madura to Trichinopoly. As there was no fitting residence for the king in the latter town, he caused the edifice now known as the Nawáb's palace to be built there, and, according to Mr. Nelson, pillaged Tirumala Náyakkan's palace at Madura in order to obtain materials for its construction.[46] In 1663 the Musalmans again invaded the south and laid siege to Trichinopoly. The town however was valiantly defended, and the invaders had to retreat, but not till they had devastated the country far and wide, burnt the crops and pillaged the villages. During the greater part of his reign Choka Náyakkan was engaged in hostilities with Ekoji, the Mahratta king of Tanjore. He was invariably unsuccessful, and at one time was left with but little of his kingdom but the fort of Trichinopoly. In 1677 the country was invaded by the king of Mysore, when, taking advantage of the confusion

Choka Náyakkan removes the capital of the kingdom from Madura to Trichinopoly.

(45) *Vide Madura Manual*, Part III, pages 121 to 176.

(46) *Madura Manual*, Part III, page 190.

that ensued, Choka Náyakkan's ministers deposed him, and placed his brother Muttu Linga on the throne in his place. His reign however was of short duration. He had placed great confidence in a Musalman named Rustam Khán, and had made him the Governor of Trichinopoly. This man betrayed his confidence, made himself master of the city, and taking Choka Náyakkan out of prison, replaced him on the throne. Rustam Khán remained in power for two years, when the Mysore army again invested Trichinopoly. During the siege Rustam Khán was led into an ambuscade and killed. Choka Náyakkan was now the undisputed king, but his power was greatly diminished and his kingdom was overrun by the Mysore army, the Musalmans and the Mahrattas of Tanjore. He died in 1682, and was succeeded by his son Ranga Krishna Muttu Vírappa, a lad of only 15 years of age, who however gave great promise of ability and vigour. Unfortunately for the country, he died in a few years and was succeeded by his posthumous son Vizia Ranga Choka Náyakkan, the kingdom being governed by Ranga Krishna's mother, Mangammál, as regent up to 1705, when the young king came of age.

Mangammál's regency.

Mangammál seems to have been a remarkably able woman, and to have ruled the country with great judgment. She built roads, planted avenues of trees, erected choultries, and generally improved the condition of the country. Many of the old lines of road lined with trees in the Trichinopoly and Madura districts are still known as Mangammál's roads, and there seems no reason to doubt that the country owes them to her. Mangammál died soon after her grandson came of age, and there is a local tradition extant both in Trichinopoly and Madura, that she was starved to death. It would seem that during the latter portion of her regency she had lived on terms of great intimacy with her prime minister, a Bráhman named Achchaya, and that at his instigation she attempted to exclude her grandson from the throne. She however failed in her attempt, and it is generally believed was imprisoned and slowly starved to death. I remark that Mr. Nelson, in his Manual of the Madura District, and Mr. Taylor, in his Oriental MSS., both state that the story current in Madura is that she was confined in a portion of the building now used there as a jail.[47] In Trichinopoly, however, a small room, near the large hall in the Nawáb's palace, which is always called Mangammál's hall, is pointed out as the place of her death. Vijaya Ranga Choka, the last of the Náyakkans, ruled the country for twenty-six years, but his reign is uninteresting and barren of incident. He appears to have largely endowed the Srírangam temple.

---

(47) *Madura Manual*, Part III, page 237; TAYLOR's *Oriental MSS.*, Vol. II., page 226.

CHAPTER VI. POLITICAL HISTORY, PART I.

I have purposely given a very brief account of the Náyakkan dynasty, as this period of the history of Trichinopoly and Madura has been already fully described in the Madura Manual, and as it does not appear advisable to relate again incidents that have been given there in minute detail, especially as the attempt that I have made to throw some little light on the history of the Chólas has already caused this portion of this work to run to, perhaps, an excessive length. I will, therefore, conclude this chapter with a description of Trichinopoly in 1719, towards the close of the rule of the Náyakkas, by Father Bouchet, then one of the Jesuit Missionaries in that city. It is translated and abridged from one of the papers in the "*Mission du Maduré*."

Description of Trichinopoly in 1719.

Trichinopoly, where the prince lives, is a very populous city and of considerable extent. It contains about 300,000 inhabitants.[48] It is the finest fortress between Cape Comorin and Golconda. Many armies have besieged it, but always unsuccessfully, and the Hindus say that it is impregnable. It is surrounded by a double wall, attached to which are sixty square towers about eighty or a hundred feet apart. The inner wall is higher than the outer and has 130 pieces of cannon of considerable size mounted on it. The space thus enclosed is divided into two fortresses, and in it there is also a high rock from which the approach of an enemy could be discerned. The arsenal is in the middle of the rock and the palace is at its foot. The interior of the fortress is a large square amphitheatre, with steps on all sides leading up to the ramparts. In addition to the towers attached to the walls round the town, there are also eighteen larger ones where provisions and ammunition, for which there is no room in the arsenal, are kept. The garrison consists of about 6,000 men and sometimes more. The ditch which surrounds the fortress is wide and deep. It is full of water, in which there are some crocodiles. This ditch was constructed at great expense, as in some places it was necessary to cut through the solid rock. Trichinopoly has four great gates corresponding to the points of the compass. Of these, however, only two are kept open now, those to the north and south. The eastern one, called the Tanjore gate, has been built up for a long time, and the western is open to the women of the palace only.[49] There is a procession round the town three times every night, first at nightfall, then at 9 o'clock, and lastly at midnight. On the first two occasions they go round with musical instruments of various kinds, but the last time in silence. The river Cauvery flows along the fortress from west to east. They

(48) This is evidently a mistake. It is quite impossible that Trichinopoly can ever have had anything like so large a population.

(49) The gate mentioned here must have been either that now known as the main-guard gate or some other gate close to it. The palace gardens formerly extended almost up to the wall of the town on that side.

have constructed a large and deep canal near Trichinopoly, out of which several small channels flow and supply the numerous large tanks that are inside the town.[50] The Trichinopoly palace is as fine as the Madura one. It consists of a suite of rooms, galleries, and inner apartments. The hall of justice is supported by high and handsome pillars. The gardens cannot be compared with those of Europe. I have, however, seen four or five fountains playing there at a time. At the entrance to this garden there is a large room open on all sides and surrounded by a rather deep ditch, which is filled with water whenever the queen comes out to get fresh air. The pillars which support this room are covered with gold flowers and tinsel of various colors.[51]

(50) This is plainly the Uyyakondán channel, a side channel from which supplies many of the tanks in the fort.

(51) The palace in Trichinopoly cannot for a moment be compared to Tirumala Náyakkan's palace in Madura. The building has been recently restored by order of Government, and converted into offices for the Tahsildar of Trichinopoly, the District Munsif, and other public officials.

CHAPTER VII.

POLITICAL HISTORY OF TRICHINOPOLY, PART II.

(FROM THE FALL OF THE NÁYAK DYNASTY TILL THE RAISING OF THE SIEGE OF TRICHINOPOLY AND THE DEATH OF CHANDA SAHIB IN 1752.)

Chanda Sahib gets possession of Trichinopoly.—Vangáru Tirumala applies to the Mahrattas.—The Mahrattas take Trichinopoly.—Nizam-úl-Mulk enters the Karnatic and captures Trichinopoly.—Anwar-úd-dín appointed Nawáb.—War between France and England.—Death of the Nizam Asáf Jah.—The English assist Muhammad Ali in the contest for the Nawábship.—Defeat of Muzuffar Jung and Chanda Sahib.—Death of Nazir Jung.—Muzuffar Jung appointed Nizam.—The English send a detachment to support Muhammad Ali.—Skirmishes near Úttattúr.—The English retreat to Trichinopoly.—The French take possession of Srírangam.—Siege of Trichinopoly by Chanda Sahib and the French.—Clive's expedition to Arcot.—Muhammad Ali solicits aid from the Mysore regent and Morari Rau.—The King of Tanjore and the Tondiman of Pudukóttai assist Muhammad Ali.—Reinforcement under Lawrence sent to Trichinopoly.—Unsuccessful attempt of the French to intercept Lawrence.—The French abandon their outposts to the south of the Cauvery.—Skirmish at Samayapuram.—Expedition under Dalton to oppose D'Auteuil at Úttattúr.—Capture of Pichándárkóvil.—Desertion of the greater portion of Chanda Sahib's army.—D'Auteuil surrenders.—Capitulation of the French under Law in Srírangam.—Death of Chanda Sahib.

VIJAYA RANGA CHOKA NÁYAKKAN died in 1731 leaving no issue, and the right to succeed to the throne became at once a subject of dispute. His widow, Mínákshi, instigated most probably by her brother Venkata Perumál Náyakkan, attempted to gain possession of the kingdom for herself. In this design she was, however, opposed by Vangáru Tirumala, son of Kumára Tirumala, who had been second in power to king Choka Náyakkan. It appears, from the History of the Karnatic Governors[1] that Mínákshi offered to adopt Vangáru's son Vijaya Kumára Muttu Tirumala as her own, but that he refused to consent to this arrangement, and assumed the crown for himself. The dispute appears to have caused a sharp contest, for Wilks states[2] that Venkata Ráyar Achári, the commander-in-chief of the forces, who supported the pretensions of Vangáru Tirumala, succeeded in forcibly entering the fortress of Trichinopoly, and was on the point of putting the Ráni to death, when the opposite party collected their forces and expelled him.

(1) TAYLOR'S *Oriental MSS.*, Vol. II, page 232.
(2) *History of Mysore*, Vol. I, page 155.

CHAPTER VII. POLITICAL HISTORY, PART II.

On this Vangáru Tirumala applied for assistance to Safdar Ali, the eldest son of Daust Ali, the Nawáb of Arcot, who accordingly marched to Trichinopoly with an army, Chanda Sahib accompanying him as his second in command. On their arrival Safdar Ali summoned all concerned to appear before him with a view to adjudicating on their dispute. They did so, and after hearing both parties he eventually decided that the kingdom did not belong to Mínákshi, as she had no male child, but to Vangáru Tirumala; but that she should continue to enjoy whatever privileges had been granted to her by her deceased husband; that her personal property and jewels should be left to her; but that all the public treasure and jewels should be handed over to Vangáru Náyakkan. He also stipulated that thirty lakhs of rupees should be paid to himself by fixed instalments; took a written agreement from Vangáru promising the due payment of the sum, and, giving it in charge to Chanda Sahib to see this promise fulfilled, returned to Arcot.

Chanda Sahib gets possession of Trichinopoly.

On his departure Mínákshi made overtures to Chanda Sahib and offered him a crore of rupees if he would not give over the kingdom to Vangáru Tirumala. He accordingly put off doing so from day to day, and eventually made an oath to the queen's brother that he would transfer the kingdom to her party, on condition of the promised crore of rupees being handed over to him. In pledge for the due payment of this sum, the queen gave him all the jewels, elephants, horses and similar property that had been left by the former kings of Madura. On this Chanda Sahib entered Trichinopoly with his troops and took possession of the city in the name of the queen.

It appears that up to this Vangáru Tirumala had been living in Trichinopoly, but that Mínákshi now sent him together with his son to Madura, and that on this Chanda Sahib returned to Arcot. It is not easy to understand the reason of these movements. The account given in the manuscripts translated by Mr. Taylor[3] is that, when Chanda Sahib heard that Vangáru Tirumala and the crowned prince had gone to Madura, he knew that he could not succeed in his design, and accordingly returned with his troops to Arcot. On this the queen retained Trichinopoly for herself, and left Tinnevelly, Madura and Dindigul with the Rámnád and Sivaganga Zemindáries under the management of Vangáru Tirumala, who, with his son, continued to live in Madura.

In 1736, however, Chanda Sahib returned again to Trichinopoly, and, having gained possession of the fort, probably by treachery, proceeded at once to wrest Madura and other provinces held by him from Vangáru Tirumala. In this attempt he was

(3) *Oriental MSS.*, Vol. II, page 233.

soon successful. Madura was captured and Vangáru fled to Sivaganga. Chanda Sahib then returned to Trichinopoly, and confined the queen as a prisoner in her own palace. On this she appears to have committed suicide by poisoning herself.

Vangáru Tirumala applies to the Mahrattas.

As a last resource against Chanda Sahib, Vangáru Tirumala applied to the Mahrattas. They gladly responded to the invitation, and a large force entered the Karnatic under Raghuji Bhonslai. The Nawáb Daust Ali marched from Arcot to oppose them, but was utterly defeated and lost his life on the 20th May 1740. Safdar Ali, who was advancing to his father's assistance, on hearing of his defeat retreated to Vellore, and Chanda Sahib, who had also taken the field, hurried back to Trichinopoly. The Mahrattas marched at once to that city and laid siege to it. The place was closely invested and the Mahrattas were careful to prevent any supplies or reinforcements reaching it. Chanda Sahib defended himself with valour, but was, notwithstanding all his efforts, obliged to surrender the town on the 26th March 1741, after it had stood a siege of three months. He, his son and his principal officers were sent as prisoners to Sattara, and the Mahrattas made one of their generals, Morari Rau, Governor of Trichinopoly, leaving him a force of 14,000 men to hold the place. About a year after this Safdar Ali, the Nawáb of the Karnatic, was murdered by Mortiz Ali, the Governor of Vellore. In consequence, however, of the general indignation excited against him by this act, he was obliged to escape from Arcot in disguise, and the army proclaimed Safdar Ali's infant son, Muhammad Khán, as his successor.

The Mahrattas take Trichinopoly.

Nizam-úl-Mulk enters the Karnatic and captures Trichinopoly.

At this juncture the Nizam, Asáf Jah, entered the Karnatic with a large army and arrived at Arcot, where he appointed one of his own generals, Abdul Khán, Nawáb. He then sent a summons to Morari Rau to surrender Trichinopoly, and, on his refusal to do so, marched at once to that city and laid siege to it. Morari Rau soon surrendered the place, and in August 1743 left the Karnatic with his Mahrattas. The Nizam then returned to Golconda, leaving Abdul Khán Governor of Arcot. On his death a few months afterwards, Anwar-úd-dín was appointed in his place, the Nizam, however, announcing that he intended to confer the nawábship on Muhammad Khán as soon as he should come of age. As this young prince was, however, murdered soon afterwards, Anwar-úd-dín was confirmed as Nawáb. In 1744 war was declared between France and England. It is not necessary to follow the varying fortunes of the contest waged between these powers in the Karnatic, except in so far as the district of Trichinopoly was affected by it. The first event in the war that it is necessary to touch on is the expedition of the English to Tanjore. In 1749 Sahoji, the Mahratta king of the city, was deposed, and his brother put in his place. The deposed prince fled to Fort St. David, and entreated

Anwar-úd-dín appointed Nawáb.

War between France and England.

the English to assist him, agreeing to hand over to them the fort of Dévikóttai, with the adjacent country, and to pay all the expenses of the war, if they would consent to do so. The English determined to accede to his prayer, and two expeditions were accordingly undertaken with a view of assisting him. The first was unsuccessful, but the second, under Major Lawrence, had the effect of inducing the king of Tanjore to come to terms and give up the fort of Dévikóttai to the English. In the meantime the French had determined to espouse Chanda Sahib's cause, and accordingly paid his ransom, on which he was released from confinement in Sattara.

Death of the Nizam Asáf Jah.

In 1748 Asáf Jah, generally known as Nizam-úl-Mulk, died and was succeeded by his son Nazir Jung. A favourite grandson, however, of the late Nizam, who was afterwards known as Muzuffar Jung, contested the succession, in doing which he was assisted by Chanda Sahib, who was himself an aspirant to the nawábship of the Karnatic then held by Anwar-úd-dín. In the contest that ensued the English espoused of the cause of Nazir Jung and Anwar-úd-dín and the French that of Muzuffar Jung and Chanda Sahib. Hostilities commenced by the invasion of the Karnatic by a large army under Muzuffar Jung and Chanda Sahib. Anwar-úd-dín advanced to oppose them, but, in a battle fought on the 23rd of July 1749 at Ambúr, fifty miles from Arcot, was utterly defeated, and lost his life. His son Muhammad Ali fled at once to Trichinopoly and applied to the English for assistance. Only 120 men were however sent to him, while Muzuffar Jung and Chanda Sahib marched from Pondicherry and entered the kingdom of Tanjore accompanied by 800 French soldiers. Dupleix had urged upon Chanda Sahib the great importance of capturing Trichinopoly and so debarring Muhammad Ali from making any further attempts to obtain the nawábship of the Karnatic. Instead however of following this advice, he advanced in the first instance against Tanjore. The king tried to gain time by negotiation, but eventually came to terms, and agreed to hand over a considerable sum of money to Chanda Sahib. Much time was however lost in obtaining possession of the stipulated sum, and before it was all paid Muzuffar Jung, having heard that Nazir Jung was marching from Golconda, broke up his camp and fled to Pondicherry. Immediately on entering the Karnatic Nazir Jung directed Muhammad Ali, who was still in Trichinopoly, to join him, and requested the English to send a body of European troops to his aid. The detachment at Trichinopoly, under Captain Cope, was, in compliance with this request, ordered to march with Muhammad Ali, and it accordingly left that city in February 1750, and joined the Nizam's army at Valdore, about fifteen miles from Pondicherry, where they were shortly afterwards reinforced by 600 more Europeans from Fort St. David under Major

The English assist Muhammad Ali in the contest for the Nawábship.

Defeat of Muzuffar Jung and Chanda Sahib.

CHAPTER VII. POLITICAL HISTORY, PART II.

Lawrence. In the meantime Muzuffar Jung and Chanda Sahib had marched out of Pondicherry, and were encamped within a short distance of Nazir Jung's army. While the hostile camps were thus situated, some of the French officers, dissatisfied with their share of the contribution paid by the king of Tanjore on the raising of the siege of his capital, threw up their commissions and left the camp. On this M. D'Auteuil, who was in command of the French troops, marched his battalion back again to Pondicherry, where he was followed by Chanda Sahib. Muzuffar Jung however gave himself up to Nazir Jung, by whom he was placed in close confinement. After the retreat of the French, Major Lawrence returned to Fort St. David, and Nazir Jung broke up his camp and marched to Arcot.

Death of Nazir Jung. Muzuffar Jung appointed Nizam.

In December 1750 Nazir Jung, while advancing to recover the fort of Gingi, which had been taken by the French, was assassinated. No sooner was his death known than the greater portion of his army offered their services to Muzuffar Jung, who was proclaimed Nawáb. On hearing of what had happened, Muhammad Ali fled at once with two or three attendants to Trichinopoly, whence he earnestly solicited aid from the English. After some delay a force of 280 Europeans and 300 sepoys, under the command of Captain Cope, was sent to assist him in February 1751. On his arrival at Trichinopoly, Cope discovered that Madura had been taken possession of by a soldier of fortune named Allam Khán, and that all communication between Trichinopoly and Tinnevelly, then a portion of Muhammad Ali's dominions, had been thus cut off. He accordingly marched at the head of a detachment to reduce the place, but was unsuccessful. Just at this juncture Muhammad Ali received intelligence that Chanda Sahib was about to march from Arcot to besiege Trichinopoly, and he accordingly renewed his application to the English in Fort St. David for assistance. This call was responded to, and in the beginning of April a body of 500 Europeans and 1,000 sepoys with eight field pieces marched from Fort St. David under the command of Captain Gingen. On their way they carried the Fort of Virudáchallam by assault, and, leaving a small garrison there, marched on towards Trichinopoly, and were soon after joined by a force of 100 Europeans from that city and 400 horse and foot of Muhammad Ali's troops under the command of his brother Abdúl Wahab Khán.

The English send a detachment to support Muhammad Ali.

After this junction the army came in sight of Chanda Sahib's force, which was then encamped near Válikandapuram, a village in the north of the Perumbalúr Taluq, on the high road from Trichinopoly to Madras. Orme states that this was a strong fortress, its principal defence being a "rock 200 feet high and about a mile in circumference at the bottom, where it is enclosed by a high and strong wall mostly cut out of the solid rock; near the summit it is enclosed by another wall, and the summit itself is surrounded by a third. Adjoining the eastern side of the rock on the plain is a fort built of stone, contiguous to which lies a town slenderly fortified with a mud wall. The river Vellár, after running due east, forms an angle about a mile to the north of Válikandapuram, where it turns to the south, and in this direction passes close by the western side of the rock, and winding round it reassumes its course to the eastward along the southern side of the fort and town."[4] Captain Gingen took up a position in a tope about a mile and a half to the east of the village, in sight of Chanda Sahib's army, which was encamped on the north of the river.

Skirmishes near Úttattúr.

On the next morning the French advanced along the bed of the river towards the fort. Captain Gingen attempted to intercept them, and a smart action ensued. The English troops were, however, seized with a panic and retreated in great confusion. To avoid total defeat, Gingen was obliged to break up his camp on the following night and proceed by forced marches to Trichinopoly. On the next evening they arrived at what Orme terms the "Straits of Úttattúr." "A part of the range of mountains which bounds the province of Arcot to the westward forms one side of these straits, and some hills about a mile to the east the other. The ground for several miles further eastward is covered with rocks which render it impassable to an army encumbered with carriages."[5] A company of 100 grenadiers under Captain Dalton was left in a village at the entrance of the straits, while the main army encamped in the valley, and a few Europeans were placed in Úttattúr to protect the rear of the camp. The enemy followed close after the retreating force, and, taking up a position within five miles of the village near the straits, advanced against the English. In the action that ensued the French and their allies forced their adversaries to retreat, and took possession of the village. Although the position in the straits was considered defensible, yet, as it was feared that Chanda Saib would send out a detachment from his main army, and, stationing it between Trichinopoly and their camp, would cut of all supplies, Captain Gingen thought it advisable to push on without delay. He accordingly broke up his camp the same night and marched at once as far as the north bank of the Coleroon, where he halted.

"This river is a principal arm of another called the Cauvery, which has its source in the mountains within thirty miles of Mangalore on the coast of Malabar, and passing through the kingdom of Mysore, runs 400 miles before it reaches Trichinopoly. About five

(4) ORME's *History of Hindustan*, Vol. I, page 172. The village is termed Volcondah in the original.

(5) ORME, Vol. I. page 174. Úttattúr is a village in the Perumbalúr Taluq, on the old road from Trichinopoly to Madras, but about two miles from the present road. The village is about two miles south of the straits.

CHAPTER VII. POLITICAL HISTORY, PART II.

miles to the north-west of this city, the Cauvery divides itself into two principal arms. The northern is called the Coleroon, and disembogues at Dévikóttai; the other retains the name of Cauvery, and about twenty miles to the eastward of Trichinopoly, begins to send forth several large branches, all of which pass through the kingdom of Tanjore, and are the cause of the great fertility of that country. For several miles after the separation, the banks of the Coleroon and Cauvery are in no part two miles asunder, in many scarcely one; and at Kóviladi,[6] a fort fifteen miles to the east of Trichinopoly, the two streams approach so near to each other, that the people of the country have been obliged to fling up a large and strong mound of earth to keep them from uniting again. The long slip of land enclosed by the two channels between Kóviladi and the place where the two streams first separate, is called the island of Srírangam, famous throughout Hindustan for the great pagoda from which it derives its name. This temple is situated about a mile from the western extremity of the island, at a small distance from the bank of the Coleroon. It is composed of seven square enclosures, one within the other, the walls of which are twenty-five feet high and four thick. These enclosures are 350 feet distant from one another, and each has four large gates with a high tower, which are placed, one in the middle of each side of the enclosure and opposite to the four cardinal points. The outward wall is nearly four miles in circumference, and its gateway to the south is ornamented with pillars, several of which are single stones thirty-three feet long and nearly five in diameter, and those which form the roof are still larger; in the inmost enclosure are the chapels. About half a mile to the east of Srírangam, and nearer to the Cauvery than the Coleroon, is another large pagoda called Jembukésvaram, but this has only one enclosure."[7]

The English retreat to Trichinopoly.

The English battalion in the first instance occupied the pagoda at Pichandarkóvil, which is situated about half a mile from the Coleroon bridge on the road to Musiri and Salem, while the rest of the army encamped along the river near the pagoda. As however great difficulty was experienced in getting provisions in this position, the army crossed the river and took possession of the Srírangam temple. This was a post that might have been defended with ease, but it was thought that the extent of the pagoda was too great to be defended by a small force, and orders were accordingly given that the whole army should cross the Cauvery and take shelter

---

(6) Coiladdy in the original In quotations from Orme, the spelling of the names of people and places in the original has in many instances not been adhered to Sentences have also been left out here and there, and other slight alterations have been made.

(7) ORME, Vol. I, pages 177 and 178.

under the walls of Trichinopoly. The following description of the fortifications of this place at this time is given by Orme:—

"The city of Trichinopoly lies about ninety miles inland from the coast, and is situated within half a mile of the southern bank of the Cauvery, and about a mile and a half south-east from Srírangam. It is a parallelogram, of which the east and west sides extend near 2,000 yards, and the north and south about 1,200. It has a double enclosure of walls, each of which are flanked by round towers, built at equal distances from one another: the outward wall is eighteen feet high and about five feet thick, without rampart or parapet: the inward is much stronger, being thirty feet high, with a rampart of stone, decreasing by large steps from the ground to the top, where it is ten feet broad, and has a thin parapet of stone about seven feet high, in which are loop-holes to fire through. There is an interval between the two walls of twenty-five feet, and before the outward a ditch of thirty feet wide and twelve deep, unequally supplied with water at different seasons, but never quite dry. In the northern part of the city stands a rock 150 feet high, from which the adjacent country is discovered for many miles round."[8]

The French take possession of Srírangam.

The English battalion encamped on the west side of the city close to the ditch, and the Nawáb's troops on the south side, while Captain Cope, with 100 of the Europeans, remained within the walls. As soon as the English and the Nawáb's army had left the island of Srírangam, the French and Chanda Sahib took possession of it. Shortly after this they sent a detachment to attack Kóviladi, a mud fort in the Tanjore District not far from the confines of the Trichinopoly District, which was the only post still held by the Nawáb's troops in that direction. Captain Gingen sent 20 Europeans and 100 sepoys to reinforce the garrison. The little fort was defended gallantly, but it had to be abandoned after a few days, as it had become so shattered as to be no longer tenable. Encouraged by this success, Chanda Sahib crossed the Cauvery, and, leaving a garrison in Srírangam, encamped with the main body of his army to the east of Trichinopoly.

Siege of Trichinopoly by Chanda Sahib and the French.

On hearing of these reverses the Government of Fort St. David determined to reinforce the troops in Trichinopoly. A detachment was accordingly sent through the Tanjore kingdom under Lieutenant Clive, and was joined by a small force from Dévikóttai under Captain Clarke. The united army, which, however, consisted of only 100 Europeans and 50 sepoys, then marched towards Trichinopoly, which they reached in safety, after a skirmish with a detachment sent by the French from Kóviladi to oppose them. Even with this reinforcement, however, the English force in Trichinopoly was only 600 strong, while the besieging army, itself

---

(8) ORME, Vol. I, page 180.

CHAPTER VII. POLITICAL HISTORY, PART II.

Clive's expedition to Arcot.

ten times as numerous as that under Muhammad Ali, was assisted by 900 French soldiers. Clive accordingly, on his return to Fort St. David in August, prevailed on the Government to give him permission to lead an expedition against Arcot, with a view of diverting a portion of Chanda Sahib's army from Trichinopoly. The success of this expedition and the capture of Arcot had the desired effect, for Chanda Sahib, on hearing of it, detached 4,000 of his troops from Trichinopoly to that town. The fort was, however, successfully defended by Clive, and after a siege of fifty days the enemy were obliged to retreat and abandon the attempt to capture it.

"During these successes in the province of Arcot, Chanda Sahib beleaguered Trichinopoly. The French battalion fixed their quarters at a village called Sarkárpálayam,[9] on the southern bank of the Cauvery, about two and a half miles from the east side of the town. The troops of Chanda Sahib, for the convenience of water, encamped likewise along the bank of the river, and to the eastward of Sarkárpálayam, which post secured one of the flanks of their camp, and at the other extremity of it, three miles distant, they raised a redoubt, on which they mounted two pieces of cannon. The French, on whom the operations of the siege principally depended, sent to their settlement of Karikal for a train of artillery ; and, in the beginning of September, raised their principal battery a little to the south of the north-east angle of the town, and at a distance of 1,200 yards from the walls. To save the fatigue of carrying on trenches between this post and the camp, they afterwards made the battery a regular redoubt by enclosing it on both flanks and in the rear with a parapet and a deep ditch ; here they mounted three 8-pounders and three mortars, which were defended by a constant guard of 100 Europeans and 400 sepoys. They likewise mounted two 18-pounders on a rock, which has ever since obtained the name of the French Rock,[10]

---

(9) Chuckly-pollam in the original. There can, I believe, be no doubt that Sarkárpálayam is the village alluded to.

(10) There is considerable difficulty in fixing the position of the rocks mentioned by Orme in his account of the several actions that took place in the vicinity of Trichinopoly. The French Rock can, however, be identified. Orme states (Vol. I, page 200) that this rock is about 2,000 yards directly east from the south-east angle of the town of Trichinopoly, and that the Erumbísvaram rock is three miles to the south-east of it (*vide* Vol. I, page 215). These two data are sufficient to determine its position, and prove that it is a little rock that is to be found about a mile to the east of Trichinopoly, situated to the north of the Tanjore road, at the point where it is crossed by the Uyyakondán channel. Its position is given with tolerable accuracy in the maps published with Orme's History. It is much more difficult, however, to decide which is the Golden and which the Sugar-loaf rock. The rock near the Central Jail is always called by Natives Ponmalai, or golden rock, and the little rock to the south-west of it is termed by them Kalludaimalai, or ass rock, and by the European residents in Trichinopoly the Fakir's rock. Orme, it

situated about 2,000 yards directly east from the south-east angle of the town; they also raised a battery of two guns on the island of Srírangam, from which they fired across the Cauvery at the northern gate of the city, to interrupt the communication of the inhabitants with the river; these guns, as well as those on the French Rock, were at too great a distance to make impression on the walls.

"To save that part of the wall against which the enemy's principal battery fired, a glacis was raised to such a height as left nothing but the parapet exposed; and the grenadiers, commanded by Captain Dalton, were posted behind this glacis. An entrenchment was flung up between the French Rock and the south-east angle of the town, in which the company of Caffres was posted, to protect from surprises the Náwáb's cavalry encamped to the south; and to oppose the enemy's battery in the island, two guns were mounted close to the southern bank of the river."[11]

Muhammad Ali solicits aid from the Mysore regent and Morari Rau.

Muhammad Ali having been now reduced to great distress from want of sufficient funds to carry on the war, determined to solicit aid from the king of Mysore, and even agreed to the demand made in behalf of this prince by his prime minister Nandiraz, that Trichinopoly and all its dependencies, down to Cape Comorin, should be given up to him as the price of his assistance. A treaty to this effect having been made, the Mysore army under Nandiraz and 4,000 Mahrattas under Morári Rau, the chief of Ghooty, marched to Karúr, and, after some delay there, set out for Trichi-

must be remembered, never talks of Fakir's rock, but only of the Fakir's tope. In Orme's maps, however, the rock near the Central Jail is called the Sugar-loaf rock, and that to the west of it the Golden rock, and what he says of their relative position in his history, shows that the maps represent his view correctly, and that he considered that the Golden rock was the more westerly of the two. In one passage especially (Vol. I, page 309) he states that the camp of our adversaries extended on each side of the Sugar-loaf rock, but further to the west than to the east; that most of the Mahrattas were encamped on the east, while the French quarters were close to the west of the rock; and that beyond these the Mysore troops extended almost as far as the Golden rock. Here it is clear that Orme puts the Golden rock to the west of the other. The true Golden rock is not unlike a sugar-loaf in shape, and might easily have been named after one by Europeans, Natives of course would never give such a name, but it is difficult to understand how any one could have called what we now term the Fakir's rock, the Golden rock. It is a little hill green almost to the top, and never looks golden, as that near the Central Jail does when the evening sun shines on it. In his description of the battle of the Golden rock (Vol. I, page 291), Orme states that the grenadiers assailed the enemy's position on this rock, and never halted till they got to the top of it. They might easily have scaled the Kalludaimalai, but it is quite impossible that they could have managed to get up the real Golden rock. There therefore seems to be no doubt that Orme has made a mistake about the names, and that what is now called the Kalludaimalai or Fakir's rock is what he terms the Golden rock, while he gives the name of Sugar-loaf rock to the real Golden rock. Colonel Malleson, in his history of the French in India, throws no light on the difficulty, but follows Orme blindly.

(11) ORME, Vol. I, pages 200 and 201.

CHAPTER VII. POLITICAL HISTORY, PART II.

nopoly. A strong party however of French troops and sepoys were sent out to oppose them to the village of Kristnáráyapuram.[12] On hearing of their arrival, Nandiraz halted his army, and applied to Muhammad Ali that a party of English should be sent to support him. Captain Cope accordingly marched to the place with a small detachment, and attempted to dislodge the French troops from the position that they had taken up. The village was surrounded by a mud wall, and on the north side touched the bank of the Cauvery, while the other sides were protected by a deep morass. In his attack on this position, Captain Cope was defeated and killed. On this disaster becoming known in Trichinopoly, Captain Dalton was sent to take the command of the detachment, and a few days after his arrival, Nandiraz and his army reached the place. It was then determined that Dalton should keep the French employed while the Mysore army hurried on to Trichinopoly. Shortly after their departure the English also broke up their camp, and without any molestation from the French in Kristnaráyápuram, rejoined their head-quarters. On this the French detachment also was recalled.

The King of Tanjore and the Tondiman of Pudukóttai assist Muhammad Ali.

As Muhammad Ali's fortunes had now improved, the number of his friends increased. First of all the king of Tanjore sent an army of 3,000 horse and 2,000 foot under the command of his General Monakji to Trichinopoly, and then the Tondiman of Pudukóttai sent another reinforcement of 400 horse and 3,000 men. With these troops the force at the disposal of Muhammad Ali was larger than that of the besiegers, and the Mysore General and Morari Rau consequently urged the English commander, Captain Gingen, to make a general onslaught on their adversaries. This, however, he declined to do till he was reinforced by a fresh detachment of English troops, for which he was then waiting.

Reinforcement under Lawrence sent to Trichinopoly.

The expected reinforcement, consisting of 400 Europeans and 1,100 sepoys, under the command of Major Lawrence, left Fort St. David in March 1752, and advancing through Tanjore, pushed on to Trichinopoly. The French force was then stationed between the Erumbísvaram[13] rock and the French Rock, the latter of which is three miles to the north-west of the former. The pagoda on the Erumbísvaram rock had been fortified and cannon placed on it.

Unsuccessful attempt of the French to intercept Lawrence.

Lawrence marched to the south of this rock and met Captain Dalton, who had been sent out from Trichinopoly to reinforce him with 200 Europeans and 400 Sepoys, between it and what Orme terms the Sugar-loaf rock. Captain Clive, who had accompanied Lawrence in this expedition, reconnoitred the position and discovered that the French had neglected to take possession of a

(12) Kistnavaram in Orme. A village in the north of the Kulittalai Taluq, about eleven miles west of Kulittalai.

(13) Elimiserum in Orme. The rock is close to the village of Tiruvarambúr, the first station on the line of railway from Trichinopoly to Tanjore.

large choultry not far from the front of their battalion. The English accordingly advanced at once on this building. They were opposed by the whole of the enemy's force and some sharp fighting ensued. The French and their allies were repulsed with considerable loss, which would have been greater had not Lawrence stopped the pursuit in order to save his troops, who had been fighting and marching all through the raging heat of an April day. Orme indeed mentions that seven of the men were struck dead by the heat during the skirmish. Major Lawrence arrived in Trichinopoly on the same evening, and at once consulted with the other Generals as to the plan of operations to be pursued. The Nawáb was anxious that a general attack should be made without delay on the enemy's camp, but so much time was lost by the Native Generals in fixing on a lucky day for the expedition that Major Lawrence determined to act without them. As, however, he did not feel strong enough to attack the French lines unassisted by his allies, he resolved to make an onslaught on Chanda Sahib's camp first.

Accordingly on the 1st of April a body of 400 men under Captain Dalton set out at night with this object. They were, however, misled by their guides and at break of day found themselves between Erumbísvaram and the French rock in the centre of all the French outposts. Discovering their danger, they began to retreat at once. They were, however, perceived by the French under Law, who, instead of seizing the opportunity that was offered to him of crushing them completely, fancied that he was no longer safe from attack while he remained to the south of the Cauvery, and not only allowed the English to escape unmolested, but determined to retreat across the river himself at once and take up his position in the Island of Srírangam.

The French abandon their out-posts to the south of the Cauvery.

Chanda Sahib pointed out to Law the folly of this course but to no avail, and the French army abandoned all their posts to the south of the Cauvery, except Erumbísvaram, and encamped in the Jembukésvaram pagoda. Some of Chanda Sahib's troops occupied the large Vishnu pagoda in the island, others were placed under the northern outer wall of that building, and the remainder took up their position to the east along the bank of the Coleroon. The natural results of the retreat of the French soon followed. Erumbísvaram was first of all captured by Captain Dalton, the garrison making but a feeble resistance, and then Major Lawrence, at Clive's suggestion, determined to divide his army into two divisions and to send one of them to the north of Trichinopoly with a view of getting possession of the posts which the enemy held in that part of the country and intercepting any reinforcements which might be sent from Pondicherry. This expedition was entrusted to Clive, who, on the night of the 6th of April, marched from

CHAPTER VII. POLITICAL HISTORY, PART II.

Trichinopoly with 400 Europeans and 700 sepoys, 3,000 Mahrattas under Innis Khân, and 1,000 of the Tanjore horse. The troops passed the Coleroon and, marching 7 miles to the north of that river, took possession of the village of Samayapuram.[14] There are two pagodas in this village about a quarter of a mile apart, one on each side of the old high road leading to Madras. The Europeans and Sepoys were placed inside these buildings, while the Mahrattas and Tanjore troops encamped round them outside.

Whilst the detachment under Clive was thus employed, a party from Srírangam took possession of the pagoda in Mannachanellúr[15] Village situated between Pichándárkóvil and Samayapuram. From its position this pagoda was the best advanced post that could be chosen by either side, and a detachment was therefore immediately sent by the English to dislodge the enemy from it. The French defended the place successfully for one day, but in the night abandoned it and escaped to Pichándárkóvil. On the next day another force succeeded in capturing Lálgudi,[16] which Orme describes as a mud fort situated about seven miles to the east of Srírangam, close to the bank of Coleroon and opposite to the eastern part of the enemy's late encampment to the south of the Cauvery. A quantity of grain sufficient to feed ten thousand men for two months was found in this place.

Law had retreated to Srírangam against the orders of Dupleix, who, on hearing of the difficulties to which his army had been reduced and Clive's expedition to Samayapuram, sent a detachment of 120 Europeans as well as 500 sepoys under M. D'Autenil to his assistance. This force reached Úttattúr on the 14th of April. As Orme remarks the fate of the two armies depended in a great measure upon the success or otherwise of this attempt to reinforce the army in Srírangam, and Clive therefore determined if possible to intercept the detachment while on the march. With this object he advanced from Samayapuram towards Úttattúr, on which D'Autenil, who had already started for Trichinopoly, retraced his steps to that village. Clive then fell back on his former position. Law, who was commanding in Srírangam, had heard of Clive's

(14) A village on the high road to Madras, about 8 miles from Trichinopoly. The two pagodas alluded to in Orme, called the Bója Ìsvaran and Máriyamman temples, are situated on the west and east sides respectively of the *old* road to Madras, which at Samayapuram runs some few hundred yards to the east of the present road. The pagoda in which Clive was so nearly killed is evidently the larger one, Máriyamman, which is almost in the centre of the village.

(15) Munsurpett in Orme. There can, I think, be no doubt that Mannachanellúr is the village referred to by Orme, as it lies on the old road to Madras between Pichándárkóvil and Samayapuram and as there is no other village in that locality which the description given in the text would suit. The pagoda is in the middle of the village by the side of the road to Turaiyúr and Salem.

(16) In the Trichinopoly Taluq, at present the station of a Sub-Magistrate.

departure but not of his return and therefore determined to surprise and cut off whatever force might have been left behind by him. With this object he despatched a force of eighty Europeans of whom forty were deserters and 200 sepoys to Samayapuram. Orme gives the following account of the skirmishing that ensued in which Clive had more than one narrow escape :—

Skirmish at Samayapuram

"The party arrived near the English camp in Samayapuram at midnight, when one of their spies informed the Commanding Officer that the troops which had marched against M. D'Auteuil had returned ; but he, imputing the information either to cowardice or treachery, gave no credit to the spy and proceeded. They were challenged by the advanced guard of English sepoys, on which the officer of the deserters, an Irishman, stepped out and told them that he was sent by Major Lawrence to reinforce Captain Clive, and the rest of the deserters speaking English likewise confirmed the assertion and persuaded the sepoys so fully that they omitted the usual precaution of asking the counter-word, which would certainly have discovered the stratagem, and sent one of their body to conduct the enemy to the head-quarters. They continued their march through a part of the Mahratta camp without giving or receiving any disturbance until they came to the lesser pagoda. Here they were challenged by the sentinels and by others who were posted in a neighbouring choultry to the north of it, in which Captain Clive lay asleep. They returned the challenge by a volley into each place, and immediately entered the pagoda, putting all they met to the sword. Captain Clive starting out of his sleep, and not conceiving it possible that the enemy could have advanced into the centre of his camp, imputed the firing to his own sepoys, alarmed by some attack at the outskirts. He however ran to the upper pagoda, where the greatest part of his Europeans were quartered, who, having likewise taken the alarm, were under arms, and immediately returned with 200 of them to the choultry. Here he now discovered a large body of sepoys drawn up facing the south, and firing at random. Their position, which, looked towards the enemy's encampment, joined to their confusion, confirmed him in his conjecture that they were his own troops, who had taken some unnecessary alert. In this supposition he drew up his Europeans within twenty yards of their rear, and then, going alone amongst them, ordered the firing to cease, upbraiding some with the panic he supposed them to have taken, and even striking others. At length one of the sepoys, who understood a little of the French language, discovering that he was an Englishman, attacked and wounded him in two places with his sword ; but, finding himself on the point of being overpowered, ran away to the lower pagoda. Captain Clive, exasperated at this insolence from a man whom he imagined to be in his own service, followed him to the gate, where,

CHAPTER VII. POLITICAL HISTORY, PART II.

to his great surprise, he was accosted by six Frenchmen. His usual presence of mind did not fail him in this critical occasion, but, suggesting to him all that had happened, he told the Frenchmen, with great composure, that he was come to offer them terms, and, if they would look out, they would perceive the pagoda surrounded by his whole army, who were determined to give no quarter if any resistance were made. The firmness with which these words were delivered made such an impression that three of the Frenchmen ran into the pagoda to carry this intelligence, whilst the other three surrendered their arms to Captain Clive and followed him towards the choultry, whither he hastened, intending to order the Europeans to attack the body of sepoys, whom he now for the first time knew to be enemies ; but these had already discovered the danger of their situation and had marched out of the reach of the Europeans, who, imagining that they did this in obedience to Captain Clive's orders, made no motion to interrupt or attack them. Soon after, eight Frenchmen, who had been sent from the pagoda to reconnoitre, fell in with the English troops and were made prisoners, and these, with the other three which Captain Clive had taken, were delivered to the charge of a Serjeant's party, who, not knowing in this time of darkness and confusion that the enemy were in possession of the lower pagoda, carried them thither, and, on delivering them to the guard, found out their error ; but such was also the confusion of the French in the pagoda that they suffered the Serjeant and his party to return unmolested. The rest of the English troops had now joined the others, and Captain Clive, imagining that the enemy would never have attempted so desperate an enterprize without supporting it with their whole army, deemed it absolutely necessary to storm the pagoda before the troops who were in it could receive any assistance. One of the two folding doors of the gateway had for some time been taken down to be repaired, and the other was strongly stapled down, so that the remaining part of the entrance would admit only two men abreast. The English soldiers made the attack and continued it for some time with great resolution, but the deserters within fought desperately, and killed an officer and fifteen men, on which the attack was ordered to cease until daybreak ; and in the meantime such a disposition was made as might prevent those in the pagoda from escaping and at the same time oppose any other body which might come to their relief. At daybreak the Commanding Officer of the French, seeing the danger of his situation, made a sally at the head of his men, who received so heavy a fire that he himself with twelve others who first came out of the gateway were killed by the volley, on which the rest ran back into the pagoda. Captain Clive then advanced into the porch of the gate to parley with the enemy, and being weak with the loss of blood and fatigue, stood with his back to the wall of the porch, and leaned, stooping forward, on the shoulders of two Serjeants. The officer of the English deserters presented himself with great insolence, and, telling Captain Clive with abusive language that he would shoot him, fired his musket. The ball missed him, but went through the bodies of both the Serjeants on whom he was leaning, and they both fell mortally wounded. The Frenchmen had hitherto defended the pagoda in compliance with the English deserters, but thinking it necessary to disavow such an outrage, which might exclude them from any pretensions to quarter, their officer immediately surrendered."[17] The sepoys who had belonged to the attacking party now retreated as fast as they could towards the Coleroon, but they were pursued by the Mahrattas under Innis Khán and cut to pieces to a man.

Expedition under Dalton to oppose D'Auteuil at Úttattúr.

M. D'Auteuil still remained in Úttattúr, where the English determined to attack him. With this object a detachment under Dalton, sent by Lawrence from Trichinopoly, marched through Samayapuram as far as a choultry within two miles of Úttattúr which they took possession of. The French attempted to dislodge them and some skirmishing resulted, the result of which was on the whole favorable to the English. On this D'Auteuil determined to retreat and accordingly marched back on Válikandapuram, while Dalton took possession of Úttattúr. He remained here for two days, when he received orders to rejoin Lawrence in Trichinopoly. He started at once, but, on reaching the bank of the Coleroon, found that the river was impassable. He therefore placed himself and the troops that he had with him under the command of Clive, who was still at Samayapuram and was then preparing to attack the French in Pichándárkóvil and Sríraugam.

Capture of Pichándárkóvil.

The first measure adopted by the attacking party was to place six cannons on the bound of the Coleroon facing the island of Srírangam and to open fire on the camp there by which they caused the greatest confusion especially among the camp followers. "The crowd first moved between the pagodas of Srírangam and Jembukésvaram towards the bank of the Cauvery, and from this side they were fired on by the guns in Trichinopoly. They then hurried to the eastward of Jembukésvaram, where, finding themselves out of the reach of danger, they began to set up their tents again. The garrison in Pichándárkóvil attempted to interrupt the cannonade, and finding that their artillery had no affect to dismount the English guns covered by the mound, they made a sally to seize them, but had not proceeded far before they received the fire of a detachment which Captain Clive had taken the precaution to post

---

(17) ORME, Vol. I, pages 223 and 225.

CHAPTER VII.
POLITICAL HISTORY, PART II.

in the way they were coming. This instantly drove them back again, not without some loss.

"During the rest of the day the English troops were employed in erecting a battery in a ruined village, about 200 yards to the north of Pichándárkóvil. The pagoda, like most others on the coast of Coromandel, is a square, of which the gateways, projecting beyond the walls, flank the angle the French had 70 Europeans, 200 Sepoys, and three pieces of cannon in the place. The attack began the next morning at daybreak from two pieces of battering cannon, which fired from embrasures cut through the wall of a brick-house ; the shock soon brought down the wall, and left the artillery-men for some time exposed, but a large body of sepoys being ordered to keep a constant fire on the parapet, the enemy were very cautious in making use either of their small arms or cannon Some time after one of the English guns burst, and killed three Europeans and wounded Captain Dalton. The breach nevertheless was made practicable by four in the afternoon, when it was determined to storm it and escalade the walls at the same time."[18] The fort was but feebly defended and was captured after a very short struggle. Several of the defendants were put to the sword by the Sepoys and fifteen Frenchmen who jumped into the river from the walls with a view of escaping were drowned. The rest of the garrison surrendered to the English.

Desertion of the greater portion of Chanda Sahib's army.

The troops in the island were spectators of the attack, but, with the exception of firing a few random shots at the English, which did no damage, they took no part in the fight. By the capture of Pichándárkóvil all communication between the army in Sríraṅgam and the country to the north of the Coleroon was cut off and, in addition to this the camp was now exposed to the fire of the English guns on all sides. Finding themselves in this position, the greater number of Chanda Ṣahib's Officers determined to leave his service. Some of them offered to join the enemy's army and the remainder applied to be allowed to return unmolested to their own countries. By the efforts of the English, these requests were acceded to. Two thousand of Chanda Sahib's horse and 1,500 foot joined Clive at Samayapuram and the greater part of the rest of the enemy dispersed homewards. One 2,000 horse and 3,000 foot were left with Chanda Sahib, and these took possession of Sríraṅgam, while the French army with 2,000 Sepoys entrenched themselves in Jembukésvaram. The English and their allies now closed round their opponents. Major Lawrence left Sarkárpálaiyam and encamped opposite to that village in the Sríraṅgam island. Clive's army abandoned Samayapuram and encamped on the north bank of the Coleroon. Monakjí, the Tanjore General, occupied the post

(18) ORME, Vol. I, pages 229 and 230.

relinquished by Lawrence, while the Mysore army remained to the west of the city.

D'Auteuil surrenders.

On hearing of these movements M. D'Auteuil left Válikandapuram, giving out that he intended to retake Úttattúr. Clive however marched at once to oppose him, leaving a strong garrison in Pichándárkóvil and a sufficient number of troops in his own camp in Samayapuram to prevent the army in Sírirangam from discovering the absence of the force that he had taken with him, which was composed of 100 Europeans, 1,000 Sepoys, and 2,000 Mahratta horse. In an action which took place in the plain near Válikandapuram D'Auteuil was defeated and obliged to fall back on the fort, into which however he was refused admittance by the Poligar who then held it. On this he was obliged to surrender at discretion. His army consisted of 100 Europeans, 400 Sepoys, and 340 Native Cavalry. Of these the Sepoys and horsemen were disarmed and set at liberty, while Clive returned to his camp on the bank of the Coleroon with the European prisoners as well as all the military stores, ammunition, &c., that had been intended for the beleaguered army in Sírirangam.

Capitulation of the French under Law in Sírirangam.

The troops in the Sírirangam island were now reduced to great distress for want of provision, and, as the defeat of D'Auteuil had deprived them of all hope of being relieved, Chanda Sahib determined to surrender, and with that view entered into negotiation with Monakji, the Tanjore General. This chief having received a considerable sum of money, and having been promised a further amount, solemnly swore to preserve Chanda Sahib's life if he gave himself up. No sooner, however, had he done so than this promise was violated and the Nawáb brutally murdered.

Death of Chanda Sahib.

Lawrence now called on the French to surrender, which, after some discussion, they agreed to do on the following terms:—That the pagoda of Jembukésvaram should be given up with all the stores, &c., in it; that the officers should give their parole not to serve against Muhammad Ali or his allies; that the private soldiers should remain prisoners; and that the deserters should be pardoned. The Sírirangam pagoda was soon afterwards surrendered, and the remains of Chanda Sahib's army were allowed to depart unmolested.

CHAPTER VIII.

POLITICAL HISTORY OF TRICHINOPOLY, PART III.

(FROM THE RAISING OF THE SIEGE OF TRICHINOPOLY AND THE DEATH OF CHANDA SAHIB IN 1752 TILL THE TREATY BETWEEN THE ENGLISH AND FRENCH IN 1754.)

The English become aware of the secret treaty between Muhammad Ali and the Mysore regent.—Defeat of the French at Bahoor.—The English determine to treat the Mysore regent as an enemy.—Dalton attacks the Mysore army in Srírangam.—The Mysore regent attempts to reduce Trichinopoly by famine.—Lawrence marches to relieve Trichinopoly.—Dupleix sends a large force to assist the besieging army.—The battle of the Golden rock.—Battle of the Sugar-loaf rock.—Capture of Uyyakondántirumalai.—Night attack on Dalton's battery.—Party of English grenadiers guarding supplies for the city cut to pieces.—The Mahrattas leave Trichinopoly.—Unsuccessful attempt of the besieging army to intercept a convoy under Lawrence.—Provisional treaty concluded between the English and French.

CHAP. VIII. POLITICAL HISTORY, PART III.

The English become aware of the secret treaty between Muhammad Ali and the Mysore regent.

Up to the surrender of the French and Chanda Sahib's death, the English had remained in ignorance of the treaty that had been entered into between the Nawáb and the Mysore regent, and the terms on which the latter had agreed to march to Trichinopoly. Muhammad Ali now confessed the whole transaction to Lawrence, stating that the promise to deliver up Trichinopoly had been extorted from him in his difficulties, and that the Mysore General must have known very well that he could not fulfil it. He then tried to put Nandiraz off by promising to give up Trichinopoly to him in two months, as soon as he could obtain some other safe fortress in which to place his family. Morari Rau was appointed umpire in the dispute, and secretly endeavoured to get possession of the bone of contention for himself. Major Lawrence determined not to interfere unless the Mysore regent attacked the Nawáb, and the English battalion prepared to return to Madras. When they had, however, got as far as Úttattúr, they were obliged to march back to Trichinopoly, as an immediate rupture between the Nawáb and Nandiraz appeared imminent. On their reappearance a temporary reconciliation was made, and Muhammad Ali gave up Srírangam and allowed a force of 200 Mysore troops to enter Trichinopoly. As however it was evident that, as soon as the English were gone, Nandiraz would attempt to seize the city, Captain Dalton was left behind with 200 Europeans and 1,500 sepoys, while the rest of the army, including 2,000 horse under Muhammad Ali, marched northward.

Defeat of the French at Bahoor.

In the meantime Dupleix, roused to fresh exertions by the defeat which the French had sustained at Trichinopoly, and having received large reinforcements from Europe, appointed Reza Sahib, Chanda Sahib's son, Nawáb of the Karnatic, and, to support his pretensions, opened negotiations with the Mysore regent and the Mahrattas. At first he was successful in his attacks on some small detachments of the English troops, but eventually he was utterly defeated by Major Lawrence at Bahoor, not far from Pondicherry. This victory, and the reduced state of Dupleix's resources, ought to have secured the complete success of the English and their allies, but unfortunately the management of the next campaign was entrusted to Muhammad Ali, who wasted the season in inaction. Nandiraz, on the first intelligence of the defeat at Bahoor, had given up all intention of keeping his compact with Dupleix; but, when he perceived that the English and the Nawáb had made so little use of their success, he determined to abandon their alliance and sent Morari Rau with all his Mahrattas, except 500, to join the French at Pondicherry. He however gave out that the Mahrattas had left him in consequence of a dispute that he had had with their chief, and attempted to hide his real intention till the arrival of some Europeans that Dupleix had promised to send to reinforce his army in Srírangam. As however his horsemen stopped all the supplies of provisions intended for the garrison in Trichinopoly, and had also showed other clear proofs of hostility, the Government of Madras saw that it was now time to treat him as a declared enemy.

The English determine to treat the Mysore regent as an enemy.

Dalton attacks the Mysore army in Srírangam.

On receiving information of this resolution, Captain Dalton, who was then in command in Trichinopoly, determined to attack the Mysore army, which was then encamped under the northern wall of the Srírangam pagoda, without delay. A night expedition, which he himself led on the 23rd of December, was so far successful that it had the effect of obliging the entire army to retreat inside the walls of the pagoda. In order to dislodge them from this position, Dalton took possession of a large choultry on the riverside directly opposite the south gate of the pagoda, had it enclosed with a strong entrenchment, and placing in this fortress one detachment of his army, posted the remainder on the opposite bank of the Cauvery, at that time dry, with four field pieces, which, as the river is not wide at this spot, could be worked with execution against any force that might attack the choultry. The enemy remained quiet for a few hours, and then advanced in great numbers from the pagoda against the detachment in the choultry. On this the guns on the opposite side of the river were at once directed against them, and with so good an effect as to

CHAP. VIII
POLITICAL HISTORY, PART III.

prevent their approaching the object of their attack. "During the cannonade a party of the Nawáb's sepoys crossed the river, and taking possession of a small choultry at a little distance to the right of the other, began to fire from this untenable post; upon which a body of 300 Mahratta horse galloped up to attack them, but before they arrived the sepoys took flight, several of them were cut to pieces, and the rest, recrossing the river, ran into the city; the Mahrattas, encouraged by this success, now galloped up towards the entrenchment of the great choultry, where they were suffered to come so near that several of them made use of their sabres across the parapet before the troops within gave fire, which then began, and, seconded by that of the four pieces of cannon on the other side of the river, killed and wounded a great number of men and horses, and obliged the enemy to retire in confusion. At this instant an officer unadvisedly took the resolution of quitting his post, and passed the river, in order to give Captain Dalton some information concerning the artillery. Some of the soldiers seeing this, imagined that he went away through fear, and, concluding that things were worse than appeared to them, followed his example, and ran out of the entrenchment; which the rest perceiving, a panic seized the whole, and they left the post with the greatest precipitation. A body of 3,000 Mysore horse, who were drawn up on the bank, immediately galloped into the bed of the river, and charging the fugitives with fury, cut down the whole party, excepting fifteen men, and then flushed with this success, made a push at Captain Dalton's division on the other side. All these motions succeeded one another so rapidly that he had hardly time to put his men on their guard, more especially as many of them had caught the panic from having been spectators of the massacre of their comrades. However some of the bravest, hearkening to his exhortations, stood firm by the artillery; their behaviour encouraged the sepoys, who made a strong fire from behind the low wall in their front, which, accompanied by the grape-shot of the four field pieces, soon abated the ardour of the enemy, and obliged them to retreat, leaving some horses whose riders fell within twenty yards of the muzzles of the guns."[1]

The English force was so seriously diminished by this disaster that Dalton was obliged to relinquish his idea of driving the enemy out of Srírangam. In order, however, to show them that he was not totally dispirited by his recent reverse, he sent a small detachment to attack a position which they had taken up in a pagoda in the village of Kumáravayalúr,[2] a few miles to the west of

(1) ORME, Vol. I, pages 270 and 271.
(2) Velore in Orme.

Trichinopoly, with a view of intercepting supplies of provisions to that city. This pagoda was surrounded by a strong stone wall, the gate in which had been blocked up with mud. The attacking party blew up this mud work, carried the place by assault, and put all the sepoys found in it to death.

The Mysore regent attempts to reduce Trichinopoly by famine.

The regent now perceived that his best chance of taking Trichinopoly was by starving the garrison out. All the supplies for the city at this time came from the Pudukóttai territory, which was then under a poligar who was in alliance with the English. To cut off these supplies, an outpost was formed at a place called by Orme the Fakir's tope, which appears to have been situated to the south-west of the little hill now called the Fakir's rock by European residents in Trichinopoly. In this camp 5,000 horse and 3,000 sepoys were placed, and all communication from this side with the city was thus cut off. Dalton had up to this been constantly assured by the Governor of this city that they had provisions in store sufficient to last the garrison for four months. As, however, all hopes of obtaining supplies from outside were now cut off, he determined to inspect the magazines personally and ascertain the accuracy of this account. On doing so, he discovered that the Governor had sold the greatest portion of the provisions to the inhabitants of the city at high prices, and that not more than enough to last for fifteen days was left. On making this discovery, he lost no time in communicating the straits to which he was reduced to Lawrence, who was then encamped with a considerable force at Trivádi. On being informed of the actual state of affairs in Trichinopoly, Lawrence started at once to the relief of the garrison.

Lawrence marches to relieve Trichinopoly.

While awaiting his arrival, Dalton, however, was not inactive. With the view of annoying the enemy in the position that they had taken up in the Fakir's tope, he erected a redoubt within cannon shot of this encampment and opened fire on it. This caused the Mysore army so much inconvenience that their General shifted his position, remaining, however, at first to the south of the Cauvery. In a few days, however, he received information of Lawrence's march to relieve the city, and on this at once retreated to Srírangam. All the enemy's posts to the south having thus been abandoned, the besieged garrison were able to obtain provisions without difficulty.

Lawrence arrived in Trichinopoly on the 6th of May without any molestation on the part of the besieging army. The entire force in the city now consisted of 500 Europeans, 2,000 sepoys and 3,000 of the Nawáb horse. At the same time, the Mysore army was reinforced by a detachment of 200 Europeans and 500 sepoys, sent by Dupleix from the camp at Trivádi. Lawrence now determined to attack the besieging force in Srírangam without

CHAP. VIII. POLITICAL HISTORY PART III.

delay. With this object, he marched his troops to Muttarasanellúr,[3] a village four miles to the west of Trichinopoly, opposite to the west end of the Srírangam island, and from there crossed the river and advanced towards the pagoda. He was, however, opposed by the Mahrattas and French, and, after twenty hours of hard fighting and marching, his men were obliged to retreat to Trichinopoly without any decisive result having been achieved. After this repulse, Lawrence abandoned the idea of driving the enemy out of the island, and directed all his attentions to securing a sufficient supply of food for the army under his command. With this object, he took possession of the camp that the Mysore army had abandoned in the Fakir's tope, and sent out agents to purchase grain in Pudukóttai and Tanjore. Nandiraz, however, did every thing to thwart him in his endeavours, and with such success, that the garrison in Trichinopoly was but scantily supplied with provisions. Lawrence was obliged to remain in this condition for five weeks, as the enemy were determined not to hazard an engagement till the arrival of reinforcements, which they were then expecting.

Dupleix sends a large force to assist the besieging army.

Soon after Lawrence's departure from Trivádi, both that fortress and Chedambaram were captured by the French, and Dupleix then turned all his attention to the operations before Trichinopoly, and ent 3,000 Mahrattas, 300 Europeans, and 100 sepoys to reinforce the besieging army. "As soon as these troops arrived, the enemy quitted Srírangam, and, crossing the Cauvery, encamped on the plain three miles to the north of Fakir's tope. Their force now consisted of 450 Europeans, 1,500 well-trained sepoys, 8,000 Mysore horse, 3,500 Mahrattas, and two companies of topasses, with 1,000 sepoys in the service of the regent, the rest of whose infantry was 15,000 peons, armed with matchlocks, swords, bows and arrows, pikes and clubs. Major Lawrence had only the 500 Europeans and 2,000 sepoys he had brought with him from the coast, and 700 of these sepoys were continually employed in the poligar's country to escort the convoys; his artillery were eight excellent 6-pounders. Of the Nawáb's horse only 100 encamped with the English, the rest remaining under the walls, and peremptorily refusing to march until they were paid their arrears.

The battle of the Golden Rock.

There are, about a mile to the south of the Fakir's tope, some high mountains called the five rocks,[4] on the summit of which the Major always kept a strong guard of sepoys, but, being obliged

(3) Moota Chellinoor in Orme.

(4) These rocks are situated to the east of the Madura road, at the point where it krosses the Kóraiyàr. They are about half a mile south-west of what is now known as the Fakir's rock.

to go into the city for the recovery of his health, the officer who commanded during his absence neglected to continue this detachment. The enemy reconnoitring, and finding this post without defence, detached in the night a strong party to take possession of it; and early the next morning their whole army was discovered in motion, assembling under the shelter of the five rocks, whilst their advanced cannon plunged into the English camp, whither the Major immediately returned, but found it impossible to regain the post. He however kept his ground until night, and then encamped about a quarter of a mile nearer the city, behind a small eminence which sheltered the troops from the enemy's artillery; they the next day quitted the camp to the north of the Fakir's tope and encamped at the five rocks. Here they had it in their power entirely to cut off the supplies of provisions coming from the poligar's country, and intercept the detachment of 700 sepoys sent to escort them; at the same time the great superiority of their numbers, and the advantage of the ground they occupied, rendered an attack upon their camp impracticable; but it was evident that if they were not soon dislodged, neither the English army in the field, nor the garrison of the city, could subsist long. To augment the distress, a strong spirit of desertion arose among the soldiery In these circumstances, even the most sanguine began to lose hope, and to apprehend that the city must be abandoned in order to save the troops from perishing by famine.

The Major had stationed a guard of 200 sepoys on a small rock situated about half a mile south-west of his camp, and nearly a mile north-east of the enemy's. M. Astruc soon discovered the importance of this post, which if he could get possession of, his artillery would easily oblige the English to decamp again and retire under the walls of the city, where, still more straitened, they would probably be reduced in a very few days to the necessity of retreating. He therefore resolved to attack the post, and marched early in the morning, on the 26th of June, with his grenadiers and a large body of sepoys; but they meeting with more resistance than was expected, he ordered the whole army to move and support them. The Major, as soon as he found the rock attacked, ordered the picket guard of the camp, consisting of 40 Europeans, to march and support his sepoys; but afterwards observing the whole of the enemy's army in motion, he ordered all his troops to get under arms, and leaving 100 Europeans to take care of the camp, marched with the rest of his force, which in Europeans did not exceed 300 battalion men with 80 belonging to the artillery, and 500 sepoys. With this small force, he hastened to reach the rock before the enemy's main body. But M. Astruc, with the party already engaged in the attack, perceiving his approach, made a vigorous effort, and before the Major had got half way, the sepoys who defended the rock were all either killed or taken prisoners, and the French colours immediately hoisted. This obliged the Major to halt, and consider what was most advisable to be done in this critical conjuncture, on which the fate of the whole war seemed to depend. There was little time for deliberation, for the French battalion were now arrived behind the rock, and their artillery from the right and left of it were firing upon the English troops; the rock itself was covered by their sepoys supported by their grenadiers; the whole Mysore army was drawn up in one great body at the distance of cannon-shot in the rear; the Mahrattas were, as usual, flying about in small detachments, and making charges on the flanks and rear of the English battalion in order to intimidate and create confusion.

In such circumstances the officers unanimously agreed in opinion with their General, that it was safer to make a gallant push, than to retreat before such numbers of enemies; and the soldiers seeming much delighted at this opportunity of having what they called a fair knock at the Frenchmen on the plain, Major Lawrence took advantage of the good disposition of the whole, and ordered the grenadiers to attack the rock with fixed bayonets, while he himself, with the rest of the troops, wheeled round the foot of it to engage the French battalion. The soldiers received the orders with three huzzas, and the grenadiers setting out at a great rate, though at the same time keeping their ranks, paid no attention to the scattered fire they received from the rock, nor made a halt until they got to the top of it; whilst the enemy, terrified at their intrepidity, descended as they were mounting, without daring to stand the shock of their onset. Some of the best sepoys followed the grenadiers, and all together began a strong fire upon the French troops, drawn up within pistol-shot below. In the meantime M. Astruc, perceiving that the left flank of his battalion would, if it remained drawn up facing the north, be exposed to the English troops, wheeling round the foot of the rock, changed his position, and drew up facing the west, in order to oppose them in front. But this movement exposed him right flank to the fire of the grenadiers and sepoys from the rock, by which his troops had already suffered considerably; when the English battalion, executing their evolution with great, address, drew up at once directly opposite to the enemy, at the distance of twenty yards.

The French troops were struck with consternation upon seeing themselves thus daringly attacked in the midst of their numerous allies, by such a handful of men; and indeed a stranger, taking a view of the two armies from the top of one of the rocks on the plain, could scarcely have believed that the one ventured to dispute a province with the other. Astruc exerted himself as a brave and active officer, and with difficulty prevailed on his men to keep their ranks until the English gave their fire, which, falling in a well-levelled discharge from the whole battalion, and seconded by a hot fire from the rock, together with a discharge of grape-shot from the first field piece that came up, threw them into irreparable disorder. They ran away with the utmost precipitation, leaving three pieces of cannon, with some ammunition carts behind them. The Mahrattas immediately made a gallant effort to cover their retreat by flinging themselves between, and some of the grenadiers, who had run forward to seize the field pieces, fell under their sabres. Animated by this success, they attacked the battalion, pushing in several charges up to the very bayonets, and endeavouring to cut down the men, who constantly received them with so much steadiness, that they were not able to throw a single platoon into disorder. At length having suffered much, and lost several of their best men by the incessant fire of the line, they desisted from their attacks, and retreated to the main body of the Mysoreans. In the meantime the French never halted until they got into the rear of the Mysore army, when their officers prevailed on them to get into order again, and drew up in a line with their allies, whence they fired their two remaining field pieces with great vivacity, although the shot did not reach above half-way.

The Major remained three hours at the foot of the rock, in order to give them an opportunity of renewing the fight; but finding that they showed no inclination to move towards him, he prepared to return to his camp, leaving them to take possession of the rock again at their peril; for since the loss of the 200 sepoys that defended it in the beginning of the action, he did not think it prudent to expose another detachment to the same risk, at such a distance from his main body. The three guns, with the prisoners, were placed in the centre, and the troops marching in platoons on each side, the artillery was distributed in the front, rear, and intervals of the column. The rear had scarcely got clear of the rock into the plain, when the whole of the enemy's cavalry set up a shout, and came furiously on, flourishing their swords as if they were resolved to exterminate at once the handful of men that opposed them. The English troops waited for the enemy, who were suffered to come sufficiently near before the signal was given to the artillery officers. The cannonade then began from eight 6-pounders, loaded with grape, and was kept up at the rate of eight or ten shot in a minute from each piece, so well directed, that every shot went amongst the crowd, as was visible by the numbers that dropped; this soon stopped their career, and turning to the right-about, they got out of reach of the guns as fast as they had come on, leaving the troops to return quietly to their camp.

CHAP. VIII. POLITICAL HISTORY, PART III.

Thus was Trichinopoly saved by a success which astonished even those who had gained it, nor was the attempt, however desperate it might seem, justified by the success alone; for as the city would inevitably have fallen if the English had remained inactive, so the loss of it would have been hastened only a few days if they had been defeated; and Major Lawrence undoubtedly acted with as much sagacity as spirit, in risking everything to gain a victory, on which alone depended the preservation of the great object of the war."[5] Orme terms this action the battle of the Golden rock.

Lawrence determined not to risk another engagement until he was joined by some English troops which had been ordered to march to his assistance through Tanjore. As however what he was most in need of was cavalry, he determined to go himself to Tanjore, and, while waiting there for the reinforcement that he expected, induce the king to furnish him with a body of horse. As soon as his army had left Trichinopoly, the officers of the Nawáb's cavalry informed Dalton that they intended to desert to the enemy, and, as he was very glad to get rid of them, they were allowed to depart unmolested. The enemy now blockaded the city on every side. Dalton, however, took the precaution of undermining the forts at Uraiyúr and Uyyakondántirumalai[6] with a view of blowing them up. Uraiyúr was completely ruined, but the explosion at Uyyakondántirumalai was not successful, and the Mysore army, finding that the fortifications of this latter place had been but little injured, took possession of it.

After Trichinopoly had been closely blockaded for a month, Lawrence started from Tanjore to the relief of the garrison, with 3,000 horse and 2,000 foot of the Tanjore troops that he had with much difficulty persuaded the king to send with him, and 170 Europeans and 300 sepoys that had at last arrived from Fort St. David. The besieging army determined to intercept Lawrence if possible, and prevent him from entering the city. With this view they stationed their cavalry in a line extending from the French rock as far as the Golden rock, while the main body of Europeans, sepoys and artillery, were stationed near the Sugar-loaf rock. In this position they were attacked by Lawrence and completely defeated. The relieving army entered the city without further opposition, and their opponents the same night broke up their camp at the Sugar-loaf rock and removed to Uyyakondántirumalai, where they entrenched themselves in a strong position. Lawrence, however, attacked them there at once, whereon they retreated in

---

(5) ORME, Vol. I, pages 289-294.

(6) Weycondah in Orme. It is a village on the road from Trichinopoly to Allitturai, and about three miles from the former town.

Chap. VIII. Political History, Part III.

disorder to Muttarasanellúr, and the English took possession of the abandoned fort.

Battle of the Sugar-loaf rock.

On the following day the besieging army was reinforced by the arrival at Sríraugam of 3,000 Mahrattas under Morari Rau, together with 400 Europeans and 2,000 sepoys. On hearing of this accession to the force opposed to him, Lawrence relinquished the small fort at Uyyakondántirumalai, and returned to his former position near the Fakir's rock, while the Mysore army left Muttarasanellúr and encamped at the five rocks. On information of the large reinforcement that the army at Sríraugam had received reaching Madras, it was determined to send all the men that could be spared to strengthen the army in Trichinopoly. Lawrence, in order to facilitate the juncture of those troops with his own, moved to the eastward and pitched his camp a little to the south-east of the French rock. On this the enemy shifted their position from the five rocks to the Sugar-loaf, their encampment extending from that point up to the Golden rock. The expected reinforcement, consisting of 237 Europeans and 300 sepoys, joined the English army towards the close of September, and, on their arrival, Major Lawrence determined to provoke the enemy to a general engagement as soon as possible, and accordingly left his encampment near the French rock and marched to the Fakir's rock. The following description of the action that ensued, known as the battle of the Sugar-loaf rock, is given by Orme :—

"The enemy's camp extended on each side of the Sugár-loaf rock,[7] but much farther to the west than to the east. Most of the Mahrattas were encamped on the east ; the French quarters were close to the west of the rock, and beyond these the Mysoreans extended almost as far as the Golden rock,[7] occupying the ground for a considerable way behind the two rocks. The rear of the camp was covered with thickets and rocky ground. The French had flung up an entrenchment in front of their own quarters, and the Mahrattas had likewise flung up an entrenchment in their front to the east of the Sugar-loaf. At the Golden rock, which commanded the left flank and the front of the ground on which the Mysoreans were encamped, the French had stationed an advanced guard of 100 Europeans, two companies of topasses, and 600 sepoys, with two pieces of cannon. Major Lawrence being apprised of these dispositions, projected his attack to take the utmost advantage of them. At the hour appointed, the army quitted the Fakir's tope, and marched in silence towards the Golden rock, the battalion consisting of 600 men, formed the van in three equal divisions ; the first was composed of the grenadier company of 100 men commanded by Captain Kilpatrick, the picket of forty by

(7) The note on the nomenclature of these rocks, which will be found in Chapter VII, should be consulted here. I believe that Orme has made a mistake regarding their names, but he is, as a rule, so wonderfully accurate in matters of local detail, that I have thought it better not to alter his text.

Captain Calliaud, and two platoons, each of thirty men, under the command of Captain Campbell. The artillery, six field pieces, with 100 artillerymen, were divided on the flanks of each division: 2,000 sepoys, in two lines, followed the Europeans, while the Tanjorine cavalry were ordered to extend to the eastward, and march even with the last line of sepoys. The moon had hitherto been very bright, but a sudden cloud now obscured it so much, that the first division of the battalion came within pistol-shot of the Golden rock before they were discovered, and, giving a very smart fire, mounted it in three places at once, whilst the enemy, who had barely time to snatch up their arms, hurried down after making one irregular discharge, and ran away to the camp with such precipitation that they left their two field pieces ready loaded with grape undischarged. Animated by this success, the men called out to be led on to the grand camp, and the Major, availing himself of their alacrity, remained no longer at the rock than was necessary to break the carriages of the enemy's guns, and to form his troops again. Their disposition was now changed: the three divisions of Europeans were ordered to march as near as they could in one line in front, through the camp of the Mysoreans, in order to fall at once upon the left flank of the French quarters; while the sepoys were divided on each flank of the battalion, but at some distance in the rear. The Tanjore cavalry had halted during the attack of the Golden rock on the plain nearly opposite to the front of the French entrenchment, and they were now instructed to move directly up to it, in order to create what confusion they could with their fire-arms and rockets. The battalion received the orders for continuing the march with loud huzzas, and the whole proceeded with the greatest confidence, as to a victory of which they were sure; the drums of the three divisions beating the Grenadier's March, the gunners with their portfires lighted on the flanks, and the sepoys sounding with no little energy all their various instruments of military music. This did not a little contribute to augment the consternation which the fugitives from the rock had spread among the Mysoreans, who were already taking flight when the English entered their camp. The Europeans marched with fixed bayonets, while the sepoys kept up a smart fire upon the swarms that were taking flight on all sides. The French discovered by the fugitives which way the attack would fall, and drew up to oppose it, facing the west. To the left of their battalion was a body of 2,000 sepoys, who inclined to the left, intending to gain the flank of the English battalion, and the same number was designed to form their right wing; but these, by some mistake in this scene of hurry and confusion, posted themselves on the Sugar-loaf rock. The English troops advancing were prevented by the interruption which they met with in the Mysore camp from keeping up in a line, so that the first division had out-marched the second, and the second the third. However, as soon as they came nigh the enemy, the hindermost quickened their pace; but nevertheless, the whole line was not completely formed before they came within twenty yards of the enemy, by which time the sepoys to the right had advanced from the rear, in order to oppose those on the enemy's left: the artillery in the hurry could not keep up with the battalion. The French artillery had for some time fired with great vivacity, but most of the shot flew too high, and killed several of the flying Mysoreans. The action commenced just as the day began to dawn. M. Astruc, with indefatigable activity, prevailed on his men to wait and receive the English fire before they gave theirs. Amongst those who suffered on this onset was Captain Kilpatrick, who commanded the division on the right; he fell desperately wounded, upon which Captain Calliaud put himself at the head of the grenadiers, and took the command of the whole division. The French sepoys on the left scarcely stood the first fire of the right wing of the English sepoys, but took flight, which Captain Calliaud perceiving, he wheeled instantly round with his division, and, gaining the left flank of the entrenchment, behind which the left of the French battalion was posted, poured in a close fire upon them; and the grenadiers pushing on with their bayonets, drove them crowding upon their centre. The whole line was already falling into confusion, when a well-levelled discharge from the centre and left of the English battalion in front completed the rout, and they ran away in great disorder to gain the other side of the bank on their right, where M. Astruc endeavoured to rally them: but the grenadiers pursuing then closely, renewed the attack with their bayonets, and put them again to flight. Every man now provided for his own safety, without any regard to order, running towards the Golden rock, as this way was the only outlet not obstructed; but, as soon as they got to some distance on the plain, they dispersed and took various routes. The left wing of the English sepoys had hitherto taken no share in the engagement, for, by keeping too much to the left of the battalion, they came to the outside of the French entrenchment, on the ground to which the Tanjorines were ordered to advance. However, as soon as they perceived the French battalion in confusion, they pushed on to the Sugar-loaf rock, and, with much resolution, attacked and dispersed the body of the enemy's sepoys posted there, who, from the beginning of the action, had employed themselves in firing random shots indiscriminately upon friends and foes." [8]

The battle was now over and the victory of the English complete. The French tents, baggage and ammunition, together with eleven guns, were taken, and their loss is estimated by Orme at not less than 300 European soldiers. Of the English force only 40 were killed or wounded. On the same evening Lawrence marched to Uyyakondántirumalai, and carried the fortified pagoda there which the French had taken possession of by assault. From Uyyakondántirumalai the English moved to the French rocks, where they took up their camp. As none of the besieging force now ventured to appear in the plain, provisions were brought in abundance to the camp, and all fear of scarcity was removed, at least for the present. Trichinopoly was now virtually out of danger, and Captain Dalton therefore gave up the command of

Capture of Uyyakondántirumalai.

(8) Orme, Vol. I, pages 309–313.

CHAP. VIII. POLITICAL HISTORY, PART III.

the city and proceeded on leave to Europe. On the approach of the monsoon in October, Lawrence increased the garrison in Trichinopoly by 400 sepoys and 150 Europeans, and marched with the remainder of his army to Kóviladi, as they could be supplied with provisions there with greater ease than in the city.

Night attack on Dalton's battery.

In the beginning of November the French at Sríraṅgam received a reinforcement of 300 Europeans and 1,000 sepoys with some cannon, and, strengthened by this reinforcement, they made their last effort of any importance to capture Trichinopoly. This was an attempt to surprise the city by a night attack upon that part of the fortifications known as Dalton's battery. This fort was situated a few hundred yards to the north-west of what is now known as the main-guard gate, but it has recently been completely demolished by the Municipality. The following graphic account of the attack is given by Orme :—

"On the 27th of November, at night, the greatest part of the enemy's army crossed the river. The Mysoreans and Mahrattas were distributed in different parties round the city, with orders to approach the ditch, and divert the attention of the garrison during the principal and real attack, which was reserved for the French troops. Of this body 600 Europeans were appointed to escalade, whilst M. Maissin, the commander, with the rest of the battalion, 200 men, and a large body of sepoys, waited at the edge of the ditch, ready to follow the first party as soon as they should get into the town. At three in the morning the first party crossed the ditch, and, planting their scaling ladders, all mounted the battery without raising the least alarm in the garrison : for although the guard appointed for the battery consisted of fifty sepoys, with their officers, and some European gunners, who were all present and alert when the rounds passed at midnight, most of them were now absent, and those who remained on the battery were fast asleep; these the French killed with their bayonets, intending not to fire until they were fired upon : but this resolution was immediately after frustrated by an unforeseen accident; for some of them, attempting to get to a slight counterwall which lines the backside of the battery, fell into a deep pit, which had been left in the body of the battery itself contiguous to that wall. None but the most tried soldiers can refrain from firing upon any unexpected alarm in the night, and upon the screaming of those who were tumbling into the hole several muskets were discharged. The French now concluding that they were discovered, imagined they might intimidate the garrison by showing how far they were already successful, and, turning two of the 12-pounders upon the battery against the town, discharged them, together with a volley of small arms, their drums beating, and their soldiers shouting. Fortunately the main-guard, the barracks of the garrison, and the quarters of the officers were in the north part of the town, not more than 400 yards from the battery. Captain Kilpatrick, who commanded, remained so ill from the wounds he had received in the last engagement, that he was unable to remove from his bed. Lieutenant Harrison, the next in command, came to him upon the alarm to receive his orders, which he gave with the usual calmness that distinguished his character on all occasions, directing Lieutenant Harrison to march instantly with the picket, reserve and the sepoys who were not already posted, to the place where the attack was made, and to order the rest of the garrison to repair to their respective alarm-posts, with injunctions not to stir from them upon pain of death. The enemy, having drawn up their scaling ladders into the battery, sent two parties down from it into the interval between the two walls: one of these parties carrying two petards, conducted by a deserter, entered the passage which led between the double walls surrounding the fort, intending to get into the town by blowing open the gate which stands in the inward rampart. The other party carried the ladders, and were appointed to escalade, whilst the main body remained upon the battery, keeping up a constant fire upon the inward rampart. But by this time the alarm was taken, and the cannon from each hand began to fire smartly into the interval between the two walls, and upon the battery. Lieutenant Harrison, with the main guard, had likewise arrived upon the rampart. The musketry of the assailants and defenders were now employed with great vivacity against each other, but with some uncertainty, having no other light to direct their aim except the frequent flashes of fire. Notwithstanding the hurry and confusion, Lieutenant Harrison had the presence of mind to station a platoon upon the rampart directly above the gate, ordering them to keep a constant fire upon the passage immediately below, whether they saw anything or not. Nothing could be more sensible or fortunate than this precaution ; for the platoon killed, without seeing them, the man who was to apply the first petard, as well as the deserter who conducted him, and both of them fell within ten yards of the gate. Those appointed to escalade, fixed their ladders on the south side, and a drummer, followed by an officer had already mounted to the top, when a party of sepoys came to this station, killed the drummer, wounded and seized the officer.and then overturning the scaling ladders, overset the men who were upon them. The ladders broke with the fall, and the assailants called for more, but were disappointed ; for the rest which had been brought were shattered and rendered useless by the grape-shot fired from the two pieces of cannon planted upon the cavalier: it was soon after found that the man who was to manage the second petard was killed. Thus defeated in all their expectations, they determined to retreat, and went up to the battery again, where the whole now resolved to make their escape ; but this, for the want of their ladders, was no longer practicable, except by leaping down eighteen feet perpendicular, either upon the rock or into the water. Desperate as this attempt appeared, nearly one hundred made the experiment; but what they suffered deterred the rest from following their example, who, in despair, turned, and recommenced their fire from the battery upon the defenders. Lieutenant Harrison, with the greatest part of his Europeans, were assembled upon the inner wall,

CHAP. VIII. POLITICAL HISTORY, PART III.

and the two bodies, separated only by an interval of twenty feet, kept up a smart fire upon each other as fast as they could load: but the defenders had the advantage of firing under the cover of parapets from a situation twelve feet higher than the enemy upon the battery, who were totally exposed from head to foot, and were likewise taken on each flank by two pieces of cannon, as well as by the fire of some parties of sepoys posted on the main rampart on each hand of the gateway. Thus galled, unable to retreat, and finding that resistance served only to expose them more, they desisted from firing, and every man endeavoured to shelter himself as he could, some in the embrasures of the battery, others behind a cavalier contiguous to it, and the rest in the interval between the two walls; the garrison, nevertheless, trusting to no appearances of security, continued to fire upon all such places in which they suspected them to be concealed. At length the day, long wished for by both sides, appeared; when the French, flinging down their arms, asked for quarter, which was immediately granted."[9]

Three hundred and sixty Europeans were taken prisoners, and it was found that 36 had been killed, and that, in addition to these, all those who had attempted to escape by jumping off the battery were more or less disabled. The number of French prisoners in Trichinopoly was so much increased by the accession of those taken in this attack, that Lawrence was obliged to increase the garrison in the city to 300 Europeans and 1,500 sepoys, which reduced the force under him to only 600 Europeans and 1,800 sepoys. The French army had recently been reinforced, and it was now stronger than the English, yet they did not dare to leave the island of Srírangam.

Party of English grenadiers guarding supplies for the city cut to pieces.

The English were at this time obliged to obtain almost all their provision from Tanjore, but, as the merchants would not venture further than Tirukáttupalli, a village eighteen miles east of Trichinopoly in the present Tanjore District, it was necessary, as soon as a sufficient quantity of supplies had been collected there, to have it conveyed under the protection of a strong escort to the camp. In February 1754 a larger convoy than usual, consisting of military stores as well as provisions, had been collected, and to guard it a detachment of the grenadier company, consisting of 100 men, together with 80 other Europeans, 800 sepoys and four guns, was sent out. They arrived without interruption at Tirukáttupalli in the evening, whence they set out with the convoy the next day, and gained Kiliyúr,[10] where they stopped for the night. The allies in Srírangam having heard of their

(9) ORME, Vol. I, pages 321 to 324.

(10) Kellicottah in Orme. I have ascertained that Kiliyúr used to be called by this name. It is situated on the confines of the Tanjore District, about ten miles from Trichinopoly.

march, sent out a force of 12,000 Mahratta and Mysore horse, 600 sepoys and 400 Europeans, with seven pieces of cannon, to intercept them. The small body of men in charge of the convoy were quite unable to contend with this overwhelming force, and were completely defeated. Fifty men were killed on the spot and the rest made prisoners, while of the eight officers in charge of the party six lost their lives. Orme remarks that this was the severest blow that the English had sustained during the war. The whole convoy, provisions, military stores, and £7,000 in cash fell into the hands of the enemy.

As soon as news of this disaster reached Madras, a detachment of 180 men was sent by sea to Dévikóttai to reinforce the garrison at Trichinopoly. As however Lawrence did not consider that they would be able to advance in safety across the Tanjore territory, and as he was unwilling to weaken the force in the city by sending a detachment to meet them, they were directed to remain at Dévikóttai for the present.

The King of Tanjore, concluding that the recent severe reverse which the English had sustained, would compel them to abandon Trichinopoly, discouraged the merchants in his territory from bringing them supplies, and they were consequently obliged to depend entirely on the Tondiman's country. In order to avoid any further losses the greatest precautions were taken in escorting the convoys to the camp. Parties of sepoys first of all were sent out about twelve miles to the south of Trichinopoly to collect the supplies together. The detachments of Europeans employed as escorts then moved about five miles from the city, where they halted and sent forward additional bodies of sepoys to bring up the supplies from the place where they had been collected. The sepoys were at this time under the command of a man named Muhammad Yusuf, who had enlisted as an ordinary sepoy under Clive, and by his courage and ability had raised himself to his present position. The routes of the several escorts were so well planned by him that for three months not one of them was interrupted. Indeed the only attack which was made on them failed signally. On the 12th of May Captain Calliaud had marched from the camp to escort one of the convoys, intending to wait for it about two miles to the south of the Sugar-loaf rock. Here he was unexpectedly attacked by a body of French 700 strong, assisted by a large force of sepoys and Mahrattas. Although greatly outnumbered, the English stood their ground, and the French, after some hard fighting, were obliged to retreat to Uyyakondántirumalai and thence to Srírangam.

The French now resolved to carry the war into the enemy's country, and thus, if possible, improve their position. They first advanced into the Tondiman's territory with a force of 3,000 Mysore sepoys and 2,000 horse, determined to devastate the entire country. The inhabitants, however, stripped their houses of everything of any value, and drove their cattle into the woods, where they also fled themselves. The invading army consequently finding nothing but empty villages to burn, beat a hasty retreat. Disappointed in Pudukóttai, they turned to the Tanjore District and captured Kiliyúr. Immediately on hearing of this loss, Lawrence, determining to march to Tanjore, and accordingly having withdrawn the detachments at Erumbísvaram and the other outposts, advanced through the woods in the Pudukóttai country. Orders were sent to the detachment, which, as has previously been mentioned, had been sent from Madras, and was now at Dévikóttai, to join him without delay at Tanjore, and this they did two days after his arrival there.

The Mahrattas leave Trichinopoly.

After the capture of Kilikóttai, the Mysore army marched to Kóviladi, and cut through the embankment that is raised near that village with a view of preventing the waters of the Cauvery from rejoining those of the Coleroon. This had the effect of at last rousing the King of Tanjore to action, and caused him to send a force of 1,500 horse at once to Tirukáttupalli to attack the Mysore army. The Mahratta general, Morari Rau, who was then at Pichándárkóvil, having withdrawn from Srírangam in consequence of a dispute that he had had with the Mysore regent, conceived that an attack on this detachment would render the King of Tanjore, already terrified by the incursions made into his kingdom by the Mysore troops and the French, willing to purchase his retreat from the country. He accordingly fell on the troops and completely defeated them, killing all except about 300 who managed to escape. On accomplishing this exploit, he wrote to the Nawáb and offered to return to his own kingdom and never bear arms again against either the English or the King of Tanjore, if he would give security for the due payment to him of Rupees 3,00,000. As Muhammad Ali was as usual in want of funds, he applied to the Tanjore king, and the Mahratta chief's terms having been eventually agreed to, he left the Karnatic with all his followers in July 1754.

Unsuccessful attempt of the besieging army to intercept a convoy under Lawrence.

The English detachment under Major Lawrence was still delayed at Tanjore, owing to the difficulties experienced in inducing the Tanjore general Monakji to join them with his cavalry. They at last started on the 16th of August, and, entering the plain to the south of Trichinopoly about a mile to the south of Erumbísvaram, attempted to pass between the Sugar-loaf rock and the French rock. The army in Srírangam, having been informed of their approach, marched to the five rocks to oppose them. They however completely failed in their attempt, and, after

CHAP. VIII.
POLITICAL HISTORY, PART III.

a sharp skirmish in which the English got the better of their adversaries, Lawrence reached Trichinopoly in safety. On his arrival he at once determined to drive the enemy from the plain to the south of the city, so as to enable the garrison to get supplies from Tanjore and Pudukóttai without hindrance. He accordingly advanced to the Fakir's rock, hoping to induce the French to fight. This, however, they would not do, but retreated to Muttarasanellúr, opposite the west end of the Srírangam island. Finding that they appeared determined to hold this position, Lawrence advanced to attack them there, and took up his camp in the pagoda in Uraiyúr. The French had inundated the fields on each side of their camp, they had the Cauvery in their rear, and had flung up an embankment, on which they had mounted several pieces of cannon in their front. M. Maissin who commanded, however, had not the firmness to hold the place, and retreated to Srírangam. On this the English took possession of the post abandoned by them, and the Tanjore horse under Monakji at the same time recaptured Erumbísvaram. As the rainy season had not set in, the English went into winter quarters in Uraiyúr.

Provisional treaty concluded between the English and French.

In September hostilities between the English and French were suspended, and on the 31st of December a provisional[11] treaty was concluded, which was not to be considered, definitive until confirmed in Europe. It was, however, decided that, until news was received in India of the answers made in Europe concerning the treaty, there should be a truce between the two nations and their respective allies, and that during the truce neither party should procure any new grant or cession of land or build any new forts. On the terms of this treaty being made known, the Mysore regent declared that, as he was not a party to it, he was not bound by its conditions, and that he was determined not to leave Srírangam without taking Trichinopoly. As the English, however, were not apprehensive of any attack that he might make on them unassisted by the French, at the request of the Nawáb, they sent a detachment in February 1755 under Colonel Heron to reduce the provinces of Madura and Tinnevelly to obedience to him. Into the results of this expedition it is, however, not necessary to enter, as they do not concern the Trichinopoly District.

The Mysore regent remained with his army in Srírangam, and occupied himself with schemes to get possession of Trichinopoly, without however making any progress towards the attainment of his object. In April he received intelligence that the Nizam Salabat Jung, assisted by French troops, was about to march to Mysore, and demand payment of the tribute which had not been

(11) *Treaties, Engagements and Sunnuds relating to India and neighbouring Countries,* compiled by C. U. AITCHISON, Vol. V, page 185.

CHAP. VIII. POLITICAL HISTORY, PART III.

paid since the date of Nizam-úl-Mulk. Alarmed at this intelligence, Nandiraz broke up his camp and returned in haste to his own country, leaving the French in possession of the island of Srírangam and the other lands which had been made over to him by the Nawáb. On hearing of the approach of the Nizam to the Karnatic, the Government of Madras sent orders to Colonel Heron to return with the troops under his command without delay to Trichinopoly, which he accordingly did in June, taking up his camp in the pagoda in Uraiyúr.

CHAPTER IX.

POLITICAL HISTORY OF TRICHINOPOLY, PART IV.

(FROM THE TREATY BETWEEN THE FRENCH AND ENGLISH IN 1754 TILL THE ACQUISITION OF THE DISTRICT BY THE ENGLISH IN 1801.)

Disturbances in Madura and Tinnevelly.—The French under M. D'Auteuil advance through Ariyalúr and Udaiyárpálayam to Sríraṅgam.—Calliaud marches from Madura to reinforce the garrison in Trichinopoly.—The French abandon Sríraṅgam.—Calliaud determines to depose the Chieftain of Turaiyúr.—Capture of Turaiyúr by Captain Smith.—The French again march towards Sríraṅgam, but retreat in consequence of their defeat at Wandiwash.—Capture of Karúr by Captain Smith.—Lally surrenders Pondicherry.—Treaty of Paris.—The Nizam and the English join against Hyder.—Hyder devastates Trichinopoly and Tanjore and marches to within a few miles of Madras.—Treaty between the English and Hyder.—Renewal of the war.—Hyder lays waste the Karnatic.—Account of his raid on Trichinopoly.—Death of Hyder.—Tippu Sahib threatens Trichinopoly.—Death of Muhammad Ali.—Discovery of treasonary correspondence between the Nawáb and Tippu Sahib.—The English assume the government of the Karnatic.—Mr. Wallace appointed the first Collector of Trichinopoly.

CHAPTER IX. POLITICAL HISTORY, PART IV.

Disturbances in Madura and Tinnevelly.

ON the ratification of the provisional treaty with the French, the Madras Government turned their attention to quelling the disturbances then prevailing in Madura and Tinnevelly. Colonel Heron had rented these two districts some years before to Makhphuz Khán, the Nawáb's elder brother. His administration of the country had, however, been a complete failure, and he was unable either to pay the Company the annual rent of the territories leased out to him, or to prevent their being plundered by the poligars. He had also failed to pay the arrears due to the sepoys left him to keep the country in order, and had consequently lost all authority over their officers, or jemadárs as they were called. In April 1756 Muhammad Yusuf was sent to Madura to introduce some order into the government of the country. From thence he marched into the Tinnevelly District with Makhphuz Khán, whom he attempted to persuade to leave the country with his troops. Makhphuz appeared to comply with this request, and went as far as Madura. No sooner, however, had he arrived there, than the jemadárs, no doubt with his connivance, revolted, and, taking possession of the city, issued invitations to all the neighbouring poligars to join them.

CHAPTER IX.
POLITICAL HISTORY, PART IV.

In October Captain Calliaud marched from Trichinopoly as far as Nattam[1] with the intention of retaking Madura, but, before he could get further, intelligence was received at Madras that war had been again declared between France and England, and orders were sent to him not to leave Trichinopoly without express permission. In November attempts were made by Lieutenant Rumbold, on the part of the English Government, to come to terms with the jemadárs, but without any success. The failure of these negotiations caused the Madras Government to entertain serious apprehensions that the French might attempt to insinuate themselves into the councils of the jemadárs, and assist them in their revolt. They accordingly revoked the order that they had sent to Calliaud not to leave Trichinopoly, and gave him permission to employ such means as he might consider necessary to recapture Madura, and to lead the expedition against that city himself. They also despatched a reinforcement to his assistance through Tanjore from Dévikótta. Calliaud accordingly started for Madura in March 1757.

The French under M. D'Auteuil advance through Ariyalúr and Udaiyárpálayam to Srírangam.

In April 1757 the Madras Government were obliged to send a detachment to Nellore under Colonel Forde, to assist the Nawáb in reducing his brother, the governor of that place, to obedience. The French Government had up to this determined to keep aloof from offensive operations against the English, pending the arrival of a large armament that they were expecting; but, when they saw the English separating their forces by attacking two places so far apart as Nellore and Madura, they conceived that the time for action had arrived. They accordingly sent a detachment of 200 Europeans and 2,000 sepoys under the command of M. D'Auteuil, with the view of invading the territories occupied by the English. D'Auteuil captured Chedambaram, and from that marched direct to Udaiyárpálayam.[2] Two years before this, shortly after the suspension of hostilities between the English and the French, the latter had sent a small detachment against the poligars of Ariyalúr and Udaiyárpálayam to force them to pay tribute. On that occasion, however, they were unsuccessful in their attempt, as the English Government ordered Captain Calliaud to march from Trichinopoly, and attack them if they persisted in their endeavour; on which the Government of Pondicherry recalled their troops. D'Auteuil now determined to make another attempt to levy a contribution from the poligar of Udaiyárpálayam. He attempted to gain time by discussion, whereupon the French attacked his fort, but were repulsed with some loss. In order to avoid a repetition of the attack, the poligar

(1) In the Mélúr Taluq of the Madura District.
(2) Called Warriorepollam in the account given by Orme of these transactions.

Calliaud marches from Madura to reinforce the garrison in Trichinopoly.

agreed to pay Rupees 40,000, taking however time to collect the money. The Pondicherry Government sent every man they could spare to reinforce M. D'Auteuil, who had moved on to Ariyalúr, and, on arrival of the reinforcement, set out at once for Srírangam with a force of 1,000 Europeans and 3,000 sepoys. On the 14th of May he joined the French garrison in the island, and fixed his camp in the pagoda of Uraiyúr. Captain Joseph Smith had expected the arrival of the French, and had done everything in his power to guard against it, by filling the fort ditch with water and repairing the ramparts. He also applied for assistance to the Rájah of Tanjore and the Tondiman, who between them sent him 600 men. The only troops, however, that he had on whom he could rely were 150 Europeans and 700 sepoys of the Company's service, and with this small force he had to protect the entire walls of the city, which were 6,400 yards in extent, besides guarding 500 French prisoners. Immediately on the arrival of the French, Captain Smith sent off to inform Captain Calliaud, who was then at Madura, of the danger in which Trichinopoly was. On receiving this intelligence, Calliaud started at once for Trichinopoly with 120 Europeans and 1,200 sepoys, leaving the rest of the troops under the command of Lieutenant Rumbold and Muhammad Yusuf, to treat with the jemadárs.

On his arrival at Iluppúr,[3] nineteen miles from Trichinopoly, Calliaud received intelligence from Captain Smith that D'Auteuil, on hearing of his approach, had quitted the station that he had occupied up to this in the pagodas of Uraiyúr, and drawn up his troops in a line extending from the Fakir's tope, round the five rocks and the Fakir's and Golden rocks, up to the French rock, by which all access to the city from the south was precluded. The troops marched from Iluppúr at two in the afternoon of the day that they had reached that village, and at six arrived at Ávúr,[4] about twelve miles from Trichinopoly, where they stopped for half an hour. From this Calliaud advanced, as if he intended to come out upon the plain, between the five rocks and the Sugar-loaf, opposite to the middle of the enemy's line. Some French spies who had accompanied the camp, confident that they now knew the route that the relieving force intended to take, escaped, bearing the intelligence to D'Auteuil. Their departure was however observed, and, as soon as they were gone, Calliaud entirely

---

(3) Eliapore in Orme. This village is situated in the extreme south of the Trichinopoly District, and separated from the rest of the taluq of that name by a portion of the Pudukóttai territory.

(4) A village about three miles from Iluppúr on the road from Trichinopoly to Pudukóttai. It was well known afterwards as one of the principal outstations of the Jesuits of the Madura Mission.

CHAPTER IX. POLITICAL HISTORY, PART IV.

changed his route and turned to the east, along the confines of the Pudukóttai woods, till he got opposite to Erumbvísaram.

The French abandon Sríraṅgam.

From this place he had to march through seven miles of rice-fields up to Trichinopoly, which he reached at dawn on the following morning. As soon as D'Auteuil discovered that his opponents had outwitted him, and that the garrison in the city had been reinforced, he recrossed the Cauvery with his whole army into the island of Sríraṅgam, and on the next day passed the Coleroon and retreated towards Pondicherry.

On the retreat of the French, Calliaud returned to Madura. In the following October, however, he received intelligence of the arrival of the French squadron that had been expected from Europe, and, leaving Muhammad Yusuf to defend Madura, which had been captured by him in August, and, if possible, recover Tinnevelly, he started at once for Trichinopoly with all the European troops that he had under his command. He was afterwards obliged, under orders received from Madras, to direct Muhammad Yusuf to follow him to Trichinopoly, and that officer accordingly marched there with the 1,000 sepoys that he had under his command. As however intelligence was received shortly after this that Hyder Ali had arrived at Dindigul, and as the commencement of the monsoon relieved the garrison in Trichinopoly from all apprehensions of an immediate attack on the part of the French, Muhammad Yusuf was directed to return to Madura.

In May 1758, with a view of strengthening the army with which he was then engaged in besieging Fort St. David, Lally recalled the French soldiers from Sríraṅgam, handing the island over to a detachment of Mysore troops from Dindigul under Hyder Ali's brother. The day after the French left, Calliaud sent Captain Smith to take possession of Jembukésvaram. The Mysore army commenced to fire on the party, but, as their cannon were answered with effect from Jembukésvaram, they abandoned Sríraṅgam and retreated to Dindigul. On this Calliaud took possession of the pagoda at once, garrisoning it with 500 sepoys. On the capitulation of Fort St. David in June, the French sent a small detachment against Dévikóttai. On its approach, the garrison in that fort abandoned it and repaired to Trichinopoly. The English being now apprehensive that, after their great success at Fort St. David, the French would attack Madras, removed their garrison from the greater nnmber of the forts held by them,, but determined not to abandon Trichinopoly till the last extremity. They, however, ordered Muhammad Yusuf to leave Palamcottah and march to Madura, where he was to hold himself in readiness to return to Trichinopoly on the first summons from Captain Calliaud. In June Lally, with

CHAPTER IX. POLITICAL HISTORY, PART IV.

a view of replenishing his coffers, despatched an army against the King of Tanjore and laid siege to his capital. The best portion of the sepoys in the Trichinopoly garrison were sent to his assistance, and the attempt of the French to capture the city was a complete failure.

Calliaud determines to depose the chieftain of Turaiyúr.

As on the retreat of the French from Tanjore, there was no longer any immediate dread of an attack being made by them on Trichinopoly, Captain Calliaud took the opportunity to strengthen his position by deposing the existing holder of the petty chieftainship of Turaiyúr, who had been set up by the French in the place of his cousin, whom they had expelled. The cause of the exiled chief was espoused by the poligars of Ariyalúr and Udaiyárpálayam, and, as these petty chieftains had always been firm in their opposition to the French, Captain Calliaud considered that it would be good policy to gratify them by reinstating him. He accordingly despatched a force of twenty Europeans under Captain Joseph Smith, and a large body of sepoys under Muhammad Yusuf, with this object. Turaiyúr was captured after some spirited skirmishing in the woods which then surrounded the village.[5] The expelled Reddi was reinstated and five companies of sepoys were left to protect him.

Capture of Turaiyúr by Captain Smith.

After the fall of Fort St. David the French under Lally captured a considerable number of the outlying forts held by the English and the Nawáb, and the Government of Madras were apprehensive that Chingleput would be attacked. They accordingly determined to recall Calliaud with all the English troops under him from Trichinopoly. He marched from the city in September, leaving the command of it to Captain Smith, with a few Europeans, most of them invalids, and a force of 2,000 sepoys, who had returned with Muhammad Yusuf from Tinnevelly. These latter, however, were in November ordered to march to the relief of Fort St. George, then besieged by the French. By their departure the garrison in Trichinopoly was so much reduced, that it was found necessary to withdraw three out of the five companies of sepoys that had been left in Turaiyúr. The exiled chief, who had gathered together a small body of men disaffected to his successor on the confines of the Mysore territory, from whence he had made several marauding expeditions into the country about Úttattúr, seized the opportunity to make an attempt to regain possession of Turaiyúr. His attack on the town was completely successful, and his rival was again expelled. On regaining his chieftainship, he professed allegiance to the Nawáb, and promised to pay him a considerable sum of money. His offer was accepted, and he was confirmed in his government.

(5) ORME, Vol. II, pages 337 340.

CHAPTER IX. POLITICAL HISTORY, PART IV.

The French again march towards Srírangam, but retreat in consequence of their defeat at Wandiwash.

In July 1759 the important fortress of Thiagar, which commanded the road through Válikandapuram to Trichinopoly, was taken by a detachment of French troops, notwithstanding that Captain Smith had sent a small force from Trichinopoly to the relief of the place. After the capture of Thiagar the French troops marched through Válikandapuram as far as Úttattúr, plundering the country through which they passed. The garrison in Trichinopoly expected that they would occupy Srírangam again, but, on Wandiwash being attacked by the English in September, they were recalled to Pondicherry. In October, however, M. Lally determined to regain the country between Úttattúr and Trichinopoly, and with this object directed a force of 900 European soldiers to assemble at Thiagar. On hearing of their arrival, the advanced guard of the English troops, which was then stationed at Úttattúr, retreated to Pichándárkóvil, on which the French marched at once through Samayapuram, and took possession of the village and pagoda of Mannachanellúr. On being informed of this, Captain Smith, who was still in command at Trichinopoly, sent out a small force to oppose them. This, however, they were unable to do successfully, and the French got possession of the Srírangam pagoda. As soon as the Government of Madras received intelligence of this movement on the part of their opponents, they determined that their entire army should take the field, and Colonel Coote, who was in command, marched at once against Wandiwash. His expedition was successful, and the reverses which the French sustained, first in the capture of Wandiwash, and afterwards in the utter defeat of their army near that village, compelled Lally to withdraw first the greater portion, and eventually the whole of the detatchment from the Srírangam island.

Hyder Ali had at this time acquired complete ascendancy in the Government of Mysore, and Lally determined to treat with him, with a view of obtaining his aid in the dangers which he saw were threatening Pondicherry. An agreement was entered into between them, by which it was arranged that the fort of Thiagar should be permanently ceded to Hyder, who, in return, undertook to assist the French with a force of horse and foot. In consequence of this treaty, a detachment of Hyder's troops arrived at Thiagar in June 1860. Shortly before their arrival, the Mysore forces stationed in Dindigul had commenced hostilities against some of the poligars dependent on Trichinopoly, and it was reported that they designed seizing on the pass of Nattam, [6] and thereby interrupting all communication between Trichinopoly and Madura. In order to prevent their succeeding in this object, Muhammad Yusuf sent a detachment from Tinnevelly to Madura,

(6) In the Mélúr Taluk of the Madura District.

and the Nawáb's troops in Trichinopoly were also directed to assemble at Nattam and guard the pass.

Capture of Karúr by Captain Smith.

As soon as information of the arrival of the Mysore troops at Thiagar was received in Trichinopoly, Captain Smith determined to create a diversion by attacking Hyder's territories to the west of Trichinopoly, which at that time extended as far as Karúr. In an expedition which he led against that fort, he was completely successful, and the Mysore garrison there was compelled to evacuate the place. Shortly after this Hyder was obliged to withdraw all his troops from the Karnatic, and on the 14th of January 1761, Lally surrendered Pondicherry to Colonel Coote. The success of the English armies in Southern India was thus complete, and, by the treaty of Paris, concluded in 1763, Muhammad Ali was recognized as Nawáb of the Karnatic.

Lally surrenders Pondicherry. Treaty of Paris.

The Nizam and the English join against Hyder.

The rapid extension of Hyder Ali's conquests after the treaty of Paris, rendered his power dangerous to the interests of the Government of Madras. Consequently, in a treaty made with the Nizam of Hyderabad in 1766, the English undertook to assist him against Hyder. Before long the Nizam, however, deserted the English and joined Hyder in his attack on the Karnatic. The confederates were defeated in several engagements, and the Nizam in February 1768 formed a new alliance with the English. Hyder, nothing daunted by this desertion, persevered in the contest alone. The fortunes of the combatants were various, but it would be out of place here to give any account of the vicissitudes of the struggle, except when the scene of the combat approached Trichinopoly District.

Hyder devastates Trichinopoly and Tanjore, and marches to within a few miles of Madras.

Towards the close of the year 1768 Fuzzul-ulla-Khán, one of Hyder's generals, was sent by him from Seringapatam to Coimbatore, and captured with ease all the forts in the possession of the English in that portion of the country. Hyder himself, on the 6th of December, marched southward, and attacked such fortresses as had not been already captured by his General. Námakkal, Karúr, Erode and Dindigul fell in rapid succession, and Major Fitzgerald, who had been despatched by Colonel Lang, then commanding the army opposed to Hyder in Mysore, to relieve the besieged towns, although he advanced by rapid marches, was on every occasion too late to do so. As he crossed the Cauvery, he was informed that Hyder had also passed that river near Karúr, and that he intended to leave Fuzzul-ulla to take that place and Erode, and to advance himself, with the main army, to Trichinopoly. As Fitzgerald considered that Erode was safe, and was well aware that Trichinopoly was virtually defenceless, the greater part of the troops in that town having been sent into the Coimbatore District, he marched there at once with a view of defending the place. On hearing of this move, Hyder altered his plans, attacked and took Karúr, and thence marched to besiege Erode. In this attack also

CHAPTER IX. POLITICAL HISTORY, PART IV.

he was successful, and before the close of the year he had recovered all the posts that had been lost in the two previous campaigns. Fuzzul-ulla was now despatched to Dindigul, and directed to invade the Madura and Tinnevelly Districts, and Hyder himself recrossed the Cauvery, marching in an easterly direction along the northern bank of that river. Major Fitzgerald, who had been obliged to detach portions of his army to both Madura and Tinnevelly, to defend those districts, was then at Mannachanellúr, and, being convinced that Hyder was without doubt marching for Madras, he determined to intercept him in his progress, and with that view advanced his army in a northerly direction. As soon, however, as Hyder became aware of this move of his adversary, he changed his course, and marched along the bank of the Coleroon, destroying all the villages that he passed. He levied a contribution of four lakhs of rupees from the Rájah of Tanjore on condition of not devastating his territory, and then retraced his steps through the Trichinopoly District, whence Fitzgerald had been obliged, through want of sufficient supplies for his troops, to retreat to Cuddalore.[7] In March 1769, Hyder marched his cavalry to within a few miles of Madras, and the Government, fearing that the town would be plundered, concluded a treaty with him in the following month, on the footing of mutual restitution of conquests.[8]

Treaty between the English and Hyder.

Renewal of the war. Hyder lays waste the Karnatic.

In 1780 Hyder again declared war on the English, and devastated the Karnatic in that and the following year. The following account of his exploits in the south in 1781 is given by Colonel Fullarton, in his account of the transactions in Southern India during the war:—

"The calamities with which the invasion of Hyder Ali in 1781 overwhelmed the Karnatic, fell heavily upon the southern countries. No sooner had the multitudes under that ravager poured down from the mountains of Mysore, than desolation extended across the Coleroon. Thousands of his plunderers overran the countries of Tanjore, Trichinopoly and Madura. The ground was at that time covered with the most luxuriant crops, which were instantly swept off, and every water-dyke and embankment was destroyed. The inhabitants who escaped the sword sought shelter in the fort, where they added misery to distress, and perished in the streets. The whole country, laid waste by fire and sword, exhibited the sad reality of a general conflagration.

Account of his raid on Trichinopoly.

At length Hyder, having left nothing to destroy in the Karnatic, and regardless of our force, which, from the time of Colonel Baillie's defeat, had never ventured from its encampment near Madras, resolved to lead in person his victorious army to the

(7) WILKS' *History of Mysore*, Vol. I, page 369.

(8) AITCHISON'S *Treaties, &c., relating to India*, Vol. V, page 120.

CHAPTER IX. POLITICAL HISTORY. PART IV.

southward. After remaining some weeks encamped within random shot of Tanjore, he proceeded to invest Trichinopoly, and threatened to fill up the ditch with the slippers of his Muhammadans. The repeated checks sustained by the Company's troops in that quarter, the corps that Hyder had cut off, and the forts he had reduced, spread a general consternation. The important and defenceless garrison of Trichinopoly seemed ready to surrender, and in that event, the southern countries must have fallen before him, had not the repulse of Sir Eyre Coote's army at Chedambaram elated Hyder with the hopes of defeating the only force that could endanger his conquest."[9] He advanced against Coote, and was completely defeated at the battle of Porto-Novo on the 1st of July 1781.

Notwithstanding Hyder's defeat, the English affairs in the south continued to be in the greatest confusion. Indeed if it had not been for the efforts of Mr. J. Sullivan, who was at that time Resident of Tanjore and Superintendent of the Assigned Revenues[10] of Trichinopoly, no order whatever could have been maintained. Hyder died in 1782, and on his death Tippu was obliged to leave the Karnatic. Colonel Fullarton, who was now in command in the south, had been directed to augment the army under his command with detachments of the troops in Tanjore, Trichinopoly and Tinnevelly. He arrived in Trichinopoly in June 1783, and, having obtained supplies of grain and ammunition there, recrossed the Cauvery and Coleroon, and took up his position at Mannachanellúr. From there he was about to march to Turaiyúr, to restore the Reddi chieftain who had been set up there by the English, and had been again turned out. Intimation, however, having reached him that an armistice had been concluded with Tippu, he was obliged to abandon this idea, and retraced his steps southwards. He then undertook an expedition against the poligars of Madura and Tinnevelly, who were then in revolt, and successfully reduced them to order. The only other event in these wars that affected Trichinopoly, took place in 1790, when Tippu marched through Karúr to that city, followed by Colonel Meadows. He made several demonstrations against the town, and laid waste the island of Srírangam, but did nothing more, and soon afterwards was obliged to leave the country.[11]

Death of Hyder.

Tippu Sahib threatens Trichinopoly.

As has already been stated, Muhammad Ali had been recognized as Nawáb of the Karnatic by the treaty of Paris in 1763. He

Death of Muhammad Ali.

(9) *A View of the English Interests in India, and an Account of the Military Operations in the southern parts of the Peninsula during* 1782–84, by WILLIAM FULLARTON, M.P., late Commander of the Southern Army on the Coast of the Coromandel, (recently printed by order of the Madras Government).

(10) By a treaty, concluded between the Nawáb and the English in December 1781, the revenues of the Karnatic had been transferred to the British Government for five years, the Nawáb receiving one-sixth of them for his private expenses.

(11) WILKS, Vol. II, page 176.

CHAPTER IX. POLITICAL HISTORY, PART IV.

had, however, contracted large debts to the English during the war, and, in consideration of these, and of the services that they had rendered him, he conferred on them certain districts, yielding an annual revenue of over four and a half lakhs of pagodas. The war with Hyder had involved the Madras Government in great pecuniary difficulties, and they therefore applied to the Nawáb for assistance. He however appealed to a treaty concluded in 1781 with the Bengal Government, by which he had been exempted from all pecuniary demands beyond the expense of maintaining ten battalions. The Government of Madras remonstrated against this treaty, and it was at length decided in December 1781, that the revenues of the Karnatic should be transferred to the British Government for five years, the Nawáb receiving one-sixth for his private expenses. The Nawáb did his best to be relieved from this agreement, and, after various treaties and engagements, it was eventually decided by the treaty of 1792, among other stipulations, that the English Government should maintain a force, for the payment of which the Nawáb should contribute nine lakhs of pagodas a year; that the country should be governed by English troops; that the English Government should collect the tribute of the poligars in the Nawáb's name, giving him credit for it in his contribution; and that, on failure of payment, the English Government should assume the management of certain districts.

Discovery of the treasonable correspondence between the Nawáb and Tippu Sahib.

Muhammad Ali died in 1795, and was succeeded by his son Umdut-úl-Umrah. The treaty of 1792 was found to have the most injurious effects. The subsidy was indeed regularly paid, but to meet his liabilities the Nawáb contracted heavy loans, and to liquidate them, assigned the revenues of his country to his creditors. On the capture of Seringapatam in 1799, a treasonable correspondence was discovered between Muhammad Ali and his son and Tippu, and, on inquiry being made into the matter, the guilt of the Nawáb was completely proved. The British Government declared itself released from the treaty of 1792, which had been thus violated, and resolved to assume the government of the Karnatic, making a provision for the Nawáb's family. Umdut-úl-Umrah died before the arrangements were concluded, and his reputed son, Ali Hossein, refused to agree to them. Negotiations were therefore opened with the nephew of the late Nawáb, Azim-úl-Dowlah, by whom the terms offered by the English were accepted. An engagement was accordingly made with him on the 31st of July 1801, by which he renounced the civil and military government of the Karnatic, and received a pension.[12] Among the territories transferred to the English by this measure, was the district of Trichinopoly, to which Mr. John Wallace was accordingly appointed as the first Collector in August 1801.

The English assume the government of the Karnatic.

Mr. Wallace appointed the first collector of Trichinopoly.

(12) AITCHISON's *Treaties, &c.*, Vol. V, pages 197–256.

CHAPTER X.

REVENUE HISTORY OF TRICHINOPOLY, PART I.

(FROM THE ACQUISITION OF THE DISTRICT BY THE ENGLISH TILL THE INTRODUCTION OF THE REVISED SETTLEMENT.)

Revenue system under the Nawáb's government.—System introduced by Mr. Wallace, the first Collector.—Fasli 1212 unfavorable.—Changes made in that year.—Fasli 1213 favourable.—Classification of soils introduced in that year.—Trichinopoly made a sub-division of Tanjore.—Mannárgudi and Chellambram Taluqs transferred to South Arcot.—Survey of the unirrigated taluqs.—Trichinopoly separated from Tanjore.—The ryots complain of the commutation prices of grain.—Disastrous floods in 1809.—Irrigated villages leased for three years in Fasli 1219.—Irrigated portions of district leased out for ten years in Fasli 1223.—Further alteration in the commutation prices of grain. —Abolition of Úttattúr and Kurumbalúr Taluqs and formation of Válikandapuram Taluq.—Great floods in Faslis 1228 and 1229.—Reduction of assessment in the wet taluqs.—Improvements in the Revenue system introduced by Mr. Dickinson when Collector.—Abolition of the "Pattukattu" system.—Alterations in the manner of making the annual settlement.—Reduction of the rates of assessment in the dry taluqs.—Account given by Mr. Puckle of the Revenue system in force previous to the introduction of the Revised Settlement.

CHAPTER X. REVENUE HISTORY, PART I.

WHEN Trichinopoly was taken possession of by the English in 1801, the district comprised the whole of its present extent, with the exception of the Manapparai division of Kulittalai Taluq, which was transferred from Madura in 1856, and the Káttuputtúr mittah in Musiri Taluq, which, till 1851, formed a portion of Salem. It also comprised the old taluqs of Mannárgudi and Chellambram, which form the present taluq of Chellambram in South Arcot, and were handed over to that district in Fasli 1215 (1805-6).

Revenue system under the Nawáb's government.

A full account of the condition of the country during the latter years of the Nawáb's government is given in Mr. Wallace's Settlement Report for Fasli 1211 (1801-1802). When the first Collector arrived in the district, he found that the whole of it, with the exception of the tracts afterwards known as the Ariyalúr, Udaiyárpálayam, Válikandapuram, Chellambram and Mannárgudi Taluqs, had been farmed out to Hussain-úl-Mulk, the brother of the Nawáb. The remainder was rented out to two Hindus named Paupayer and Chinniya Mudali. The real governor of the country however was Arunáchalla Pillai, Hussain-úl-Mulk's manager. Mr. Wallace states that this man, originally employed as a writer in Trichinopoly, owed his advancement from this post to being the uncontrolled ruler

CHAPTER X. REVENUE HISTORY, PART I.

of the province, "not less to a minute knowledge of every village in it, than to an unprincipled spirit of intrigue, and to those qualities which are so particularly required in native management, implicit obedience to the mandates of his employer, alacrity in projecting bad measures, and unrelenting cruelty in executing them."

Under the Nawáb's government, the revenue had been collected in the irrigated taluqs by a division of the produce with the ryots. As a general rule, the crops were equally divided between the Government and the cultivators, after a deduction of five per cent. of the gross produce had been made for reaping expenses. This was the ordinary rate of division (*váram*), but in lands irrigated from tanks and also in those which, from their position, were liable to have the crops damaged by inundations, the ryots were allowed to take 55 to 58 per cent. of the gross produce. In newly formed wet lands the cultivator's share (*kudiváram*) was 60 per cent., and in those irrigated by picottahs and other mechanical contrivances, it varied from 65 to 68¾ per cent. The allowances (*sutantrams*) paid to the village artificers, karnams, watchers, cultivating slaves (*Pallars*), and others varied from 23 to 28 per cent. of the gross produce, and were paid by the inhabitants alone out of their share.

In the dry portions of the country, the revenues were collected in some villages according to the sorts of grains cultivated, while in others the assessment varied according to the nature of the soil. The demands were, however, made in a most arbitrary manner, and were invariably increased if the outturn of the crops happened to be better than usual. The collections in these villages were made in money and not in kind, as in the wet villages.

The sale of grain was a strict monopoly, the price being fixed by the manager. All importation was forbidden, and it was an offence, punishable by exorbitant fines, even to lend a neighbour such small quantities of grain as he might require for his immediate support. The grain was taken from the cultivators at the rate of 7 and 8 fanams[1] per kalam,[2] and sold back to them from Government granaries kept up in different parts of the district, at 9 and 10 fanams per kalam.

In some remarks that he makes on the system of government prevailing in Trichinopoly before the English got possession of the country, Mr. Wallace remarks that, under the system then in force, the people never knew when the demands on them would cease. The so-called fixed assessments seemed to have been imposed merely with the view of inducing the ryots to cultivate, in the hope that nothing beyond the settled amount in money or grain would be exacted

(1) There were 30 fanams to the pagoda, so that 1 fanam equalled 1 Anna 10½ Pies of our present currency.

(2) The kalam contained 39 measures o 100 cubic inches.

from them. In this hope they were, however, invariably disappointed, and he asserts that, if any one year the revenues were actually collected according to the fixed rates, this was done merely with the view of inducing the ryots, by this apparent moderation, to increase the extent of their cultivation in the succeeding year, and thus give the managers or their sub-renters an opportunity of doubling their exactions.[3]

System introduced by Mr. Wallace, the first Collector.

In framing a scheme of settlement for the district for the first fasli that it was under English management, Mr. Wallace first of all commuted the payments in kind in the irrigated villages into a money rate. To this change the ryots, he states, expressed extreme aversion, their main objection to it being that they were afraid that they would find great difficulty in disposing of the amount of grain which would be thrown on their hands as soon as the new system was introduced. In answering this objection, Mr. Wallace acknowledged that he was well aware that the district produced more grain that the inhabitants could consume, but stated that he felt no doubt that no difficulty would be found in exporting it as soon as the monopoly was done away with.[4]

As soon as the payments in kind had been commuted into a money rent, an account was prepared, showing the extent of land cultivated in each village, the necessary information being obtained from the villagers themselves. An average of the gross produce for five years was taken as the basis of the settlement, and with the exception of cases where, from peculiar causes, a larger share had previously been allowed to the ryots, an equal division of the crops between the Government and the villagers was determined on. In fixing the price for which the ryots should purchase back the Government share of the gross produce, the Collector met with considerable difficulty, as a free sale of grain had never been allowed in the district, except during the short period for which the management of it had been assumed by the Company during the war with Hyder Ali. He was therefore obliged to refer to the prices prevailing in neighbouring districts, from a consideration of which the commutation price of the several grains was eventually fixed at the following rates, in the several wet taluqs, for a kalam of 12 mercals.[5]

(3) Jamabandi Report for Fasli 1211, paragraph 157.

(4) Jamabandi Report for Fasli 1211, paragraphs 181–184.

(5) The mercal originally contained 128 pollams, or the weight of 312 Arcot doodies, of one-year-old horse-gram. Subsequently Mr. Wallace raised its capacity to 130, and eventually to 133 pollams.—*Appendix A to Mr. Puckle's Report as Deputy Director of Revenue Settlement, dated 28th October 1860.*

CHAPTER X. REVENUE HISTORY, PART I.

Grains.	Kónád.	Vettukatti.	Aylúr.	Lálgudi.
Kár[6]	9 Fanams.	7 Fanams.	7 Fanams.	7 Fanams.
Pishánam	9¼ ,,	7⅜ ,,	7½ ,,	8 ,,
Válán	6⅜ ,,	6 ,,	6 ,,	6½ ,,

The settlement for Fasli 1211 was made by Mr. Wallace with each village separately, the principles on which it was based being explained by him in person to the ryots. At the same time, an inquiry was made as to the cultivation carried on in each village, with the view of ascertaining how the settlement that had just been introduced would work in particular instances, and relaxing or increasing the demands made on the ryots accordingly. Mr. Wallace's settlement made no change in the rates of assessment charged on dry lands, and, as far as possible, none of the established local usages in revenue matters were altered by him.[7]

Fasli 1212 unfavourable.

The following fasli (1212 or A.D. 1802-3) was an unfavourable one. Notwithstanding that more land was brought under the plough than had ever been cultivated previously, yet the want of rain, and the late date at which the freshes came down the Cauvery, rendered the exertions of the ryots of little or no avail, and both the wet and dry crops were to a great extent lost. In spite of the unfavourable nature of the season, there was, however, a considerable increase in this year both in the extent of land cultivated and in the revenue. This, Mr. Wallace states, was due to a large number of the ryots who had left the country when it was under the Nawáb's government, having returned to it again when it came under English rule. He remarks that since 1796, the district had become greatly depopulated owing to the constant disturbance, created by the leading poligars, and the vexatious and oppressive government of the Nawáb's agent, which had driven numbers of the people to take refuge in the neighbouring districts.[8]

Changes made in that year.

In his report for this fasli, Mr. Wallace divides the district into taluqs in the following manner: Western Division, comprising Aylúr, Vettukatti, Lálgudi and Kónád; Northern Division, Turaiyúr, Válikandapuram, Úttattúr and Kurumbalúr; and Eastern Division, Mannárgudi, Chellambram and Srímustam. In this year

(6) Kár is an inferior description of paddy, consumed as a rule by the lower classes.

Pishánam, more generally known as Samba, is a better sort of paddy, used by the middle and higher classes. It is, as a rule, a six months' crop.

Válán (derived from *vál*, a tail) is a bearded description of paddy, eaten principally by the labouring classes.

(7) Jamabandi Report for Fasli 1211, paragraph 207.

(8) Jamabandi Report for Fasli 1212, paragraph 26.

the lands in the wet taluqs were measured. As, however, the measurement was made entirely by the village karnams, and was not checked by properly trained surveyors, it was almost useless.[9] A change was also made in the commutation price of grain, the following rates being fixed for the four wet taluqs :—

Grains.	Rate per Kalam.
Kár	$8\frac{1}{2}$ Fanams.
Pishánam	$9\frac{1}{2}$,,
Válán	7 ,,

Fasli 1213 favourable.

The following season (Fasli 1213, A.D. 1803-4) was a much more favourable one. The crops under the lands irrigated by the Cauvery and Coleroon were universally abundant, while the yield on the dry lands was fair. In his settlement for this year, Mr. Wallace gives the following figures to show the extent to which the revenue of the province had increased since it came under English rule.

Fasli.	Revenue.
1210	490,171 Star Pagodas.
1211	505,660 ,,
1212	525,648 ,,
1213	561,926 ,,

He states that although the revenue had increased, yet material relief had been given to the people. The commutation price of grain had been lowered, the rates of assessment in the upland taluqs reduced, the revenue paid by each ryot accurately defined, and every possible step taken to inspire confidence and encourage industry. He adds that existing channels, tanks and sluices had been repaired and new ones constructed.[10]

Classification of soils introduced in that year.

In Fasli 1213 an attempt was for the first time made to classify the soils in the district. The following scale was adopted in the irrigated villages :—

Soils yielding 45 kalams and upwards per cawni, Karasal (black), 1st sort.

Do.	40 to 45 kalams	do.	do.	(black), 2nd sort.
Do.	35 to 40 do.	do.		Sheval (red), 1st sort.
Do.	30 to 35 do.	do.		do. (red), 2nd sort.
Do.	25 to 30 do.	do.		Manal (sand), 1st sort.
Do.	20 to 25 do.	do.	do.	(sand), 2nd sort.
Do.	10 to 20 do.	do.		Kalar (soda soil), 1st sort.
Do.	5 to 10 do.	do.	do.	(soda soil), 2nd sort.

(9) Paragraph 11 of Settlement Report by Mr. Dickinson for Fasli 1236.
(10) Settlement Report for Fasli 1213, paragraphs 85 and 86.

CHAPTER X. REVENUE HISTORY, PART I.

The dry lands were divided into five descriptions, namely, (1) Karasal, (2) Padugai (river deposit), (3) Sheval, (4) Manal, and (5) Kalar; each class was divided into two sorts, and the rates of assessment for each class and sort were then fixed.[11]

In the same year the commutation price of grain was again altered, and the following rates introduced :—

Grains.	Aylúr and Vettukatti Rate per Kalam.	Kónád and Lálgudi Rate per Kalam.
	Fanams.	Fanams.
Kár	8	$8\frac{1}{2}$
Pishánam	9	9
Válán	7	7

In April 1804 Mr. Wallace was appointed as a commissioner to inquire into the state of affairs in Tanjore; and Mr. Kinloch, who had been Head Assistant Collector in the district since the English had taken possession of it, was directed to perform the duties of Collector of Trichinopoly during the absence of the permanent incumbent.

From Mr. Kinloch's Settlement Report for Fasli 1214 (1804-5) we learn that the year was by no means a favourable one. The freshes down the Cauvery were late, the tanks were insufficiently supplied, and the rainfall was deficient.

Trichinopoly made a sub-division of Tanjore. Mannárgudi and Chellambram Taluqs transferred to South Arcot.

In June 1805 the Trichinopoly District was made a sub-division of Tanjore, and placed under the management of the principal Collector of that district, who was at that time Mr. Wallace, the first Collector of Trichinopoly. Mr. Young was appointed Sub-Collector, in immediate charge of the district. In the same year the Mannárgudi and Chellambram Taluqs were transferred to South Arcot.

Survey of the unirrigated taluqs.

In Fasli 1215 (1805-6) the karnams were again directed to measure the lands in their villages, and to bring to account all excess cultivation. They were also ordered to classify the several fields according to the system that had been adopted in the previous year.[12]

In Fasli 1216 (1806-7) the dry taluqs in the district were surveyed, principally with the view of having the fields measured according to a rod of 24 English feet, and not of 21 feet, as had been done up to that time. In his Settlement Report for Fasli

(11) Settlement Report for Fasli 1214, and paragraph 13 of Report for 1236.
(12) Settlement Report for Fasli 1236, paragraph 13.

CHAPTER X. REVENUE HISTORY, PART I.

1236 (1836-37), Mr. Lushington states that the only effect of this second survey was to create confusion, because, while the accounts in the Collector's office were kept according to it, in the villages the old measurements continued to be adhered to. As regards the survey of the wet villages, which, as has been already stated, was made in Fasli 1212 (1812-13), Mr. Lushington remarks that he looked upon it as utterly untrustworthy. He had ascertained that in some villages the karnams, who, it must be remembered, were the sole surveyors, in order to favour the ryots, did not bring the total extent cultivated to account ; while in others, with a view of carrying favour with the district authorities, they entered a larger extent of land than there really was.[13]

While on this subject, it may be as well to remark that Mr. Puckle was of opinion that the old survey (*pymaish*) was of no great value, as the system of measuring and numbering the fields differed in nearly every taluq. In some the survey measurements were calculated according to a rod of 24 English feet, while in reality the actual measurements of the fields were taken according to the human foot. In some instances the fields were numbered consecutively, in others a series of numbers were allotted to the several descriptions of wet, dry, and garden land, while in some the survey numbers were altogether disregarded by the karnams.[14]

Trichinopoly separated from Tanjore.

In August 1808 Trichinopoly was again separated from Tanjore, and formed into a separate district, Mr. G. Garrow being appointed Collector. He, however, did not remain long in charge of the district, as he was removed in June 1809. He was succeeded in October 1809 by Mr. G. F. Travers, the district having been in the meantime in the charge of the Head Assistant Collector, Mr. R. H. Young.

The ryots complain of the commutation prices of grain.

Up to Fasli 1218 (1808-9) the average market price of grain in the district had been above the commutation rates fixed by Mr. Wallace. In that year, however, it fell so considerably, that the cultivators found the greatest difficulty in disposing of their surplus produce. The result was, that the ryots began to clamour against the system of ready-money payments, in which they had up to this quietly acquiesced. The mirasidárs of seventy-one villages refused to accede to the terms of the existing rent, complaining that the produce of their land had been estimated at far too high a standard, while the rate at which they had to dispose of their surplus grain was one, or in some cases two, fanams below the commutation rates.[15] In no part of the district were the complaints

(13) Settlement Report for Fasli 1236, paragraphs 26 and 60.

(14) Paragraph 12 of Appendix A attached to Report as Deputy Director of Revenue Settlement, dated 28th October 1860.

(15) Settlement Report for Fasli 1218.

CHAPTER X. REVENUE HISTORY, PART I.

louder than in the Lálgudi Division, and, as Mr. Travers considered that there could be no doubt that the landholders in that part were hardly treated, in being obliged to pay a higher commutation rate than that imposed in Aylúr and Vettukatti, he reduced the rate paid by them by half a fanam.[16]

In this year it was discovered that the classification of the soils in the district was most inaccurate, and that consequently the rates of assessment had been calculated on wrong data. This discovery necessitated so many alterations and amendments in the rates, and the fields were so often changed from one class to another, that Mr. Dickinson, writing in 1827, states that the result was that but few traces of the original classification were left.[17]

Disastrous floods in 1809

In December 1809, owing to extraordinary high freshes, the Cauvery and Coleroon burst their banks and flooded the whole country. In consequence of the disputes that they had had with the Government as to commutation prices, the ryots had left large quantities of their grain stacked in the fields, and the result was that the damage caused by the flood was greater than it would have been in an ordinary year, and large quantities of grain were destroyed. Mr. Travers states that the country was covered with water as far as the eye could reach, and that even high-lying fields were submerged. The Uyyakondán channel burst in several places, and it was only with the greatest difficulty that it was repaired.[18] The troubles experienced by the Collector in making his annual settlement with the ryots, were even greater in this fasli than in the previous one, and we find him complaining, in a letter to the District Magistrate, that a number of the leading inhabitants had placed themselves under the protection of that officer, and refused to attend the Collector's office when summoned there for annual settlement.

Irrigated villages leased for three years in Fasli 1219.

In this fasli (1219) the irrigated villages were leased out for a term of three years. The Bráhman landholders, who owned their greater portion of the lands in these villages, refused at first to take up the leases, and did their best to thwart the Collector in every way. Mr. Travers then attempted to get strangers to take the leases, but with no success, as all the Bráhmans were in league against the new-comers, and had it in their power to ruin them by leaving their fields uncultivated. At last, however, he was able, by promises of remission of assessment and assistance, to induce a few strangers to come forward, and the Bráhmans, finding themselves forced either to take the leases or give up their lands for three years,

(16) Settlement Report for Fasli 1219, paragraph 19.
(17) Jamabandi Report for Fasli 1236, paragraph 16.
(18) Letter from Collector to Board, dated 19th January 1810.

came to terms with the Collector, and agreed to accept the leases proposed by him.[19]

Irrigated portions of the district leased out for 10 years in Fasli 1223.

From the Collector's Settlement Report for the following year (1810-11), we learn that the condition of the landholders in the irrigated portions of the district had become very bad, owing to the continued low price of grain which had then prevailed since Fasli 1216, or for over four years. The commutation price was much higher than the market price, and, as a result, the ryots had become poorer year by year, and had been obliged to part with whatever little personal effects they might have to enable them to meet the Government demand. Mr. Travers in this report gives the following explanation of the landholders of the fertile valley of the Cauvery and Coleroon having become so impoverished. He shows that as a rule, the wet lands were held by Bráhmans, who, however, took no part in the cultivation of the soil, but left it entirely to predial slaves (*Pállars*). The agreement between the landholders and the Government, was that the latter should take half the produce, commuted into specie, at the rate fixed by Mr. Wallace in 1801. Of the 50 per cent. of the produce left, the landholders had to give between from 25 to 27 per cent. to the Pállars and the village servants, and they were thus left with from 25 to 23 per cent. for their own support. This allowance Mr. Travers considered was sufficiently large, provided the price of grain prevailing in the market was any thing like equal to the commutation price; but stated that when, as had then been the case for three seasons, there was a loss of two or three gold fanams on every kalam of paddy, almost the whole of the 25 or 23 per cent. of the produce left to the landholder went to make up the loss sustained by him in converting the Government share into specie.[20] The result of the Collector's representation was that, in order to improve the condition of the landholders, the irrigated portions of the district were leased out for a term of ten years (Faslis 1223—1232), the rent to be paid for each village being fixed at the average collections from it during the previous twelve years.[21]

Further alteration in the commutation prices of grain.

Mr. Travers was succeeded as Collector of Trichinopoly by Mr. C. M. Lushington in March 1815. In the following year there was no change for the better in the condition of the people, and the Board of Revenue, in consequence of petitions that had been presented to them by the leading landholders of the irrigated villages in the district, called on the Collector to report if the amount of rent in the decennial leases had been fixed too high, and

(19) Settlement Report for Fasli 1219, paragraphs 21 to 29.

(20) Settlement Report for Fasli 1220, paragraphs 4 to 8.

(21) Settlement Report for Fasli 1223, and General Report of the Board of Revenue, Vol. 20, paragraphs 770 to 802.

CHAPTER X. REVENUE HISTORY, PART I.

if the fall of the price of grain complained of in the petitions, was likely to be permanent or merely temporary.[22] In his reply, Mr. Lushington points out that while Mr. Travers had, in introducing the decennial settlement, given it as his opinion that its success would depend on whether the market price of grain remained at least as high as 7 gold fanams (13 a. 3 p.) per kalam or not,[23] the price had, as a matter of fact, fallen to $5\frac{2}{16}$ gold fanams per kalam. He further showed, that if the entire produce for Fasli 1225, deducting 27 per cent. for the cultivation charges, had been sold at the prices then current, the amount realized would have been actually less than the Government demand, and that it was, therefore, impossible for the ryots to fulfil their engagements.[24] He accordingly proposed that when the market price fell below 7 gold fanams per kalam, a corresponding reduction should be made in the assessment. He was of opinion that the fall in prices that had been complained of, was likely to continue, and ascribed it to a series of abundant harvests, and the considerable importation of grain from Tanjore that had resulted on the removal of the old restrictions on free trade. The Collector's letter shows that in his opinion the importation of grain should be prevented, but he hesitated to recommend this retrograde measure, from a doubt of its finding acceptance with the Board.[25]

In the following year (A.D. 1816-17) the north-east monsoon almost totally failed, and this disaster, added to a murrain among the cattle, increased the poverty of the cultivating classes, and caused a large number of them to leave the district in the hope of bettering their condition elsewhere. In Fasli 1227 (1817-1818) the Taluqs of Úttattúr and Kurumbalúr were abolished, and out of the greater portion of the villages that had been included in them, together with the jaghire of Ranjangedi that had recently been resumed by the Government, consisting of 36 villages, the Taluq of Válikundapuram was formed.[26] At this period the district was sub-divided as follows: Wet taluqs, Aylúr, Vettukatti, Kónád and Lálgudi; Dry taluqs, Turaiyúr, Ariyalúr, Válikandapuram and Udaiyárpálayam.

Abolition of Kurumbalúr and Úttattúr Taluqs, and formation of Válikandapuram Taluq.

The following season (Fasli 1228, A.D. 1817-18) is described by the Collector as having been a peculiarly disastrous one. At the commencement of the cultivation season, the freshes in the Cauvery and Coleroon were greater than had been ever known before, and

Great floods in Faslis 1228 and 1229.

---

(22) Settlement Report for Fasli 1225, paragraph 21.
(23) Letter from Collector to Board, dated 8th September 1814.
(24) Settlement Report for Fasli 1225, paragraph 22.
(25) Settlement Report for Fasli 1225, paragraphs 24-27.
(26) Settlement Report for Fasli 1227, paragraphs 38-41.

CHAPTER X. REVENUE HISTORY, PART I.

the result was that these rivers were breached in no less than 837 places. The amount of sand deposited over the fields, as a consequence of the inundation, was so great, that Mr. Lushington was of opinion that some of the wet lands would not be able to be cultivated again for years. Scarcely had the breaches been repaired, when cholera and fever broke out, principally among the cultivating slaves (Pállars), and carried away 8,000 people according to the Collector's estimate. The value of the crops lost was calculated to have reached as high a figure as four lakhs of rupees.[27] On the recommendation of the Collector, the Government, in this fasli, sanctioned a reduction of 15 per cent. on the assessment in the dry taluqs.

In Fasli 1229 (1819-20) the country suffered even more from inundations than it had done in the previous years. Fifty-five villages, chiefly in the Lálgudi Taluq, were swept away, and the first crop of paddy in them was totally lost. The inhabitants of Samayapuram, a village on the Madras trunk road, seven miles north of Trichinopoly, had to be carried in boats to that town, as the whole of the intervening country was under water. In Chintámani, one of the suburbs of Trichinopoly, not only were the crops utterly lost, but many of the villagers were drowned. As in the previous year, the floods were succeeded by a pestilence.[28]

Reduction of assessment in the wet taluqs.

The two following seasons (Faslis 1230-1231) were so favourable that the people began to recover rapidly from the state of destitution to which they had been reduced by the disasters of the previous years. Notwithstanding this improvement, however, the district was found to be still so exhausted, that in the latter of these years, Mr. Lushington got permission to cancel the decennial leases, which were to have run on till the end of Fasli 1232, and take the district under his own direct management. As experience had shown that the assessment on the irrigated lands was higher than the people could pay, the following reductions were introduced into the four wet taluqs:—

Taluqs.	No. of Villages reduced 40 per cent.	Number reduced 30 per cent.	Number reduced 20 per cent.	Number reduced 12 per cent.	Total.
Kónád	4	7	97	..	108
Lálgudi	..	6	173	..	179
Vettukatti	..	..	2	33	35
Aylur	..	..	..	32	32
Total ..	4	13	272	65	354

(27) Settlement Report for Fasli 1228, paragraphs 2–15.

(28) Settlement Report for Fasli 1229, paragraphs 2–4.

CHAPTER X.
REVENUE HISTORY, PART I.

Mr. Lushington, in making this reduction, expressly declared that the assessment in the wet taluqs would no longer be calculated according to the description of crop grown, but merely with reference to the class of the land. He also exempted second-crop cultivation from extra charge.[29] In the following year (Fasli 1232) these principles were adhered to, and they were also adopted by Mr. Saunders, who succeeded Mr. Lushington as Collector in August 1823, when making the settlement for Fasli 1233. In Fasli 1234 (1824-25), however, the old system was reverted to; second crop was again charged, and the assessment from that time up to the introduction of the new settlement was levied, both according to the class of the land (*taram*) and the crop raised on it.[30] In Fasli 1236 pattás were for the first time issued by the Collector to each ryot. Up to this it had been the custom for the Collector to settle with the headman of each village the amount to be paid by the community, leaving it to the tahsildar and village officers to decide what portion of the total assessment should be borne by each cultivator. This was now altered, and an attempt was made towards introducing the system of giving pattás individually to ryots. As will, however, be seen further on, this change was not firmly established till some years later.[31] Among the many improvements in the revenue system, introduced by Mr. Dickinson in this year, was one in the method according to which the village karnams were paid. The practice that had existed up till then was that, although the amount to be paid to these officials was entered in the several pattás given to the ryots, yet it was not collected by the tahsildar or his subordinates. The karnams were obliged to get their pay as they could from the ryots, and the result was, that they were either exposed to vexatious delay in obtaining their fees, or were induced to show some irregular favour to those who paid them promptly. This system was now put an end to, and the fees to village officials were henceforth collected by the tahsildar along with the ordinary assessment.[32]

Improvements in the revenue system introduced by Mr. Dickinson when Collector.

The season of 1237 (1827-28) was an unfavourable one. In the month of May the district was visited by a severe storm. The bunds of many of the tanks were breached, and large numbers of cattle perished. The Uyyakondán channel also burst, and sixteen villages under it had to be left uncultivated.[33] During the next

(29) Settlement Report for Fasli 1236, paragraphs 17,18 and 19.

(30) Settlement Report for Fasli 1236, paragraph 20, and Appendix A to Mr. Puckle's Report as Deputy Director of Revenue Settlement, dated 28th October 1860, paragraph 28.

(31) Settlement Report for Fasli 1236, paragraphs 56 and 57.

(32) Settlement Report for Fasli 1237, paragraphs 28–82.

(33) Settlement Report for Fasli 1237, paragraphs 2 and 3.

few years there was a gradual rise in the price of grain, and in Fasli 1240 it exceeded the commutation rates.

Abolition of the "Pattukattu" system.

In his Settlement Report for Fasli 1240, the Collector, Mr. Nelson, who had succeeded Mr. Cameron, represented the evils of what was known as the *pattukattu* system to the Board, and strongly urged its discontinuance. The main principle of this system was that, whatever land was once brought by a ryot under the plough, became from thenceforward his *pattukattu*, and no part of it could, at any time, be relinquished by him. This system was not universal throughout the district, but prevailed in the case of wet and dry lands in irrigated villages in irrigated taluqs, and in dry lands in unirrigated taluqs, but was not the custom in the case of dry villages in irrigated taluqs, or of wet lands in unirrigated taluqs. In the same report Mr. Nelson states that the entire revenue system of the district was full of anomalies; that in no two taluqs did the same rules for conducting the annual settlement prevail; and that one taluq (Válikandapuram) had three distinct sets of revenue rules for the three divisions of which it was then composed.[34] The result of this representation was that, in the following year, the assessment was levied in the unirrigated taluqs only on the land actually cultivated, the result being a loss of assessment to the extent of over 46,000 Rupees.[35] The portions of "pattukattu" land that had been relinquished were, however, for the most part taken up by other ryots during the following seasons.

In Fasli 1243 (1833-34) the lands of revenue defaulters were for the first time put up for sale. Orders were given for the sale of lands for which Rupees 15,000 were due. Of this sum Rupees 7,500 were paid in before the sale commenced, and 5,800 Rupees were obtained from the land sold; but the balance of about Rupees 1,700 could not be realized, as, in consequence of the high rate at which the land was assessed, no one would bid even half the upset price for it.[36]

In the next few years there was a steady increase in the area of cultivation, 3,740 cawnies more having been brought under the plough in Fasli 1245 than in Fasli 1242. There were still, however, no less than 440,000 cawnies of waste land in the dry taluqs, of which the Collector considered that at least 50,000 were fit for cultivation, a large portion of it being land of the best quality.[37]

Alterations in the manner of making the annual settlement.

The annual settlement was at this time conducted in the following manner: First of all the extent of each ryot's cultivation

(34) Settlement Report for Fasli 1240, paragraph 13.
(35) Settlement Report for Fasli 1241, paragraph 23.
(36) Settlement Report for Fasli 1243, paragraphs 52 and 53.
(37) Settlement Report for Fasli 1246, paragraph 20.

CHAPTER X. REVENUE HISTORY, PART I.

was ascertained from the karnam's accounts, and as soon as this had been done, the items entered against each individual were added together, and the total entered in what was called the *Motta-pattá* which was given by the Collector at the settlement to the head of the village (*Maniyagár*). Each ryot afterwards received a separate pattá, which was given to him after the settlement was over, either by the Collector, or, in case he was unable to distribute them all, by the tahsildar.[38] It was not, however, till Fasli 1253 (1843-44) that the distribution of the pattás to the ryots individually was made by the Collector himself during the settlement, instead of being postponed to the end of the fasli, when it was useless, as had been the custom up till then.[39] During the next few years the seasons were, as a rule, favourable, and prices gradually fell, till in Fasli 1261 (1851-52) they were once more above the commutation rates.[40]

In the month of March in the following year a violent hurricane swept over the district, and, according to the account given by the then Collector Mr. John Bird, caused great damage to a number of the most important irrigation works, injured a large extent of crops, both wet and dry, destroyed numbers of the cattle, and swept away thousands of coccanut and other fruit trees.[41] In consequence of the large extent of land that had to be left waste, or on which the crops were destroyed, prices again began to rise steadily. The losses sustained by the people in consequence of this hurricane were so great, that in Fasli 1263 (1853-54) Government sanctioned an advance (*takávi*) of 40,000 Rupees to enable the ryots to carry on the cultivation.

Reduction of the rates of assessment in the dry taluqs.

In February 1855 the Board of Revenue sanctioned a considerable reduction in the rates of assessment then prevailing in the four unirrigated taluqs. In Udaiyárpálayam and Ariyalúr the rates on dry land were reduced to nine-sixteenths of the full assessment, in Válikandapuram to five-eighths, and in Turaiyúr to three-fourths. No reduction was made in the rates on irrigated land in Udaiyárpálayam or Turaiyúr, but in Ariyalúr and Válikandapuram these rates were reduced in the case of all who had previously paid the full assessment to three-quarters of the old rates.[42] In the following year, a reduction of 4 Annas per rupee of the full assessment on garden lands was sanctioned in Turaiyúr and Udaiyárpálayam, and 6 Annas per rupee on land of the same description in Ariyalúr and Válikandapuram.

(38) Settlement Report for Fasli 1246, paragraph 28.

(39) Settlement Report for Fasli 1253, paragraph 8.

(40) Settlement Report for Fasli 1261, paragraphs 5 and 6.

(41) Settlement Report for 1262, paragraph, 3, and letters from Collector to Board, dated 28th March and 28th April 1853.

(42) Proceedings of the Board of Revenue, dated 1st February 1855.

CHAPTER X. REVENUE HISTORY, PART I.

The immediate effect of this reduction was a decrease of assessment to the amount of 2,38,436 Rupees, but, in his report for Fasli 1266 (1856-57), the Collector, Mr. John Bird, reported that, notwithstanding that the season had been an unfavourable one, the lowering of the rates had caused a great extension of cultivation.[43]

In Fasli 1266 (1856-57) the rates of assessment in both the irrigated and unirrigated taluqs were again altered, and further reductions sanctioned, and in Fasli 1268 (1858-59) the new settlement, an account of which is given in the next chapter, was commenced.

Account given by Mr. Puckle of the revenue system in force previous to the introduction of the revised settlement.

The revenue system in force previous to the introduction of the revised settlement was one of the most complicated that it is possible to conceive, as the rates of assessment varied not only with the soil, but also with the crop, and the condition of the person by whom the crop was grown.

In the irrigated taluqs the soil was classed as (1) nunjah, (2) pattukattu-punjah and garden, and (3) ordinary garden land. The nunjah was divided into six classes, each of which was assessed at four different rates for single, and ten for double-crop land ; the pattukattu-punjah and garden consisted of portions of land upon too high a level to be converted into nunjah, and were originally, under the Muhammadan government, rented to the inhabitants at merely nominal rates as a set-off against the exorbitant assessment on the irrigated lands. The ordinary garden was divided into six classes of soil, which were charged according to their relative value.

In the Turaiyúr Taluq the lands were classed as (1) karasal (black), (2) sheval (red), (3) manal (sand), and (4) kalar (soda), and were divided into nunjah, punjah and tóttakál (garden). The nunjah was sub-divided into (1) ayen or actual nunjah, and (2) nunjah taram punjah (wet land cultivated with dry crops). Some villages paid nunjah panavarisai (or a nunjah rate for any crop grown). The punjah was divided into (1) tavasam, and (2) 1 ánam, or grains of superior or inferior yield, and the former was again subdivided into five different kinds.

The garden land consisted of single and double crop, the former being assessed in some cases according to four different kinds of produce, and in others according to eleven varieties of soil ; while the latter was charged at twenty-seven different rates, according to the produce grown. Again, these rates varied with the condition of the cultivator, for the ulkudi, or resident ryot, paid full assessment, while the purakkudi, or stranger, paid three-quarters, and the mahájanam, Bráhman, paid but one-half.

(43) Settlement Report for Fasli 1266, paragraph 10.

CHAPTER X. REVENUE HISTORY, PART I.

In Válikandapuram Taluq the land was classed as nunjah, punjah and tóttakál (garden), and in some village the nunjah rates were charged on the crops, and in others on the several kinds of soil. The tax on the crop, or "payirtírvah" as it was called, was sub-divided into fifteen rates, each of which was again divided into "mudaladi," first crop, and "táladi," second crop. The punjah land was in some villages classed according to the soil, and in others according to the crop, which was sub-divided into "kadir," full crop, "mukkálpayir," three-quarters of a crop, and "araipayir," half a crop, which were respectively chargeable with six different rates of assessment. There were, besides, additional rates for the different kinds of rice and tobacco.

The garden land was divided into single and double crop, the former being chargeable with eleven, and the latter with seven different rates of assessment.

In Ariyalúr Taluq the soil was classed as black and sand, and divided into nunjah and punjah only. In some villages the tax was levied on the crop grown, and in others on four descriptions of cultivation, viz., garden produce, "kadir," full crop; "mukkálpayir," three-quarters crop; and "araipayir," half crop; kadir being again sub-divided into three classes. In this taluq the resident ryot was charged with full tírvah, the Bráhman, the stranger, and sukavási (*i.e.*, a resident but not a pattádár) with three-quarters, stranger with nine-sixteenths, and "zemindári kumbatam" (zemindár's cultivation) eight-sixteenths.

In Udaiyárpálayam Taluq the soil was classed as black and sand, the former of which contained six and the latter seven subdivisions. Nunjah and punjah paid alike, while garden was separately assessed. The resident ryot was charged full tax, the stranger, Bráhman, and sukavási three-quarters, and others who held land on favourable terms but nine-sixteenths.[44]

The relative values, however, of the several descriptions of soil and crop varied in nearly every village to such an extent that there were in the dry taluqs alone 899 different rates for unirrigated and 384 for irrigated lands.[45]

---

(44) This description of the Revenue system in force previous to the introduction of the revised settlement is taken, with slight alterations, from an account of the Revenue History of the district by Mr. Puckle, which forms Appendix A attached to his letter as Deputy Director of Revenue Settlement, to the Director, dated 28th October 1860. This account has been of the greatest assistance to me in writing this chapter.

(45) Letter from Mr. J. Bird, as Collector, to Board, dated 25th October 1851.

CHAPTER XI.

REVENUE HISTORY OF TRICHINOPOLY, PART II.

(THE NEW SETTLEMENT.)

Report of the Deputy Director of Revenue Settlement, Mr. Puckle, proposing a scheme for the revision of the assessment of the district.—Remarks of the Director, Mr. Newill, on Mr. Puckle's scheme.—Criticism passed by the Board of Revenue on Mr. Newill's proposals.—Mr. Newill's reply to the remarks of the Board.—Proceedings of the Board forwarding the proposals for a revised settlement to Government.—Government determine not to pass orders on these proposals till the receipt of further information from the Deputy Director.—Mr. Puckle's report giving the required information.—Remarks of the Director, Mr. R. E. Master, on Mr. Puckle's report.—Proceedings of the Board of Revenue, sending all the papers connected with the revised settlement for the orders of Government.—Reference to the Secretary of State regarding the nature of the revised settlement to be introduced.—Reply from the Secretary of State to this reference.—Final orders of Government sanctioning the introduction of the new settlement.—Report from Mr. Puckle showing the immediate results of the introduction of the revised assessment.

CHAPTER XI. REVENUE HISTORY, PART II.

THE survey of the Trichinopoly District was commenced in Fasli 1264 (1854-55) by a party under Captain Priestly, and the settlement by Mr. Puckle, then Deputy Director of Revenue Settlement, in Fasli 1268 (1858-1859).

Trichinopoly was one of the first districts into which the revised settlement was introduced, having been preceded in this respect by only the Mannárgudi and Chellambram Taluqs of South Arcot and the Western Delta of the Godavery District. Partly for this reason, and partly because the several authorities to whose province it fell to criticise Mr. Puckle's scheme took widely divergent views as to the manner in which the district should be dealt with, and the rates of ássessment that should be introduced, the revised settlement of this district has given rise to more discussion than that of any other. It therefore appears advisable to insert here an analysis of this discussion, and a brief account of the results of the settlement as far as they have been ascertained up to this.

On the 28th of October 1860 Mr. Puckle submitted his scheme for the revision of the assessment of the district to Mr. Newill, who was then the Director of Revenue Settlement.[1] At this time the district was divided into nine taluqs, of which Mr. Puckle classes

(1) Deputy Director of Revenue Settlement to Director, dated 28th October 1860.

CHAPTER XI. REVENUE HISTORY, PART II.

Report of the Deputy Director of Revenue Settlement, Mr. Puckle, proposing a scheme for the revision of the assessment of the district.

five, Vettukatti, Kónád, Lálgudi, Musiri and Manapparai as Nírárambam, or irrigated; and four, Turaiyúr, Válikandapuram, Ariyalúr and Udaiyárpálayam as Kádárambam, or upland. He remarks that, although Manapparai cannot be called an irrigated taluq, yet it has been included in the Nírárambam portion for convenience of classification, as it is unlike all the Kádárambam taluqs, while in natural features and quality of soil it resembles the high lands of Vettukatti and Kónád. As the maps and records relating to only four of the taluqs, Udaiyárpálayam, Ariyalúr, Válikandapuram and Turaiyúr, had been received when the Deputy Director's scheme was drawn up, the survey areas could be made use of for those taluqs only, and the karnams' measurements had to be followed for the remaining taluqs.

Classification.

The classification of the upland taluqs was commenced according to the following scale, which had been previously adopted for South Arcot:—

	Class.
Islands and other alluvial deposits	1
Permanently improved lands and garden lands near village sites	2
Best regur mixed with vandal or sand	3
Regur of ordinary quality	4
Inferior regur mixed with bad ingredients ..	5
Best mussab, rich in vandal	6
Good mussab	7
Ordinary mussab	8
Inferior mussab	9
Best red earth	10
Ordinary do.	11
Worst do.	12
Regur and mussab not fit for tarams 5 and 9 ..	13
Sandy or stony lands	14
Pure sand or gravel	15

Experience, however, afterwards showed that there were no rich alluvial lands in Trichinopoly, and that the first exceptional series was not required. It was also found necessary to add a third sort to each of the third, fourth, and fifth classes to include a very poor description of black soil, peculiar to some of the taluqs in the district, which could not be fairly classified according to the previously existing scale. The ninth, tenth, eleventh, twelfth, thirteenth, and fourteenth classes were struck out as inapplicable to Trichinopoly. For Manapparai and the dry villages in the irrigated taluqs it was considered necessary to add an extra sort to each of the seventh and eighth classes to avoid over-estimating the value of an inferior description of red soil that was found to abound in that part of the country, and was much mixed with saltpetre and other deleterious ingredients. The following classification for both wet and dry land was eventually adopted by Mr. Puckle for the northern taluqs and Manapparai, as well as for the dry villages of the four irrigated taluqs :—

Description of Soil.	Class.	Sort.	Primary Taram.	
			Wet.	Dry.
Best garden land	2	1	1	1
Best nattavoi and more ordinary garden land ..	2	2	2	3
Best loamy regur	4	1		2
Best clay regur	3	1		
Ordinary loamy regur	4	2	3	4
Best loamy red soil	7	1		
Ordinary clay regur	3	2	4	5
Best sandy regur	5	1		
Ordinary sandy regur	5	2		
Do. loamy red soil	7	2	5	6
Best sandy red soil	8	1		
Do. red clay	6	1		
Inferior loamy regur	4	3	6	7
Ordinary red clay	6	2		
Inferior clay regur	3	3		
Do. sandy regur	5	3	7	8
Ordinary sandy red soil	8	2		
Inferior loamy red soil	7	3	8	9
Do. sandy red soil	8	3		

The following classification was adopted for the river-irrigated villages of Kónád, Vettukatti, Lálgudi and Musiri, the cultivable area of which is composed of black soil and river deposit :—

Description of Soil.	Class.	Sort.	Primary Taram.
Best loamy regur much mixed with river deposit ..	4	1	2
Ordinary do. do. ..	4	2	3
Best clay do. do. ..	3	1	
Ordinary clay do. do. ..	3	2	4
Best sandy do. do. ..	5	1	
Ordinary do. do. ..	5	2	5
Inferior loamy regur much mixed with limestone ..	4	3	6
Do. clay regur mixed with soda	3	3	

The following rates, proposed by Mr. Puckle in consultation with the Director of Revenue Settlement, as the commutation prices of the principal grains grown in the district, were eventually accepted by both the Board of Revenue and Government :—

Commutation prices.

	Per Harris Kalam of 24 Madras Measures.
Paddy (*Oryza sativa*)	8 Annas.
Chólum (*Sorghum vulgare*)	12 ,,
Cumbu (*Holcus spicatus*)	10 ,,
Rági, (*Eleusine corocana*)	10 ,,
Varagu (*Paspalum scrobiculatum*)	6 ,,

CHAPTER XI. REVENUE HISTORY, PART II.

The grounds on which these rates were selected are given fully in Mr. Puckle's report.

The gross produce was ascertained by numerous experiments in the staple products of each variety of soil, and the conclusions arrived at in the case of paddy were checked by a series of accounts exhibiting the gross produce of every field in the wet villages of Lálgudi and Musiri Taluqs from Fasli 1244 to 1250. The yield of the principal dry grains, chólum, cumbu, rági and varagu was also ascertained by actual experiment.

A deduction of 20 per cent. on account of unfavourable seasons was made from the gross produce of the principal dry grains, but it was considered unnecessary to provide for this contingency in the case of paddy, as the Government had sanctioned a remission for all wet crops that might perish through accident or failure of the requisite water-supply. "The ryots," Mr. Puckle remarks, "are so anxious to overrate the expense of cultivation that in some instances they represent themselves to be cultivating at a loss, and in few cases will they admit that the net produce is more than sufficient to meet the Government demand. In the items of ploughing and manuring, they assume that every field is repeatedly ploughed and highly manured, while, in practice, it is customary to thoroughly plough and manure but a small portion of each holding; for the cultivating season is very limited, and the resources of a village are not sufficient to meet any sudden and greatly increased demand for labour. Consequently the greater portion of the land is simply turned over with the plough two or three times, and the little manure procurable is trodden into but a small percentage of the fields." Mr. Puckle states that it was found impossible to frame an estimate of the cultivation expenses with any great degree of accuracy, but that the tables drawn up by him were, he considered, tolerably correct, and exhibited a fair calculation of the gross and net produce of each class of soil generally throughout the district.

Existing rates of assessment.

Mr. Puckle gives the following account of the various rates of assessment that were to be found in the district previous to the introduction of the revised settlement. "If the different rates of assessment in each taluq of Trichinopoly be added together, their total sum amounts to no less than Rupees 3,741. These vary from 25 Rupees to an anna and a half for irrigated, and from 22 Rupees to about one anna per acre for unirrigated land. They are not, however, graduated on any fixed scale, or classed according to any system whatsoever, but appear to have been merely the arbitrary imposition of the persons to whom these taluqs were formerly rented out. In some villages of the upland taluqs, the assessment varies according to the nature of the soil, and in others according to the crop produced. In some it is levied on both soil and crop, and in others the whole of the dry lands are charged at one universal rate. It thus frequently happens that thousands of acres of good land are left uncultivated, owing to the inability of the ryots to pay the tax peculiar to that locality, often as much as 5 Rupees; while, perhaps, in a village but a few miles distant, the very same sort of soil is charged at but 1 or 2 Rupees per acre. As might be expected, this state of things gives rise to frauds innumerable. The village officers, who are generally the principal land-owners, have the power of falsifying the accounts to almost any extent, with but a very small chance of detection."

The following statement, taken from Mr. Puckle's report, shows the highest and lowest rates of assessment on wet, dry and garden lands in each taluq of the Trichinopoly District, before the introduction of the revised settlement:—

Taluqs.		Wet.			Dry.			Garden.		
		No. of Rates.	Highest Rates.	Lowest Rates.	No. of Rates.	Highest Rates.	Lowest Rates.	No. of Rates.	Highest Rates.	Lowest Rates.
			RS. A. P.	RS. A. P.		RS. A. P.	RS. A. P.		RS. A. P.	RS. A. P.
Kónád ...	Wet villages. Dry do.	107	6 2 11	0 4 10	75	2 0 6	0 1 2	33	5 12 7	0 5 9
Vettukatti.	Wet do. ...	225	17 7 9	0 4 3	36	6 11 8	0 1 9	25	5 10 1	0 2 1
	Dry do. ...	31	5 10 8	0 6 1	56	2 6 1	0 2 8	20	3 1 2	0 10 6
Musiri ...	Wet do. ...	397	17 0 9	0 11 9	14	1 12 11	0 3 4	70	6 0 9	0 9 4
	Dry do. ...	35	6 9 5	0 14 1	46	1 12 11	0 2 10	56	6 0 9	0 8 5
Lálgudi ...	Wet do. ...	742	16 11 9	0 2 7	112	6 9 5	0 2 9	82	6 0 9	0 3 0
	Dry do. ...	28	7 1 0	0 14 1	119	3 11 2	0 2 9	74	6 0 9	0 9 8
Turaiyúr ...	Dry	187	25 4 7	0 13 9	231	4 14 3	0 9 1	208	21 1 4	1 15 3
Ariyalúr ...	Do.	19	8 4 9	1 8 0	32	4 3 5	0 11 8	28	9 6 5	0 12 0
Udaiyárpálayam.	Dry ...	28	11 15 10	1 13 1	16	5 4 0	0 10 11	15	7 7 0	1 8 0
Válikandapuram	... ...	105	21 3 10	1 2 0	238	4 12 0	0 6 2	131	10 4 3	1 15 4
Manapparai	... ...	72	7 3 6	0 15 5	24	2 2 7	0 5 8	24	3 15 6	2 8 5

Proposed standard rates of assessment.

The following scale of money rates for wet and dry land was calculated on an average struck between one-fourth the gross and half the net produce of each variety of soil. "These average values again," Mr. Puckle states, "nearly coincide with 30 per cent. of the gross produce which represents the Government demand upon the land. Both the first and last tarams are to be considered as exceptional, for, though they only include a small area of actual classification, they are nevertheless indispensable for the subsequent adjustment of the tarams of such lands as require their assessment to be raised or lowered, according to their grades of irrigation, or on account of advantages or disadvantages of situation with reference to roads and market towns."

"Upwards of two-thirds of the area of the dry lands is assessed at rates varying from 1 to 3 Rupees, and half of that of the wet lands at from Rupees $3\frac{1}{2}$ to 6 Rupees per acre. It was originally intended to take 8 Annas for dry and $2\frac{1}{2}$ Rupees for wet as the lowest rates, but the insertion of one still lower, in either case, was subsequently found necessary to allow of the reduction of a taram in favour of certain lands south of the Cauvery, that could not otherwise be equitably assessed even at the lowest ordinary rates."

Proposed Rates.

Wet.				Dry.			
Class.	Sort.	Primary Taram.	Rate per Acre.	Class.	Sort.	Primary Taram.	Rate per Acre.
			RS. A. P.				RS. A. P.
2	1	1	7 0 0	2	1	1	3 8 0
2	2	2	6 0 0	4	1	2	3 0 0
4	1			2	2	3	2 8 0
3	1			3	1		
4	2	3	5 0 0	4	2	4	2 0 0
7	1			7	1		
3	2	4	4 0 0	3	2	5	1 8 0
5	1			5	1		
5	2			5	2		
6	1	5	3 8 0	6	1	6	1 0 0
7	2			7	2		
8	1			8	1		
4	3	6	3 0 0	4	3	7	0 12 0
6	2			6	2		
3	3			3	3		
8	2	7	2 8 0	8	2	8	0 8 0
5	3			5	3		
7	3	8	2 0 0	7	3	9	0 6 0
8	3			8	3		

Grouping of the villages.

The following tables show the manner in which Mr. Puckle grouped the villages in the district. His reasons are fully given in his report, but they are too lengthy to insert here. "In forming these groups," he says, "I have been assisted by the Náttukarnams[2] and other revenue officers of long experience, as well as by the most intelligent of the villagers themselves, who are universally well acquainted with the relative value of each of the groups of villages into which they have been accustomed to subdivide the country in their immediate neighbourhood. They seem also to be well aware of the advantages that each group may happen to possess in its irrigation, vicinity to market-towns, or productive power of the land; and, as I have had the opportunity of acquiring considerable local experience, and am personally well acquainted with the situation, requirements, and advantages or

(2) நாட்டுக்கர்ணம் so called as they were the karnams of a நாடு or mágánam, that is to say, of a small division of a taluq comprising ten or fifteen villages. The representatives in a tahsildar's office of the karnams of all the villages in a mágánam were styled náttukarnams. There were two náttukarnams for each mágánam, *i.e.*, a head náttukarnam and his deputy. Their duty chiefly consisted in examining the cultivation accounts received from each village, and estimating the extent of land under each kind of grain for the whole mágánam. On the introduction of the revised settlement the services of these officers were dispensed with.

disadvantages of each group, I feel confident that the relative value assigned to each is as nearly correct as it is possible to be without drawing minute distinctions, and thus multiplying the number of the groups to an inconvenient extent." CHAPTER XI. REVENUE HISTORY, PART II.

Grouping of the Villages.

WET.

Taluqs.	Number of Villages.				
	First Group.	Second Group.	Third Group.	Fourth Group.	Fifth Group.
Kónád	13	67	23	..	45
Vettukatti	14	16	..	..	22
Lálgudi	..	138	60	..	7
Musiri	..	24	7	..	24
Manapparai	..	..	..	..	32
Ariyalúr	..	..	14	111	..
Válikandapuram	..	..	..	76	..
Udaiyárpálayam	..	..	6	133	..
Turaiyúr	..	..	27	101	..
Total ..	27	245	137	421	130

DRY.

Taluqs.	Number of Villages.		
	First Group.	Second Group.	Third Group.
Kónád	..	..	157
Vettukatti	..	..	63
Lálgudi	230	..	..
Musiri	55	..	..
Manapparai	33	..	..
Ariyalúr	190	39	..
Válikandapuram	..	127	9
Udaiyárpálayam	225	..	..
Turaiyúr	114	15	2
Total ..	847	181	231

Mr. Puckle remarks that the settlement operations had tended rather to revise than to reduce the existing rates of assessment, for that, although all those for unirrigated land above Rupees 3-8-0 and those for irrigated above 8 Rupees had been reduced to those maximum rates, yet, on the other hand, the assessment had been raised in many cases where the land paid but a nominal tax. "This was however unavoidable as the revenue system of the district is, with some modifications, that of the Muhammadan government, and the varying and arbitrary taxation of the former renters of these taluqs is still retained up to the present time. In Udaiyárpálayam the wet and dry lands, previous to Fasli Financial results of the new settlement.

CHAPTER XI. REVENUE HISTORY, PART II.

1264, have always been charged alike, and though the dry rates were then reduced, no alteration was made in those for wet lands. The new classification has therefore slightly raised the assessment in the first-class wet lands, but has lowered it in all other parts of the taluq. In Ariyalúr and Válikandapuram it has been lowered, but in Turaiyúr there is hardly any alteration. The assessment on dry land has been reduced in every taluq." Mr. Puckle was of opinion that the total loss of land revenue for the entire district, consequent on the revision of assessment, would not be more than 50,000 Rupees. "To this must be added 67,478 Rupees, the amount of the collections on account of *Katlai-silavu* and grazing-tax, thus making the total remission about $1\frac{1}{4}$ lakhs of Rupees. As a set-off against this reduction there is, in the four northern taluqs, 220,232 acres of cultivable waste, assessed at 3,12,387 Rupees, much of which will, no doubt, be taken up now that it can be obtained upon easy terms.

The greater portion of the agricultural community will greatly benefit by the revision of assessment, and be induced to extend their cultivation, while in the exceptional cases, where a merely nominal tax has been raised by the classification, it is optional to the ryots to pay the assessment or to give a rázinámáh for such portion of their land as they find themselves unable to cultivate."

Remarks of the Director, Mr. Newill, on Mr. Puckle's scheme.

In his letter[3] sending on Mr. Puckle's scheme to the Board of Revenue, Mr. Newill proposed considerable alterations in it. Of these, the most important was in the grouping of the villages, for which he suggested the following arrangement:—

—		River Irrigation.		Tank Irrigation.			Total.	Punjah Villages.		Total.
		1st.	2nd.	3rd.	4th.	5th.		1st.	2nd.	
Kónád ..	River irrigation ..	80	..	24	..	..	149	..	157	157
	Tank do.	..	..	..	..	45				
Vettukatti ..	River do.	30	..	..	..	..	52	..	63	63
	Tank do.	..	..	..	..	22				
Lálgudi ..	River do.	..	138	33	..	..	205	230	..	230
	Tank do.	..	..	27	..	7				
Musiri ..	River do.	..	24	7	..	..	55	55	..	55
	Tank do.	..	..	..	..	24				
Ariyalúr ..	Vellár and Coleroon irrigation	..	..	14	..	..	125	229	..	229
	Tank irrigation ..	..	..	..	111	..				
Udaiyár-pálayam.	Coleroon do.	..	..	6	..	..	139	225	..	225
	Tank do.	..	..	..	133	..				
Válikanda-puram ..	Do. do.	..	..	..	76	..	76	136	..	136
Turaiyúr ..	Do. do.	..	..	27	101	..	128	129	2	131
Manapparai.	Do. do.	..	..	..	..	32	32	33	..	33
	Total ..	110	162	138	421	130	961	1,037	222	1,259

(3) Director of Revenue Settlement to Board, No. 649, of the 20th April 1861.

CHAPTER XI. REVENUE HISTORY, PART II.

It will be remarked that the effect of this alteration was to move a large number of the villages in the district into a group higher than that assigned to them by Mr. Puckle. Sixty-seven villages in Kónád and sixteen in Vettukatti were advanced from the second to the first wet group. The third dry group was abolished altogether, 222 of the villages in it being put in the second group, and the remaining nine in the first. The 181 villages placed by Mr. Puckle in the second group were all moved into the first.

Mr. Newill accepted Mr. Puckle's commutation prices, and proposed the following scale of money rates :—

Punjah.	Classes.		Nunjah.	Classes.				
	1st.	2nd.		1st.	2nd.	3rd.	4th.	5th.
	RS. A.	RS. A.		RS. A.	RS. A.	RS. A.	RS. A.	RS. A.
1	3 8	3 0						
2	3 0	2 8	1	9 0	8 8	7 0	6 8	6 0
3	2 8	2 0	2	8 0	7 8	6 0	5 8	5 0
4	2 0	1 8	3	7 0	6 8	5 0	4 8	4 0
5	1 8	1 0	4	6 0	5 8	4 0	3 12	3 8
6	1 0	0 12	5	5 0	4 8	3 8	3 4	3 0
7	0 12	0 8	6	4 0	3 12	3 0	2 12	2 0
8	0 8	0 6	7	3 8	3 4	2 8	2 4	2 0
9	0 6	0 6	8	3 0	2 12	2 0	2 0	2 0

He observes that he has rated the river-irrigated lands in Trichinopoly somewhat higher than those in the newly-settled taluqs in South Arcot for the following reason: "The Chellambram Taluq is irrigated by the lower anicut on the Coleroon branch after a supply is taken off from the Cauvery by the upper anicut for the Trichinopoly Taluq, and altogether the irrigation is better in the latter, while the great Trichinopoly market also places the neighbourhood on a more favourable footing." The Director proposed to assess the dry lands lower than it was intended to do in Godavery, as the inferiority of the soil in Trichinopoly and other local circumstances called for a difference.

Financial result of the settlement proposed by the Director.

The following table shows the result of the settlement proposed by Mr. Newill :—

CHAPTER XI.
REVENUE HISTORY, PART II.

Taluqs.		As per Jamabandi of Fasli 1268.		As per New Settlement.	
		Extent.	Assessment.	Extent.	Assessment.
1		2	3	4	5
		ACRES.	RS.	ACRES.	RS.
Kónád	Dry	23,707	17,504	25,834	18,509
	Irrigated ...	32,726	1,78,951	32,916	1,69,137
Vettukatti ...	Dry	69,150	40,147	74,619	35,173
	Irrigated	10,866	73,054	11,891	62,041
Lálgudi	Dry	36,704	59,487	34,079	49,924
	Irrigated	31,464	1,82,226	31,017	1,74,134
Musiri	Dry	41,473	42,694	39,874	37,926
	Irrigated	11,433	71,222	13,992	76,055
Ariyalúr	Dry	54,648	1,12,508	87,596	1,56,593
	Irrigated	4,577	26,221	5,868	27,706
Udaiyárpálayam.	Dry	32,654	66,774	43,952	61,667
	Irrigated	3,262	41,569	8,622	37,891
Turaiyúr ...	Dry	75,037	1,17,039	91,309	1,34,881
	Irrigated	3,236	43,666	13,849	70,202
Válikandapuram.	Dry	52,201	1,10,612	70,855	1,30,670
	Irrigated	4,126	25,076	4,895	22,884
Manapparai ...	Dry	40,242	51,132	44,293	45,127
	Irrigated	2,742	7,652	2,116	6,750
Total ...	Dry ...	425,816	6,17,897	512,411	6,70,470
	Irrigated ...	114,432	6,49,637	125,166	6,46,800
Grand Total ...		540,248	12,67,534	637,577	13,17,270

Taluqs.		Comparison		Assessment on the Area in occupation as per New Rates.	Comparison of Columns 3 and 8.
		Of Columns 2 and 4.	Of Columns 3 and 5.		
		6	7	8	9
		ACRES.	RS.	RS.	RS.
Kónád	Dry	+ 2,127	+ 1,005	17,039	— 465
	Irrigated	+ 190	— 9,814	1,68,866	— 10,085
Vettukatti ...	Dry	+ 5,469	— 4,974	32,500	— 7,647
	Irrigated	+ 1,025	— 11,013	58,576	— 14,478
Lálgudi	Dry	— 2,625	— 9,563	53,718	— 5,769
	Irrigated	— 447	— 8,092	1,78,332	— 3,894
Musiri	Dry	— 1,599	— 4,768	38,332	— 4,362
	Irrigated	+ 2,559	+ 4,833	63,447	— 7,775
Ariyalúr	Dry	+ 32,948	+ 44,085	97,626	— 14,882
	Irrigated	+ 1,291	+ 1,485	21,449	— 4,772
Udaiyárpálayam.	Dry	+ 11,298	— 5,107	45,749	— 21,025
	Irrigated	+ 360	— 3,678	35,942	— 5,627
Turaiy úr ...	Dry	+ 16,272	+ 17,842	1,10,883	— 6,156
	Irrigated	+ 5,613	+ 26,536	41,819	— 1,847
Válikandapuram.	Dry	+ 13,654	+ 20,058	96,245	— 14,367
	Irrigated	+ 769	— 192	19,276	— 5,800
Manapparai ...	Dry	+ 4,051	— [illegible]05	41,709	+ 9,423
	Irrigated	— 626	— 902	8,754	— 1,102
Total ...	Dry ...	+ 86,595	+ 52,573	5,33,801	— 84,096
	Irrigated ...	+ 10,734	— 2,837	5,96,461	— 53,176
Grand Total ..		+ 97,329	+ 49,736	11,30,262	—1,37,272

This statement shows that, if the ryots continued to keep in their pattás all the land held by them before the settlement, and paid the new rates on it, the revenue would be increased by Rupees 49,736. Mr. Newill, however, pointed out that it was not to be expected that all the land then claimed but not paid for, or assessed at a merely nominal rate, would be retained by the cultivators when the new rates were imposed on it, and that, if the proposed rates were levied on no greater extent of land than that actually paid for in Fasli 1268, there would be a deficiency of Rupees 137,000. Mr. Newill, however, was of opinion that this was not a fair index of the probable results for the following reasons. First of all there was in places a considerable extent of concealed cultivation, which would be brought to account; in the next place, tracts of land, the assessment on which had been prohibitory from its arbitrary and excessive character, would be readily taken up under the new settlement; and lastly, some portion at least of the lands to which the ryots then retained a claim by payment of merely nominal rates, would continue to be held by them on the regular assessment.

"The immediate results of the new settlement will thus," Mr. Newill remarks, "depend upon the ryots on its introduction, and any calculation of the extent to which they will hold the lands in question can only be in a measure conjectural. But there is a prospect of the full standard being reached at an early period, while there are further ample resources for the increase of revenue by the extension of cultivation."

Mr. Newill observes that Mr. Puckle had estimated that the settlement, as proposed by him, would result in a decrease of about half a lakh of rupees, and then points out that, if the *Katlai-silavu*, or fees to village servants, amounting to about 70,000 Rupees, was given up, as well as the grazing-tax, the total reduction of assessment would be about one and a quarter lakhs of rupees. In order to prevent the loss of revenue consequent on the introduction of the revised settlement being so great, he therefore proposed a settlement by which there would be an increase of 50,000 Rupees. Against this increase, however, he points out that there would be a loss of Rupees 6,800 on account of *Katlai-silavu*, and about 7,000 on account of grazing-tax. The actual deficiency would therefore be about 19,000 Rupees. He was of opinion that, possibly, in the first year there might be a further falling off of 50,000 Rupees or 60,000 Rupees, but had no doubt that the sweeping away of the many impediments to the extension of cultivation that then existed, and the fixing of the assessment on a sound footing, would afford so great a stimulus to the extension of agricultural operations, that eventually there would be no loss of revenue.

Criticism passed by the Board of Revenue on Mr. Newill's proposals.

The Board of Revenue[4] in reviewing these papers, commenced by observing that Mr. Newill's report was so meagre and unsatisfactory on many points that, before they submitted it to Government, they were compelled to call on him for further and fuller information.

They then proceed to criticise his scheme. They remark that the revenue history of Trichinopoly shows that from the first the

(4) Proceedings of the Board of Revenue, No. 5,989, dated 1st November 1861.

land assessment was too high, and marked with extraordinary anomalies, and that the consequence was that large portions of the district, up till lately, had remained unoccupied. It therefore appeared to them that it required in a peculiar degree to be dealt with in a liberal spirit, whereas Mr. Newill had treated it with less consideration than other districts more favourably situated. As an instance of this, it is pointed out that only two classes were proposed for dry lands, and that the Director had placed almost all the villages in the first group, including thirty-three villages in Manapparai Taluq, the soil of which had been described as being of the poorest description. It is also remarked that, although Mr. Newill had stated that his classification of the lands differed from Mr. Puckle's, yet he had not explained in what the difference consisted, or on which it was grounded.

The Board proceed to observe that the Director had stated that, in forming his calculations, one-fifth had been deducted from the gross produce of dry lands for vicissitudes of season; but that, in the case of wet lands, no allowance had been made, as the vicissitudes of the season were created or influenced by the nature of the irrigation, and that this had been provided for in the classification of the villages. The Board remark that in South Arcot a deduction of from 15 to 25 per cent. of the gross produce had been allowed to cover losses from the season in both wet and dry lands ordinarily situated, and a still further deduction on inferiorly irrigated lands; and that in the fertile alluvial lands of the Godavery Delta a deduction of 17 per cent. had been allowed. Mr. Newill was directed to explain his reasons for treating Trichinopoly differently from these districts, and to show how the wet lands were provided for in the classification of villages, and on what grounds 20 per cent. was considered a sufficient deduction on dry lands.

It was then pointed that in the western taluqs of the Godavery Delta the highest ordinary combined punjah and water-rate was 8 Rupees an acre. In the settled taluqs of South Arcot it was 8½ Rupees, while in Trichinopoly 9 Rupees had been fixed as the highest assessment for the first rate of a first-class village, and 8½ Rupees for the first rate of a second-class village. The Board observed that the Godavery delta and the Mannárgudi and Chellambram Taluqs in South Arcot possessed greater advantages than the irrigated portions of Trichinopoly, both in respect of fertility of soil and proximity to good markets. They remarked that it was difficult to understand on what principle Mr. Newill had fixed the rates of assessment on wet lands so high, and pointed out that the then Acting Collector of the district, Mr. McDonell, considered that these rates were excessive, and that a recorded opinion of Mr. Bird, who was for many years Collector of Trichinopoly, showed that he, too, held the same view. The following statement made by Mr. Puckle in his report on the settlement was then quoted in corroboration of the statement that the irrigated portions of Trichinopoly were not as favourably situated as the taluqs in South Arcot already mentioned. "The river-irrigated lands of Trichinopoly are peculiarly situated, being immediately contiguous to the great rice-producing country of Tanjore, and far distant from any seaport, or, excepting Trichinopoly itself, from any large market town. The ryots have not the means of exporting their surplus grain to any considerable extent, and a comparison of the advantages of situation of the irrigated taluqs of Trichinopoly and those of South Arcot is decidedly in favour of the latter."

The Board then direct the Director to reconsider his classification of the irrigated lands, with a view to the rates being modified and reduced. They further remark that they considered that Mr. Newill's dry rates were too high, if the discontinuance of the practice of granting remissions was contemplated. Taking into consideration "the great vicissitudes of the seasons, the total failure of the rains, or the lateness at which they fall, the repeated blights and other accidents to which dry cultivation is exposed, the heavy expenses to which the ryots are subjected in cultivating their lands sometimes three and four times a season, the poverty of the soil and the necessity which consequently arises for fallows," they arrived at the conclusion that 25 per cent. of the gross produce would be a sufficient demand from ordinary dry lands. The Director was, therefore, ordered to reconsider this point, and, if necessary, reduce his assessment on dry lands.

Mr. Newill's reply to the remarks of the Board.

In his reply[5] to these proceedings, Mr. Newill remarked that the Board's main objection to the settlement proposed by him appeared to be that it had been pitched at too high a standard, especially when compared with that fixed for the settled taluqs in South Arcot. He however pointed out that, if the average assessment on wet and dry lands in Trichinopoly and those taluqs in South Arcot was taken, it would be found that there was a difference of 6 Annas on wet lands and 8½ Annas on dry in favour of Trichinopoly. He then added that it should be borne in mind that, pending the introduction of the settlement, reductions of assessment had been made in the Kádárambam taluqs of Trichinopoly, which had lowered the land revenue from 15½ lakhs of Rupees to 12½ lakhs, while his settlement would reduce it by about 137,000 Rupees more, or 4½ lakhs below what it stood at a few years previously. It therefore appeared to him that the district had been dealt with in a sufficiently liberal spirit.

Mr. Newill then proceeded to give his reasons for altering the Deputy Director's grouping. "Mr. Puckle," he remarks, "says that

(5) Director of Revenue Settlement to Board, No. 101, of the 29th January 1862.

the villages in Kónád and Vettukatti, placed by him in the second group, are little inferior to those of the first group, and that the lands are very rich and the crops produced excellent. Nevertheless he proposed for the second group of villages in these taluqs a reduction of half a taram. The remedy for this inconsistency was, therefore, applied in merging the second group into the first, and, even after doing this, there is a decrease of about 17,000 Rupees and 13,000 Rupees in the first group of the two taluqs. On a general view of the case, the distinction of three dry groups appeared uncalled for, and the principle was adopted of throwing all villages under ordinary circumstances into one general group, reserving a second group for those with any marked disadvantages. There may be minor distinctions such as do not warrant the reduction of a whole taram, but it is unnecessary to multiply the rates so as to provide for such small differences."

The Director therefore proposed to transfer thirty-nine villages in the Ariyalúr Taluq into the first group, remarking that this would only place the taluq on the same footing as Mr. Puckle had put Udaiyárpálayam, and that he knew no reason why they should be treated differently. Even with this modification, there would be a reduction of Rupees 15,000 or 13 per cent. in the dry assessment for Ariyalúr Taluq. He further proposed to move all the villages in Válikandapuram into the first group, as there appeared to him to be no sufficient ground for putting them into a lower group than the adjacent taluqs. The result of the settlement proposed by the Director for these villages would therefore be to reduce the assessment by 14,000 Rupees, or 12 per cent., against a reduction of 27,000, or 46 per cent., according to Mr. Puckle's scheme. In reply to the objection raised by the Board to the thirty-three villages in Manapparai being put in the first group, Mr. Newill stated that they were so placed by Mr. Puckle, and remarked that the soil was doubtless poor, but that this was met in the classification, and that they were not considered to be in so unfavourable circumstances as to warrant their transfer to the second group.

The Board had asked on what grounds 20 per cent. was considered a sufficient deduction on dry lands for vicissitudes of seasons. To this Mr. Newill replied that the conclusion was necessarily arrived at on general considerations, and could not be supported by definite calculations showing any fixed proportion as the average extent of failure of produce. In Chellambram Taluq, in South Arcot, 25 per cent. had been allowed on this account, but the dry land there was limited in extent and the district of Trichinopoly was considered generally. The survey also in Trichinopoly included within the fields a smaller extent of unproductive portions of land than they did elsewhere, provision having been made for marking off in separate lots all channels, &c., of a certain size.

Mr. Newill then replies to the remarks made by the Board contrasting the maximum wet rate in Trichinopoly with that introduced in Godavery and South Arcot. He observes that a comparison of the maximum rates is not a proper index of the relative bearing of the assessment. It was only on some exceptional land in Trichinopoly that a rate higher than that introduced in South Arcot was imposed. In Godavery the maximum rate was the "dry assessment plus the universal water-rate, which latter necessarily treats both good and bad soils alike, and obviously creates a lower maximum than is derived by the process of forming regular wet rates."

CHAPTER XI.
REVENUE HISTORY, PART II.

As regards the objection taken to a 9 Rupees rate having been proposed for Trichinopoly, while 8½ Rupees was the highest introduced into the settled taluqs in South Arcot, the Director stated that he believed that there were lands in Trichinopoly more productive than anything to be found in these taluqs. Some of these were then paying 22 Rupees per acre, and he therefore considered that, if rates of 8½ Rupees and 9 Rupees were levied on them, they would not be burdensome. He then went into some particulars to prove that the assessment on river-irrigated land in South Arcot was really lower than that proposed for Trichinopoly, but, as he had been directed by the Board to reduce his rates, he eventually proposed the following scale :—

Number.	First Group.		Second Group.		Third Group.		Fourth Group.		Fifth Group.	
	RS.	A.	RS.	A.	RS.	A.	RS.	A.	RS.	A.
1 ..	8	8	7	8	7	0	6	8	6	0
2 ..	7	8	6	8	6	0	5	8	5	0
3 ..	6	8	5	8	5	0	4	8	4	0
4 ..	5	8	4	8	4	0	3	12	3	8
5 ..	4	8	4	0	3	8	3	4	3	0
6 ..	3	12	3	4	3	0	2	12	2	8
7 ..	3	4	2	12	2	8	2	4	2	0
8 ..	2	12	2	4	2	0	2	0	2	0

The financial effect of this modification of the rates would be, Mr. Newill stated, a reduction of Rupees 40,450, or 12 per cent., below his original proposal for the four irrigated taluqs, and 31,428, or 9 per cent., below Mr. Puckle's estimate. The Director's former proposal involved a loss of Rupees 1,37,272 on the total assessment of the district. This sum would now be raised to 17,77,722, and, if Mr. Puckle's scheme of grouping was accepted in preference to Mr. Newill's, to a little over two lakhs.

The Board had remarked that the dry rates proposed were too high, and had suggested that they should be fixed at 25 per cent. of the gross produce. Mr. Newill pointed out that this would be a fundamental change in the basis of the settlement, and that the Secretary of State had decided that the assessment should not be based on any proportion of the gross produce, but on the net produce. He then gave some further reasons for considering that the dry rates should not be reduced.

Proceedings of the Board forwarding the proposals for a revised settlement to Government.

The Board of Revenue,[6] in submitting to Government the Director's proposal for a revised settlement of the Trichinopoly District, considered Mr. Newill's answers to the criticisms passed by them on his first report at some length, and eventually arrived at the conclusion that Mr. Puckle's grouping for wet and dry villages, and his rates for dry lands and Mr. Newill's revised rates for wet lands should be adopted, on the distinct understanding that the village-cess and road-tax were included in the land-tax thus assessed. Before however the proceedings embodying these views were sent on to Government, a letter from Mr. Master, the Acting Director of Revenue Settlement, enclosing another letter from Mr. Puckle, was received, which caused the Board to append certain paragraphs to these proceedings, modifying them to a certain extent.

In the letter[7] just mentioned, Mr. Puckle brought to notice that the new survey had resulted in a much greater increase of area than had been anticipated, and gave it as his opinion that the result of the introduction of the survey measurements, and the revised assessment, would have the effect of increasing the revenue derived from the district by about a lakh of rupees instead of reducing it, as it had been expected would be the result. On this Mr. Master remarked[8] that, *primâ facie*, the mere fact of the area proving larger than was supposed, was no reason for interfering with the rates per acre, if the calculations by which they had been arrived at were correct and fair; but that, since it was generally admitted that the Trichinopoly District was too heavily assessed and needed relief, the circumstance that the new rates would, instead of affording the relief, actually increase the burden of taxation, demanded that these rates would not be adopted without careful consideration.

Mr. Puckle, in his letter to the Director, had remarked that the precise financial results of the new assessment could not be ascertained until a register had been prepared for every village, exhibiting the area and assessment of every individual field, and had proposed that, to enable Government to have before them an accurate estimate of the probable financial result of the introduction of the new assessment, village registers should be prepared with every column complete, except that the proposed rates should

---

(6) Proceedings of the Board of Revenue, No. 2,234, of the 5th April 1862.

(7) Deputy Director of Revenue Settlement to Officiating Director, No. 8, of 3rd April 1862.

(8) Director of Revenue Settlement to Board, No. 154-36, of 7th April 1862.

be entered in pencil only, so that they might be altered if necessary. Mr. Master pointed out, in modification of this plan, that the financial results of the settlement might be calculated, as soon as the survey areas were received, by taking the gross area coming under each class and sort from the abstract appended to the classification accounts, and calculating the assessment on them without ascertaining that on each field. To this the Board of Revenue agreed, and directed that, as soon as the survey areas were available, village area statements should be prepared, showing the financial results according to Mr. Puckle's original rates, Mr. Newill's modified rates, and again according to these rates reduced ten and twenty per cent. "The Government," it is remarked, "will then be in a position to determine with more safety and satisfaction what assessment shall be imposed."[9]

Before these proceedings were disposed of by Government another very important question connected with the revised assessment came before the Board. In a letter[10] to the Director of Revenue Settlement, Mr. Puckle proposed that the charge for second-crop should be altogether abolished. He was of opinion that, in consequence of the excess of area brought to light by the survey, which would have to be charged for in future, and the numerous instances in which the nominal rates hitherto paid would be raised, it was very doubtful if the existing charge on the river-irrigated lands would be materially reduced by the introduction of the new settlement, unless some relief, such as that proposed by him, was granted. Mr. Master, in sending on this proposal to the Board,[11] did not support it, as it appeared to him to be questionable whether, instead of attempting to correct rates confessedly too high by abolishing a separate and distinct item of assessment, the proper course would not be to reduce the rates themselves to the necessary limit. Mr. Puckle had urged that, as long as the second-crop charge existed, vexatious interference with the agricultural operations of the ryots would be unavoidable; but Mr. Master was of opinion that this objection would not hold good if a consolidated double-crop assessment was adopted, as Mr. Newill had proposed. The Board of Revenue, in forwarding these letters to Government in continuation of their previous proceedings regarding the new settlement proposed for Trichinopoly District, made the following remarks[12] :—

(9) Proceedings of the Board of Revenue, No. 2,234, of the 5th April 1862, paragraph 69.

(10) Deputy Director of Revenue Settlement to Director, No. 30, of 6th June 1862.

(11) Director of Revenue Settlement to Board, No. 825-54, of 20th June 1862.

(12) Proceedings of Board of Revenue, No. 4,663, of the 18th July 1862.

CHAPTER XI. REVENUE HISTORY, PART II.

"If Mr. Puckle's proposal is founded on good grounds, it affords an additional evidence that the proposed rates for single-crop wet land in Trichinopoly are too high. The Board fully concur in his objections to a distinct charge for a second crop, as tending to perpetuate uncertainty and most mischievous interference, while it checks enterprise and encourages fraud; but Mr. Puckle's proposal is in fact to relieve land possessing superior advantages of irrigation at the expense of those less favourably circumstanced, for, if land ordinarily capable of producing two crops cannot bear a consolidated rate, one-third higher than that charged on single-crop land, it can scarcely admit of doubt that the basis of that assessment on the double-crop land, viz., the rate for single-crop land of the same class, must be too heavy.

"The Board cannot support Mr. Puckle's proposal to take no account of second crops in assessing the Government demand on the land. They adhere to the views they have already expressed in favour of a consolidated assessment on double-crop land in lieu of a distinctive charge for a second crop, and they do not doubt that when the basis of the whole, the assessment for the first crop, which forms the whole charge on single-crop land, has been reduced to a fair and reasonable rate, the addition of one-third of that rate in the case of river-irrigated double-crop lands, and of one-fourth in that of similar tank lands and lands in the upland taluqs, to form the consolidated rate, will not result in producing a burdensome assessment, or one which the ryot will not willingly accept.

"The Board would lay it down, as a principle to be invariably and liberally applied, that no land which cannot safely bear a consolidated double-crop rate from its advantages of position and means of irrigation of a permanent character, should, under any circumstances, be charged for a second crop."

Government determine not to pass orders on these proposals till the receipt of further information from the Deputy Director.

The Government in G.O., No. 1,692, R.D., of the 8th August 1862, decided not to pass orders on the proposed settlement until the receipt of the statements which the Board had, on Mr. Puckle's suggestion, directed should be prepared, shewing the financial results of the revised assessment calculated on the new survey areas.

Mr. Puckle's report, giving the required information.

On the 28th of the following November, Mr. Puckle reported[13] to the Director of Revenue Settlement on the financial results of the new settlement, forwarding at the same time the statements that had been called for by the Board of Revenue. The Deputy Director had been instructed to prepare accounts showing the effect of introducing his own original rates; these, as altered by Mr. Newill, and also as reduced 10 and 20 per cent. The financial results of these several rates are given in the enclosures to

(13) Deputy Director of Revenue Settlement to Director, dated 28th November 1862.

Mr. Puckle's report, but he did not recommend that any of them should be introduced, but that, in their stead, the rates originally proposed by him, reduced by 13 per cent. for irrigated and 11 per cent. for unirrigated lands, should be adopted for the following reasons. He remarks that Mr. Newill's modification of his rates had reduced the assessment proposed by him by 6 and 14 per cent. on the first and second irrigated groups respectively, but had made no corresponding reduction either in the case of the three remaining irrigated groups or of the dry lands in the district. As these clearly demanded as much consideration as the rich villages in the valley of the Cauvery, Mr. Puckle reverted to the rates originally proposed by him, reducing them by 13 per cent. in irrigated and 11 per cent. in dry lands as a set-off against the unprofitable area that must be fairly allowed for and yet could not be deducted from each field. The Board had directed that 10 per cent. should be deducted in all measurement of cultivated areas for unfruitful or barren land, but, as a reduction at this rate would have caused uneven fractions of rupees and annas in every taram, Mr. Puckle proposed to modify it as just stated. The rates finally proposed by the Deputy Director are shown in the following table :—

Taram.	Irrigated.					Dry.		
	1st Group.	2nd Group.	3rd Group.	4th Group.	5th Group.	1st Group.	2nd Group.	3rd Group.
	RS. A.	RS. A.	RS. A.	RS. A.	RS. A.	RS. A.	RS. A.	RS. A.
1	8 0	7 8	6 0	5 8	5 0	3 4	3 0	2 12
2	7 0	6 8	5 0	4 8	4 0	2 12	2 8	2 4
3	6 0	5 8	4 0	3 12	3 8	2 4	2 0	1 12
4	5 0	4 8	3 12	3 8	3 0	1 12	1 8	1 4
5	4 0	4 0	3 4	3 0	2 8	1 4	1 0	0 14
6	3 8	3 4	3 12	2 8	2 4	0 14	0 12	0 10
7	3 0	2 12	2 4	2 4	2 0	0 10	0 8	0 6
8	2 8	2 4	2 0	2 0	2 0	0 6	0 6	0 6
9	..	..	..	..	..	0 6	0 6	0 6

Mr. Puckle remarks that, although 8 Rupees was given in his list as the highest assessment to be levied on any single crop in the district, yet it was not intended that this rate should be levied anywhere. It was included in the classification merely to express the money-value of the 2—1 in the technical language of the Settlement Department. As, however, there was none of this 2—1, or permanently-improved wet land, in either the first or second groups, Rupees 7, the rate proposed for the second taram, first group, would be the highest actually levied for a single crop and Rupees 9-6-0 for a permanent double-crop land. Further, even this moderate rate would be quite exceptional, as the great bulk of the area assessed as permanent double crop fell into the third and fourth tarams and would therefore be charged for at from 5 Rupees to 8 Rupees per acre in the first three groups, and at even lower rates in the two remaining ones.

The Deputy Director's report related to only seven of the nine taluqs into which the district was then divided, as the necessary statements for Udaiyárpálayam and Ariyalúr had not been completely prepared when it was submitted. The land-revenue of these seven taluqs for the previous year was 11½ lakhs. Of this amount 6,15,614 Rupees had been paid for irrigated and 5,21,203 Rupees for unirrigated land. Mr. Puckle calculated that the remission proposed by him would be altogether 2,16,550 Rupees, of which 77,237 Rupees would be the amount reduced on wet land and 1,39,313 Rupees on dry.

The following are the most important points connected with the mode of registering lands adopted by the Settlement Department in Trichinopoly as given by Mr. Puckle:—

I. The entire cultivation area of the district was divided into irrigated and dry, instead of irrigated, dry, and garden as it had been up till then.

II. All lands supplied by Government water direct from rivers, tanks, or channels or by picottah labor from Government wells or other sources of supply yielding sufficient water for the production of wet crops were registered as irrigated.

III. Irrigated lands possessing a twofold source of supply, such as a tank and a well, a river-channel and a tank, &c., were entered as permanently-improved.

IV. Lands entirely dependent upon local rainfall or irrigated by private wells and tanks or from Government wells that yielded enough water to raise only dry grains or vegetables were registered as dry.

V. No lands were entered as permanently improved unless they had some means of irrigation. Fields irrigated by baling were, as a general rule, registered as wet, but in some localities where the water-supply was sufficient to produce only a dry crop they were entered as permanently-improved dry.

VI. Topes irrigated with Government water were entered as wet, but those not thus irrigated as dry according to the classified value of the soil. Topes planted under the rules of 1848 were classed as dry.

Up to the time of the introduction of the settlement it had been the custom to enter all lands held in common by the villagers rateably in undivided pattás. Thus fifty men might have shares in a plot of land not ten acres in extent which was not divided into fields but cultivated in common, the produce being divided by mutual agreement. One man might get one-third of the produce and another one-fiftieth, but, whatever was the amount of the share received, a proportionate extent of the common land was entered in each holder's pattá. Mr. Puckle proposed to abolish this system and issue but one *samudáyam* pattá, with the names of all the shareholders, to the headman of the village, leaving the value of the several shares and the amount of assessment due by individuals to be apportioned among them by themselves.

As regards the question of imposition of a consolidated cess as assessment for a second crop, Mr. Puckle stated that, as the Board had required that this cess should be fixed on only such lands as were likely to produce a second crop in ordinary seasons with almost perfect certainty, he had prepared lists of all fields cultivated with a second crop during three consecutive faslis, and after striking out first those irrigated solely by picottah labor; secondly, those which formed but fractional parts of a survey block; and, thirdly, those that were so exceptional that the second-crop assessment of the village in which they were situated would be less than 10 Rupees per annum, he had finally entered as permanent double crop only such a portion of the remainder as had borne a double crop at least twice during three successive seasons. Besides the area thus assessed as permanent double crop, there were many fields irrigated by picottah labor that sometimes yielded a second crop of paddy, but more frequently one of dry grains or garden-produce. These Mr. Puckle excluded from the imposition of the consolidated cess, in consideration of the expense incurred in raising water, and the consequent disadvantage that their owners labored under in comparison with those more fortunate ryots who drew their water-supply direct from a tank or river-channel. He left it for the Board to decide, whether those lands which had not been classed as permanent double crop, but which nevertheless yielded an occasional second crop, should continue to be charged second-crop assessment. He however remarked that, if it should be deemed inexpedient to sacrifice a certain source of revenue by exempting from all extra charge such lands as produced an occasional second crop, he begged to suggest that, instead of retaining the existing method of taxation on even a portion of the irrigated lands, it might be preferable to increase the area of permanent double crop by including all lands thus cultivated in the previous year rather than continue the imposition of a fluctuating charge, which would not only involve the annual alteration or renewal of a considerable percentage of the pattás, but would also expose the ryots to a continuance of the existing system of vexatious interference on the part of the revenue subordinates, which he believed

CHAPTER XI. REVENUE HISTORY, PART II.

to be a far greater evil than any slight over-assessment in individual cases, where a second crop might be charged for, though it could not be invariably produced.

As regards the financial results of the introduction of the new settlement, Mr. Puckle stated that the reduction that he had proposed in the assessment of the seven taluqs then reported on amounted to 3,04,330 Rupees. As a set-off, however, against this reduction, there were in the district 309,207 acres of cultivable waste assessed at 2,18,602 Rupees, and he expected that a large extent of this land would be taken up as soon as the proposed light assessment was introduced. The application of the new rates to the two taluqs, Ariyalúr and Udaiyárpálayam, not reported on in this letter, would, it was estimated by Mr. Puckle, effect a further reduction of about 60,000 Rupees. The available sources of revenue in these taluqs were, however, 130,000 acres of cultivable waste not then assessed, but which at the low rate of 8 Annas an acre would, it was calculated, yield a revenue of Rupees 65,000, and large tracts of jungle which had not been surveyed, but which, Mr. Puckle considered, would no doubt be cleared and cultivated at no very distant period.

Remarks of the Director, Mr. R. E. Master, on Mr. Puckle's report.

Mr. R. E. Master, the Director of Revenue Settlement, in forwarding this report to the Board of Revenue,[14] observed that it appeared to him to be an objectionable feature in the scale of rates for irrigated lands proposed by Mr. Puckle, that 7 Rupees would become the maximum rate for the best lands watered by the Cauvery, whereas in the adjoining district of South Arcot the maximum was Rupees 8-8-0, and land similar in quality. and not superior in point of irrigation was assessed at Rupees 7-8-0. He therefore proposed to raise the rates to a slight degree in the first group. As regards the dry assessment, he pointed out that Mr. Puckle had proposed to reduce the rates originally recommended by him in the same manner as he had reduced the wet rates, so that the loss of revenue under this head would be 1,39,313 Rupees instead of Rupees 80,882 as at first expected. Mr. Master calculated that, if the altered rates were introduced, only 5 per cent. of the entire dry area would be assessed at a higher rate than Rupees 1-12-0, that 19 per cent. would be charged Rupees 1-12-0 or Rupees 1-8-0, and that 37 per cent. would come under the six-anna rate, the average rate being Annas 14-6 on cultivated dry land and Annas 10-8 on waste. As this appeared to him to be a very low average, and as the adoption of the rates originally proposed would give relief to the ryots to the extent of 15 per cent., he proposed to revert to them.

---

(14) Director of Revenue Settlement to Board, No. 1,558-87, of the 31st December 1862.

CHAPTER XI. REVENUE HISTORY, PART II.

Proceedings of the Board of Revenue sending all the papers connected with the revised settlement for the orders of Government.

The Board of Revenue, in reviewing these letters and submitting the proposed settlement for the orders of Government, made the following remarks on it.[15] The circumstances of the district are stated to be as follows:—"An inland position, a shallow and comparatively poor soil, indifferent irrigation even as regards the Cauvery-irrigated land, a limited and very fluctuating market and a barbarous revenue system under which the taxation is based on the crop and varies with every change of cultivation and with the caste and even the residence of the ryot. It is essentially an unirrigated district, nine-tenths of its lands being under dry grain cultivation, and 52 per cent. of the culturable area consisting of the poorest clay and gravelly soils of the Karnatic. The channels from the Cauvery upper anicut are at so high a level that only when the river is in tolerable flood does the water run down them, and much labor and expense is incurred by the ryots in forming korambus, or mud dams, to divert the stream into the channel. The irrigated cultivation is very generally dependent on picottah and well irrigation; the population are industrious but poor; emigration has thinned the number of agricultural laborers; in a word, the district is one that eminently needs relief although its present state is improved and improving. Under a moderate though fair settlement of the land-tax, the Board are sanguine that it will rapidly progress."

The Board go on to observe that they believed that the revision that had been made of the rates had resulted in proposals which might safely be adopted with advantage to all concerned as calculated to attain the end in view, namely, that the assessment should be fixed and so moderate as to render remissions unnecessary, except in years of great and extraordinary drought.

After a conference with the Director and Deputy Director of Revenue Settlement and the then Collector of the district, the Board proposed the following rates, which it was stated had the entire approval of these officers, and would, it was believed, be acceptable to the people and ultimately advantageous to the interests of the State.

Irrigated per Acre for a Single Crop.

Taram or Class of Land.	First Group of Villages.		Second Group of Villages.		Third Group of Villages.		Fourth Group of Villages.		Fifth Group of Villages.	
	RS.	A.	RS.	A.	RS.	A.	RS.	A.	RS.	A.
1	8	0	7	8	6	0	5	8	5	0
2	7	0	6	8	5	0	4	8	4	0
3	6	0	5	8	4	0	3	12	3	8
4	5	0	4	8	3	12	3	8	3	0
5	4	8	4	0	3	4	3	0	2	8
6	3	8	3	4	2	12	2	8	2	4
7	3	0	2	12	2	4	2	4	2	0
8	2	8	2	4	2	0	2	0	2	0

(15) Proceedings of the Board of Revenue, No. 1,270, of 3rd March 1863.

CHAPTER XI. REVENUE HISTORY, PART II.

For lands classed as permanent double crop a consolidated assessment, one-third higher than the proposed rates in the Nírárambam and one-fourth higher in the Kádárambam Taluqs, was to be imposed, and on lands classed as doubtful of two crops a consolidated assessment formed by the addition of half rupee to these rates.

The fluctuating charge for an occasional second crop it was proposed should be abolished totally, and with it all the vast opportunities the system afforded, in the opinion of the Board, for bribery, corruption, oppression, and fraud and the excessive labor that it entailed for most meagre results.

Unirrigated per Acre.

Taram or Class of Land.	First Group of Villages.	Second Group of Villages.	Third Group of Villages.
	RS. A.	RS. A.	RS. A.
1	3 4	3 0	2 12
2	2 12	2 8	2 4
3	2 4	2 0	1 12
4	1 12	1 8	1 4
5	1 4	1 0	0 14
6	0 14	0 12	0 10
7	0 10	0 8	0 6
8	0 6	0 6	0 6
9	0 6	0 6	0 6

These rates are identical with those proposed by Mr. Puckle, with the exception of the fifth nunjah taram in the first group of villages to which 8 Annas per acre was added to get rid of an anomaly pointed out by Mr. Master of rating this class of land at the same amount in the first and second groups. To this addition Mr. Puckle did not object, and the rest of his rates for wet lands were eventually approved of by Mr. Master, whose objections to the rates for the first group had been based on an assumed similarity between Trichinopoly and the adjoining district of South Arcot in quality of soil and circumstances of situation, which the Board considered did not really exist, as

Trichinopoly was, in their opinion, in an inferior position in both these respects.

Mr. Master had proposed a considerable addition to Mr. Puckle's dry rates, but, after discussing the subject with the Deputy Director, the Collector of the district, and the Board, he withdrew his objections because, as observed in the Board's Proceedings, further consideration showed that his proposed rates would in reality result in an addition to the tax on dry lands as compared with the settlement of Fasli 1271, a result which it is stated that neither he nor the Board contemplated or considered the district able to bear. In regard to the charge for a second crop on irrigated land the Board remark that they "advocate strongly the adoption of the consolidated assessment proposed, in lieu of a fluctuating charge with all its attendant evils and the abuses to which it gives rise, in obtaining by a most expensive process financial results of comparatively trifling importance. The retention of the temporary charge for second crop necessitates an annual examination of lands sown and much inquisitorial interference, which at all times are evils to be deprecated, even if under the present system they cannot be altogether avoided. It is the desire of the Board to reduce to the minimum this interference, which is the source of bribery, corruption, and oppression, and under the revised assessment there will be no necessity for any inspection of cultivation for the first crop. If the recommendation now made for abolishing the temporary charge for second crop be adopted, the necessity will altogether cease."

To obtain a consolidated assessment for the Trichinopoly District, Mr. Newill had proposed an addition of one-third to the single-crop rates on double-crop land under the Cauvery irrigation. The Board supported this proposal for the Cauvery irrigated double crop lands, and proposed an addition of one-fourth of the single-crop rate to form a consolidated assessment for two-crop lands in the Kádárambam and under tanks.

Corrected by survey, the area charged with second-crop assessment in the seven taluqs reported on by Mr. Puckle in Fasli 1271 was found to be 31,101 acres, of which 21,563 acres were classed by Mr. Puckle as permanent double crop. There therefore remained 9,538 acres liable under the then existing system to an occasional charge for second crop when raised, which, at the average rate of Rupees 1-8-0 per acre, would produce about Rupees 14,000 in the event of the whole area being so cultivated in any one year. The Board however were of opinion that it would

CHAPTER XI. REVENUE HISTORY, PART II.

in reality never produce a revenue return approaching to this amount.

The Board then proceed to observe as follows :—

"In consideration of the trifling amount of revenue at stake and of the great evils inherent in the system of a temporary charge for a second crop, the Board would have advocated the entire relinquishment of the charge rather than that recourse should be had to an expedient which they cannot too strongly denounce; but they are unwilling to risk the chance of introducing a cause for contention as to the right to use surplus water when such may be present, and they therefore propose, as a reasonable compromise, that an addition of Annas 8 per acre shall be made to the single-crop assessment to form a consolidated rate for all land classed by the Deputy Director as 'doubtful of two crops,' and that all further charge for occasional second crops shall be absolutely excluded from the revenue system of the district. This measure the Board believe will greatly conduce to the outlay of private capital in the improvement of means of irrigation, and thereby to the stability of the Government revenue, for the ryots will be able to sink wells in their wet lands without the possibility of being charged extra for water as if it were brought from the Government source of irrigation."

On all the papers connected with the revision of the assessment in Trichinopoly coming before Government, Sir W. Denison, who was then Governor of Madras, took exception to Mr. Puckle's calculations in several particulars, and especially objected to the proposed commutation prices and to the assessment not being based on a definite proportion of the *net* produce. The whole question was therefore referred for the decision of the Secretary of State for India.[16]

Reply from the Secretary of State to this reference.

In his reply to this reference from the Government of Madras, the Secretary of State remarked[17] that Sir W. Denison had stated that the main points in his argument were as follows :—

First.—The adoption of the *net* produce instead of the *gross* as the unit of which Government should take a fraction.

Second.—The adoption of one-third as the fraction to be taken.

Third.—That the commutation rate should be 12 Annas per Harris kalam of paddy.

As regards the first of these points, the Secretary of State remarked that the Court of Directors, in their despatch of the 17th

(16) Letter to the Right Honorable the Secretary of State for India, No. 113, of the 26th October 1863.

(17) Letter from the Secretary of State for India, No. 7, dated 24th February 1864.

December 1856, in conveying their sanction of the revised survey and settlement of the Madras Presidency, had directed that the assessment should be proportioned to the *net* and not to the *gross* produce, and that this principle had been upheld in the Secretary of State's despatch of the 15th December 1858. Adhering to this view, the Secretary of State therefore directed that in the revision of the assessment in Trichinopoly the *net* and not the *gross* produce should be adopted as the unit of which Government was to take a fraction.

Chapter XI. Revenue History, Part II.

As regards the second point, namely, whether one-third or one-half should be adopted as the fraction to be taken, the Secretary of State decided that the share of the *net* produce which might fairly be taken as the due of Government should be assumed at one-half, but that this proportion was "not to be worked out pedantically or with any pretence to mathematical accuracy, but to be kept in view by every Settlement Officer in forming his assessments."

With reference to the third point, the Secretary of State observed that, as all the authorities that had given their opinion, with the exception of the Governor, had considered that 8 Annas per Harris kalam was a fair commutation rate, he had no hesitation in deciding that that rate should be adopted as the commutation rate for paddy, a proportionate rate being assumed for the grains on which the assessment of the dry lands was calculated.

Final orders of Government sanctioning the introduction of the new settlement.

On the receipt of this despatch orders[18] were passed on the whole question. Government remarked that they did not consider it necessary to enter into the details of the original operations or of the various assessments that had been laid before them. They accepted Mr. Puckle's calculations of the gross and net produce, his scheme of grouping and the proposed commutation rates. In accordance with the instructions received from the Secretary of State, the Government assessment was fixed at a moiety of the net produce, subject to a deduction of 10 per cent. for unprofitable fields of which the survey did not take account. The following rates were fixed for each class of land and group of villages, a reasonable discretion, however, being left to the settling officer in applying them in particular instances.

---

(18) G.O., No. 577, of the 5th April 1864, R. D.

CHAPTER XI.
REVENUE HISTORY, PART II.

Irrigated.

Primary Taram.	Class.	Sort.	First Group.	Second Group.	Third Group.	Fourth Group.	Fifth Group.
			RS. A.	RS. A.	RS. A.	RS. A.	RS. A.
1	..	..	9 4	8 12 0	7 4	6 12 0	6 4
2	2	2	8 0	7 8	6 0	5 8	5 0
	4	1	7 8	7 0	5 8	5 0	4 8
3	..	..	6 8	6 0	4 8	4 0	3 8
4	..	..	5 8	5 0	3 8	3 4	3 0
5	..	..	4 8	4 0	3 0	2 12	2 8
6	..	..	3 8	3 4	2 8	2 4	2 0
7	..	..	3 0	2 12	2 0	1 12	1 8
8	..	..	2 8	2 4	1 8	1 4	1 0

Unirrigated.

Primary Taram.	Class.	Sort.	First Group.	Second Group.	Third Group.
			RS. A. P.	RS. A. P.	RS. A. P.
1	..	..	3 8 0	3 2 0	2 12 0
2	..	..	2 12 0	2 8 0	2 4 0
3	..	..	2 4 0	2 0 0	1 12 0
4	3	1	2 0 0	1 12 0	1 10 0
	4	2	1 12 0	1 10 0	1 8 0
	7	1			
5	..	..	1 8 0	1 4 0	1 0 0
6	..	..	1 0 0	0 13 0	10 0 0
7	..	..	0 10 0	0 9 0	0 8 0
8	..	..	0 8 0	0 7 0	0 6 0
9	..	..	0 6 0	0 5 0	0 4 0

The Government then proceeded to pass orders on some minor points connected with the settlement.

Second-crop cultivation.

All the wet land had been rated as single crop, and half the assessment was to be charged in addition to the rate for the first crop when a second crop was raised. The Board of Revenue and the Settlement Officers had proposed to charge a consolidated rate for second-crop cultivation to be paid whether a supply of water was available or not on all lands which were almost certain of getting such a supply in at least two out of every three years. The consolidated rate proposed was one-third of the single-crop assessment in irrigated taluqs and one-fourth in unirrigated. As regards this proportion, the Government remarked that the principle of a consolidated double-crop assessment had much to recommend it and that it was worth while giving up one-sixth of the full charge to attain it. It however did not appear why, if one-third was a fair rate in irrigated taluqs, one-fourth should be proposed for unirrigated. "The lands," it is remarked, "are grouped and classified in both on the same principle, and thus difference in soils and character of irrigation is provided for and the same care is taken to rate as double crop only such lands as are likely to produce a second crop in ordinary seasons with almost perfect certainty. It is therefore unnecessary liberality to commute at a lower rate in the upland than in the other taluqs." The Government go on to observe that the same arguments that supported the consolidation of the second-crop charge on permanent double-crop land also supported the additional proposal made by the Board of Revenue to compound for the irrigation of those lands which were supplied with less certainty. It was, however, considered that the rate proposed, 8 Annas per acre, was out of the question and had been fixed in disregard of all principles. The Board had described the charge for occasional double crop as affording vast opportunities for bribery, corruption, oppression, and fraud and as entailing excessive labor for most meagre results, but the Government considered that this was an overdrawn picture. They did not see why the charge for doubtful irrigation should not be fixed on the same principle as the permanent second-crop assessment, *i.e.*, in the ratio of the uncertainty of the water-supply, at one-fourth or one-fifth of the first-crop rate, and directed that in all cases there should be a minimum charge of not less than 1 Rupee as the very smallest sum for which Government could be at the cost of supplying water.

Village servants' fees.

The total amount of the fees paid to the village servants in the district at the time of the introduction of the revised settlement amounted to Rupees 1,18,666.[19] This sum included what was called the "*Katlai-silavu*," amounting to Rupees 63,790,[19] which was an allowance supposed to be paid by the ryots to the Karnams as a remuneration for the oil, cadjans, &c., used in the preparation of the settlement accounts, and as batta during their absence from their villages on public business. In reality, however, the Karnams generally throughout the district were solely dependent on this cess for remuneration for their official work.[20] The cess was levied in various ways, and the amount to be paid was apportioned

---

(19) Proceedings of the Board of Revenue, No. 7,752, of the 3rd December 1864.

(20) Collector of Trichinopoly, to Board of Revenue, No. 133, of the 19th August 1856.

CHAPTER XI. REVENUE HISTORY, PART II.

among the ryots according to their means. In the Kádárambam Taluqs and in the dry villages in Kónád, Musiri, and Lálgudi the amount to be paid by each ryot was entered in his pattá and collected with the Government assessment. In the wet villages in the Nírárambam taluqs, and in the dry villages in Válikandapuram, it was not entered in the pattás, but paid in kind to the Karnams by the ryots themselves. In the Manapparai Taluq, transferred from Madura District in 1856, it did not exist, and the Karnams there were remunerated by grants of Inám land. The Government directed that, on the introduction of the settlement, the *Katlai-silavu* should cease to be collected, but that the other fees paid to the village officials, amounting to about five per cent. on the assessment, should continue to be levied. It was determined that, as soon as a law was enacted for the purpose, these fees should be formally commuted, and that, in the mean time, an addition of five per cent. on the assessment should be charged in lieu of them and entered in the pattás.

Report from Mr. Puckle showing the immediate results of the introduction of the revised assessment.

The Government Order, sanctioning the introduction of the revised assessment, was passed on the 5th of April 1864, and the actual settlement, according to the new rates, was commenced by Mr. Puckle on the 10th of the following May. In applying the revised rates he dealt with the occupation of Fasli 1273 (1863-64). The settlement for that year on the old rates was Rupees 15,82,074 and the new assessment was Rupees 11,94,018, being a reduction of Rupees 3,88,056, which was made up of the following items.[21]

Items.	Assessment of Years previous to Settlement.	Settlement.	Decrease by Settlement.	Percentage of Reduction.
	RS.	RS.	RS.	RS.
Single crop irrigated ..	6,89,364	5,26,634	1,63,230	24
Do. dry	6,84,335	5,38,376	1,46,459	21
Do. garden ..	98,573	80,167	18,506	19
Second crop irrigated ..	84,287	48,841	35,446	42
Do. garden ..	24,415	..	24,415	100
Total ..	15,82,074	11,94,018	3,88,056	25

To secure uniformity throughout the district the area irrigated directly from tanks or river-channels, as also by water raised from

(21) Letter from Deputy Director of Revenue Settlement, to Director, dated 30th May 1865.

large Government wells, was everywhere assessed as permanently-improved irrigated land in the first and second classes only. Other lands, having only a direct supply from a tank or river-channel, were assessed as ordinary irrigated lands from the third class downwards. Lands supplied with water by picottah labor or by baling from any Government well, tank, stream, or channel were assessed as permanently-improved dry lands or gardens in the first and third classes only. Lands without any kind of irrigation, as also those supplied with water from private tanks or wells, were assessed as ordinary dry land in the second, fourth, and lower classes. The following table shows the area and assessment of the cultivated lands in the district, both irrigated and dry, under each money-rate as assessed by Mr. Puckle:— CHAPTER XI. REVENUE HISTORY, PART II.

Irrigated.			Dry.		
Rate.	Area in Acres.	Assessment in Rupees.	Rate.	Area in Acres.	Assessment in Rupees.
RS. A.			RS. A.		
7 8	967	7,249	3 8 ..	9,616	33,656
7 4	23	167	3 2 ..	3,081	9,634
7 0	2,296	16,070	2 12 ..	1,277	3,510
6 12	770	5,201	2 8 ..	613	1,532
6 8	3,164	20,572	2 4 ..	10,062	22,643
6 4	7	42	2 0 ..	1,315	2,629
6 0	19,608	1,17,645	1 12 ..	36,509	63,896
5 8	4,068	22,374	1 10 ..	33,125	53,829
5 0	19,899	99,539	1 8 ..	45,292	67,942
4 8	8,449	38,026	1 4 ..	25,907	32,384
4 0	13,076	52,307	1 0 ..	197,978	1,97,987
3 8	12,245	42,850	0 13 ..	18,704	15,197
3 4	7,600	24,704	0 10 ..	31,795	19,876
3 0	8,116	24,351	0 9 .	17,364	9,768
2 12	3,480	9,569	0 8 ..	66,032	33,020
2 8	14,456	36,140	0 7 ..	10,644	4,657
2 4	676	1,521	0 6 ..	107,061	40,152
2 0	3,115	6,230	0 5 ..	1,426	446
1 12	122	212	0 4 ..	23,130	5,785
1 8	878	1,316	..	..	..
1 0	548	548	..	..	..
Total ..	123,563	5,26,633	..	640,931	6,18,543

The highest rate imposed on irrigated land was, it will be remarked, Rupees 7-8-0 per acre; the average rate was Rupees 4-4-0 per acre, about 40 per cent. of the total area being rated at 5 Rupees per acre and upwards. The average assessment on dry land, including garden cultivation, was almost exactly Rupee 1. The average assessment on garden cultivation was Rupees 2-11-0, and on ordinary dry cultivation 14 Annas per acre.

The ryots readily accepted the terms on which Government had directed that a consolidated cess should be charged for permanent double crop raised on wet lands, and agreed to compound for even Second crop.

CHAPTER XI. REVENUE HISTORY, PART II.

a larger area than had been expected. Garden lands were not compounded for as permanent double crop, as the cess levied on cultivation of this nature was in the revised settlement confined to wet lands; but Mr. Puckle was of opinion that garden lands along channel banks should be made to pay for an occasional second crop if supplied with water from a Government source for the following reasons:—"For though not generally better off than gardens irrigated from wells, yet at the very time that the channels are low and water is most precious everywhere, picottahs are busily at work exhausting the channels and effectually cutting off the water-supply from those who would gladly pay for it. For every acre of garden thus irrigated by baling a corresponding area of wet land lower down the stream is prevented from growing a second crop; and, therefore, as it is but fair that those who get the water should pay for it, if occupants of garden land think fit to cultivate a second crop by raising water from river-channels, they should do so on precisely the same terms as other ryots who cultivate wet lands." In this view the Board of Revenue and Government coincided, and Mr. Puckle's proposals were accordingly carried out.

"To make up for the present reduction," Mr. Puckle remarks, "there are 402,703 acres of culturable waste assessed at 3,68,352 Rupees, as well as 130,000 acres not yet surveyed or classified, mostly in the Perambalúr and Udaiyárpálayam taluqs. The ryots are so anxious to take up land that the revenue of the district is now likely to increase even more rapidly than it has done since the general remission in 1854. But it is not only by the cultivation of waste land that the revenue will be increased, but by the extension of irrigation, occasional second crop, ready-money collections, &c., and the ratio of increase for the next three years will probably amount to nearly a lakh of rupees per annum. In five years time the reduction will certainly be made up, and the revenue will amount to even more than it did before the settlement."

Mr. Puckle concludes his final report on the Trichinopoly revised settlement with the following remarks:—"Each entry in the registers has been taken from the Karnam's accounts, and has been tested by passing through many processes, and the results arrived at have been finally submitted to the scrutiny of the ryots themselves. The latter, however, look more to total figures than to detailed entries, and, with all precautions taken, some errors will still be found. For the recent change of system was too good an opportunity to be lost by those who hoped to gain petty benefits by misrepresenting the actual state of things, and thus no doubt some irrigated lands are registered as dry, some patches of garden are rated unduly low, and deductions are made for waste that does not actually exist; but these and similar errors will be at once brought to light if a thorough and complete examination of every field in the district be made by competent and trustworthy offices, as soon as they are provided with the settlement maps and registers.

"The field and village boundary marks that actually exist at present have been made over to the Collector's care, but many marks once erected have now entirely disappeared. There is, however, no difficulty in determining the exact position of any boundary mark by the aid of the map and register, and steps should be taken to redemark every field as permanently as possible; with the fields thus demarked and with map and register in hand, a European officer may proceed to any village and satisfy himself as to the condition of any field or number of fields without asking a single question or having recourse to the Karnam for aid."

In reviewing[22] the Deputy Director's report, the Board of Revenue remarked that they saw no reason to question the reasonableness of Mr. Puckle's estimation that in five years the revenue of the district would exceed what it was before the introduction of the revised assessment. The Government also, in the order[23] passed on these papers, stated that they entertained no doubt that the district, unless it was visited by a succession of exceptionally adverse seasons, would rapidly advance in wealth in consequence of the simple and moderate character of the new land-tax, and that, within the period of five years fixed by Mr. Puckle, its entire revenue would considerably exceed its former standard while the condition of the people would be materially improved. In accordance with a proposal that had been made by the Board of Revenue, Government, in the same Order, directed that the District Road Cess Act (Madras Act III of 1866) should be extended to the whole of the Trichinopoly District from the commencement of the current fasli and fixed the rate of assessment at 6 Pies in every rupee on the annual rent-value of all land. It was ordered that as the land-tax on the ryotwári lands under the new settlement included 2 per cent. for road-cess, a further charge of 2 Pies only should be levied on such lands, but that all other lands should be charged 6 Pies.

An account of the results of the new settlement, as far as they have been ascertained up to this, is given in the next chapter.

(22) Proceedings of the Board of Revenue, No. 3,641, of the 28th May 1866.
(23) G.O., No. 2,523, R.D., of the 19th September 1866.

CHAPTER XII.

REVENUE HISTORY OF TRICHINOPOLY, PART III.

THE RESULTS OF THE REVISED SETTLEMENT AND THE REVENUE HISTORY OF THE DISTRICT SINCE ITS INTRODUCTION.

Revision of the Village Establishment.—Examination instituted by Mr. Banbury with a view to the detection of evasions of revenue.—Mr. Banbury's report regarding the causes of the evasions.—Financial results of the settlement.—Proposal to redemarcate the district.—List of the Collectors of Trichinopoly.

CHAPTER XII. REVENUE HISTORY, PART III.

Revision of the Village Establishment.

THE most important alteration that has been made in the revenue administration of the district since the introduction of the new settlement is the revision of the Village Establishment. In the order sanctioning the introduction of the new settlement Government directed that the cess known as *katlai silavu*, an account of which has already been given, should be abolished; that the other village fees which had hitherto been paid should be continued; and that, pending a law providing for the commutation of these fees, an addition of five per cent. should be made to the assessment in lieu of them.[1] The proposed enactment was passed as Act IV of 1864 (Madras) on the 26th August 1864, and was extended to Trichinopoly District from the 1st January 1865, the cess leviable under it being one anna on every rupee of assessment and water-rate, or $6\frac{1}{4}$ per cent. of the land revenue.[2] In the following June some further orders were passed by Government regarding the *katlai silavu*, and it was directed that, as the revised assessment was *inclusive* of this cess, in case the collections made under the Village Cess Act fell short of the cost of the revised Village Establishment when introduced, the deficiency should be met from the ordinary land revenue to an extent not exceeding Rupees 63,790, the amount of the abolished cess.[3]

In September 1868 the Board of Revenue directed the Collector of Trichinopoly to draw up a scheme for the revision of the Village Establishment of the district.[4] In his reply to these Proceedings Mr. Banbury, who was then Collector, reported that the number of villages that would be affected by the new establishment was 1,255, of which 111 however were uninhabited. In the remaining 1,144 villages there were 9,758 village officials bearing the following designations :—

(1) G.O., No. 577, of the 5th April 1864, paragraphs 20–22.
(2) G.O., No. 2,267, of the 16th December 1864.
(3) G.O. of the 30th June 1865, paragraphs 12 and 13.
(4) Proceedings of the Board of Revenue, No. 6,265, of the 2nd September 1868.

2,662 Pattámaniyagàrs (Village Heads).
814 Karnams.
3,813 Vettiyáns.
1,794 Taliáries (Village Watchmen).
174 Shroffs.
18 Vattaráyasams (Clerks under Revenue Inspectors).
185 Tandalkárans (Village Collectors performing the duties partly of Peons and partly of Shroffs).
6 Úr Sévagans (Village Peons).
59 Múppans (Water Distributors).
85 Níránies (Do).
2 Kondiótties (Impounders of Stray Cattle).
19 Pannaigárans (Assistant Manigars).

Mr. Banbury proposed to dispense with the services of all these officials, except the Pattámaniyagàrs, Karnams, Vettiyáns, Taliáries, and Vattaráyasams. The Board in the orders passed on this letter agreed with the Collector, except as regards the Vattaráyasams, whom they directed should also be dispensed with as the pay of Clerks for Revenue Inspectors could not be charged to Village Service Funds. Mr. Banbury proposed to form the 1,255 villages in the district into 702 groups, but the Board considered that the grouping had been carried too far, and directed the Collector to revise his proposals in this particular. As regards the question as to how far the post of Karnam and Maniyagàr were to be considered hereditary, the Board in the same Proceedings directed that the office of Karnam should continue to be non-mirássi, but that in practice the next heir of the last incumbent, duly qualified in education, character, and conduct, should always have the preference over others. When however a Karnam was convicted of any serious offence involving moral turpitude the claim of his family was to lapse. The same rule was to be followed in the case of Maniyagàrs.[5]

In his reply to these Proceedings, Mr. Banbury proposed to raise the number of clubbed villages to 810.[6] The Board[7] approved of the amended scheme and the following village establishment was eventually sanctioned by Government[8] :—

Office.	No.	Cost per Annum.
		RS.
Karnams	810	68,604
Maniyagars	870	36,498
Vettiyáns	864	31,104
Taliáries	964	34,704
Total ..	3,508	1,70,910

(5) Proceedings of the Board of Revenue, No. 2,056, of the 24th March 1869.
(6) Collector to Board, No. 89, of 30th April 1869.
(7) Board's Proceedings, No. 6925, of 15th September 1869.
(8) G.O., No. 965, of 19th June 1870, R.D.

CHAPTER XII. REVENUE HISTORY, PART III.

One Karnam was to be allotted to each village, and these officers were to receive pay according to the following scale per mensem:—

	RS.
In villages the revenue of which was above Rs. 4,000 ..	9
Do. do. of above Rs. 2,000 and less than Rs. 4,000	8
Do. do. of above Rs. 1,000 and less than Rs. 2,000	7
Do. do. of under Rs. 1,000	6

The Maniyagárs, who were to be also the Village Munsifs, were to receive Rupees 3-8-0 per mensem, and the Taliáries and Vettiyáns Rupees 3 each. The cost of this establishment was estimated, as already stated, at Rupees 1,70,910 per annum. To meet this expenditure the following funds were available:—It was calculated that the Village Service Cess would produce Rupees 96,365 per annum, and this cess was when necessary to be supplemented by grants from the General Village Service Fund which was to consist of (1) the annual deduction from the revenue of the district instead of the abolished *katlai silavu* amounting to Rupees 63,790; (2) the amount that would be realized by the enfranchisement of the Service Ináms estimated at Rupees 9,544; (3) the interest derived from the amount of the fund that had accumulated up till then, calculated to be about Rupees 75,000 a-year.

The revised Village Establishment was introduced in October 1870. The actual amount realized by the enfranchisement of the Village Service Ináms was Rupees 9,639. The proceeds of the Village Service Cess are about Rupees 1,15,000 a-year, and the balance standing to the credit of the General Service Fund on the 31st March 1876 was Rupees 72,406.

Examination instituted by Mr. Banbury with a view to the detection of evasions of revenue.

Towards the conclusion of his final report on the settlement of the district, Mr. Puckle had remarked that, notwithstanding all the precautions taken, the change of system introduced by the new settlement had been too good an opportunity to be lost, and that there could be no doubt that in some cases irrigated lands had been entered as dry, deductions made for waste that did not exist, &c., but that these errors could easily be brought to light by a thorough examination of the fields made as soon as the maps and registers had been prepared.[9] Acting on this suggestion the Collector, Mr. Banbury, in 1869, commenced a complete examination (*azmaish*) of the entire district with the view of detecting any frauds or mistakes that might have been

(9) Letter from Deputy Director of Revenue Settlement to Director, dated 30th May 1865, paragraph 62.

committed. The inquiry at first progressed but slowly owing to the limited staff available for employment on it, but in March the Government sanctioned the temporary transfer of the Salem Settlement Party to Trichinopoly to assist in the examination.[10] The *azmaish* went on through the whole of that year and was finished in Fasli 1280 (1870-71), the result being that a large extent of concealed cultivation was discovered, various other frauds and mistakes detected, and no less than Rs. 2,39,990 brought to account as the direct result of the examination.

CHAPTER XII. REVENUE HISTORY, PART III.

Mr. Banbury's report regarding the causes of the evasions.

In G.O., No. 418, of the 8th March 1871, Government directed Mr. Banbury, who was then Director of Revenue Settlement, to submit a report on the evasions of revenue detected by means of the examination set on foot by him when Collector, showing how there came to be opportunity for them and how they might be guarded against for the future. In his reply to this order[11] Mr. Banbury commenced by enumerating the frauds that had been detected as follows :—

I. False *porambokes*, or portions of fields untruly asserted to be uncultivable, and thus deducted from the area of the survey fields.

II. Wet lands falsely entered as dry.

III. Garden lands irrigated by baling and fraudulently declared to be dry.

IV. Waste land cultivated but not brought to account.

V. Water-rate not charged upon dry lands, both Government and Inám, to which Government water had been taken.

VI. Second crop raised on single crop wet lands, both Government and Inám, but not brought to account.

VII. Cultivation upon prohibited spots, such as channel-banks, village-sites, burning-grounds, &c., the assessment upon which should have been brought to *Sivāy Jamā* or extra sources.

Of these items, the three first were frauds which, when detected, were set right for ever and could not occur again. Mr. Banbury makes the following remarks regarding them :—

False porambokes.

" There is no doubt that the ryots took greatly to heart the discovery of excess areas in their holdings by the survey, and tried their utmost to do away with what they disapproved of and dreaded as likely eventually to enhance their assessment. In Trichinopoly, in collusion with the Karnams, the ryots made out that channels and other unprofitable plots, beyond those which had already been properly allowed for, had been unfairly included in

---

(10) G.O., No. 717, of the 17th March 1869.

(11) Director of Revenue Settlement to Chief Secretary to Government, No. 971-28, of the 10th June 1872.

CHAPTER XII. REVENUE HISTORY, PART III.

their holdings, and should consequently also be deducted from the occupied area. In this they were partially successful.

"The two next items—wet lands fraudulently entered as dry and garden lands irrigated by baling fraudulently entered as dry—were similarly incorrectly recorded owing to the untrue representation of the Karnams and landholders. These evasions were duly corrected and brought to their proper heads together with any other lands which the examinations showed had been changed into wet, or garden irrigated by baling, subsequent to the introduction of the new settlement.

"The next cases," Mr. Banbury remarks, "comprised items of concealment which it was intended should be brought to light by the annual *azmaish* or examinations; but in respect to which, owing to this check being now unavoidably little more than nominal, advantage was taken to defraud the State.

1*st.*—Waste cultivated but not brought to account. Patches of waste land were in some cases newly entered upon, and in others surreptitiously annexed to existing cultivation without being brought to account. In some instances this was owing to the connivance of the Karnam; in others to his apathy or his ignorance of the real boundaries of the fields." In cases where the scrutiny set on foot by Mr. Banbury showed that the cultivation had been going on upon these tracts for two or three years, assessment was levied from the introduction of the settlement. Mr. Banbury remarks that the only remedy for this kind of fraud is a strict *azmaish.*

2*nd.*—Water-rate not charged upon dry lands to which Government water is taken. "This is an evasion," Mr. Banbury observes, "which like the next item, second crop not brought to account, is the Karnam's opportunity. A rigid examination is the only method by which this fraud can be checked, although when a channel is improved it is, of course, only natural that the settling officer should look for better results under the head of water-rate. It may also be said that this item of evasion is more frequently brought to notice by petitions than any other, as the fact of water being surreptitiously taken, or baled away when the supply is diminishing, engenders envy and discord resulting in a representation to the authorities."

3*rd.*—Second crop raised on wet lands, but not brought to account. This item of revenue, Mr. Banbury remarked, must always be most difficult to realize, and he considered that, in order to guard against fraud under this head, there should in Trichinopoly be two examinations, one at the end of July, when the first crop is just beginning to grow, and another at the end of December, when the second crop will be pretty clearly distinguishable.

Mr. Banbury went on to observe that the extension of the compounding system was the best method of meeting the difficulty and of securing the revenue without worry to the people or opportunities for trickery. Much of the wet land in Trichinopoly, he pointed out, had been compounded for at one-third and one-fourth of the first-crop assessment by Mr. Puckle with the consent of the ryots, and thus, although the area upon which the second crop was to be levied was greatly circumscribed, still the ryots and karnams did not let the opportunity slip, and second crops were raised on the uncompounded lands free from any demand. To make the system more effectual, he considered that compounding should be introduced throughout the wet lands in the taluqs, descending even to one-fifth where the water-supply was scanty, but with the proviso that the rate of composition should never be below one rupee, except when the water was raised by picottahs or other appliances, in which cases deduction might be made.

The last item to be considered was cultivation of *poramboke*. These encroachments, "so peculiarly delightful to the mind of the Indian cultivator," would, in Mr. Banbury's opinion, doubtless continue to the end of the chapter. "Boundary stones, or even theodolite stations, are altogether ignored when a piece of road, channel, village-site, or other *poramboke* is to be added each year, bit by bit, to the neighbouring cultivation. In out-of-the-way localities this annexation goes on apace, and even roads are altogether appropriated by the adjoining cultivators. The examinations showed that the Trichinopoly ryots had not been backward in this work of aggression, and the assessment on the areas thus discovered was brought to "*Siváy Jamá*" with prohibitation against future cultivations, except in a few cases where it was found that the permission might be safely granted."

The effects of the examination that he had made would, Mr. Banbury considered, no doubt last for some time, but he was of opinion that, after the lapse of five years or so, it would be advisable to institute a similar investigation, more especially as the spread of cultivation on waste dry lands might, by that time, certainly be looked for.

Mr. Banbury's report was referred to the Board of Revenue for their remarks, and, in their Proceedings on the subject, it was observed that the water charge on second-crop cultivation, both in Ryotwári and Inám land, was evidently extensively evaded wherever the consolidated charge for watering a second crop had not been introduced. As the advantages of this composition were universally acknowledged, the Board considered that there could be no hardship in insisting on the universal adoption of the consolidated two-crop water charge in all tracts where a second crop was often

CHAPTER XII. REVENUE HISTORY, PART III.

grown, and that the ryots might be not unfairly coerced into it by the alternative of having to pay the full charge upon water taken for a second-crop.[12] Government, however, were not prepared to sanction the plan of coercion recommended by the Board, but directed that every opportunity should be taken of extending the system of compounding.[13]

The following statement shows the extent to which second-crop assessment was compounded for at the settlement and in each year since in the several taluqs in the district :—

Fasli.	Trichinopoly Taluq.		Musiri Taluq.		Kulittalai Taluq.		Perumbalúr Taluq.		Udaiyár-pálayam Taluq.		Total.	
	Extent.	Assessment.	Extent.	Assessment.	Extent.	Assessment.	Extent.	Assessment.	Extent.	Assessment.	Extent.	Assessment.
	ACS.	RS.	ACS.	RS.	ACS.	RS.	ACS.	RS.	ACS.	RS.	ACS.	RS.
1274* ..	14,062	23,272	5,825	8,811	5,655	9,492	3,538	5,583	327	355	29,407	47,513
1275 ..	5	5	..	..	7	14	..	..	..	..	12	19
1276 ..	..	..	..	..	17	21	..	..	..	..	17	21
1277 ..	..	..	..	..	..	..	..	..	..	..	..	..
1278 ..	..	..	77	158	..	..	..	..	..	..	77	158
1279 ..	27[illegible]	249	713	1,029	228	378	2,376	2,679	365	394	3,958	4,729
1280 ..	13[illegible]	240	359	408	46	54	58	60	53	71	654	833
1281 ..	18	40	80	118	..	..	14	18	..	..	112	176
1282 ..	40	80	58	67	..	..	11	15	..	..	109	162
1283 ..	19	170	7	12	10	18	10	17	..	..	118	217
1284 ..	142	539	8	8	21	21	9	13	1	1	181	582
1285 ..	49	92	4	3	..	..	16	34	..	..	69	129
1286 ..	46	89	20	35	..	..	..	..	..	..	66	124
Total ..	14,867	24,776	7,151	10,649	5,984	9,998	6,032	8,419	746	821	34,780	54,663

* Settlement year.

Financial results of the settlement.

It will be remembered that Mr. Puckle, in his final report regarding the settlement, had expressed his belief that in five years the reduction of assessment caused by it would certainly be made up and that the revenue would amount to even more than it did before its introduction, and the Board of Revenue and Government expressed their agreement with him in this view.[14] This expectation has unfortunately not been borne out by experience. For the first few years after the introduction of the settlement there was a steady rise in revenue, but since then the figures have fluctuated, and at the end of Fasli 1285 (1875-76), although eleven years had then

(12) Proceedings of the Board of Revenue, No. 1,696, of the 26th August 1872.

(13) G.O., No. 1,498, of the 28th October 1872.

(14) Letter from the Deputy Director of Revenue Settlement to the Director, dated 30th May 1865, paragraph 54 ; Proceedings of the Board, No. 3,641, of the 28th May 1866, paragraph 7 ; and G.O., No. 2,523, of the 19th September 1866, paragraph 5.

elapsed since the settlement, the *collections* were still Rupees 1,47,305 below what was realized in the year previous to its introduction.[15] Much has been written regarding the failure of the revenue to show that elasticity that was expected, and many causes have been assigned for the disappointing result. In his Settlement Report for Fasli 1281 (1871-72) the then Collector of the district, Mr. Pennington, showed that the land revenue had fallen Rupees 38,340 when compared with the previous year, Fasli 1280 (1870-71), or Rupees 1,59,533 when compared with that of the year immediately preceding the settlement, and ascribed this fall to large relinquishments of land caused by a failure of rain in August 1871. Explanation was called for, and Mr. Pennington reported at length on the subject to the Board.[16] In their Proceedings reviewing the Collector's letter the Board observed that the year regarding which explanation had been called for, Fasli 1281 (1871-72), showed much greater relinquishments of land than usual, smaller acquisitions, and less second-crop cultivation. The Collector had explained that the land was so lightly assessed that the cultivators were continually tempted to take up more than they could manage. This was specially the case immediately after the new settlement was introduced, and the occupied area was being gradually reduced in consequence. It rose from 727,000 acres in Fasli 1273 to 800,000 acres in Fasli 1274, the settlement year. Since then it had risen to 1,032,000 acres, and it was then 993,000 acres. Another reason for large relinquishments was that the cultivators were in the habit of throwing up land for the years during which it must lie fallow. These two causes were permanent, but the chief cause, *viz.*, the failure of rain in August 1871, was temporary. The ryots, it was said, saw reason to expect a bad season and gave up their land knowing that they would be able to get it again if the season turned out to be favorable. The Board were disposed to think that the difference of revenue in Faslis 1280 and 1281, viz., Rupees 38,348, had been sufficiently accounted for and need cause no alarm, especially as the effect of the discovery of concealed cultivation by Mr. Banbury was still felt in Fasli 1281.

As regards the large decrease that had taken place since the settlement, the Board remarked that from Fasli 1259 to Fasli 1268 the revenue was not stationary, and even declined a little. Faslis 1269 to 1273 were years of rising prices and exceptional prosperity, so that the rapid increase from 14 lakhs to 16½ lakhs was not to be

---

(15) The collections under Land Revenue and Land Revenue Miscellaneous for Fasli 1273 (the year before the settlement) were Rupees 16,94,103-10-11, and for Fasli 1285 Rupees 15,46,798. I have compared these two years and excluded Fasli 1286, as in that year the district suffered to a considerable extent from famine.

(16) Letter from Collector to Board, No. 51 of 24th March 1873.

CHAPTER XII. REVENUE HISTORY, PART III.

wondered at; but it might well be doubted that the revenue would have been maintained at the level of Fasli 1273 even if there had been no settlement. The settlement caused a great—and the Board feared an unnecessarily great—diminution, but the area of occupied land and the revenue had been steadily increasing since. The figures of Faslis 1279 and 1280 were abnormally high because of the large quantity of concealed cultivated land brought to account by Mr. Banbury, much of which, as might have been expected, was given up directly afterwards. The occupied area and revenue probably reached their normal condition in Fasli 1281, and the increase of 24 per cent. in occupation and in revenue since the settlement was considered to be reassuring.[17] In the order passed on these Proceedings, Government remarked that they still held the opinion expressed in G.O., No. 2,523, of the 19th September 1866, to the effect that, in consequence of the simple and moderate character of the new land-tax, the district would steadily advance in wealth and that the condition of the people had been materially improved.[18]

In the following year there was again a decline in the land revenue of the district, and the Director of Revenue Settlement, Mr. Banbury, in sending on to the Board his annual report regarding those districts that have been settled by his department, made the following remarks on the subject:—

He observed that, strange to say, in Trichinopoly, where the assessment had been so liberally lightened, the revenues did not exhibit the increase year by year that might be reasonably expected, although prices kept up and the seasons were favorable. The land revenue of the past fasli stood at Rupees 38,505 below that of the previous twelve months, and there still remained a sum of Rupees 1,98,038 to be made good before the revenue demand would touch that of the year previous to the new régime.

Mr. Pennington, the Collector, it was stated, had assigned three causes for these disheartening results:—

(1.) The springing up of a most deleterious grass in the dry lands owing to heavy rains.

(2.) The retention in their pattás of more land than the ryots can cultivate.

(3). The fact that much land had been taken up on speculation. The Collector had added that the real cause had yet to be ascertained. "No doubt," Mr. Banbury observed, "the matter is very perplexing, as lands are relinquished which now pay less than they did before the new settlement. It can, I think, only be accounted for by the last of the above reasons, and is owing to large tracts of

(17) Proceedings of the Board of Revenue, No. 925, of the 3rd June 1873.

(18) G.O., No. 724, of the 12th July 1873.

dry land having been taken up under the expectation that the assessment would be decreased, and the venture prove remunerative. The first anticipation was realized no doubt, but the second has ended in disappointment, and thus the lands have been abandoned. Under the old régime a ryot probably cultivated a little area well, and under the new a larger area badly, so that he has had to restrict his operations. It has, I believe, been urged that the examinations into concealed cultivation, which I made as Collector in Faslis 1278 and 1279, tended to increase rázinámáhs and to decrease second-crop wet culture. Mr. Pennington does not, however, allege this as a reason, and it can hardly be one, as lands surreptitiously occupied, which the ryots had to pay for owing to the "Azmaish," would have been thrown up long ere Fasli 1282, and although the ryots are glad enough to get a second crop if they can without paying for it, still the knowledge that they were likely to have to do so owing to the examinations would not have deterred them from raising this second crop, the average assessment on which is under Rupees 2-8-0 per acre."[19]

In their review of this report the Board remarked that the financial aspect of the district was still disappointing. "So much," it is observed, "has been written regarding the Trichinopoly settlement and its results that the Board need only point out that the main cause of the falling off in dry is to be attributed to the relinquishment of lands which were taken up very extensively when the rates were reduced as a venture that has not turned out to be so favorable as was anticipated. Any reduction in "wet" can only be recouped by extended irrigation works, as, speaking generally, there is but little wet waste wherewith to make good the amount foregone on the cultivated area. Thus the settlement officers of the present day are apparently very careful that the rates on the wet lands, particularly those of high agricultural value, are not unduly reduced."[20]

The Board have in this last paragraph hinted at what, in the opinion of almost all the officials, whether European or Native, employed of late years in the district, was the real mistake made in the new settlement, namely, that the rates imposed on the lands in the irrigated valley of the Cauvery were not high enough. It is generally considered that the rates on dry lands have not been unreasonably reduced. The soil of these lands is, as a rule, by no means very good throughout the district, and the rainfall is very precarious. In fact a good dry crop is in all the taluqs the exception, and an indifferent or bad one the rule. The irrigated lands

(19) Letter from Director of Revenue Settlement to Board, No. 2,773-96, of the 17th December 1873.

(20) Board's Proceedings, No. 205, of the 3rd February 1874.

along the Cauvery and its channels however are, with few unimportant exceptions, simply magnificent. Regarding this point there seems to have been some misapprehension when the scheme for a revised settlement was under consideration. For example the Board of Revenue, in the last Proceedings passed by them on the subject, before the final orders of Government were passed, include among the "circumstances of the district" "indifferent irrigation even as regards the Cauvery-irrigated lands" and "a limited and a very fluctuating market." They also observed that the channels from the Upper Anicut are at so high a level that it is only when the river is in tolerable flood that the water runs down them, and that much labor and expense is incurred by the ryots in forming *korambus* to divert the stream into the channels.[21] The foregoing, it will be generally acknowledged, is a more unfavorable view of the irrigated portions of the district than the facts actually warrant. The Cauvery is a river that seldom or ever fails; one year no doubt is better than another, but the worst is on the whole very favorable. For example in Fasli 1286 (1876-77) the famine year, when the supply of water in the Cauvery was decidedly scanty and great apprehensions were entertained that it would not be sufficient to enable the wet crops in Tanjore District to reach maturity, the irrigated lands along the Cauvery in Trichinopoly gave Revenue Officers no cause for anxiety, and excellent crops were obtained, by the sale of which enormous prices were realized. No doubt there was more trouble with the *korambus* than usual, and there were disputes between some of the ryots of Musiri and Kulittalai Taluqs and those of Trichinopoly as to the periods during which these should be cut. This, however, did not occur till February, and the crops at stake were in reality only a limited extent of second-crop paddy, principally in the Lálgudi Division at the end of channels taken off at the Upper Anicut. The great mass of the irrigated lands were not affected by this, and were safe throughout. From the early revenue history of the district we learn, no doubt, that the lands under the Cauvery were frequently flooded, and great injury caused to the soil by the deposits of sand with which they were, in consequence, covered. Since the river however has been properly embanked, such floods are unknown. It must not be forgotten that, although Government had, in sanctioning the scheme for the revised settlement, fixed the highest rates of wet land at Rupees 9-4-0, Rupees 8-12-0, and Rupees 8,[22] yet that no lands were actually assessed at these rates, the highest imposed being Rupees 7-8-0 per acre. In Tanjore and Tinnevelly rates, in many cases more than twice the amount of those imposed in Trichinopoly, are levied on land not generally of a superior quality to

(21) Board's Proceedings, No. 1.270, of the 3rd March 1863, paragraphs 2 and 5.
(22) G.O., No. 577, of the 5th April 1864, paragraph 9.

those to be found in the irrigated portions of this district, and are, it is believed, paid with ease, and it may therefore, on the whole, be reasonably presumed that the rates imposed on the irrigated lands along the Cauvery in Trichinopoly might safely be enhanced to a considerable extent. The South Indian Railway traverses the district in two directions, so that there is now no danger of a market not being found for whatever amount of grain it can produce.

The period of thirty years for which the new settlement is to run will expire in the official year 1893-94, and it will then be open to Government to revise it.

The following statement shows the *actual collections* under Land Revenue and Land Revenue, Miscellaneous, for a number of years previous to the settlement and since then up till now [23] :—

Year.	Land Revenue.			Land Revenue Miscellaneous.			Total.		
	RS.	A.	P.	RS.	A.	P.	RS.	A.	P.
1264 (1854-55)	12,01,740	5	7	3,486	6	1	12,05,226	11	8
1265 (1855-56)	12,29,401	15	11	3,040	15	2	12,32,442	15	1
1266 (1856-57)	13,95,430	10	0	3,238	9	9	13,98,669	3	9
1267 (1857-58)	13,50,308	9	4	2,137	5	2	13,52,445	14	6
1268 (1858-59)	13,58,676	11	11	3,475	14	2	13,62,152	10	1
1269 (1859-60)	15,14,480	6	8	9,770	2	9	15,24,250	9	5
1270 (1860-61)	16,89,984	11	11	8,723	2	1	16,98,707	14	0
1271 (1861-62)	15,72,481	14	1	19,216	12	7	15,91,698	10	8
1272 (1862-63)	16,75,135	11	5	16,753	0	0	16,91,888	11	5
1273 (1863-64)	16,70,598	3	10	23,505	7	1	16,94,103	10	11
1274 (1864-65)*	12,84,318	0	0	26,434	0	0	13,10,752	0	0
1275 (1865-66)	13,37,329	3	0	42,662	10	11	13,79,991	13	11
1276 (1866-67)	13,89,576	6	5	54,351	0	2	14,43,927	6	7
1277 (1867-68)	13,41,485	4	6	43,138	6	0	13,84,623	10	6
1278 (1868-69)	14,59,486	3	9	59,222	5	3	15,18,708	9	0
1279 (1869-70)†	14,75,932	14	9	1,94,276	10	0	16,70,209	8	9
1280 (1870-71)	16,28,602	3	5	98,065	13	0	17,26,668	0	5
1281 (1871-72)	13,82,819	9	8	75,461	4	9	14,58,280	14	5
1282 (1872-73)	14,39,251	2	2	87,778	5	0	15,27,029	7	2
1283 (1873-74)	13,58,126	5	3	66,874	9	0	14,25,000	14	3
1284 (1874-75)	14,81,806	14	11	83,609	10	3	15,65,416	9	2
1285 (1875-76)	14,46,488	0	0	1,00,310	0	0	15,46,798	0	0
1286 (1876-77)	12,95,397	0	0	77,929	0	0	13,73,326	0	0

* Settlement year.

† Year in which concealed cultivation was brought to account by Mr. Banbury.

Proposal to redemarcate the district.

Not long after the introduction of the new settlement it was found that considerable mistakes had been made in the survey of the district, and inconvenience was also felt owing to the fields having been demarcated with earthen mounds which had rapidly disappeared. These defects were brought to notice more than once, and eventually Government sanctioned the redemarcation of two

(23) It must be remembered that the figures given here represent the *actual collections*. I think that they will be found to be accurate. It was found impossible to get trustworthy figures previous to Fasli 1264.

CHAPTER XII. REVENUE HISTORY, PART III.

villages in the district by the Survey Department as a preliminary to the redemarcation of the entire district.[24]

The villages selected were Kulittalai and Kallapalli, both in the Kullittalai Taluq. The redemarcation was carried out by Captain Cloete, whose report regarding its results was sent on to the Director of Revenue Settlement through the Director of Revenue Survey. Mr. Puckle, who was then Director of Revenue Settlement, in sending on this letter to the Board of Revenue, remarked that, as the Board were aware, there were but few demarcation marks standing in the Trichinopoly District. Some taluqs had been surveyed without demarcation, others demarcated with earthen mounds, and only in a few instances had stones been erected as field-marks. In the villages which had been demarcated as an experiment there were no field-marks to be found, but Captain Cloete, it was stated, had experienced no difficulty in tracing the survey fields in the irrigated lands, the edges forming the boundaries of these fields not having been shifted since the survey. In the dry lands it was stated that greater difficulty had been experienced more especially in the river-bed, but that the people knew their own fields which were mostly gardens supplied by baling, and practically a Revenue Officer would have little difficulty in tracing the survey fields in the dry lands also. The errors discovered by Captain Cloete in the survey were, Mr. Puckle considered, mostly trifling and to be accounted for partly by the absence of marks on the ground and partly by the method of computation in use when the survey of Trichinopoly was made.

To redemark the villages would, Mr. Puckle remarked, cost Rupees 150 per square mile or three lakhs for the entire district. Redemarcation would of course necessitate resurvey, and resurvey would necessitate resettlement. The district had been surveyed and settled only eleven years previously, and it was early yet to think of repeating these processes. The Survey Department had pressing work to perform elsewhere, and the expediency of completing the survey of the entire Presidency before returning to resurvey any district was therefore urged. Captain Cloete had shown that the survey maps and settlement registers were quite sufficient to enable him to trace the fields throughout the irrigated lands, and Mr. Puckle considered that the probabilities were that, with the aid of known fields and the topographical details shown in the maps, there were virtually not five per cent. of the fields in each village that could be distinctly traced. Even these could be guessed near enough, and an outlay of three lakhs of rupees, it was urged, was out of all proportion to the benefit to be derived by securing accuracy in the definition of a few dry fields here and

(24) G.O., No. 1,219, R.D., of the 25th September 1874.

CHAPTER XII. REVENUE HISTORY, PART III.

there. Mr. Puckle therefore recommended that Trichinopoly should be left as it was till the completion of the settlement and survey of the other districts of the Presidency.[25]

In their Proceedings reviewing this letter the Board remarked that they were not so sanguine as Mr. Puckle seemed to be as to the ease with which the fields could be identified from the survey maps and the extent to which these could be utilized for practical purposes; but, as they were unable to suggest any more economical means of attaining the end in view, they endorsed Mr. Puckle's recommendation.[26] The Government took the same view of the question, and all idea of redemarcating or resurveying the district during the currency of the present settlement has now been abandoned. Since the date of this discussion there is nothing of the importance to record regarding the revenue history of the district.

List of the Collectors of Trichinopoly.

The following is a list of the officers who have held the post of Collector of Trichinopoly up to the present time :—

J. Wallace, August 1801 to April 1804.

P. Kinlock, Head Assistant Collector in charge, April 1804 to June 1805.

R. H. Young, Sub-Collector in immediate charge of the district during the time that it was joined with Tanjore, June 1805 to June 1808.

G. Garrow, August 1808 to June 1809.

R. H. Young, Head Assistant Collector in charge, June 1809 to October 1809.

G. F. Travers, October 1809 to March 1815.
C. M. Lushington, March 1815 to August 1823.
G. W. Saunders, August 1823 to November 1826.
H. Dickinson, November 1826 to December 1828.
N. S. Cameron, January 1829 to February 1831.
R. Nelson, March 1831 to April 1832.
H. M. Blair, April 1832 to May 1838.
W. C. Ogilvie, May 1838 to February 1839.
A. P. Onslow, February 1839 to March 1847.
W. Elliot, March 1847 to November 1848.
A. P. Onslow, November 1848 to December 1848.
E. Maltby, December 1848 to March 1851.
J. Bird, March 1851 to August 1858.
M. J. Walhouse, September 1858 to November 1858.
J. Bird, November 1858 to April 1860.
Æ. R. McDonell, May 1860 to February 1863.
M. J. Walhouse, February 1863 to January 1864.

(25) Letter from Director of Revenue Settlement to Board, No. 1,441-40, dated 15th July 1875.

(26) Proceedings of the Board of Revenue, No. 2,419, of the 26th August 1875.

CHAPTER XII.
REVENUE HISTORY, PART III.

J. Fraser, January 1864 to April 1864.
Æ. R. McDonell, April 1864 to February 1866.
C. N. Pochin, February 1866 to September 1866.
G. VansAgnew, September 1866 to October 1866.
G. Banbury, October 1866 to March 1867.
G. VansAgnew, March 1867 to December 1867.
C. T. Longley, December 1867 to October 1868.
G. Banbury, October 1868 to January 1870.
W. M. Cadell, January 1870 to December 1870.
W. McQuhae, December 1870 to April 1871.
W. S. Whiteside, April 1871 to April 1872.
A. McC. Webster, April 1872 to July 1872.
J. B. Pennington, July 1872 to May 1875.
H. Sewell, May 1875.

In all twenty-nine Collectors in seventy-seven years, giving an average tenure of office of about two years and seven months for each officer.

CHAPTER XIII.

REVENUE ADMINISTRATION, ABKÁRI, SALT, STAMPS, POSTAL DEPARTMENT, METRICAL SCALES.

REVENUE ADMINISTRATION—Revenue Divisions.—Tahsildars.—Deputy Tahsildars.—Revenue Inspectors.—Village Officials.—District Hukumnámáh. ABKÁRI—Abkári Revenue up to 1875.—The Excise System.—Manufacture of Arrack.—Toddy Farms—Number of Shops in the District. SALT. STAMPS. POSTAL DEPARTMENT. METRICAL SCALES.

REVENUE ADMINISTRATION.

CHAP. XIII. REVENUE ADMINISTRATION, &c.

Revenue divisions.

THE Collector has authority throughout the whole of the district in revenue matters; but, for convenience of administration, the district is split up into divisions, each of which is placed under a separate officer. The Head Assistant Collector is in charge of Musiri and Kulittalai, his head-quarters being at Musiri. The Deputy Collector, on general duties, is in charge of Perumbalúr and Udaiyárpálayam, his head-quarters being at Ariyalúr in the latter taluq. If there is an Assistant Collector in the district who has passed the lower standard, he, as a rule, is placed in revenue charge of Trichinopoly Taluq. If there is no qualified Assistant, a Temporary Deputy Collector is generally in charge of the taluq. Of late years the Collector has almost never had any direct revenue charge. In addition to the officers already mentioned, there is another Deputy Collector employed in the district, who is in charge of the Treasury, and remains permanently in Trichinopoly.

Taluqs.

Previous to the year 1861 the district was divided into the following nine taluqs: Kónád, Lálgudi, Musiri, Turaiyúr, Vettukatti, Manapparai, Válikandapuram, Ariyalúr, and Udaiyárpálayam. In 1861 Mr. Pelly's scheme for the revision of taluqs and taluq establishments was introduced, and the number of taluqs reduced from nine to five. The old Lálgudi and Kónád Taluqs were amalgamated and formed into the present taluq of Trichinopoly, with head-quarters at Trichinopoly; Vettukatti and Manapparai were joined together in one taluq, Kulittalai, with head-quarters

CHAP. XIII. REVENUE ADMINISTRATION, &c.

at the village of that name. Out of the old Musiri and Turaiyúr Taluqs the new Musiri Taluq was formed, with head-quarters at Musiri ; while Válikandapuram, Ariyalúr and Udaiyárpálayam were divided into two new taluqs, Perumbalúr, with head-quarters at the village of the same name, and Udaiyárpálayam, head-quarters at Jeyamkondasólapuram.

Tahsildars.

The following statement shows the grades to which the several taluqs in the district belong :—

Taluq.	Grade.	Salary of Tahsildar.
Trichinopoly	1st ..	250 Rupees per mensem.
Musiri	2nd ..	225 do. do.
Kulittalai	3rd ..	200 do. do.
Perumbalúr	4th ..	175 do. do.
Udaiyárpálayam	5th ..	150 do. do.

Each Tahsildar has an establishment, consisting of a Sheristadar on Rupees 60 a month, nine Clerks, two of whom draw 20 Rupees and the rest Rupees 15 a month, and a Pound Clerk on Rupees 10 a month, who is paid from Local Funds, and is charged with the supervision of the Pound accounts. In the office of the Kulittalai Tahsildar there is also an Úrani and a Chattram Clerk on Rupees 6 each. Both these officials are paid from Local Funds, and have to look after the accounts of the chattrams and úranis in the south-west portion of that taluq, transferred from Madura District in 1856, to which mániyam lands are attached. There is a Shroff attached to each Tahsildar's office on Rupees 15, and a Deputy Shroff also in Trichinopoly and Musiri on Rupees 10. There is a Dufterbund on Rupees 7 in each taluq office.

Deputy Tahsildars.

In Trichinopoly Taluq there are two Deputy Tahsildars, both of the first class, drawing Rupees 100 a month each, stationed in Trichinopoly Town and Lálgudi. In Musiri there is one First-class Deputy Tahsildar stationed in Turaiyúr ; in Kulittalai one of the second class, with a salary of Rupees 70 a month, stationed at Manapparai ; and in Udaiyárpálayam, one of the same class, stationed at Kílapaluvúr. There is no Deputy Tahsildar in Perumbalúr Taluq. Up to January 1873 the Lálgudi Deputy Tahsildar was second class, and the Manapparai first class. Each Deputy Tahsildar has an establishment of two Clerks on Rupees 15 each, and one Dufterbund on Rupees 7, with the exception of the Kílapaluvúr Deputy Tahsildar, who has only one Clerk and a Dufterbund.

The following statement gives some particulars regarding the Revenue Inspectors employed in the district :—

CHAP. XIII. REVENUE ADMINISTRATION, &c.

Revenue Inspectors.

Taluq.	Grade of Inspector.	Salary.	Head-quarters.	Number of Villages, including Inám and Zemindári, in each Range.
		RS.		
Trichinopoly	1st ..	30	Allúr	118
Do.	2nd ..	25	Manachanellúr ..	128
Do.	3rd ..	20	Púválúr	94
Do.	" ..	20	Kundur	96
Musiri	1st ..	30	Eragudi	36
Do.	2nd ..	25	Chettikulam ..	40
Do.	3rd ..	20	Musiri	64
Do.	" ..	20	Kannanúr	41
Kulittalai	1st ..	30	Nangapuram ..	34
Do.	2nd ..	25	Kulittalai	35
Do.	3rd ..	20	Kistnaráyapuram ..	46
Perumbalúr	1st ..	30	Ranjengedi ..	82
Do.	2nd ..	25	Perumbalúr ..	75
Do.	3rd ..	20	Kolattúr	90
Udaiyárpálayam ..	1st ..	30	Kílapaluvúr ..	135
Do. ..	2nd ..	25	Kuruvalappar-kóvil.	85
Do. ..	3rd ..	20	Tamaraipúndi ..	149
Do. ..	" ..	20	Palúr	114

In Kulittalai Taluq the Deputy Tahsildar does the work of a Revenue Inspector in 19 Government, 17 inám, and 100 zemindári villages, and in Musiri Taluq the Deputy Tahsildar does similar work in 32 Government, 4 inám, and 17 zemindári villages.

Village officials.

An account of the reorganisation of the village establishment introduced in 1870 has already been given in Chapter XII. There are only four descriptions of village officials paid by Government in the district. These are the village headman or maniyagàr, who collects the revenue, and who also, as a Village Magistrate and Munsif, settles petty criminal cases and civil disputes; the accountant or karnam, who keeps the revenue accounts; the taliári or village watchman; and the vettiyán, who may be described as a village peon.

District Hukumnámáh.

There is at present no sanctioned hukumnámáh for the district. When the new settlement was introduced, the Collector was directed to draw up a revised set of rules suitable to the altered state of affairs. Considerable delay took place, and at last Mr. Banbury, in his letter to the Board of Revenue, No. 270, of the 27th November 1866, sent up a hukumnámáh with notes and suggestions. This letter was recorded in Proceedings, No. 6,569, of the 2nd September 1869, because the Board had, in their Proceedings of the 17th August 1869, No. 6,134, circulated a draft hukumnámáh, with the proposal that it should be in force throughout the Presidency, a separate supplement being added for each district, containing such

CHAP. XIII. REVENUE ADMINISTRATION, &c.

revenue rules as might be peculiar to it. Eventually the Board abandoned the idea of a general hukumnámáh.

ABKÁRI.

Abkári revenue up to 1875.

Under the head of Abkári are included (1) the taxes levied on the manufacture and sale of arrack, (2) the tax levied on the sale of toddy, and (3) the amount realized from licenses granted for the manufacture and sale of country beer, and for the sale of European spirits. The abkári revenue of the Trichinopoly District was only Rupees 16,000 in 1830-31, and fell to 13,373 in 1840-41, but rose again to Rupees 24,000 in 1850-51, and to Rupees 25,000 in 1860-61. In 1865-66 the amount realized under this head was Rupees 1,06,000, and in 1866-67, Rupees 1,19,000. In 1869 the toddy and arrack farms were sold by taluqs on a three years' contract for Rupees 1,46,600 a year, and in 1872, on similar terms, for Rupees 1,40,400 a year.[1]

The Excise system.

From the commencement of Fasli 1285 (1875-76) two great changes were made in the abkári system in force in the district. These were the introduction of the excise system of raising the arrack revenue, and the separation of the arrack and toddy farms.[2] Under the excise system the exclusive privilege of manufacturing and selling arrack is assigned to a contractor, selected on tender made after public notification. Distillation is not permitted, except at certain selected places, where a sufficient gauging establishment is kept up at the contractor's expense. The revenue is paid in the shape of an excise duty on each gallon of liquor issued from the distillery, at rates fixed with reference to strength, and the contractor is obliged to guarantee that the total amount paid by him as excise duty shall not fall below a specified sum. The Trichinopoly arrack farm for Faslis 1285 to 1287 was sold to Messrs. Parry and Co., who guaranteed to pay Rupees 1,10,000 annually. The sum actually paid by them as excise duty did not in any year exceed the guaranteed amount. For the three faslis commencing with 1288 the arrack farm has again been sold to Messrs. Parry and Co., who have guaranteed to pay 1,12,000 a year. The following important alteration is to be introduced into the excise system in this district from the commencement of Fasli 1288. In addition to the rate of excise duty paid at the time of the issue of the liquor from the distillery, a surcharge of duty at 8 Annas per gallon is to be levied on all spirits sold under the license in shops within the limits of what is known as the cantonment farm, which includes the whole of the Trichinopoly and Srìrangam Munici-

(1) Mr. Dalyell's Report on the Abkári system of the Madras Presidency, dated 22nd April 1874. Appendix D, page 26.

(2) G.O., No. 1,520, of the 8th December 1874.

palities and a few shops outside their boundaries, and a separate guarantee has to be given by the renter that the amount of such surcharge shall not be less than Rupees 15,000. The following statement shows the prescribed rates of excise duty, and the maximum and minimum prices of arrack directed to be in force from the commencement of Fasli 1288.

—	Spirits, 30° under Proof.				
	Rate of Excise Duty per Imperial Gallon.	Maximum Price		Minimum Price	
		Per Imperial Gallon.	Per Dram.	Per Imperial Gallon.	Per Dram.
	RS. A. P.	RS. A. P.	RS. A. P.	RS. A. P.	RS. A. P.
Arrack sold within the limits of the Cantonment Farm.	2 4 0	4 0 0	0 1 4	3 8 0	0 1 2
Arrack sold in the rest of the district.	1 12 0	3 8 0	0 1 2	3 0 0	0 1 0

—	Spirits, 60° under Proof.				
	Rate of Excise Duty per Imperial Gallon.	Maximum Price		Minimum Price	
		Per Imperial Gallon.	Per Dram.	Per Imperial Gallon.	Per Dram.
	RS. A. P.	RS. A. P.	RS. A. P.	RS. A. P.	RS. A. P.
Arrack sold within the limits of the Cantonment Farm.	1 4 0	2 12 0	0 0 11	2 4 0	0 0 9
Arrack sold in the rest of the district.	1 0 0	2 8 0	0 0 10	2 0 0	0 0 8

Manufacture of arrack.

The following account of the manner in which the arrack sold by Messrs. Parry and Co. is manufactured, is given by their agent:—

The ingredients used are either cane-juice, sugar, treacle from cane-sugar, palmyra-jaggery or treacle from palmyra-sugar, the bark of the velvélam (*Acacia leucophlœa*) and water. About 20 gallons of water go to 100 lbs. of jaggery and 12 lbs. of velvélam bark. When fermentation has ceased, which is generally after thirteen or fifteen days, the wash is distilled, the outturn of spirit varying very much, according to quality of material used and the state of the weather. On an average, a candy of jaggery gives 35 gallons of arrack.[3]

(3) Letter from Agent to Messrs. Parry and Co. to Collector, dated 10th November 1877.

CHAP. XIII. REVENUE ADMINISTRATION, &c.

Toddy farms.

Both cocoanut and palmyra toddy are consumed in the district, but the former is much more generally drunk than the latter. The following statement shows the amount realized by the sale of the toddy farms since they were separated from the arrack farms:—

—	Fasli 1285 to 87. For each Fasli.	Fasli 1288 to 90. For each Fasli.
	RS.	RS.
Trichinopoly Taluq and Cantonment ..	35,050	50,050
Musiri	1,650	8,600
Kulittalai	2030	7,500
Perumbalúr	530	1,600
Udaiyárpálayam	530	2,350
Total ..	39,790	70,100

Number of shops in the district.

The following statement shows the number of arrack and toddy shops in the district in Fasli 1286 (1876-77) :—

Taluq.	Area in Square Miles.	Population.	Number of Arrack Shops sanctioned.	Number of Toddy Shops sanctioned.	Total Number of Shops.	Population per Shop.	Number of Shops per 10 Square Miles.
Trichinopoly	519	306,461	123	47	170	1,802	3·33
Musiri	667	257,174	109	24	133	1,933	2·01
Kulittalai	930	228,313	94	58	152	1,502	1·63
Perumbalúr	690	170,567	89	8	97	1,758	1·40
Udaiyárpálayam	777	237,893	77	9	86	2,766	1·12
Total for the whole District.	3,583	1,200,408	492	146	638	1,881	1·78

SALT.

There is no licit manufacture of salt in the Trichinopoly District, but in certain localities the law has hitherto been more or less evaded by the surreptitious manufacture of earth-salt which it is believed is also smuggled over the boundary of the native State of Pudukottai where it is a State monopoly.

Earth-salt is manufactured in the following manner: earth impregnated with salt (known as salt-earth) is collected, put into earthen pots, and dissolved in water. The water is afterwards strained off, and either boiled till only the salt remains, or poured on flat stones or hard stony ground, and left till the moisture is evaporated by the sun.

Act II of 1878 (Madras), which declares that to make earth-salt, with intent to defraud the public revenue, or to be in possession of salt-earth for the purpose of manufacturing earth-salt, shall be deemed to be an offence under Regulation I of 1805 (Madras), was extended to the Trichinopoly District on the 31st of May 1878.

In addition to the earth-salt manufactured as such, edible salt is produced in the manufacture of saltpetre, which is carried on to a considerable extent in this district. According to a return sent to the Madras Salt Commission in 1876, it would appear that there were then 188 works in the district where saltpetre was made, at which 13,719 maunds of saltpetre were manufactured yearly, the outturn of the salt produced in consequence being 698 maunds.

STAMPS.

Statement No. 9 given in the appendix, shows the revenue under the head of stamps for a series of ten years. This revenue is derived from the sale of stamped papers under Act XVIII of 1869 (the General Stamp Act), and Act VII of 1870 (the Court Fees Act). The following statement shows the stations in the district at which there are stamp vendors licensed to sell stamps :—

Taluqs.	No.	Stations.
Trichinopoly	6	Collector's Office, Trichinopoly. District Court, do. District Munsif's Court, Trichinopoly. Tahsildar's Office, do. Do. Srírangam. Do. Lálgudi.
Musiri	3	Musiri. Turaiyúr. Alattudaiyámpatti.
Kulittalai	3	Tahsildar's Office, Kulittalai. District Munsif's Court, Kulittalai. Do. Manapparai.
Perambalúr	1	Perumbalúr.
Udaiyárpálayam	4	Ariyalúr. Kilapaluvúr. Jeyamkondasólapuram. Udaiyárpálayam.

In addition to the above, all Taluq Sheristadars are ex-officio stamp vendors at their respective head-quarters.

CHAP. XIII. REVENUE ADMINISTRATION, &c.

POSTAL DEPARTMENT.

The following is a list of the imperial post offices in the district. There are no district post offices.

Head Offices.	Sub-Offices.	Receiving Offices.
Trichinopoly. Kulittalai.	Ariyalúr. Iluppúr. Irungalúr. Jeyamkondasólapuram. Lálgudi. Manapparai. Musiri. Perumbalúr. Srírangam. Teppakulam (Trichinopoly Fort). Turaiyúr. Kilapaluvúr.	Trichinopoly Fort. Uraiyúr.

The administration of the district post is vested in the Revenue Department, but the detailed management of it has, in this district, been handed over to the Postmaster-General, who, in communication with the Collector, has the charge of the practical working of the post, the necessary funds being provided by the Collector in his annual revenue budget.

The following statement shows the routes of the imperial and district post, and the stations on the several lines in the Trichinopoly District :—

No. of Lines.	Routes from and to.	Miles.	Stages.	Stations.
	District.			
1	Kulittalai to Turaiyúr.	19	4	1, Kulittalai ; 2, Musiri ; 3, Kannanúr ; and 4, Turaiyúr.
2	Manapparai to Iluppúr.	15	2	1, Manapparai ; 2, Iluppúr.
	Imperial.			
3	Trichinopoly to Jeyamkondasólapuram.	62	13	1, Trichinopoly; 2, Srírangam; 3, Pudúchattram; 4, Lálgudi ; 5, Vellanúr ; 6, Vadugarpéttai ; 7, Kallagam ; 8, Kilapaluvúr ; 9, Poyúr ; 10, Kudikádu ; 11, Managhirri ; 12, Udaiyárpálayam ; and 13, Jeyamkondasólapuram.
4	Kilapaluvúr to Perumbalúr.	25	5	1, Kilapaluvúr; 2, Ariyalúr; 3, Kunnam; 4, Pérali; and 5, Perumbalúr.

In Kulittalai Taluq there are village receiving-houses at the following places :—Vadiyam, Karuvappanáykenpéttai, Kallapalli, Lálapéttai, Mahádánapuram, Kristnaráyapuram, Kattapalli, Manavási, Kattalai, Nangapuram, Poyámani, Vettuváytalai and Siváyam.

In these villages either the village schoolmaster or the munsif is allowed 2 Rupees a month for taking charge of the village letter-box, which they clear whenever a district post peon calls at the village, and hand the letters over to him to be taken to the Kulittalai post office, whence they are transmitted to their destination. The boxes are cleared twice a week. Village receiving-houses have not as yet been opened, except in Kulittalai Taluq.

The following statement shows the number of covers received for delivery in the several post offices in the district in 1877:—

Names of Post Offices.	Number of Covers received for Delivery.	Percentage of Covers consigned to the Dead Letter Office.				Remarks.
		Unclaimed.		Refused.		
Trichinopoly	460,000	449	1·161	1,663	4·317	No record is kept of the number of letters posted for despatch.
Kulittalai	82,800	38	1·141	169	5·354	
Srírangam	45,600	26	·634	327	8·633	
Ariyalúr	9,619	7	·803	40	4·738	
Iluppúr	3,177	..	..	..	..	
Irungalúr	3,851	4	1·195	8	2·053	
Jeyamkondasólapuram.	18,351	15	1·021	86	5·937	
Kílapaluvúr	7,734	10	1·644	36	4·524	
Lálgudi	13,485	2	·188	85	7·533	
Manapparai	12,236	14	1·346	52	5·179	
Musiri	25,212	5	·244	29	1·443	
Perumbalúr	20,234	12	·686	78	5·046	
Teppakulam (Trichinopoly Fort).	19,356	6	·386	76	5·120	
Turaiyúr	19,727	9	·528	48	2·703	
Total ..	741,382	597	16·777	2,697	62·580	

METRICAL SCALES.

The following are the weights used in the district :—

180 Grains = 1 Tólá, or a rupee's weight.
3 Tólás = 1 Palam.
40 Palams = 1 Viss.
50 Palams = 1 Túk.
25 Palams = 1 Pucka Seer.
4 Túks (or 600 Tólás) = 1 Tulám.
8 Viss = 1 Maund.
20 Maunds = 1 Páram.

Grain and salt are, as a rule, bought and sold throughout the district according to the local measure (padi) of 116 tólás,—4 padis make 1 mercal and 12 mercals one kalam. In Udaiyárpálayam an half padi containing 65 tólás, and in Turaiyúr a half mercal containing 240 tólás are used.

The following statement shows the equivalents in imperial seers of 80 tólás of the local measures of the different food-grains and of salt :—

Stations.	Name of Measure.	How used locally.	Assumed normal Contents.	Rice, 1st Sort.	Rice, 2nd Sort.	Paddy, 1st Sort.	Paddy, 2nd Sort.	Horse-gram.	Chólum.	Cumbu.	Varagu.	Rági.	Sált.	Wheat.	Ulundu.
			Tólás.												
Trichinopoly .. .. .. Musiri .. .. Kulittalai .. .. .. Perumbalúr .. .. .. Lálgudi .. .. .. Manapparai	Padi.	Liberally heaped.	116	1·44	1·45	1·21	1·21	1·54	1·40	1·27	1·29	1·31	1·62	1·32	1·51
Udaiyárpálayam .. .. Kílapaluvúr	HalfPadi	Liberally heaped.	65	0·81	0·81	0·63	0·63	0·84	0·78	0·71	0·72	0·73	0·90	0·72	0·83
Turaiyúr	Half Mercal.	Liberally heaped.	240	3·00	3·01	2·30	2·30	3·04	2·80	2·57	2·65	2·71	3·26	2·65	3·02

For oil a measure called a vísam is used, 16 of which equal one ádam. A vísam full of oil is supposed to weigh $1\frac{1}{4}$ pucka seers, or $31\frac{1}{4}$ palams.

The English measures of land are used in the ryotwári villages, as they have all been surveyed by the Revenue Survey Department. Elsewhere the following measures prevail: 100 gulies = 1 cawni. This cawni, in irrigated villages, is equivalent to 1·1 English acres and to 1·32 in unirrigated. The measures of time are a náligai equal to 24 minutes, a jámam equal to $7\frac{1}{2}$ náligais or 3 hours, and a day equal to 8 jámams or 24 hours. The English measures of distance are the only ones used.

CHAPTER XIV.

ZEMINDA'RIS AND THE KA'TTUPUTTU'R MITTAH.

Earliest information extant regarding the Poligars of Turaiyúr, Udaiyárpálayam and Ariyalúr.—Capture of Turaiyúr by the English in 1758.—History of the Poliyams from 1758 to 1801.—Mr. Wallace's proposals regarding the Poliyams.—Sanads granted to the Poligars.—Sale of the Ariyalúr Zemindári.—Poligars of Marungápuri and Kadavúr.—The Káttuputtúr Mittah.

CHAP. XIV. ZEMINDÁRIS, &c.

Earliest information extant regarding the Poligars of Turaiyúr, Udaiyárpálayam and Ariyalúr.

I HAVE not been able to obtain any trustworthy information regarding the Poliyams of Turaiyúr, Udaiyárpálayam and Ariyalúr previous to 1752. We learn from Orme's History that during the siege of Trichinopoly in that year, a detachment of the Mysore army, assisted by some French troops, overran the Poliyam of Turaiyúr, deposed the reigning chieftain, and put one of his cousins in his place. In 1755, the new chief having neglected to pay the tribute demanded from him, a detachment of French troops and sepoys was sent from Pondicherry to punish him. After some opposition, the French took Turaiyúr, deposed the chief, and reinstated his predecessor. From Turaiyúr they marched against the Poligars of Ariyalúr and Udaiyárpálayam. Captain Calliaud, however, who then commanded in Trichinopoly, advanced against them, and they consequently left the poligars unmolested, and returned to Pondicherry.[1] In 1756 the Poligar of Turaiyúr again failed to pay his tribute, and was accordingly deposed by the French, his immediate predecessor taking his place.[2]

Capture of Turaiyúr by the English in 1758.

In the following year the Poliyam of Udaiyárpálayam was invaded by the French, and the poligar forced to pay a tribute of 40,000 Rupees.[3] The Poligar of Turaiyúr, whom the French had expelled in 1757, was befriended by the Poligars of Ariyalúr and Udaiyárpálayam, and in 1758 Captain Calliaud, who still commanded the English in Trichinopoly, in order to gratify these chiefs, who had always been firm opponents of the French, determined to reinstate their friend. He accordingly sent a detachment under Captain Joseph Smith to attack Turaiyúr.

The following account of the assault on this place is given by Orme: "The wood of Turaiyúr stretches twenty miles along the foot of the western mountains, and extends from them ten miles into the

(1) ORME, Vol. I, page 396.
(2) ORME, Vol II, page 118.
(3) ORME, Vol. II, page 209.

plain ; the wood is in most parts seven miles across, and encloses an open space about three miles square. In this area are the habitation of the Reddi, which is a spacious building, a town, gardens, arable lands, and immediately under the hills a very large tank, computed to be seven miles in circumference. The attacking force knew that the path before them had defences in various parts, and that the whole of the fighting-men would be in these stations. Captain Smith therefore sent off four companies of sepoys, with Rama Náyak, a jemadár, on whom Muhammad Isuf had reliance, to enter the wood at a considerable distance on the right, under the conduct of the guides, who undertook to lead them to the town through a secret path, of which there are several in the wood, known only to the inhabitants. The first barrier was a winding passage between two thick-set hedges of thorn, leading into the straiter path of the wood, but choked at both ends with brambles laid for the occasion. Nevertheless the enemy abandoned this post, although very defensible, without resistance.

The coffres led, followed by the Europeans ; they by one of the 6-pounders with limber-boxes only ; and the sepoys marched in the rear, excepting a few who remained to guard the other 6-pounder, the spare ammunition and the baggage, which were left at the skirt of the wood ; the line proceeded more than a mile in the path without interruption, but at length was fired upon from a breastwork of brick on the right, from which the enemy were soon dislodged, and retired through the bushes to the west ; but as they were intent in carrying off their wounded, the musketry galled them a good deal as they were going away. Moving onward, the line soon received a smart fire from a second breastwork like the first ; but the coffres obliged the enemy to quit this station also, on which they retired to their main body. A few of the line were wounded in driving them from these defences. The coffres continued to move on in front, and out-marched the rest of the line, when, by a sudden turning in the road, they came unexpectedly at once within pistol-shot of the enemy's principal post. This was a strong wall of brick, fourteen feet high, divided into rampart and parapet, and in the parapet were several tiers of loop-holes. It stretched across the path, and some yards beyond it on each hand, and had a return of the same construction at each extremity, but falling back, instead of projecting to flank the main wall; and in the return on the left stood the gateway. This work was surrounded by a strong hedge of thorn, which, continuing on the sides, joined the main wood to some distance in the rear. As soon as the coffres appeared at the turning, the enemy testified their numbers and their courage by shouting, the din of instruments, and a strong fire of their match-locks, which, with the surprise, panic-struck the coffres. They ran back in the path, and were immediately followed by

CHAP. XIV. ZEMINDÁRIS, &c.

numbers of the enemy issuing from the thickets on the left. There was no time to inquire the cause. Captain Smith immediately led on the Europeans, who soon drove the enemy back into the wood, who did not escape through the barrier of thorns before the wall. Both were now attentively examined; and, whilst some endeavoured to tear up the hedge in front, others tried to get round the flanks of it into the wood; but none succeeded, and several were wounded. The field-piece was then advanced, and fired until all its ammunition was expended, without taking any effect on the parapet or intimidating the enemy, whose match-locks had wounded five of the six artillerymen serving the gun, and more of the other Europeans, who likewise had expended most of their cartridges. It was now 7 o'clock and began to grow dark, when all the blacks, whether coffres, sepoys, or lascars, took advantage of this protection and slunk away back into the path out of the reach of danger, excepting Muhammad Isuf, one servant of Captain Smith's, and one corporal of the lascars. A supply of ammunition had been sent for from the skirt of the wood as soon as the troops came to the wall; but from the distance it could not be expected for some time, during which Captain Smith ordered the Europeans to fire their muskets now and then against the parapet, as well to convince the enemy that they were determined not to relinquish the attack, as to divert the chance of their discovering the party with Rama Náyak, whose arrival, too long delayed, had for some time created much doubt and anxiety. At 8 o'clock more ammunition came up, when the firing of the field-piece and musketry was renewed with great vivacity, and was equally returned by the enemy. Soon after firing was heard in the rear of the wall, and the sound of *Deen Deen* echoed from every part of the wood. They were already in the path, advancing at full pace; the troops on the rampart were flying, and met their fire, after which all resistance ceased, and Rama Náyak breaking down the gate, let in his friends from without. There remained three miles of the path to the town, but impeded with no more defences, nor were the thickets on either hand so close. The troops were gathered, the sepoys and coffres who had kept back came on, and all proceeded to the town, which they found abandoned. The reigning Reddi and all his people had escaped to the hills, excepting a few men, who could not move, having been blown up with gunpowder intended to load a field-piece, which they were dragging to the wall in the pass. The delay of Rama Náyak's party had been caused by the timidity of his guides, who, on some fright, left them soon after they entered the wood to find their way as they could. Of 70 Europeans, 4 were killed and 28 wounded in the attack. Muhammad Isuf was shot through the arm, but, binding up his wound, continued on the ground until all was over. A great number of scaling ladders were found at the Reddi's house, which had been prepared and were lying in readiness for the French to escalade Trichinopoly when they should see the opportunity. The natives of this district have little resemblance to any others in the Karnatic ; they have large bloated heads, pot bellies and small limbs. The climate is very unhealthy to strangers, and this is imputed to the nature of the water. The detachment continued in the town a week, and during this short stay, Captain Smith, all his officers, and most of the other Europeans fell ill. Three companies of sepoys with three sergeants were left to protect the reinstated Reddi, and the main body of the detachment returned to Trichinopoly."[4]

The country about Turaiyúr is still well wooded, but the forest, which appears to have surrounded the village at the time of which Orme wrote, has completely disappeared. The place is slightly feverish, and Natives complain of the water ; but Orme's description of the people is, by no means, applicable now. On the contrary, the Reddis of Turaiyúr are fine hardy fellows, and the best ryots in the district.

The chief of Turaiyúr, who had been ejected by the detachment under Captain Smith, escaped to Mysore, where he was joined by all those who were dissatisfied with the existing state of things. From the post that he had taken up, he plundered the country between Turaiyúr and Úttattúr. When, in November 1758, Muhammad Isuf had to march from Trichinopoly to the relief of Fort St. George, three out of the five companies that had been left in Turaiyúr had to be recalled to Trichinopoly. The deposed Poligar took advantage of the opportunity, and captured the town. He then submitted to the Nawáb, who accepted his offers, and confirmed him in the government.[5]

History of the Poliyams from 1758 to 1801.

An account of the varying fortunes of these poligars from the date where Orme's history comes to a conclusion to the acquisition of the district by the English Government is given in a report addressed by Mr. Wallace, the first Collector of the district, to the Board of Revenue. From this account, it appears that in the year 1773 the Turaiyúr Poligar quarrelled with his son, who, fearing that his father had a design on his life, left the country and proceeded to lay his case before the Nawáb in Madras. On his agreeing to raise the peishcush of the poliyam, which till then had been 1,50,000 Rupees, to 1,75,000 Rupees, the young chief was sent back in 1786 to Turaiyúr as poligar, and his father was removed to

(4) Orme, Vol. II, pages 3373-40. A few unimportant abbreviations and alterations have been made in this extract. The *Coffres* or *Caffres* mentioned here are stated by Orme (Vol. I, page 81) to have been slaves, natives of Madagascar or the Eastern Coast of Africa. It may perhaps be presumed that for *Coffres* should be read *Kaffirs*.

(5) Orme, Vol. II, pages 465-467.

Madras. The old man, however, resorted to the same means that had been employed by his son for getting the management of the poliyam, and offered to increase the peishcush to 2,00,000 Rupees if the estate was placed under his authority. His offer was accepted, and he was restored to the poliyam in 1787. In 1789 however the son, by the offer of 1,00,000 Rupees as a present to the Nawáb, and on engaging to pay the same peishcush as his father had agreed to, was again reinstated. The country had suffered by these repeated changes of authority, and the disturbances which naturally attended them, and the young chief was unable to fulfil his engagements. He was accordingly removed in 1793, and his father, for the third time, placed in the management of the poliyam, having previously engaged to pay a peishcush of 2,75,000 Rupees. The poliyam in its impoverished state was of course unable to pay this increased tribute, and in 1795 the old chief and his son became reconciled, and, seeing that they had no chance of being able to meet the Nawáb's demands, left the country and took refuge in Tanjore, where the old man soon afterwards died. His son, taking advantage of the disturbances which broke out in 1796 in Udaiyárpálayam, and profiting by the distracted state of the country under the Nawáb's authority, determined to make an attempt to regain Turaiyúr. He accordingly collected a considerable number of men, and, being aided by the adherents of the family, laid waste all parts of the poliyams. The Nawáb, seeing how fruitless and expensive it was to contend with the expelled chief, who, although not absolute master of the country, had yet sufficient power to prevent its being cultivated, resolved to come to terms. As the poligar's resources had by this time been nearly exhausted by the length of the contest, he listened to the overtures made him and agreed to retire to Tanjore, having first obtained the Nawáb's promise to allow him 1,000 Rupees monthly for his subsistence, and to permit him to levy annually an assessment on the inhabitants of Turaiyúr, which was to bear a proportion of 25 per cent. to the amount of the revenue collected by the State. This arrangement continued in force till the assignment of the Karnatic to the Company.

The families of the Udaiyárpálayam and Ariyalúr poligars appear to have held uninterrupted possession of their poliyams until the year 1765, when the Nawáb, assisted by a party of English troops, attacked the forts of Ariyalúr and Udaiyárpálayam, and, after a slight resistance on the part of the chiefs, drove them and their families from the poliyams. The cause of this attack is said to have been a refusal on the part of the poligars to contribute their quota of men and money for the reduction of Madura. Previous to the expulsion of the poligar, Udaiyárpálayam is said to have yielded to its chief an annual revenue of about a lakh of star pagodas, out of which a peishcush of 10,000 Rupees was paid annually to the Nawábs of the Karnatic. Ariyalúr yielded the poligar about one-fifth less than Udaiyárpálayam, and was charged with a peishcush of 20,000 Rupees. The expelled poligars took refuge first in Tanjore and then in Mysore until 1780, when Hyder, taking advantage of their claims to their poliyams, and the influence which they still possessed over their people, sent them with a party of his troops into the poliyams. With this assistance the poligars found it not difficult to expel the Nawáb's troops, and to re-establish their authority in the country. From this period the poligars held undisturbed possession of their estates till 1783, when Mr. Sullivan persuaded them to separate themselves from Hyder, and became, during the first assignment of the southern countries, the renters of their respective districts. A short time before the restoration of the Nawáb's authority, the poligars were imprisoned at Trichinopoly on account of their having failed in the punctual payment of their tribute. After a confinement of about two years, they were released and permitted to reside in their poliyams, which were however rented out for three years to the chief servant of the Udaiyárpálayam family. When however only one year of this lease had expired, all authority was again taken from the poligars, and the districts were placed under the management of the Nawáb's servants. In this situation they remained, until a short period before the assignment of the Karnatic in 1790, when the Ariyalúr poligar was again imprisoned on a suspicion of having meditated an insurrection in the district. On the assumption of the country in 1790, the poligars were placed in the management of the poliyams as renters, and they continued to act as such until the restoration of the country to the Nawáb, when the Ariyalúr poligar fled to Tanjore, and the Udaiyárpálayam chief went to Madras to endeavour to establish his claim to his ancestral estate. After many fruitless attempts on the part of the poligars to regain their poliyams, the entire management of the revenues of these estates was, in 1798, handed over to an agent of the Nawáb, a monthly allowance of Rupees 1,000 being paid to the Poligar of Udaiyárpálayam and of 700 Rupees to the Poligar of Ariyalúr. This system continued in force till Trichinopoly was made over to the Company in 1801.[6]

Mr. Wallace's proposals regarding the poliyams.

Mr. Wallace concludes his report regarding the poligars by proposing that they should be restored to their poliyams on the footing of zemindárs, and should pay a peishcush equal to two-thirds of the value of their zemindáris, and that, till this arrangement could be carried out, they should receive a monthly allowance for their support.

(6) Letter from Collector of Trichinopoly to Board of Revenue, dated 30th May 1802, paragraphs 5–33.

CHAP. XIV. ZEMINDÁRIS, &c.

In the orders passed on this letter, the Board of Revenue directed that, as it was intended to extend to the poliyams in the district of Trichinopoly the system by which zemindári rights would be conferred on their possessors, for the purpose of facilitating the introduction of that system, the poliyams of Turaiyúr, Ariyalúr, and Udaiyárpálayam should be continued under the Collector's management, and that he should ascertain the value of the lands comprised in them, and the extent to which the poligars might, at any time, have been considered bound to render military service to the State. The Collector was also ordered to report the amount of commutation that he would propose for that service, and the peishcush that he would recommend should be assessed on the poligars in perpetuity. He was further instructed to disarm all the adherents of the poligars. Until the information required before the poliyams could be assessed was collected, an allowance of 10 per cent. on the net revenue of their respective estates was sanctioned for these poligars, which the Board desired the Collector to pay to them, with arrears calculated at the same rate, from the day the Karnatic was ceded to the Company.[7]

Sanads granted to the poligars.

The matter seems to have rested on this footing till 1816, when Government directed that the poligars should not be restored to the entire possession of their poliyams, but should receive merely the villages in which they lived, together with a number of other villages surrounding their head-quarters, of an annual value equivalent to 10 per cent. of the gross collections from the entire poliyams. These villages were to be subjected to the payment of a nominal peishcush.[8] In accordance with these orders, a *sanad-i-milkiat-istimrar* was given to each of the poligars on the 23rd December 1817, and they were thus constituted zemindárs under Regulation XXV of 1802. In these estates the ordinary Hindu law of inheritance prevails. They can be sub-divided and alienated in the same manner as other real property, and Government has no power of regulating the succession to them.

The Zemindárs of Turaiyúr are Reddis, and of Telugu extraction. The Zemindárs of Ariyalúr and Udaiyárpálayam, however, are Kallars by caste, and, till they received their present sanads, held their estates as arasukávalgárs. An account of their kával duties will be found in Chapter XVIII under the head of Police. As has been there shown, the poligars were relieved from the performance of all police duties from the time that their present estates were handed over to them on zemindári tenure.

Sale of the Ariyalúr zemindári.

In 1871 twenty-seven villages in the Ariyalúr zemindári were sold by orders of the Civil Court in satisfaction of debts incurred by the Zemindár, and in 1873 the remaining thirty villages

(7) Proceedings of the Board of Revenue, dated 14th August 1802.
(8) Proceedings of the Board of Revenue, dated 22nd April 1816.

were sold for the same reason.[9] The estate is now held by a number of petty proprietors, whose names are registered in the Collector's office, but who have no sanads. The *sanad-i-milkiat-istimrar* granted by Government is in the possession of the zemindár, who however is a pauper, and has lost the whole of his ancestral estate.

Poligars of Marungápuri and Kadavár.

There are two poliyams, Marungápuri and Kadavúr, in the southern portion of Kulittalai Taluq, which were transferred to Trichinopoly District from Madura in 1856. These estates were at that time unsettled poliyams, *i.e.*, poliyams for which no sanads had been granted.

There has recently been a very protracted litigation regarding the succession to the Marungápuri poliyam, a brief account of which will be given here, as, by the judgment passed by the Privy Council in the case, some important questions regarding the succession to unsettled poliyams have been decided.

The Zemindár of Marungápuri died in 1864, and his half-brother (a minor) was nominated to succeed him by Government. The senior widow of the deceased zemindár claimed the estate as his heir, asserting that the minor nominated by Government was illegitimate. The case came on for trial in the Civil Court, Trichinopoly, where it was decided that the Marungápuri zemindári was an unsettled poliyam, and that, therefore, the right to decide as to the succession to it was vested in Government. The widow's claim was accordingly dismissed.[10] On appeal to the High Court, it was decided that the poliyam was an ancestral hereditary estate, which had devolved through several generations in the ordinary course of legal succession. It followed, therefore, that the right of succession contested in the suit depended upon whether the minor nominated by Government was legitimate or not, and an issue to that effect was sent down to the Trichinopoly District Court for trial.[11] The District Court decided that the boy was legitimate, and this view was upheld on appeal in the High Court and the Privy Council.[12] The decision of the High Court that the poliyam was an ancestral hereditary estate was also confirmed, on appeal, by the Judicial Committee of the Privy Council.[13]

(9) Proceedings of the Board of Revenue, No. 1,751, of the 3rd September 1873; G.O., No. 1,074, of the 6th October 1873; and G.O., No. 142, of the 23rd October 1873.

(10) Original Suit, No. 130 of 1868, in the Civil Court of Trichinopoly.

(11) Decision of the High Court in R.A., No. 129 of 1869.

(12) Judgment of the Judicial Committee of the Privy Council on the appeal of Pedda Ammani and another *v.* the Zemindár of Marungápuri from the High Court of Madras, delivered 14th January 1874.

(13) Judgment of the Judicial Committee by the Privy Council on the appeal of the Collector of Trichinopoly *v.* Lekkamani and the zemindár of Marungápuri from the High Court of Madras, delivered 14th March 1874.

CHAP. XIV. ZEMINDÁRIS, &c.

A *sanad-i-milkiat-istimrar* was offered to, and accepted by, the Zemindár of Kadavúr in 1871. No sanad has been given to the Zemindár of Marungápuri, so that his estate is still an unsettled poliyam. Both these zemindárs are of Telugu extraction, and of the Tottiya Náyak caste. Their families are believed by them to have come from Ghooty in Bellary District.

The Káttuputtúr mittah.

Káttuputtúr is the only mittah in the district. It was created by Government in 1802, and given to one Saruvóthama Rau, the then Head Sheristadar of the Salem Collectorate. He sold the estate in 1810 to one Gunnamareddi, who, in his turn, sold it to Annayar and Saptha Rishi Reddi in 1813. These men are the ancestors of the present owners, and ever since the estate was sold to them it has been enjoyed by two joint proprietors, one of whom is a Bráhman and the other a Reddi. The mittah was transferred from Salem District to Trichinopoly in 1851.[14] The revenue of the estate was Rupees 16,303 in 1802 and 30,144 Rupees in 1876.

Statement No. 8 given in the appendix shows the revenue of the several zemindáris in the district, and of the Káttuputtúr mittah and the peishcush paid yearly by them.

---

(14) Extract from Minutes of Consultation, No. 382, of the 17th April 1851.

CHAPTER XV.

PUBLIC WORKS DEPARTMENT. THE ANICUTS. RAILWAYS.

PUBLIC WORKS DEPARTMENT RANGES—Public Works Department Establishment.—Expenditure under Imperial and Provincial Funds.—Expenditure under Local Funds. THE ANICUTS—The Upper Anicut.—The Cauvery Regulating Dam.—The Lower Anicut. LINES OF RAIL—Traffic Returns.

PUBLIC WORKS DEPARTMENT.

CHAPTER XV. P. W. DEPT., &c.

Public Works Department Ranges.

THE general supervision of the public works in the district is vested in the District Engineer. The district is divided into three ranges as follow:—

Range No. I, comprising Trichinopoly and Kulittalai Taluqs.

Range No. II, comprising Musiri and Perumbalúr Taluqs.

Range No. III, comprising Udaiyárpálayam Taluq.

Range No. I is at present in charge of an Executive Engineer, whose head-quarters are at Trichinopoly. He has four Overseers under his supervision. Range No. II is under an Assistant Engineer, with head-quarters at Musiri. Three Overseers are employed in this range. Range No. III is at present in charge of a Sub-Engineer, whose head-quarters are at Udaiyárpálayam, and who has one Overseer under him.

Public Works Department Establishment.

The District Engineer has an establishment consisting of a Head Clerk on Rupees 70 a month, an Accountant on Rupees 40, a Writer on Rupees 30, and a Draughtsman and Estimator on Rupees 45. The Officer in charge of No. I Range has an Accountant on Rupees 50, a Clerk on Rupees 30, and a Draughtsman and Estimator on Rupees 40. In No. II Range an Accountant on Rupees 50 and a Draughtsman and Estimator on Rupees 40 are entertained, and in No. III Range an Accountant on Rupees 40.

Expenditure under the Imperial and Provincial Funds.

Statement No. 16 given in the appendix shows the expenditure on public works from Imperial and Provincial Funds for a period of five years. In the descriptive notices of the several taluqs given in Chapter I, an account is given of the more important irrigation channels and tanks under the supervision of the Public Works Department, and of the revenue under them. The annual allotment for the upkeep of these works and construction of others of a similar nature is paid from Imperial Funds.

CHAPTER XV. P. W. DEPT., &c.

Expenditure under Local Funds.

All the roads maintained by the Local Fund Board are under the charge of the Public Works Department, with the exception of the unfinished road from Manapparai to Puttánattam, which is at present under the Revenue Department. For the upkeep of these roads, which are in all 533¼ miles in length, the maintenance allowance handed over to the Public Works Department for the year 1877-78 was Rupees 76,570. A list of these roads is given in Chapter XVI under the head of Local Funds, and a detailed account of them in the descriptive notices of the taluq through which they run, to be found in Chapter I.

THE ANICUTS.

The anicuts.

There are three anicuts, or large masonry dams, across the Cauvery and Coleroon rivers, two of which are in the district of Trichinopoly, while the third is in Tanjore. Of these, that locally known as the upper anicut has been built across the Coleroon at the point where that river separates from the Cauvery, at the head of the island of Srírangam. The lower anicut is also across the Coleroon, and is situated almost at the point where the river leaves Trichinopoly District and enters South Arcot. The grand anicut is in Tanjore. It has been built across the Cauvery at a distance of about ten miles to the east of Trichinopoly Town.

The following is a brief account of the objects for which the two of these works that are situated in this district were built, and the nature of their construction. For further particulars, reference may be made to a Report on Irrigation in Southern India, by Colonel Baird Smith of the Bengal Engineers, published in 1856 by order of the Government of India, from which the greater part of the information now given has been derived.

The upper anicut.

Shortly after Trichinopoly came into the possession of our Government, it was observed that the bed of the Coleroon was gradually deepening, while that of the Cauvery was rising. The effect of the change was a constantly-increasing difficulty in securing sufficient water in the Cauvery for the irrigation of Tanjore. In 1803 Captain Caldwell predicted that in the course of not many years the Cauvery would be dry and Tanjore District ruined. Various expedients were adopted from time to time to arrest the evil, but with only partial and temporary effect, and the consummation foretold by Captain Caldwell at one time seemed impending. At this juncture Colonel (now General Sir Arthur) Cotton, of the Madras Engineers, proposed to construct an anicut across the head of the Coleroon where it branches off from the Cauvery, and this work was accordingly carried out in 1836, and has completely answered the purposes for which it was intended. This anicut, known as the upper anicut, although situated in Trichinopoly

District, was designed for the benefit of Tanjore, and has always remained under the supervision of the Public Works Department officers of that district.

In its original form the upper anicut consisted of a simple bar of masonry 750 yards in length, divided into three parts by the interposition of two small islands formed in the bed of the stream. The northern portion is 7 feet 4 inches, and the remainder 5 feet 4 inches in height. The body of the dam is of brick masonry coped with cut-stone, there being 1 foot in height of the latter material and 6 feet 4 inches or 4 feet 4 inches of the former according to position. The thickness throughout is 6 feet. This bar, forming the obstructive portion of the dam, rests on a foundation of masonry 3 feet deep, built on three lines of walls 6 feet in exterior diameter, and sunk to a depth of 6 feet in the sandy bed of the river. In rear of the bar there is an apron of masonry 21 feet broad, and covered with cut-stone 1 foot in thickness, carefully laid in hydraulic cement. Below the apron a mass of rough-stone, from 9 to 12 feet broad and 4 feet deep, has been formed to protect the junction of the apron and river-bed. Twenty-two openings of sluices, originally 2 feet in width by 3½ in length, are distributed throughout the length of the dam, their sills being on the same level as the apron or the bed of the stream. The object of this arrangement is to afford free passage to the sand, and, if possible, to prevent the bed of the Coleroon above the dam being raised by deposits.

The Cauvery regulating dam.

In consequence of the construction of the anicut, a greatly increased volume of water was thrown into the Cauvery during freshes, and this led to great erosion of the banks and deepening of the bed. Simultaneously with these effects, the Coleroon branch was obstructed by heavy deposits and sand-banks above the dam; the deep channel, which formerly followed the left bank of the river, was thrown across to the right; and, in a word, there seemed reason to apprehend an inversion of the former relations of the two branches, the Cauvery becoming the main stream, and the Coleroon ceasing to obtain its due share of water. This would have led to disastrous results in Tanjore, and measures were accordingly adopted to obtain entire command over the bed of the Cauvery. The first of these measures, executed in 1843 on the recommendation of Colonel Sim of the Engineers, was to lower the central portion of the Coleroon dam 2 feet. This was done on a length of about 700 feet, and, of course, added considerably to the volume of the Coleroon; still, however, the enlargement of the head of the Cauvery continued, the banks were cut away, and there was great difficulty in preserving the narrow part of the island that separated the two branches. These effects were specially noted in 1844, and sanction was finally given to the construction of a masonry regulating dam across the mouth of the Cauvery, a work suggested by Colonel Sim at the same time as he proposed to lower the crown of the Coleroon dam. This work, consisting of a bar of masonry 650 yards in length carried across the mouth of the Cauvery, was executed in 1845. The level of the crown at the central portion was the same as that of the river-bed, while 150 feet at each flank were raised from 1 foot to 18 inches above it. The ordinary precautions were adopted to secure the foundations, and strong wing walls protected both flanks. The means thus adopted have proved sufficient to control the two rivers, and the regulation of the beds and the distribution of the water are as nearly complete as could be desired. The construction of a bridge for foot-passengers over the entire length of the anicut has added greatly to its general utility.

A small bungalow has been built close to the northern end of the anicut, which is a favourite place of residence of the Collectors of Trichinopoly, and there is also another bungalow under the charge of the Tanjore Public Works Department officers situated at the southern end in the Srírangam island.

The lower anicut.

Another effect of the upper anicut, to which it is necessary to advert here, is the influence of the work on the volume of the river across which it is thrown, and on the irrigation dependent upon it. The principle on which the division of the water in the main stream was based being that none should flow over the Coleroon dam until the wants of the Tanjore District had been provided for, it is clear that, in average conditions of the river, the practical effect of this arrangement would be to divert nearly the entire volume of the main stream into the Cauvery, and thus to leave the channels from the Coleroon dependent on the drainage, escape-water, springs in the bed of the river, or other minor sources of supply. These combined had been found to furnish a volume sufficient for the irrigation on the Lower Coleroon; but, as the abstraction of so large a portion of the former supply of the river by means of the dam would of course very much lower its surface-level, all the old channels in South Arcot would have been thrown out of use, and the levels of the village water-courses wholly deranged. A dam across the Coleroon at the point where it enters South Arcot, of such height as to restore the old surface-level of the water, became, therefore, absolutely necessary. It was supplementary to the upper dam, and the sole motive for its construction was to re-establish in South Arcot the state of things destroyed by the construction of that work. This dam, known as the lower anicut, was built across the river at a point about seventy miles below where the Coleroon leaves the Cauvery, and consists of a bar of masonry 8 feet high and 8 feet broad, but having a hollow space 3 feet by 4 feet in the centre, arched over and filled with rammed sand. It is provided with twenty-three under-sluices, giving 69 feet of waterway in a total breadth of 1,901½ feet, and has an apron of masonry in rear 2 feet thick and 24 feet broad, and covered with 1 foot additional of cut-stone; while in front and rear rough, loose stones of large dimensions are employed to protect the junctions of the work with river-bed.

The lower anicut was constructed simultaneously with the upper one in 1836, and was at first made only six feet in height. In 1837 two feet were added to the height, and, by the floods of that season, a formidable breach was made in the work from the failure of the apron in rear, wherein some inferior materials had been inadvertently employed. The accident was immediately repaired, and the work has, since that period, given but little trouble, while it has effected its purpose in maintaining the irrigation of Chellambram Taluq in South Arcot and a small portion of Tanjore in a very satisfactory manner.

RAILWAYS.

Lines of rail.

The South Indian Railway traverses the district from east to west, running through Trichinopoly and Kulittalai Taluq, a distance of 55¼ miles. It also runs from Trichinopoly through the south-eastern portion of Kulittalai Taluq, and thence into the Madura District, a distance of 37¾ miles. The portion of the line from Trichinopoly to Negapatam was opened in March 1862, from Trichinopoly to Erode in July 1866, and from Trichinopoly to Madura in September 1875. In 1876 the South Indian Railway carried to and from the several stations in the district 1,073,692 passengers and 42,965 tons of goods. Trichinopoly is the head-quarters of the Chief Engineer of the South Indian Railway.

Traffic returns.

The following statement gives the inwards and outwards traffic under each article or group of articles for the several stations on the South India Railway in Trichinopoly District for 1876:—

Article.	Tiruvarambúr.		Trichinopoly Junction.		Trichinopoly Fort.		Elamanúr.		Kulittalai.		Lálápéttai.		Kattalai.		Kolattúr.		Manapparai.		Vaiyampatti.		Total.	
	Inwards.	Outwards.	Inwards.	Outwards.	Inwards.	Outwards.	Inwards.	Outwards.	Inwards.	Outwards.	Inwards.	Outwards.	Inwards.	Outwards.	Inwards.	Outwards.	Inwards.	Outwards.	Inwards.	Outwards.	Inwards.	Outwards.
—	1	2	3	4	5	6	7	8	9	10	11	12	13	14	15	16	17	18	19	20	21	22
	TONS.	TONS.	TONS.	TONS.	TONS.	TONS.	TONS.	TONS.	TONS.	TONS.	TONS.	TONS.	TONS.	TONS.	TONS.	TONS.	TONS.	TONS.	TONS.	TONS.	TONS.	TONS.
Areca nuts	...	...	...	...	385·77	68·36	...	...	32·38	1·98	2·71	...	·28	...	...	...	9·70	1·16	...	...	430·84	71·50
Cloths	·15	...	...	...	473·68	43·61	·09	·17	8·19	2·31	·25	...	·10	1·57	1·09	...	7·93	2·43	10·10	4·35	501·58	54·44
Cotton	...	...	...	...	6·58	1·11	...	...	1·21	...	...	...	..	...	...	...	...	...	...	...	7·79	1·11
Curry-stuff	...	...	...	...	824·83	730·21	...	...	7·93	·58	...	2·98	4·90	25·87	...	...	1·41	·51	·01	...	839·08	760·15
Fruits and Vegetables ...	6·33	·45	...	...	265·43	735·12	...	1·34	2·39	·05	71·84	75·45	44·12	37·72	...	...	...	·67	...	·46	390·11	851·26
Grains of all kinds ...	201·55	20·40	...	...	7,999·23	4,140·37	...	104·95	21·78	484·67	224·80	557·31	61·37	208·60	31·50	19·15	93·32	40·76	·86	4·34	8,634·71	5,580·55
Granite stones	...	...	...	...	131·15	901·70	...	...	...	7·90	·77	...	33·51	...	33·15	273·17	...	...	5·27	·25	203·85	1,182·92
Oil and Ghee	...	...	...	...	297·71	338·70	...	...	...	11·26	10·05	12·31	...	·21	...	...	...	137·79	...	1·17	307·76	501·44
Oil-cakes	...	...	...	...	74·77	1,077·66	...	...	...	1·5	...	5·20	1·72	12·40	...	...	...	10·99	·02	...	76·94	1,107·32
Salt	...	...	...	...	3,843·13	664·17	...	...	128·44	...	416·76	5·20	249·64	123·85	...	...	88·80	·42	...	...	4,726·77	793·64
Seeds of all kinds ...	...	·13	...	...	1,657·61	870·22	14·39	6·16	5·42	20·56	7·06	13·20	·28	12·36	...	·15	3·37	13·92	4·59	5·04	1,692·72	941·74
Sundries	27·75	88·13	...	...	7,713·03	3,252·41	38·49	2·89	83·51	24·43	93·75	78·14	57·71	27·33	34·95	29·92	197·21	86·00	31·44	60·96	8,277·84	3,650·21
Tobacco	...	...	...	...	643·63	65·73	·37	...	·07	·04	1·01	...	2·61	1·98	...	...	...	·25	1·22	2·49	648·91	70·49
Hides	...	1·10	...	...	446·64	43·06	...	·39	...	...	8·69	3·20	134·62	·07	·16	·27	...	20·68	...	·71	590·11	69·48
Total ...	236·08	110·21	...	...	24,763·19	12,932·34	53·34	115·90	291·32	555·28	837·69	752·99	590·86	451·96	100·85	322·66	401·74	315·58	53·51	79·77	27,328·58	15,636·78

CHAPTER XVI.

LOCAL FUNDS.

LOCAL FUNDS RAISED UNDER ACT IV OF 1871—Local Fund Board.—Sources from which the funds are derived.—Objects to which the funds can be applied.—Roads. —Education.—Dispensaries.—Vaccination.—Sanitation.—Chattrams and other Charitable Institutions.—Public Bungalows. SPECIAL LOCAL FUNDS—Jungle Conservancy Fund.—Pound Fund.—Village Service Fund.—Irrigation Cess Fund.

LOCAL FUNDS RAISED UNDER ACT IV OF 1871.

Local Fund Board.

THE whole of the Trichinopoly District, with the exception of the Trichinopoly and Srírangam Municipalities, has been constituted a Local Fund Circle under Act IV of 1871 (Madras). The Collector is ex-officio President of the Local Fund Board, the other official members being at present the Head Assistant Collector, who is also Vice-President, the District Engineer, the Public Works Department Officer in charge of No. I Range, the Inspector of Schools, 3rd Division, the Deputy Inspector of Schools, the Civil Surgeon, Trichinopoly, the Deputy Collector on general duties, and the Collector's Sheristadar. There are also nine non-official members.

Sources from which the funds are derived.

The funds administered by the Local Fund Board are derived principally from a cess levied at the rate of one anna in the rupee on all occupied land in the Circle and tolls. Minor receipts are the contribution from the Surplus Pound Fund, Ferry and Fish Rents, and the proceeds of the sale of the loppings, fruit, &c., of avenue trees. Up to 1873 the Trichinopoly Municipality levied tolls on all the roads leading into the town. In that year, however, these tolls were handed over to the Local Fund Board, and the toll-gate that had previously been erected at the southern end of the Cauvery Bridge was transferred to a point a few hundred yards north of the Coleroon Bridge, where Roads Nos. 4 and 1 join Road No. 3. By this means all the traffic to and from the Srírangam island is taxed. Half of the proceeds of the tolls levied on the roads leading to Trichinopoly and Srírangam is handed over to the Trichinopoly Municipality as a yearly contribution from the Local Fund Board, while of the remainder Rupees 1,000 a year is given to the Srírangam Municipality. A toll has also been established on the bridge across the Ayyár River over which Road No. 1 passes. The entire proceeds of this toll are credited to the Local Fund Board.

CHAP. XVI. LOCAL FUNDS.

Objects to which the funds can be applied.

The objects to which the funds raised under the Local Fund Act can be applied are the following :—(1) The construction, repair, and maintenance of roads and communications. (2) The diffusion of education, and, with this object in view, the construction and repair of school-houses, the maintenance of schools either wholly or by means of grants-in-aid, the inspection of schools and the training of teachers. (3) The construction and repair of hospitals, dispensaries, lunatic asylums, choultries, markets, tanks and wells, the payment of all charges connected with the objects for which such buildings have been constructed, the training and employment of vaccinators and medical practitioners, the sanitary inspection of towns and villages, the cleansing of the roads, streets and tanks, and any other local works of public utility calculated to promote the health, comfort, or convenience of the people. Two-thirds of the land-cess and the net proceeds of all tolls must be applied to the first of these objects.

Roads.

The following is a list of the roads kept up by the Local Fund Board in the Circle with the amount of maintenance allotted for them in the year 1878-79 :—

	RS.
Road No. I from Trichinopoly to Salem *viâ* Musiri, 39 miles..	8,750
Road No. II from Trichinopoly to Ahtúr in Salem District *viâ* Turaiyúr, 39 miles ..	3,900
Road No. III from Trichinopoly to Madras *viâ* Perumbalúr, 45 miles	12,600
Road No. IV from Trichinopoly to Mannárgudi in South Arcot *viâ* Udaiyárpálayam, 62 miles	8,100
Road No. V from Trichinopoly to Combaconam *viâ* the Grand Anicut, 9 miles ..	1,080
Road No. VI from Trichinopoly to Kovalagudi *viâ* Sarkárpálayam, 9 miles	550
Road No. VII from Trichinopoly to Tanjore *viâ* Tiruvarambúr, 12 miles	1,800
Road No. VIII from Trichinopoly to Pudukóttai, 6 miles	600
Road No. IX from Trichinopoly to Madura, 42 miles	11,300
Road No. X from Trichinopoly to Dindigul, 41 miles	4,900
Road No. XI from Trichinopoly to Karúr in Coimbatore District, 40 miles	7,040
Road No. XII from Káttuputtúr to Valayapatti on Road No. I, 5 miles	500
Road No. XIII from Musiri to Turaiyúr, 17 miles	1,700

CHAP. XVI.
LOCAL FUNDS.

	RS.
Road No. XV[1] from Tirumanúr *viâ* Ariyalúr and Perumbalúr to Ahtúr in Salem District, 46 miles	4,250
Road No. XVII from Madanakurichi on the bank of the Coleroon *viâ* Jeyamkondasólapuram to Rajéndrapatnam, 31 miles ..	1,550
Road No. XVIII from the Lower Anicut to the Vellár Anicut, 12 miles	1,800
Road No. XIX from Pullambádi to Aramanaikurichi. 14 miles	1,050
Road No. XX from Sirudayúr *viâ* Sengariyúr along the bank of the Coleroon to the Lower Anicut, 18 miles	900
Road No. XXI from Samayapuram on Road No. III to Irungalúr, 2 miles	100
Road No. XXII from Tiruvarambúr Station *viâ* Lalgudi to Edaiyáthamangalam, 9¼ miles	630
Road No. XXIII from Trichinopoly to Allitúrai, 4 miles	500
Road No. XXV from Kulittalai to Kóvilpatti *viâ* Manapparai, 32 miles	2,970

Education.

Act IV of 1871 gives Government the power of levying a tax on houses for the support of local schools, but this tax has never as yet been imposed in any villages in Trichinopoly Circle. An account of the schools kept up or assisted by the Local Fund Board is given in Chapter XX under the head of Education.

Dispensaries.

There are two branch dispensaries at Musiri and Ariyalúr supported by the Local Fund Board. Annual grants are also made by the Board to the Municipal Hospitals in Trichinopoly and Srírangam and to the S.P.G. Mission Dispensary at Irungalúr.

Vaccination.

A Deputy Inspector of Vaccination and a staff of five First-class and eleven Second-class Vaccinators are maintained from Local Funds.

The following statement shows the work done by this establishment for the last four years :—

Particulars.	1874-75.	1875-76.	1876-77.	1877-78.
Number of persons vaccinated ..	21,188	14,792	20,096	15,615
Do. of successful cases ..	20,091	14,195	19,630	12,721

(1) As the roads in the district are numbered at present, there are no roads numbered as No. 14, No. 16, or No. 24.

CHAP. XVI. LOCAL FUNDS.

Sanitation.

Grants are made every year by the Local Fund Board for deepening and repairing existing wells and constructing new ones, These grants are, as a rule, supplemented by contributions from the villagers. In 1876-77 Rupees 15,163 were spent on these objects in the Circle. For the last three years the Local Fund Board has also made considerable grants towards the sanitation of certain of the larger villages in the Circle. A sum of 8,000 Rupees was allotted for this purpose in 1877-78, which was distributed as follows: Lálgudi, Musiri, Turaiyúr, Kulittalai, Ariyalúr, and Udaiyárpálayam, Rupees 1,000 each; Perumbalúr, 700 Rupees; Manapparai and Jeyamkondasólapuram, Rupees 500 each; and Kílapaluvúr Rupees 300. Out of these grants latrines and dust-bins have been built, carts engaged to remove night-soil and rubbish, and other measures calculated to improve the sanitary condition of the villages carried out. The general appearance of these villages has been greatly improved by the expenditure thus incurred.

Chattrams and other charitable institutions.

The following is a list of the principal chattrams and other charitable institutions that have either been transferred to the Local Fund Board under the provisions of Section 10 of Act IV of 1871, or have been established by the Board since the introduction of the Act. In Trichinopoly Taluq Shadikkán and Kolattúr Chattrams. The latter of these chattrams has been built by the Local Fund Board close to the Kolattúr Railway Station from funds transferred from a ruined chattram on the Dindigul Road known as Chetti Chattram. In Musiri Taluq Puduperiyammápálayam Chattram. In Kulittalai Taluq the chattrams at Kalpatti, Kóvilpatti, Manapparai, Puttánattam, Koraipatti, and the two chattrams at Tógamalai. Of the two Tógamalai Chattrams, one, known as Mayen Chetti Chattram, situated in the town, is now in ruins, but an estimate to rebuild it has been sanctioned. The other building, known as Tandappan Chetti Chattram, is at a distance of about a mile from the village. It is in good order, but, as it is off the present line of road, is almost useless to travellers. In Udaiyárpálayam Taluq the chattram known as Puduchávadi and that at Kistnapuram in Perumbalúr have also been transferred to the Local Fund Board. A new chattram has been built at Padalúr in Perumbalúr Taluq out of Local Funds. There is a water-pandal in Puduvádi in Kulittalai Taluq which has been transferred to the Local Fund Board. There are also eighty-four *úranies* or ponds under the Board. These are all situated in the Manapparai Division of Kulittalai Taluq, and have small portions of Mániyam land attached to them for their support.

Travellers' Bungalows.

There are at present but three public bungalows in the Circle kept up out of Local Funds. These are at Manapparai on the Dindigul Road and Kóvilpatti and Tuvarankurichi on the Madura

Road. The Local Fund Board have proposed to take over the buildings at Pudupálayam, Manavási, Tottiyam, Válikandapuram, Toramangalam, Tuvágudi, Nágamangalam, and Samayapuram which were formerly used as public bungalows, but the sanction of Government to the transfer has not as yet been obtained.

Statement No. 17, given in the appendix, shows the receipts and expenditure of the Local Funds constituted under Act IV of 1871 for a series of five years.

SPECIAL LOCAL FUNDS.

The following is a list of the Special Local Funds in the district. They are all under the control of the Board of Revenue. (1) Jungle Conservancy Fund, (2) Pound Fund, (3) Surplus Pound Fund, (4) Village Service Fund, (5) Irrigation Cess Fund. Statement No. 18, given in the appendix, shows the receipts and disbursements under these funds for a series of five years.

Jungle Conservancy Fund.

The object of this fund is the conservation and extension of village jungles. Its income is derived from a tax levied on fuel, firewood and bamboos, the proceeds of the sale of trees, and fees levied from charcoal-burners. The fund is applied principally to the maintenance of existing plantations and topes and the formation of new ones.

The following are the most important of the Jungle Conservancy Rules at present in force in the district [2] :—

The Tahsildars and Sheristadars of Musiri, Kulittalai, Perumbalúr, and Udaiyárpálayam Taluqs and the Deputy Tahsildars of Turaiyúr, Manapparai, and Kílapaluvúr alone are authorized to issue licenses for felling timber, fuel, bamboos, &c., and for burning charcoal, and to collect seigniorage. The village rangers are authorized to issue licenses and collect seigniorage on bullock, ass, or head-loads only. Any one entering the jungles for the purpose of felling wood, &c., or burning charcoal, must previously obtain a license which he must produce, when required, by any Forest or Revenue Officer, and any person found felling wood or burning charcoal in the Government forests or jungles without a license is declared to be liable, in addition to the confiscation of the wood felled by him, to prosecution under the Penal Code for theft or mischief. Charcoal-burners are required to put out their fires before leaving the jungles, and no Government hills can be set on fire without express permission. The " Malaiyálies " (natives of the hills) are declared to have a right to fell wood for their own use free of all charge. All persons wishing to fell

(2) The rules are published in full in the District Gazette of the 1st April 1876.

CHAP. XVI. LOCAL FUNDS.

timber in Government forests are required to pay seigniorage in advance into one of the taluq treasuries at the following rates, on which they are entitled to receive from the Tahsildar a numbered license (in duplicate).

	RS.	A.	P.
Bamboos, cart-load	1	0	0
Do. head-load	0	0	6
Do. donkey-load	0	1	0
Charcoal, cart-load	1	8	0
Do. head-load	0	2	0
Do. bullock-load	0	4	0
Do. donkey-load	0	2	0
Fuel, cart-load of 1,000 lbs.	0	6	0
Do. head-load	0	0	3

Every license must be produced before the ranger named in it, who is directed to retain the duplicate of the license and return the original to the holder to serve him as a permit. The rangers are obliged to send monthly to the Tahsildar all licenses retained by them. The original license, which serves as a permit till the holder takes home the wood, &c., is eventually handed over to the Munsif of the village to which the wood is taken.

The following are the rules under which free felling is allowed:—

Villagers are entitled to wood for their agricultural implements and erection of cow-sheds, &c., free of seigniorage and to firewood for their own use, but they are required to obtain a free pass before felling it.

A permit must be obtained before entering the forest or jungle for the purpose of felling or removing timber, &c., and persons found felling or removing wood, &c., without a permit are declared to be liable to be dealt with as ordinary offenders, notwithstanding that with a permit they might be entitled to fell free. The following officers are authorized to issue free passes under the Forest Conservancy Rules:—

The Collector of the district.
The Forest Officer in charge.
All Revenue Officers in charge of a division or part of a division.
All Tahsildars and Deputy Tahsildars.
Forest Overseers.
Village Rangers.[3]

A supply of free licenses in duplicate, signed and sealed by the Forest Officer in charge, is supplied to each of these officers, the

(3) There are 27 Rangers in Musiri Taluq, 15 in Kulittalai, 5 in Perumbalúr, and 24 in Udaiyárpálayam.

original of which is issued to applicants, and the duplicate sent to the ranger in charge of the village in which the felling is to take place to enable him to get back the original on the expiry of the time allowed and check the quantity felled with that entered in the pass. All officers issuing free licenses have to keep a register of the licenses granted by them, in order to prevent the same person obtaining a second pass before a sufficient time has elapsed since the issue of the first one.

CHAP. XVI. LOCAL FUNDS.

Ryots holding Government land are entitled to have the following wood, &c., free under the Forest Conservancy Rules under the orders of the Divisional Officers :—

Timber of the unreserved classes and bamboos for erection of their houses when destroyed by fire or other exceptional causes.

Timber of the unreserved classes and bamboos for sheds.

Timber of the unreserved classes and bamboos for all agricultural purposes and head-loads and bandy-loads of firewood on obtaining a free permit.

The following statement shows in detail the receipts and expenditure under the head of Jungle Conservancy for a period of three years :—

Receipts.				Expenditure.			
Items.	1874-75.	1875-76.	1876-77.	Items.	1874-75.	1875-76.	1876-77.
	RS.	RS.	RS.		RS.	RS.	RS.
Tax on fuel, firewood, and bamboos.	2,084	1,942	2,593	Formation of new plantations and topes.	219	54	..
Rent of jungles ..	179	12	105	Improvement and maintenance of topes.	10,433	8,800	6,331
Sale of trees ..	2,996	2,863	4,469				
Fees from charcoal-burners.	232	444	675	Commission for collection.	227	158	146
Miscellaneous ..	2,870	1,955	64	Miscellaneous charges.	168	5	9
				Establishment at the Presidency.	..	86	47
				Cost of supervision.	354	802	493
Total ..	8,361	7,216	7,906	Total ..	11,401	9,905	7,026

Pound Fund. Surplus Pound Fund.

The income of the Pound Fund is derived from fines levied on stray cattle and the proceeds realized by the sale of unclaimed cattle. The fund is expended on the pay of the establishment kept up on account of the pounds and the repair of existing and construction of new pounds. Fifty per cent. of the fees levied on stray cattle forms the remuneration of the pound-keepers, the Village Munsif being always the pound-keeper for his village. The watchmen employed to guard the pounds get 15 per cent. of

CHAP. XVI. LOCAL FUNDS.

these fees. There is a clerk on Rupees 10 per mensem in each Tahsildar's Office, who is also paid out of this fund. The unexpended balance of the Pound Fund is transferred quarterly to the Surplus Pound Fund, one half of which is handed over to the Local Fund Board and the Municipalities, while the remainder goes towards the support of the Government Farms at Sydapet.

The following statement shows in detail the receipts and expenditure of the Pound Fund for three years :—

Receipts.				Expenditure.			
Items.	1874-75.	1875-76.	1876-77.	Items.	1874-75.	1875-76.	1876-77.
	RS.	RS.	RS.		RS.	RS.	RS.
Fines levied on stray cattle.	9,328	9,586	10,135	Establishment ..	2,519	3,029	5,086
Sale proceeds of unclaimed cattle.	836	844	1,030	Charges for constructing and repairing pounds.	933	279	439
Miscellaneous ..	14	99	8	Miscellaneous ..	17	1	..
				Transferred to Surplus Pound Fund.	7,206	8,000	5,105
Total ..	10,178	10,529	11,173	Total ..	10,675	11,309	10,630

Village Service Fund.

An account of the establishment of the Village Service Fund and of the objects for which it was introduced has been given already in Chapter XII.

The following statement shows the receipts and expenditure of this fund for three years :—

Receipts.				Expenditure.			
Items.	1874-75.	1875-76.	1876-77.	Items.	1874-75.	1875-76.	1876-77.
	RS.	RS.	RS.		RS.	RS.	RS.
Deduction from Land Revenue credited to the fund for payment of Village Establishment.	63,790	63,790	63,790	Payments to Village Officers.	1,70,251	1,70,137	1,58,868
Cess under Act IV of 1864.	1,09,492	1,15,224	94,189				
Revenue of enfranchised ináms.	8,691	14,790	528				
Miscellaneous ..	14,283	131	53				
Total ..	1,96,256	1,93,935	1,58,560	Total ..	1,70,251	1,70,137	1,58,868

Irrigation Cess Fund.

This fund is derived from a voluntary cess paid by the ryots holding lands under certain river channels in lieu of the customary labor that they are liable to be called on to supply under Act I of 1858. This cess is at present levied in 296 Government and 15

Inám villages in Trichinopoly Taluq, and 14 villages along the Ponnéri Channel in Udaiyárpálayam. The inhabitants of some of the villages along the Cauvery Channels in Musiri Taluq have recently requested that it might be extended to their lands, and inquiries are now being made as to whether the ryots of all the river-irrigated villages in Musiri and Kulittalai Taluqs could not be induced to consent to its introduction into their villages. This voluntary cess was introduced in the Lálgudi Division of Trichinopoly Taluq in 1857, and is levied there at the rate of two annas for every acre irrigated under main channels and one anna under surplus channels. In the villages where it is in force in the rest of the taluq three annas are paid per acre under main channels and two annas under surplus channels. Most of these villages are those under the Uyyakondán Channel, and the cess was introduced into them in 1866. The cess was first levied in the villages irrigated under the Ponnéri Channel in Udaiyárpálayam Taluq in 1877, and is there paid at the rate of six annas an acre.

The following is an account of the management of the irrigation under channels where the cess is levied:—

The whole system, from the river to the village channels, is under the control of the revenue authorities. As soon as water is let into a village channel, it comes under the control of the villagers themselves, and is regulated by custom, any disputes being settled by the Tahsildar. Each main channel has its establishment of shutter-men, divers, and coolies with a Maniyagár over them, and the most important channels have also an Amín to superintend the conservancy. When the river is full, the Conservancy Establishment is employed in letting into the channel as much water as will suffice to supply all the villages without injuring the banks. Each village channel has its head sluice at the main channel, and the shutters at these heads are regulated according to the requirements of each village under the superintendence of a maistry, who has the charge of the whole or half the length of the main channel according to its importance. In the case of smaller channels this work is managed by the Channel Maniyagár. Each shutter-man is in charge of the regulating sluices of three or four branch channels. When the river goes down, *korambus* or mud dams are raised across the river to divert the water into the channels. It is at this time that the greatest care is required in the distribution of the water. The shutters of the branch channels are generally let down at this season, the water that escapes through the apertures between them, or in some cases through openings left by the removal of one or two of them, is all that is allowed to enter the branch channels. The remaining shutters are chained or locked, the keys being, as a rule, left in charge of the Tahsildar. In those

CHAP. XVI. LOCAL FUNDS.

cases where chains and locks are not provided, as in small channels where there are no regulating sluices, the Maistry or the Maniyagár, as the case may be, shuts up the village channels by mud dams, and opens them according to the wants of each village and in proportion to the supply in the main channel.[4] The cost of the establishment required to carry out this system is defrayed from the Irrigation Cess Fund.

(4) Letter from Collector to Board, No. 210, of 21st August 1875.

CHAPTER XVII.

MUNICIPALITIES.

TRICHINOPOLY—Municipal limits.—Filling in of the moat.—Markets.—Latrines. —Water-supply.—Conservancy.—Lighting.—Roads.—Vaccination. SRIRANGAM —Municipal limits.—Sanitation.—Roads.—New works.—Lighting.—Vaccination.

TRICHINOPOLY.

Municipal limits.

THE old Municipal Act (X of 1865, Madras) was introduced into Trichinopoly on the 1st of November 1866. The following villages are included within municipal limits: Sengulam, Puttúr, Abishégapuram, Uraiyúr, Pándamangalam, Virupákshipuram, Tirutándóni, Suttupannai, Dévadánam, Dáránallúr, Varaganéri, Chintámani, Vadavúr, Periya Vadavúr, Chinna Vadavúr, Tennúr, Nattarasápallivásal and Trichinopoly itself. The military cantonment, or rather the civil and military station, for strictly speaking there is no cantonment in Trichinopoly, is also a portion of the Municipality. It lies to the south of the fort, and is about one and a half miles distant from it. Shortly after the introduction of the Municipal Act into Trichinopoly, it was proposed to separate the cantonment from the remainder of the Municipality; but this idea was eventually abandoned. In order, however, to ensure that the interests of the military residents are not overlooked, the Government have directed that a military officer shall be Vice-President, and, as a general rule, the holder of this post is appointed on the recommendation of the Brigadier-General commanding the station.

Filling in of the moat.

One of the first tasks that engaged the attention of the Commissioners on the introduction of the Municipality, was the demolishing of the old ramparts round the town, and the filling in of the moat with the clay and debris thus made available. Previous to the commencement of this work the moat and wall constituted a mass of filth surrounding the fort on every side. The ramparts were overgrown with prickly-pear, and were naturally largely resorted to by the inhabitants instead of latrines. The ditch was the receptacle of all the liquid filth and sewage of the town, which was left there to vitiate the atmosphere all round. Frequent complaints had been made by the military authorities of the state in which the walls and moat were allowed to remain, and

CHAP. XVII. MUNICIPALITIES.

it was urged that the prevalence of cholera almost every year among both the military and civil population was due in great measure to the neglect of the conservancy of these parts of the town. The Government accordingly, in the commencement of the year 1866, directed that large gangs of convicts should be placed under the orders of the Collector with a view of putting an end to the nuisance complained of. A quantity of the prickly-pear was accordingly removed, and a portion of the moat filled in. The work, however, was never taken systematically in hand till the Municipality directed their attention to it. Since then it has been steadily proceeded with, large sums being spent on it every year, and it is now almost completed. The only piece of the moat now unfilled in is a portion of that on the north side of the town, and it is expected that this small remainder of this great task will soon be completed. Sir Charles Treveleyan, in a minute written in January 1860, suggested that the moat when filled in should be laid out as a boulevard, and this suggestion has been followed. Trees have been planted over the greater extent of the reclaimed land, and a wide road laid out, running completely round the fort. When the trees have grown, and the road is metalled throughout, the drive round will be a pleasant one. The moat reclamation has been an expensive work. It was estimated by the Public Works Department, before the introduction of the Municipality, that it would cost Rupees 22,000 ; but, exclusive of what was spent before their labours commenced, the Commissioners have already expended over 55,000 Rupees on it, and will probably have to lay out about 2,000 Rupees more before it is finished.

Markets.

The next in importance of the new works carried out by the Municipality is the market, situated on a portion of the reclaimed moat to the south of the fort. It was commenced in 1867 and finished in the following year. The total expenditure on this work up to 1874 was over 20,000, and the average income up to that date Rupees 3,924, that for the year previous to that having been as high as Rupees 4,752, or over 20 per cent. on the expenditure. Since 1874 considerable improvements have been made in the market. It has been enlarged to almost double its original size at a cost of Rupees 2,807, the portion thus added being used as a grain market and by petty vendors. Butchers' stalls have been constructed at a cost of Rupees 2,422, and a terrace, containing additional shops, has been erected outside the old portion of the building, on which a sum of Rupees 1,631 has been expended. The income derived from the market has been considerably increased in consequence of these extensions of the building, and in 1876-77 it was leased out for Rupees 7,222. At a distance of a few hundred yards from the fort market another one has been constructed, in which straw and firewood are sold, and there are also two smaller markets, one in Uraiyúr and one in Marsackpétta near the cantonment for the convenience of the inhabitants of those parts of the town. A large clock-tower has been erected in front of the fort market.

Latrines.

Before the introduction of the Municipality ten latrines were built round the town under the orders of Government. These buildings consisted of merely four brick walls, enclosing a small piece of ground, and contained no separate compartments of any description whatever. In addition to these, the Municipality have constructed 48 latrines. Of the total number available at present 30 are for males and 28 for females; 17 have brick walls, and 41 only mud ones. Up to 1873 no attempt was made to introduce dry-earth conservancy into the Municipality. Since then two latrines on that system have been built. Considerable difficulties are, however, experienced in working dry-earth latrines, and they are very expensive. It is therefore very doubtful if it will be possible to introduce them generally throughout the town, at least for some time to come.

Water-supply.

A considerable number of the tanks with which the fort is studded are supplied with water from an irrigation channel called the Uyyakondán, which leaves the Cauvery at a distance of some miles above Trichinopoly, and, flowing across the greater portion of that taluq and through the town itself, eventually falls into a large tank in the village of Valavandánkóttai, about ten miles to the east of Trichinopoly. An open channel from the Uyyakondán supplies the tanks, and the water flowing through it is open to contamination from filth of every description during almost the whole of its course. In order to avoid this, it was at one time proposed to cover the channel in at a cost of Rupees 14,000. The project was, however, abandoned partly owing to the expense, and partly because it became evident that it would be of but little use to expend such a large sum on preserving the water from impurity while running through the branch channel, as long as the main channel from which it flows was allowed to collect filth during its entire course through the town. Many projects have been suggested to remove the evils just mentioned. One of these is to construct an aqueduct from the Uyyakondán, from the point where it enters the town above the artillery barracks, and carry the water across by means of it in a straight line to Sundra Dass Tank, the first of the receptacles in the fort that it supplies. The Commissioners are thoroughly investigating this project, and have had the necessary levels taken. It is, however, very doubtful if they will be able, for many years to come, to afford the funds necessary to carry it out. The Sanitary Commissioner, when he inspected the town in 1870, gave it as his opinion that the water

CHAP. XVII. MUNICIPALITIES.

of the channel was sufficiently pure for domestic uses, and that, if care was taken in the conservation of the banks of the channel and in the prevention of the fouling of the stream, no harm could result from its use. This, however, has not as yet been done, and the banks are used as a latrine during the greater portion of their course. In consequence of the accumulation of silt in them, it is necessary to clear out periodically the masonry reservoirs in the fort, into which the water from this channel flows.

Conservancy.

For conservancy purposes the town is divided into four divisions, to each of which there is attached a Nuisance Inspector and some Peons. One of the Commissioners also is in charge of each of these divisions, and is expected to carry out the wishes of the body of which he is a member throughout it. His special duty is to attend to sanitation, and direct prosecutions under the conservancy clauses of the Act when necessary. The Vice-President is, as a rule, in charge of the cantonment.

One of the greatest difficulties that the Commissioners have had to contend with in their attempts to improve the conservancy of the town, is the question of the best means of removing the sewage water. At present a practice prevails in several of the streets of leading the liquid sewage in a masonry channel across the street side-drains into a cess-pit, which is sometimes almost in the centre of the street, and is almost entirely concealed from view. Every one acknowledges that this system is a bad one. As remarked by the present Sanitary Commissioner, when alluding to this subject, it can scarcely be good for the public health that the soil of the old town should be saturated continually with house-filth. It is, however, most difficult to devise a scheme to obviate what all agree is an evil. The objections to open side-drains for the removal of sewage water, are even greater than these cess-pits, and the great difficulties in the way of procuring glazed earthenware pipes, added to the enormous expense that their introduction would entail, have prevented the adoption of what would otherwise be the best mode of removing the sewage water.

Lighting.

The lighting of the town is still not good, although it has been greatly improved of late years. The extent indeed of the Municipality is so great, that it is very doubtful if it will ever be possible to light all the streets and roads within its limits well, without expending on this object a far greater sum of money than it is advisable to devote to it. There are altogether 231 lamps in the town, of which 96 are placed on iron lamp-posts procured from England, and the remainder on wooden and stone ones. Kerosine oil is now burnt in all these lamps.

Roads.

Thirty-eight miles of road have to be kept up by the Municipality. Of these twenty-nine miles are metalled, and nine unmetalled. The expenditure incurred on the construction and repairs of roads for 1875-76 was Rupees 6,114. The condition of the roads, within municipal limits, is on the whole good. Owing, however, to the high winds that prevail in Trichinopoly during June, July and August, they generally get greatly out of order in these months, and it is only by a considerable expenditure every year that they can be kept in repair.

Vaccination.

Five Vaccinators are employed by the Municipality. The First-class Hospital Assistant attached to the Municipal Hospital superintends their operations, and pays batta to the mothers of the children vaccinated. The number of operations performed by the Vaccinators amounted to 2,424 successful cases in 1875-76, and 1,268 in 1876-77. First-calss Vaccinators are paid a fixed salary of Rupees 15 a month, and those of the Second-class Rupees 10.

An account of the Municipal Hospital is given in Chapter IV. Statement No. 20, given in the appendix, shows the receipts and disbursements of the Municipality for a series of five years.

SRÍRANGAM.

Municipal limits.

The Municipal Act (III of 1871) was introduced into Srírangam on the 1st November 1871. The following are the names of the villages and hamlets included within municipal limits: Srírangam, Palapattarai, Pudutirnattu, Virésvaram Kithapuram, Mélúr, Jembukésvaram, Kondayampéttai, Kylasaváhana tope, Latchamara tope, Sandanádikattlai, Timmaráyasamudram and Tiruvannávanallúr.

Sanitation.

Since the introduction of the Municipality considerable efforts have been made by the Commissioners towards the improvement of the sanitary condition of the town. The roads have been sectioned, the side-drains cleared out, dust-bins erected, and three latrines on the dry-earth system built. These latrines are outside the walls, as suitable sites could not be procured inside. The crying want of the town, however, is the removal of the cess-pool nuisance, and this the Commissioners from want of funds and other causes have not as yet been able to accomplish. Indeed the difficulty felt in almost all native towns in abolishing the cess-pool system is aggravated in Srírangam by special circumstances, which will be briefly detailed. Of the seven enclosures of which the pagoda and town of Srírangam[1] consist, the fifth, sixth, and seventh, or the three outer ones, alone are occupied by houses. In the fifth enclosure there are 211 dwelling-houses and 17 bazaars, in the sixth 726 houses and 80 bazaars. The houses in these enclosures are almost exclusively occupied by Bráhmans. In the seventh enclosure there are 1,012 houses and 60 bazaars. In this enclosure

(1) A description of the temple and town of Srírangam will be found in Chapter XXI.

CHAP. XVII. MUNICIPALITIES.

some of the houses are terraced and some thatched. They are inhabited by all classes, with the exception of Pariahs, Chucklers and Musalmans. The houses in the fifth and sixth enclosures are almost all terraced-buildings with a small yard behind, between the houses and the enclosure wall, which is of stone. In these yards there are, as a rule, a well to supply water for domestic purposes, and two cess-pits. Into one of these pits the sewage water from the houses flows, while the other is filled with night-soil. The first plan for removing the night-soil that suggested itself to the Commissioners, was to employ scavengers, who should go from house-to-house with conservancy carts. This idea was abandoned, as it was believed that the people would strongly object to scavengers passing through their houses, as they would have been obliged to do owing to there being no back-entrances. It was then proposed to open a lane three feet wide running between the stone enclosure walls and the houses. This scheme involved the construction of a wall running parallel to the enclosure wall and the construction of a door in it for every house. The estimated cost of carrying out the scheme was 37,000, and, as about the time that the plans for introducing it were completed the professional tax was abolished, the Commissioners came to the conclusion that the funds at their disposal were inadequate to carry it out, and the idea had to be abandoned.

Roads.

Twelve miles of road are kept up by the Municipality, of which $2\frac{1}{3}$ miles are metalled and $9\frac{2}{3}$ unmetalled. The amount spent on the maintenance of roads in 1877-78 was Rupees 1,049.

New works.

The principal new works constructed by the Commissioners since the introduction of the Municipality are an hospital, an account of which has been given in Chapter IV, a bridge erected at a cost of Rupees 3,786 across the large irrigation channel known as the Nát-Váykkál, and steps, which cost Rupees 5,631, leading down to the Cauvery river, used by those who go there to bathe or to wash their clothes.

Lighting.

The town is fairly well lighted by means of 107 kerosine oil-lamps, most of which have been placed on stone-posts.

Vaccination.

One Vaccinator is employed by the Municipality. The following statement shows the work turned out by him in the last five years :—

Years.	Successful Cases.	Unsuccessful Cases.	Total.
1872-73	340	3	343
1873-74	385	17	402
1874-75	761	73	834
1875-76	476	33	509
1876-77	585	46	631

CHAPTER XVIII.

POLICE AND JAILS.

POLICE—Police under Native rule.—The Kával system.—The Police placed under the Magistracy.—Reorganization of the Police Department.—Strength of Police Force.—Distribution of Police throughout the district.—Police Stations.—Village Police.

JAILS—Opening remarks.—Distribution of Prisoners in the Central and District Jails.—Religion and Age.—Previous occupation.—The Remission system.—Education.—Employment of Prisoners.—Jail Offences.—Scales of Diet.—Mortality in the Central and District Jails.—Cost of Prisoners.—Subsidiary Jails.

POLICE.

CHAP. XVIII. POLICE AND JAILS.

THE following account of the system of police prevailing in the country when first under English management, is abridged with a few alterations from an excellent report drawn up by Mr. Wallace when Collector of the district. He remarks that, previous to our acquisition of the district, the police of the country appeared to have been vested in a body of people distinguished officially by the name of kávalgárs or watchers. "The kávalgárs," he writes, "are a bold, hardy, predatory race, living generally in jungles and fastnesses. They are composed of various tribes, such as Udaiyán, Tévan, Padaiyáchi, Kavundan, Nayinár, &c. In many places their habits are well described by the name of *kallans*[1] or robbers, by which they are distinguished. They appear to have attended their chiefs to the field in time of war, and at all times to have practised open depredation as well as private theft. Strength and violence, cunning, and dexterity appear to have been their leading characteristics. Their employment as the protectors of the country must be considered rather as a payment for exemption from their outrages by the districts in which they were employed, than as the just opposition of the authority of the state to the crimes and vices of this lawless part of the community.

"Such appear to have been the hands into which the police of these countries under the reigns of the native princes, during the last century, had been committed. From a police so constituted nothing worth imitating can possibly be learned. The best police system of those times appears to have been that adopted by

(1) Frequently mentioned in Orme's History as "*Colleries*."

CHAP. XVIII. POLICE AND JAILS.

Muhammad Isúf and other Muhammadan commanders, who, by the terror excited by their energetic though cruel and arbitrary vigilance, drove theft and murder from their usual haunts, and rendered, for a time, these tribes, if not humane and civilized, at least less daring and violent than they had been.

"The vigilance manifested by many of the Nawáb's managers was closely followed, if not by the immediate and direct influence of our civil government, at least by the distribution of a considerable portion of our military power through the various districts of the southern provinces. The presence of regular troops, commanded by European officers, was also well calculated in those turbulent times to keep down the spirit of licentiousness which had engrossed the government of the whole of the southern districts.

"The Muhammadan authority and our own arms gave the first check to the kával system, and the gradual introduction of our civil government into the various provinces of the southern parts of the peninsula deprived that system of its remaining active evils, although the passive defects of the institutions still remain.

"The officers of the kával system of police are distinguished by different appellations, each signifying the rank or duty of the person on whom it is conferred.

1st.—The *Arasukávalgár* signifies a prince or chief who holds a kával. Tondiman[2] and the Poligars of Ariyalúr and Udaiyárpálayam are distinguished by the appellation of Arasukávalgár.

2nd.—*Ménkávalgár* signifies the head or chief kávalgár of a district. Individuals holding the kával of one or more villages are termed Ménkávalgárs. The Arasukávalgárs have Ménkávalgárs under them in charge of particular districts.

3rd.—The term *Kudikávalgárs* is applied to the ryots of a village or district when they are kávalgárs either in their own village or in other villages or districts. Their responsibility and duties are similar to that of Ménkávalgárs and Arasukávalgárs.

4th.—*Visárippukáran* is the person placed by the Mén or Kudikávalgár in charge of particular villages or districts. They are the temporary servants of the Ménkávalgár.

5th.—*Kulapandu* or Taliári is the village watchman under the Arasu, Mén or Kudikávalgár. In some instances they are independent, and then they are the only police officers of the village.

---

(2) The ancestor of the present Rajah of Pudukóttai.

"The offices of arasukávalgár, of ménkávalgár when not held under an arasukávalgár, and in general of taliári, are hereditary. The kudikával is inherent in the ryots of the village to which it belongs. The ménkávalgárs, when employed by the arasukávalgárs, the visárippukárans in all cases, and in some few instances the taliáris, are removable at the pleasure either of the sirkár or of their employers. The right of removal of the arasukávalgárs and independent ménkávalgárs appears not to have been exercised of late years by the Nawáb in Trichinopoly, but since the establishment of the Company's Government the independent ménkávalgárs have been removed in more than one instance. The conduct of the arasukávalgárs has not been such as to require a similar exertion of authority. The duties and obligation of the kávalgárs may be very briefly described. The arasu and ménkávalgárs as well as the kudikávalgárs are responsible for all thefts committed after sunset and before sunrise in the villages of their respective jurisdictions; if they do not produce the thieves they are responsible for the amount stolen, but, if they can trace the thieves into the limits of another kávalgár, it is understood that on sufficient proof thereof, the latter becomes responsible for the amount stolen or for the production of the thieves. This duty and responsibility is demanded as well in towns and in villages, and it extends to all property belonging to resident inhabitants, as well to that which is kept in houses and also to cattle and standing and reaped crops. The performance of these duties is enforced not by written regulations, but by the continuation of the usages of late years, and the occasional orders of the public officers. The utmost vigilance and attention of the sirkár is constantly necessary to render the kával system at all useful and efficacious, to oblige the kávalgárs to keep up the necessary number of taliáris, and to enforce the obligation of payment for thefts in default of the production of the thieves.

"The kával establishment in Trichinopoly is maintained, first by a portion of the crops being set aside and given up to the kávalgárs, secondly by a portion of the cultivated lands being given up to the kávalgárs, and thirdly by assessments in money being levied on the people. As far as regards the share of the crops set apart for the kávalgárs, the charge falls jointly on Government and the agricultural class of the people, the deductions being made in common with the other general allowances called swatantarams from the gross produce of the lands. Where this system is observed, a small portion of the part of the *swatantarams* allotted for police charges goes to the taliáris direct, but the greater portion goes to the arasu, mén or kudikávalgárs, who from it discharge the allowances of their visárippukárans and taliáris, and make good the thefts committed within their respective limits.

CHAP. XVIII. POLICE AND JAILS.

"When a portion of the cultivated lands is given up to the kávalgárs, a system of payment peculiar to certain parts of Trichinopoly, the whole expense of the police falls on Government, for the inhabitants cultivate the land and receive their portion of the produce, while the kávalgárs receive that portion of it which would fall to the sirkar were the lands under amáni. In cases of this kind the arasukávalgárs receive the whole of the funds allotted to the support of the police establishment, and with it defray the wages of their visárippukárans and taliáris.

"The system of levying a money assessment for the support of the police is only observed in certain large towns, the inhabitants of which, by paying trifling tax on each house, contribute to the preservation of their property. The amount is paid to the méṇkávalgár, who, out of it, defrays the expenses of taliáris. The assessment is very light.

"It will be observed from the foregoing remarks, first, that the funds allotted for the police establishment are in general variable, as they depend on the abundance of the crops and the extent of the cultivation; secondly, that the expense of the kával system is borne, with a trifling exception, by the sirkár and the agricultural class. The amount of the kával funds may be estimated in Trichinopoly at 19,022 Star Pagodas 3 Fanams and 22 Cash, which is a sum fully adequate to the expense of a most efficient police, but which procures, under the present mode of administering this department, advantages in no way proportionate to the amount expended.

"Under the government of the Nawábs of the Karnatic the kavalgars were a bold, turbulent, disorderly class of people, who, instead of protecting the country, plundered it, and instead of putting down internal commotions, excited them. The orders of the Collectors were frequently disregarded by these people, and in many cases they have been known to oppose the Nawábs and our government by force. In 1796 the Poligar of Udaiyárpálayam attacked and repulsed our troops with the loss of an officer and some of his men, and it was only in his capacity as kávalgár of the district that the poligar was enabled to offer this opposition, for he had not for thirty years been recognized as chief of it. It was entirely by means of his ménkávalgárs, visárippukárans and taliáris, that he was enabled to excite a commotion among the people, and to oppose openly and effectively the whole force which the Nawáb could bring against him, aided by a considerable detachment of our troops.

"I cannot learn that the spirit of turbulence and opposition which the kávalgárs manifested under the latter years of the Nawábs' and Rajahs' government proceeded from any acts of oppression or injustice on the part of those governments; on the contrary, their weakness and inefficiency appear to have given activity to the vices inherent in the kával system.

"If, since the Company's authority has been finally established in these provinces, the turbulent character of the kávalgárs has not manifested itself, and if, on the contrary, they have shown due obedience to Government and an alacrity in the discharge of their duties previously unknown, the change in my opinion should be attributed not to the extinction of their former spirit, nor to the introduction among them of habits of obedience, but to the fear of that punishment which they feel would follow the commission of any open breach of their duty as subjects and officers of Government. But it is not a fit state of things when those who are paid for preserving peace and tranquillity are prevented from open acts of violence and outrage merely by the dread of punishment.

"From the foregoing remarks it will be seen that open outrages are not now committed by the kávalgárs. I believe, however, that in many cases, and I know that in some, the kávalgárs are concerned in the thefts and robberies which are committed even now but too frequently. While I state this, I must, on the other hand, say that I have found some of the kávalgárs very active in endeavouring to detect thieves; but such are the defects of the system, that they are not always successful."[3]

In 1816 the Board of Revenue directed that the Poligars of Ariyalúr, Udaiyárpálayam and Turaiyúr should be exonerated from all police duties, and obliged to relinquish all allowances hitherto paid for their performance.[4] The kával system has since then been completely abolished throughout the district, except in Trichinopoly cantonment, where a remnant of it is still to be found. This consists in the custom that prevails of having a kávalgár or watchman of the Kallan caste employed to guard each house. These men are professional thieves, but are employed on an understanding that they are to protect the houses guarded by them from the depredations of their fellow castemen, and to be held responsible for all property lost. As a matter of fact it is, however, impossible to enforce this supposed responsibility, and the kávalgárs are concerned in almost every theft that occurs in the station. Frequent efforts have been made to put a stop to this utterly vicious system, but these have up to this been unsuccessful.

Not long after the English got possession of the district the police were placed under the Judge, but when, by the passing of Regulation XI of 1816, the Collector and his revenue subordi-

(3) Letter from the Principal Collector of Tanjore and Trichinopoly to the Secretary to the Police Committee, Fort St. George, dated 29th September 1805.

(4) Proceedings of the Board of Revenue, dated 22nd April 1816.

CHAP. XVIII. POLICE AND JAILS.

nates became Magistrates, they were at the same time entrusted with the supervision of the police. As a matter of practice this supervision was, as a rule, left in the hands of the Tahsildars. This system cannot be said to have worked well, and the disclosures brought to light by the Torture Commission in 1855 hastened its abolition.

The new police.

The organization of the present police system was commenced in 1858, and it was introduced into Trichinopoly in 1860. The strength of the police employed in the district on the 31st March 1876 was as follows:—

Superintendent	1
Inspectors	13
Sub-Inspectors	3
Constables (general duty)	563
Jail Guards	105

Distribution of the police.

The following statement shows the manner in which the police are distributed throughout the district:—

Divisions.		Number of Inspectors.	Strength of all Grades.	Number of Stations.
A.	Reserve, Jails, &c.	..	227	..
B.	Town	1	135	4
C-I.	Trichinopoly Taluq ..	1	67	10
C-II.		1	41	6
D-I.	Udaiyárpálayam do. ..	1	41	6
D-II.		1	32	5
E.	Perambalúr do.	1	58	8
F-I.	Musiri do. ..	1	38	5
F-II.		1	35	5
G-I.	Kulittalai do. ..	1	44	6
G-II.		1	38	6

Police stations.

Below are given the names of the several police stations according to the divisions in which they are situated:—

A.—Reserve.

Huzúr Treasury.
Head-quarter Office.
Orderlies—Sessions and Magistrates' Courts.

B.—Fort Station.

Uraiyúr.
Dark's Bridge.
Cantonment.

C-I.—Rural.

Tuvágudi.
Manikandam.
Kóppu.
Iluppúr.
Arasangudi.
Suraiyúr.
Gundúr.
Velúr.
Kolattúr.

C-II.—Lálgudi.

Srírangam.	Samayapuram.
Sengaraiyúr.	Váytalai.
Pullambádi.	

D-I.—Jeyamkondasólapuram.

Rájéndrapatnam.	Mínsurutti.
Udaiyárpálayam.	Támaraipúndi.
Madanakurichi.	

D-II.—Ariyalúr.

Vikkramam.	Ánandavádi.
Kílapaluvúr.	Tirumánúr.

E.—Perambalúr.

Rangangedi.	Pádálúr.
Aduthorai.	Pasumbalúr.
Arumbávúr.	Kádúr.
Sáttanúr.	

F-I.—Musiri.

Tottiyam.	Kannanúr.
Mangalam.	Harikistnavári.

F-II.—Turaiyúr.

Tiruppattúr.	Pulivalam.
Uppiliyapuram.	Chettikulam.

G-I.—Kulittalai.

Kattalai.	Siváyam.
Tógamalai.	Séngal.
Lálápéttai.	

G-II.—Manapparai.

Tuvarankurichi.	Valanádu.
Puttánattam.	Palaviduthi.
Kallupatti.	

The Village Police consists of 964 taliáris or village watchmen on salaries of Rupees 3 a month each. These officers assist the regular police in the prevention and detection of crime. They are, however, under the supervision of the Revenue Department and not of the Superintendent of Police. They are appointed and dismissed by the Divisional Officers. Village Police.

CHAP. XVIII. POLICE AND JAILS.

JAILS.

(*Contributed by* W. A. SYMONDS, Esq., *Acting Superintendent of Central Jail, Trichinopoly*, 1871–77.)

Opening remarks.

I have not been able to find in the oldest records of the District Court or the Collector's Office any allusion either to the ancient criminal law of the Chóla and Náyak kings, or even to the modern criminal law of the Nawábs. I must, therefore, refer those interested in this subject to Manu for the Hindu criminal law, and to Muhammadan law writers for information as to what was done with criminals in the time of the Nawábs. I may, however, mention that the long period prior to that of the British assumption was a *pre*-jail period. It has been said that the first thing an Englishman does, upon settling in a new place, is to build a church and a jail. In those days, though they could not do without churches, they did without jails. The imprisonment of criminals was unknown both to the early Hindu kings and the Nawábs. Minor offences were punished by fine and mutilation, serious offences with death. In the early part of the British supremacy, when our penal code was nominally that of the Musalmans, it was the duty of the Muhammadan law assessor to determine what length of imprisonment was to be considered equal to such and such a mutilation. Thus, "the prisoner, having been found guilty, is sentenced to lose an eye, *i.e.*, he is to be imprisoned for five years." This was the substance of the *futwa*.

The first British jail at Trichinopoly was a building which is situated on the eastern boulevard, and is now used for the purposes of a lock and a leper hospital, but was, till quite of late years, the lunatic asylum of the southern division. This building may possibly be suited to its present inmates, but it was a bad place for the insane, and a worse for prisoners, these last having been overcrowded to such an extent as to tax the defective ventilation to the utmost.

The inevitable result, high mortality, led, in 1848, to the building of the present District Jail, which has for the last few years been restricted to prisoners sentenced to short terms of rigorous imprisonment and to simple imprisonment, and to security and under-trial prisoners, and to civil debtors. Formerly there was, here as elsewhere, the same overcrowding, with the same terrible consequences. I need not dwell upon familiar details. Yet I may remark, in passing, that nothing worse has been recorded by Howard than existed in some Indian jails of old days.

All this is changed for the better, and there is now at Trichinopoly a large Central Jail, which it becomes my duty briefly to describe. It is situated in the vicinity of the Golden Rock, which is about the healthiest site that could have been selected.

Round it runs a wall nearly seventeen feet in height. The jail is built upon the radial principle, almost every part of it being commanded by the central tower. It is capable of accommodating 982 males and 86 females, at an average of 40 superficial feet per prisoner, and is provided with separate barracks for females and juveniles, the former being under the charge of a matron. The system of conservancy is that of dry earth.

Distribution of prisoners in the Central and District Jails.

The following general summary shows the distribution of the prisoners confined in the Trichinopoly Central and District Jails during the year 1876, and the succeeding statement their religion, age, and previous occupation :—

1	2	3			4			5			6		
Place of Confinement.	Classes of Prisoners.	Remained at the commencement of the Year.			Received during the Year.			Total.			Discharged from all Causes.		
		M.	F.	Total.	M.	F.	Total.	M.	F.	Total.	M.	F.	Total.
Central Prison.	Convicts ..	893	29	922	543	86	629	1,436	115	1,551	447	68	515
	Civil ..	..	..	..	..	..	..	..	..	..	..	..	..
	Under-trial.	..	..	..	..	..	..	..	..	..	..	..	..
	Security ..	..	..	..	..	..	..	..	..	..	..	..	..
	Insane ..	..	..	..	..	..	..	..	..	..	..	..	..
	State ..	..	..	..	..	..	..	..	..	..	..	..	..
District Jail.	Convicts ..	124	..	124	342	..	342	466	..	466	368	..	368
	Civil ..	..	..	..	29	1	30	29	1	30	27	..	27
	Under-trial.	24	..	24	85	6	91	109	6	115	101	5	106
	Security ..	1	..	1	..	..	..	1	..	1	1	..	1
	Insane ..	..	..	..	..	..	..	..	..	..	..	..	..
	State ..	..	..	..	..	..	..	..	..	..	..	..	..

Place of Confinement.	Classes of Prisoners.	7 Remaining at end of the Year.			8 Daily Average Number of each Class.			9 Total Daily Average of whole Jail.		
		M.	F.	Total.	M.	F.	Total.	M.	F.	Total.
Central Prison.	Convicts ..	99	47	1,036	963·20	41·07	1004·27	963·20	41·07	1004·27
	Civil ..	..	..	..	..	..	..			
	Under-trial.	..	..	..	..	..	..			
	Security ..	..	..	..	..	..	..			
	Insane ..	..	..	..	..	..	..			
	State ..	..	..	..	..	..	..			
District Jail.	Convicts ..	98	..	98	114·64	..	114·64	123·92	·59	124·51
	Civil ..	2	1	3	3·11	·05	3·16			
	Under-trial.	8	1	9	5·38	·54	5·92			
	Security ..	..	..	..	·79	..	·79			
	Insane ..	..	..	..	..	..	..			
	State ..	..	..	..	..	..	..			

CHAP. XVIII.
POLICE AND JAILS.

Religion and age.

1	2														3							
	Religion.														Age.							
	A.						B.		C.		D.		E.		A.		B.		C.		D.	
Jails.	Christians.																					
	a.		b		c.																	
	Europeans.		Eurasians.		Natives.		Muhammadans.		Hindus.		Budhists and Jains.		All other Classes.		Under 16.		16 to 40.		40 to 60.		Above 60.	
	M	F.	M	F.	M	F.	M	F.	M.	F.	M	F.	M	F.	M	F.	M.	F.	M.	F.	M	F.
Trichinopoly Central	2	..	2	..	13	3	19	4	927	87	..	..	..	9	3	2	495	29	107	9	14	..
Do. District.	..	..	1	..	2	..	26	..	..	..	35	..	..	15	2	..	..	82	206	9	21	1

Previous occupation.

	4										5		
	Previous Occupation.												
	Males.						Females.						
Jails.	A.	B.	C.	D.	E.	F.	G.	H.	I.	J.	Total.		
	Of Independent property.	Agriculturists.	Non-Agriculturists.	Domestic Servants.	Government Servants.	No Occupation.	Married.	Unmarried.	Widows.	Prostitutes.	M.	F.	Total.
Trichinopoly Central	5	294	252	67	40	209	32	4	17	41	998	94	1,092
Do. District.	26	522	134	2	45	3	..	..	..	..	466	..	466

The excellent sanitary arrangements of our central jails, the employment of matrons, and segregation of juveniles are all indications of marked improvement in the general management of our convicts.

The remission system.

Another sign of the same reform is the introduction of the remission system, which enables a well-disposed prisoner to abridge his sentence by industry and good behaviour combined. This system has now been working in its entirety for nearly seven years, and has proved a great boon both to the convicts and to those in charge of them. Since its introduction there has been a steady diminution in the frequency and severity of punishments for breaches of jail discipline, and an equally steady increase in the outturn of all measurable work. The progress of non-measurable work is also noticeable, as evidenced by the comparatively small number of convicts so employed who are reported for idleness now-a-days. But it is in the manufactures that the beneficent operation of the remission system is most clearly to be traced. For instance, where men used to weave a maximum of eight yards of police cloth *per diem*, they now weave thirty, and so forth.

I proceed to briefly describe the *modus operandi* of the remission system.

The sentence is represented by marks, at the rate of six marks a day, and every convict sentenced to rigorous imprisonment for eighteen months and upwards is credited with an additional mark or half-mark per diem for extra industry; but, before being permitted to earn any extra marks, the convict must undergo a period of probation equal to one-sixth of the sentence, and while under probation he is put to the harder description of prison labour. In no case can the period of probation be less than one-sixth of the sentence, but it may be longer, as any convict who misconducts himself is liable to be fined a certain number of marks, which will retard his advancement by an equivalent number of days. When a convict has passed through his term of probation, he is admitted into the third-class, and may then commence to earn extra marks towards a partial remission of his sentence; should he be very industrious, and not be reported for any breach of jail rules, he is allowed to earn one extra mark per diem; for lesser industry he would be allowed one half-mark per diem. A convict must remain in the third-class for at least six months, after which, if he has earned the prescribed number of marks, he is promoted to the second-class. He must remain at least four months in the second-class, after which period, if he has not forfeited any marks by misconduct or idleness, he is promoted to the first-class. When the convict has earned in the first-class the prescribed number of marks, which cannot be done without earning full marks every day for one year, he becomes eligible for appointment to the lowest grade of convict servant. Besides the ordinary remission he may earn in this class, he is allowed to reckon additional remission at the rate of one month a year. After a year's service in this grade, he is eligible for the post of convict warder, in which he may earn additional remission at the rate of two months a year. The remaining grade of convict servant is that of work overseer, whose privileges are the same as those of convict warder. No remission is granted for conduct only, as it is on condition of good conduct that convicts are allowed to earn remission by their industry. If, therefore, their conduct is bad, they are liable to be fined a certain number of marks, and will forfeit by ill-conduct the remission they may have gained by their industry. Reconvicted prisoners are not debarred from earning remission, and in this respect the previous career and character of the prisoner make no difference.

The hope of earning remission has not only been found to afford a strong incentive to continuous industry and good conduct, and a powerful auxiliary in the maintenance of discipline, but has been attended by economy and increased efficiency in the details of jail management. There has not yet been time to test whether the habits of industry formed in jail are maintained after release, nor does our present system of unconditional release give means of observation. A system of surveillance after release is one of the latest achievements of civilized communities.

The only point on which doubts as to the remission system have arisen concerns its extension to life-convicts. On the one hand, the objection is advanced that there should be no interference with a sentence intended to separate the criminal from society for ever. On the other hand, it is urged that to withdraw all hope from this class of prisoners is to render them desperate and to deprive the jail authorities of the services of a class of men who, under the operation of the remission rules, are found specially useful. In the application of the remission system to this class of convicts, twenty years is considered the equivalent of a life-sentence. By this I do not mean that it is proposed to release life-convicts, as a matter of course, as soon as ever they have earned the full complement of marks which it is possible for one sentenced to twenty years' imprisonment to gain. So far from this being the case, the release of life-convicts even after the expiration of twenty full years of imprisonment, though not unknown, is rare, and is then conceded by virtue of the prerogative of mercy vested in the Governor in Council. It has, however, been found necessary to fix an arbitrary limit to the period which affords a basis for the calculation of the marks that are commuted into days. Thus, the only advantage, under the remission system, upon which, *ceteris paribus*, a life-prisoner can reckon as a matter of right, is the privilege of promotion to the highest convict grades attainable, *viz.*, those of warder and work overseer.

The subjoined statement shows the employment of convicts as prison officers during the year 1876 :—

1	2		3		4		5		6	
Jails.	Average Number of Prisoners of all Classes.		Total Number employed as Prison Officers.		Average Number employed.		Ratio of Column 5 to Column 3.		Number reduced or otherwise punished.	
	M.	F.	M.	F.	M.	F.	M.	F.	M.	F.
Trichinopoly Central ..	963·20	41·07	167	4	101·00	3·00	10·48	7·30	21	..
Do. District ..	123·92	·59	37	..	6·59	..	5·31	..	2	..

From the remission system to the education of prisoners is a natural transition. This is a question attended with many difficulties. Education has indisputably a powerful effect in repressing the more brutal forms of crime, but its softening and subduing influences here act rather in the way of prevention than of cure. Education is hence of greater potency as a civilizer of free agents than as a reformatory instrument within the walls of a jail. The other difficulties are of a more practical kind. Under existing orders, all the inmates of a jail are to be placed under instruction; consequently, there must be a considerable number who, by reason of their advanced age and entire ignorance, cannot be expected to learn. Again, there is the difficulty of getting competent teachers from amongst the convicts, and the disadvantage of employing badly-paid free teachers, such men being likely to introduce forbidden articles, and to serve as means of communication between prisoners and the world outside the jail. Lastly, there is the insufficiency of the time which can be spared for the purpose of education, without undue interference with the hours of labour, and the increased trouble of supervision caused by schools held at night, when both convict teachers and jail employés are tired with a hard day's work. Then, the bulk of the jail population consists of those who, on release, depend, for the means of subsistence, on manual labour, and, to this class, the having learnt some trade or handicraft is of course more useful than a smattering of book knowledge.

CHAP. XVIII.
POLICE AND JAILS.
Education.

The gradual recognition of these facts has led to the limiting of the teaching of adult criminals to a single hour of elementary instruction in reading, writing, and arithmetic *per diem*. Three hours a day are set apart for juveniles.

The annexed statement shows the state of education of the convicts imprisoned in and released from the Trichinopoly Central and District Jails during the year 1876:—

1		2						3		4		5		6						7					
Number imprisoned during the Year.		Of those in Column 3 there were						Daily Average Number of Convicts.		Daily Average Number under Instruction.		Number released during the Year.		Of those in Column 5 there were						Number released during the year after more than Six Months in Jail.					
		Unable to Read or Write.		Able to Read or Write a little.		Able to Read or Write well.								Unable to Read and Write.		Able to Read and Write a little.		Able to Read and Write well.		Able to Read and Write a little.		Unable to Read and Write well.		Able to Read and Write well.	
M.	F.	M.	F.	M	F.	M	F.	M.	F.	M.	F.	M.	F.	M.	F.	M.	F.	M	.F	M	F.	M.	F.	M	F.
105	65	79	65	15	..	11	..	963·20	41·07	919·31	..	252	66	43	66	122	..	87	..	23	10	135	..	75	..
342	..	244	..	82	..	16	..	114·64	..	96·00	..	359	..	193	..	94	..	72	..	48	..	8	..	2	..

CHAP. XVIII. POLICE AND JAILS.

Employment of prisoners.

I now turn to the employment of prisoners. The advance of this branch of jail administration has kept pace with other improvements. So long as jail accommodation was contracted, and the sound policy of appealing, not merely to the fears, but also to the hopes of convicts was ignored, progress in this direction was unattainable. With the extension of jail buildings and the introduction of the remission system, it has been found practicable to provide very considerable variety of intramural labour to suit the different classes of prisoners and the several stages of imprisonment. Indeed, the labour of our central jails may now be said to be entirely intramural, even the farm lands which are attached to some of these prisons being effectually enclosed.

The employment of convicts sentenced to rigorous imprisonment is as essential a part of our penal system as is the loss of liberty or the prohibition of indulgences. For the right understanding, therefore, of the rules regulating the distribution of prison labour, it will be well to consider the principles of punishment by imprisonment.

The primary object of such punishment is to deter from crime both criminals *in esse* and criminals *in posse*, the latter of course by force of example. Its next object is to reform the criminal himself.

In the case of the short-sentenced prisoner, the first object is best attained by making him pass the whole of his sentence in separate (not solitary) confinement, with unpalatable food and ultra penal labour. The second and third conditions are not wanting, but there are financial impediments to separation. However, it is hoped these may be gradually removed. Already partial experiments towards separating convicts from each other have been begun at the Presidency Prison and the Coimbatore Central Jail.

The reform of the short-sentenced prisoner is hardly to be looked for from the brief influences that can be brought to bear upon him in jail. Yet his reform may sometimes remotely result from the single useful lesson it is possible to teach him while there, the lesson that prison life is a life of expiation.

The case of the long-sentenced prisoner is similar, with an important difference. Him, too, both for the sake of society, and for his own sake, is it imperative to make so feel the penalty of jail as shall lead him to look back upon his prison life with loathing, and thus deter him from the repetition of crime. By parity of reasoning it would, at first sight, seem as if this primary object of punishment could be best attained by precisely the same process of stringent discipline as attends the short-sentenced prisoner throughout his incarceration. And this is true with certain limitations. That is to say, such discipline is even more called for in the case of the long-sentenced prisoner, and, since its *in terrorem* and *ad castigandum* conditions could not, with safety to health, be made more punitive than they already are, it would appear as if the only alternative was to prolong their duration. But here the analogy ends. For punishment pursued beyond a certain point, besides tending to demoralize those who inflict it, defeats its own purposes, because, as beings can suffer only according to their capacity, it then perforce becomes inoperative. Consequently, the extreme penalties of jail, by which phrase I desire to denote isolation (where practicable) and expiatory labor, are inflicted upon the long-sentenced prisoner for a certain well considered period only, that period being the part of his sentence already described as his probation. In our central jails male prisoners going through this period of probation are put to grain-grinding, stone-breaking, breaking cocoanuts with a wooden mallet, excavating wells with the pick-axe, and turning an oil-mill. All these forms of labour being tasked, are sufficiently trying and irksome to secure a good measure of punishment. They strain the muscles, perceptibly quicken the breath, sensibly open the pores of the skin, and demand unflagging attention. In like manner, task work in grain-grinding and grain-pounding is exacted from female convicts undergoing their probation.

I consider grain-grinding to be one of the very best kinds of punitive labour, superior even to the crank, because remunerative, while equally severe and monotonous. In the other forms of penal labour mentioned, unless carried on under such conditions of isolation as will prevent communication or distraction, it is more difficult to obviate the tendency of the prisoner to move slowly, hit lightly, and stop often. They admit of an inequality of exertion arising more from the various dispositions than the physical capacities of the prisoners. In the grinding of grain every man exerts himself equally.

After a preliminary course of stringent punishment, which, besides acting as a deterrent from crime, is thought to prepare the criminal for reformation, the long-sentenced prisoner is gradually transferred to industrial employment in association, such as weaving of various descriptions, working in leather and rattan, rope and mat and carpet-making, carpentry, and printing and book-binding. It seems generally agreed upon, that, while such occupation is wholly unfit for those offenders who are undergoing a short sentence or are working out the first stage of their imprisonment, industrial employment may properly follow the more penal labour, and that it then exercises some moral influence upon the mind of the convict, though the extent and value of the influence are

CHAP. XVIII. POLICE AND JAILS.

obviously not susceptible of direct proof. The forms of industrial labour in vogue have been determined by the demands of the state, preference being given to those kinds which are the most severe, require least instruction, have the great advantage of being easily measured, and, with these qualifications, are most profitable. Thus, the uniform of the entire police force and many articles required by other public departments are manufactured in the jails of the Madras Presidency. In the Trichinopoly Central Jail thousands of yards of police cloth are annually woven, and thousands of pairs of police sandals are annually made. At this jail much excellent carpentry and gunny work is also every year turned out for different public departments.

Judged by the above standard, the weaving of gunny is an excellent form of industrial labour. It can be perfectly learnt in a few weeks, it pays, and it exercises a great number of muscles. The dressing of stones is also to be recommended as requiring little space, and as being severe, easily learnt, unfavourable to communication, and comparatively profitable.

The employment of prisoners in the district jail differs chiefly from that of prisoners in the central jail in not being so strictly intramural. Some of the manufactures above detailed are carried on, to a more modified extent, in the district jail, but the prisoners in this jail are also largely employed in quarrying and carting stone and lime, in digging gravel, and excavating tanks and wells. On some occasions gangs are hired by Municipalities, and, in rare instances, the employment of convict labour on useful public works has been sanctioned by the Government without charge. The prisoners of the Trichinopoly District Jail, for example, have frequently (though not of late years) been placed at the disposal of the local Municipality free of charge, and have done good work in helping to reclaim the moat and to demolish the walls of the old fort.

It is sometimes urged against labour at manufactures within the prison walls, that it is an undue competition with private capital and labour. But it is evident that the form of labour most for the interest of those on whom the cost of the prison falls is that which produces the largest return for the cost of maintenance, provided, of course, that a profitable return from industrial employment is not elevated into the test of prison efficiency. This danger guarded against, though individuals may be affected, it is plain that any labour which is not so productive as it might be made, is a form of loss to the community. It is better to employ the prisoners on what will not interfere with free labour only if there is at last equal profit.

The gradually-relaxed discipline and slowly-accumulated rewards of what may be called the industrial stage having succeeded what may be called the penal stage *par excellence*, the long-sentenced prisoner upon whom their separate teachings have not been thrown away, as evidenced by continuous industry and good conduct, is, in the last stage of his imprisonment, usually made first a maistry and then a warder or work overseer, with the view of entrusting him, before release, with some of the privileges and responsibilities of a free man, in order to fit him for a return to a law-abiding community. Whether or not this final part of the process of our prison system is productive of reformation of character to the degree which is expected from it, its tendency is unquestionably towards the inculcation of habits of self-respect and self-control; and there can be little doubt that the great majority of long-termed prisoners who prove themselves worthy of being thus utilized are found good and useful servants. At the same time, it must be admitted that in Indian jails convict servants are employed in the maintenance of discipline and the superintendence of work to an extent altogether unknown in other parts of the world, and there are some authorities to whom it seems utterly incompatible with the position of a convict under punishment to give him such a status, and thus to place him in a position of responsibility, and to entrust him with control over others. In Ceylon, prisoners who have served at least two-thirds of their sentence with credit are even promoted to the grade of jail constable.

The proportion in which prison officers are employed as above is one maistry to every twelve convicts, and one warder or work overseer to every fifty.

This notice of the distribution of prison labour would not be complete did I fail to take account of the manner in which it is influenced by caste, and of the kindred recognition of that most tenacious of national institutions in the department of convict diet. I have elsewhere said that the majority of the criminal population of our jails is composed of men who, on release, must earn their livelihood by manual labour, and that to this class instruction in some handicraft or trade is of more use than a smattering of book-knowledge. Of course there will always be a prejudice against men who have once been the inmates of a jail, while, if they go where they are not known, the fact of their being strangers will operate only less prejudicially against the chance of their obtaining employment. To these obstacles, which are more or less common to all parts of the civilized world, must be added an obstacle peculiar to India, namely caste prejudice, one tendency of it being to prevent a man from taking up any trade or adopting any occupation other than the calling of his particular caste. It may, indeed, be doubted whether the articles thus produced would ever find a ready sale. If they were articles of food, the producer would certainly have the melancholy satisfaction of consuming them himself. For instance, what Hindu, with any pretensions to respectability, would dream of eating the coarse sugar (commonly called jaggery) made out of the sap of the palmyra, if it had been thus converted, not by the Shánárs, whose caste calling is the cultivation of this tree, but by Pariahs? But—to return to the point—the only recognition of caste in the jails of the Madras Presidency is the provision of suitable cooks for all classes of prisoners, and the exemption from scavengering and shoe-making of all except Pariahs, Chucklers, Yanádies and Koravars.

It appears to me that the recognition of caste within these carefully-considered limits may be briefly defended in two ways.

The defence may be based on the unquestionable difference between English rank and Hindu caste. The former is social, the latter essentially religious. This being the case, so long as caste-prisoners are put to such kinds of labour as entail loss of dignity alone, they are in no worse a position than that of any noble felon when made to pick oakum. For example, even Bráhmans will not lose caste by coir-twisting or grain-grinding, though they will consider their social dignity lowered by such labour. But put them to shoe-making or scavengering, and they will lose caste.

I should, however, feel inclined to base the defence, not so much on the difference between English rank and Hindu caste, as on the principle of law that the judge cannot sentence the criminal to any punishment not prescribed in the Penal Code, and that the superintendent of a jail cannot inflict any punishment not prescribed in the sentence. The maximum he can inflict is "rigorous imprisonment," and this has never been interpreted to mean anything beyond loss of liberty, hard labour, and the prohibition of indulgences. There is no crime for which the punishment prescribed is loss of caste. Putting aside the case of life-convicts, to deprive of caste prisoners committed for a certain definite term of years, thus rendering it impossible for them ever after to have any intercourse with Native society, or even with their own wives and children, would be to inflict upon them a heavier punishment than even imprisonment for life. To most high-caste prisoners death itself would seem preferable to such dishonour. Indeed, I am of opinion that if we were to compel Bráhmans to eat food cooked by a Pariah, or to work upon a dead skin, so many of them would commit suicide that the trouble of taking care of this class of prisoners would be greatly diminished.

The first of the following statements shows the employment of the convicts in the Trichinopoly Central and District Jails during the year 1876; the second shows the results of their employment:— **CHAP. XVIII. POLICE AND JAILS.**

1		2		3		4						5		
Average Number sentenced to Labour.		Average Number not sentenced to Labour.		Average Number of Effectives.		Employment.						Ratio per cent. Column 5 of those employed		
						A.	B.	C.	D.	E.	F.			
						Prison Officers.	Prison Servants.	Building and Repairing Jail.	On Jail Garden.	On Manufactures.	Extramural.	As Prison Officers.	As Prison Servants.	On Manufactures.
M.	F	M.	F.	M.	F.									
962·00	40·00	1·00	1·00	768·00	31·00	104	192	134	84	187	98	13·01	24·03	23·40
112·00	..	3·00	..	96·00	..	7	34	24	21	6	4	7·29	35·41	6·25

1						2					3			4			5
Credits.						Debits.											
A.	B.	C.	D.	E.	F.	A.	B.	C.	D.	E.	A.	B.	C.	A.	B.	C.	
Cash received for Labour or Articles sold during the Year.	Value of Manufactured Goods supplied for Government purposes.	Value of Manufactured Goods remaining in Store.	Value of Raw Material in Store.	Value of Plant and Machinery.	Total Credits.	Value of Manufactured Goods in Store on 1st January.	Value of Raw Material in Store on 1st January.	Value of Plant and Machinery in Store on 1st January.	Cash expended on Raw Material, Plant, &c., during the Year.	Total Debits.	Excess of Credits or Profit.	Average Profit per Head of Effectives	Excess of Debits or Loss.	Excess of 3 A. over 4 D. or Cash Profit.	Average Cash Profit per Head of Effectives.	Excess of 4 D, 3 A. or Cash Loss.	Amount of Out-Standing Bills due to Jails.
373	..	54	..	20	449	71	..	25	..	96	351	4	..	373	4	..	229
3,331	..	529	191	119	4,170	430	359	81	1,499	2,369	1,801	4	..	1,832	4	..	129

I have not yet done with the penal side of jail-life. Hard, irksome, incessant labour does not exhaust it. The labour test of prison discipline, though indispensable to an unrelenting exclusion of comfort, is not all-sufficient. It needs to be supplemented by coarse food and by a planned and regulated deprivation of liberty amounting to much more than mere watch and ward. With the subject of convict diet I shall deal separately hereafter. In this place I desire to remark that, from a disciplinary point of view, an enforced subordination and strict obedience to rules are of perhaps equal importance with the labour test. Such little things as rigid

CHAP. XVIII. POLICE AND JAILS.

punctuality in all the operations of the day, marching in step, keeping together in compact squads, preserving strict silence, and the like, maintain a state of activity and attention, tend to diminish the mischief of intercourse, accustom the prisoners to the word of command and teach them self-restraint, and thus must prove valuable aids to any system of prison-discipline. An almost military precision ought to pervade every part of the routine of a jail. To enforce a system so strict is, of course, not easy. Indispensable an adjunct to prison-discipline as is the hope of reward, there must be also fear of punishment. Without adequate punishment it is impossible to reduce those who have defied the law to a condition of complete subordination and control. I have already dealt in detail with the scheme of rewards, which chiefly affects long-term prisoners. I will now state the method of punishing offences against prison-discipline.

Jail offences.

Criminal offences committed in jail, such as attempts to escape and petty thefts and assaults, are, except in serious cases, ordinarily treated as offences against prison discipline ; but the vast majority of offences against prison regulations fall under the heads of refractory and disorderly conduct, idleness and intentional mismanagement of work, the possession of forbidden articles, and other forms of wilful disobedience. Under the Madras Jails Act (V of 1869) these offences are, with one exception, punishable by stripes not exceeding one hundred and fifty with a cat-o'-nine-tails, by restriction of diet in the manner prescribed by Government, and by separate confinement for not more than seven days for each offence. The exception is that of idleness and intentional mismanagement of work, where the utmost that can be inflicted in the way of corporal punishment in the most contumacious case is sixty lashes, though the Act seems to contemplate "in the instance of a prisoner pertinaciously refusing to work," a maximum of severity in respect of restriction of diet, declaring that the allowance may be "reduced in such degree as may be consistent with his support until he shall perform the work required from him." However, the present rules for the restriction of diet do not go to this length. Under these rules, which have of course the force of law, Europeans and East Indians may be sentenced to bread and water, and Natives to conjee (rice gruel) for any period not exceeding three days at a time, during which they are subject to the lightest kind of labour, such as picking coir. All prisoners of whatever nationality may also be sentenced to half-rations for any period not exceeding seven days at a time, during which they are subject to labour of medium severity, such as twisting coir. The judicial punishment of solitary confinement and the jail punishment of separate confinement further carry with them a diminution of the ordinary rations by one-third. Female prisoners and persons committed to prison or custody in a civil jail are exempted from corporal punishment, which, in the case of juveniles, is inflicted with a light rattan, after the manner of school-discipline, the maximum number of cuts being limited to eighteen. Both in their case and in that of adults, who are flogged on the shoulder-blades, corporal punishment is not inflicted unless the Medical officer of the jail states in writing that the prisoner can bear it without danger to his general health, nor except in the presence of the Superintendent and some Medical subordinate. Neither can any sentence of restriction of diet or of separate or solitary confinement be carried out except upon a similar medical certificate, and the Superintendent and Medical officer are bound to note, in their respective journals, any injurious effect that may be observed on the mind or health of prisoners thus confined.

No person who has been punished under the provisions of the Madras Jails Act can be punished for the same offence, in any other way, or by any other authority than the superintendent of the jail, who is legally bound to record the particulars of any such offence and punishment in a prescribed form.

The following statement shows the offences committed by, and the punishments inflicted on, the convicts in the Trichinopoly Central and District Jails during the year 1876 :—

1	2		3		4								5													6
					Breaches of Jail Rules.								Punishments inflicted.													
													A.		B. By Jail Officers.									C.		
															a.		b.		c.		d.	e.				
Jails.	Average Number of Convicts.		Criminal Offences.		Smoking or having Possession of Forbidden Articles.		Offences relating to Work.		Other Offences against Prison Discipline.		Total Offences.		By Criminal Courts.		Separate Confinement.		Reduced Diet.		Separate Confinement with Reduced Diet.		Corporal Punishment.	Other Punishments.		Total Punishments.		Ratio of Column 6 C. to Column 3.
	M.	F.	M.	F.	M.	F.	M.	F.	M.	F.	M.	F.	M.	F.	M.	F.	M.	F.	M.	F.		M.	F.	M.	F.	
Trichinopoly Central ...	963·20	41·07	..	..	60	..	23	..	64	..	147	..	..	..	9	..	4	..	..	..	55	69	..	147	..	14·63
Trichinopoly District ...	114·64	..	1	..	1	..	3	..	18	..	36	..	1	..	1	..	7	..	9	..	17	2	..	37	..	32·27

I cannot quit this subject without expressing my regret at the frequency of corporal punishment in Indian jails. The use of this coarse, rough and ready, time and trouble-saving expedient almost to the exclusion of other modes of coercion is, in large measure, attributable to the barrack-like construction of our jails, both district and central, and to their insufficient provision for separate confinement, one of the most effective of the limited punishments at our disposal. Again, restriction of diet without seclusion of the offender is almost impracticable, as, if left in

CHAP. XVIII. POLICE AND JAILS.

association with others, he can generally manage to get extra food somehow or other. We are thus thrown back upon the lash, which has no doubt a demoralizing effect upon the offender subjected to it, tending to lessen his self-respect and to render him callous, though not of course to the extent observable in countries where the growth of individualism is greater, and the sense of the degradation of personal correction is hence more developed. It is only as a preventive, and as, in some cases, likely to inflict less moral injury on the prisoner than confinement among criminals, that whipping should be resorted to even as a judicial punishment. With the projected improvement in the construction of our jails, flogging will take its proper place in the disciplinary code of a prison, namely as the ultimate resort where every other means of coercion has failed.

Scales of diet.

The following table exhibits the scales of diet in force in the Trichinopoly Central and District Jails, which are, with slight variations, those in force elsewhere :—

1		2							3						
		Diet Scale of Labouring Prisoners.							Diet Scale of Non-Labouring Prisoners.						
No.	Articles.	Monday.	Tuesday.	Wednesday.	Thursday.	Friday.	Saturday.	Sunday.	Monday.	Tuesday.	Wednesday.	Thursday.	Friday.	Saturday.	Sunday.
		oz.	oz.	oz.	oz.	oz.	oz.	oz.	oz.	oz.	oz	oz.	oz.	oz.	oz.
21	Rice	..	..	..	..	..	..	26	..	..	..	..	..	..	20½
	Rági	24	24	..	24	..	24	..	19⅕	19½	..	19½	..	19½	..
	Chólum	..	..	24	..	24	..	..	..	..	19½	..	19½	..	..
	Cumbu	..	..	..	..	..	..	..	..	..	..	..	..	..	..
	Dholl	2	2	2	2	2	2	2	2	2	2	2	2	2	2
	Mutton	3	..	5	..	5	..	..	2½	..	4	..	4	..	..
	Fish	..	..	..	..	..	..	..	..	..	..	..	..	..	..
	Butter-milk or tyre.	..	10	..	10	..	10	10	..	10	..	10	..	10	10
	Ghee or oil ..	½	½	½	½	½	½	½	½	½	½	½	½	½	½
	Tamarind	½	½	½	½	½	½	½	½	½	½	½	½	½	½
	Salt	1	1	1	1	1	1	1	1	1	1	1	1	1	1
	Curry-powder ..	½	½	½	½	½	½	½	½	½	½	½	½	½	½
	Vegetable	4	4	4	4	4	4	4	4	4	4	4	4	4	4
	Onions	½	½	½	½	½	½	½	½	½	1	½	¼	¼	½
	Garlic Grs.	30	..	30	..	30	..	..	30	..	30	..	30	..	..
	Firewood lbs.	2	2	2	2	2	2	2	2	2	2	2	2	2	2

Prisoners convicted oftener than once do not receive any ration of rice, but get fourteen instead of twelve meals of dry grain per week. In all jails great care is taken to provide a daily issue of wholesome vegetables, and the same amount of condiments is issued throughout the Presidency. The introduction of the present scale, of which dry grains are the staple article, has improved the health of the prisoners, yet serves a punitive purpose, being far less palatable than former scales, where rice preponderated over dry grains.

It is not only in the dietary, but also in the water-supply and cleanliness of prisoners that real care has of late years been enforced. In fact, our jails have undergone a complete sanitary reformation, and what were pest-houses, converting sentences of imprisonment into sentences of death, have now become healthy places of confinement. In connection with this subject it may be well to note the precautions in force against the influence of epidemics prevailing throughout the Presidency upon the health of the prison-population. Every central jail is provided with an observation block, where prisoners on arrival are entirely separate from the rest of the inmates, and they are there detained for periods varying according to the sanitary condition of the places whence they have been sent. The arrangements for observation in most of the district jails consist of temporary sheds erected in the vicinity of the prison. This is the case with the Trichinopoly District Jail.

Mortality in the central and district jails.

The subjoined statement shows the sickness and mortality among the convicts in the Trichinopoly Central and District Jails during the year 1876:—

1			2			3			4			5			6		
Capacity of the Jail Barracks at 40 Superficial Feet per Head.			Average Daily Strength.			Maximum Population on any one Day.			Number admitted into Hospital.			Daily Average Number of Sick.			No. of Deaths in and out of Hospital.		
M.	F.	Total.	M.	F.	Total.	M.	F.	Total.	M.	F.	Total.	M.	F.	Total.	M	F.	Total.
982	86	1,068	973·20	41·07	1,004·27	1,048	41	1,097	315	14	229	13·89	78	14·67	27	..	27
180	18	198	123·92	·59	124·51	155	2	157	130	..	130	4·91	..	4·91	7	..	7

7														
Ratio per cent. of Average Strength.														
A.			B.			C.			D.			E.		
Of Admissions into Hospital.			Of Daily Average Number of Sick.			Of Deaths from Cholera.			Of Deaths from all other Causes both in and out of Hospital.			Of Deaths from all Causes both in and out of Hospital.		
M.	F.	Total.	M.	F.	Total.	M.	F.	Total.	M.	F.	Total.	M.	F.	Total.
32·73	34·08	32·76	1·44	1·89	1·46	..	..	..	..	..	..	2·80	..	2·68
104·90	..	104·40	3·96	..	3·94	3·22	..	3·21	2·42	..	2·40	5·64	..	5·62

CHAP. XVIII. POLICE AND JAILS.

Cost of prisoners.

What the prisoners of the Trichinopoly Central and District Jails cost the State in the year 1876 may be learnt from the following statement, but it should be explained that civil debtors and under-trials are omitted, the former being supported from subsistence money paid by creditors and the latter from funds provided in the budget under Law and Justice:—

1	2							3		4		5	
	Average Number of Prisoners.							Rations.		Establishment.		Police Guard.	
								A.	B.	A.	B.	A.	B.
Jails.	Convicts.	Civil.	Under-trial.	Security.	Insane.	State.	Total.	Total Cost.	Cost per Head of Average Strength, excluding Civil Prisoners and Under trial.	Total Cost.	Cost per Head of Average Strength	Cost per Head of Average Strength	Total Cost.
								RS.	RS. A. P.	RS.	RS. A. P.	RS. A. P.	RS.
Trichinopoly Central ..	1,003	..	..	..	..	..	1,003	1,247	42 0 2	13,075	13 0 7	11 11 1	11,727
Do. District ..	119	4	6	1	..	..	103	4,410	36 12 0	2,074	22 14 0	14 2 6	1,840

6			7		8		9	10
Hospital Charges.			Clothing.		Contingencies.			
A.	B.	C.	A.	B.	A.	B.		
Total Cost.	Cost per Head of Average Strength.	Cost Per Head of Average Number Sick.	Total Cost.	Cost per Head of Average Strength, excluding Civil Prisoners and Under-trial.	Total. Cost.	Cost per Head of Average Strength, excluding Civil Prisoners and Under-trial.	Grand Total expended.	Total Cost per Head of Average Strength.
RS.	RS. A. P.	RS. A. P.	RS.	RS. A. P.	RS.	RS. A. P.	RS.	RS. A. P.
891	0 14 3	58 10 8	4,436	4 6 9	2,228	2 3 7	74,498	74 4 5
265	2 0 1	52 3 2	541	4 8 3	555	4 10 0	10,581	81 6 3

Subsidiary jails.

The following statement shows the number of prisoners confined in the subsidiary jails of the Trichinopoly District during the year 1876 :—

Taluqs.	Subsidiary Jails.	Residence of what Officer or Officers.	Number the Jail will hold.		Number remaining 31st Dec. 1875.		Number remaining 31st Dec. 1876.		Average Daily Number during the Year.		Greatest Number at any one time.		Remarks.
			M.	F	M	F	M	F	M.	F.	M	F	
Trichinopoly	Trichino-poly.	District, Assistant and Cantonment Magistrates, and one 2nd and two 3rd-class Magistrates.	71	4	10	..	1	..	17·03	2·68	25	8	The prisoners confined in the old Fort Sub-jail were transferred to the Sub-jail attached to the District Jail during the year.
	Lálgudi ..	2nd-class Magistrate.	24	12	..	..	16	..	15·09	1·55	24	4	
Musiri ..	Musiri ..	Head Assistant Magistrate, one 2nd and one 3rd-class Magistrate.	10	4	1	..	13	1	1·80	·31	13	7	The surplus prisoners were kept in the cells for under-trial prisoners.
	Turaiyúr.	3rd-class Magistrate.	26	12	..	..	..	..	·20	·02	9	5	
Kulittalai ..	Kulittalai.	2nd and 3rd-class Magistrates.	38	20	1	..	5	1	6·32	1·84	19	3	
	Manap-parai.	3rd-class Magistrate.	24	10	3	..	6	1	2·56	·08	14	1	
Perambalúr.	Peramba-lúr.	2nd and 3rd-class Magistrates.	15	15	4	..	12	2	2·00	..	12	2	
Udaiyár-pálayam.	Jeyam-kondasó-lapuram.	2nd and 3rd-class Magistrates.	12	12	..	..	12	..	4·43	1·40	12	4	
	Kilapalu-vúr.	2nd-class Magistrate.	20	10	6	..	..	..	2·03	·04	18	2	
		Total ..	240	99	26	..	55	5	51·46	7·92	..	..	

The subject of the accommodation afforded for prisoners under trial in subsidiary jails attracted the attention of the Government of Madras in the year 1869. A committee was appointed to report on the existing condition of these buildings, and the inquiry revealed the pressing urgency for increased accommodation. The old subsidiary jails were too small, horribly deficient in ventilation, and extremely unhealthy. The present subsidiary jails are suitable buildings, sufficient in size, thoroughly ventilated, and providing for the separation of the sexes, a rare provision formerly. Indeed, so complete has been the success of Government in this direction that the subsidiary jails, which used to be positively dangerous to life, are now the healthiest places of confinement in

CHAP. XVIII. POLICE AND JAILS.

the Presidency, and, in connection with this subject, it may be mentioned that a similar improvement has been made throughout the country in respect of police lock-ups, where the same stringent provisions for adequate space and ventilation, and for the separation of the sexes have been carefully enforced.

The following statement shows the sickness and mortality in the subsidiary jails of the Trichinopoly District during the year 1876:—

Subsidiary Jails.	Average Daily Number of Prisoners during the Year.		Number remaining 31st December 1875.		Cholera.				Small-pox.				Fevers.				Dysentery.				Other Diseases.				Total Admissions.		Total Deaths.		Number remaining 31st December 1876.		Average Daily Sick during the Year.	
					Admitted.		Died.		Admitted.		Died.		Admitted.		Died.		Admitted.		Died.		Admitted.		Died.									
	M.	F.	M	F	M	F	M	F	M	F	M	F	M	F	M	F	M	F	M	F	M	F	M	F	M	F	M	F	M	F	M.	F.
TRICHINOPOLY.																																
Trichinopoly ..	17·03	2·68											3				2				1				6						.01	..
Lálgudi ..	15·09	1·55																													..	..
Musiri ..	1·80	·31												1												1					..	..
Turaiyúr ..	·20	·02																													..	..
Kulittalai ..	6·32	1·84			1		1																		1		1				..	..
Manapparai ..	2·56	·08																													..	..
Perumbalúr ..	2·00	..			2		1																		2		1				..	..
Joyamkondasólapuram.	4·43	1·40																													..	..
Kílapaluvúr ..	2·03	·04																													..	..
Total ..	51·46	7·92			3		2						3	1			2				1				9	1	2				·01	..

The necessity of working the prisoners undergoing short sentences of less than a month in the subsidiary jails has been constantly in view, but there are great practical difficulties in this matter. The prisoners are few in number in each jail, they are chiefly of a class that can only be employed in the rudest kind of works, and there are few facilities in the immediate vicinity of these jails for utilizing the labour of their inmates. With the exception of stone-breaking, little has been done in the employment of these prisoners.

Here I might stop. But, before concluding, I desire to combat the notion held by many European Judges and Magistrates, and by still more police officers, that our jails are not merely undeterrent, but positively attractive to criminals. I shall have written to very little purpose, if what I have already said on the subject of prison discipline does not point in the opposite direction. Still, it may be asked why, if punishment is sufficiently secure, it has proved inadequate to arrest an undoubtedly constant increase of crime. Now, notwithstanding the period of general though gradual improvement which, if I have not overstated my case, we have entered upon, I am very far from believing that prison discipline is yet as stringent as it ought to be. But I am still further from thinking that the explanation of an admitted increase of crime is to be found in the inefficacy of our penal system alone. There are several stumbling-blocks in the way of such a conclusion. Before bewailing the laxity of jail discipline, I should wish to be sure of the effect of much recent legislation and of many administrative changes. Certainty of detection being more deterrent than severity of punishment, the question of the efficiency of the police would also claim attention. Then there are stupendous social as well as economic forces at work, the results of which could not be ignored in any searching analysis of the statistics of crime. To fathom the causes of the growth of the jail-population it would, above all, be necessary to estimate the general effect of the movement that is unquestionably going on towards the individualization of the collective rights and responsibilities which have hitherto regulated Native society. The people of India are not prone to lay themselves open to the onward moving forces in the world around them, but they are notwithstanding being gradually steeped in the disintegrating solvents of Western civilization, and, under its influence, they must become less and less able to acquiesce in traditional methods of action and in the respectabilities of time-hallowed institutions, while nothing has as yet supplied their place in the popular mind. A period of transition in which archaic ties and sanctions are surely, though slowly disappearing, is likely to be attended by an increase of crime until fresh controlling forces come into play.

CHAPTER XIX.

CIVIL AND CRIMINAL JUSTICE.

CIVIL—District Court.—List of Judges of Trichinopoly.—District Munsifs.—Cantonment Court of Small Causes.—Village Munsifs.—Revenue Courts.—Registration. CRIMINAL—Session Court.—District Magistrate.—Divisional Magistrate.—Cantonment Magistrate.—Subordinate Magistrates.—Honorary Magistrates—Justices of the Peace.—Village Magistrates.—Statistics.

CIVIL.

CHAP. XIX. CIVIL AND CRIMINAL JUSTICE.

District Court.

THE principal Civil Court in Trichinopoly is the District Court which has both original and appellate jurisdiction. This Court is presided over by the District Judge who under Section 27 of the Madras Civil Court's Act (III of 1873) is vested with general control over all the Civil Courts of whatever grade in the district subject however to rules prescribed by the High Court. On the original side the jurisdiction of the District Judge extends, subject to the rules contained in the Code of Civil Procedure, to all original suits and proceedings of a civil nature. The following statement shows the result of the trial of civil suits in the District Court on the original side for a series of 3 years :—

Years.	Suits remaining on the 1st January.	Filed in each year included in suit remanded or re-admitted	Received by Transfer.	Total for Disposal.	Transferred to other Courts.	Plaint rejected or returned.	Dismissed for Default.	Uncontested. Withdrawn with leave.	Uncontested. Compromised.	Uncontested. Decreed on Confession.	Uncontested. Decreed ex parte. For Plaintiff.	Uncontested. Decreed ex parte. For Defendant.	Contested. Judgment for Plaintiff in whole or part.	Contested. Judgment for Defendant.	Total. Total disposed of.	Pending at the end of year.	Pending Over 2 Months.	Pending Over 4 Months.	Pending Over 12 Months.	Average duration of Suits in days. Contested.	Average duration of Suits in days. Uncontested.	Referred to Arbitration.
1	2	3	4	5	6	7	8	9	10	11	12	13	14	15	16	17	18	19	20	21	22	23
1874 ...	8	26	5	39	...	...	4	...	3	...	2	...	8	8	25	14	3	6	...	160	55	...
1875 ...	14	29	3	46	2	1	...	1	5	2	...	...	9	9	26	18	3	10	2	208	101	1
1876 ...	18	13	2	33	...	...	...	...	3	1	...	...	12	9	25	8	4	2	...	358	44	...

The appeals from decrees and orders of the several District Munsifs in the district lie to the District Court. The District Judge also hears all appeals preferred from judgments passed by the Revenue Courts in the district under Act VIII of 1865 (Madras). The following statement shows the appellate work of the District Court for a period of 3 years :—

Years.	Appeals remaining on the 1st January.	Instituted in each year including appeals remanded or remitted.	Received by Transfer.	Total for Disposal.	Transferred.	Dismissed for Default under Sections 5 and 6, Act XXIII, 1861.	Withdrawn, compromised, or decreed on Confession.	Uncontested. Confirmed.	Uncontested. Modified.	Uncontested. Reversed.	Contested. Confirmed.	Contested. Modified.	Contested. Reversed.	Total disposed of.	Pending at the end of year.	Pending. Over 4 Months.	Pending. Over 12 Months.	Remanded.	Objections under Section 348 of Civil Procedure Code.	Objections allowed.
1	2	3	4	5	6	7	8	9	10	11	12	13	14	15	16	17	18	19	20	21
1874 ...	99	181	1	281	...	16	8	6	...	...	86	1	37	154	127	56	...	7	...	...
1875 ...	127	311	...	438	...	7	3	7	1	...	83	75	47	233	215	84	1	16	...	...
1876 ...	215	327	...	542	..	10	12	12	...	1	108	7	37	187	355	227	34	9	...	...

The following statement shows the extent to which Trichinopoly District has contributed to the civil work of the Presidency for a period of 5 years :—

Years.	No. of Appealable Suits instituted in Courts subordinate to the District Court.	No. of Appeals preferred in the District Court.	No. of Regular Appeals preferred in the High Court.	No. of Special Appeals preferred in the High Court.
1872 ..	2,234	162	7	23
1873 ..	2,354	108	9	34
1874 ..	2,205	181	7	24
1875 ..	2,399	311	8	19
1876 ..	2,749	327	11	90

From 1803 to 1843 Trichinopoly was the head-quarters of the southern Provincial Court, which was presided over by three Judges and had jurisdiction throughout Trichinopoly, Tanjore, Salem, Coimbatore, Madura, and Tinnevelly Districts. In September 1843 the Provincial Court was abolished, and a Civil and Session Judge was appointed for the Trichinopoly District alone. The following is a list of the officers who have held the post of Judge of Trichinopoly since that date :—

G. S. Greenway, September 1843—November 1845.
W. Harrington, November 1845—December 1847.
E. Story, December 1847—May 1848.
G. S. Greenway, June 1848—March 1850.
T. E. J. Boileau, March 1850—September 1850.
J. Rohde, September 1850—March 1851.
J. H. Davidson, March 1851—November 1851.

G. S. Greenway, November 1851—June 1852.
G. M. Swinton, July 1852—September 1852.
G. S. Greenway, October 1852—June 1853.
T. J. P. Harris, June 1853—October 1858.
R. G. Clarke, October 1858—April 1860.
T. J. P. Harris, May 1860—January 1866.
A. E. R. McDonell, February 1866—January 1867.
F. M. Kindersley, January 1867—June 1867.
W. McQuhae, June 1867—December 1867.
R. Davidson, December 1867—September 1868.
W. M. Cadell, September 1868—December 1869.
R. Davidson, December 1869—August 1873.
E. F. Webster, August 1873—April 1878.
F. Brandt, April 1878.

District Munsifs.

As there is at present no Subordinate Judge in Trichinopoly the Civil Courts next in importance to the District Court are those of the District Munsifs. There are at present three of these Courts in the district, which are stationed at Trichinopoly, Kulittalai, and Perambalúr. The Trichinopoly District Munsif has jurisdiction over the whole of Trichinopoly Taluq with the exception of seventy-two villages; the Kulittalai Munsif has jurisdiction over Musiri and Kulittalai Taluqs as well as the villages of Trichinopoly Taluq not under the Trichinopoly Munsif, and the Perambalur Munsif over Perambalúr and Udaiyárpálayam Taluqs. The original jurisdiction of the District Munsifs extends to all suits, the value of which does not exceed Rupees 2,500. They have no appellate jurisdiction. At present all the District Munsifs in Trichinopoly are invested with Small Cause jurisdiction over suits up to Rupees 50 in value. The following statement shows the result of the trial of civil suits in the Courts of the several District Munsifs for 3 years :—

CHAP. XIX.
CIVIL AND CRIMINAL JUSTICE.

Court.	Suits remaining on the 1st January.	Filed in the Year.	Received by Transfer.	Total for Disposal.	Transferred to other Courts.	Plaint rejected or returned.	Uncontested.						Contested.		Total.	Pending at the end of the Year.	Pending.			Average duration of Suits in Days		Referred to Arbitration.
							Dismissed for Default.	Withdrawn with Leave.	Compromised.	Decreed on Confession.	Decreed *ex parte* For Plaintiff.	Decreed *ex parte* For Defendant.	Judgment for Plaintiff in whole or part.	Judgment for Defendant.	Total disposed of.		Over 2 Months.	Over 4 Months.	Over 12 Months.	Contested.	Uncontested.	
1	2	3	4	5	6	7	8	9	10	11	12	13	14	15	16	17	18	19	20	21	22	23
1874.																						
Trichinopoly. Original ..	402	1,007	9	1,418	2	..	25	17	330	41	222	3	147	38	823	593	147	156	74	161	90	..
Trichinopoly. Small Causes.	41	845	5	891	..	..	21	4	285	123	198	..	126	44	801	90	3	..	..	17	13	..
Kulittalai. Original ..	167	383	2	552	7	..	15	..	37	9	105	25	174	24	389	156	27	32	21	65	34	..
Kulittalai. Small Causes.	47	641	..	688	1	..	7	..	30	37	195	162	168	52	651	37	..	..	..	15	7	..
Perambalúr. Original ..	639	724	..	1,363	6	..	114	3	234	146	198	27	260	105	1,087	270	88	168	14	249	90	..
Perambalúr. Small Causes.	32	641	..	673	5	..	102	..	72	54	133	4	81	61	624	44	..	..	..	20	15	..
1875.																						
Trichinopoly. Original ..	593	995	48	1,636	64	4	31	7	367	23	224	4	180	172	1,008	564	184	206	14	148	130	1
Trichinopoly. Small Causes.	90	864	..	954	..	..	28	1	171	160	203	..	221	67	851	103	1	..	..	22	20	..
Kulittalai. Original ..	156	597	140	893	17	..	25	6	83	12	136	39	320	92	713	163	32	13	..	72	38	..
Kulittalai. Small Causes.	37	733	3	773	3	..	12	..	89	37	165	169	191	54	720	50	..	..	..	12	9	..
Perambalúr. Original ..	270	524	..	794	110	..	7	8	142	31	117	6	128	124	563	121	110	9	2	256	42	..
Perambalúr. Small Causes.	44	421	..	465	7	..	5	1	110	32	82	76	64	43	413	45	45	..	..	..	..	..
1876.																						
Trichinopoly. Original ..	564	1,041	1	1,606	..	2	19	12	332	26	176	..	193	155	913	693	199	312	4	181	135	..
Trichinopoly. Small Causes.	103	750	..	853	..	..	27	2	288	91	213	..	109	72	802	51	..	..	..	31	28	..
Kulittalai. Original ..	163	861	..	1,024	..	..	2	7	82	24	156	31	439	104	845	179	34	5	..	75	32	..
Kulittalai. Small Causes.	50	1,006	..	1,056	..	..	12	..	180	62	290	120	253	90	1,007	49	..	..	..	15	16	..
Perambalúr. Original ..	121	707	..	828	3	..	11	4	244	80	138	47	163	80	767	58	56	2	..	92	28	..
Perambalúr. Small Causes.	45	466	..	511	..	..	14	2	151	60	105	51	50	51	484	27	27	..	..	..	..	..

CHAP. XIX.
CIVIL AND CRIMINAL JUSTICE.

Cantonment Court of Small Causes.

The Cantonment Magistrate is invested under Section 7 of Act I of 1866 (Madras) with powers of a Court of Small Causes for the trial of suits up to Rupees 500 in value. He has jurisdiction within the limits of the cantonment only. The following statement shows the result of the trial of small causes in his Court for 3 years :—

Years.	Suits remaining on the 1st January.	Filed in each Year.	Received by Transfer.	Total for Disposal.	Transferred to other Courts.	Plaint rejected or returned.	Uncontested. Dismissed for Default.	Uncontested. Withdrawn with Leave.	Uncontested. Compromised.	Uncontested. Decreed on Confession.	Uncontested. Decreed ex parte. For Plaintiff.	Uncontested. Decreed ex parte. For Defendant.	Contested. Judgment for Plaintiff in whole or part.	Contested. Judgment for Defendant.	Total. Total disposed of.	Pending at the end of the Year.	Pending. Over 2 Months.	Pending. Over 4 Months.	Pending. Over 12 Months.	Average duration of Suits in Days. Contested.	Average duration of Suits in Days. Uncontested.	Referred for Arbitration.
1	2	3	4	5	6	7	8	9	10	11	12	13	14	15	16	17	18	19	20	21	22	23
1874 ...	1	60	...	91	...	...	4	15	1	18	8	...	40	4	90	1	1	...	...	6	3	...
1875 ...	1	126	...	127	...	...	6	...	14	31	10	...	60	6	127	...	...	...	...	6	3	...
1876 ...	...	114	...	114	...	...	12	...	20	10	42	...	25	5	114	...	...	...	...	6	4	...

Village Munsifs.

The maniyagár or headman of each village is its Munsif under Regulation IV of 1816, and is empowered to try suits for sums of money or personal property, the amount or value of which does not exceed Rupees 10. No appeal lies from the decision of a Village Munsif. The following statement shows the result of the trial of petty suits by the Village Munsifs in the district for 3 years :—

Years.	Suits remaining on the 1st January.	Filed in each Year.	Received by Transfer.	Total for Disposal.	Transferred to other Courts.	Plaint rejected or returned.	Uncontested. Dismissed for Default.	Uncontested. Withdrawn with Leave.	Uncontested. Compromised.	Uncontested. Decreed on Confession.	Uncontested. Decreed ex parte. For Plaintiff.	Uncontested. Decreed ex parte. For Defendant.	Contested. Judgment for Plaintiff in whole or part.	Contested. Judgment for Defendant.	Total disposed of.	Pending at the end of the Year.	Pending. Over 2 Months.	Pending. Over 4 Months.	Pending. Over 12 Months.	Average duration of Suits in Days. Contested.	Average duration of Suits in Days. Uncontested.	Referred to Arbitration.
1	2	3	4	5	6	7	8	9	10	11	12	13	14	15	16	17	18	19	20	21	22	23
1874 ...	1,470	3,565	...	5,035	...	...	1,329	302	590	278	671	7	426	103	3,706	1,329	471	367	31	96	47	...
1875 ...	1,329	3,247	...	4,576	...	...	1,008	560	220	164	999	14	437	77	3,479	1,097	286	87	65	218	153	...
1876 ...	1,097	3,148	...	4,245	...	...	1,052	554	294	186	1,085	23	399	75	3,668	577	197	36	...	21	139	...

There are 1,241 Village Munsifs in the district. Of these 36 exercised their powers in 1874, 40 in 1875, and 23 in 1876. The Trichinopoly Town Munsif gets a salary of Rupees 40 a-month, and tries on an average about 2,529 cases a year.

CIVIL AND CRIMINAL JUSTICE.

Revenue Courts.

The Collector, Head Assistant Collector, Deputy Collector on General Duties, and the Assistant Collector (when in charge of a division) exercise judicial powers under Regulation XII of 1816, Regulation IX of 1822, Regulation VI of 1831, and Act VIII of 1865 (Madras). The following statement shows the number and nature of the suits filed before the Revenue Officers in the district under these enactments for 3 years :—

Nature of the Suits filed.	Number of Cases in the several Courts.														
	1874.					1875.					1876.				
	Collector.	Head Assistant Collector.	Assistant Collector.	Deputy Collector.	Temporary Deputy Collector.	Collector.	Head Assistant Collector.	Assistant Collector.	Deputy Collector.	Temporary Deputy Collector.	Collector.	Head Assistant Collector.	Assistant Collector.	Deputy Collector.	Temporary Deputy Collector.
Claims connected with boundary and cultivation disputes, Regulation XII of 1816, Section 4.	..	..	..	..	..	..	..	..	..	..	..	..	..	..	..
Claims to hereditary offices or their emoluments, Regulation VI of 1831, Section 3.	..	..	..	..	..	..	..	..	..	..	..	1	..	..	..
Suits to establish or contest right to enhancement or abetment of rent, or to determine amount of rent, Madras Act VIII of 1865, Sections 8, 9, 10, and 11.	..	70	11	1	..	..	33	7	223	..	..	32	11	120	..
Suits relating to ejectment, Section 12.	..	..	..	..	..	..	1	..	..	..	..	..	..	..	..
Suits regarding illegal exaction, distraint, &c., Sections 5, 17, 20, 35, 36, 49, and 80.	..	2	..	..	..	..	12	1	120	..	..	..	..	8	..

Whenever the provisions of Act IV of 1864 (Madras) is extended to any district or part of a district, all fees, contributions, and allowances collected, &c., under Regulation VI of 1831, absolutely cease. This Act was extended to all the Government villages in Trichinopoly from the 1st of January 1875. It, however, does not apply to Zemindári and Inám villages.

Statement No. 14, given in the Appendix, shows the number and value of all suits disposed of in the Civil and Revenue Courts in the district for a series of 10 years.

Registration.

The following is the establishment entertained in the district for the purposes of carrying out the provisions of the Registration Act (III of 1877). Up to 1875 the Treasury Deputy Collector

CHAP. XIX. CIVIL AND CRIMINAL JUSTICE.

was the District Registrar, and drew an allowance of Rupees 100 a-month as such. In that year a special Registrar was appointed who is also the Sub-Registrar for Trichinopoly Taluq, with the exception of Lálgudi Division, which is under a special Sub-Registrar stationed at Lálgudi. Another special Sub-Registrar stationed at Kulittalai has jurisdiction through the whole of Musiri and Kulittalai Taluqs, with the exception of the divisions of the Turaiyúr and Manapparai Deputy Tahsildars. The former of these till 1878 was under the Deputy Tahsildar as an official Sub-Registrar, but in that year a special Sub-Registrar was appointed. The Deputy Tahsildar is Sub-Registrar for Manapparai. The Taluq Sheristadars of Perambalúr and Udaiyárpálayam are the Sub-Registrars for their taluqs, and hold their office at Perambalúr and Jeyamkondasólapuram, respectively. There are at present in the district four special Sub-Registrars, including the District Registrar, and three official Sub-Registrars.

The following statement shows the number of documents registered in the district for a series of 4 years :—

Year.	Book I, Instruments relating to Immovable Property.	Book IV, Miscellaneous Register.	Total.
1873-74	6,220	389	6,609
1874-75	6,135	377	6,512
1875-76	7,383	487	7,870
1876-77	7,940	484	8,424

The following statement gives the receipts and expenditure on account of registration in the several offices in the district for the years 1875-76 and 1876-77 :—

Office.	No. of Documents registered in Books I, III, and IV.	Amount of Ordinary Fees.			Amount of other Receipts.			Total Receipts.			Total Expenditure.		
		RS.	A.	P.	RS.	A.	P.	RS.	A.	P.	RS.	A.	P.
1875-76.													
Trichinopoly Registrar's Office.	3,767	5,478	14	0	946	3	0	6,425	1	0	5,403	7	4
Lálgudi Sub-Registrar's Office.	1,480	2,087	2	0	313	6	0	2,400	8	0	1,242	6	6
Turaiyúr Sub-Registrar's Office.	570	836	11	0	75	7	0	912	2	0	407	12	4
Kulittalai Sub-Registrar's Office.	1,279	1,862	9	0	289	5	0	2,151	14	0	1,050	0	8
Manapparai Sub-Registrar's Office.	381	483	4	0	31	6	0	514	10	0	254	8	4
Jeyamkondasólapuram Sub-Registrar's Office.	222	322	0	0	26	3	0	348	3	0	202	7	9
Perambalúr Sub-Registrar's Office.	198	320	8	0	56	5	0	376	13	0	195	11	8
Total for the whole District.	7,897	11,391	0	0	1,738	3	0	13,129	3	0	8,756	6	7

Office.	No. of Documents registered in Books I, III, and IV.	Amount of Ordinary Fees.	Amount of other Receipts.	Total Receipts.	Total Expenditure.
1876-77.		RS. A. P.	RS. A. P.	RS. A. P.	RS. A. P.
Trichinopoly Registrar's Office.	4,074	5,972 5 0	1,174 8 6	7,146 13 6	5,432 12 7
Lálgudi Sub-Registrar's Office.	1,550	2,187 13 0	355 14 6	2,543 11 6	1,270 2 2
Turaiyúr Sub-Registrar's Office.	551	847 8 0	87 12 3	935 4 3	424 14 1
Kulittalai Sub-Registrar's Office.	1,408	2,049 12 0	449 8 6	2,499 4 6	1,272 12 5
Manapparai Sub-Registrar's Office.	423	536 8 0	17 14 0	554 6 0	612 11 8
Jeyamkondasólapuram Sub-Registrar's Office.	266	359 12 0	65 10 0	425 6 0	215 2 8
Perambalúr Sub-Registrar's Office.	182	284 8 0	44 10 0	329 2 0	200 4 6
Total for the whole District.	8,454	12,231 2 0	2,195 13 9	14,433 15 9	9,077 12 1

CRIMINAL.

Session Court.

The District Judge, in the exercise of his criminal jurisdiction, is styled the Session Judge, and presides over the Session Court. This Court cannot take cognizance of any offence as a Court of original jurisdiction unless the accused person has been committed to it by a competent Magistrate, except in the case of certain offences triable exclusively by the Session Court and committed before it or under its own cognizance (*vide* Section 472 of the Civil Procedure Code). The system of trial by jury has not been extended to Trichinopoly, and all Session cases are tried with the aid of assessors, whose finding, however, the Judge has the power to set aside in case he disagrees with it. The Session Judge hears appeals from the decisions of all the First-class Magistrates in the district. For magisterial purposes the district is divided into three divisions. The District Magistrate exercises all the powers of a Magistrate throughout the district, and is in direct magisterial charge of one division consisting of Trichinopoly Taluq. The Magistrates under him in this division are the Taluq Magistrate who is also the Tahsildar. This officer is a Second-class Magistrate, and has jurisdiction throughout the whole of the taluq, excepting the Trichinopoly Cantonment. The Taluq Sheristadar and Third-class Magistrate, the Town Sub-Magistrate, who has third-class powers and jurisdiction in Trichinopoly town and its adjoining suburbs, in all 52 villages, and the Lálgudi Sub-Magistrate who has second-class powers and jurisdiction in 131 villages. Appeals from the decisions of these Magistrates lie to the District Magistrate. The Head

District Magistrate. Divisional Magistrate. Cantonment Magistrate. Sub-Magistrates.

CHAP. XIX. CIVIL AND CRIMINAL JUSTICE.

Assistant Magistrate has first-class powers and is in charge of another division comprising Musiri and Kulittalai Taluqs, and has under his supervision in Musiri the Taluq Magistrate, who has second-class powers and jurisdiction throughout the taluq, the Taluq Sheristadar and Third-class Magistrate and the Turaiyúr Sub-Magistrate, who has third-class powers and jurisdiction in 126 villages, and in Kulittalai the Taluq Magistrate, who has second-class powers and jurisdiction throughout the taluq, the Taluq Sheristadar and Third-class Magistrate and the Manapparai Sub-Magistrate, who has third-class powers and jurisdiction in 163 villages. The appeal from the decisions of these Magistrates lie to the Head Assistant Magistrate. The Deputy Magistrate on General Duties has first-class powers, and is in charge of another division which consists of Perambalúr and Udaiyárpálayam Taluqs. The Magistrates under him are in Perambalúr the Taluq Magistrate, who has second-class powers and jurisdiction throughout the taluq, and the Taluq Sheristadar and Third-class Magistrate, and in Udaiyárpálayam the Taluq Magistrate, who has second-class powers and jurisdiction over the whole taluq, the Taluq Sheristadar and Third-class Magistrate, and the Kílapaluvúr Sub-Magistrate who has second-class powers and jurisdiction in 191 villages. Appeals from these Magistrates lie to the Deputy Magistrate. When there is an Assistant Magistrate in the district who has passed the lower standard he is, as a rule, invested with first-class powers. At present there is an unpassed Assistant who has third-class powers and a Temporary Deputy Magistrate with first-class powers who has no direct charge, but tries cases referred to him by the District Magistrate. Trichinopoly Cantonment is in the charge of a First-class Magistrate styled the Cantonment Magistrate who, within the limits of his jurisdiction, has the powers of a Magistrate in charge of a division of a district. The Cantonment Magistrate is subordinate to the District Magistrate and has no appellate jurisdiction. Trichinopoly is a second-class Cantonment Magistracy. There are altogether twenty-one paid Magistrates in the district, of whom 5 have first-class powers, 7 second-class, and 9 third-class.

Honorary Magistrates.

There are also unpaid Honorary Magistrates appointed under Section 9 of the Civil Procedure Code for Trichinopoly town. These Magistrates sit twice a week as a bench, with the Town Sub-Magistrate as their President, for the summary trial of offences coming within Sections 277, 278, 279, 285, 286, 289, 290, 292, 293, and 294 of the Penal Code, and offences against the Municipal Act and the conservancy clauses of the Police Act punishable with fine or with imprisonment for a term not exceeding one month. The following statement shows the number of cases tried by the bench of Honorary Magistrates in Trichinopoly in 1875, 1876, and 1877 :—

—	Filed.		Number of Persons.					Disposed of.	
	Cases.	Persons.	Dismissed.	Discharged.	Convicted.	Acquitted.	Otherwise disposed of.	Cases.	Persons.
1875	491	518	4	..	465	37	..	479	506
1876	1,279	1,757	39	..	1,588	140	..	1,260	1,727
1877	1,598	2,584	106	..	2,316	88	..	1,538	2,510

Justices of the Peace.

The undermentioned officers in the district have been appointed Justices of the Peace by Government under Act II of 1869 :—

The District Magistrate, the
Head Assistant Magistrate, and
The Cantonment Magistrate.

The following statement shows the cases tried by the Justices of Peace in the district in 1875, 1876, and 1877 :—

Magistrates.	1875.					1876.					1877.				
	Cases.	Persons.	Committed.	Convicted.	Discharged.	Cases.	Persons.	Committed.	Convicted.	Discharged.	Cases.	Persons.	Committed.	Convicted.	Discharged.
District Magistrate..	..	..	..	..	..	..	..	..	..	..	..	..	..	..	..
Head Assistant do...	..	..	..	..	..	1	1	..	..	1	..	..	..	..	..
Cantonment do. ..	3	3	..	3	..	2	2	..	1	1	3	3	..	3	..

Village Magistrates.

The head of every village is the Village Magistrate, and as such is empowered by Regulation XI of 1816 to take cognizance of petty offences of assault and abusive language, and to confine the offenders in the village choultry for not more than twelve hours, or, if they are of the lower castes, to put them in the stocks for not more than six hours. Regulation IV of 1821 extends the above provisions to the punishment of petty thefts not attended with aggravating circumstances, where the value of the property stolen does not exceed 1 Rupee.

CHAP. XIX. CIVIL AND CRIMINAL JUSTICE.

The following statement shows the number of cases tried under these Regulations for 3 years:—

Years.	Number of Village Magistrates.	Number who exercised their powers.	Number of Cases tried.
1874	1,241	573	774
1875	1,241	419	487
1876	1,241	401	446

Statistics.

The following statement shows the result of appeals in the criminal cases in the district for 3 years:—

Courts.	Number of Persons.										Pending.	
	Appeals remaining on the 1st January.	Filed in the Year.	Total for Disposal.	Appeals rejected.	After perusal of Records. Sentence confirmed.	After perusal of Records. Sentence modified.	After perusal of Records. Sentence reversed.	Otherwise disposed of by Transfer, Death, &c.	Total of Columns 5 to 9.	Further Enquiry or Evidence ordered.	Cases.	Persons.
1	2	3	4	5	6	7	8	9	10	11	12	13
1874.												
Session Court	2	77	79	27	40	..	11	..	78	..	1	1
District Magistrate	6	218	224	3	117	..	86	18	224	..	..	..
Head Assistant Magistrate ..	12	108	120	..	81	4	33	..	118	2	1	2
Assistant Magistrate	..	..	..	..	..	..	..	..	..	..	..	..
Deputy Magistrate	..	8	8	..	6	..	..	..	6	..	2	2
1875.												
Session Court	1	46	47	24	12	..	9	..	45	..	2	2
District Magistrate	..	120	120	14	35	23	18	12	102	3	7	18
Head Assistant Magistrate ..	2	93	95	8	23	6	16	..	53	3	9	42
Assistant Magistrate	2	47	49	23	20	..	..	6	48	..	..	..
Deputy Magistrate	17	66	83	35	19	2	24	2	82	..	1	1
1876.												
Session Court	2	44	46	36	7	1	1	1	46	..	..	..
District Magistrate	18	161	179	10	118	9	16	7	160	6	5	19
Head Assistant Magistrate ..	42	112	154	..	91	..	57	..	148	9	2	6
Assistant Magistrate	..	..	..	..	..	..	..	..	..	..	..	..
Deputy Magistrate	1	106	107	31	22	14	40	..	167	..	..	..

The following statements show the operations of the Criminal Courts in the district for 3 years:—

1874.

1	2		3		4		5	6	7	8	9	10		11	
	Preliminary Enquiries.														
Courts.	Pending on the 1st January 1874.		Received during the Year.		Total pending and received.		Number of Persons.					Total disposed of.		Pending.	
	Cases.	Persons.	Cases.	Persons.	Cases.	Persons.	In Cases referred to other Magistrates.	In complaints dismissed under Sec. 147, C.P.C.	Discharged under Sec. 195, C.P.C.	Committed for Trial.	Otherwise disposed of by Death, &c.	Cases.	Persons.	Cases.	Persons.
Session Judge	..	..	..	..	..	..	..	..	..	..	..	..	..	..	..
District Magistrate	..	..	1	3	1	3	..	3	..	..	..	1	3	..	..
Head Assistant Magistrate	1	2	10	27	11	29	13	9	4	3	..	11	29	..	..
Assistant Magistrate	..	..	5	11	5	11	7	..	..	2	2	5	11	..	..
Deputy Magistrate	..	..	1	5	1	5	5	..	..	..	..	1	5	..	..
Assistant Magistrate	..	..	3	13	3	13	..	1	..	10	2	3	13	..	..
Cantonment Magistrate	..	..	3	3	3	3	..	1	..	2	..	3	3	..	..
Trichinopoly Taluq Magistrate	..	..	11	20	11	20	..	3	8	6	..	10	17	1	3
Trichinopoly Shtdr. & 3rd-Cl. Magt. ..	..	..	..	..	..	..	..	..	..	..	..	..	..	..	..
Trichinopoly Town Sub-Magistrate ..	..	..	6	18	6	18	..	2	4	7	..	5	13	1	5
Lálgudi Sub-Magistrate	..	..	13	25	13	25	..	..	13	5	..	11	18	2	7
Musiri Taluq Magistrate	..	..	1	1	1	1	..	..	..	1	..	1	1	..	..
Musiri Shtdr. & 3rd-Cl. Magt.	..	..	..	..	..	..	..	..	..	..	..	..	..	..	..
Turaiyúr Sub-Magistrate	..	..	2	14	2	14	..	..	..	7	7	2	14	..	..
Kulittalai Taluq Magistrate	..	..	7	31	7	31	..	..	8	21	2	7	31	..	..
Kulittalai Shtdr. & 3rd-Cl. Magt.	..	..	..	..	..	..	..	..	..	..	..	..	..	..	..
Manapparai Sub-Magistrate	..	..	4	6	4	6	..	1	..	5	..	4	6	..	..
Perambalúr Taluq Magistrate	..	..	24	35	24	35	..	3	9	15	8	24	35	..	..
Perambalúr Shtdr. & 3rd-Cl. Magt. ..	..	..	4	7	4	7	..	..	..	7	..	4	7	..	..
Udaiyárpálayam Taluq Magistrate ..	..	..	6	21	6	21	..	2	6	13	..	6	21	..	..
Udaiyárpálayam Shtdr. & 3rd-Cl. Magt. ..	..	..	3	9	3	9	..	..	3	6	..	3	9	..	..
Kilapaluvúr Sub-Magistrate	..	..	1	1	1	1	..	..	1	..	..	1	1	..	..
Total ..	1	2	105	250	106	252	25	25	52	110	21	102	237	4	15

1874—(*Continued*).

Courts.	12		13		14		15	16	17	18	19	20	21		22	
	Trials.															
	Pending on the 1st January 1874.		Received during the Year.		Total pending and received.		Number of Persons.						Total disposed of.		Pending.	
	Cases.	Persons.	Cases.	Persons.	Cases.	Persons.	In complaints dismissed under Secs. 147, 205, 208, C.P.C.	Discharged under Sec. 215, C.P.C.	Convicted.	Acquitted.	Otherwise disposed of by death, &c.	Referred to other Magistrates.	Cases.	Persons.	Cases.	Persons.
Session Judge	1	4	50	125	51	129	..	..	52	75	..	2	51	129	..	..
District Magistrate	..	..	141	531	141	531	241	16	59	6	2	207	141	531	..	..
Head Assistant Magistrate	8	20	381	1,599	389	1,619	212	30	84	14	..	1,276	388	1,616	1	3
Assistant Magistrate	3	12	239	624	242	636	61	38	56	35	27	404	236	621	6	15
Deputy Magistrate	2	2	109	296	111	298	23	42	76	48	37	72	111	298	..	..
Assistant Magistrate	1	16	84	298	85	314	47	18	52	95	61	..	75	273	10	41
Cantonment Magistrate	2	2	443	565	445	567	135	10	350	29	43	..	445	567	..	..
Trichinopoly Taluq Magistrate	7	7	404	1,110	411	1,117	194	505	161	197	36	..	392	1,093	19	24
Trichinopoly Shtdr. & 3rd-Cl. Magt.	..	..	402	1,204	402	1,204	40	589	134	383	51	..	395	1,197	7	7
Trichinopoly Town Sub-Magistrate	5	9	967	2,263	972	2,272	350	126	210	1,384	172	..	955	1,242	17	30
Lálgudi Sub-Magistrate	..	..	379	1,310	379	1,310	694	69	369	151	..	..	373	1,285	6	25
Musiri Taluq Magistrate	..	..	142	393	142	393	111	31	63	24	155	..	136	384	6	9
Musiri Shtdr. & 3rd-Cl. Magt.	..	..	96	296	96	296	69	55	87	37	48	..	96	296	..	..
Turaiyúr Sub-Magistrate	..	..	186	566	186	566	56	63	255	46	146	..	186	566	..	..
Kulittalai Taluq Magistrate	..	..	219	679	219	679	89	234	144	70	130	3	215	670	4	9
Kulittalai Shtdr. & 3rd-Cl. Magt.	..	..	135	372	135	372	13	57	175	75	52	..	135	372	..	..
Manapparai Sub-Magistrate	1	1	179	590	180	591	67	48	225	59	187	..	177	586	3	5
Perambalúr Taluq Magistrate	3	67	237	643	240	710	117	40	252	49	252	..	240	710	..	..
Perambalúr Shtdr. & 3rd-Cl. Magt.	..	..	58	208	58	208	15	8	60	59	68	..	58	208	..	..
Udaiyárpálayam Taluq Magistrate	5	32	240	923	245	956	365	33	98	68	333	15	236	912	9	44
Udaiyárpálayam Shtdr. & 3rd-Cl. Magt.	..	..	77	250	77	250	33	33	50	42	16	76	77	250	..	..
Kílapaluvúr Sub-Magistrate	2	2	214	604	216	606	138	14	107	30	296	4	214	589	2	17
Total ..	40	174	5,382	15,449	5,422	15,623	3,072	2,059	3,110	2,976	2,092	1,860	5,422	14,395	90	229

1875.

1	2		3		4		5	6	7	8	9	10		11	
	Preliminary Enquiries.														
Courts.	Pending on 1st January 1875.		Received during the Year.		Total pending and received.		Number of Persons.					Total disposed of.		Pending.	
	Cases.	Persons.	Cases.	Persons.	Cases.	Persons.	In Cases referred to other Magistrates.	In Complaints dismissed under Sec. 147, C.P.C.	Discharged under Sec. 195, C.P.C.	Committed for Trial.	Otherwise disposed of by Death, &c.	Cases.	Persons.	Cases.	Persons.
Session Judge	..	..	..	..	..	..	..	..	..	..	..	..	..	..	..
District Magistrate	..	..	3	5	3	5	2	1	..	2	..	3	5	..	..
Head Assistant Magistrate	..	..	6	14	6	14	2	..	9	3	..	6	14	..	..
Assistant Magistrate	..	..	5	9	5	9	5	..	4	..	..	5	9	..	..
Deputy Magistrate	..	..	2	13	2	13	13	..	..	..	..	2	13	..	..
Cantonment Magistrate	..	..	1	1	1	1	..	..	..	1	..	1	1	..	..
Trichinopoly Taluq Magistrate	1	3	11	30	12	33	1	1	3	27	..	11	32	1	1
Trichinopoly Shtdr. & 3rd-Cl. Magt. ..	..	..	3	3	3	3	..	1	..	2	..	3	3	..	..
Town Sub-Magistrate	1	5	11	19	12	24	..	1	10	10	..	9	21	3	3
Lálgudi Sub-Magistrate	2	7	3	6	5	13	..	6	6	1	..	5	13	..	..
Musiri Taluq Magistrate	..	..	6	7	6	7	..	2	..	3	1	5	6	1	1
Musiri Shtdr. & 3rd-Cl. Magt.	..	..	1	1	1	1	..	..	..	1	..	1	1	..	..
Turaiyúr Sub-Magistrate	..	..	3	3	3	3	..	..	..	3	..	3	3	..	..
Kulittalai Taluq Magistrate	..	..	14	29	14	29	3	4	6	12	2	12	27	2	2
Kulittalai Shtdr. & 3rd-Cl. Magt.	..	..	4	5	4	5	..	1	1	1	2	4	5	..	..
Manapparai Sub-Magistrate	..	..	4	7	4	7	..	3	..	3	..	3	6	1	1
Perambalúr Taluq Magistrate	..	..	11	36	11	36	..	1	7	14	14	11	36	..	..
Perambalúr Shtdr. & 3rd-Cl. Magt.	..	..	..	..	..	..	..	..	..	..	..	..	..	..	..
Udaiyárpálayam Taluq Magistrate	..	..	11	47	11	47	..	34	6	7	..	11	47	..	..
Udaiyárpálayam Shtdr. & 3rd-Cl. Magt. ..	..	..	5	21	5	21	..	16	5	..	..	5	21	..	..
Kílapaluvúr Sub-Magistrate	..	..	2	6	2	6	..	..	1	5	..	2	6	..	..
Total ..	4	15	106	262	110	277	26	71	58	95	19	102	269	8	8

1875—(*Continued*).

Courts.	12		13		14		15	16	17	18	19	20	21		22	
	Trials.															
	Pending on the 1st January 1875.		Received during the Year.		Total pending and received.		Number of Persons.						Total disposed of.		Pending.	
	Cases.	Persons.	Cases.	Persons.	Cases.	Persons.	In Cases referred to other Magistrates.	In Complaints dismissed under Secs. 205, 147, & 208, C.P.C.	Discharged under Sec. 215, C.P.C.	Convicted.	Acquitted.	Otherwise disposed of.	Cases.	Persons.	Cases.	Persons.
Session Judge	..	..	52	102	52	102	..	..	..	36	38	1	43	75	9	27
District Magistrate	..	..	70	179	70	179	110	39	..	15	2	8	69	175	1	4
Head Assistant Magistrate	1	3	65	164	66	167	39	61	16	28	18	..	65	162	1	5
Assistant Magistrate	10	41	167	585	177	626	309	72	34	75	107	13	171	610	6	16
Deputy Magistrate	..	..	123	463	123	463	396	43	1	20	1	1	122	462	1	1
Cantonment Magistrate	..	..	477	640	477	640	..	143	29	337	38	93	477	640	..	..
Trichinopoly Taluq Magistrate	19	24	293	811	312	835	139	356	120	158	56	..	309	829	3	6
Trichinopoly Shtdr. & 3rd-Cl. Magt. ..	7	7	253	691	260	698	1	377	191	125	1	..	258	695	2	3
Town Sub-Magistrate	17	30	1,725	2,819	1,742	2,849	..	330	196	1,406	371	484	1,707	2,787	35	62
Lálgudi Sub-Magistrate	6	25	356	1,249	362	1,274	..	435	186	391	257	..	360	1,270	2	4
Musiri Taluq Magistrate	6	9	198	558	204	567	..	124	84	112	20	218	202	558	2	9
Musiri Shtdr. & 3rd-Cl. Magt.	..	..	93	308	93	308	1	27	28	75	34	143	93	308	..	..
Turaiyúr Sub-Magistrate	..	..	271	765	271	765	..	68	44	256	100	294	270	762	1	3
Kulittalai Taluq Magistrate	4	9	127	389	131	398	2	70	90	132	76	16	124	386	7	12
Kulittalai Shtdr. & 3rd-Cl. Magt.	..	..	126	372	126	372	11	22	68	224	34	..	124	359	2	13
Manapparai Sub-Magistrate	3	5	123	334	126	339	4	26	13	110	47	130	123	330	3	9
Perambalúr Taluq Magistrate	..	..	292	781	292	781	..	180	28	253	18	291	288	768	4	13
Perambalúr Shtdr. & 3rd-Cl. Magt.	..	..	83	222	83	222	..	17	2	98	50	55	83	222	..	..
Udaiyárpálayam Taluq Magistrate ..	9	44	364	1,126	373	1,170	5	435	155	241	41	292	372	1,169	1	1
Udaiyárpálayam Shtdr. & 3rd-Cl. Magt. ..	..	..	101	461	101	461	..	80	22	147	16	191	100	456	1	5
Kílapaluvúr Sub-Magistrate ..	2	17	301	919	303	936	13	175	35	185	68	452	300	928	3	8
Total ..	89	213	5,255	5,939	5,744	14,152	1,030	3,080	1,342	4,424	1,393	2,682	5,660	13,951	84	201

1876.

1	2		3		4		5	6	7	8	9	10		11	
	Preliminary Enquiries.														
Courts.	Pending on the 1st January 1876.		Received during the Year.		Total pending and received.		Number of Persons.					Total disposed of.		Pending.	
	Cases.	Persons.	Cases.	Persons.	Cases.	Persons.	In Cases referred to other Magistrates.	In Complaints dismissed under Sec. 147, C.P.C.	Discharged under Sec. 195, C.P.C.	Committed for Trial.	Otherwise disposed of by Death, &c.	Cases.	Persons.	Cases.	Persons.
Session Judge	..	..	..	..	..	..	..	..	..	..	..	..	..	..	..
District Magistrate	..	..	6	11	6	11	10	..	..	..	1	6	11	..	..
Head Assistant Magistrate	..	..	17	69	17	69	64	..	2	3	..	17	69	..	..
Assistant Magistrate	..	..	1	1	1	1	..	..	..	1	..	1	1	..	..
Deputy Magistrate	..	..	5	6	5	6	1	1	..	4	..	5	6	..	..
Cantonment Magistrate	..	..	3	4	3	4	..	..	3	1	..	3	4	..	..
Trichinopoly Taluq Magistrate	1	1	4	9	5	10	1	..	3	5	1	5	10	..	..
Trichinopoly Shtdr. & 3rd-Cl. Magt. ..	..	..	4	7	4	7	..	..	1	6	..	4	7	..	..
Trichinopoly Town Sub-Magistrate ..	11	13	26	53	37	66	..	..	26	23	..	24	49	13	17
Lálgudi Sub-Magistrate	7	19	18	62	25	81	..	9	31	8	2	17	50	8	31
Musiri Taluq Magistrate	1	1	15	29	16	30	..	3	10	17	..	16	30	..	..
Musiri Shtdr. & 3rd-Cl. Magt.	..	..	1	10	1	10	..	10	..	..	..	1	10	..	..
Turaiyúr Sub-Magistrate	..	..	10	19	10	19	..	..	13	6	..	10	19	..	..
Kulittalai Taluq Magistrate	2	2	2	6	4	8	..	..	6	1	1	4	8	..	..
Kulittalai Shtdr. & 3rd-Cl. Magt.	..	..	8	31	8	31	..	1	12	16	2	8	31	..	..
Manapparai Sub-Magistrate	1	1	11	25	12	26	..	1	17	5	..	12	26	..	..
Perambalúr Taluq Magistrate	..	..	6	8	6	8	..	1	5	2	..	1	8	..	..
Perambalúr Shtdr. & 3rd-Cl. Magt. ..	..	..	..	..	..	..	..	..	..	..	..	..	..	..	..
Udaiyárpálayam Taluq Magistrate	..	..	13	37	13	37	3	27	9	1	..	13	37	..	..
Udaiyárpálayam Shtdr. & 3rd-Cl. Magt. ..	..	..	2	2	2	2	..	1	1	..	..	2	2	..	..
Kilapaluvúr Sub-Magistrate	..	..	3	19	3	19	..	..	3	16	..	3	19	..	..
Total ..	23	37	155	408	178	445	79	54	142	115	7	152	397	21	48

CHAP. XIX. CIVIL AND CRIMINAL JUSTICE.

1876—(*Continued*).

Courts.	12		13		14		15	16	17	18	19	20	21		22	
	Trials.															
	Pending on the 1st January 1876.		Received during the Year.		Total pending and received.		Number of Persons.						Total disposed of.		Pending.	
	Cases.	Persons.	Cases.	Persons.	Cases.	Persons.	In Cases referred to other Magistrates.	In Complaints dismissed under Secs. 147, 205, 208, C.P.C.	Discharged under Sec. 215, C.P.C.	Convicted.	Acquitted.	Otherwise disposed of.	Cases.	Persons.	Cases.	Persons.
Session Judge	9	27	52	96	61	123	..	..	..	72	44	1	57	117	4	6
District Magistrate	1	4	71	103	72	107	49	14	2	29	12	..	71	106	1	1
Head Assistant Magistrate	1	5	316	1,243	317	1,248	1,154	26	14	49	4	..	316	1,247	1	1
Assistant Magistrate	6	16	45	152	51	168	..	46	36	36	24	3	42	145	9	23
Deputy Magistrate	1	1	192	554	193	555	88	172	25	90	111	61	191	547	2	8
Cantonment Magistrate	..	..	414	541	414	541	..	155	7	326	15	38	414	541	..	..
Trichinopoly Taluq Magistrate	3	6	310	689	313	695	148	196	103	192	41	1	308	681	5	14
Trichinopoly Shtdr. & 3rd-Cl. Magt. ..	2	3	267	842	269	845	13	316	156	165	64	..	262	814	7	31
Trichinopoly Town Sub-Magistrate ..	35	62	2,090	3,496	2,125	3,558	..	397	150	2,077	489	370	2,088	3,483	37	75
Lálgudi Sub-Magistrate	2	4	487	1,813	489	1,817	..	815	228	522	203	..	474	1,768	15	49
Musiri Taluq Magistrate	2	9	270	830	272	839	..	341	117	82	39	243	266	822	6	17
Musiri Shtdr. & 3rd-Cl. Magt.	..	..	70	228	70	228	..	20	68	39	8	93	70	228	..	..
Turaiyúr Sub-Magistrate	1	3	291	824	292	827	..	168	82	156	79	340	291	825	1	2
Kulittalai Taluq Magistrate	7	12	215	572	222	584	..	70	121	211	97	60	210	559	12	25
Kulittalai Shtdr. & 3rd-Cl. Magt.	2	13	134	445	136	458	..	11	127	142	93	135	136	458	..	..
Manapparai Sub-Magistrate	3	9	254	572	257	581	2	67	93	114	102	181	250	559	7	22
Perambalúr Taluq Magistrate	4	13	241	568	245	581	5	74	94	211	34	163	245	581	..	..
Perambalúr Shtdr. & 3rd-Cl. Magt. ..	..	..	94	371	94	371	1	22	37	218	45	48	94	371	..	..
Udaiyárpálayam Taluq Magistrate ..	1	1	476	1,468	477	1,469	38	617	138	149	66	440	467	1,444	10	25
Udaiyárpálayam Shtdr. & 3rd-Cl. Magt. ..	1	5	132	491	133	469	2	64	20	128	62	219	132	495	1	1
Kílapaluvúr Sub-Magistrate	3	8	305	937	308	945	2	160	11	180	65	504	301	895	7	23
Total ..	84	201	6,726	16,808	6,810	17,009	1,502	3,751	1,629	5,188	1,697	2,900	6,685	16,686	125	323

The following statement shows the extent to which the district has contributed to the criminal work of the Presidency for a series of 5 years :—

Years.	Number of Persons convicted by the Sub-Magistrates.	Number of Persons who appealed to the District or Divisional Magistrates.	Number of Persons convicted by the Divisional and District Magistrates.	Number of Persons who appealed to the Session Court.	Number of Persons convicted by the Session Court.	Number of Persons who appealed to the High Court.
1872 ..	4,334	435	657	78	72	50
1873 ..	4,051	347	559	46	35	38
1874 ..	4,230	352	677	77	52	19
1875 ..	3,913	327	476	46	37	7
1876 ..	4,559	379	530	44	72	22

Statement No. 15, given in the appendix, shows the number of persons tried, convicted, and acquitted, and the amount of property lost and recovered in connection with criminal offences for a series of 10 years.

CHAPTER XX.

EDUCATION.

Higher Education.—Middle Education.—Lower Education.—Local Fund Schools.—Private Lower-class Schools aided under the Salary System.—Lower-class Result Schools.—Muhammadan Education.—Female Education.—Normal School.—Statement showing the number of Schools in the district, with reference to the agency by which they are managed.

CHAPTER XX. EDUCATION.

In giving an account of the system of education pursued in the Trichinopoly District, the best course seems to be to follow the classification of schools adopted by the Educational Department.

Higher education.

There is no institution in the district educating up to the B.A. standard, and but one up to the F.A. This is the S.P.G. High School in Trichinopoly. This school is one of the most important of the Aided Collegiate Schools, and one of the largest educational institutions in the Presidency. There were 664 pupils in the school on the 31st March 1874, 702 on the 31st March 1875, and 783 on the 31st March 1876. Of those receiving instruction on the latter date, 30 were in the collegiate, 186 in the higher, and 389 in the lower department. The total cost to Government on account of the school for the official year 1875-76 was as follows:—

Collegiate Department.	Higher. Department.	Middle Department.	Lower Department.	Total.
RS. A. P.	RS. A. P.	RS. A. P.	RS. A. P.	RS. A. P.
1,501 10 5	1,919 10 1	1,822 13 4	523 13 4	5,767 15 2

In the years 1872—76 (both inclusive) 11 pupils from the school passed the F.A. examination at the Madras University, while 96 matriculated during the same period. The strength of the school lies in its middle department, which numbers more pupils than the corresponding departments in the Combaconum College and the Tanjore High School added together. Till a few years ago this school was in great want of proper school-house accommodation. In 1875, however, a suitable building was erected for this purpose on one side of the *teppakulam* in the fort, the cost of which was defrayed by subscriptions given by the leading Native gentlemen in the district. **CHAPTER XX. EDUCATION.**

The only taluq school in the district is that at Srírangam. The following table gives some particulars regarding this school :— **Middle education.**

Number of Teachers.	Highest Class.	No. of Pupils on the 31st March.				
		1872.	1873.	1874.	1875.	1876.
6	V.	137	141	150	179	156

The cost to Government each year per pupil during the same period was 3 Annas 10 Pies. This school is doing very well, but suffers very much from want of a good school-house. It is at present held in a mantapam, which is in every respect most unsuitable for the purposes to which it is applied.

The middle-class schools in the district, aided under the Salary Grant System, may be divided into those under Mission management and those not so situated. Of the former description there is only one at present, the Wesleyan Mission School in Trichinopoly town. The following statement gives certain information regarding this school :—

Number of Teachers.	Highest Class.	No. of Pupils on the 31st March.		
		1874.	1875.	1876.
6	IV.	135	144	148

The cost to Government on account of the middle department of this school in 1875-76 was Rupees 972, and on account of the lower department Rupees 300.

The following table gives information regarding the three Middle-class Salary Grant Schools in the district not under Mission management :—

Name of Schools.	Number of Teachers.	Highest Class.	No. of Pupils on the 31st March.		
			1874.	1875.	1876.
Kulittalai	4	IV.	72	95	130
Turaiyúr	3	IV.	49	32	33
Lálgudi	3	IV.	64	32	57

The cost of these schools for 1875-76 was as follows : Kulittalai, Rupees 1,451 ; Turaiyúr, Rupees 251 ; and Lálgudi, Rupees 286.

CHAPTER XX. EDUCATION.

The Kulittalai Grant-in-aid School is doing very well indeed, and is thoroughly appreciated by the people of the place. In 1876 the leading inhabitants of the village petitioned that the school should be converted into a Taluq School, but this request, although supported by the Director of Public Instruction, was negatived by Government. In 1870 there were 32 Middle-class Salary Grant-in-aid Schools in the district. The number, however, of the pupils attending these schools gradually fell off, and 29 of them were consequently closed between 1870 and 1875.

Lower education.

The following statement gives some statistics regarding the system of lower education prevailing in the district for the years 1874-75 and 1875-76:—

—	On 31st March 1875.								On 31st March 1876.							
	Local Fund or Municipal Schools.	Scholars.	Result System Schools.	Scholars.	Unaided Schools.	Unaided Scholars.	Total. Schools.	Total. Scholars.	Local Fund or Municipal Schools.	Scholars.	Result System Schools.	Scholars.	Unaided Schools.	Unaided Scholars.	Total. Schools.	Total. Scholars.
Trichinopoly Local Fund Circle ...	...	...	111	2,779	85	1,499	196	4,278	21	852	54	1,229	106	2,363	181	4,4441
Trichinopoly Municipality ...	..	...	9	368	8	301	17	669	...	...	12	477	10	294	22	77
Srírangam Municipality	...	...	5	237	2	45	7	282	...	...	5	207	2	67	7	274

A brief account of these schools will now be given.

Local Fund Schools.

No schools under the Madras Education Act, Act VI of 1863, were ever established in this district. On the introduction of Act IV of 1871, the Madras Local Funds Act, a scheme of school unions for the Trichinopoly Circle was drawn up and submitted to the Board of Revenue for consideration. Before, however, orders could be passed on it, a Government order issued on the 28th March 1873, abolished the house-tax which it had been intended to levy for the support of union schools, and with it the proposed scheme fell to the ground. After considerable discussion, it was eventually decided to establish Local Fund Schools on what is known as the Combined System, under which the remuneration of the teachers consists partly of fixed salaries and partly of result grants earned under the ordinary rules. The scheme proposed by the Local Fund Board was sanctioned in G.O., No. 858, of the 17th April 1875, and 23 schools were opened on this plan in the official year 1875-1876.

On the 31st March 1877 there were 33 Local Fund Schools on the Combined System in the circle. The following table gives certain information regarding these schools:—

Taluqs.		Schools.	Number of Pupils on 31st March 1877.	Number of Teachers.	Cost to Local Funds for 1876-77.
					RS.
Trichinopoly.	1	Ángarai	29	1	227
	2	Lálgudi	51	2	235
	3	Manachanallúr	30	1	161
	4	Váytalai Gúdalúr	56	1	118
	5	Tirupláturai	10	1	108
	6	Váládi	27	1	269
	7	Pichándárkóvil	26	1	72
Kulittalai.	8	Nangapuram	16	1	141
	9	Kistnaráyapuram	43	1	157
	10	Lálápéttai	21	1	106
	11	Kattalai	36	2	291
	12	Mahádánapuram	22	1	93
	13	Kulittalai	64	2	200
Musiri.	14	Musiri	65	2	238
	15	Tottiyam	42	1	275
	16	Káttuputtúr	64	2	240
	17	Turaiyúr	46	2	247
	18	Settikulam	15	1	98
	19	Uppilyapuram	30	1	71
	20	Eragudi	29	1	99
Perumbalúr.	21	Perambalúr	49	2	268
	22	Kurumbalúr	63	2	288
	23	Esanai	45	2	288
	24	Arumbavúr	32	1	61
	25	Tondamándurai	34	1	64
Udaiyárpálayam.	26	Ariyalúr	22	1	155
	27	Udaiyárpálayam	81	2	285
	28	Jeyamkondasólapuram	41	1	158
	29	Kílapaluvúr	54	2	238
	30	Ulaiyúr	32	1	53
	31	Vánatiriyánpatnam	23	1	48
	32	Tirumánúr	50	1	54
	33	Karuppúr	30	1	42

The fixed salary of the masters in these schools is Rupees 6 where there are less than 30 pupils, and Rupees 7 if the number exceeds that figure. An assistant master on Rupees 5 is appointed whenever a school has more than 30 boys. The Result Grants earned by the school are divided between the head and assistant masters in proportion to their salaries. These grants are paid to schools on the Combined System at only half the maximum rate given to ordinary Result Grant schools. The fees charged are 2 Annas per mensem for boys in the lowest class, reading for the First Standard, 3 Annas for the second, and 4 Annas when a class is formed for the Third Standard. Contingent expenses are charged against fees, and the balance distributed among the masters in the same proportion as the Result Grants. Whenever there is a Local Fund School in a village, Results Grants are not paid to any other school in the same village; but if the accommodation in a Local Fund School is found

CHAPTER XX. EDUCATION.

insufficient, additional Local Fund Schools may be opened in the place.

Private Lower-class Schools aided under the Salary System.

There are three Mission schools in the district that come under this head. These are the S.P.G. Schools in Uraiyúr, Tennúr and the Fort Trichinopoly, which serve as feeders to the S.P.G. High School of which mention has already been made. The following statement gives some particulars regarding these schools:—

Schools.	No. of Pupils on 31st March		Highest Class on 31st March		Cost to Trichinopoly Municipality for 1875-76.
	1875.	1876.	1875.	1876.	RS.
S.P.G. School, Uraiyúr	57	40	IV.	II.	150
Do. Tennúr	32	27	III.	II.	66
Do. Fort Trichinopoly.	50	40	II.	II.	66

There is only one school of the description under consideration in the district that is not under Mission management. This is the Hindu Aided School, Trichinopoly Fort. There were 63 boys in this school on the 31st March 1876, and the amount of the grant paid to it for the year by the Trichinopoly Municipality was Rupees 147. This school is well officered and systematically conducted. It suffers, however, from bad school-house accommodation.

Lower-class Result Schools.

The annexed statement gives the number of lower-class schools and the scholars taught in them in the Trichinopoly Local Fund Circle and the two Municipalities for the year 1875-76. Mission schools are distinguished from those under other management, and aided from unaided institutions:—

—	Mission Schools.							Schools other than Mission.							Total.						
	Aided.		Un-aided.		Total.		Amount of Grant paid.	Aided.		Un-aided.		Total.		Amount of Grant paid.	Aided.		Unaided.		Total.		Amount of Grant paid.
	Schools.	Scholars.	Schools.	Scholars.	Schools.	Scholars.	RS.	Schools.	Scholars.	Schools.	Scholars.	Schools.	Scholars.	RS. A. P.	Schools.	Scholars.	Schools.	Scholars.	Schools.	Scholars.	RS. A. P.
Trichinopoly L. F. Circle.	16	349	9	187	25	536	671	38	880	97	2,176	135	3,056	1,090 0 0	54	1,229	106	2,363	160	3,592	1,767 0 0
Trichinopoly Municipality.	4	181	2	59	6	240	414	8	296	8	235	16	531	418 8 0	12	477	10	294	22	771	832 8 0
Srírangam Municipality.	...	...	...	...	...	...	...	5	207	2	67	7	274	336 0 0	5	207	2	67	7	274	336 0 0

Muhammadan education.

There is one Government school in Trichinopoly, intended especially for Muhammadans. It was started in 1873, and is located in a room over the post office in the building attached to the main-guard gate in the fort. On the 31st March 1875 there were 73 boys in this school and 65 on the 31st March 1876. Its cost is defrayed from Provincial funds, the charge on which on account of it for 1875-76 was Rupees 454-11-6. Tamil, Hindustani and English are taught in this school which has been on the whole successful so far, and has, it is believed, had the effect of creating a desire among the Musalman population for education.

Female education.

There is only one Middle-class Girls' School in the district on the Salary Grant-in-aid System. This is the school attached to the Roman Catholic convent in the Trichinopoly cantonment. There were 73 pupils in this school on the 31st March 1876, the amount of the grant paid to it from Provincial funds being Rupees 600 per annum. There is also a Lower-class Girls' School in Srírangam, which was opened in January 1875. The number of girls in this school on the 1st of March 1876 was 50. The girls were favourably reported on by the Inspector of Schools in that year. It costs the Srírangam Municipality Rupees 207-6-7 a year. The Vice-President and other members of the Municipality take considerable interest in this school, and there is every reason to expect that it will prove a success. There is also a girls' school in Trichinopoly fort known as Lady Hobart's Girls' School. It was opened in 1874, and is held in a portion of the old Nawáb's palace. The number of girls receiving instruction in it on the 31st March 1876 was 59, and the cost to Provincial funds on account of it, for a year, is Rupees 132. In addition to these there is a girls' school at Irungalúr under the management of the S.P.G. Missionary there, Mr. Kohloff, in which there were 63 pupils in 1876. There are also girls' schools in Porattagudi and Viragalúr under Roman Catholic management, the grants to which are paid out of Provincial funds.

Normal School.

Trichinopoly is one of the districts comprised in the range of the Inspector of the Fourth Division. The Normal School, however, in Trichinopoly, is under the supervision of the Inspector of the Third Division. There were in this school on the 31st March 1876 29 normal and 129 practising pupils. The cost of this school is defrayed altogether from Local Funds. It is held in the audience hall in the Nawáb's palace, which was repaired and rendered suitable for this purpose in 1878.

Statement No. 19, given in the appendix, shows the progress of education in the district for a period of ten years, and the annexed statement gives the number of schools according to the agency by which they are managed, and the standard of the instruction imparted in them for the year 1875-76 :—

Statement showing the Number of Schools in the District in 1875-76, with reference to the Agency by which they are managed.

Classification of Schools.	Government Colleges and Schools.		Schools under Municipalities and Local Fund Boards, and Committees under the control of Government.		Private Colleges and Schools — Receiving Grants-in-Aid — From Provincial Funds.		From Local Funds.		From Municipal Funds.		From Provincial Funds.		From Local Funds.		From Municipal Funds.			Schools under Inspection but not receiving Aid.							
	Number of Institutions.	Pupils.	Schools under Municipalities and Local Fund Boards, and Committees under the control of Government.	Pupils.	Established by Missionary Societies.	Pupils.	Established by Missionary Societies.	Pupils.	Established by Missionary Societies.	Pupils.	Established by other than Missionary Societies.	Pupils.	Established by other than Missionary Societies.	Pupils.	Established by other than Missionary Societies.	Pupils.	Total Pupils.	Established by Missionary Societies.	Pupils.	Established by other than Missionary Societies.	Pupils.	Total Number of Private Colleges and Schools.	Total Pupils.	Total Colleges and Schools.	Total Pupils.
College	...	...	...	...	1	783	...	...	...	...	...	...	...	...	...	...	783	...	...	...	...	1	783		
Middle	1	156	...	...	1	148	...	...	...	...	3	220	...	...	...	...	368	...	...	...	...	4	368		
Lower	1	65	15	544	...	...	15	301	7	288	...	...	33	753	14	566	1,908	11	246	105	2,369	185	4,523	232	7,562
Normal	1	154	...	...	...	...	..	...	...	...	...	...	...	...	...	...	...	...	...	...	...	...	...		
Mixed Lower	...	...	6	308	...	...	1	48	...	...	3	109	5	127	...	...	284	...	...	...	...	9	284		
Girls' do.	...	...	1	50	5	230	...	...	...	...	1	22	...	...	...	...	252	2	75	...	...	8	327		

Statement showing the Number of Schools in the District, with reference to the Standard of the Instruction imparted in them.

Colleges.		Boys' Schools.								Mixed Schools.								Girls' Schools.								Normal Schools.			
	Number of Pupils.	Higher-class Schools.	Number of Pupils.	Middle-class Schools.	Number of Pupils.	Lower-class Schools	Number of Pupils.	Total Schools.	Total Pupils.	Higher-class Schools.	Number of Pupils.	Middle-class Schools.	Number of Pupils.	Lower-class Schools.	Number of Pupils.	Total Schools.	Total Pupils.	Higher-class Schools.	Number of Pupils.	Middle-class Schools.	Number of Pupils.	Lower-class Schools.	Number of Pupils.	Total Schools.	Total Pupils.	Number of Schools.	Number of Pupils.	Total Schools.	Total Pupils.
1	783	...	...	5	524	201	5,132	207	6,439	...	...	...	...	15	592	15	592*	...	...	...	...	9	377	9	377	1	154	232	7,562

* Of these 30 are girls.

CHAPTER XXI.

ANCIENT TEMPLES AND BUILDINGS.

Srírangam.—Jembukésvaram.—Buildings on the Trichinopoly Rock.—Gangaikandapuram.—Jaina Images.

Of the temples in the Trichinopoly District the most important, from every point of view, is the great pagoda in the Srírangam island, dedicated to Vishnu, to which frequent allusions are made in the historical portion of this work. An interesting account of this temple, and a criticism on its architectural merits, is given by Mr. Fergusson in his History of Indian and Eastern Architecture.

Chap. XXI. Ancient Temples, &c. Srírangam.

As prefatory to this account, Mr. Fergusson's remarks on the manner in which most Dravidian temples, and among others Srírangam, have grown up, and his explanation of the cause of their leading defects, may be inserted here. In commenting on the temple at Tiruvalúr, he remarks that "the nucleus of the building was a small village temple containing a double shrine, dedicated to Siva and his consort, standing in a cloistered court with one gópuram in front." "So far," he says, "there is nothing to distinguish it from the ordinary temples found in every village. It however at some subsequent period became sacred or rich, and a second or outer court was added with two gópuras, higher than the original one, and containing within its walls numberless little shrines and porches. Additions were again made at some subsequent date, the whole being enclosed in a court 940 feet by 701 feet, this time with five gópuras and several important shrines." He then goes on to observe that as an artistic design, nothing can be worse than the plan on which the temple has been built. "The gateways, irregularly placed in a great blank wall, lose half their dignity from their positions; and the bathos of their decreasing in size and elaboration, as they approach the sanctuary, is a mistake which nothing can redeem. We may admire beauty of detail, and be astonished at the elaboration and evidence of labour, if they are found in such a temple as this; but as an architectural design it is altogether detestable." "The temple which has been most completely marred by this false system of design is that at Srírangam, which is certainly the largest, and, if its principle of design could be reversed, would be one of the finest temples in the south of India. Here the central enclosuro is quite as small and as insignificant as that at Tiruvalúr, and except that its dome is gilt, has nothing to distinguish it from an ordinary village temple. The next enclosure, however, is more magnificent. It encloses the hall of 1,000 columns, which measures some 450 feet by 130 feet. The number of columns is, I believe, sixteen in front by sixty in depth, or 960 altogether; but I do not feel sure there is not some mistake in my observations, and that the odd 40 are to be found somewhere. They consequently are not spaced more than ten feet apart from centre to centre; and as at one end the hall is hardly over 10 feet high, and in the loftiest place only 15 or 16 feet, and the pillars spaced nearly evenly over the floor, it will be easily understood how little effect such a building really produces. They are, however, each of a single block of granite, and all carved more or less elaborately. A much finer portico stretches across this court from gópura to gópura; the pillars in it are much more widely spaced, and the central aisle is double that of those on the sides, and crosses the portico in the centre, making a transept; its height, too, is double that of the side aisles. It is a pleasing and graceful architectural design; the other is only an evidence of misapplied labour. The next four enclosures have nothing very remarkable in them, being generally occupied by the Bráhmans and persons connected with the temple. Each, however, has, or was intended to have, four gópuras, one on each face, and some of these are of very considerable magnificence. The outer enclosure is, practically, a bazaar filled with shops, where pilgrims are lodged and fed and fleeced. The wall that encloses it measures 2,475 feet by 2,880 feet, and, had its gópuras been finished, they would have surpassed all others in the south to the same extent as these dimensions exceed those of any other known temple. The northern gópura, leading to the river and Trichinopoly, measures 130 feet in width by 100 feet in depth; the opening through it measures 21 feet 6 inches, and twice that in height. The four jambs or gate-posts are each of a single slab of granite, more than 40 feet in height, and the roofing slabs throughout measure from 23 feet to 24 feet.[1] Had the ordinary brick pyramid of the usual proportion been added to this, the whole would have risen to a height of nearly 300 feet. Even as it is, it is one of the most imposing masses in Southern India, and probably—perhaps, because it never was quite finished—it is in severe and good taste throughout.

Looked at from a distance, or in any direction where the whole can be grasped at once, these fourteen or fifteen great gate-towers

(1) These measurements are not perfectly accurate. The outer wall surrounding the temple measures 3,072 feet by 2,521. The unfinished gópura mentioned by Mr. Fergusson, is the southern one and not the northern. The fine granite gate-posts in it measure 36 feet × 3 feet × 3 feet. The roofing slabs are sixteen in number, the dimensions of the largest being 33 feet × 5 feet 7 inches × 5 feet 4 inches and the smallest 31 feet × 5 feet × 5 feet 10 inches.

cannot fail to produce a certain effect, but even then it can only be by considering them as separate buildings. As parts of one whole, their arrangement is exactly that which enables them to produce the least possible effect that can be obtained either from their mass or ornament. Had the four great outer gópuras formed the four sides of a central hall, and the others gone on diminishing, in three or four directions, to the exterior, the effect of the whole would have been increased in a surpassing degree. To accomplish this, however, one other defect must have been remedied: a gateway even 150 feet wide in a wall nearly 2,000 feet in extent is a solecism nothing can redeem; but had the walls been broken in plan or star-shaped, like the plans of Chalukyan temples, light and shade would have been obtained and due proportions of parts, without any inconvenience. But if the Dravidians ever had it in them to think of such things, it was not during the 17th and 18th centuries, to which everything in this temple seems to belong."[2]

Of the justice of the foregoing criticism there can be but little doubt. Almost every European visitor to the temples is disappointed with them, and the cause appears to be that assigned by Mr. Fergusson. As one drives up to the unfinished gópura on the south side, which is the usual entrance, and then through it goes on into the first enclosure, the gópuras look fine, and the general appearance of the buildings is striking; but they lead up to nothing, and the centre of the building is mean and uninteresting. The hall of the 1,000 pillars is excessively ugly, and possessed of no artistic or architectural merits whatever. A good view of the whole building can be obtained from the top of the unfinished gópura, and a still better one from the large gópura near the hall just mentioned. The island of Srírangam is very well wooded, and cocoa trees grow close up to the outside hall of the town, and are also scattered about through it. This adds greatly to the beauty of the scene. From the large gópura, the rivers Cauvery and Coleroon can also be seen flowing round the island, but they are not visible from the unfinished gópura as the trees intercept the view.

The entire mass of buildings consists of seven enclosures, in the centre of which is the shrine of the divinity known as Ranganáda-swámi. This shrine is surrounded by a wall measuring 240 feet by 181. The second enclosure is 426 feet by 295 feet, and the third 767 feet by 503 feet. Europeans are not allowed to enter these enclosures. The fourth, in which is the 1,000 pillar mantapam, to which the idol is brought every year at the great festival known as *Vaikunta Ékádési*, measures 1,235 feet by 849 feet. Over the

(2) History of Indian and Eastern Architecture, page 346–350.

gates at the entrances to this enclosure are three gópuras, of which the eastern one is the finest in the whole temple. It is known as as the *vellai* or white gopura, and is 146 feet 6 inches in height. There are altogether fifteen gópuras in the entire group of buildings. Of these there are four in each of the three outer walls and three in the one next in order. There is at present no gate or gópura on the western side of this enclosure, but tradition states that there was a gate there formerly, but that it was blocked up because a number of the inhabitants of the portion of the town near it had entered through it and plundered the pagoda. The gate over which is the vellai gópura leads into a yard to the south of the 1,000 pillar mantapam, in which the only respectable specimens of stone-carving in the temple are to be found. Even these, however, are by no means remarkable, and are not for a moment to be compared with those in the great pagoda in Madura. During the annual festival, which has been already mentioned, this yard is covered by a pandal erected every year at a cost of about 3,000 Rupees. In booths round this pandal, which is handsomely decorated, are to be seen various figures of gods and other mythical personages. Among the groups of images, that of a very sallow-faced Collector administering justice, surrounded by peons with a prisoner in fetters in front of him, is never omitted. Running round this enclosure there is a street, in which there are ordinary dwelling-houses and shops. The fifth wall measures 1,653 feet by 1,270 feet. Outside it is a second street, and then a wall of 2,108 feet in length by 1,846 feet in breadth. This wall is surrounded by a third street, and then comes the seventh and last wall, which measures 3,072 feet by 2,521 feet. This wall is built of fine cut-stone, and is 20 feet 8 inches in height and 6 feet broad at the top.

The great annual festival at Srírangam, which has been already mentioned, takes place in December or January, and lasts for about twenty days. On the two most important days, known as *Mogini* and *Ékádési*, great crowds assemble, in some years as many as 20,000 pilgrims having been known to congregate there on these occasions.

About half a mile to the east of the famous Vishnu pagoda in the Srírangam island there is another remarkable temple dedicated to Siva, and known by the name of Jembukésvaram.[3]

Jembukésvaram.

Jembukésvaram is a compound of the words Jembu, a name of the tree known in Tamil as Nával (*Eugenia jambolana*) and Ísvara, a name of Siva. The image of the deity in this pagoda is placed under a Jembu tree, which is much venerated, and is said to be several hundred years old; and it appears not improbable that the generally received opinion that the pagoda takes its name from the tree is well founded.

(3) This temple is also known as Tiruvánaiká, or the sacred grove of the elephant.

Mr. Fergusson has given it as his opinion that this building far surpasses the larger temple in the same island in beauty as an architectural object. "The first gateway of the outer enclosure," he says, "is not large, but it leads direct to the centre of a hall containing some 400 pillars. On the right these open on a tank fed by a perpetual spring, which is one of the wonders of the place. The corresponding space on the left was intended to be occupied by the 600 columns requisite to make up the 1,000, but this never was completed. Between the two gópuras of the second enclosure is a very beautiful portico of cruciform shape leading to the door of the sanctuary, which, however, makes no show externally, and access to its interior is not vouchsafed to the profane. The age of this temple is the same as that of its great rival, except that, being all of one design, it probably was begun and completed at once, and, from the simplicity of its parts and details, may be earlier than the great buildings of Tirumalla Náyak. If we assume A.D. 1600, with a margin of ten or fifteen years either way, we shall probably not err much in its date."[4]

Mr. Fergusson is not quite correct in his enumeration of the pillars in the large hall. There are in reality 796 of them, and if to these those round the little tank that adjoins the hall are added, of which there are 142, the total reaches 938. There are five enclosures in the building. Of these the first or inner one, in which the Vimana is, measures 123 feet by 126 feet, with a wall 30 feet high round it. The second is 306 feet by 197, with a wall 35 feet high. There is a gópura 65 feet high in this enclosure, and several small mantapams. The third enclosure is 745 feet by 197, surrounded by a wall 30 feet high. There are two gópuras in it, in height 73 feet and 100 feet respectively. There is a cocoa tope in this portion of the building, in which there is a small tank and temple, to which the image from the great Vishnu pagoda in the Srírangam island is brought for one day in the year. The hall and tank described by Mr. Fergusson are in the fourth enclosure, which measures 2,436 feet by 1,493. The wall surrounding it is 35 feet in height and 6 feet in thickness. The fifth or outer enclosure contains four streets of houses. There is a small gópura over the western entrance, which, there is little doubt, is not more than from fifty to seventy years of age.

There are a number of inscriptions to be found in various parts of the building. They are, however, of no great use from a historical point of view, as they are simply accounts of grants of land made to the pagoda from time to time, and as they are, with one exception, without dates. One of them, however, is stated to have been written in the year Sáliváhana S. 1403 or A.D. 1481-82. If this inscription can be relied on, we must conclude that the

(4) History of Indian and Eastern Architecture, page 365.

Chap. XXI. Ancient Temples, &c.

temple is nearly 400 years old. It is generally believed to have been built before the large Vishnu temple near it.

The Jembukésvaram pagoda is not a rich one. It would appear that it had an endowment of 64 villages in A.D. 1750. In 1820, however, it owned only 15 villages. In 1851 an annual money allowance of Rupees 9,450 was given to the pagoda in lieu of its lands, and this sum is now paid to the trustees every year. The building is in many parts rapidly falling into ruins, and is filthy in the extreme. The funds available for its maintenance would be quite sufficient to keep it in good order if they were devoted to their proper object, but this, it is needless to state, is not the case.

Buildings on the Trichinopoly rock.

There are some buildings on and round the Trichinopoly Rock (*Tháyumánaswámi-malai*) that are deserving of notice. The ascent to the rock is by a covered stone staircase, the entrance to which is on the south side of the rock. At the head of the first flight of steps a street runs completely round the rock, by the sides of which a number of houses have been built. At the head of the last flight of steps that is covered in there is a temple to Siva. Close to this is a cave-like room, cut out of the rock, which was formerly used as an arsenal. After this point the remainder of the ascent is by means of steps cut in the rock itself, and on the summit there is a small Pillaiyár (Belly-god) pagoda. Every year in August a feast is held at this temple, for which a large number of persons assemble. A serious accident happened at this festival in 1849. Large crowds had congregated together for the festival, and had all got up to the summit of the rock in safety. "When, however, the time for descending arrived, some confusion unfortunately occurred, apparently from an eagerness on the part of the crowd to get down quickly. In the struggle some persons fell, dragging down others, which led to such a panic-struck rush, that the stone staircase became impassable from the heaps of dead and dying, while some thousands of persons still remained on the top of the rock."[5] Order was restored with difficulty by the District Magistrate, who, with the assistance of the military, stopped the panic, and brought the people down gradually. The rock was not, however, cleared till 3 o'clock in the morning, and it was calculated that at least 250 people lost their lives on the occasion.

Gangaindakapuram.

There is another very remarkable, although comparatively speaking unknown, temple in the district. This is the one close to Gangaikandapuram, a village about six miles to the east of Jeyamkondasólapuram, the head-quarters of the Tahsildar of the Udaiyárpálayam taluq. The building consists of one large enclosure measuring 584 feet by 372 feet. This enclosure was evidently once well fortified, with a strong stone wall surrounding it and

(5) Letter from District Magistrate to Government, dated 22nd August 1849.

batteries at the four corners. In 1836, however, these batteries were almost entirely destroyed and the wall removed by some Vandal members of the Public Works Department, who required the stones as materials for the dam across the river Coleroon, known as the lower anicut, which was then under construction. In the place of the old wall a low one of stone has been built round two sides of the enclosure, but the other sides have been left open. The Vimana in the centre of this courtyard is a very conspicuous building, and strikes the eye from a great distance. The pyramid surmounting it reaches a height of 174 feet. There are six gópuras or gate pyramids in different parts of the building. Of these, that over the eastern entrance to the main enclosure was evidently once a very fine one, being built all of stone, except at the very top, and not of brick, like those in Srírangam and most of the other temples in the south. It is now almost completely in ruins. There were a large number of mantapas and small buildings all round the centre edifice, but most of these have been pulled down and the materials carried off, and the rest are all more or less in ruins. All the lower part of the centre building is covered with inscriptions, but these have not as yet, it is believed, been deciphered. In a letter published in the *Pall Mall Gazette*, Dr. Caldwell has remarked that he has reason to hope that future inquiry will firmly establish a supposition formed by him, that this temple is one of the great, if not the greatest of, parent Hindu temples. He also states that he believes that the old and splendid temple of Tanjore is probably merely a model of it. There is a well in the temple enclosure, into which, according to tradition, the water of the Ganges once flowed. Hence the name of the place, Gangaikandapuram, or the place that the Ganges visited. It is not, however, quite certain that this derivation is correct. The place is sometimes called Gangaikandasólapuram, which would mean the place or city of the Chóla named Gangaikandasóla. Tradition says that the village near the temple was once the capital of the Chóla kings, and the ruins of the building said to have been their palace are still to be seen.

Jaina images.

There are a few vestiges of the Buddhists, or more probably of the Jains, in the district. The following description of one of the most remarkable of these is given in a paper by Mr. Walhouse, who acted for a time as Collector of Trichinopoly, in the *Indian Antiquary* for September 1875 :—

"About two miles south of Kulittalai, on a wide open plain, a remarkable rocky ridge crops up. It may be 200 or 300 yards long, of no great height, and strewn with enormous boulders, one of which, situated at the western end of the ridge, is the most remarkable and striking example of the kind I have ever seen, being a colossal rounded mass nearly 30 feet high, poised on its smaller end, so as to resemble a pear or top upright when viewed from the

CHAP. XXI. ANCIENT TEMPLES, &c.

east, but presenting a different aspect and shape on each quarter. Its enormous mass, and the very small stand it rests on, make it an astonishing object viewed from any side. The eastern end of the ridge terminates in a precipitous pile, crowned with another vast boulder, square and broad, also very striking, but of less interest than the other. Between the two the ridge is covered with an agglomeration of immense masses, some of colossal size, under one of which runs a long deep cave. The point of antiquarian interest in the ridge consists in a square entablature that is cut on the eastern face of the first-mentioned boulder. It is well cut, in perfect preservation, and represents Buddha seated with attendants on each side. This lonely memorial of a vanished faith is entirely ignored and unnoticed by the present population. No legend even attaches to it; the herdsmen grazing their cattle on the plain have no name for it, that I could discover at least; and it remains a mute witness of Buddhist or Jaina ascendancy. Though calling it a representation of Buddha,[6] it may also be one of Jaina Manus or Tírthankaras, which does not seem improbable, considering how long the Jaina faith prevailed in the neighbouring Pándyan kingdom of Madura."

This interesting carving is situated within the limits of Siváyam village, close to the road from Kulittalai to Manapparai. Mr. Walhouse, in the same paper, mentions as the only other relic of the Jaina faith that he could hear of in the district, a large Buddhist or Jaina image, exceeding life-size, that lies prostrate under a hedge near the Vellár river, not far from the point where it is crossed by the high road from Trichinopoly to South Arcot. The image is covered with the blown sand from the river-bed, having only the head and shoulders exposed. In addition to these, however, I have met with three other figures in different parts of the district that I have but little doubt are of Jaina origin. One of these lies half-buried in the sand close to the road from Lálgudi to Pulambádi. The other two are in Jeyamkondasólapuram, the head-quarters of the Tahsildar of Udaiyárpálayam Taluq. One is situated just outside the village on the bund of a tank, and the other is at the side of one of the lanes. Certain ceremonial observances are performed in honour of the former by the villagers, because they believe that tears drop from its eyes whenever rain is wanted. The other is entirely neglected. There are no traditions extant among the people as to the origin of these figures. They all three closely resemble the image remarked by Mr. Walhouse in the bed of the Vellár.

---

(6) It appears to represent Buddha in what Colonel Yule designates the western attitude, as a mendicant, both hands resting in the lap with the palms upwards the begging pot, as is often the case, omitted.

CHAPTER XXII.

PUDUKOTTAI.

General description of the country.—Political history up to 1803.—Grant of the fort and district of Kilánelli to the rajah.—Political history from 1807 to 1839.—Accession of the present rajah in 1839.—System of administration introduced in 1854.—Political history since 1854.—Administration.—Land tenures.—Ináms.—Revenue and Finance.—Police and Jails.—Registration.—Public works.—Education.—Vaccination.—Results of the census.—Pudukóttai town.

CHAP. XXII. PUDUKÓTTAI.

General description of the country.

The Pudukóttai territory resembles in its general features those parts of the Karnatic which depend chiefly on rain-fed tanks for their irrigation, and consists of wide plains of barren or sparsely-cultivated land, perhaps somewhat more undulating than other parts of the plains of Southern India, and more interspersed with picturesque rocky hills. In the south-west corner hills and jungles become the prevailing features of the landscape, and the country is extremely wild and rugged; but elsewhere cultivation has made successful inroads on the jungles, and rain-fed tanks, nearly 3,000 in number, some of which are of considerable magnitude, are met with. One of these tanks irrigates as much as 2,000 acres of land. The area of the country is not even approximately known with any degree of certainty. It is generally given in the reports as about 1,046 square miles; but, considering the hilly character of the south-west corner, it seems not unlikely that the area given in Pharoah's Gazetteer, 1,380 square miles (which was adopted in the Census report), is more nearly correct than the official return which does not profess to take into account the unexplored hills and jungles. The population was 316,695, according to the census of 1871, which divided over an area of 1,380 square miles gives 229·5 inhabitants per square mile. The climate is similar to that of the surrounding districts; perhaps from being more open and nearer the sea it may be a few degrees cooler than Trichinopoly. No account has ever been kept of the rainfall, but it is probably much the same as that of the neighbouring districts.[1]

Political history up to 1803.

The British Government has no treaty with Pudukóttai, the rajah of which is exempt from tribute, and has courts of justice independent of all European superintendence. Our first connection

(1) Report by Mr. Pennington when Political Agent of Pudukóttai, to the Chief Secretary to Government, dated 23rd April 1875. This report has been of the greatest assistance to me in writing this chapter, and much of the information given here is derived from it.

CHAP. XXII. PUDUKÓTTAI.

with the ancestors of the present rajah, then known as Tondiman, was formed during the wars in the Karnatic in the eighteenth century. An account of the several transactions in which Tondiman rendered us assistance during these wars has been already given in the Political history of the district, and it is, therefore, not necessary to refer to them again. It will be sufficient to mention that, during the siege of Trichinopoly by the French in 1752 and 1753, our troops in the city were more than once solely dependent on the provisions received from the Pudukóttai territory, and that, if it had not been for the ready and efficient manner in which Tondiman came to our aid and furnished us with supplies, it can scarcely be doubted that we should have been obliged to capitulate.[2] Subsequently he was very serviceable in the wars with Hyder Ali and in the operations against the rebellious usurpers of the zemindári of Shivaganga in Madura District. The rajahs of Pudukóttai are of the Kallar caste, and a report furnished to Government by Mr. Wallace, the first Collector of Trichinopoly, on the Police of that district and Tanjore shows that at the time (1805) Tondiman was an *Arasukávalgár*, and that he held his land on the same tenure as the Poligars of Ariyalúr and Udaiyárpálayam, the ancestors of the present Zemindárs of those places.[3]

Grant of the fort and district of Kılánelli to the rajah.

In 1803 Tondiman, as a reward for his services, solicited favourable consideration of a claim preferred by him to the fort and district of Kílánelli, situated in the southern portion of Tanjore. He founded his claim on a grant made of the country to him by Pradaba Sing, Rajah of Tanjore, and it appeared that engagements had been afterwards entered into by Colonel Braithwaite, General Coote, and Lord Macartney, on the faith of which he had retaken the fort from Hyder Ali. In consideration of these facts the Government of Madras ceded the fort and district of Kílánelli to Tondiman in 1803 by the following grant :—

Grant of the Fort and District of Kílánelli to Tondiman.

Captain Blackburne, the Resident at Tanjore, having communicated to me an explanation of the nature of the claims which you stated by my desire to that officer, I have, in consequence, caused particular inquiry to be made respecting the grounds of your right to the district of Kílánelli, and the result of the information which I have received, combined with the testimonies which have been brought to my attention of the fidelity and attachment to the interests of the Honorable Company's Government which have marked the

(2) ORME's *History*, Vol. I, pages 272, 273, 346, &c.

(3) Letter from the Principal Collector of Tanjore and Trichinopoly, to the Secretary to the Police Committee, Fort St. George, dated 29th September 1805. An account of the duties of *Arasukávalgárs*, and of the nature of the tenure on which they held their lands, is given in Chapter XVIII. under the head of Police.

conduct of yourself and your ancestors, have determined me to cede to you the possession of that territory, for the purpose of recompensing the services of your family, and of affording a distinguished example of the disposition of the Company's Government to reward with liberality those persons who adhere with fidelity to its interests and confidence in its protection.

I shall, in consequence, direct measures to be taken for defining the limits of the district of Kílánelli according to its extent, when formerly in your possession, in order that it may be separated from the territory of the province of Tanjore, and transferred to you.

It is my intention that you and your descendants shall hold the district in perpetual lease, subject to the tribute of an elephant to be presented annually to the British Government. But as the orders, whi about to issue on this subject, must be dependent on the order confirmation of the Honorable Court of Directors, you will not consider the arrangement to be permanent until it shall have been ratified by the Honorable Court of Directors. In the mean time, however, I shall direct that you shall be placed in possession of the afort of Kílánelli, and that you shall enjoy the revenues of the district until the final decision of the Court of Directors on your claim shall have been made known to this Government.

With respect to the honorary marks of distinction which Captain Blackburne has informed me that you are desirous of possessing, I have determined that you and your descendants shall be permitted to assume the distinguishing marks of two gold chobdar-sticks conformably to the wish which you have expressed on that subject; and as token of my approbation I have desired that two gold-sticks of that description shall be prepared and presented to you in my name.

What more?

FORT ST. GEORGE, (Signed) CLIVE.

8th July 1803.

The cession of Kílánelli was confirmed by the Court of Directors, and Tondiman was informed of the fact in the following letter :—

"You were informed by a letter from Lord Clive, dated the 8th July 1803, of the tenure on which his Lordship was pleased to place you in possession of the district of Kílánelli, as a reward for your fidelity and that of your family to the British Government.

The subject having been referred to the Honorable the Court of Directors, agreeably to the intention stated in Lord Clive's letter, I have now to acquaint you that I have received the decision of the Honorable Court on that reference, and that the grant of Kílánelli to you and your family has been confirmed by the Court of Directors, subject, however, to the express condition that the district shall not be alienated, and that it shall revert to the Company upon satisfactory proof being given that the inhabitants labor under any oppressive

CHAP. XXII. PUDUKÓTTAI.

system of management. Provided that the above conditions shall be observed you and your descendants will continue in the uninterrupted possession of the district in question.

What more ?

FORT ST. GEORGE, (Signed) BENTINCK.
7th March 1806."[4]

The grant of Kílánelli was made subject to the yearly tribute of an elephant. The tribute, however, was not insisted upon, and in 1836 was formally excused.

Political history from 1807 to 1839.

Rajah Vijaya Ragunatha Tondiman died on the 1st February 1807, leaving two sons, the elder of whom aged eleven, succeeded. During the minority of the young chief, the Resident at Tanjore exercised a strict superintendence over the affairs of the State, and procured a reformation of system in the Revenue, Police, and Judicial Departments, besides interfering to prevent particular acts of injustice. As the rajah increased in age this interference was gradually lessened till about 1817 when he was placed in charge of the whole administration.

Rajah Vijaya Ragunátha Rai Tondiman Bahadúr died in 1825, and was succeeded by his younger brother Rajah Ragunátha Tondiman, who died on the 13th July 1839. During his incumbency a question of jurisdiction having arisen between the Magistrate of Trichinopoly and Tondiman in 1834 it was decided by the Governor-General in Council that the subjects of petty states like Pudukóttai, should be always amenable to the British Courts for crimes and heinous offences committed within the British territory, but that this practice should not be reciprocal, such a distinction being a proper prerogative of the paramount power. It was at the same time ruled, however, that the delivery of heinous criminals, subjects of other states, who may have fled into the British territories, is entirely unobjectionable; and that a native subject of the British Government charged with a crime committed in another state, and apprehended before he had effected his escape into British territory, can be tried in that state. In consideration of the good character of Tondiman's Government the concession was made to him that on a special order of the Madras Government, for which application was to be made in each and every case, native British subjects charged with offences committed in Pudukóttai and apprehended in British territory might be delivered over to be dealt with by the rajah's courts. By Act I of 1849, however, this concession was cancelled, and it was rendered imperative that British subjects charged with offences in Pudukóttai and apprehended

(4) AITCHISON'S *Treaties, &c.*, Vol. 5, pages 331–333.

within British limits should be tried by British tribunals, inasmuch as the Pudukóttai territory contains no court established by the authority of the Governor-General in Council.[5]

Accession of the present Rajah in 1839.

On the decease of Rajah Ragunátha Tondiman in 1839, his son, Rajah Ramachendra Tondiman Bahadúr, the present chieftain, who was then ten years of age, succeeded. Up to 1841 the administration was conducted by the widow of the late ruler, assisted by two ministers, but in that year, in consequence of representations of injustice preferred by relations of the rajah, the Resident of Tanjore was directed to reside at Pudukóttai as much as possible during the minority of the Tondiman and to take the immediate superintendence and control of the business of the country, which was, however, continued to be conducted by the rajah's ministers.

In the same year the Residency of Tanjore was abolished, and the charge of the Political Agency for Pudukóttai was entrusted to the Collector of Madura, a post held at that time by Mr. John Blackburne. Towards the end of the year 1844 the present rajah took the management of the affairs of the state into his own hands, his ministers being instructed to report direct to him but to keep the Political Agent informed regarding all disbursements of money and cases in which public servants were dismissed. In April 1847 Mr. Parker succeeded Mr. J. Blackburne as Collector and Political Agent.

System of administration introduced in 1854.

In 1854 some of the rajah's nobles (Sérveikárs or Sirdars) stirred up a sort of rebellion in the state, and his mismanagement of the country was consequently brought so prominently to the notice of Government that they resolved to deprive him of all share in the direct administration of affairs, and established the form of government which has subsisted with slight modifications to the present time.

In submitting his final report on the disturbances, which had just been quelled by the aid of British troops, Mr. Parker, the Political Agent, whilst exonerating the rajah from any charge of oppression such as might have in some measure justified the revolt, yet gave it as his opinion that the people had just cause of complaint against him for his shameful conduct of public business, and, therefore, recommended that he should be deprived of all share in the direct management of the finances, and that the following regulations should be laid down for the government of the country :—

1st.—That the Sirkele should be made responsible to the Political Agent alone, who should be entitled to object, if he saw cause, to all appointments and dismissals.

(5) Report by Mr. Parker, Collector of Madura and Political Agent for Pudukóttai, No. 102, of the 27th May 1854.

CHAP. XXII. PUDUKÓTTAI.

2ndly.—That, subject to the directions of the Political Agent, the Sirkele should have the sole control of the finances of the State, the rajah being restricted to the stated sums allotted to his different items of expenditure.

3rdly.—That the Political Agent should be required to make to Government a full yearly report of the mode, satisfactory or otherwise, in which the affairs of the state had been carried on in the preceding year, the conduct of the rajah, the administration of justice, and the progress made in the liquidation of the rajah's debts.

4thly.—That certain jaghires belonging to relatives of the rajah should be placed under the control of the Sirkele.

5thly.—That the Political Agent should be empowered to cause the expulsion from the territory of such persons as he might know to be endeavoring to corrupt the mind of the rajah and lead him into expense.

6thly.—That the Political Agent should be authorized to forbid all sowcars and shopkeepers from lending money or delivering goods on trust to the rajah and his brother, and that the Courts of Justice should be debarred from receiving suits for debts due by these individuals, and from issuing any process for the recovery of debts against service lands of every description.[6]

Government in their Order, No. 395, dated 17th October 1854, approved of all the Agent's proposals, except the first and sixth. As to the first they observed that they were unwilling to deprive the Tondiman altogether of his authority, as that would tend to render him still more useless and to confirm his bad habits. It was, therefore, arranged that he should exercise the power of appointment and dismissal by his Sirkele, subject to the revision of the Political Agent. The system thus introduced, which is still in force, is (1) That the rajah through the Diwán or Sirkele should appoint and dismiss all officials subject to the revision of the Political Agent. (2) That subject to the Agent the rajah shall manage the finances, the rajah being restricted to his privy purse allowances. (3) That there shall be a full yearly report of the affairs of the State. (4) That the Political Agent may expel from the territory all disorderly persons and evil counsellors.

Lastly, in view to engage him in a position of dignity, the rajah was to preside over the chief court with a Judge and the Sirkele as co-adjutors, it being open to the Political Agent, on any well-founded representation of injustice being wilfully done to parties by wrong decrees, to call for explanation and, if necessary,

(6) Letter from Political Agent to the Chief Secretary to Government No. 199, dated 1st September 1854.

use his influence with the rajah, and recommend what should be done.[7]

Political history since 1854.

Since the rajah attained his majority the Government of Madras has more than once interposed to insist on his regulating his expenditure, and to remind him that the Honorable Court of Directors in 1805 made it a condition that the grant to Tondiman of the district of Kílánelli should be liable to resumption upon satisfactory proof being given that the inhabitants labored under any oppressive system of government, and to warn him that, should he continue regardlessly in his ruinous course of living, the British Government would be compelled either to withdraw the Political Agent from all connection with him, or to take the Pudukóttai country under their own control and management, and to assign the rajah a personal allowance not to be exceeded on any plea. The rajah having, in despite of all warnings, continued in a course of reckless extravagance, and contracted fresh debts as fast as with the aid of the Political Agent his old ones were cleared off, Government in 1859, as a mark of their displeasure, resolved to withhold the title of Excellency from him.[8]

In 1862 the following sanad was granted to the rajah by the Governor-General of India:—

Sanad granted to the Rajah of Pudukóttai, dated 11*th March* 1862.

"Her Majesty being desirous that the Governments of the several Princes and Chiefs, who now govern their own territories, should be perpetuated, and that the representation and dignity of their houses should be continued, in fulfilment of this desire this sanad is given to you to convey to you the assurance that, on failure of natural heirs, the British Government will recognize and confirm any adoption of a successor made by yourself or by any future chief of your State that may be in accordance with Hindu law and the customs of your race.

"Be assured that nothing shall disturb the engagement thus made to you so long as your house is loyal to the crown and faithful to the conditions of the treaties, grants, or engagements which record its obligations to the British Government.

"(Signed) CANNING."

In 1865 the Political Agency was transferred from the Collector of Madura to the Collector of Tanjore. In 1870 the title of Excellency was restored to the rajah.[9] On the 18th September

(7) Letter from Political Agent, to Chief Secretary to Government, dated 23rd April 1875, paragraphs 9 to 14, and the Government Order passed on this letter (No. 703, of the 15th October 1875, paragraph 4).

(8) G.O., No. 326 of the 25th May 1859.

(9) G.O., No. 54 of the 16th February 1870.

CHAP. XXII. PUDUKÓTTAI.

1874 the Political Agency was transferred to the Collector of Trichinopoly, and a few months afterwards Mr. Pennington, who then held that post, was directed by Government to reside for two or three months in Pudukóttai, make himself personally acquainted with the working of all the principal branches of the administration, Revenue, Police, Civil and Criminal Justice and Public Works and, after having made a complete scrutiny into the state of the country, submit a full report thereon with the recommendations that occurred to him.[10]

Mr. Pennington's report, furnished in reply to this order, gives a complete account of the system of administration in force in the State as well as suggestions for its improvements.[11] Among other recommendations he strongly urged that the rajah should be removed from all direct share in the administration of justice, but Government, in the order passed on his report, stated that they were unwilling to take any course that might palpably disgrace the rajah. As, however, it appeared probable that there would be no great difficulty in inducing him to retire voluntarily from the chief court, the Political Agent was directed to try to bring this about. Mr. Pennington had described, in detail, the several circumstances relating to the rajah's indebtedness, and the various orders that had been issued on the subject. Into this question the Government observed that it was then unnecessary to go as it had been recently definitely decided[12] that the surplus revenues belonged to the State, that they must be used in improving the territory and the administration in its various branches, that the rajah had his civil list and his privy purse, and was entitled to nothing more. The settlement that had lately been sanctioned for the payment of the rajah's debts was declared to be the last that would be allowed, and this, it was observed, was perfectly well understood by all concerned.[13] The rajah has not as yet retired from the appeal court. In 1877 the rajah adopted his eldest daughter's third son, and this adoption has been recognized and confirmed by the Viceroy.[14]

Administration.

The chief administrative officer of the State is the Sirkele who draws a salary of Rupees 350 a month. In addition to his work as Diwán and as a member of the Appellate Court this officer conducts the revenue business of the country through an officer known as the Head Karbar besides having also the direct management of the jaghires belonging to certain relations of the rajah.

(10) G.O., No. 448 of the 3rd November 1874.

(11) Letter from Political Agent to Government, dated 23rd April 1875.

(12) G.O., No. 138 of the 4th March 1875.

(13) G.O., No. 703 of the 15th October 1875, paragraphs 5 and 6.

(14) Letter from the Secretary to the Government of India read in G.O., No. 46, of the 23rd January 1878.

The State is divided into three taluqs—Kolattúr, Alangudi, and Tirumayam—for each of which there is a Tahsildar and a Deputy Tahsildar. The principal Court of Justice is the Appellate Court composed of the Rajah, the Sirkele, and the Appellate Judge, who erceives a salary of Rupees 200 a month. The other officers employed in the administration of justice are a District Magistrate and a Civil and Session Judge on Rupees 200 each, three Sub-Magistrates on Rupees 80, three on Rupees 35, a Town Sub-Magistrate on Rupees 50, and on the Civil side three Munsifs on Rupees 80, and a Small Cause Court Judge on Rupees 70. There are no Village Magistrates. The principles of law as laid down in the Courts in British India are applied in the Pudukóttai Courts, and the rulings of the Madras High Court are considered binding on them. CHAP. XXII. PUDUKÓTTAI.

Land tenures.

An account of the land tenures prevailing in Pudukóttai is given in Mr. Pennington's report, of which mention has been made already. Out of the total area of the state, which has been estimated at 669,332 acres, only 115,177 acres are fully assessed, about 300,000 are either held entirely free of assessment, or are charged with only a nominal quit-rent. 130,000 are occupied for public purposes of various kinds, and 8,224 are held in lieu of salary by various classes of persons whose sole duty appears to be to wait upon the rajah. About 116,000 acres are waste. The full assessed land is classed under the following heads :—

	ACRES.
Várapat or amáni (where the ryot pays a share of the produce)	22,742
Tírvapat (assessed with money rates) ..	53,995
Land held on conditional leases ..	38,528

In the case of the amáni lands, the Government share is fixed at 50 per cent. of the gross produce on wet lands, and $33\frac{1}{3}$ on dry land, after deducting the *swatantrams* (fees to village servants, &c.,) which are fixed at $12\frac{1}{2}$ per cent. Mr. Pennington described the evils of the amáni system as follows :—

"In the first place the ryots have no hereditary right to the enjoyment of the amáni lands they cultivate, and though, as a matter of fact, they generally are allowed to hold them year after year they have very little interest in improving them, as they only enjoy half the result of their extra labor and expense, and are, at the same time liable to be deprived of them on the ground that the lands were not properly manured, that they did not cultivate at proper times, that the crops were not watched, and (worst of all) for disobedience of the orders of the village officers. Moreover, a pernicious practice has arisen of putting up even amáni lands to competition, and if an outsider at any time offers to pay what is called *swámibógam* in

CHAP. XXII. PUDUKÓTTAI. addition to the authorized *mélváram* fixed by the grandfather of the present rajah the cultivating ryot is asked if he is willing to pay at the enhanced rate, and, if not, the land may be given to a perfect stranger."

The only attempt ever made to introduce a permanent ryotwári settlement into Pudukóttai was during the time that Mr. Blackburne was Political Agent. It was extended to only about fifty villáges, and, while the rates introduced for irrigated lands were too low, those for unirrigated were unduly high. Mr. Pennington proposed that the amáni lands should be regularly surveyed and settled by the Madras Survey and Settlement Departments, and Government approved of this suggestion and directed that the survey and settlement should be extended to all assessed lands.

The following account is given of the land classed as Tírvapat. These lands are divided into two classes; the first is called *mámúl kadamai*, or land occupied for a long time without any cowle or deed of contract. There is no uniform rate of assessment on land held on this tenure, the nanjah rates varying from Rupees 3 to Rupees 6 per kurukkam of 500 gulies (an acre being 302½ gulies) and the punjah from 10 Annas to Rupees 2. The second description is known as *nilaitta kadamai* or lands granted on permanent tenure. Lands which have been long waste and tracts covered with jungle are usually given on this tenure by means of progressive cowles where the land is unusually difficult of reclamation. When an offer (*karárnamá*) is made for land of this description a notice (*istiyár*) is issued inviting competition for the land, and at the end of a month a cowle is granted to the highest bidder, no matter who he may be. As regards the third class of lands, namely, those held under conditional leases, we learn from Mr. Pennington's report that large blocks of land and sometimes whole villages were leased out for a fixed amount for a definite term of years. In this case the amount of lease was fixed either at the highest revenue on record or by putting the land to public auction. The term of such leases was formerly ten years, but it had recently been reduced to five years.

Ináms. Under this head are three jaghires or estates granted for the support of the near relatives of the rajah. These are the *Chinna Aramanai Jaghire* belonging to the rajah's nephew, yielding a revenue of about 55,000 Rupees, the *Mél-Aramanai* Jaghire attached to the family of Rajah Gopál Tondiman, a son of the rajah's great great-grandfather by a second wife, and the *Manavarti Jaghire* or estate attached to the ladies of the palace which is at present enjoyed by the rajah's two wives. The total area of these jaghires is given as about 110,000 acres. In addition to the above there are 95,627 acres attached to temples and 9,584 to almshouses as inám. There are also about 100,000 acres held on various inám tenure rates, more than half of which have the obligation of military service attached to them. These service lands are at present resumable at the will of the reigning rajah No survey of the inám lands has ever been undertaken.

Revenue and finance.

The following statement shows the revenue of the Pudukóttai State for the last three faslis (revenue years) :—

Revenue.

Items.	Fasli 1284.	Fasli 1285.	Fasli 1286.
	RS.	RS.	RS.
Land revenue	3,04,918	2,91,220	2,48,177
Moturpha house, shop and loom taxes ..	18,411	18,537	18,333
Abkári	9,719	11,669	11,106
Salt monopoly	5,577	6,581	3,994
Income from jungles	653	809	1,116
Miscellaneous	194	174	170
Extra sources (interest on loans, &c.) ..	21,853	15,953	14,778
Total ..	3,61,325	3,44,943	2,97,674

An account of the system under which the land revenue is raised has been given already. The tax on houses and trades (known as moturpha) is levied in the following manner :—Terraced houses are assessed at 1 Rupee per annum, tiled houses at 8 Annas, thatched houses at 4 Annas, and huts at 6 Pies. Shops and bazaars are charged at the rate of Rupees 3, 2, 1, and 8 Annas, according to their importance. Silk looms pay 1 Rupee each, other looms 12 Annas, and oil-mills 2 Rupees per annum. The abkári revenue is derived from a monopoly of the right to manufacture and sell arrack and toddy which is leased yearly. The manufacture of earth-salt is a Government monopoly, from which a small revenue is derived. There are no stamp duties in Pudukóttai.

Police and Jails.

A Police force was introduced into Pudukóttai in 1875, which is governed by an Act closely modelled on the Madras Police Act (XXIV of 1859). The Police are placed under the Trichinopoly District Police Superintendent who receives Rupees 100 a month for the work of supervising them. The force is composed of 4 Inspectors, 20 Head Constables, and 152 Constables. There is one jail for long-sentenced prisoners at Pudukóttai, which is in charge of a Jailor on Rupees 20 under the orders of the Joint Magistrate or Deputy Karbar. All prisoners sentenced to fifteen days' imprisonment or more are sent to this jail. It is proposed to build subsidiary jails at the head quarters of the Tahsildars, but this has not been done as yet.

CHAP. XXII. PUDUKÓTTAI.

Registration.

A Registration Act, drawn up on the model of the Registration Act then in force in British India, was introduced into Pudukóttai in 1876. A District Registrar supervises the working of the Act, and each of the three Tahsildars is also a Sub-Registrar for his taluq.

Public Works.

There are three main lines of road in the State. These run from Pudukóttai to Trichinopoly, Tanjore, and Madura. In 1875 the condition of these roads was deplorable, most of the bridges and culverts were in ruins, and the roads were almost impassable, except in fine weather. Since then an Overseer on the Madras Establishment has been employed as Superintendent of Public Works, and by this means considerable improvements have been made. The road between Trichinopoly and Pudukóttai has been metalled and put in good order, and the repair of the two other main roads has been commenced; very much, however, in this direction remains to be done. The tanks throughout the country have been greatly neglected and are in urgent need of repair.

Education.

But little has been done in the way of education as yet in the State. The rajah keeps up a school at Pudukóttai town, in which English is taught up to the Matriculation standard, and there are three vernacular schools in the taluqs.

Vaccination.

Vaccination was introduced into Pudukóttai early in the present century when Sir W. Blackburne was Political Agent. Till of late years, however, but little was done towards extending vaccine operations. At present three Vaccinators are employed, and the following statement shows the work done by them in the last three years:—

Years.	Successful.	Unsuccessful.	Total.
Fasli 1284 (1875-76)	2,941	173	3,114
„ 1285 (1876-77)	4,165	117	4,282
„ 1286 (1877-78)	3,909	124	4,033

The operations of the Vaccinators are supervised by a pensioned Hospital Assistant, who is in charge of the rajah's hospital in Pudukóttai.

Results of the Census.

The population of Pudukóttai, according to the census of 1871, was returned as follows:—

Males.		Females.	Total.	Proportion of Females to every 100 Males.
151,929	..	164,766	316,695	108·4

The annexed statement gives certain details regarding the distribution of the population :—

Area in Square Miles.	Number of Taluqs.	Number of Villages.	Number of Houses.	Total Population.	Average Number of Houses to a Square Mile.	Average Number of Houses to a Village.	Average Number of Persons to a Square Mile.	Average Number of Persons to a House.	Average Number of Persons to a Village.	Average Number of Persons to a Taluq.
1,380	3	1,279	77,638	316,695	56·2	60·7	229·5	4·07	247·6	105·565

The following table shows the distribution of the people according to nationality :—

Hindus.	Muhammadans.	Native Christians.	Europeans.	Eurasians.	Total.
296,829	8,506	11,328	8	24	316,695

Pudukóttai Town.

The only town of any importance in the State is Pudukóttai itself which is returned, according to the last census, as having a population of 13,978. Pudukóttai is an unusually clean, airy, and well-built town. This is due to Rajah Vijaya Ragunátha Rai Bahadúr (who died in 1825) having pulled down the whole of the old town which was built with narrow and tortuous lanes and rebuilt it in regular streets, a large number of the houses being tiled. This great improvement was carried out at the suggestion of Sir William Blackburne, who was at that time Resident of Tanjore and Political Agent for Pudukóttai.

APPENDIX.

No. 1.—*Statement showing the Number of Villages and Hamlets in the District of Trichinopoly as they stood in Fasli* 1284 (1874-75).

Taluks.	Area in Square Miles.	Government.				Zemindári.				Inám.				Total.					
		Inhabited.		Uninhabited.		Inhabited.		Uninhabited.		Inhabited.		Uninhabited.		Inhabited.		Uninhabited.		Total.	
		Number of Villages.	Number of Hamlets.	Number of Villages.	Number of Hamlets.	Number of Villages.	Number of Hamlets.	Number of Villages.	Number of Hamlets.	Number of Villages.	Number of Hamlets.	Number of Villages.	Number of Hamlets.	Number of Villages.	Number of Hamlets.	Number of Villages.	Number of Hamlets.	Number of Villages.	Number of Hamlets.
1	2	3	4	5	6	7	8	9	10	11	12	13	14	15	16	17	18	19	20
1. Trichinopoly ..	519	338	146	48	6	..	..	..	..	40	30	10	2	378	176	58	8	436	184
2. Musiri	667	184	265	5	..	20	20	2	..	20	11	3	..	224	296	10	..	234	296
3. Kulittalai ..	930	97	567	2	75	111	289	5	69	33	46	3	6	241	902	10	150	251	1,052
4. Perumbalúr ..	690	185	46	31	20	18	..	4	..	9	..	..	..	212	46	35	20	247	66
5. Udaiyárpálayam	777	344	91	20	..	95	21	5	..	17	2	1	..	456	114	26	..	482	114
Total ..	3,583	1,148	1,115	106	101	244	330	16	69	119	89	17	8	1,511	1,534	139	178	1,650	1,712

No. 2.—*Statement of Population arranged with reference to Caste, according to the Census of* 1871.

Nationality.	Caste.	Population.		
		Males.	Females.	Total.
Hindus ..	Bráhman	15,854	15,574	31,428
	Kshattriya	1,849	1,825	3,674
	Chetti	10,649	10,806	21,455
	Vellálan or Agriculturist	96,985	103,868	200,853
	Idaiyan or Shepherd	29,912	31,319	61,231
	Kammálan or Artisan	14,175	14,296	28,471
	Kannakkan or Writer	138	156	294
	Kaikalan or Weaver	17,168	17,259	34,427
	Vannian or Labourer	194,898	203,512	398,410
	Kusavan or Potter	3,244	3,188	6,432
	Sátáni (mixed castes)	59,107	63,225	122,332
	Sembadavan or Fisherman ..	11,908	12,466	24,374
	Shánán or Palmyra climber ..	2,375	2,444	4,819
	Ambattan or Barber	6,590	6,496	13,086
	Vannán or Washerman	6,091	6,206	12,297
	Others	23,059	23,040	46,099
	Pariahs	77,168	79,891	157,059
	Total Hindus ..	571,170	595,571	1,166,741
Muhammadans	Labbay	5,849	5,697	11,546
	Mapilah	1	..	1
	Arab	278	351	629
	Sheik	6,389	6,491	12,880
	Syud	1,024	1,066	2,090
	Pathan	1,044	1,066	2,110
	Moghul	161	177	338
	Others	1,259	1,171	2,430
	Total Muhammadans ..	16,005	16,019	32,024
Europeans ..	....	457	166	623
Eurasians ..	....	287	343	630
Others ..	....	215	175	390
	Total Population ..	588,134	612,274	1,200,408

The total number of Native Christians in the district is 50,822.

No. 2-A.—*Statement showing the Male Population with reference to Occupation according to the Census of* 1871.

Major Headings.	Minor Headings.	Number of Males employed.
Professional	Government service	2,507
	Military	3,862
	Learned professions	1,576
	Minor do.	8,829
Domestic	Personal service	13,572
Commercial	Traders	15,492
	Conveyers	1,673
Agricultural	Cultivators	219,271
Industrial	Dress	16,973
	Food	8,425
	Metals	4,853
	Construction	4,539
	Books	50
	Household goods	2,754
	Combustibles	200
Indefinite and non-productive.	Labourers	70,587
	Property	490
	Unproductive	2,163
	Others	2,443
	Total ..	380,259

No. 2-B.—*Statement showing the Number of Houses, the Population, and the Agricultural Stock in each Taluk.*

Items.	Number of Houses.					Population.			Agricultural Stock.						
	Terraced.	Tiled.	Thatched.	Unspecified.	Total.	Males.	Females.	Total.	Tilling Cattle.	Cows.	She-Buffaloes.	Sheep.	Ploughs.	Horses.*	Ponies.*
1. Trichinopoly ..	6,065	5,033	40,433	..	51,531	146,691	158,039	304,730	42,792	22,163	13,953	73,892	22,473	..	..
2. Musiri	857	144	55,175	..	56,176	122,103	133,029	255,132	38,444	28,879	16,051	172,217	18,789	..	..
3. Kulittalai ..	651	130	60,905	..	61,686	112,640	115,027	227,667	67,010	39,450	11,265	117,648	35,355	..	..
4. Perumbalúr ..	217	136	23,903	..	24,256	84,156	85,562	169,718	26,485	35,895	1,400	212,387	11,393	..	..
5. Udaiyárpálayam..	42	1,765	27,935	23	29,765	119,998	117,895	237,893	28,740	35,688	10,522	164,516	14,307	..	..

* Horses and ponies are not used for agricultural purposes in Trichinopoly District.

No. 3.—*Statement of Rent Roll for Fasli* 1284 (1874-75).

Pattás.	Single Pattás.		Joint Pattás.		Total Pattás.	
	Number.	Assessment.	Number.	Assessment.	Number.	Assessment.
		RS.		RS.		RS.
Below 10 Rupees	98,400	2,85,522	6,400	20,934	104,800	3,06,456
Above 10 do. but below 30 Rupees..	23,245	3,53,065	1,367	22,441	24,612	3,75,506
Do. 30 do. do. 50 do. ..	5,114	1,75,651	369	13,804	5,483	1,89,455
Do. 50 do. do. 100 do. ..	2,611	1,70,566	229	16,079	2,840	1,86,645
Do. 100 do. do. 250 do. ..	1,009	1,48,316	114	20,190	1,123	1,68,506
Do. 250 do. do. 500 do. ..	218	74,315	33	11,929	251	86,244
Do. 500 do. do. 1,000 do. ..	70	47,097	15	10,244	85	57,341
Do. 1,000 do.	29	43,379	9	14,067	38	57,446

APPENDIX.

No. 4.—*Statement showing the different Sources of Irrigation belonging to Government.*

Taluks.	Tanks.			Channels.			Anicuts.			Wells.		
	Number of Tanks.	Average Extent of Cultivation within the last Five Years.	Assessment including all Charges for Water, &c.	Number of Channels	Average Extent of Cultivation within the last Five Years.	Assessment including all Charges for Water, &c.	Number of Anicuts.	Average Extent of Cultivation within the last Five Years.	Assessment including all Charges for Water, &c.	Number of Wells.	Average Extent of Cultivation within the last Five Years.	Assessment including all Charges for Water, &c.
			RS.			RS.			RS.			RS.
1. Trichinopoly ..	264	11,396	28,392	540	62,977	3,31,708	1	882	3,477	1,098	1,880	5,535
2. Musiri ..	53	8,737	48,197	59	13,290	80,070	..	..	..	4,703	7,092	22,708
3. Kulittalai ..	307	4,934	1,50,134	56	14,227	73,987	..	..	..	2,908	7,531	14,713
4. Perumbalúr ..	216	7,926	46,841	65	619	3,197	..	..	..	1,597	1,996	6,887
5. Udaiyárpálayam	405	8,907	31,759	12	4,288	16,029	..	..	..	188	942	2,852

No. 5.—*Statement showing the Rainfall for a Series of Ten Years in the District of Trichinopoly.*

Faslis.	Official Years.	July.	August.	September.	October.	November.	December.	January.	February.	March.	April.	May.	June.	Total.
		Inches.	Inches.	Inches.	Inches.	Inches.	Inches.	Inches.	Inches.	Inches.	Inches.	Inches.	Inches.	Inches.
1276 ..	1866-67	2·03	2·42	3·35	9·70	1·8	5·55	..	·03	..	·89	2·40	·43	27·98
1277 ..	1867-68	2·17	2·73	·86	11·44	..	·23	5·70	2·05	·04	·13	4·27	1·76	32·27
1278 ..	1868-69	4·77	2·64	5·83	8·13	·35	·35	·43	·44	·07	3·22	2·92	·73	29·88
1279 ..	1869-70	2·44	4·68	3·76	7·37	9·27	3·53	1·52	..	·27	·93	·52	4·78	39·07
1280 ..	1870-71	·99	7·05	4·02	8·56	6·44	2·40	1·59	1·15	..	·69	4·48	1·23	38·60
1281 ..	1871-72	·89	3·04	5·00	7·05	8·74	1·82	..	·01	·03	1·17	4·61	1·39	33·75
1282 ..	1872-73	5·89	5·50	5·55	5·96	9·37	3·71	..	4·39	..	2·92	2·66	..	45·95
1283 ..	1873-74	1·33	2·96	2·83	14·36	2·29	1·57	..	·35	·01	1·39	2·35	2·92	32·36
1284 ..	1874-75	1·94	3·92	4·33	6·53	8·95	2·44	·27	..	·13	1·73	3·27	1·32	34·83
1285 ..	1875-76	·80	3·92	4·36	6·99	3·42	1·26	..	..	·38	·52	4·33	1·06	27·04

No. 6.—*Statement showing the Prices of Grain and Salt for a Series of Ten Years in the District of Trichinopoly.*

Faslis.	Official Years.	Rice, 1st sort, per Garce.*	Rice, 2nd sort, per Garce.	Paddy, 1st sort, per Garce.	Paddy, 2nd sort, per Garce.	Chólum, per Garce.	Cumbu, per Garce.	Rági, per Garce.	Varagu, per Garce.	Horse-gram, per Garce.	Ulundu, per Garce.	Wheat, per Garce.	Salt, per Garce.
		RS.	RS.	RS.	RS.	RS.	RS.	RS.	RS.	RS.	RS.	RS.	RS.
1276	1866-67 ..	603	563	283	258	272	286	287	149	392	669	808	293
1277	1867-68 ..	450	423	211	194	190	207	203	140	260	605	680	298
1278	1868-69 ..	422	379	196	180	184	192	198	137	250	565	488	286
1279	1869-70 ..	383	341	175	158	160	156	161	97	197	411	592	321
1280	1870-71 ..	291	262	131	117	124	110	108	101	154	311	639	321
1281	1871-72 ..	297	260	131	115	113	110	110	66	174	277	494	327
1282	1872-73 ..	317	285	141	125	135	130	124	100	219	185	263	202
1283	1873-74 ..	348	315	157	140	191	180	169	133	261	457	533	320
1284	1874-75 ..	372	325	167	148	175	159	158	111	235	355	400	320
1285	1875-76 ..	373	350	165	144	160	167	167	125	236	343	430	345

* A garce is equivalent to 400 mercals, and each mercal contains 8 Madras measures of 117 tólás each.

No. 7.—*Statement showing the Particulars of Cultivation for a Series of Ten Years.*

Faslis.	Cultivable Extent.	Area occupied. Dry. Extent.	Area occupied. Dry. Assessment.	Area occupied. Wet. Extent.	Area occupied. Wet. Assessment.	Charge for Water, Second crop Assessment, Additional Assessment, Road Cess, &c.	Total Assessment.	Deduct Remissions.	Remainder.	Add Miscellaneous Items.	Total Ryotwari Demand.	Revenue from Permanently-settled Estates.	Jodi on Shrotriyam Villages.	Total Land Revenue Demand.	Arrears previous Years.	Total Demand of the Year.	Gross Collections (including Remissions).	Balance at the end of the Fasli.
1	2	3	4	5	6	7	8	9	10	11	12	13	14	15	16	17	18	19
	ACRES.	ACRES.	RS.	ACRES.	RS.	RS.	RS.	RS.	RS.	RS.	RS.	RS.	RS.	RS.	RS.	RS.	RS.	RS.
1275 ...	1,313,561	712,683	6,77,552	124,745	5,28,962	83,789	12,90,303	38,065	12,52,238	46,127	12,98,365	49,889	8,996	13,57,250	88,807	14,46,057	13,79,991	66,066
1276 ...	1,313,561	761,781	7,22,592	126,023	5,32,988	1,16,947	13,72,527	68,529	13,03,998	49,126	13,53,124	49,889	9,016	14,12,029	66,066	14,78,095	14,44,898	33,197
1277 ...	1,313,561	805,111	7,59,336	126,786	5,35,280	1,23,563	14,18,179	1,16,148	13,02,031	46,712	13,48,743	49,889	12,619	14,11,251	33,197	14,44,448	13,85,118	59,330
1278 ...	1,313,561	823,267	7,74,058	127,500	5,37,721	1,44,624	14,56,403	79,217	13,77,186	61,052	14,38,238	49,889	12,619	15,00,746	59,330	15,60,076	15,20,436	39,640
1279 ...	1,313,561	912,164	8,54,770	133,821	5,61,189	1,81,485	15,97,444	81,034	15,16,410	2,39,056	17,55,466	49,889	12,689	18,18,044	39,640	18,57,684	16,70,782	1,86,902
1280 ...	1,313,561	897,088	8,38,192	134,488	5,63,203	1,79,993	15,81,388	83,169	14,98,219	72,826	15,71,045	49,889	12,699	16,33,633	1,86,902	18,20,535	17,31,283	89,252
1281 ...	1,372,001	857,761	8,02,230	135,375	5,65,697	3,24,225	16,92,152	3,60,488	13,31,664	88,950	14,20,614	49,899	12,659	14,83,172	89,252	15,72,424	14,60,234	1,12,190
1282 ...	1,372,001	808,108	7,54,622	135,520	5,66,093	3,29,925	16,50,640	2,93,652	13,56,988	88,825	14,45,813	49,899	12,688	15,08,400	1,12,190	16,20,590	15,27,337	93,253
1283 ...	1,372,001	814,463	7,64,973	135,667	5,66,706	3,12,148	16,43,827	2,82,947	13,60,880	60,812	14,21,692	49,899	12,691	14,84,282	93,253	15,77,535	14,27,994	1,49,541
1284 ...	1,372,001	811,163	7,60,329	135,798	5,67,059	3,21,395	16,48,783	2,76,814	13,71,969	77,910	14,49,879	49,899	12,691	15,12,469	1,49,541	16,62,010	15,67,968	94,042

No. 7-A.—*Statement showing the Area under the principal Crops cultivated in the District in Fasli* 1285 (1875-76).

Taluks.	Rice.	Rági.	Chólum.	Cumbu.	Varagu.	Dholl.	Horse-gram.	Samai.	Millet.	Bengal-gram.	Ulundu.	Green-gram.	Mochai.	Oil seeds.	Cotton.	Indigo.
	ACRES.	ACRES.	ACRES.	ACRES.	ACRES.	ACRES.	ACRES.	ACRES.	ACRES.	ACRES.	ACRES.	ACRES.	ACRES.	ACRES.	ACRES.	ACRES.
Trichinopoly ..	69,894	15,027	15,267	12,835	15,089	2,531	6,184	2,978	163	6	178	..	851	1,602	7,628	372
Musiri	15,960	24,662	36,396	52,098	20,727	18,355	2,745	2,199	1,761	186	87	1,598	1,188	7,066	6,807	7
Kulittalai ..	16,131	8,891	74,330	27,381	15,584	3,602	10,757	19,560	311	..	203	489	603	5,864	63	..
Perumbalúr ..	6,890	31,933	8,484	23,556	53,521	1,075	2,592	52	79	351	1,075	1,072	861	5,876	24,839	148
Udaiyárpálayam.	25,132	23,494	5,699	41,323	40,882	2,465	2,744	20	58	106	829	435	431	3,913	7,191	151
Total ..	134,007	104,007	140,176	157,193	145,803	28,028	25,022	24,809	2,372	649	2,372	3,594	3,934	24,321	46,528	678

No. 8.—*Statement showing the Particulars of the several Tenures other than Ryotuári.*

Names of the Zemindáris and Inám Villages.	The entire Beriz of the Estate.			Peishcush or Quit-rent.		
Zemindáris.	RS.	A.	P.	RS.	A.	P.
Turaiyúr	40,022	2	0	700	0	0
Káttuputtúr (Mittah)	30,234	15	6	15,901	7	11
Marungápuri	68,436	9	1	20,586	15	6
Kadavúr	44,062	9	0	13,410	10	6
Udaiyárpálayam	63,080	2	5	642	15	4
Ariyalúr	42,618	5	7	700	0	0
Inám Villages enfranchised.						
(*Trichinopoly Taluk.*)						
Aiyakalayanpattavarti	535	10	0	110	12	0
Kadiyakurichi	1,408	10	0	178	0	0
Kándalúr	672	5	0	0	4	0
Kumbakudi	918	2	0	0	4	0
Panjappúr	487	10	0	27	0	0
Mudikandam	412	0	0	193	8	0
Navalpatti	5,897	12	0	0	10	0
Vadavúr	543	4	0	50	8	0
Tiruchandurai	2,004	6	0	250	0	0
Navalúr Kottapattu	1,600	1	0	185	0	0
Súraiyúr	8,932	6	0	1	12	0
Sengulam	964	9	0	85	6	0
Pódávúr	667	0	0	40	0	0
Turakudi	450	1	0	54	4	0
Periyakaruppúr	2,231	13	0	716	0	0
Samayapuram	1,799	1	0	18	8	0
Kíramangalam	1,102	10	0	586	0	0
Puliyúr	767	7	0	45	0	0
Rájámpálayam	809	10	0	0	6	0
Kalpálayam	1,934	6	0	0	6	0
Ammapéttai	745	9	0	1	0	0
Kolattúr	4,054	12	0	412	4	0
Ariyavúr	528	5	0	55	14	0
Tirutavaturai Kattalai	160	0	0	159	0	0
Uttamanambi	97	11	0	90	0	0
Péttaiváytalai	870	1	0	43	12	0
Kistnasamudram	1,573	0	0	..		
Ulkadai Ariyamangalam	755	9	0	..		
Puttúr	806	3	0	..		
Vélayudankudi	156	8	0	..		
Nágamangalam	725	8	0	..		
Méykkudi	728	9	0	..		
Kottapatti	545	7	0	..		
Kolakattakudi	173	7	0	..		
Majara Palankávéri	126	4	0	..		
Mattúr	1,027	6	0	..		
Chinnavadavúr	32	2	0	..		
Nattadsápalli	87	6	0	..		
Tenéripatti	3,202	10	0	..		
Uluntuni	691	1	0	..		
Púlánkudi	1,155	6	0	..		
Kámánáyakkanpálayam	27	0	0	..		
Ulkadai Ariyavúr	93	5	0	..		
Terkuchattram	277	0	0	..		
Kilamárimangalam	244	7	0	..		
Elandapatti	758	0	0	..		

No. 8.—*Statement showing the Particulars of the several Tenures other than Ryotwári*—(Continued).

Names of the Zemindáris and Inám Villages.	The entire Beriz of the Estate.			Peishcush or Quit-rent.		
Inám Villages enfranchised—(Continued).						
(*Musiri Taluk.*)	RS.	A.	P.	RS.	A.	P.
Múvéli	549	5	0	167	0	0
Umayapuram	827	4	0	281	3	0
Tirunáráyanapuram	1,036	15	0	187	8	0
Kidáram	1,655	4	0	342	12	0
Válvélputtúr	1,723	0	0	340	4	0
Jayankondán	862	2	0	150	0	0
Kárappudaiyánpatti	1,000	3	0	100	0	0
(*Kulittalai Taluk.*)						
Suriyanúr	468	6	0	36	10	2
Talinji	788	13	0	94	0	0
Puludéri	772	15	0	97	10	0
Alattúr	745	11	0	107	0	0
Seppalapatti	438	13	0	40	0	0
Pudangupatti	574	0	0	4	4	0
Ponnambalampatti	315	14	0	34	12	0
Múkkureddipatti	478	11	0	60	0	0
Edaiyapatti	384	2	0	47	0	0
Kappampatti	145	4	0	18	7	0
Sigampatti	608	7	0	77	8	0
Mondipatti	923	11	0	76	0	0
Chattrapatti	513	5	0	67	0	0
(*Perumbalúr Taluk.*)						
Púlámbádi	354	1	0	60	0	0
Áduturai	225	6	0	35	0	0
Málavaráyanallúr	237	1	0	68	0	0
Kulapádi	1,019	10	0	117	7	3
Kurumbúr	603	6	0	116	10	5
Eraiyasamudram	515	9	0	376	2	0
Alanguli	350	12	0	112	0	0
Agaram	557	15	0	378	8	0
Úttattúr	2,852	13	0	10	8	0
(*Udaiyárpálayam Taluk.*)						
Amanakkantóndi	164	3	3	20	0	0
Kulotanganallúr	457	8	0	145	0	0
Govindaputtúr	1,355	10	6	396	11	0
Kasánkóttai	485	13	3	116	10	4
Kalingaráyapuram	56	1	0	11	11	3
Darmasamudram	74	10	6	46	10	0
Kurichinattam	519	2	6	149	0	0
Seruvalúr	640	2	6	93	[illegible]	[illegible]
Kóman	797	11	0	186	1[illegible]	[illegible]
Veluppanankurichi	1,102	6	3	281	5	0
Kumáramangalam	255	5	3	23	6	0
Tirumánúr	1,294	8	4	396	10	0
Tirumaluvádi	1,167	15	0	233	9	2
Mélapaluvúr	1,120	4	3	245	0	0
Kílapaluvúr	2,856	5	0	466	11	0
Sirukadambúr	1,153	6	0	273	0	0
Uraiyúr	519	1	0	204	1	0
Áttukurichi	598	9	0	278	8	0
Sríraman	1,120	4	4	179	0	0

No. 8.—*Statement showing the Particulars of the several Tenures other than Ryotwári*—(Continued).

Names of the Zemindáris and Inám Villages.	The entire Beriz of the Estate.			Peishcush or Quit-rent.		
Unenfranchised.						
(*Trichinopoly Taluk.*)	RS.	A.	P.	RS.	A.	P.
Sembangulam	2,060	3	0	..		
Páganúr	1,219	7	0	..		
Periyanáyagichattram	497	1	0	..		
Kómákudi	1,142	5	0	..		
(*Musiri Taluk.*)						
Okkarai	3,881	9	0	..		
Sénappanallúr	2,841	11	0	..		
Kámáchipuram	1,092	11	0	..		
Puduvannápálayam	879	13	0	..		
Mávalingai	1,645	12	0	..		
Tirupattúr	1,878	9	0	..		
Aváravalli	379	14	0	..		
Tiruppanghili	5,245	4	0	..		
Abinimangalam	1,762	15	0	..		
Koppamapuri	1,390	15	0	..		
Sokkanádapuram	557	15	0	..		
Karattámpatti	1,207	11	0	..		
Muttámpatti	749	4	0	..		
Kamachipatti	464	13	0	..		
Manamédu	646	11	0	..		
Venkatanallúr	183	7	0	..		

No. 9.—*Statement showing the Collections under the several Heads of Revenue in the District of Trichinopoly for a Series of Ten Years.*

Faslis.	Official Years.	Land Revenue.	Abkári.	Income Tax.	License Tax.	Professional and Trade Tax.	Stamps.	Total.
		RS.	RS.	RS.	RS.	RS.	RS.	RS.
1275 ..	1865-66..	13,79,991	1,10,263	6,421	..	..	86,809	15,83,484
1276 ..	1866-67..	14,44,898	1,11,428	681	5,324	..	80,383	16,42,714
1277 ..	1867-68..	13,85,118	1,27,008	..	7,100	..	93,685	16,12,911
1278 ..	1868-69..	15,20,436	1,21,254	943	..	5,958	1,09,340	17,57,931
1279 ..	1869-70..	16,70,782	1,39,234	28,808	..	..	1,05,222	19,44,046
1280 ..	1870-71..	17,31,283	1,48,219	49,709	..	..	98,043	20,27,254
1281 ..	1871-72..	14,60,234	1,36,270	15,682	..	..	1,12,660	17,24,846
1282 ..	1872-73..	15,27,337	1,60,565	9,429	..	..	1,22,252	18,19,583
1283 ..	1873-74..	14,27,994	1,40,439	7	..	..	1,21,227	16,89,667
1284 ..	1874-75..	15,67,969	1,26,814	..	..	..	1,38,280	18,33,063

Nos. 10, 11, 12, *and* 13 *are blank for the Trichinopoly District, as it has no Seaports.*

No. 14.—*Statement showing the Number and Value of Suits disposed of in the Civil and Revenue Courts for a Series of Ten Years.*

Years.	Number of Suits disposed of in different Courts.													
	Ordinary Suits.								Small Causes.					
	Village Munsifs'.	Revenue Courts.	District Munsifs'.	Principal Sadar Amins' or Subordinate Judges'.	Judges of Small Cause Courts as Principal Sadar Amins.	Civil Judges' and Judicial Commissioner's.	Total Number of Suits.	Total Value in Rupees.	District Munsifs', Assistant Agent's and Assistant Commissioner's.	Principal Sadar Amins' or Subordinate Judges'.	Judges of Small Cause Courts.	Civil Judges' and Judicial Commissioner's.	Total Number of Small Causes.	Total Value in Rupees.
1	2	3	4	5	6	7	8	9	10	11	12	13	14	15
								RS. A. P.						RS. A. P.
1866 ..	3,656	..	3,245	..	..	47	6,948	*	1,355	..	130	..	1,485	*
1867 ..	4,607	..	1,449	..	..	91	6,147	*	1,996	..	213	..	2,209	*
1868 ..	5,012	..	1,442	..	..	63	6,517	*	2,177	..	133	..	2,310	*
1869 ..	4,862	..	5,073	..	..	55	9,990	*	1,889	..	143	..	2,032	*
1870 ..	5,472	19	1,993	..	..	62	7,546	12,20,279 0 0	1,765	..	131	..	1,896	48,830 0 0
1871 ..	4,295	23	1,683	..	..	88	6,089	9,35,963 0 0	1,355	..	89	..	1,444	36,117 0 0
1872 ..	4,259	57	2,114	..	..	95	6,525	5,37,618 0 0	1,936	..	121	..	2,057	49,860 0 0
1873 ..	3,650	154	1,721	18	..	37	5,580	8,95,794 0 0	1,814	65	105	..	1,984	58,573 0 0
1874 ..	3,706	131	2,299	3	..	25	6,164	5,14,308 7 9	2,076	74	90	..	2,240	66,216 8 8
1875 ..	3,479	128	2,281	..	..	26	5,917	8,77,995 2 8	1,984	..	127	..	2,111	56,305 6 6
Total ..	42,998	512	23,303	21	...	589	67,423	49,81,957 10 5	18,347	139	1,282	..	19,768	3,15,901 15 2

* These particulars cannot be obtained.

No. 15.—*Statement of Persons tried, convicted, and acquitted, and of Property lost and recovered for a Series of Ten Years.*

Nature of Offences.	1866. No. of Persons tried during the Year.	1866. Acquitted or Discharged.	1866. Convicted.	1866. Remaining under Trial.	1866. Property: Stolen.	1866. Property: Recovered.	1867. No. of Persons tried during the Year.	1867. Acquitted or Discharged.	1867. Convicted.	1867. Remaining under Trial.	1867. Property: Stolen.	1867. Property: Recovered.
					RS.	RS.					RS.	RS.
1. Murder	1	..	1	*	41	29	6	..	6	..	..	..
2. Culpable Homicide.	4	4	..	..	..	..	5	3	2	..	..	..
3. Rape	3	1	2	..	..	..	3	2	1	..	..	..
4. Hurts and Assaults.	1,376	847	529	..	..	..	1,084	635	449	..		..
5. Other Offences against person.	46	26	20	..	32	32	31	12	19	..	506	..
6. Dacoity	91	64	27	..	10,381	205	41	9	32	..	3,88[illegible]	
7. Robbery	6	4	2	..	768	3	27	3	24	..	1[illegible]	[illegible]43
8. House-breaking ..	73	26	47	..	15,799	1,235	59	19	40	..	1[illegible]	1,765
9. Theft	552	223	329	..	18,174	4,759	731	305	426	..	17,444	1,898
10. Other Offences against property.	606	335	271	..	2,834	320	521	274	247	..	6,515	1,016
11. Other Offences against Penal Code.	626	264	362	..	..	..	1,178	324	854	..	..	..
Total ..	3,384	1,794	1,590	..	48,029	6,583	3,686	1,586	2,100	..	43,244	4,831
12. Special and Local Laws.	2,570	433	2,137	..	134	111	2,771	549	2,222	..	1,127	98
Total ..	5,954	2,227	3,727	..	48,163	6,694	6,457	2,135	4,322	..	44,371	4,929

—	1868. No. of Persons tried during the Year.	1868. Acquitted or Discharged.	1868. Convicted.	1868. Remaining under Trial.	1868. Property: Stolen.	1868. Property: Recovered.	1869. No. of Persons tried during the Year.	1869. Acquitted or Discharged.	1869. Convicted.	1869. Remaining under Trial.	1869. Property: Stolen.	1869. Property: Recovered.
					RS.	RS.					RS.	RS.
1. Murder	8	3	5	..	..	..	1	1	..	..	28	..
2. Culpable Homicide.	2	1	1	..	..	..	4	2	2	..	..	..
3. Rape	..	..	..	..	..	..	..	..	..	..	..	..
4. Hurts and Assaults.	977	563	414	..	..	..	789	512	277	..	..	..
5. Other Offences against person.	45	29	16	..	41	6	97	39	58	..	..	..
6. Dacoity	56	29	27	..	3,406	219	69	36	33	..	3,638	662
7. Robbery	13	4	9	..	416	163	4	..	4	..	126	14
8. House-breaking ..	84	23	61	..	12,289	465	87	34	53	..	8,874	988
9. Theft	598	302	296	..	17,295	3,293	575	199	376	..	12,020	3,130
10. Other Offences against property.	433	229	204	..	4,626	461	495	257	238	..	2,541	769
11. Other Offences against Penal Code.	835	363	472	..	..	..	1,097	431	666	..	..	..
Total ..	3,051	1,546	1,505	..	38,073	4,607	3,218	1,511	1,707	..	27,227	5,563
12. Special and Local Laws.	2,622	493	2,129	..	105	82	3,014	626	2,388	..	132	103
Total ..	5,673	2,039	3,634	..	38,178	4,689	6,232	2,137	4,095	..	27,359	5,666

* This column cannot be filled in for years previous to 1872.

No. 15.—*Statement of Persons tried, convicted, and acquitted, and of Property lost and recovered for a Series of Ten Years*—(Continued).

Nature of Offences.	1870.						1871.					
	No. of Persons tried during the Year.	Acquitted or Discharged.	Convicted.	Remaining under Trial.	Property Stolen.	Property Recovered.	No. of Persons tried during the Year.	Acquitted or Discharged.	Convicted.	Remaining under Trial.	Property Stolen.	Property Recovered.
					RS.	RS.					RS.	RS.
1. Murder	4	..	4	..	24	15	4	1	3	..	21	..
2. Culpable Homicide	2	..	2	..	..	..	9	5	4	..	..	..
3. Rape	2	..	2	..	..	..	1	1	..	..	..	..
4. Hurts and Assaults	713	367	346	..	..	..	865	483	382	..	..	..
5. Other Offences against person.	26	9	17	..	..	..	112	35	77	..	..	..
6. Dacoity	41	5	36	..	4,485	739	36	15	21	..	2,765	55
7. Robbery	4	..	4	..	485	408	28	7	21	..	2,220	114
8. House-breaking ..	111	36	75	..	10,652	1,868	123	18	105	..	9,700	1,604
9. Theft	544	173	371	..	11,469	4,051	686	272	414	..	11,194	3,095
10. Other Offences against property.	382	212	170	..	1,870	301	533	280	253	..	2,869	562
11. Other Offences against Penal Code.	1,101	507	594	..	..	..	1,299	710	589	..	..	..
Total ..	2,930	1,309	1,621	..	28,985	7,382	3,696	1,827	1,869	..	28,769	5,430
12. Special and Local Laws.	3,509	556	2,953	..	122	81	4,721	706	4,015	..	159	79
Total ..	6,439	1,865	4,574	..	29,107	7,463	8,417	2,533	5,884	..	28,928	5,509
—	1872.						1873.					
					RS.	RS.					RS.	RS.
1. Murder	18	9	9	..	1,586	910	14	7	7	..	14	3
2. Culpable Homicide	2	1	1	..	..	..	1	..	1	..	..	..
3. Rape	1	1	..	..	..	..	1	..	1	..	10	..
4. Hurts and Assaults.	931	524	407	..	..	..	807	435	372	..	..	..
5. Other Offences against person.	60	36	23	1	25	19	90	48	37	5	..	..
6. Dacoity	25	11	14	..	1,361	309	16	9	7	..	1,148	21
7. Robbery	19	7	12	..	388	67	24	6	15	3	314	80
8. House-breaking ..	125	30	95	..	7,673	1,330	93	24	64	5	10,064	1,674
9. Theft	675	232	440	3	10,529	2,587	744	252	468	24	16,200	4,239
10. Other Offences against property.	1,251	788	455	8	792	514	835	651	169	15	3,059	1,774
11. Other Offences against Penal Code.	627	179	444	4	..	..	504	186	307	11	..	..
Total ..	3,734	1,818	1,900	16	22,354	5,736	3,129	1,618	1,448	63	30,809	7,791
12. Special and Local Laws.	4,814	688	4,126	..	140	92	4,734	445	4,271	18	81	64
Total ..	8,548	2,506	6,026	16	22,494	5,828	7,863	2,063	5,719	81	30,890	7,855

No. 15.—*Statement of Persons tried, convicted, and acquitted, and of Property lost and recovered for a Series of Ten Years*—(Continued).

Nature of Offences.	1874. No. of Persons tried during the Year.	1874. Acquitted or Discharged.	1874. Convicted.	1874. Remaining under Trial.	1874. Property: Stolen.	1874. Property: Recovered.
					RS.	RS.
1. Murder	10	7	3	..	8	6
2. Culpable Homicide.	3	..	3	..	..	..
3. Rape	4	3	1	..	..	..
4. Hurts and Assaults.	698	330	68	..	..	..
5. Other Offences against person.	137	72	60	5	17	..
6. Dacoity	77	42	28	7	8,271	158
7. Robbery	16	3	10	3	493	74
8. House-breaking ..	118	20	92	6	14,732	3,802
9. Theft	603	146	420	37	10,191	3,948
10. Other Offences against property.	647	475	161	11	3,713	865
11. Other Offences against Penal Code	629	147	431	51	..	..
Total ..	2,942	1,245	1,577	120	37,425	8,853
12. Special and Local Laws.	4,655	339	4,312	4	78	64
Total ..	7,597	1,584	5,889	124	37,503	8,917

Nature of Offences.	1875. No. of Persons tried during the Year.	1875. Acquitted or Discharged.	1875. Convicted.	1875. Remaining under Trial.	1875. Property: Stolen.	1875. Property: Recovered.
					RS.	RS.
1. Murder	13	12	..	1	141	
2. Culpable Homicide.	2	2	..	..	..	..5
3. Rape	..	..	..	..	..	..
4. Hurts and Assaults.	939	459	480	..	..	..
5. Other Offences against person.	99	60	38	1	..	..
6. Dacoity	41	6	14	21	11,278	56
7. Robbery	14	1	13	..	682	87
8. House-breaking ..	117	8	104	5	13,521	1,388
9. Theft	475	89	370	16	10,081	3,620
10. Other Offences against property.	662	493	163	6	7,837	944
11. Other Offences against Penal Code	1,036	297	618	121	..	..
Total ..	3,398	1,427	1,800	171	43,540	6,100
12. Special and Local Laws.	3,562	258	3,300	4	53	44
Total ..	6,960	1,685	5,100	175	43,593	6,144

No. 16.—*Statement showing the Expenditure on Public Works from Imperial and Provincial Funds for a Series of Five Years.*

Years.	Imperial.				Provincial.			
	Military.	Civil Buildings.	Agricultural.	Total.	Civil Buildings.	Communications.	Miscellaneous Public Improvements.	Total.
New Works.	RS. A. P.	RS. A. P.	RS. A. P.	RS. A. P.	RS. A. P.	RS. A. P.	RS. A. P.	RS. A. P.
1871-72	1,271 10 0	..	7,269 9 5	8,541 3 5	21,814 5 0	..	..	21,814 5 0
1872-73	10,692 7 6	..	3,848 10 4	14,541 1 10	22,040 2 6	..	..	22,040 2 6
1873-74	15,279 6 0	..	4,416 5 9	19,695 11 9	21,994 7 6	..	..	21,994 7 6
1874-75	18,802 15 7	..	4,575 6 5	23,378 6 0	48,054 14 2	2,673 15 8	..	50,728 13 10
1875-76	11,965 3 7	..	9,612 13 11	21,578 1 6	6,239 6 1	..	..	6,239 6 1
Total ..	58,011 10 8	..	29,722 13 9	87,734 8 6	1,20,143 3 3	2,673 15 8	..	1,22,817 2 11
Repairs.								
1871-72	10,747 12 5	..	85,255 1 2	96,002 13 7	1,847 8 9	..	..	1,847 8 9
1872-73	11,374 8 0	..	64,500 1 0	75,874 9 0	7,332 12 7	..	..	7,332 12 7
1873-74	13,240 7 10	..	40,406 5 10	53,646 13 8	1,692 10 8	..	..	1,692 10 8
1874-75	15,519 5 4	..	68,051 7 4	83,570 12 8	6,933 8 8	12,359 12 0	57,641 15 1	76,935 3 9
1875-76	2,990 7 0	..	56,409 0 2	59,399 7 2	38,766 13 11	..	33,517 5 0	72,284 2 11
Total ..	53,872 8 7	..	3,14,621 15 6	3,68,494 8 1	56,573 6 7	12,359 12 0	91,159 4 1	1,60,092 6 8
Grand Total ..	1,11,884 3 3	..	3,44,344 13 3	4,56,229 0 7	1,76,716 9 10	15,033 11 8	91,159 4 1	2,82,909 9 7

No. 17.—*Statement showing the Receipts and Expenditure of*

Receipts.	1871-72.	1872-73.	1873-74.	1874-75.	1875-76.
	RS.	RS.	RS.	RS.	RS.
1. Balance	17,495	9,328	39,950	42,772	49,456
2. Provincial Grants for Roads ..	34,730	44,210	50,960	50,960	42,165
3. Provincial Grant to Schools ..	..	..	..	..	..
4. Provincial Grant for general purposes.	..	..	..	..	..
5. Surplus Pound Fund	5,500	5,591	3,300	3,500	5,647
6. Avenue	..	..	132	1,787	1,578
7. Fishery Rents	3,068	4,721	4,623	3,312	4,765
8. Miscellaneous	..	..	..	..	..
9. Road Cess under Act III of 1866 ..	48,408	5,086	795	217	197
10. Land Cess under Act IV of 1871 ..	31,527	1,28,406	1,13,895	1,13,822	1,32,904
11. Tolls Act IV of 1871	..	1,509	1,817	30,992	29,498
12. House Tax	..	..	..	..	..
13. Fees in Schools and Training Institutions.	..	..	..	..	672
14. Contributions	..	..	240	300	195
15. Educational Receipts	..	..	..	..	..
16. Sale of Elementary Books	..	..	..	..	..
17. Fees from Travellers' Bungalows ..	..	231	133	160	78
18. Balance of Bungalow Fund	..	1,171	158	..	..
19. Fines and Penalties	..	..	..	..	40
20. Sale of other Property	..	..	..	..	19
21. Public Works Receipts	..	1,095	26	558	202
22. Public Works Refund of Expenditure.	..	..	286	..	..
23. Miscellaneous	..	36	8,382	87	11
24. Miscellaneous Debt Account ..	..	70	..	1,101	1,385
25. Ferry Rent	7,515	6,854	6,383	5,867	7,414
26. Choultries and Markets, &c. ..	1,925	2,123	1,954	1,875	3,469
27. Grass Rent	..	21	28	2	17
28. Contribution for Works unconnected with Schools or Endowed Foundations.	..	..	..	40	4,007
Total ..	1,32,673	2,01,124	1,93,112	2,14,580	2,34,263
Total including Balance ..	1,50,168	2,10,452	2,33,062	2,57,352	2,83,719

Local Funds under Act IV of 1871 for a Series of Five Years.

Expenditure.	1871-72.	1872-73.	1873-74.	1874-75.	1875-76.
New Works.	RS.	RS.	RS.	RS.	RS.
1. Communications { By P.W.D. ..	33,753	43,926	46,743	53,090	50,447
By Other Agency ..	1,185	1,344	865	750	..
2. Educational .. { By P.W.D. ..	..	..	..	..	..
By Other Agency ..	..	..	..	..	..
3. Sanitary and Miscellaneous. { By P.W.D. ..	603	268	283	194	2,480
By Other Agency ..	130	170	153	664	500
4. Tolls .. .. { By P.W.D. ..	..	..	..	484	180
By Other Agency ..	..	..	..	179	..
Repairs.					
5. Communications { By P.W.D. ..	71,745	74,823	78,158	77,199	77,747
By Other Agency ..	174	1,584	14	..	..
6. Educational .. { By P.W.D. ..	..	..	..	..	..
By Other Agency ..	..	..	..	..	..
7. Sanitary and Miscellaneous. { By P.W.D. ..	16	..	18	1,243	2,405
By Other Agency ..	200	231	150	155	547
8. Tolls .. .. { By P.W.D ..	..	..	..	..	..
By Other Agency ..	..	..	..	..	9
9. Public Works Department supervision.	19,120	28,470	35,021	33,053	33,315
10. Petty Establishment	4,661	4,358	5,379	921	733
11. Contributions to Municipalities, &c. ..	..	..	200	15,532	14,835
12. Tolls and Ferries	..	104	46	2,696	..
13. Miscellaneous	..	..	..	2,473	..
14. Tools and Plant	68	1,659	2,860	2	2,336
Total Grant I ..	1,31,655	1,56,937	1,69,890	1,88,635	1,85,534
15. Payment for Inspection	1,263	2,198	2,116	1,096	1,524
16. Local Fund Schools	..	..	..	..	1,605
17. Purchase of Books, &c.	..	..	..	..	16
18. Salary Grants	..	299	469	285	..
19. Results do.	1,540	2,683	1,908	4,248	4,147
Total Grant II ..	2,803	5,180	4,493	5,629	7,292
20. Hospitals and Dispensaries	..	..	..	..	750
21. Vaccine Establishment	2,546	2,444	2,437	2,632	3,105
22. Sanitary Establishment, cleansing Tanks and Wells.	..	..	2,024	1,936	1,247
23. Choultries' Establishment, &c. ..	713	671	652	2,084	654
24. Travellers' Bungalow Establishment.	..	153	247	283	139
25. Contributions to Municipalities ..	2,358	2,733	8,108	3,293	8,414
Total Grant III ..	5,617	6,001	13,468	10,228	14,309
26. Establishment at the Presidency and in the Collectors' and Local Fund Boards' Offices and Contingencies.	765	2,314	2,439	2,297	2,118
27. Write-backs of Incorrect Credits of District Road Fund and Balances.	..	..	..	..	560
Total Grant IV ..	765	2,314	2,439	2,297	2,678
28. Miscellaneous Debt Account	..	70	..	1,107	1,379
Total Expenditure ..	1,40,840	1,70,502	1,90,290	2,07,896	2,11,192
29. Balance	9,328	39,950	42,772	49,456	72,527
Grand Total ..	1,50,168	2,10,452	2,33,062	2,57,352	2,83,719

No. 18.—*Statement showing the Receipts and Expenditure for Special Funds for a Series of Five Years.*

—	1871-72.					1872-73.		
	Balance at the beginning of the Year.	Receipts during the Year.	Total.	Expenditure during the Year.	Balance at the end of the Year.	Receipts during the Year, including Balance.	Expenditure during the Year.	Balance at the end of the Year.
1	2	3	4	5	6	7	8	9
	RS.	RS.	RS.	RS.	RS.	RS.	RS.	RS.
1. Jungle Conservancy Fund.	6,805	8,260	15,065	3,316	11,749	20,922	4,776	16,146
2. Nanal Grass Fund*..	3,717	1,324	5,041	1,953	3,088	6,614	862	5,752
3. Cattle Pound Fund..	6,814	8,071	14,885	7,642	7,243	15,430	12,827	2,603
4. Public Bungalow Fund.†	1,167	709	1,876	413	1,463	..	..	..
5. Village Service Fund.	81,284	1,05,622	1,86,906	2,36,211	49,305	1,92,968	1,71,181	21,787
6. Irrigation Cess Fund.	6,490	9,418	15,908	8,167	7,741	20,360	8,720	11,640
Total ..	1,06,277	1,33,404	2,39,681	2,57,702	18,021	2,56,294	1,98,366	57,928

—	1873-74.			1874-75.			1875-76.		
	Receipts during the Year, including Balance.	Expenditure during the Year.	Balance at the end of the Year.	Receipts during the Year, including Balance.	Expenditure during the Year.	Balance at the end of the Year.	Receipts during the Year, including Balance.	Expenditure during the Year.	Balance at the end of the Year.
	10	11	12	13	14	15	16	17	18
	RS.	RS.	RS.	RS.	RS.	RS.	RS.	RS.	RS.
1. Jungle Conservancy Fund.	21,892	11,419	10,473	18,834	11,401	7,270	14,486	9,905	4,521
2. Nanal Grass Fund.*	10,999	32	10,967	15,016	2,796	12,220	13,658	12,220	1,438
3. Cattle Pound Fund.	11,095	8,507	2,588	12,766	10,675	2,091	12,620	11,309	1,311
4. Public Bungalow Fund.†	..	..	..	..	..	..	..	..	..
5. Village Service Fund.	1,85,213	1,64,379	20,834	2,17,090	1,70,251	48,607	2,42,542	1,70,137	72,405
6. Irrigation Cess Fund.	21,578	10,440	11,138	23,210	9,662	13,548	28,469	17,732	10,737
Total ..	2,50,777	1,94,777	56,000	2,86,916	2,04,785	83,736	3,11,775	2,21,303	90,472

* This fund was transferred to the head of Irrigation Revenue in 1877-78.

† Transferred to the Local Fund Board from the commencement of the year 1872-73—(G.O., No. 412, of the 4th April 1872).

No. 19.—*Statement showing the Progress of Education in Trichinopoly District for a Series of Ten Years.*

Description of Schools.		1866-67.			1867-68.			1868-69.			1869-70.		
		No. of Schools.	Number of Pupils.		No. of Schools.	Number of Pupils.		No. of Schools.	Number of Pupils.		No. of Schools.	Number of Pupils.	
			Boys.	Girls.		Boys.	Girls.		Boys.	Girls.		Boys.	Girls.
A.—*Government Schools.*													
1. Maintained from Imperial or Provincial Funds.	Higher.	..	..	..	..	..	..	..	..	..	..	..	..
	Middle.	2	315	..	2	357	..	2	349	..	1	145	..
	Lower.	..	..	..	..	..	..	..	..	..	..	..	..
2. Maintained from Local or Municipal Funds.	Higher.	..	..	..	..	..	..	..	..	..	..	..	..
	Middle.	..	..	..	..	..	..	..	..	..	..	..	..
	Lower.	..	..	..	..	..	..	..	..	..	..	..	..
	Total ..	2	315	..	2	357	..	2	349	..	1	145	..
B.—*Schools Aided.*													
1. By Salary Grants ..	Higher.	2	533	..	2	553	..	2	626	..	4	261	..
	Middle.	11	355	..	18	520	..	31	953	7	11	330	..
	Lower.	2	..	46	3	..	65	4	..	107	13	350	..
2. By Result Grants ..	Higher.	..	..	..	..	..	..	..	..	..	..	..	..
	Middle.	..	..	..	..	..	..	..	..	..	..	..	..
	Lower.	..	..	..	..	..	..	..	..	..	..	..	..
3. Combined Salaries and Result Grants.	Higher.	..	..	..	..	..	..	..	..	..	..	..	..
	Middle.	..	..	..	..	..	..	..	..	..	..	..	..
	Lower.	..	..	..	..	..	..	..	..	..	..	..	..
	Total ..	15	888	46	23	1,073	65	37	1,579	114	28	941	..
C.—*Schools under Inspection for Result Grants but not aided.*	Higher.	..	..	..	..	..	..	..	..	..	..	..	..
	Middle.	..	..	..	..	..	..	..	..	..	..	..	..
	Lower.	7	177	..	5	54	1	4	61	..	..	..	..
	Total ..	7	177	..	5	54	1	4	61	..	..	..	..
Number of successful candidates for the Uncovenanted Civil Service Examinations educated in the district			23			34			23			18	
Number of successful candidates for Special Tests			9			13			17			24	
Number of successful candidates for Matriculation and F. A. ..			10			9			18			14	

No. 19.—*Statement showing the Progress of Education in Trichinopoly District for a Series of Ten Years*—(Continued).

Description of Schools.		1870-71. No. of Schools.	1870-71. Number of Pupils. Boys.	1870-71. Number of Pupils. Girls.	1871-72. No. of Schools.	1871-72. Number of Pupils. Boys.	1871-72. Number of Pupils. Girls.	1872-73. No. of Schools.	1872-73. Number of Pupils. Boys.	1872-73. Number of Pupils. Girls.
A.—*Government Schools.*										
1. Maintained from Imperial or Provincial Funds.	Higher ..	..	..	..	..	..	..	..	..	..
	Middle ..	1	146	..	1	137	..	1	141	..
	Lower ..	..	..	..	..	..	..	..	..	..
2. Maintained from Local or Municipal Funds.	Higher ..	..	..	..	..	..	..	..	..	..
	Middle ..	..	..	..	..	..	..	..	..	..
	Lower ..	..	..	..	..	..	..	..	..	..
Total ..		1	146	..	1	137	..	1	141	..
B.—*Schools Aided.*										
1. By Salary Grants ..	Higher ..	2	564	..	2	489	..	2	639	..
	Middle ..	46	1,298	..	8	510	..	10	330	..
	Lower ..	24	752	..	27	537	..	11	263	..
2. By Result Grants ..	Higher ..	..	..	..	..	..	..	..	..	..
	Middle ..	1	..	29	1	..	30	1	..	30
	Lower ..	32	710	25	48	1,140	..	118	2,677	..
3. Combined Salaries and Result Grants.	Higher ..	..	..	..	..	..	..	..	..	..
	Middle ..	..	..	..	..	..	..	..	..	..
	Lower ..	..	..	..	..	..	..	..	..	..
Total ..		105	3,324	54	73	2,676	30	142	3,909	30
C.—*Schools under Inspection for Result Grants but not aided.*	Higher ..	..	..	..	..	..	..	..	..	..
	Middle ..	..	..	..	..	..	..	..	..	..
	Lower ..	4	83	..	34	805	..	42	697	..
Total ..		4	83	..	34	805	..	42	697	..
Number of successful candidates for the Uncovenanted Civil Service Examinations educated in the district			17			10			36	
Number of successful candidates for Special Tests			21			16			30	
Number of successful candidates for Matriculation and F. A.			13			8			22	

No. 19.—*Statement showing the Progress of Education in Trichinopoly District for a Series of Ten Years*—(Continued).

Description of Schools.		1873-74. No. of Schools.	1873-74. Number of Pupils. Boys.	1873-74. Number of Pupils. Girls.	1874-75. No. of Schools.	1874-75. Number of Pupils. Boys.	1874-75. Number of Pupils. Girls.	1875-76. No. of Schools.	1875-76. Number of Pupils. Boys.	1875-76. Number of Pupils. Girls.
A.—*Government Schools.*										
1. Maintained from Imperial or Provincial Funds.	Higher ..	..	..	..	..	..	..	..	..	..
	Middle ..	2	251	..	2	252	..	2	221	..
	Lower ..	..	..	..	..	..	..	..	..	..
2. Maintained from Local or Municipal Funds.	Higher ..	..	..	..	..	..	..	..	..	..
	Middle ..	..	..	..	..	..	..	..	..	..
	Lower ..	..	..	..	..	..	..	..	..	..
Total ..		2	251	..	2	252	..	2	221	..
B.—*Schools Aided.*										
1. By Salary Grants ..	Higher ..	1	575	..	1	702	..	1	783	..
	Middle ..	8	299	..	5	330	..	4	368	..
	Lower ..	9	240	..	8	298	87	4	170	109
2. By Result Grants ..	Higher ..	..	..	..	..	..	..	..	..	..
	Middle ..	1	..	30	1	..	56	1	..	64
	Lower ..	120	2,593	..	148	3,004	..	149	3,633	148
3. Combined Salaries and Result Grants.	Higher ..	..	..	..	..	..	..	..	..	..
	Middle ..	..	..	..	..	..	..	..	..	..
	Lower ..	..	..	..	..	..	..	21	818	14
Total ..		139	3,707	30	163	4,334	143	179	5,772	335
C.—*Schools under Inspection for Result Grants but not aided.*	Higher ..	..	..	..	..	..	..	..	..	..
	Middle ..	..	..	..	..	..	..	..	..	..
	Lower ..	62	1,029	..	93	1,765	..	60	1,459	..
Total ..		62	1,029	..	93	1,765	..	60	1,459	..
Number of successful candidates for the Uncovenanted Civil Service Examinations educated in the district			27			31			20	
Number of successful candidates for Special Tests			25			28			57	
Number of successful candidates for Matriculation and F. A.			18			33			38	

No. 20.—*Statement showing the Receipts and Expenditure of the several Municipal Commissions for a Series of Five Years.*

Years.	Municipal Towns.	Receipts. Rate on Houses and Lands.	Trade Tax.	Tolls.	Tax on Carriages and Animals.	Registration of Carts.	Licenses.	Fines.
		RS. A. P.	RS. A. P.	RS. A. P.	RS. A. P.	RS. A. P.	RS. A. P.	RS. A. P.
1870-71	Trichinopoly ..	7,437 7 8	9,089 6 0	18,902 1 10	6,355 9 4	1,998 2 8	750 7 8	206 8 0
1871-72 (11 months only)	Do. ..	10,564 10 10	10,815 0 0	17,037 4 2	4,797 4 0	1,042 0 0	651 8 0	1,951 14 0
1872-73	Do. ..	13,776 15 8	11,427 8 0	16,430 8 3	5,697 12 0	1,654 0 0	848 8 0	898 7 8
1873-74	Do. ..	12,274 10 4	8,734 0 0	19,464 0 0	5,713 12 0	1,664 4 0	1,064 8 0	429 8 0
1874-75	Do. ..	16,003 4 0	..	14,000 0 0	6,046 8 0	1,706 4 0	1,145 0 0	568 13 1
*1st November 1871 to 31st March 1872.	Srírangam ..	1,388 12 0	410 9 0	..	..	..	55 4 0	75 6 0
1872-73	Do. ..	5,997 15 0	778 15 0	..	..	..	347 6 6	179 13 0
1873-74	Do. ..	5,684 7 0	2,683 5 0	..	495 4 0	297 0 0	386 8 0	282 2 0
1874-75	Do. ..	5,660 0 6	1,273 0 0	..	662 0 0	351 0 0	397 0 0	216 3 0
	Total ..	78,788 3 0	45,211 11 0	85,833 14 3	29,768 1 4	8,712 10 8	5,646 2 2	4,808 10 9

* This Municipality was established on the 1st November 1871.

No. 20.—*Statement showing the Receipts and Expenditure of the several Municipal Commissions for a Series of Five Years*—(Cont.)

Years.	Municipal Towns.	Receipts—(*Continued*).					Expenditure.	
		State Contribution.	Arrears, including Balance.	Miscellaneous.	Other Receipts and Advances recovered.	Total.	New Works.	Repairs.
		RS. A. P.	RS. A. P.	RS. A. P.	RS. A. P.	RS. A. P.	RS. A. P.	RS. A. P.
1870-71	Trichinopoly ..	13,141 10 0	12,782 6 1	7,074 14 9	5,268 15 8	83,007 9 8	6,474 4 5	13,300 6 1
1871-72 (11 months only)	Do. ..	3,028 0 0	9,021 4 6	7,105 7 5	3,653 7 1	69,667 12 0	13,664 1 0	11,367 11 9
1872-73	Do. ..	6,228 0 0	12,384 11 0	9,832 0 3	6,117 0 7½	85,295 7 5½	25,837 5 1	6,224 14 2
1873-74	Do. ..	1,429 4 9	11,788 11 1½	10,245 3 1	15,503 2 4	88,310 15 7¼	34,809 2 2½	6,529 11 0
1874-75	Do. ..	6,538 6 10	2,754 6 5	20,678 5 9	7,465 8 3	76,906 8 4	15,873 9 4	7,275 0 2
1st November 1871 to 31st March 1872.	Srírangam ..	..	1,666 14 0	1 9 0	..	3,598 6 0	136 0 6	..
1872-73	Do. ..	950 0 0	4,861 2 6	97 5 10	..	13,212 9 10	444 14 6	395 8 11
1873-74	Do. ..	6,809 6 7	8,224 8 3	151 1 0	..	25,013 9 10	9,116 8 9	423 6 10
1874-75	Do. ..	7,435 14 3	4,592 14 8	153 3 0	..	20,741 3 5	3,822 15 4	1,114 0 2
	Total ..	45,560 10 5	68,076 14 6½	55,339 2 1	38,008 1 11¼	4,65,754 2 2	1,10,178 13 1½	46,630 11 1

No. 20.—*Statement showing the Receipts and Expenditure of the several Municipal Commissions for a Series of Five Years*—(Cont.)

Years.	Municipal Towns.	Expenditure—(*Continued*). Conservancy.	Police.	Establishments.	Miscellaneous.	Total.	Balance.
		RS. A. P.	RS. A. P.	RS. A. P.	RS. A. P.	RS. A. P.	RS. A. P.
1870-71	Trichinopoly ..	17,419 10 9	21,081 0 1	5,473 11 6	14,640 2 1	78,389 2 11	4,618 6 9
1871-72 (11 months only) ..	Do. ..	8,554 14 4	..	13,029 10 1	16,658 3 1	63,274 8 3	6,393 3 9
1872-73	Do. ..	12,617 13 5	..	18,316 8 7	16,321 1 3	79,317 10 6	5,977 12 11½
1873-74	Do. ..	12,459 4 4	..	20,999 10 11	12,857 8 11	87,655 5 4½	655 10 3
1874-75	Do. ..	8,788 12 10	..	20,515 5 7	17,339 11 0	69,792 6 11	7,114 1 5
1st November 1871 to 31st March 1872.	Srírangam ..	488 12 8	..	489 7 4	203 14 0	1,318 2 6	2,280 3 6
1872-73	Do. ..	1,190 3 6	..	1,957 11 11	1,439 10 9	5,428 1 7	7,784 8 3
1873-74	Do. ..	2,511 8 9	..	4,429 3 1	2,983 3 3	19,463 14 8	5,549 11 2
1874-75	Do. ..	1,804 10 2	..	4,683 4 1	3,975 6 7	15,400 4 4	5,340 15 1
	Total ..	65,835 10 9	21,081 0 1	89,894 9 1	86,418 12 11	4,20,039 9 0½	45,714 9 1½

INDEX.

H.

I.

J.

K.

L.

M

N.

O.

P.

TRICHINOPOLY GAZETTEER

TRICHINOPOLY GAZETTEER

BY

LEWIS MOORE

VOLUME 2

STATISTICAL APPENDIX

COSMO PUBLICATIONS

2000 INDIA

TABLE OF CONTENTS.

* These tables are *nil.*

I.—Area, Population, etc., in 1911.

Locality.	Area in square miles.	Number of			Population.			Population (both sexes) in 1901.	Percentage of variation (of population).		Density of population per square mile, 1911.
					1911.						
		Towns.	Villages.	Occupied houses.	Total.	Males.	Females.		1891—1901.	1901—1911.	
(1)	(2)	(3)	(4)	(5)	(6)	(7)	(8)	(9)	(10)	(11)	(12)
KARUR DIVISION.											
Karur	612	2	92	54,646	241,252	116,696	124,556	220,843	+ 4·3	+ 9·2	394
Kulittalai	901	1	229	57,717	285,206	139,131	146,075	263,331	+ 8·1	+ 8·3	317
NAMAKKAL DIVISION.											
Namakkal...	691	2	343	71,266	311,333	151,272	160,061	299,506	+ 4·4	+ 3·9	451
Musiri	762	1	156	68,326	311,835	150,114	161,721	294,383	+ 4·2	+ 5·9	409
ARIYALUR DIVISION.											
Perambalur	674	...	127	36,616	219,932	107,296	112,636	204,257	+ 4·7	+ 7·7	326
Udaiyarpalaiyam	753	2	227	49,087	318,444	155,265	163,179	300,708	+ 3·5	+ 5·9	423
TRICHINOPOLY DIVISION.											
Trichinopoly	542	2	197	77,022	419,027	203,092	215,935	382,091	+ 5·9	+ 9·7	773
District Total ...	4,935	10	1,371	414,680	2,107,029	1,022,866	1,084,163	1,965,119	+ 5·0	+ 7·2	427

II.—Variation in Population since 1891.

Towns. (1)	Population. 1911. (2)	1901. (3)	1891. (4)	Percentage of variation of population. 1891—1901. (5)	1901—1911. (6)
The whole district...	2,107,029	1,965,119	1,871,476	5·0	7·2
KARUR TALUK.					
Karur *	17,674	12,769	10,750	18·7	38·4
Pallappatti	9,277	8,452	7,653	10·4	9·7
KULITTALAI TALUK.					
Kulittalai	6,767	8,197	6,286	30·4	—17·4
NAMAKKAL TALUK.					
Namakkal ...	5,196	6,843	6,341	7·9	—24·1
Sendamangalam ...	9,196	13,584	13,354	1·7	—32·3
MUSIRI TALUK.					
Turaiyur	13,249	12,870	7,467	72·3	2·9
UDAIYARPALAIYAM TALUK.					
Ariyalur	7,904	7,370	6,730	9·5	7·2
Udaiyarpalaiyam ...	6,759	7,553	7,739	— 2·4	—10·5
TRICHINOPOLY TALUK.					
Srirangam * ...	24,799	23,039	21,632	6·5	7·6
Trichinopoly † ...	123,512	104,721	90,609	15·6	17·9

* Represents a Municipal Town.
† Represents a Municipality and Cantonment.

III.—Roads.

Year.	Mileage of roads maintained. Metalled.	Unmetalled.	Total.
1911-12	984	145	1,129

NOTE.—The territorial limits of the district were revised with effect from November 1910.

IV.—List of Travellers' Bungalows.

Serial number. (1)	Taluks and stations. (2)	By whom maintained. (3)	Nearest railway station, if any, and the distance from it. (4)	Nature of accommodation. (5)
	KARUR DIVISION.			
	Karur Taluk.			
1	Noyal	L.F.D.	Noyal, 5 furlongs.	Two rooms, two bath rooms and verandahs front and back, one kitchen, one stable with three stalls and one latrine.
2	Karur	P.W.D.	Karur, ¾ mile.	Two sets of rooms furnished.
3	Anaipalaiyam ...	Do.	Karur, 10 miles.	A small thatched shed having only one room.
	Kulittalai Taluk.			
4	Manapparai ...	L.F.D.	Manapparai, 1 furlong.	An arched terraced building with two accommodations, one big hall, two store rooms, two bath rooms and verandah in front with separate kitchen and stables.
5	Kovilpatti ...	Do.	Manapparai, 8 miles.	An arched terraced building with two accommodations, one hall, one room, two bath rooms and a thatched verandah on all sides, a separate kitchen, one bandy stall and stables.
6	Puduppalaiyam.	Do.	Kulittalai, 3 miles.	A tiled building with two rooms, two bath rooms with front verandah, one rear verandah room, a separate new kitchen, new stables and a well. There is also a kitchen for caste people.
7	Panjappatti ...	P.W.D.	Kulittalai, 13½ miles.	One room at centre and two side bath rooms. Not furnished.
8	Kattalai ...	Forest Department.	Kattalai, 50 yards.	Tiled building with two rooms, two bath rooms, stables and out-houses tiled. Furnished.
9	Vaiyampatti ...	Do.	Vaiyampatti, 1½ miles.	Tiled building with two rooms and bath rooms. Out-houses and stables also tiled. Furnished.
10	Kalpatti chatram.	Do.	Kalpatti, 1½ miles.	One room and two bath rooms tiled. Out-houses tiled; stables thatched. Furnished.

IV.—List of Travellers' Bungalows—*cont.*

Serial number. (1)	Taluks and stations. (2)	By whom maintained. (3)	Nearest railway station, if any, and the distance from it. (4)	Nature of accommodation. (5)
	NAMAKKAL DIVISION.			
	Namakkal Taluk.			
11	Namakkal ...	L.F.D.	Pugalur, 19 miles. Cauvery should be crossed by ferry.	Two compartments, each has one hall and one bath room with verandah all round, one kitchen with four rooms, one stable for three horses, one carriage and one latrine.
12	Valaiyappatti ...	Do.	Lalapet, 18 miles.	One hall with a bath room and a one side verandah, one shed for kitchen and one stable.
	Musiri Taluk.			
13	Turaiyur ...	L.F.D.	Kulittalai, 20 miles.	Two halls, two bath rooms, one kitchen and stables.
14	Musiri	P.W.D.	Kulittalai, 3 miles.	One room, two side rooms and bath rooms, kitchen and stables, etc.
15	Kannanur ...	Do.	Kulittalai, 15 miles.	Do do.
16	Sobanapuram ...	Forest Department.	Kulittalai, 32 miles.	Thatched building; two rooms and two bath rooms with thatched out-houses and stables. Furnished.
17	Sengattuppatti on the Pachchamalais.	Do.	Kulittalai, 40 miles.	Thatched building; two rooms and two bath rooms with thatched out-houses and stables. Furnished.
18	Kulivaluvappatti on the Kollimalais.	Do.	Karur, 40 miles.	Two rooms and two bath rooms corrugated iron roofed. Out-houses and stables thatched. Furnished.
	ARIYALUR DIVISION.			
	Perambalur Taluk.			
19	Tirumanur ...	P.W.D.	Tanjore, 12 miles.	Two rooms, two bath rooms, two store rooms, kitchen and stables.
20	Malaiyalappatti.	Forest Department.	Trichinopoly, 55 miles.	Tiled building with one room and a bath room. Out-houses and stables tiled. Furnished.

IV.—List of Travellers' Bungalows—*cont.*

Serial number.	Taluks and stations.	By whom maintained.	Nearest railway station, if any, and the distance from it.	Nature of accommodation
(1)	(2)	(3)	(4)	(5)
	ARIYALUR DIVISION—*cont.*			
	Perambalur Taluk —cont.			
21	Toramangalam.	L.F.D.	Trichinopoly Fort, 34 miles.	One front hall, one rear hall, two bath rooms, two kitchens and four stables.
22	Veppantattai ...	Do.	Trichinopoly Fort, 42 miles.	One hall, one bath room, one private room, one kitchen and two stables.
23	Padalur ...	Do.	Trichinopoly Fort, 23 miles.	One hall and one bath room with a verandah on three sides.
	Udaiyarpalaiyam Taluk.			
24	Ariyalur ...	L.F.D.	Tanjore, 26 miles.	One hall, one bath room, one kitchen and two stables.
25	Kilappaluvur ...	Do.	Tanjore, 20 miles.	It is a thatched building and is not fit for occupation. Stables are also thatched and are leaky.
26	Jayankondam ...	Do.	Kumbakonam, 20 miles.	One hall, one bath room, one kitchen and one stable with two stalls. All these are thatched.
27	Nandiyar anicut.	P.W.D.	Budalur, 9 miles.	Two rooms, two bath rooms, kitchen and stables.
	TRICHINOPOLY DIVISION.			
	Trichinopoly Taluk.			
28	Tiruvallarai rest shed.	L.F.D.	Trichinopoly Fort, 11 miles. Srirangam Road station is nearer by three miles, but Coleroon and Cauveri will have to be crossed.	Main building with one room and verandah all round, one kitchen and one stable with two stalls.

IV.—List of Travellers' Bungalows—*cont.*

Serial number. (1)	Taluks and stations. (2)	By whom maintained. (3)	Nearest railway station, if any, and the distance from it. (4)	Nature of accommodation. (5)
	TRICHINOPOLY DIVISION—*cont.*			
	Trichinopoly Taluk—cont.			
29	Samayavaram ...	L F.D.	Trichinopoly Fort, 8 miles.	Main building with two halls and two bath rooms and thatched sun shade on three sides, one cook house with three rooms and a verandah in front and one stable with three stalls.
30	Manthurai rest shed.	Do.	Trichinopoly Fort, 9 miles.	Main building with one room with verandah on three sides, one bath room, one kitchen and one stable with two stalls.
31	Pettaivayttalai.	P.W.D.	Pettaivayttalai, ½ mile.	Two sets of rooms. Only one room furnished. Tiled building.

Charges per diem : As. 8 for a single person and As. 12 for married couple and As. 4 for use of stables or for pitching tents in the compound when no use is made of the bungalow or rest house. For halts of less than 4 hours a fee of As. 4 for a single person and As. 6 for a married couple is charged.

V.—Religions in 1911.

Taluks.	Hindus.			Musalmans.			Christians.			Others.		
	Total.	Males.	Females.	Total.	Males.	Females.	Total.	Males.	Females.	Total	Males.	Females.
(1)	(2)	(3)	(4)	(5)	(6)	(7)	(8)	(9)	(10)	(11)	(12)	(13)
Karur Division.												
Karur	228,219	111,265	116,954	11,900	4,872	7,028	1,133	559	574	...	...	...
Kulittalai	260,057	126,911	133,146	11,328	5,465	5,863	13,821	6,755	7,066	...	...	...
Namakkal Division.												
Namakkal	307,151	149,159	157,992	3,621	1,838	1,783	561	275	286	...	...	...
Musiri	302,623	145,693	156,930	4,390	2,126	2,264	4,822	2,295	2,527	...	...	...
Ariyalur Division.												
Perambalur	207,495	101,136	106,359	8,141	3,994	4,147	4,296	2,166	2,130	...	...	...
Udaiyarpalaiyam	302,686	147,580	155,106	2,545	1,277	1,268	13,213	6,408	6,805	...	...	...
Trichinopoly Division.												
Trichinopoly	345,621	167,313	178,308	23,828	11,974	11,854	49,507	23,751	25,756	71	54	17
District Total ...	1,953,852	949,057	1,004,795	65,753	31,546	34,207	87,353	42,209	45,144	71	54	17

VI.—Vital Statistics.

Taluks.	Ratio per 1,000 of population of			
	Births.		Deaths.	
	1911.	1912.	1911.	1912.
Karur Division.				
Karur	29	27	18	18
Kulittalai	29	28	18	20
Namakkal Division.				
Namakkal	31	31	17	21
Musiri	29	32	21	26
Ariyalur Division.				
Perambalur	33	32	24	22
Udaiyarpalaiyam	37	40	25	31
Trichinopoly Division.				
Trichinopoly	28	27	24	23
Town Circles.				
Trichinopoly	31	31	31	29
Srirangam	26	28	31	29
Karur	32	33	30	30
District Average ...	31	31	22	24

Note.—(1) This table includes statistics relating to Europeans and Eurasians.
(2) Karur and Namakkal Taluks were newly added to this district with effect from 15th November 1910.

VII.—Causes of Death.

(Average of the statistics for the two years 1911 and 1912.)

Taluks. (1)	Ratio of deaths per 1,000 of population from Cholera. (2)	Small-pox. (3)	Plague. (4)	Fever. (5)	Dysentery and Diarrhœa. (6)	All other causes. (7)	Total. (8)
KARUR DIVISION.							
Karur	4	1	...	5	2	24	36
Kulittalai	3	1	...	10	1	25	40
NAMAKKAL DIVISION.							
Namakkal	2	1	...	12	2	23	40
Musiri	3	1	...	11	2	26	43
ARIYALUR DIVISION.							
Perambalur	2	...	...	4	1	35	42
Udaiyarpalaiyam ...	5	1	...	17	2	27	52
TRICHINOPOLY DIVISION.							
Trichinopoly	5	1	...	7	1	29	43
TOWN CIRCLES.							
Trichinopoly	3	4	...	7	9	36	59
Srirangam	3	4	...	11	6	30	54
Karur	5	...	...	11	11	45	72
District average ...	2	...	...	5	1	14	22

NOTE.—The territorial limits of the district were revised in November 1910.

VIII.—Castes, Tribes and Races in 1911.

Caste, Tribe or Race.	Strength.		
	Males.	Females.	Total.
I. HINDU AND ANIMIST CASTES.			
(a) *Tamil.*			
Agamudaiyan	2,159	2,381	4,540
Ambalakaran	69,154	72,488	141,642
Ambattan	10,258	10,908	21,166
Andi	2,323	2,698	5,021
Brahman	21,747	22,561	44,308
Chetti	12,309	13,519	25,828
Idaiyan	22,235	25,372	47,607
Irula	3,293	3,489	6,782
Kaikolan	19,205	20,575	39,780
Kallan	13,486	14,244	27,730
Kammalan	25,002	26,377	51,379
Kuravan	3,444	3,575	7,019
Kusavan	6,606	6,652	13,258
Malaiman	7,809	8,401	16,210
Malayali	6,317	6,613	12,930
Muttiriyan	15,153	15,533	30,686
Nattaman	35,799	38,034	73,833
Pallan	70,044	74,811	144,855
Palli	91,492	97,879	189,371
Pandaram	4,274	4,768	9,042
Paraiyan	80,267	88,698	168,965
Sembadavan	1,173	1,202	2,375
Shanan...	6,291	6,521	12,812
Sudarman	14,921	15,091	30,012
Uppiliyan	5,116	5,582	10,698
Urali	20,501	21,855	42,356
Valaiyan...	4,264	4,556	8,820
Valluvan...	3,258	3,432	6,690
Vaniyan	6,740	6,951	13,691
Vannan	10,342	10,959	21,301
Vedan	1,257	1,297	2,554
Vellala	162,376	168,286	330,662
Vettuvan	10,493	11,563	22,056
(b) *Telugu.*			
Balija	24,923	25,704	50,627
Brahman...	2,953	3,059	6,012
Chakkiliyan	32,669	32,886	65,555
Devanga...	2,575	2,457	5,032
Kamma	4,060	4,232	8,292
Kapu	25,111	26,917	52,028
Komati	5,951	5,822	11,773
Odde	17,888	18,513	36,401
Sale	5,355	5,706	11,061
Tottiyan...	12,690	12,822	25,512
Vadugan	4,512	5,285	9,797
(c) *Malayalam* ...	*Nil.*	*Nil.*	*Nil.*

VIII.—Castes, Tribes and Races in 1911—*cont.*

Caste, Tribe or Race.	Strength.		
	Males.	Females.	Total.
I. HINDU AND ANIMIST CASTES — *cont.*			
(*d*) *Canarese.*			
Brahman	2,179	2,419	4,598
Kurumban	17,387	18,367	35,754
(*e*) *Oriya*	*Nil.*	*Nil.*	*Nil.*
(*f*) *Other Madras Languages.*			
Patnulkaran	3,429	3,923	7,352
II. MUSALMAN.			
Labbai	16,727	20,072	36,799
Pathan	2,530	2,383	4,913
Saiyad	2,019	1,977	3,996
Sheik	8,862	8,601	17,463
III. CHRISTIAN.			
Indian Christian	41,618	44,545	86,163
IV. OTHERS...	20,320	21,602	41,922
Total ...	1,022,866	1,084,163	2,107,029

IX.—Classification of area and principal crops in fasli 1322 (1912–13).

Items.	Karur Division.		Namakkal Division.		Ariyalur Division.		Trichinopoly Division.	District Total.
	Karur Taluk.	Kulittalai Taluk.	Namakkal Taluk.	Musiri Taluk.	Perambalur Taluk.	Udaiyarpalaiyam Taluk.	Trichinopoly Taluk.	
(1)	(2)	(3)	(4)	(5)	(6)	(7)	(8)	(9)
	ACS.	ACS.	ACS.	ACS.	ACS.	ACS.	ACS.	ACS.
Government (Ryotwari) Land	312,898	307,914	217,787	422,830	394,986	319,774	275,986	2,252,175
Minor inam	45,784	34,774	3,026	9,695	13,116	12,604	14,228	183,227
Whole inam	9,101	52,039	16,534	10,150	9,114	18,790	56,928	172,656
Zamindari	23,994	181,843	201,616	48,096	14,029	130,336	...	599,914
Total area by survey ...	391,777	576,570	438,963	490,771	431,245	481,504	347,142	3,157,972
Forests	1,901	24,655	33,817	62,355	69,408	17,714	7,571	217,421
Not available for cultivation	41,906	116,717	83,776	92,034	22,920	90,240	78.787	526,380
Culturable waste other than fallow ...	2,020	27,519	58,719	54,779	46,830	50,082	13,219	253,168
Current fallows	112,240	138,059	47,328	51,736	57,989	52,908	75,707	535,967
Net area cropped	233,710	269,620	215,323	229,867	234,098	270,560	171,858	1,625,036
Area shown in village accounts ...	391,777	576,570	438,963	490,771	431,245	481,504	347,142	3,157,972
Irrigated by Government canals	16,457	12,881	9,886	15,803	1,268	8,290	67,967	132,552
Do. by private canals	...	32	5,001	491	..	...	...	5,524
Do. by tanks	720	12,793	10,925	11,394	10,102	13,748	22,856	82,538
Do. by wells	21,944	20,434	14,452	24,533	10,314	1,205	5,485	98,367
Do. by other sources...	227	141	882	2,536	7,282	131	114	11.313
Total area irrigated ...	39,348	46,281	41,146	54,757	28,966	23,374	96,422	330,294

Area under—								
Cereals and pulses—								
Rice	18,187	37,027	37,666	42,451	16,820	41,152	103,203	296,506
Cholam	26,153	88,505	43,331	49,098	39,317	17,039	18,508	281,951
Cambu	112,636	36,273	110,329	75,331	54,057	40,296	14,076	442,998
Ragi	11,318	14,436	16,702	29,613	35,015	24,279	18,299	149,662
Others	15,611	79,563	29,503	41,750	60,954	80,509	21,639	329,529
Total ...	183,905	255,804	237,531	238,243	206,163	203,275	175,725	1,500,646
Oil-Seeds—								
Til or gingelly	32,432	8,942	4,059	3,060	3,634	4,705	682	57,521
Ground-nut	2,987	943	3,239	2,131	11,964	55,932	4,440	81,636
Castors	1,086	8,571	605	2,576	759	342	831	14,770
Others	4	106	46	318	553	891	200	2,118
Total ...	36,509	18,569	7,949	8,085	16,910	61,870	6,153	156,045
Condiments and spices	3,512	2,327	3,577	3,288	13,074	7,245	3,136	36,159
Sugarcane, etc.	589	260	2,241	997	1,255	989	1,532	7,863
Cotton	24,672	5,101	17,973	5,786	8,716	1,576	2,699	66,523
Indigo, etc.	...	43	89	157	578	6	743	1,611
Drugs and narcotics—								
Tobacco	1,887	530	286	36	236	948	17	3,940
Others	31	130	668	118	114	4	69	1,755
Total ...	1,918	660	954	154	350	952	707	5,695
Fodder crops...	...	40	7,326	9	...	150	...	7,525
Orchards and garden produce	3,082	5,342	3,677	4,055	721	2,068	9,840	28,785
Miscellaneous non-food crops	22	144	73	1,647	1,170	2,456	1,613	7,125
Total area cropped ...	254,209	288,290	281,390	262,421	248,932	280,587	202,148	1,817,977
Deduct area cropped more than once ...	20,499	18,670	66,067	32,554	14,834	10,027	30,290	192,941
Net area cropped ...	233,710	269,620	215,323	229,867	234,098	270,560	171,858	1,625,036

X.—Reserved Forest and area proposed for reservation (in square miles) on 30th June 1913.

Taluks.	Reserved Forest.	Area proposed for reservation.	Total of columns 2 and 3.	Area of Taluk.	Percentage of column 4 to cultivated area.
(1)	(2)	(3)	(4)	(5)	(6)
KARUR DIVISION.					
Karur	2·97	...	2·97	612·14	1·02
Kulittalai	38·52	1·52	40·04	900·89	9·5
NAMAKKAL DIVISION.					
Namakkal	52·84	4·47	57·31	714·45	17·2
Musiri	95·04	10·10	105·14	762·18	29·3
ARIYALUR DIVISION.					
Perambalur	108·45	...	108·45	673·82	29·7
Udaiyarpalaiyam ...	27·68	0·78	28·46	753·21	6·7
TRICHINOPOLY DIVISION.					
Trichinopoly	10·86	0·97	11·83	542·41	4·40
Total ...	336·36	17·84	354·20	4,959·10	13·9

Net revenue realized under forests during

	RS.
1911–12	63,960
1912–13	71,398

XI.—Classification of area and money rates according to the last settlement.

(Part 1. Area under each money rate.)

Dry.

Particulars of money rates.	Karur Division.	Namakkal Division.	Ariyalur Division.		Trichinopoly Division.
	Kulittalai Taluk.	Musiri Taluk.	Perambalur Taluk.	Udaiyarpalayam Taluk.	Trichinopoly Taluk.
(1)	(2)	(3)	(4)	(5)	(6)
RS. A.	ACS.	ACS.	ACS.	ACS.	ACS.
7 0* ...	...	...	...	..	...
5 0* ...	300	27	...	...	277
5 0 ...	25	...	...	...	70
4 0 ...	395	1,578	55	75	1,087
3 8 ...	...	23	519	14	..
3 0 ...	1,000	555	171	2	2,382
2 12 ...	...	1	852	...	...
2 8 ...	468	1,640	104	658	2,354
2 4 ...	...	217	383	178	980
2 0 ...	360	13,052	20,283	3,232	7,699
1 12 ...	...	3,900	48,444	3,363	5
1 10 ...	57	3,995	11,822	30,564	7,780
1 8 ...	542	543	..	449	1,988
1 6 ...	...	667	46,089	1,394	...
1 4 ...	363	142	..	346	562
1 2 ...	33,421	130,519	16,947	171,578	29,191
1 0 ...	196	...	...	12	182
0 14 ...	...	9,552	29,890	...	756
0 12 ...	672	20,941	15,779	886	23,344
0 10 ...	...	5,711	52,272	...	82
0 9 ...	61,964	35,504	10,546	1,896	9,213
0 8 ...	...	641	24,704	36	...
0 7 ...	110,133	12,892	1,073	77	25,413
0 6 ...	...	88	7,663	...	...
0 4 ...	18,286		4,994	...	8,540
Special rate.					
3 0 ...	6	58	33	41	21
1 0 ...	4	...	...	...	...
Grand Total.	228,187	242,246	292,623	214,796	121,876

* Padugai special rates.

NOTE.—Particulars for Namakkal and Karur Taluks are furnished separately.

XI.—Classification of area and money rates according to the last settlement—*cont.*

(Part 1. Area under each money rate)—*cont.*

Wet.

Particulars of money rates.	Karur Division.	Namakkal Division.	Ariyalur Division.		Trichinopoly Division.
	Kulittalai Taluk.	Musiri Taluk.	Perambalur Taluk.	Udaiyarpalayam. Taluk.	Trichinopoly Taluk.
(1)	(2)	(3)	(4)	(5)	(6)
RS. A.	ACS.	ACS.	ACS.	ACS.	ACS.
14 0 ...	...	...	...	...	...
12 0 ...	645	157	...	...	1,006
11 0 ...	...	...	...	...	...
10 8 ...	...	..	...	...	0·33
10 0 ...	2,800	1,011	...	...	9,959
9 8 ...	...	...	...	...	...
9 0 .	1,749	2,590	...	..	15,286
8 12 ...	...	...	...	..	3
8 8 ...	..	18	166	4	1
8 4 ...	...	...	...	...	...
8 0 ...	2,291	2,743	526	...	10,996
7 8 ...	...	...	...	...	4
7 4 ...	...	3	...	...	17
7 0 ...	1,635	2,727	...	15	8,612
6 8 ...	...	934	1,493	233	1
6 0 ...	483	1,462	409	1,734	8,699
5 4 ...	...	2,608	899	433	156
5 0 ...	617	141	...	2,992	3,356
4 12 ...	...	2,233	2,918	850	2,362
4 8 ...	582	...	...	300	410
4 4 ...	668	1,815	490	1,663	1,427
4 0 ...	858	...	...	211	224
3 12 ...	143	2,279	1,102	3,059	3,472
3 8 ...	508	1,381	10	1,229	428
3 4 ...	258	251	232	2,484	1,932
3 0 ...	2,909	122	11	36	5,680
2 12 ...	6	233	541	...	118
2 8 ...	587	459	7	2	1,632
2 0 ...	...	60	162	...	74
1 12 ...	35	7	...	...	1,042
1 8 ...	...	...	...	...	...
1 4 ...	170	...	...	...	361
Special rate.					
2 8 ...	...	12	...	...	...
2 0 ...	...	29	...	...	...
Grand Total.	16,944	23,275	8,966	15,245	77,258·33

NOTE.—Particulars for Namakkal and Karur Taluks are furnished separately.

XI.—Classification of area and money rates according to the last settlement—*cont.*

(Part 1. Area under each money rate in the Karur taluk.)

Money rates. (1)		Occupied. (2)	Unoccupied. (3)	Total. (4)
RS.	A.	ACS.	ACS.	ACS.
		Wet.		
9	4 ...	......	0·33	0 33
6	14 ...	31·53	0·46	31·99
5	12 ...	47·69	...	47·69
4	10 ...	221 93	0·50	222·43
4	0 ...	482·04	4·13	486 17
3	8 ...	155·77	0·67	156·44
Total ...		938·96	6·09	945·05
		Permanent double crop lands.		
17	4 ...	876·24	0 40	876·64
13	14 ...	592·58	0·31	592·89
10	5 ...	939 15	0·78	939·93
8	10 ...	875·46	4·01	879 47
6	15 ...	1,042·82	1·97	1,044·79
6	0 ...	64 60	3·16	67·76
		Compounded at ¦ of single crop.		
11	9 ...	722·87	3·13	726·00
8	9 ...	2,139·18	1·70	2,140·88
7	3 ...	2,185·88	3·79	2,189·67
5	12 ...	2,085·99	3·45	2,089·44
5	0 ...	1,717·14	1·48	1,718 62
4	6 ...	309·70	1·10	310·80
Total ...		13,551·61	25·28	13,576·89
		Dry.		
1	11 ...	1,677·83	25·56	1,703·39
1	6 ...	13,450·19	154·37	13,604·56
1	2 ...	48,314·01	348·51	48,662·52
0	13 ...	89,525·85	851·05	90,376·90
0	9 ...	90,731·74	1,069·81	91,801·55
0	7 ...	11,285·05	148·90	11,433·95
Total ...		254,984·67	2,598·20	257,582 87

XI.—Classification of area and money rates according to the last settlement—*cont.*

(Part 1. Area under each money rate in the Namakkal taluk.)

Dry.			*Wet.*		
Particulars of money rates.	Occupied.	Unoccupied.	Particulars of money rates.	Occupied.	Unoccupied.
RS. A.	ACS.	ACS.	RS. A.	ACS.	ACS.
2 12	718·85	1·16	11 12	1,034·39	4·10
2 0	10,730 07	16·40	10 12	761·14	2·09
1 6	30,772·27	393·70	9 0	881 67	9·22
1 2	47,126·44	1,312·94	8 8	213·63	...
0 14	3,450·60	4,518 40	8 0	1,004.35	1·19
0 9	2,417·21	1,207·16	7 4	842·18	5·32
0 7	15,087·09	544·00	6 12	770·45	13·32
0 6	......	7,251·69	5 10	2,625·82	22·75
Special rate.			4 8	1,440 94	23·81
2 4	8·56		3 6	736·15	2·76
			2 12	560 55	6·73
			2 4	527 20	23·93
			1 12	29·46	
Total ...	110,311·09	15,245·50	Total ...	11,427·93	115·22

NOTE.—The constitution of Namakkal taluk was changed with effect from 15th November 1910. The above figures are for the taluk as it stood at the time of the introduction of settlement rates. Figures for the revised area are not available.

XI.—Classification of area and money rates according to the last settlement—*cont.*

(Part 2. Classes and sorts included under each money rate in the reclassified tract.)

Dry.

Soil. Class. (1)	Soil. Sort. (2)	First Group. Taram. (3)	First Group. Rate. (4)
			RS. A.
I	1	1	7 0*
I II	2 1	2	5 0*
I	1	2	5 0
I II	2 1	3	4 0
I II III	3 2 1	4	3 0
I II III IV	4 3 2 1	5	2 8
I II III IV VII	5 4 3 2 1	6	2 0
II III IV V VII VIII	5 4 3 1 2 1	7	1 8
III IV V VII VIII	5 4 2 3 2	8	1 4
IV V VII VIII	5 3 4 3	9	1 0
V VII VIII	4 5 4	10	0 12
V VIII	5 5	11	0 8

Wet.

Soil. Class. (5)	Soil. Sort. (6)	First Class. Taram. (7)	First Class. Rate. (8)	Second Class. Taram. (9)	Second Class. Rate. (10)	Third Class. Taram. (11)	Third Class. Rate. (12)
			RS. A.		RS. A.		RS. A.
II	1-A.	1	14 0	...	...	...	...
II	1	2	12 0	3	10 0	4	9 0
I II	1 2	3	10 0	4	9 0	5	8 0
I II IV	2 3 1	4	9 0	5	8 0	6	7 0
I II III IV VII	3 4 1 2 1	5	8 0	6	7 0	7	6 0
I II III IV V VII VIII	4 5 2 3 1 2 1	6	7 0	7	6 0	8	5 0
I III IV V VII VIII	5 3 4 2 3 2	7	6 0	8	5 0	9	4 8
III IV V VII VIII	4 5 3 4 3	8	5 0	9	4 8	10	4 0
III V VII VIII	5 4 5 4	9	4 8	10	4 0	11	3 8
V VIII	5 5	10	4 0	11	3 8	12	3 0

* Padugai Special rates.

NOTE.—Particulars for Karur and Namakkal taluks are furnished separately.

XI. —Classification of area and money rates according to the last settlement—*cont.*

(Part 2. Classes and sorts included under each money rate in the non-reclassified tract.)

Dry.											Wet.																
Soil.		First Group.			Second Group.			Third Group.			Soil.		First Class.			Second Class.			Third Class.			Fourth Class.			Fifth Class.		
Class.	Sort.	Taram.	Rate.		Taram.	Rate.		Taram.	Rate.		Class.	Sort.	Taram.	Rate.		Taram.	Rate.		Taram.	Rate.		Taram.	Rate.		Taram.	Rate.	
(1)	(2)	(3)	(4)		(5)	(6)		(7)	(8)		(9)	(10)	(11)	(12)		(13)	(14)		(15)	(16)		(17)	(18)		(19)	(20)	
			RS.	A.		RS.	A.		RS.	A.				RS.	A.		RS.	A.		RS.	A.		RS.	A.		RS.	A.
II	1	1	4	0	2	3	8	3	3	0	II	1	1	11	0	2	10	8	5	8	8	7	8	0	9	7	4
II	2	5	2	8	6	2	4	7	2	0	II	2	3	9	8	4	8	12	10	7	0	11	6	8	12	6	0
IV	1	3	3	0	4	2	12	5	2	8	IV	1	4	8	12	6	8	4	11	6	8	12	6	0	13	5	4
III	1	6	2	4	7	2	0	8	1	12	III	1															
IV	2										IV	2	8	7	8	10	7	0	13	5	4	14	4	12	15	4	4
VII	1	7	2	0	8	1	12	9	1	10	VII	1															
III	2										III	2															
V	1	9	1	10	10	1	6	11	1	2	V	1	11	6	8	12	6	0	15	4	4	16	3	12	17	3	8
V	2										V	2															
VI	1										VI	1															
VII	2	11	1	2	12	0	14	13	0	12	VII	2	13	5	4	14	4	12	17	3	8	18	3	4	19	3	0
VIII	1										VIII	1															
IV	3										IV	3															
VI	2	13	0	12	14	0	10	15	0	9	VI	2	15	4	4	16	3	12	19	3	0	20	2	12	21	2	8
III	3										III	3															
V	3	15	0	9	16	0	8	17	0	7	V	3	17	3	8	18	3	4	21	2	8	22	2	0	23	1	12
VIII	2										VIII	2															
VII	3										VII	3															
VIII	3	17	0	7	18	0	6	19	0	4	VIII	8	19	3	0	20	2	12	23	1	12	24	1	8	25	1	4

NOTE.—Particulars for Karur and Namakkal Taluks are furnished separately.

XI.--Classification of area and money rates according to the last settlement—*cont*

(Part 2. Classes included under each money rate in the Karur taluk.)

Table of wet rates.

Class and sort.					Assessment.									
					First Class.				Second Calss.			Third Class.		
III.	IV.	V.	VII.	VIII.	Taram.	Single crop.	Permanent double crop.	Compounded at ¼.	Taram.	Single crop.	Compounded at ¼.	Taram	Single crop.	Compounded at ¼.
(1)	(2)	(3)	(4)	(5)	(6)	(7)	(8)	(9)	(10)	(11)	(12)	(13)	(14)	(15)
						RS. A.	RS. A.	RS. A.		RS. A.	RS. A.		RS. A.	RS. A.
...	1	...	...	...	1	13 12	20 10	17 3	2	11 8	14 6	3	9 4	11 9
1	2	...	1	...	2	11 8	17 4	14 6	3	9 4	11 9	4	6 14	8 9
2	3	1	2	1	3	9 4	13 14	11 9	4	6 14	8 9	5	5 12	7 3
3	4	2	3	2	4	6 14	10 5	8 9	5	5 12	7 3	6	4 10	5 12
4	5	3	4	3	5	5 12	8 10	7 3	6	4 10	5 12	7	4 0	5 0
5	...	4	5	4	6	4 10	6 15	5 12	7	4 0	5 0	8	3 8	4 6
...	...	5	...	5	7	4 0	6 0	5 0	8	3 8	4 6	9	2 14	3 9

Table of Dry rates.

Class and sort.					First Group.		Second Group.		Third Group.	
III.	IV.	V.	VII.	VIII.	Taram.	Assessment.	Taram.	Assessment.	Taram.	Assessment.
(1)	(2)	(3)	(4)	(5)	(6)	(7)	(8)	(9)	(10)	(11)
						RS. A.		RS A.		RS. A.
1	1	...	...	...	1	2 4	2	1 11	3	1 6
2	2	...	1	...	2	1 11	3	1 6	4	1 2
3	3	1	2	1	3	1 6	4	1 2	5	0 13
4	4	2	3	2	4	1 2	5	0 13	6	0 9
5	5	3	4	3	5	0 13	6	0 9	7	0 7
...	...	4	5	4	6	0 9	7	0 7	8	0 5
...	...	5	...	5	7	0 7	8	0 5	9	0 4

XI.—Classification of area and money rates according to the last settlement—*cont.*

(Part 2. Classes and sorts included under each money rate in the Namakkal taluk.)

Dry lands in the resettled villages.

Soil classification.					First group.				Second group.				Third group.				Fourth group.			
					Occupied.		Waste		Occupied.		Waste.		Occupied.		Waste.		Occupied.		Waste.	
III	IV	V	VII	VII	Taram.	Rate.	Taram.	Rate.	Taram.	Rate.	Taram.	Rate.	Taram.	Rate.	Taram.	Rate.	Taram.	Rate.	Taram.	Rate.
(1)	(2)	(3)	(4)	(5)	(6)	(7)	(8)	(9)	(10)	(11)	(12)	(13)	(14)	(15)	(16)	(17)	(18)	(19)	(20)	(21)
						RS. A.		RS. A.		RS. A.		RS. A.		RS. A.		RS. A.		RS. A.		RS. A.
..	1	...	...	...	3	3 6	4	2 12	4	2 12	5	2 0	5	2 0	6	1 6	6	1 6	7	1 2
1	2	...	1	A	4	2 12	5	2 0	5	2 0	6	1 6	6	1 6	7	1 2	7	1 2	8	0 14
2	...	1	2	1	5	2 0	6	1 6	6	1 6	7	1 2	7	1 2	8	0 14	8	0 14	9	0 9
...	...	2	...	2	6	1 6	7	1 2	7	1 2	8	0 14	8	0 14	9	0 9	9	0 9	10	0 7
...	3	...	...	...	7	1 2	8	0 14	8	0 14	9	0 9	9	0 9	10	0 7	10	0 7	11	0 6
3	...	3	...	...	8	0 14	9	0 9	9	0 9	10	0 7	10	0 7	11	0 6	11	0 6	12	0 5
...	...	...	3	3	9	0 9	10	0 7	10	0 7	11	0 6	12	0 5	13	0 4	12	0 5	13	0 4

XI.—Classification of area and money rates according to the last settlement—*cont.*

(Part 2. Classes and sorts included under each money rate in the Namakkal taluk)—*cont.*

Wet lands in the resettled villages.

Soil classification.						First Class.		Second Class.		Third Class.		Fourth Class.		Fifth Class.		Sixth Class.	
II	III	IV	V	VII	VIII	Taram.	Rate.	Taram.	Rate.	Taram.	Rate.	Taram.	Rate.	Taram.	Rate.	Taram.	Rate.
(1)	(2)	(3)	(4)	(5)	(6)	(7)	(8)	(9)	(10)	(11)	(12)	(13)	(14)	(15)	(16)	(17)	(18)
							RS. A.		RS. A.		RS. A.		RS. A.		RS. A.		RS. A.
1	...	...	...	...	...	1	11 12	2	10 12	3	9 8	5	8 8	7	7 4	...	...
2	...	1	...	...	...	2	10 12	3	9 8	5	8 8	7	7 4	9	6 4	...	...
...	...	2	...	1	...	4	9 0	6	8 0	8	6 12	10	5 10	11	4 8	12	3 6
...	1	...	1	2	1	6	8 0	8	6 12	10	5 10	11	4 8	12	3 6	13	2 12
...	2	...	2	...	...	8	6 12	10	5 10	11	4 8	12	3 6	13	2 12	14	2 4
...	...	...	...	...	2	10	5 10	11	4 8	12	3 6	13	2 12	14	2 4	15	1 12
...	...	3	3	3	...	11	4 8	12	3 6	13	2 12	14	2 4	15	1 12	16	1 6
...	3	...	...	...	3	12	3 6	13	2 12	14	2 4	15	1 12	16	1 6	17	1 0

XI.—Classification of area and money rates according to the last settlement—*cont.*

(Part 2. Classes and sorts included under each money rate in the Namakkal taluk)—*cont.*

[Money-rate table for dry lands in the villages of Namakkal taluk settled for the first time in fasli 1315.]

Soil classification.		Third Group.		Fourth Group.		Fifth Group.		Sixth Group.	
VII	VIII	Taram.	Rate.	Taram.	Rate.	Taram.	Rate.	Taram.	Rate.
(1)	(2)	(3)	(4)	(5)	(6)	(7)	(8)	(9)	(10)
			RS. A		RS. A.		RS. A.		RS. A.
1	1	6	1 6	7	1 2	8	0 14	9	0 9
2	2	7	1 2	8	0 14	9	0 9	11	0 6
3	3	8	0 14	9	0 9	11	0 6	12	0 5
4	4	10	0 7	11	0 6	12	0 5	13	0 4
5	5	12	0 5	12	0 5	13	0 4	14	0 3

XII.—Rainfall.

Names of rain-gauge stations. (1)	Average rainfall (1870—1909) in inches in January. (2)	February. (3)	March. (4)	April. (5)	May. (6)	June. (7)	July. (8)	August. (9)	September. (10)	October. (11)	November. (12)	December. (13)	Whole year. (14)
Karur Taluk.													
Aravakurichi (a)	0·36	0·34	0·47	1·70	3·28	0·98	0·49	1·65	2·83	6·22	3·47	1·93	24·02
Karur	0·23	0·20	0·23	1·44	3·49	1·25	0·95	3·20	3·87	6·12	3·67	1·35	26·00
Sendamangalam *	0·55	0·36	0·19	1·58	5·10	1·31	2·35	4·51	7·09	5·68	3·06	0·92	32·70
Kulittalai Taluk.													
Kulittalai	0·46	0·28	0·28	1·44	3·93	1·09	1·08	2·68	4·10	6·93	4·69	1·90	28·86
Manapparai †	0·66	0·38	0·53	1·74	3·17	1·35	1·21	3·19	5·18	6·63	4·49	3·08	31·61
Marungapuri ‡	1·97	0·28	0·20	1·60	4·42	1·84	1·50	5·20	5·00	6·73	3·91	2·28	34·93
Namakkal Taluk.													
Namakkal	0·20	0·13	0·47	1·49	4·06	1·38	1·95	4·14	4·46	5·38	3·39	0·95	28·00
Paramati §	0·29	0·23	0·37	1·54	3·62	1·06	0·98	3·15	3·54	5·36	3·15	1·26	24·75
Thathiengarpettai ‖	1·48	0·30	0·63	1·48	4·88	0·72	0·85	4·46	6·86	6·25	3·10	1·71	32·72
Musiri Taluk.													
Musiri	0·51	0·31	0·28	1·54	3·68	1·24	1·15	3·10	4·42	7·99	4·97	2·11	31·30
Settikulam ‖	1·68	0·68	0·33	1·37	4·65	1·36	1·38	5·48	7·02	7·43	4·89	2·96	39·23
Turaiyur †	0·51	0·40	0·49	1·44	4·06	1·48	1·28	3·48	5·81	7·17	3·90	2·18	32·20
Uppiliyapuram ‡	1·67	0·34	0·55	1·06	5·12	1·83	2·59	4·28	4·58	7·39	3·30	1·84	34·55

(a) 1883—1909 * 1895—1909. † 1884—1909. ‡ 1902—1909. § 1879—1909. ‖ 1901—1909.

XII.—Rainfall—*cont.*

Names of rain-gauge stations.	Average rainfall (1870–1909) in inches in												
	January.	February.	March.	April.	May.	June.	July.	August.	September.	October.	November.	December.	Whole year.
(1)	(2)	(3)	(4)	(5)	(6)	(7)	(8)	(9)	(10)	(11)	(12)	(13)	(14)
Perambalur Taluk.													
Perambalur	0·70	0·62	0·46	1·39	3·77	1·91	1·82	5·08	5·79	7·88	6·39	3·33	39·14
Udaiyarpalaiyam Taluk.													
Ariyalur *	0·72	0·63	0·30	1·07	3·30	1·27	2·11	5·19	6·75	7·38	5·81	4·04	38·57
Kilappaluvur *	0·80	0·58	0·33	1·74	3·63	1·16	1·92	7·10	6·49	8·38	6·36	4·52	43·01
Udaiyarpalaiyam—Jayankondasholapuram.	0·86	0·61	0·29	1·05	2·80	1·56	2·75	5·04	5·69	7·46	7·95	5·10	41·16
Trichinopoly Taluk.													
Iluppur *	0·59	0·35	0·30	1·37	2·75	1·44	1·34	4·54	5·28	6·46	4·52	3·12	32·06
Lalgudi *	0·63	0·44	0·26	1·52	2·96	1·01	1·01	3·99	5·22	6·77	4·91	3·16	31·88
Trichinopoly	0·56	0·53	0·35	1·83	3·02	1·32	1·25	4·13	4·66	7·18	5·14	2·70	32·67
District Average ...	0·53	0·39	0·35	1·46	3·53	1·35	1·57	4·03	4·79	6·85	4·96	2·48	32·29

* 1884—1909.

XIII.—Holdings, Cultivation and Demand in Fasli 1322 (1912-13).

Taluks.	Total holdings.						Cultivation including waste charged.				Miscellaneous revenue.	Total Ryotwar Demand.	Land Cess.	Total demand of Land Revenue Ryotwar, Miscellaneous and Cesses.
	Dry.		Wet.		Total.		Dry.		Wet.					
	Extent.	Assessment.	Extent.	Assessment.	Extent.	Assessment.	Extent.	Assessment including water-rate.	Extent.	Assessment including second crop charge.				
	(2)	(3)	(4)	(5)	(6)	(7)	(8)	(9)	(10)	(11)	(12)	(13)	(14)	(15)
KARUR DIVISION.	ACS.	RS.	ACS.	RS.	ACS.	RS.	ACS	RS.	ACS.	RS.	RS.	RS.	RS.	RS.
Karur	255,462	2,04,896	14,514	1,16,733	269,976	3,21,629	255,462	2,08,111	14,510	1,17,416	21,331	3,14,852	23,286	3,68,138
Kulittalai	217,984	1,27,522	16,628	1,21,102	234,612	2,48,624	217,984	1,33,154	16,564	1,37,985	27,395	2,95,261	20,592	3,15,853
NAMAKKAL DIVISION.														
Namakkal	112,991	1,24,192	11 535	1,03,369	124,526	2,27,491	112,991	1,25,180	11,520	1,03,330	18,305	2,29,823	15,447	2,45,270
Musiri	215,732	2,24,836	24,263	1,60,591	239,995	3,85,427	215,732	2,39,171	24,018	1,72,753	30,584	4,30,558	27,655	4,67,213
ARIYALUR DIVISION.														
Perambalur	230,337	2,66,300	9,330	52,233	239,667	3,18,533	230,337	2,79,014	9,330	53,440	52,158	3,84,481	24,047	4,08,528
Udaiyarpalaiyam ...	202,572	2,49,032	15,331	67,907	217,903	3,16,939	202,572	2,61,500	15,302	69,813	27,732	3,61,305	23,318	3,84,623
TRICHINOPOLY DIVISION.														
Trichinopoly ...	106,599	1,10,275	76,883	5,86,607	183,482	6,96,882	106,599	1,27,310	76,876	6,32,230	52,739	7,54,808	48,957	8,03,765
HUZUR COLLECTIONS.	...	...	...	...	...	...	...	...	...	...	..	...	...	...
Total ...	1,341,677	13,06,983	168,484	12,08,542	1,510,161	25,15,525	1,341,677	13,76,440	168,120	12,86,967	2,30,244	28,10,088	1,83,302	29,93,390

XIV.—Revenue payable by permanently-settled estates in Fasli 1322 (1912–13).

Serial number.	Taluks and estates.	Peishcush.	Land-cess.	Miscellaneous revenue.	Total.
(1)	(2)	(3)	(4)	(5)	(6)
		RS.	RS.	RS.	RS.
	KARUR DIVISION.				
	Karur Taluk.				
1	Andippatti	4,684	759	749	6,192
2	Erumappatti	482	161	52	695
	Total ...	5,166	920	801	6,887
	Kulittalai Taluk.				
1	Kadavur	13,411	2,547	153	16,111
2	Marungapuri	20,590	3,881	210	24,681
	Total ...	34,001	6,428	363	40,792
	NAMAKKAL DIVISION.				
	Namakkal Taluk.				
1	Namakkal	7,874	1,141	...	9,015
2	Kondichettipatti	1,844	252	...	2,096
3	Muttanchetti	7,508	577	...	8,085
4	Lathivadi	3,180	284	...	3,464
5	Ponneri	2,135	219	...	2,354
6	A. Valavandi	2,629	419	...	3,048
7	Muttugapatti	4,930	1,044	...	5,974
8	Tippramahadevi	2,357	180	...	2,537
9	Erumaippatti	4,296	378	...	4,674
10	Palaiyapalaiyam	3,150	384	...	3,534
11	Thottamudaiyanpatti	1,252	115	...	1,367
12	Pavitram	3,249	255	...	3,504
13	Singalam kombai	786	90	...	876
14	Pudukkottai	4,943	436	...	5,379
15	Tusur	6,192	631	...	6,823
16	Mettuppatti	1,667	182	...	1,849
17	Periyapallamparai	3,475	898	...	4,373
18	Belukurichchi	1,368	295	...	1,663
19	Tirumalagiri	964	148	...	1,112
20	Melapatti	404	51	...	455
21	Uppukombai	2,735	342	...	3,077
22	Tuttikulam...	2,425	224	...	2,649
23	Marurpatti	1,784	263	...	2,047
24	Talambadi	1,486	239	...	1,725
25	Minnampalli	1,702	260	...	1 962
26	Pottanam	1,989	219	...	2,208
27	Mudalaippatti	3,485	265	...	3,750
28	Nallipalaiyam	1,946	163	...	2,109
29	Tummankurichchi	2,724	190	...	2,914
30	Marappanayakampatti	2,715	203	...	2,918

XIV.—Revenue payable by permanently-settled estates in Fasli 1322 (1912-13)—*cont.*

Serial number. (1)	Taluks and estates. (2)	Peishcush. (3)	Land-cess. (4)	Miscellaneous revenue. (5)	Total. (6)
	NAMAKKAL DIVISION—*cont.*	RS.	RS.	RS.	RS.
	Namakkal Taluk—cont.				
31	Tolur	3,556	305	...	3,861
32	Sendamangalam	711	90	...	801
33	Bommasamudram	657	77	...	734
34	Periyakulam	1,717	223	...	1,940
35	Ponnarkulam Bit I	610	86	...	696
36	Do. Bit II	470	58	...	528
37	Do. Bit III	102	27	...	129
38	Do. Bit IV	38	10	...	48
39	Solasiramani	5,347	536	...	5,883
40	Tidumal	5,238	518	..	5,756
41	Kudacherri west	1,913	297	...	2,210
42	Do. east	1,633	204	...	1,837
43	Gonur	3,248	387	...	3,635
44	Perunkurichchi	3,340	250	...	3,590
45	Kupperikkapalaiyam	2,026	128	...	2,154
46	Pillur	4,514	536	...	5,050
47	Kirambur	1,816	177	...	1,993
48	Rasampalaiyam	1,816	176	...	1,992
49	Selur	4,340	518	885	5,743
50	Tindamangalam	1,389	190	...	1,579
51	Nallagavundanpalaiyam	1,448	197	...	1,645
52	Eranapuram	882	85	...	967
53	Kollukattipalaiyam	1,346	129	...	1,475
54	Kodur	1,072	118	...	1,190
55	Taligai	973	94	...	1,067
56	S. Valavandi	3,125	294	...	3,419
57	S. Palappatti	3,135	316	352	3,803
58	Naravalur—Tottipalaiyam ...	173	19	...	192
	Total ...	1,43,829	16,392	1,237	1,61,458
	Musiri Taluk.				
1	Kattupputtur	15,894	1,560	29	17,483
2	Turaiyur	700	2,913	175	3,788
	Total ...	16,594	4,473	204	21,271
	ARIYALUR DIVISION.				
	Perambalur Taluk.				
1	Alagiripalaiyam	8	36	...	44
2	Allinagaram	17	81	27	125
3	Arunagirimangalam	18	38	...	56
4	Attur	53	119	10	182
5	Badirgudi	33	32	...	65
6	Bhujangarayanallur	17	84	45	146
7	Ilandangudi	22	60	6	88

XIV.—Revenue payable by permanently-settled estates in Fasli 1322 (1912–13)—*cont.*

Serial number. (1)	Taluks and estates. (2)	Peishcush. (3)	Land-cess. (4)	Miscellaneous revenue. (5)	Total. (6)
	ARIYALUR DIVISION—*cont.*	RS.	RS.	RS.	RS.
	Perambalur Taluk—cont.				
8	Kilamattur	15	90	8	113
9	Makkaikulam	40	31	...	71
10	Mangalam	8	35	2	45
11	Melamattur	81	220	13	314
12	Melasubbarayapuram	1	7	...	8
13	Mukundapuram	2	14	...	16
14	Nochchikulam	20	45	10	75
15	Peraiyur	17	90	50	157
16	Ramalingapuram	27	48	9	84
17	Ramanathapuram	13	62	...	75
18	Rasulabad	7	28	...	35
19	Siranattam	5	38	...	43
20	Sitaramapuram	5	30	...	35
21	Tondappadi	21	106	8	135
22	Usennagaram	17	87	10	114
	Total ...	447	1,381	198	2,026
	Udaiyarpalaiyam Taluk.				
1	Ammakulam	26	40	10	76
2	Ariyalur	53	231	122	406
3	Aspabad	5	23	1	29
4	Eruthukkarampatti	9	46	18	73
5	Govindapuram	18	75	2	95
6	Hanumanthapuram	1	8	42	51
7	Hastinapuram	8	32	4	44
8	Jayaramapuram	42	63	4	109
9	Kallankurichchi	10	49	5	64
10	Kayarlabad	24	114	42	180
11	Kollapuram	3	13	...	16
12	Koneriraysapuram	9	39	13	61
13	Krishnapuram	77	55	7	139
14	Kurumbanchavadi	7	30	14	51
15	Mahalingapuram	8	24	5	37
16	Mallur	17	66	4	87
17	Manakkal	35	91	2	128
18	Manakkudi	11	55	3	69
19	Maravanur	8	51	6	65
20	Muttunayakkanpatti	4	20	...	24
21	Nallakkapalaiyam ...	3	19	5	27
22	Papanseri	17	68	2	87
23	Ravuttanpatti	30	88	10	128
24	Srinivasapuram	16	85	7	108
25	Subbarayapuram	25	116	21	162
26	Tamaraikkulam	10	58	25	93
27	Tavuttayikulam	24	29	10	63
28	Tirumalarayapuram	2	16	6	24

XIV.—Revenue payable by permanently-settled estates in Fasli 1322 (1912-13)—*cont.*

Serial number. (1)	Taluks and estates. (2)	Peishcush. (3)	Land-cess. (4)	Miscellaneous revenue. (5)	Total. (6)
	ARIYALUR DIVISION—*cont.*	RS.	RS.	RS.	RS.
	Udaiyarpalaiyam Taluk—cont.				
29	Udaiyarpalaiyam	665	11,864	243	12,772
30	Usenabad	25	92	2	119
31	Valajanagaram	47	150	13	210
32	Varanavasi	39	73	9	121
33	Velur	13	65	2	80
34	Venkatakrishnapuram	6	28	1	35
35	Venkataramapuram	3	15	...	18
36	Venkataramanapuram	10	43	1	54
	Total ...	1,310	13,934	661	15,905
	District total ...	2,01,347	43,528	3,464	2,48,339

XV.—Demand, Collection and Balance of current Land Revenue and Cesses (in thousands of rupees).

Taluks.	Demand.		Collected or written off.		Balance.	
	Fasli 1321.	Fasli 1322.	Fasli 1321.	Fasli 1322.	Fasli 1321.	Fasli 1322.
(1)	(2)	(3)	(4)	(5)	(6)	(7)
KARUR DIVISION.						
Karur	373	376	370	375	3	1
Kulittalai	358	360	358	360	...	...
NAMAKKAL DIVISION.						
Namakkal	417	416	409	407	8	9
Musiri	489	492	483	487	6	5
ARIYALUR DIVISION.						
Perambalur ...	404	412	385	409	19	3
Udaiyarpalaiyam ...	402	405	398	402	4	3
TRICHINOPOLY DIVISION.						
Trichinopoly	799	806	795	802	4	4
Huzur Collections ...	2	4	2	4	...	...
District Total ...	3,244	3,271	3,200	3,246	44	25

NOTE.—The territorial limits of the district were revised in November 1910.

XVI.—Remissions (in thousands of rupees).

Taluks.	Waste remitted.						Other seasonal remissions (excluding fixed remissions).		
	Dry.			Wet.					
	Fasli 1321.	Fasli 1322.	Total.	Fasli 1321.	Fasli 1322.	Total.	Fasli 1321.	Fasli 1322.	Total.
(1)	(2)	(3)	(4)	(5)	(6)	(7)	(8)	(9)	(10)
KARUR DIVISION.									
Karur ...	...	...	...	...	...	...	3	1	4
Kulittalai ...	...	...	...	1	1	2	1	2	3
NAMAKKAL DIVISION.									
Namakkal	...	...	...	...	...	...	3	6	9
Musiri ...	...	...	...	2	1	3	2	1	3
ARIYALUR DIVISION.									
Perambalur ...	...	...	...	...	...	...	...	...	...
Udaiyarpalaiyam.	...	...	...	1	...	1	...	...	...
TRICHINOPOLY DIVISION.									
Trichinopoly...	...	...	...	2	...	2	1	...	1
District Total...	...	...	...	6	2	8	10	10	20

NOTE.—The territorial limits of the district were altered with effect from 15th November 1910.

XVII.—Land Improvement and Agriculturists Loans.

Taluks.	Total amount advanced under the Land Improvement and Agriculturists Loans Acts in		Total including outstanding balance at the beginning of Fasli 1321.	Total recovered.
	Fasli 1321.	Fasli 1322.		
(1)	(2)	(3)	(4)	(5)
KARUR DIVISION.	RS.	RS.	RS.	RS.
Karur	13,125	15,125	1,11,303	14,176
Kulittalai ...	5,735	5,350	62,677	12,363
NAMAKKAL DIVISION.				
Namakkal ...	6,495	8,675	56,938	11,231
Musiri	4,185	4,475	63,832	12,900
ARIYALUR DIVISION.				
Perambalur ...	28,788	51,780	1,76,030	14,056
Udaiyarpalaiyam.	11,518	3,650	96,690	26,346
TRICHINOPOLY DIVISION.				
Trichinopoly ...	16,160	8,115	74,582	10,350
District Total ...	86,006	97,170	6,42,052	1,01,422

NOTE.—The territorial limits of the district were revised in November 1910.

XVIII.—Prices in seers per rupee.

Fasli.	Karur Division.				Namakkal Division.				Ariyalur Division.			Trichinopoly Division.		District Average.
	Karur Taluk.		Kulittalai Taluk.		Namakkal Taluk.		Musiri Taluk.		Perambalur Taluk.	Udaiyarpalaiyam Taluk.		Trichinopoly Taluk.		
	Karur.	Aravakurichchi.	Kulittalai.	Manapparai.	Namakkal.	Paramathi.	Musiri.	Toraiyur.	Perambalur.	Udaiyarpalaiyam.	Kilappaluvur.	Trichinopoly.	Lalgudi.	District Average.
(1)	(2)	(3)	(4)	(5)	(6)	(7)	(8)	(9)	(10)	(11)	(12)	(13)	(14)	(15)
	Rice (second sort).													
1313	14·3	13·8	13·5	12·6	13·6	14·5	11·2	14·5	13·3	12·7	12·0	12·0	12·2	13·3
1314	12·3	10·9	12·0	10·4	11·9	12·5	12·3	12·2	10·7	11·4	11·1	10·6	10·8	11·5
1315	9·19	9·15	8·88	7·54	9·35	8·91	9·09	8·71	8·10	9·05	8·71	8·38	8·23	8·71
1316	9·5	9·2	9·1	6·9	8·8	8·7	8·7	8·1	7·5	7·9	7·7	8·2	8·1	8·3
1317	8·9	8·4	8·5	6·6	8·5	7·7	8·6	8·4	7·2	7·7	7·4	7·7	7·7	7·9
1318	7·7	8·1	7·6	6·2	7·0	7·0	7·5	8·1	6·6	7·3	6·9	6·9	7·3	7·2
1319	7·9	8·8	8·8	6·8	8·2	8·9	9·0	7·5	7·8	7·9	7·4	7·6	7·2	8·0
1320	9·2	9·8	9·6	8·5	9·0	9·9	10·3	8·6	8·8	9·5	7·4	8·5	8·1	9·0
1321	7·9	8·5	8·2	7·5	7·7	8·6	7·6	8·4	8·0	8·0	7·9	7·5	7·4	7·9
1322	5·8	7·4	6·6	6·3	6·2	6·6	6·2	7·1	6·7	6·9	6·2	6·6	6·7	6·6

XVIII.—Prices in seers per rupee—*cont.*

Fasli.	Karur Division.				Namakkal Division.				Ariyalur Division.			Trichinopoly Division.		District Average.
	Karur Taluk.		Kulittalai Taluk.		Namakkal Taluk.		Musiri Taluk.		Perambalur Taluk.	Udaiyarpalaiyam Taluk.		Trichinopoly Taluk.		
	Karur.	Aravakurichchi.	Kulittalai.	Manapparai.	Namakkal.	Paramatti.	Musiri.	Toraiyur.	Perambalur.	Udaiyarpalaiyam.	Kilappaluvur.	Trichinopoly.	Lalgudi.	
(1)	(2)	(3)	(4)	(5)	(6)	(7)	(8)	(9)	(10)	(11)	(12)	(13)	(14)	(15)
Paddy (first sort).														
1313	20·3	18·6	19·0	20·6	20·4	...	20·9	...	...	...	...	19·0	...	19·8
1314	16·8	15·0	16·1	17·2	16·4	...	17·5	...	...	...	...	16·5	...	16·5
1315	12·70	12·71	13·17	12·81	12·07	...	13·39	...	...	...	...	12·91	...	12·82
1316	14·2	12·5	...	11·8	13·3	...	13·1	...	...	...	...	12·9	...	13·0
1317	12·4	11·6	...	11·6	12·1	...	12·2	...	...	...	...	11·7	...	11·9
1318	11·7	10·1	...	10·1	10·1	...	11·0	...	...	...	...	10·7	...	10·6
1319	12·6	12·4	...	...	12·0	...	12·9	11·1	...	...	...	12·1	...	12·2
1320	13·5	13·3	...	...	13·9	...	14·9	12·9	...	...	...	13·9	...	13·7
1321	12·1	12·4	...	...	11·5	...	12·2	12·6	...	...	...	12·1	...	12·2
1322	9·9	11·2	...	...	8·7	...	10·5	11·0	...	...	...	10·1	...	10·2

Paddy (*second sort*).

1313	22·7	20·7	23·1	...	22·0	22·0	22·1	23·1	24·4	22·5	21·3	19·7	...	22·1
1314	18·6	16·9	20·2	...	17·6	18·6	19·5	19·7	19·3	19·7	19·9	16·9	...	18·8
1315	14·26	14·47	14·14	...	13·83	13·40	14·57	14·13	14·40	15·22	14·24	13·23	...	14·17
1316	14·8	13·9	14·5	...	14·1	13·0	14·1	12·6	12·8	13·5	13·1	13·2	..	13·6
1317	14·1	13·1	13·1	...	13·1	11·6	13·6	13·3	12·4	12·9	12·4	12·1	...	12·9
1318	12·6	12·3	10·9	11·9	10·8	10·2	12·1	12·4	11·1	12·2	11·8	11·0	...	11·6
1319	13·9	13·7	12·3	12·0	12·9	12·8	14·7	12·2	13·2	13·6	11·7	12·6	...	13·0
1320	15·8	15·3	14·2	14·1	15·3	15·7	16·3	14·1	14·9	16·1	11·7	14·4	...	14·8
1321	13·1	13·7	12·2	12·9	12·4	12·6	13·7	13·9	13·4	13·6	13·8	12·5	...	13·2
1322	11·3	12·1	10·4	10·6	9·1	9·8	11·7	12·2	10·9	11·6	10·3	11·3	...	10·9

Horsegram

1313	25·4	...	22·9	22·7	27·5	26·8	22·9	23·7	21·2	19·5	19·5	23·4	20·8	23·0
1314	18·0	13·6	17·5	20·2	18·2	19·3	16·7	17·0	15·8	16·4	16·2	16·9	15·7	17·0
1315	12·01	...	11·68	10·57	13·78	11·72	12·12	11·98	10·92	11·73	11·15	12·00	11·39	11·75
1316	14·0	...	12·3	12·3	14·1	13·2	12·8	11·7	11·8	12·7	10·2	13·7	12·6	12·6
1317	17·6	...	16·1	16·5	16·2	15·5	15·6	12·9	14·7	14·1	11·9	16·5	15·3	15·2
1318	12·6	12·4	12·2	12·5	12·5	12·3	11·8	11·3	11·3	11·1	11·9	12·0	11·2	11·9
1319	10·8	10·4	10·1	10·3	10·8	10·0	10·0	9·4	9·9	9·5	11·9	10·6	9·7	10·3
1320	13·5	12·7	12·1	12·3	13·0	13·4	12·5	12·5	11·8	12·0	11·9	13·6	11·9	12·5
1321	14·7	13·6	13·4	12·0	14·6	13·8	13·8	12·7	12·8	13·0	12·0	14·6	12·2	13·3
1322	13·0	13·6	13·2	12·0	12·1	12·0	13·5	12·8	12·4	13·1	11·9	13·2	12·6	12·7

Cholam.

1313	26·2	26·9	...	31·3	28·4	26·6	26·4	31·1	...	...	...	26·0	...	27·9
1314	19·1	18·6	17·4	23·4	21·1	20·7	29·0	28·3	...		...	20·6	...	22·0
1315	12·39	12·44	15·94	14·54	12·94	13·06	...	18·19	...	...	...	13·71	..	14·15
1316	12·6	11·8	14·6	12·6	12·1	12·2	. .	16·7	...	.	...	13·4	...	13·3
1317	13·0	14·1	16·1	14·1	12·6	12·6	...	16·5	...	...	...	14·2	...	14·2
1318	11·6	12·6	12·6	13·4	11·0	11·2	14·1	14·5	..	...	...	13·0	11·8	12·6
1319	11·8	12·6	11·8	13·5	11·4	10·7	...	15·1	...	...	...	12·7	...	12·5
1320	13·2	13·3	11·0	14·7	14·8	14·5	18·1	18·1	...	...	...	14·8	...	14·7
1321	12·0	12·6	11·8	13·8	13·6	15·2	16·7	16·6	...	...	...	13·6	...	14·0
1322	9·0	11·3	10·4	12·3	9·7	10·3	13·6	18·8	...	...	...	11·7	...	11·9

XVIII.—Prices in seers per rupee—*cont.*

Fasli.	Karur Division.				Namakkal Division.				Ariyalur Division.			Trichinopoly Division.		District Average
	Karur Taluk.		Kulittalai Taluk.		Namakkal Taluk.		Musiri Taluk.		Perambalur Taluk.	Udaiyarpalaiyam Taluk.		Trichinopoly Taluk.		
	Karur.	Aravakurichchi.	Kulittalai.	Manapparai.	Namakkal.	Paramathi.	Musiri.	Toraiyur.	Perambalur.	Udaiyarpalaiyam.	Kilappaluvur.	Trichinopoly.	Lalgudi	
(1)	(2)	(3)	(4)	(5)	(6)	(7)	(8)	(9)	(10)	(11)	(12)	(13)	(14)	(15)
							Cambu.							
1313	20·7	27·1	...	...	26·4	24·8	26·6	22·8	23·0	22·2	21·9	...	...	24·6
1314 ...	19·6	18·0	...	...	19·8	18·7	21·1	20·0	20·1	18·6	17·2	...	...	19·2
1315	13·23	13·53	...	...	13·70	12·64	13·89	14·97	16·68	13 81	15·71	...	..	14·24
1316	15·4	12·5	...	...	12·8	14·4	11·4	11·5	13 2	11·0	11·3	...	...	12·6
1317	13·0	13·9	...	...	12·7	13·3	13·6	13·3	11·9	10·0	10·5	...	..	12·5
1318	11·0	12·0	...	...	11·1	10·8	12 0	13·2	12·2	10·4	11·0	...	9·4	11·3
1319	10·0	12·5	...	...	11·5	12·0	12·4	11·0	12·7	...	11·0	...	...	11·6
1320	12·8	13·5	...	...	13·5	13·0	14 4	14·7	14·4	14·3	11·0	12·4	...	13·4
1321	13·1	13·8	...	...	12·8	11·9	13·7	16·2	14·0	13·5	13 0	12·5	...	13·5
1322	10·0	12·1	...	...	9·6	8·6	11·6	12·7	12·1	10 7	10·8	11·2	...	10·9

Ragi.

1313	...	34·1	...	...	31·2	32·3	27·9	28·3	28·6	...	...	26·9	...	29·9
1314	...	21·1	...	...	23·0	23·9	23·0	24·3	21·8	...	...	21·0	...	22·6
1315	...	14·40	...	...	14·52	14·12	14·61	16·66	17·55	...	...	14·71	...	15·22
1316	...	13·4	...	...	12·5	13·7	12·6	13·4	13·5	...	...	13·4	...	13·2
1317	...	16·2	...	...	14·5	14·4	14·8	14·4	13·4	...	...	13·9	...	14·5
1318	13·1	13·8	12·0	...	11·7	12·0	13·5	13·9	13·2	...	...	13·1	11·3	12·8
1319	12·8	14·6	12·6	...	12·7	13·0	15·0	12·3	13·9	...	...	13·7	...	13·4
1320	15·2	15·4	13·3	...	16·1	16·9	17·1	17·7	15·2	14·2	...	16·0	...	15·7
1321	15·1	16·4	12·9	...	15·3	15·5	15·1	18·0	15·7	14·7	...	14·8	...	13·4
1322	11·5	13·8	11·8	...	10·8	10·9	13·0	14·3	13·6	12·7	...	12·9	...	12·5

Salt.

1313	15·9	15·5	15·1	14·9	15·4	15·1	14·6	14·4	14·5	16.0	14·5	15·0	14·6	15·0
1314	14·2	13·8	14·9	15·0	13·6	13·7	14·1	14·2	13·6	15·5	13·6	14·5	13·9	14·2
1315	16·29	15·78	17·64	18·14	16·02	15·95	16·59	16·36	16·67	17·73	15·37	17·55	16·08	16·63
1316	18·0	17·1	19·2	19·1	17·7	16·9	17·5	17·2	17·4	17·7	16·5	19·3	17·7	17·8
1317	22·2	19·6	23·6	20·2	20·4	19·2	20·0	20·6	19·8	22·0	21·4	21·7	21·7	21·0
1318	22·4	19·4	23·8	20·4	19·8	19·7	19·8	20·2	19·8	21·8	21·3	21·4	21·4	20·9
1319	21·7	20·5	22·9	20·4	20·1	17·3	19·9	20·6	19·8	19·1	22·6	21·7	21·1	20·6
1320	22·1	20·7	22·7	20·4	20·0	17·7	19·9	20·8	19·8	19·9	22·6	21·3	20·9	20·7
1321	21·4	20·6	21·9	20·4	19·9	17·6	20·0	21·0	19·8	20·2	22·6	21·2	21·1	20·6
1322	21·2	21·0	22·7	20·5	19·7	17·7	19·9	20·6	19·1	20·0	22·4	22·0	21·1	20·6

Varagu.

1313	...	...	...	...	...	...	...	35·6	...	42·7	...	...	...	39·2
1314	...	...	...	...	...	...	...	30·3	...	36·5	...	...	...	33·4
1315	...	...	...	...	...	...	...	22·71	...	23·09	...	...	...	22·90
1316	...	...	...	...	...	...	...	18·2	...	19·4	...	...	...	18·8
1317	...	...	...	...	...	...	...	18·5	...	19·6	...	...	...	19·1
1318	...	...	...	...	...	...	...	15·1	...	18·5	...	...	...	16·8
1319	...	...	...	...	...	...	...	...	...	18·4	...	...	...	18·4
1320	...	...	...	...	...	...	...	...	...	21·1	...	...	...	21·1
1321	...	...	...	...	...	...	...	...	...	...	...	...	...	...
1322	...	...	...	...	...	...	...	...	...	...	...	...	...	...

XIX.—Income-tax.

(Part IV. "Other sources" only.)

Taluks.		Rs. 1,000 to 1,500.		Rs. 1,500 to 2,000.		Above Rs. 2,000.		Total.		Incidence of tax.		Objection petitions.	
		Number of assessees.	Amount of tax.	Number of assessees.	Amount of tax.	Number of assessees.	Amount of tax.	Number of assessees.	Amount of tax.	Per head of assessees.	Per head of population.	Number.	Percentage of these wholly or partially successful.
(1)		(2)	(3)	(4)	(5)	(6)	(7)	(8)	(9)	(10)	(11)	(12)	(13)
KARUR DIVISION.			RS.		RS.		RS.		RS.	RS. A. P.	RS. A. P.		
Karur ...	1911-12 ...	62	1,416	31	1,155	41	3,760	134	6,331	47 3 10	0 0 5	36	19·1
	1912-13 ...	58	1,376	51	1,967	43	4,420	152	7,763	51 1 1	0 0 6	57	26·8
Kulittalai ...	1911-12 ...	75	1,812	31	1,169	30	2,912	136	5,893	43 5 3	0 0 4	58	72·4
	1912-13 ...	92	2'120	44	1,708	33	3,050	169	6,878	40 11 2	0 0 5	88	78·9
NAMAKKAL DIVISION.													
Namakkal ...	1911-12 ...	61	1,460	31	1,162	61	7,773	153	10,395	67 15 0	0 0 6	57	19·2
	1912-13 ...	70	1,600	39	1,463	60	7,558	169	10,621	62 13 6	0 0 6	60	33·3
Musiri ...	1911-12 ...	75	1,644	29	1,099	73	8,880	177	11,623	65 10 8	0 0 7	97	32·9
	1912-13 ...	70	1,608	34	1,337	71	8,430	175	11,375	65 0 1	0 0 7	56	37·5
ARIYALUR DIVISION.													
Perambalur ...	1911-12 ...	33	756	16	623	17	1,570	66	2,949	44 10 11	0 0 3	45	40·0
	1912-13 ...	32	736	14	439	18	1,885	64	3,060	47 13 0	0 0 3	27	22·2

Udaiyarpalaiyam.	1911-12 ...	94	2,032	32	1,204	27	2,906	153	6,142	40	2	4	0	0	4	59	30·5
	1912-13 ...	108	2,260	35	1,351	25	3,026	163	6,637	40	11	6	0	0	4	75	21·3
TRICHINOPOLY DIVISION.																	
Trichinopoly	1911-12 ...	233	5,820	139	5,243	126	18,122	498	29,185	58	9	8	0	1	1	190	20·5
	1912-13 ...	260	6,094	148	5,670	131	19,533	539	31,297	58	1	0	0	1	2	189	35·9
District Total ...	1911-12 ...	633	14,940	309	11,655	375	45,923	1,317	72,518	55	1	0	0	0	7	542	46·9
	1912-13 ...	685	15,794	365	13,935	381	47,902	1,431	77,631	54	3	11	0	0	7	552	50·2

Note.—The territorial limits of the district were revised in November 1910.

XX.—Abkāri and Opium.

	1911-1912.	1912-1913
Country spirits.		
Number of retail shops licensed ...	372	368
Issues in imperial proof gallons ...	80,069	101,205
Number of persons per retail shop.	5,664	5,726
Gross receipts from duty ... Rs.	4,76,631	6,01,341
Do. rentals ,,	2,01,523	2,44,072
Toddy.		
Number of retail shops licensed ...	444	438
Number of persons per shop ...	4,746	4,810
Gross receipts from tree-tax Rs.	2,74,350	2,94,853
Do. rentals ,,	4,14,929	4,39,049
Ganja—Bhang.		
Number of retail shops licensed ...	22	18
Quantity sold in seers	2,550	3,091
Number of persons per shop ...	95,774	117,057
Gross receipts from duty ... Rs.	21,297	29,457
Do. rentals ,,	9,790	11,578
Opium.		
Number of retail shops licensed ...	14	11
Quantity sold in seers	355	340
Number of persons per shop ...	150,502	191,548
Gross receipts from duty ... Rs.	7,677	9,420
Do. rentals ,,	8,644	10,832

Note.—The territorial limits of the district were revised with effect from 15th November 1910.

XXI.—Revenue Receipts.

	1911-1912. RS.	1912-1913. RS.
Land Revenue	30,28,379	29,97,703
Stamps	6,65,278	7,05,403
Excise	14,15,303	16,42,214
Income-tax, including penalties ...	1,36,416	1,52,929
Forests (*a*)	1,43,839	1,62,085
Registration (*b*)	1,20,350	1,37,338
Opium	16,321	20,252
Salt (*c*)	3,701	3,738

(*a*) The figures are for fasli years.

(*b*) The figures under registration are for calendar years.

(*c*) The figures are for Trichinopoly Division.

Note.—The territorial limits of the district were revised with effect from 15th November 1910.

XXIII.—Income and Expenditure of Local Boards in 1912–13.

——	District Board.	Taluk Boards including unions in them.				Total.
		Karur.	Namakkal.	Ariyalur.	Trichinopoly.	
(1)	(2)	(3)	(4)	(5)	(6)	(7)
REVENUE AND RECEIPTS.	RS.	RS.	RS.	RS.	RS.	RS.
Land Revenue—						
House-tax ...	...	4,615	17,663	8,344	4,292	34,914
Rents, etc., of fisheries	...	1,998	1,096	793	5,860	9,747
Miscellaneous ..	...	8	339	37	24	408
Local rates—						
Cess on land ...	1,17,769	26,470	34,624	31,651	25,025	2,35,539
Railway cess ...	...	...	..	...	...	
Interest—						
On Government securities, etc.	5,961	42	11	21	7	6,042
Law and Justice—						
Courts of Law—						
Fines under Police and other Acts	...	201	667	371	306	1,545
Education—						
School fees ...	...	10,003	8,562	2,721	8,142	29,428
Contributions ...	1,871	10,672	12,032	11,730	11,295	47,600
Other receipts ...	...	147	111	1	35	294
Medical—						
Hospital receipts.	...	...	...	...	..	..
Contributions ...	1,189	287	623	296	209	2,604
Other receipts ...	3	271	869	408	481	2,032
Minor departments—						
Veterinary, etc., receipts.	1,116		..	...	...	1,116
Miscellaneous—						
Choultry receipts.	...	1,639	157	2,660	377	4,833
Market and slaughter-house receipts.	...	13,263	13,702	4,288	2,863	34,116
Contributions ...	23	160	50	25	100	358
Other receipts ...	2,586	688	568	366	748	4,956
Railways—						
Net receipts ...	...	...	...	...	...	
Civil works—						
Ferry receipts ...	39,572	...	...	...	...	39,572
Tolls	1,06,995	...	...	...	...	1,06,995
Contributions—						
Contribution from Government.	66,575	13,500	7,000	7,500	4,000	98,575
Other Contributions.	19,294	13,332	522	805	1,743	35,696
Debt, deposit and advances.	84,994	3,159	4,087	2,105	2,552	96,897
Total Receipts ...	4,47,948	1,00,455	1,02,683	74,122	68,059	7,93,267
EXPENDITURE.						
Refunds—						
Land Revenue and local rates.	92	83	...	76	624	875

XXIII.—Income and Expenditure of Local Boards in 1912-13—*cont.*

—	District Board.	Taluk Boards including unions in them.				Total.
		Karur.	Namakkal.	Ariyalur.	Trichinopoly.	
(1)	(2)	(3)	(4)	(5)	(6)	(7)
	RS.	RS.	RS.	RS.	RS.	RS.
EXPENDITURE—*cont.*						
Interest—						
On loans, etc. ...	...	...	...	...	...	...
General Administration—						
General establishment of Local Funds.	8,769	3,441	5,984	3,977	2,295	24,466
Other expenditure	...	...	...	...	...	...
Education—						
Secondary schools	...	9,834	9,892	...	7,685	27,411
Elementary schools.	...	16,523	25,414	22,379	15,766	80,082
Other schools ...	2,282	...	69	...	...	2,351
Other expenditure	200	...	...	...	...	200
Medical—						
Hospital and dispensaries.	6,366	6,003	11,690	5,551	5,806	35,416
Vaccination ...	1,635 *	1,714	2,114	2,276	1,029	8,768
Sanitation ...	...	3,797	10,657	6,336	3,297	24,087
Plague	3,748	...	...	...	...	3,748
Other epidemics.	13	287	481	562	222	1,565
Other expenditure	1,269	...	...	...	...	1,269
Minor department—						
Public exhibition and fairs.	...	...	...	...	...	...
Veterinary and other charges.	2,095	...	...	...	...	2,095
Superannuation, etc.—						
Pensions, gratuities, etc.	3,424	141	295	112	108	4,080
Stationery and Printing—						
Stationery supplied from central stores.	...	...	...	...	...	...
Printing work at Government and private presses.	1,804	...	482	135	224	2,645
Miscellaneous—						
Markets and slaughter houses.	...	460	650	170	165	1,445
Choultries ...	...	1,545	225	882	93	2,745
Lighting ...	...	873	2,833	1,973	886	6,565
Other expenditure	300	69	152	148	64	733
Railways—						
Construction of railways and other expenditure	...	...	...	...	...	...

* Cost of vaccine lymph.

XXIII.—Income and expenditure of Local Boards in 1912-13—*cont.*

—	District Board.	Taluk Boards including unions in them				Total.
		Karur.	Namakkal	Ariyalur.	Trichinopoly.	
(1)	(2)	(3)	(4)	(5)	(6)	(7)
	RS.	RS.	RS.	RS.	RS.	RS.
Civil works—						
Civil buildings ...	2,955	4,433	6,755	8,033	4,384	26,560
Communications.	2,38,288	11,446	19,964	12,354	13,213	2,95,265
Sanitary works and other works of public improvements.	*Nil.*	7,608	7,105	13,580	10,378	38,671
Establishment, Tools and plant.	32,157	1,914	2,806	2,293	1,782	40,952
Contributions ...	32,600	3,000	...	...	...	35,600
Other expenditure	1,400	..	...	132		1,532
Debt, deposit and advances.	70,272	5,381	3,778	1,979	2,364	83,774
Total Expenditure.	4,09,669	78,552	1,11,346	82,948	70,385	7,52,900

XXIV.—Income and Expenditure of Municipalities in 1912-13.

—	Trichinopoly.	Srirangam.	Karur.
	RS.	RS.	RS.
Opening balance ...	52,830	11,757	26,269
RECEIPTS.			
Tax on buildings and lands ...	69,180	15,906	9,800
Water and drainage tax on buildings and lands	49,882	5,008	...
Tax on vehicles with springs, animals and carts	14,198	6,158	3,032
Tax on arts	13,221	1,086	1,277
Tolls	24,430	4,170	6,097
Tax on private menial and domestic servants	...	...	...
Realizations under special Acts ...	282	4	1,273
Rent of lands, buildings, etc., and sale proceeds of lands, etc. ...	6,380	1,786	6,098
Conservancy receipts	14,154	2,929	2,034
Fees and revenue from—			
Educational institutions	237	...	13,214
Medical do. ...	337	102	54
Markets and slaughter-houses ...	35,531	877	1,595
License fees	3,822	1,876	752
Other fees	11,583	73	644
Fines under municipal and other Acts	2,428	1,542	259
Interest on investments and premium on loans	2,827	1,604	...
Grants and contributions from—			
Government	80,238	8,361	17,659
Local Boards	5,195	870	1,209
Other sources	8,300	180	...
Recoveries for services rendered to private individuals	15,113	2,253	1,427
Miscellaneous	704	142	503
Sale-proceeds of Government securities and realizations of sinking fund	845	146	...
Loans	...	...	...
Advances recovered	29,562	3,878	34
Total Receipts ...	3,88,449	58,951	66,961
Total including balance ...	4,41,279	70,708	93,230

XXIV.—Income and Expenditure of Municipalities in 1912-13—*cont.*

—	Trichinopoly.	Srirangam.	Karur.
	RS.	RS.	RS.
EXPENDITURE.			
Grant 1—			
Communications	25,109	207	3,143
Buildings	14,544	1,323	5,081
Miscellaneous public improvements	34,968	11,160	9
Drainage	2,072	44	746
Water-supply	58,465	89	459
Establishment	15,458	581	396
Tools and plant and other stores.	362	53	...
Contributions for public works ...	550	...	...
Grant 2—			
Education	16,024	2,768	17,977
Grant 3—			
Hospitals and dispensaries ...	17,436	3,598	4,170
Vaccination	674	249	243
Registration of births and deaths.	1,046	130	129
Conservancy, road cleaning and road-watering	57,805	13,750	9,062
Contributions	363	65	823
Plague charges	2,200	6	203
Veterinary charges	...	...	...
Grant 4—			
Lighting	9,928	3,219	1,236
Markets and slaughter-houses ...	2,061	...	...
Choultries and travellers' bungalows	199	...	81
Avenues	68	71	74
Public garden, survey of land, fire, pounds and other charges.	7,335	2,130	1,143
Grant 5—			
Supervision and management ...	13,328	2,647	1,897
Repayment of debt	12,246	111	701
Interest on debt	13,219	...	378
Discount on investment		40	...
Advances	6,797	120	10
Refunds	79	35	19
Investments	10,000	6,100	...
Total Expenditure ...	3,22,406	48,496	47,980
Closing balance ...	1,18,874	22,213	45,250
Total including balance ...	4,41,280	70,709	95,230

XXV.—Education in 1911.

Taluks.	Number of literates.		Literates per thousand of population.		Literates in English.	
	Males.	Females.	Males.	Females.	Males.	Females.
(1)	(2)	(3)	(4)	(5)	(6)	(7)
KARUR DIVISION.						
Karur	16,177	1,238	139	10	1,101	22
Kulittalai	15,939	651	115	4	726	3
NĀMAKKAL DIVISION.						
Nāmakkal	16,044	926	106	6	727	16
Musiri	21,244	1,105	142	7	573	3
ARIYALUR DIVISION.						
Perambalur	10,032	499	93	4	142	3
Udaiyarpalaiyam ...	19,840	609	128	4	396	14
TRICHINOPOLY DIVISION.						
Trichinopoly	53,906	7,727	265	35	10,893	989
District Total ...	153,182	12,755	150	12	14,558	1,050
Hindus	134,158	9,451	141	9	11,868	85
Musalmans	10,063	511	319	15	706	12
Christians	8,915	2,789	211	62	1,981	953
Others	46	4	852	235	3	...

XXVI.—Schools and Scholars on the 31st March 1913.

Class of institutions.	Number of Institutions.						Number of Scholars.		
	Government.	Municipal.	Local Fund.	Aided.	Unaided.	Total.	Males.	Females.	Total.
(1)	(2)	(3)	(4)	(5)	(6)	(7)	(8)	(9)	(10)
PUBLIC.									
Arts colleges ...	...	...		2	...	2	999	...	999
Professional colleges—									
(a) Secondary schools for boys.	...	1	3	9	...	13	6,882	15	6,897
(a) Secondary schools for girls	...	...	...	6	...	6	52	692	744
(b) Higher Elementary schools for boys	...	1	3	2	...	6	994	35	1,029
(b) Higher Elementary schools for girls	3	...	...	1	...	4	7	708	715
(c) Lower Elementary schools for boys ...	1	22	280	566	243	1,112	38,711	3,183	41,894
(c) Lower Elementary schools for girls	4	1	5	36	5	51	59	3,726	3,785
Training schools for masters ...	1	...	2	1	...	4	178	...	178
Training schools for mistresses ...	...	...	...	2	...	2	...	34	34
Other special schools	...	...	...	5	6	11	399	82	481
Total ...	9	25	293	630	254	1,211	48,281	8,475	56,756
PRIVATE.									
Advanced	...	...	...	...	...	15	218	..	218
Elementary ...	...	...	..	...	...	252	4,563	699	5,262
Total ...	...	...	...	...	...	267	4,781	699	5,480
Grand Total ...	9	25	293	630	254	1,478	53,062	9,174	62,236

(a) Includes European high and middle schools.
(b) Relates to Elementary Schools with standards above the fourth.
(c) Relates to Elementary schools with standards up to and including the fourth and Elementary schools with standards below the fourth and European primary schools.

XXVII.—Expenditure on Schools in 1912-13.

Nature of schools.	Expenditure on all classes of Schools.		Colleges.		Secondary Schools.		Higher Elementary Schools.		Lower Elementary Schools.		Training Schools.		Technical and Industrial Schools.	
	Total.	Net.	Total Expenditure.	Net Expenditure.	Total Expenditure.	Net Expenditure.	Total Expenditure.	Net Expenditure.	Total Expenditure.	Net Expenditure.	Total Expenditure.	Net Expenditure.	Total Expenditure.	Net Expenditure.
(1)	(2)	(3)	(4)	(5)	(6)	(7)	(8)	(9)	(10)	(11)	(12)	(13)	(14)	(15)
	RS.	RS.	RS.	RS.	RS.	RS.	RS.	RS.	RS.	RS.	RS.	RS.	RS.	RS.
Government ...	21,441	20,861	...	...	...	...	5,793	5,528	4,407	4,206	11,241	11,127	...	...
Local Board ...	1,09,901	78,038	...	...	27,419	3,367	4,273	3,006	75,993	69,449	2,216	2,216	...	...
Municipal ...	25,574	12,292	...	...	14,952	2,173	2,080	1,843	8,542	8,276	...	...	...	...
Aided	4,71,048	1,28,585	1,66,020	57,865	1,61,755	19,890	2,655	1,142	94,889	23,403	13,425	822	32,304	25,463
Unaided ...	15,939	990	...	...	...	...	...	...	11,196	1,370	...	...	4,743	−380
Private ..	17,802	4,612	...	...	5,567	2,872	..	...	12,235	1,740	...	...	...	...
District Total ...	6,61,705	2,45,378	1,66,020	57,865	2,09,693	28,302	14,801	11,519	2,07,262	1,08,414	26,882	14,165	37,047	25,083
Receipts (taken in abatement of charges in working out net expenditure) from—														
Provincial funds.	...	1,18,798	...	33,302	...	30,926	...	615	...	35,714	...	12,234	...	6,007
Local funds ...	...	...	...	...	...	...	...	...	...	...	...	...	...	...
Municipal funds.	...	9,930	...	...	...	...	...	129	...	9,703	...	98	...	...
School fees ...	...	2,78,038	...	74,553	...	1,44,757	...	2,538	...	50,943	...	...	...	5,247
Subscriptions ...	...	8,689	...	300	...	4,855	...	...	...	2,455	...	369	...	710
Endowments ...	...	585	...	...	...	585	...	...	...	...	...	...	...	...
Other sources ...	...	287	...	...	...	268	...	...	...	3	...	16	...	...

XXVIII.—Hospitals and Dispensaries in 1912.

Name of hospital or dispensary.	Whether Government, Local Fund, Municipal or Private.	In-patients. Number of beds available for: Men.	In-patients. Number of beds available for: Women.	In-patients. Daily average number treated: Men.	In-patients. Daily average number treated: Women.	In-patients. Daily average number treated: Children.	In-patients. Daily average number treated: Total.	Out-patients. Average daily attendance: Men.	Out-patients. Average daily attendance: Women.	Out-patients. Average daily attendance: Children.	Out-patients. Average daily attendance: Total.	Total number of patients treated both in-door and out-door.	Total expenditure during the year.
(1)	(2)	(3)	(4)	(5)	(6)	(7)	(8)	(9)	(10)	(11)	(12)	(13)	(14)
													RS.
Aravakurichi	Local Fund ...	...	..	...	...	...	..	18·16	6·10	11·91	36·17	6,707	1,983
Ariyalur	Do. ...	4	4	0·49	0·54	...	1·03	26·10	14·77	16·33	57·20	11,757	3,166
Iluppur	Do. ..	...	...	...	..	...	..	14·52	4·93	8·27	27·77	5,458	1,586
Jayankondasholapuram ...	Do. ...	...	.	...	...	...	...	25·22	8·38	10·52	44·12	10,774	10,222
Karur	Municipal ...	4	4	2·20	0·51	0·54	3·25	49·59	10·09	18·49	78·17	14,390	3,158
„ Branch (women and children's dispensary) ...	Do. ...	...	...	...	...	...	...		43·49	35·22	78·71	10,384	2,492
Kattuputtur	Local Fund ...	..	..	...	...	...	...	37·43	21·34	23·98	82·75	13,985	8,892
Kulittalai	Do. ...	...	...	...	...	...	...	36·18	12·46	16·71	65·35	11,829	2,124
Lalgudi	Do. ...	...	...	..	...	...	...	53·17	23·74	25·37	102·28	21,993	2,568
Manapparai	Do. ...	...	...	...	...	..	...	21·59	9·61	13·11	44·31	7,850	2,013
Musiri	Do. ...	2	2	0·70	0·44	...	1·14	38·25	16·16	19·60	74·01	12,574	2,722
Nāmakkal	Do. ...	4	4	2·00	0·80	...	2·80	54·46	14·59	26·57	95·62	15,709	3,455
Perambalur	Do. ...	...	...	...	...	...	...	38·52	14·32	13·90	66·74	14,327	2,862
Sendamangalam	Do. ...	...	...	...	..	...	..	25·76	13·08	20·03	58·87	8,030	1,850
Srirangam	Municipal ..	12	12	6·44	2·33	0·04	8·81	68·83	25·44	38·43	127·70	26,917	5,000
Trichinopoly	Do. ...	55	43	48·10	30·84	3·32	82·26	158·74	91·82	73·32	323·88	63,732	19,827
Turaiyur	Local Fund ...	...	...	...	..	...	...	43·02	16·53	24·27	83·82	12,296	2,011
Vellur	Do. ..	...	...	...	...	..	...	17·70	7·04	7·75	32·49	5,956	1,509
Woriur	Municipal ...	...	...	...	...	...	...	93·50	69·93	63·42	226·90	32,026	3,854
Irungalur	Private aided.	5	5	3·00	2·00	0·40	5·40	8·64	7·80	11·84	28·28	10,003	1,683
District Total ...		86	74	62·93	37·46	4·30	104·69	821·38	431·72	479·04	1,735·14	316,697	82,477

XXIX.—Vaccination.

Taluks and Municipalities.	Number of persons successfully vaccinated.		Registered birth rate per 1,000 of population in		Average number of successful cases of vaccination on children under one year during the two years ending 1912-13.
	1911–12.	1912–13.	1911.	1912.	
(1)	(2)	(3)	(4)	(5)	(6)
KARUR DIVISION.					
Karur	5,393	6,608	29	27	2,583
Kulittalai	7,342	7,537	29	28	3,590
NĀMAKKAL DIVISION.					
Nāmakkal	7,451	10,011	31	31	3,685
Musiri...	7,361	7,822	29	32	3,677
ARIYALUR DIVISION.					
Perambalur	5,742	5,064	33	32	2,837
Udaiyarpalaiyam	9,999	9,163	37	40	3,543
TRICHINOPOLY DIVISION.					
Trichinopoly	7,278	6,678	28	27	3,115
MUNICIPALITIES.					
Trichinopoly	5,978	5,061	33	33	3,619
Karur	537	568	34	35	416
Srirangam	1,201	1,198	27	26	684
Total for the District ...	58,282	59,710	31	31	27,749

NOTE.—The territorial limits of the district were revised in November 1910.

XXX.—Civil Justice.

(Average of the statistics for the two years 1911-12.)

Class of court. (1)	Number of all original suits disposed of. (2)	Average value of suits of which value was estimable in money. (3)	Number of appealable decrees passed in disposed of cases. (4)	Appeals preferred. (5)	Appeals decided. (6)	Decisions confirmed. (7)	Percentage of decisions confirmed to total disposals. (8)
		RS.					
Village Courts	6,718	53	..	...	...	...	...
Revenue Courts	617	211	511	47	41	9	22
District Munsifs' Courts...	18,827	1,778	3,892	530	446	219	49
Subordinate Judges' Courts.	1,664	10,988	62	13	11	4	36
District Judge's Court ...	5	4,100	...	...	...	...	...

NOTE.—The territorial limits of the district were revised in November 1910.

XXXI.—Criminal Justice.

(Number of persons convicted of certain offences in each of the years 1911-12.)

Offence. (1)	1911. (2)	1912. (3)
Murder	...	...
Culpable homicide	...	...
Hurts and assaults	388	432
Other offences against the person	29	37
Dacoity	...	...
Robbery	6	14
House-breaking	27	21
Cattle theft	110	101
Other theft	235	253
Other offences against property	249	226
Offences against public tranquillity (Chapter VIII)	242	185
Other offences against the Penal Code	544	661
Total ...	1,830	1,930
Security for keeping the peace and for good behaviour	101	91
Offences under the Madras Salt Act (IV of 1889)	...	2
Offences under the Madras Abkāri Act (I of 1886)	302	267
Offences under the Madras Forest Act (V of 1882).	292	178
Offences under the Madras District Municipalities Act (IV of 1884)	1,488	1,604
Other offences against special and local laws ...	7,189	9,045
Grand Total ...	11,202	13,117

NOTE.—The territorial limits of the district were revised in November 1910.

XXXII.—Work of Criminal Courts.

(Average of the statistics for the years 1911 and 1912.)

Class of courts. (1)	Original cases instituted. (2)	Number of appeals received. (3)
Village Magistrates	311·5	...
Bench "	8,588·5	...
Special "	13·5	...
Stipendiary Subordinate Magistrate	7,588·5	...
Deputy, Assistant and Joint Magistrates ...	453·5	388
District Magistrate	9	335
Court of Session	8	10

NOTE.—The territorial limits of the district were revised in November 1910.

XXXIII.—Police and Jails in 1912.

Taluks.	Number of Police.		Police force.						Number of known depredators.	Number of Sub-Jails.	Total accommodation in them.
	Stations.	Outposts.	Inspectors.	Sub-Inspectors.	Head Constables.	Constables.	Police Talaiyaries.	Revenue Talaiyaries.			
(1)	(2)	(3)	(4)	(5)	(6)	(7)	(8)	(9)	(10)	(11)	(12)
KARUR DIVISION.											
Karur	3	2	1	4	11	84	...	149	164	2	40
Kulittalai	6	2	1	6	14	95	...	155	*303	2	35
NĀMAKKAL DIVISION.											
Nāmakkal	6	2	1	9	18	100	...	282	164	2	24
Musiri	4	3	1	5	13	74	...	...	49	2	35
ARIYALUR DIVISION.											
Perambalur ...	4		1	4	9	58	...	175	39	1	18
Udaiyarpalaiyam ...	5	2	1	5	12	84	...	258	59	2	19
TRICHINOPOLY DIVISION.											
Trichinopoly ...	7	2	2	9	40	235	...	366	205	2	72
District Total ...	35	13	8	42	117	730	...	1,385	983	13	243

* Including suspects.

NOTE.—There is also a Central Jail in Trichinopoly town.